DANIEL DEFOE
a reference guide
1731-1924

A
Reference
Guide
to
Literature

Everett Emerson
Editor

DANIEL DEFOE
a reference guide
1731-1924

SPIRO PETERSON

G.K.HALL &CO.

70 LINCOLN STREET, BOSTON, MASS.

Library of Congress Cataloging-in-Publication Data

Peterson, Spiro.
   Daniel Defoe, a reference guide, 1731–1924.

   (A Reference guide to literature)
   Includes indexes.
   1. Defoe, Daniel, 1661?–1731—Bibliography.   I. Title.
II. Series.
Z8221.P47   1987   [PR3406]   016.823′5   86-22963
ISBN 0-8161-8157-8

This publication is printed on permanent/durable acid-free paper
MANUFACTURED IN THE UNITED STATES OF AMERICA

For
Yerevan

The Author

Spiro Peterson was born in New Haven, Connecticut, and educated at Trinity College (A.B., 1947) and Harvard University (Ph.D., 1953). He is a professor of English at Miami University, where he teaches the eighteenth-century novel. His publications, in both seventeenth- and eighteenth-century literature, have appeared in such journals as PMLA, Philological Quarterly, Huntington Library Quarterly, and Eighteenth-Century Studies, and in the Augustan Reprint Society. He has published a book, The Counterfeit Lady Unveiled and Other Criminal Fiction of Seventeenth Century England. A Selection Edited with Forewords and Notes (Garden City, New York: Doubleday & Co., 1961). From 1972 to 1982 he was dean of the Graduate School and Research at Miami University; and from 1964 to 1972, chair of the Department of English.

Contents

Preface

Over more years than I like to remember, I have been collecting
and annotating books and articles on Daniel Defoe from the year of
his death (1731) to the present. It was not until March 1977, however, that my general interest became focused upon the specific project, namely, to prepare an annotated bibliography for the Reference
Guide to Literature series of G.K. Hall & Co. It was not until the
past year that I was able to determine the scope of this volume by
fixing on the ending date 1924. The purpose of the reference guide
is to annotate all the books, translations, monographs, articles,
dissertations, verses and films about Defoe for the years 1731-1924;
and to organize these items alphabetically under the year of first
publication, in order to illustrate the history and development of
the subject author's reputation.

The scope of the present volume was limited to 1924 on the basis
of annotated bibliographies available now. In 1977 there were four
comprehensive bibliographies of writings about Defoe: Henry Clinton
Hutchins's, in CBEL (1941)*; Maximillian E. Novak's, in New CBEL
(1971), and his Bibliographical Guide (1974), and William L. Payne's
"Annotated Bibliography" (1975). In addition, there was Pat Rogers's
important Critical Heritage (1972), which first endeavored to trace
large patterns in eighteenth- and nineteenth-century criticism of
Defoe. Soon thereafter followed Rogers's Robinson Crusoe (1979); the
introduction, reprinted articles by scholars worldwide, and bibliography of Heidenreich and Heidenreich (1982); the listing of articles
in periodicals, 1950-1980, in Hammerschmidt (1983); and especially
John A. Stoler's Daniel Defoe: An Annotated Bibliography of Modern
Criticism, 1900-1980 (New York and London: Garland Publishing, Inc.,
1984). My reference guide supplements Stoler's Bibliography. The
two works, in fact, overlap for the years 1900-1924, but differ substantially in format, editorial philosophy, coverage and comprehen-
siveness for these years.

In preparing the reference guide I have followed the G.K. Hall
guidelines for the series, and present the annotated bibliography in
the standard G.K. Hall & Co. format. It may be useful, here, to repeat some of the guidelines and to call attention to a few procedures
which deliberately depart from the guidelines, and to explain my

*For the expanded titles, see "References Abbreviated in the Text."

reasons for doing so. More important, in this context, I need to
state a few principles of annotating philosophy which may be appropriate to a reference guide for Daniel Defoe.

The first of these principles follows from my earlier comment on
scope. In limiting this reference guide to the years 1731-1924, I
feel constantly obligated to know equally well the criticism and
scholarship for the years 1925-1985 both because I was led frequently
to search for items that might otherwise have gone undiscovered and
because I gained invaluable perspective thereby in writing annotations for the earlier period. For the years 1731-1924, as I shall
try to show in my Introduction, writers responded to Defoe as a man
or as an author and novelist in what appear to be cycles of almost
complete neglect (from his death to Chalmers's Life of Daniel De Foe,
1785) and of critical elation arising generally from the publication
of the major biographies (for instance, by Walter Wilson, John Forster, William Lee, Thomas Wright, William P. Trent, Paul Dottin) or
from a profoundly influential work of criticism (such as Minto's
Defoe, 1879). Within the reference guide there are approximately
1565 items that have some claim to importance as criticism and scholarship published about Daniel Defoe, predominantly in English (1325),
but also in French (133) and German (92), Russian (7) and Dutch (4),
and single items in Italian, Swedish, Eskimo, and Japanese. In sharp
contrast to these figures are the estimates for the number of items
published during the years 1925-1985. In a grand total of 2,631
items for this later period, the number for each year becomes astonishingly greater, beginning in 1957, although there are high points
in the years 1931 and 1951. Reflected in the data for 1925-1985 are
other important phenomena: (1) the entrance of Defoe criticism and
scholarship broadly into the international arena, with studies
published in the Japanese language; and (2) their alignment with
sophisticated critical theory such as feminism or Marxism.

Working with an author whose reputation has been influenced
by the popularity and fame of a single book has led me, very early
in the work, to a second principle of editorial philosophy. I aimed
to include as legitimate pieces of criticism the literally hundreds
of prefaces, introductions, and forewords to editions of Robinson
Crusoe--in English, French, and German. Quite fortunately, I was
able to accomplish this task by working in the truly fine Hubbard
Imaginary Voyage Collection, Department of Rare Books and Special
Collections, University of Michigan Library, and to have the generous
assistance of the library staff in locating Robinson Crusoe editions.
The principle applies to the preliminaries of all the frequently
reprinted novels and to all the rare book libraries that responded to
my endless pleas for help. It led also to the problem of my having
to incorporate into a few annotations, after the word "reprinted,"
a long list of publication year dates. By collating the prefatory
texts, I tried to determine apparently discrete reprintings. The
list of year dates cannot be definitively accurate; it can only be
suggestive of how frequently the item may have been republished.
Generally, if it is an edition of Robinson Crusoe, the work may be

found in the Hubbard Imaginary Voyage Collection. I must also point out, however, that I have used Defoe editions wherever I could locate them.

Immersed in the older writings about Defoe, I could not avoid observing that a mysterious synergism between biography and criticism appears to be at work, and that it was clearly self-defeating to keep the two neatly separate. This experience grew into a strong conviction, and has led me to a third principle: to allow considerable latitude for including works predominantly biographical. Accordingly, while I have not eliminated any work because it is exclusively biography, I have always placed the emphasis in the annotations on the critical implications of biography. As a fourth principle of editorial philosophy, I should mention that in order to cope with what is perhaps the largest canon of any author in the world, and with a select number of important books about Defoe, I have used my "References Abbreviated in the Text," listing alphabetically the shortened titles of "Defoe's Works" and the "Secondary Works" which recur frequently in the annotations. For quick reference to "Defoe's Works" I make use of selected titles from John Robert Moore's A Checklist of the Writings of Daniel Defoe (2d ed. Hamden, Conn.: Archon Books, 1971), at the same time remaining aware of the corrections and revisions to this important work. I have found the device of the abbreviations list enormously helpful in permitting wide-ranging discussion of the problems and issues raised in the annotations. To minimize the inconvenience to the reader, I suggest that the abbreviations be scanned so that they can be readily understood when they appear in the entries. Section B, "Secondary Works," has a further benefit in that it provides, at a glance, a listing of the bibliographies.

Appropriate, pertinent, and perhaps necessary are a few statements about the three parts of the reference guide. First, among the preliminaries are the Preface which states the main principles adopted for the collecting, identifying, dating, annotating, and organizing the items from 1731 through 1924; the Acknowledgements; the Introduction which identifies major trends in the criticism and literary reputation of Defoe, the writer and the man; and "References Abbreviated in the Text."

Second, on dates in general, I make every effort to date each item accurately, and place it under the correct year of publication, admitting now and then an honest doubt (1820? or ca.1750) and always locating the item after the year given. One item only (J.F. Bunting) has not been dated, and therefore appears at the end. Another item (Peeping Tom), dated 1840-1857, follows after the items for the year 1840, after an item dated 1840-1843. Items consisting of a number of volumes published over more than one year are listed after items published in the first year. For other irregularities, my practice is to place items incompletely dated after the longer time-interval: 19--, after 1924; 179-, after 1799.

An entry number is assigned to each book or article, made up of the publication year plus the number identifying the item within the alphabetical sequence of that year. Thus, not infrequently, items are listed out of strict chronological order in a given year. For each entry I follow the standard practice of incorporating three kinds of information: citation, annotation, record of selected reviews and reprintings.

Citation. Where an item has been searched for, and no copy has been located, I list it with an asterisk (*) immediately before the entry number. Such notation should be taken to mean that although there does exist, somewhere, a specific reference to the author and title, I have not been able to locate a copy. The "unlocated" item I distinguish carefully from the "unexamined" item which has been located, but may not be available for one reason or another. Even more difficult than either the "unlocated" or "unexamined" items are the few which I must, at this time, describe as "ghosts." Generally, the ghosts are items in the form of comments that are well-known, even quoted, traceable to important persons, but no farther: Jean François Marmontel (Wilson's Memoirs of Defoe, 1830), Alphonse Daudet (Wright, 1894), William Pitt (father or son), Samuel Johnson (on Captain Singleton), and the anonymous Ohio colonist who drew courage from his Robinson Crusoe (1833.2).

For articles in citations I have assigned authorship on the basis of the best evidence available, and have indicated the source of the information. The author for an anonymous article in a nineteenth-century periodical, for instance, may be identified in a later reprinting of his collected works or in the Wellesley Index. For titles of periodicals I have avoided acronyms or abbreviations, and cite them as they appear in the MLA Directory of Periodicals (New York: Modern Language Association of America, 1981). For books in citations, I use the word "Reprint" to indicate that I have not been able to use the first edition published in the year of the entry, but have used the later edition as identified.

Annotation. For each book or article I sum up the main point(s) and characterize the view or stance taken by the author in an objective or non-evaluative manner. I rely upon quotations, perhaps more than customary, because I strongly believe that these capture the tone and flavor of the original. Only on a few rare occasions do I call attention to a serious error through a bracketed editorial insertion, or give balance to a statement through a cross-reference. Titles of Defoe's works, always in their brief forms, are cited as they appear in my "References Abbreviated in the Text" or Moore's Checklist. Editions of both single and collected works are annotated when they include introductions or prefaces with critical, biographical, or bibliographical content; or when they have special significance in the publication of texts.

Reviews and Reprintings. Reviews are annotated only when they pertain to significant works of criticism or scholarship, and also

have an importance in their own right as providing new information
or taking strong positions, or only when they are by important people
whose views are always of interest. The "reprinting" record, at the
end of an annotation, is as accurate as I could make it, representing
information drawn from various sources: CBEL, New CBEL, National
Union Catalog, and other miscellaneous bibliographies. It should not
be assumed that each year-date represents a reprinting which I have
personally examined. Through collation I endeavor to list together
the exact reprintings of an item, and identify the reprintings that
contain substantial revisions of the original, and characterize the
latter briefly with respect to kinds of changes in the text.

Third, I make use of two separate indexes. The "Author, Title
Index" accesses names of authors, editors, translators, and reviewers, but only selected titles of books and articles in periodicals.
Editors of significant works are included, as are reviewers, whose
comments have special merits or convey new information. Since the
reference guide makes a deliberate effort to list translations that
have a critical uniqueness or an ethnic relevance, these are indexed
under the Defoe work being translated, the translator's name, and the
foreign language. The "Subject Index" lists all important authors,
titles, and subjects discussed in the annotations. All references
are by entry number rather than by pages.

Headings in the "Subject Index" are intended to be comprehensive
and thus immediately useful to the reader. Very rarely do they make
reference to material not discussed in the annotation. The principle
of a single alphabetical listing generally applies throughout the
"Subject Index." Certain primary headings, it should be noted, are
given subheadings. Such is the case with the subject-author, Daniel
Defoe, where subheadings are created for Bibliography, Biographies,
Letters, Manuscripts, Library, and Writings. Specific works by
Defoe--novels, memoirs, histories, tracts, pamphlets, poems or verse
satires--are entered under their individual titles as primary headings in their brief forms. For each novel, appropriate subheadings
have been created, as determined by the critical interests displayed
in the annotations for that novel. The intent is to communicate
clearly the different categories of scholarship and criticism available, and provide access to these titles through the entry numbers.
Here, as elsewhere in the two indexes, I have resorted to personal
judgments in creating appropriate listings and in placing the entry
numbers. I therefore urge considerable caution through a reminder
that the indexes can never be specific enough to meet the needs of
every reader, and should never substitute for the reference guide
itself.

Acknowledgments

To many people and institutions I express my thanks. I think first of Miami University where I have taught since 1952, and benefited from the enlightened leadership of presidents John D. Millett, Phillip R. Shriver, and Paul G. Pearson. I think next of the Edgar W. King Library and its dedicated director, Donald E. Oehlerts. To Sarah Barr, Interlibrary Loan Librarian, I am most grateful for her expert skills in searching for Daniel Defoe items, literally, all over the world. To her and Karen Clift I am most thankful, too, for their constant good cheer. For its congeniality as a place to work and strengths in juvenile literature, I acknowledge the Walter Havighurst Special Collections Library and the knowledgeable staff, Helen Ball, Catherine deSaint-Rat, Frances McClure, and Elizabeth Brice. For never failing assistance I thank William Wortman, Humanities Librarian.

Outside of Oxford, Ohio, I have benefited most from the Department of Rare Books and Special Collections at the University of Michigan Library, from the courtesy and cooperation of former heads, Harriet C. Jameson, Karla M. Vandersypen, and Helen S. Butz, and from the current head, Robert J. Starring. I am especially grateful to the farsightedness of Lucius L. Hubbard who brought together the Hubbard Imaginary Voyages Collection. My indebtedness to this Collection is just barely hinted at by the large number of prefaces, introductions, and "biographical notices" which I annotated from its Robinson Crusoe editions.

I have regularly visited the libraries nearby, and have been assisted greatly by being able to work in collections at the University of Cincinnati, Ohio State University, Indiana University (including the Lilly Library), University of Kentucky, University of Louisville, and University of Illinois. I express my thanks also to the Cincinnati Public Library, Boston Public Library (especially, the Department of Rare Books and Manuscripts, for its Defoe Collection), New York Public Library, and Cleveland Public Library; to the Library of Congress, British Library, and Bibliothèque nationale; to the Watkinson Library of my alma mater, Trinity College (Hartford); to the Weidner and Houghton libraries of Harvard University; to the Sterling Memorial Library and Beinecke Rare Book and Manuscript Library of Yale University; and to the American Antiquarian Society (Worcester).

Since this reference guide was intended to be international in scope, I sought and received considerable help and advice from foreign language consultants at Miami University: Peter E. Carels (German), Andre L. deSaint-Rat (Russian), Peter Tiersma (Dutch), Raymond R. Fleming (Italian), Ruth H. Sanders (Swedish), Inka M. Blazek (Czech), and Timothy J. Rogers (Spanish). For all the foreign language items I have taken the bibliographical responsibility--searching, locating, identifying--and have annotated all the French books and articles. Professor Carels annotated the next largest group, the items in German; and his initials appear within parentheses at the end of each annotation. I use the same procedure to record the contributions of the other foreign language consultants. I am especially grateful to Professor Sungkyu Cho, Yonsei University (Seoul, Korea), for his work in examining the oriental literatures. While his efforts have uncovered only one Japanese item published before 1924, he has found a large number of Japanese, Chinese, and Korean items for the period 1925-1985. For the Danish, Hungarian, and Polish languages, I have not located any works published before 1925. Nevertheless, I record that the search was made, and express thanks, respectively, to Professors Anni and Thomas Reed Whissen, Wright State University; Professor Andrew Kerek, Miami University; and Mrs. Mira Miller, Kettering (Ohio).

I would like to express my thanks for support of my research at Miami University to the Faculty Research Committee; to C. Barry Chabot, Chair, Department of English; Stephen M. Day, Dean, College of Arts and Science; and E. Fred Carlisle, Provost. From the very beginning of my work on the reference guide, I recall, with gratitude, the encouragement of Professor Joseph Katz, General Editor, Reference Guides in Literature, G.K. Hall & Co.; and the perennial good cheer and advice of my field editor, Professor Everett Emerson, University of North Carolina. For her fine work on the Subject Index I thank Janet K. Ziegler. For help far beyond the call of family, I thank Ellen Peterson, Stacey Peterson and Tim Race, and Town and Amy Peterson. It is impossible, finally, to express my abiding gratitude to Yerevan Peterson, who shared with me every pain and joy--except by dedicating the volume to her.

Daniel Defoe:
The Making of a Tradition

By the year 1924 the main lines of the critical tradition had
been firmly established. What that tradition might be--particularly
in the criticisms of British writers through William Minto's Defoe
(1879)--we have a very good idea from Pat Rogers's Critical Heritage
(1972). To this impressive assessment of Defoe's literary reputation
we can add a considerable number of new names of British and American
critics, and their critical insights; we can predicate some major
realignments owing to French and German criticism. But essentially
the main lines of development in the tradition are firmly in place.

The tradition starts with the assumption that Daniel Defoe
(1659?-1731) is overwhelmingly important as the author of Robinson
Crusoe (1719), but that in the early years (especially in France) the
book, specifically its first part, was far more important than the
author--a kind of anonymous masterpiece whose creator might be John
Arbuthnot, Richard Steele, or Robert Harley. The tradition recognizes that Defoe gradually, at times painfully, achieves recognition
for at least six other major works of the imagination: Memoirs of
a Cavalier (1720), Captain Singleton (1720), Moll Flanders (1722),
Journal of the Plague Year (1722), Colonel Jack (1722), and Roxana
(1724). Critics never ceased to marvel at his productivity and versatility. Deeply ingrained into the tradition were certain biographical assumptions, held up to William Lee's Defoe (1869), that Defoe
suffered a crisis in 1715 in which he retired from active politics
into literature, or that, in the last few years of his life, as an
aging writer, he suffered from poverty and neglect, and the fierce
hostility of an unidentified enemy. Certain distinctive characteristics were central to the tradition: a fresh and unique style,
variously described as natural, plain, homely, colloquial; an air of
authenticity; an irrepressible habit of impersonation which could
function equally well in non-fictional contexts, such as the Shortest-Way with the Dissenters, as in Mrs. Veal or the Journal of the
Plague Year; a verisimilitude or a new realism (Ian Watt would call
it "realism of presentation," as opposed to "realism of assessment");
credible characters or personages drawn from an ordinary or familiar
world; and a plot that was hardly recognizable as such or generally
negligible. With the tradition full-blown, as one encountered it for
the first time in Sir Walter Scott's brilliant essay (1827.2), one
can only admire how rapidly our understanding of Defoe and his works

has grown--from the first meager efforts at biography by Theophilus
Cibber and Robert Shiels (1753.1) and the scholarly George Chalmers
(1785.1; 1790.1) and from the critical efforts of Jean-Jacques
Rousseau (1762.2), James Beattie (1783.1), and Hugh Blair (1783.2),
to place a somewhat anonymous <u>Robinson Crusoe</u> into a larger, even
worldwide, perspective.

For any other writer, searching for critical interpretations
of the novels might be no more than an academic exercise. For
Defoe, that is emphatically not the case. Very quickly we discover
that we are also witnessing, indirectly, the emergence of the novel
as a literary form and all the profound theory that accompanies
such an event. We discover how persistent was the appeal of certain
writings, at certain times, in certain countries. We discover, particularly with <u>Robinson Crusoe</u>, that we are engaged not just in
understanding a single author and his work, but in comprehending the
creative process itself and in pursuing a cultural phenomenon, European and worldwide, psychological and historical, mythic and generic.
To a more limited extent, the same issues arise with <u>Moll Flanders</u>
and <u>Journal of the Plague Year</u>. For a novelist like Defoe, traditional criticism unfolds differently for each individual novel in
the form of central themes and issues; and these are made accessible
through the Subject Index as secondary headings under the titles of
the novels. Relating to the different traditions, certain questions
arise naturally from the 1565 entries of the <u>Reference Guide</u>. What
is the criticism by British writers like? How insular is it, or how
responsive to influences from abroad? What are its central concerns
and preoccupations? How does British criticism change, reshape, or
transform itself with new information from biography or new knowledge
of the canon? How does fiction relate to, or evolve from, fact? Why
the profound interest, on the continent, in Robinsonades, Utopian fan-
tasies, <u>voyages imaginaires</u>, true voyage narratives? When, and how,
does critical interest shift from <u>Robinson Crusoe</u> to the "secondary
novels"? Why the fascination with the picaresque? Criminal biographies? What new directions are taken by the French, German, and
Russian critics? Do we discern qualitative differences (and similarities) among the continental critics, as compared with their British
counterparts? How does a lively interest in the canon of Defoe--
identifying his authentic works with varying degrees of certainty--
start, and spread itself from Chalmers (1790.1) to Dottin (1924.7)?

The <u>Reference Guide</u> does not examine such questions narrowly.
In the "References Abbreviated in the Text" I select out thirty-nine
primary works which include the major novels, but also controversial
pieces, some still in the limbo of the Defoe canon, such as <u>Capt.
George Carleton</u> and <u>Madagascar</u>. In all, there are twenty-one items
that have close affinities to fictional narrative. The <u>Reference
Guide</u> is emphatically not belletristic. While focusing on criticism
of the novels, it includes as well critiques of the political, economic, religious, sociological, geographical, and supernatural works;
it brings together biography and bibliography as well as criticism.

Although it does not accept Moore's Checklist (2d ed., 1971) as the final word on Defoe's canon, the Reference Guide does use Moore's work as a base, and sets in relief the judgments on canon by Chalmers, Wilson, Lee, Trent, and Dottin. The Reference Guide tries to treat every printed commentary, in every language, about every fiction-related work listed among the 566 items in Moore's Checklist.

Writers responded to Defoe as a man or as an author in emphatic ways, in no uncertain terms, in clearly defined positions or attitudes toward him. Critics and scholars, biographers and politicians, novelists and men of letters could no more be neutral toward him than could his contemporary antagonists, Charles Lesley or John Oldmixon. Both as a person and writer, he represented something in letters about which one must take a stand and, often, an extreme position. Most writers were admiring of Defoe; saw him as a fellow artist, confronting and resolving artistic problems in perilous times. Not infrequent were the hostile and unsympathetic critics who daringly unfolded their standards, and sounded the trumpets, against coarseness, vulgarity, immorality in Moll Flanders and especially Roxana. Now and then, some critic raised his voice even against the author's limited artistic vision.

A clear tradition of distinctive criticism differentiates itself in England, randomly at first, under William Godwin (1807.1) and Charles Lamb (1807.2; 1830.4-6); it becomes stronger toward mid-century and apparently impervious to French and German criticism. John Gibson Lockhart (1820.4) views Defoe as a national writer, to be contrasted with such equals as Fielding, Smollett, Le Sage, and Scott. C. Barker (1821.1), using mature critical language, continues in the same vein. Then follow the admirable Scott with his full-scale criticism (1827.2) that regards Defoe from the perspective of a fellow-practitioner, and places him in a continental framework through comments on the Gusto Picaresco; William Hazlitt (1830.3), completely separating biography and fiction by means of what he calls Defoe's "world of abstraction"; and the marvellous Coleridge (1836.4), his insights among the marginalia in a copy of Robinson Crusoe shining through garbled texts, but clearly focusing upon a mythic interpretation: "Defoe's excellence it is, to make me forget my specific class, character, and circumstances, and to raise me while I read him, into the universal man." At the mid-century mark are John Forster (1845.4; 1855.3), with his conception of Defoe as "the great Middle-class English character" and his dramatic (but mistaken) notion of Defoe's retirement in 1715 from "the world Without to the world Within"; John Cordy Jeaffreson (1856.3), expressing great sympathy for the fiction, in the Dublin University Magazine, while at the same time unable to suppress a strong [Victorian] bias toward its immorality; and William Caldwell Roscoe (1856.9), whom the Wellesley Index identifies as the author of the brilliant piece of criticism in the National Review, urging the theory that the novel has become "the characteristic literature of modern man" and as our personal liberty increases, it preoccupies itself with characterization, but that in this respect Defoe failed because he was too distracted by the petty actions of his times. With Roscoe's essay one must, indeed, pause. For not only does Pat Rogers claim that with this essay "Defoe criticism may be said to have come of age" (Critical Heritage, p. 21), he also regards it most highly. One could even say that the essay is perhaps the best summation of traditional criticism, exceeding even the great essay by Leslie Stephen (1868.20). Our only disagreement seems to be that Pat Rogers has reason to believe that the author is Walter Bagehot, and I find the evidence pointing to William Caldwell Roscoe, as in his collected works (1860.9). For sheer virtuosity of critical perception and pungency of statement, Roscoe's essay remains unrivalled, as in the description of Defoe's imagination as the reverse of Shakespeare's "universal solvent," or the comparison of Jane Austen's handling of domestic life with Defoe's, ending with this beautiful iconoclasticism: "De Foe goes down the ragged lanes, tramps through gorse and heather, sits by the side of the duckpond, and studies the aspects of the dunghill" (Critical Heritage, p. 131).

Heady, indeed, were the decades in the second half of the nineteenth century, with some of the finest traditional criticism making its appearance in rapid succession: Masson (1859.11), Stephen (1868.20), Lee (1869.16), W.H.D. Adams (1871.1; 1886.2), and Saintsbury (1878.9). While global shocks were emanating from the discovery of five (then six) letters in the State Paper Office (1864.7), written in Defoe's hand, revealing that in the years of so-called retirement after 1715, he was not placidly given in to a life of the mind and literature; he was frenetically engaged by a Whig ministry to disable and enervate Tory and Jacobite journals. Lee told the story in the most favorable light, and adroitly dodged the issue of outrageous duplicity that most everyone else read into Defoe's conduct. Others remembered the much earlier charges against Defoe for plagiarism and unscrupulous treatment of Alexander Selkirk. Such charges continued to reverberate in the numerous prefaces and introductions of popular editions of Robinson Crusoe, and they had an incalculable effect on readers of all ages with respect to Defoe's reputation. In the years after Lee's biography and "newly discovered writings," reprinted in two thick volumes, the misconduct was ingeniously moved forward even to Defoe's first collaboration, in 1704, with Robert Harley. Out of this new biographical information, Minto fashioned the famous dictum: "He was a great, a truly great liar, perhaps the greatest liar that ever lived," and he explicated the novels, and summed up Defoe's theory of fiction, as "lying like the truth" (1879.5). And many years later, the great American scholar of Defoe, William P. Trent (1912.18), thoroughly shaken by his experiences in researching his author's life and works, reached the powerful new conclusion that from the trauma of his pillorying, Defoe became not "a shameless and wholesale liar," but "a consummate casuist who was often his own chief dupe." Nevertheless, to Trent, Defoe was "the greatest of plebeian geniuses." The connection between biography and criticism continued to be vibrant throughout the first quarter of the twentieth century.

The profound effect that Defoe had upon other novelists or
writers has never been adequately appraised. To sense this kind of
artistic or professional sympathy by one practitioner for another,
one need only examine the names of literary personages who, at one
time or other, express admiration for Defoe the novelist, or give
generously of their insights into the work or thought of a fellow
artist. Very rarely there is downright hostility. Listed in chronological order, on the basis of the date for the first printed
comment, are the following: Tobias Smollett, Henry Fielding, Oliver
Goldsmith, Clara Reeve, Benjamin Franklin, Sir Walter Scott, William
Williams, Mary Shelley, Charles Dickens, Edgar Allan Poe, William
Harrison Ainsworth, Frederick Marryat, James Fenimore Cooper, George
Borrow, Anna Eliza Bray, Herman Melville, Honoré de Balzac, Nathaniel
Hawthorne, Walter Savage Landor, George Eliot, Charles Reade, Wilkie
Collins, Jules Verne, Thomas Hardy, Edward Everett Hale, Arthur Conan
Doyle, William D. Howells, Oscar Wilde, Robert Louis Stevenson,
Alphonse Daudet, John Masefield, Virginia Woolf, and Willa Cather.

Side by side are the great and the less great authors, and the
English, French, and Americans. Impressive though the roll-call
may be, it does not convey any depth of feeling or acuteness of
self-perception, as when Dickens comments in a private letter (1856)
to Forster that "Robinson Crusoe should be the only instance of an
universally popular book that could make no one laugh and could make
no one cry" (1872-1874.1). Nor does the list suggest why it is that
a novelist like Borrow creates a narrator Lavengro who has been deeply influenced by Robinson Crusoe and by the old appleseller's book,
The Blessed Mary Flanders (1851.3). Gabriel Betteredge, in Wilkie
Collins's The Moonstone (1868.7), is perhaps the supreme example of
the Crusoe-like character who constantly seeks wisdom in his Robinson
Crusoe. Hardy's The Hand of Ethelberta (1875-1876.1) was commissioned as a serial for Cornhill Magazine by the editor Leslie Stephen.
The main character Ethelberta or Mrs. Petherwin is a creative writer,
one strongly influenced by Defoe. Commenting upon her method, she
asserts that "a modern critic has well observed of De Foe that he
had the most amazing talent on record for telling lies. . . ." Since
the words are directly quoted from Leslie Stephen's essay (1868.20),
he must be the "modern critic." At once we become aware of subtle
crosscurrents of influence from Stephen to Hardy and a latent cre-
ativity in Defoe's serving (for a number of writers) as a novelist's
novelist.

"Each age," writes the French critic Karl Hillebrand (1866.3),
"has its own philosophy of history; if Bossuet has given that of the
XVIIth century; Hegel that of the XIXth; it is in Robinson that one
will find that of the XVIIIth." In what specific ways does Robinson
Crusoe sum up the philosophy of history for the eighteenth century?
One does feel the overwhelming presence of this book everywhere.
Books, articles, prefaces, introductions, biographical notices,
letters, even songs and illustrations--all speak out eloquently on

the diversity of interpretations that critics give to Robinson Crusoe. Certainly, all the conventional approaches are addressed as a
glance at the entry Robinson Crusoe in the Subject Index reveals. In
addition, among the themes or motifs, one identifies a strong interest in Robinson Crusoe as an allegory, parable, or symbolic work; as
a representation of man's endless struggle in the state of nature, or
of Crusoe personifying civilization, empire, the Anglo-Saxon race,
humanity, or man. Robinson Crusoe seems constantly to be reaching
out for mythic interpretation. As the Robinsonades proliferate all
over Europe, they, too, give off flashes of insight, retroactively,
upon the mythic powers of their progenitor. And so Robinson Crusoe
is found to bear kinship with Homer's Iliad or Odyssey, Prometheus,
Don Quijote. More specifically, the German bibliographer Johann
C.L. Haken describes Robinson Crusoe as "the history of mankind and
its progressive culture in miniature" (1805-1808.1). Coleridge
and others take Crusoe himself as the "universal representative"
(1836.4); Taine discerns in Crusoe a will and enthusiasm which formerly produced sea-kings in England, and now produce emigrants and
squatters in Australia or America (1863.5); and Hermile Reynald
describes the old Robinson as "an allegorical painting" that has
"an imprint of all the preoccupations which England then experienced"
(1878.8). The finest example, perhaps, of Robinson as "the mythic
man" is again the work of a Frenchman, Eugène Melchior de Vogüe
(1895.39). Here, every possible mythic connection is discovered in
Crusoe, ending with the "symbolic tableau" of the prostrate Friday,
Crusoe's foot planted on his head, showing him the prototype of the
ruthless conqueror and empire-builder.

In the years following Defoe's death, French criticism starts
for Robinson Crusoe in 1734, and includes altogether some 100 entries; it starts for Moll Flanders in 1816 and includes ten entries.
For each of the other five novels, with Philarète Chasles's splendid
essay on English pseudonyms, critical interest was first expressed
in 1844 and never exceeded eight critical entries (for Roxana). Not
only are the French critics numerous, they are the bright lights of
the Parisian world of criticism, and they publish in the most sophisticated journals. The list is in the order of first publication:
De Moncrif, Rousseau, Grivel, Taine, Hillebrand, Battier, Reynald,
Beljame, Cherbuliez, Pellissier, Jusserand, Eugène Muller, Marcel
Schwob, Vogüe, Augustin Filon, Edmond Pilon, Chinard, Mann, Bastide,
Dekobra, and Dottin. With fine intuitions and a unique sensitivity
not always accessible to their English counterparts, the French
critics add resonant voices to the tradition. To change the meta-
phor, at some of the most illuminating points along this trajectory,
one catches glimpses of how perfectly paired are the French critical
stances toward Defoe's novels and national literary phenomena: for
instance, Rousseau's exclusive choice of Robinson Crusoe for Émile
(1862.2), Garnier's selection of the same book for his Voyages imaginaires (1787-1789.1), Zolaesque readings of Moll Flanders in the
last decade of the nineteenth century (1890.14).

Clearly different, much less persistent, still making a unique contribution to the tradition, are the strains of criticism emanating from the main cultural centers of Germany. Once the criticism, as distinct from translations, gained a separate identity, it attracted illustrious scholars, philologists and linguists, bibliographers and literary historians, economists and political theorists--in short, scholars of a socio-political orientation rather than belletristic critics. Nonetheless, the roll-call of names, listed in the order of first publication, reads most impressively: Haken, Boll, Hettner, Ullrich, Wagner, Ermel, Fischer, Kippenburg, Biltz, Geissler, Hippe, Rötteken, Horten, Prica, Wackwitz, Dibelius, Brandl, Brüggeman, Polak, Meyer, Hübener, Liljegren, Shöffler, Richard Schmidt, and Schücking.

The interest in Robinson Crusoe as a Robinsonade never slackens, beginning with Johann Gottfried Schnabel's Die Insel Felsenburg (1731.8) and continuing for some sixty items. Aside from bare citations (1833.6), there is no major study (before 1925) by a German scholar or critic of any secondary novels. The publications of Hermann Ullrich (as in J.H. Schutt's bibliography, English Studies 13 [1931]:87-89) are almost exclusively concerned with Robinson Crusoe. F. Bergmeier, in 1905.2, shows interest in the written sources of the Journal of the Plague Year, and Wilhelm Dibelius, in his Englische Romankunst (1910.5), regards the novels as picaresque narrations, with gropings toward psychological analysis, but there is, astonishingly, little more.

German scholarship focused on Robinsonades and especially their philosophical significance. Controversy, it seems, breaks out in the oddest places. In the very work, Die Insel Felsenburg (1731-1743), where the term "Robinsonaden" is used for the first time, a debate arises over whether or not such tales should necessarily be true. Later, in Robinson der Jüngere (1779-1780.1), displaying a similar penchant for truth, J.H. Campe expresses dissatisfaction with "old Robinson's history," disagrees with Rousseau about the assistance that Crusoe obtained from the arts, and thus starts a major pedagogical disagreement. Again, Johann Rudolf Wyss, participating in a still later phase of the same controversy, rivals the original in popularity with his Schweizerische Robinson (1812-1813.1); he takes the radically altered story now more deeply into children's literature and creates his own constellation of scholarship and criticism. Karl Marx, in Das Kapital (1867.6), observes that Robinson Crusoe on his island has been "a favorite theme with political economists," and he constructs his famous paradigms of Crusoe as "independent modern man" to balance the dependent man of the middle ages. In sheer breadth of sweeping generalization, Marx can only be matched by Rousseau. Yet, in the making of the tradition, one notes that not a single critic or scholar, German, French, English, or American, makes reference to Marx's brilliant reading of Robinson Crusoe. Only a hint at it may be found in the controversy that broke out, in 1920, as Gustav Hübener posed a dichotomy between the philosophical view

of Defoe as an idealized heroic figure, prevalent in German scholarship, and the realistic unflattering view of him in Anglo-American
scholarship; Hübener then offered a third view, of both Robinson and
Defoe, as models of the early middle class, combining a stringent
capitalism and the artisan's self-sufficiency. Ultimately, the
controversy drew in the traditionalist Ullrich and S.B. Liljegren
on opposing sides. The great contributions of the German scholars
were of a different order, namely, Ullrich's monumental bibliography,
Robinson und Robinsonaden (1898.16) and his study of the "world-
book," Defoes "Robinson Crusoe" (1924.22).

Even with this wide ranging of scholarship and criticism over
almost two centuries and in six foreign languages, one feels inadequate to convey the seminal qualities of Robinson Crusoe and perhaps
two other works of the imagination, Moll Flanders and Journal of the
Plague Year. The criticism will simply have to speak for itself. On
other matters, the Defoe pieces both reflect and interpret the times,
as for example, the persistent habit of turning Robinson Crusoe into
pantomime, burlesque, or comedy, or the connections with graphic
arts, for instance, Hogarth's interest in Moll Flanders (1747.1) or
the many elaborate illustrations of Robinson Crusoe. When a number
of critics, such as Leslie Stephen, begin to detect a similarity
between Defoe's objectivity or realism and the new art of photography
(1868.20), we soon become aware of how readily an old master opens up
new vistas in the making of a tradition.

References Abbreviated in the Text

Titles of Defoe's works which appear frequently in the annotations are abbreviated as in the selected listings below (Section A); the place of publication is London unless otherwise specified, and the date of publication is given within parentheses. Inasmuch as the titles at the right are necessarily shortened ones, the curious reader who wishes to know complete titles should consult John Robert Moore's Checklist of the Writings of Daniel Defoe (2d ed. Hamden, Conn.: Archon Books, 1971). Only in a few instances are titles worded differently, as they appear in the books or articles being annotated, and this then will be to make a special point. In addition to the primary works, the important secondary works often mentioned in the annotations are abbreviated in the second listing (Section B). Secondary works dated before 1925 are annotated in their appropriate places in the Reference Guide.

A. Defoe's Works

Appeal to Honour and Justice	An Appeal to Honour and Justice, Tho' it be of His Worst Enemies. By Daniel De Foe (1715)
Capt. George Carleton	The Memoirs of an English Officer, Who serv'd in the Dutch War in 1672. To the Peace of Utrecht, in 1713. . . . By Capt. Carleton (1728)
Captain Singleton	The Life, Adventures, and Pyracies, of the Famous Captain Singleton (1720)
Colonel Jack	The History and Remarkable Life of the truly Honourable Col. Jacque, Commonly Call'd Col. Jack (1722)
Compleat English Gentleman	The Compleat English Gentleman by Daniel Defoe. Edited by Karl D. Bülbring. London: David Nutt, 1890
Complete English Tradesman	The Complete English Tradesman (1726; for 1725)
Conjugal Lewdness	Conjugal Lewdness: Or, Matrimonial Whoredom (1727)

Consolidator The Consolidator: Or, Memoirs Of Sundry Transactions From the World in the Moon (1705)

Due Preparations Due Preparations for the Plague As well for
Soul as Body (1722)

The Dumb The Dumb Philosopher; or Great Britain's Wonder
Philosopher (1719)

Duncan Campbell The History of the Life and Adventures of
Mr. Duncan Campbell (1720)

Essay upon An Essay upon Projects (1697)
Projects

Family Instructor The Family Instructor. In Three Parts (1715).
The Family Instructor. In Two Parts, vol. 2
(1718)

Farther Adventures The Farther Adventures of Robinson Crusoe;
of Robinson Crusoe Being the Second and Last Part Of His Life
(1719)

General History A General History Of The Robberies and Murders
of the . . . Of the most notorious Pyrates (1724)
Pyrates

History of . . . The History of the Remarkable Life of John
John Sheppard Sheppard (1724)

History of the The History of the Union Of Great Britain.
Union Edinburgh (1709)

Hymn to the A Hymn to the Pillory (1703)
Pillory

Journal of the A Journal of the Plague Year: Being Observa-
Plague Year tions or Memorials, Of the most Remarkable
Occurrences, As well Publick as Private, Which
happened in London During the last Great Visitation In 1665 (1722)

Life of Jonathan The Life of Jonathan Wild, From His Birth to
Wild his Death (1725)

Madagascar Madagascar: or, Robert Drury's Journal, During
Fifteen Years Captivity on that Island (1729)

Memoirs of a Memoirs of a Cavalier: Or A Military Journal
Cavalier Of the Wars in Germany, And the Wars in England; From the Year 1632, to the Year 1648
(1720)

Memoirs of Majr. Alexander Ramkins	The Memoirs of Majr. Alexander Ramkins, A Highland-Officer, Now in Prison at Avignon (1718)
Mesnager	Minutes of the Negotiations of Monsr. Mesnager At the Court of England, Towards the close of the last Reign (1717)
Moll Flanders	The Fortunes and Misfortunes of the Famous Moll Flanders, &c. (1722)
Mrs. Veal	A True Relation of the Apparition of One Mrs. Veal (1705)
Narrative . . . John Sheppard	A Narrative of All the Robberies, Escapes, &c. of John Sheppard (1724)
New Voyage Round the World	A New Voyage Round the World, By a Course never sailed before (1725)
Reformation of Manners	Reformation of Manners, A Satyr (1702)
Religious Courtship	Religious Courtship: Being Historical Discourses On The Necessity of Marrying Religious Husbands and Wives only. As Also of Husbands and Wives being of the same Opinions in Religion with one another (1722)
Review	Defoe's Review. Edited by Arthur Wellesley Secord. 22 vols. Facsimile Text Society. New York: Columbia University Press, 1938.
Robinson Crusoe	The Life and Strange Surprizing Adventures of Robinson Crusoe, Of York, Mariner (1719)
Roxana	The Fortunate Mistress: Or, A History Of The Life And Vast Variety of Fortunes Of Mademoiselle de Beleau, Afterwards Call'd The Countess de Wintselsheim, in Germany (1724)
A Second Volume (1705)	A Second Volume of the Writings Of the Author Of the True-Born Englishman (1705)
Serious Reflections ... of Robinson Crusoe	Serious Reflections During The Life and Surprising Adventures of Robinson Crusoe, With His Vision Of the Angelick World (1720)
Shortest-Way with the Dissenters	The Shortest-Way with the Dissenters: Or Proposals for the Establishment Of The Church (1702)

Tour

A Tour Thro' the Whole Island of Great Britain
(vol. 1, 1724; vol. 2, 1725; vol. 3, 1726)

True and Genuine
Account . . .
Jonathan Wild

The True and Genuine Account of The Life and
Actions of the Late Jonathan Wild (1725)

True-Born
Englishman

The True-Born Englishman. A Satyr (1701)

True Collection

A True Collection of the Writings Of The Author
of The True Born English-man. Corrected by
himself (1703)

B. Secondary Works

Aitken's Romances
and Narratives

Romances and Narratives by Daniel Defoe.
Edited by George A. Aitken. 16 vols. London:
J.M. Dent & Co., 1895.

Baker's History
of the English
Novel

Baker, Ernest A. The History of the English
Novel. Vol. 3, The Later Romances and the
Establishment of Realism. London: H.F. &
G. Witherby, 1929.

Ballantyne's
Memoir of Defoe
(1809)

Ballantyne, John. "A Biographical Memoir of
Daniel De Foe." In The Life and Adventures of
Robinson Crusoe. Edinburgh: John Ballantyne &
Co.; London: John Murray, 1809, 1:i-xvii.

Bibliothèque
nationale

"Daniel Defoe." In Catalogue générale des
livres imprimés de la bibliothèque nationale.
Auteurs. Ministère de l'Instruction Publique
et des Beaux-Arts. Paris: Paul Catin, 1930,
36:988-1011; 1960-1964. Paris: Bibliothèque
Nationale, 1966, 3:440-41.

Boston Public
Library Catalog

A Catalog of the Defoe Collection in the Boston
Public Library. Boston: G.K. Hall & Co.,
1966.

Brigham (1957)

Brigham, Clarence S. "Bibliography of American
Editions of Robinson Crusoe to 1830." Proceed-
ings of the American Antiquarian Society
(October 1957). Reprint. Worcester, Mass.:
American Antiquarian Society, 1958, pp. 137-83.

British Library
General Catalogue

"Defoe (Daniel)." In The British Library
General Catalogue of Printed Books to 1975.
London, Munich, New York, Paris: K.G. Saur,
1981, 79:118-89.

Burch (1932) Burch, Charles Eaton. "British Criticism of Defoe as a Novelist: 1719-1860." Englische Studien 67, no. 2 (1932):178-98.

Burch (1934) Burch, Charles Eaton. "Defoe's British Reputation, 1869-1894." Englische Studien 68, no. 3 (1934):410-23.

CBEL H[utchins], H[enry] C[linton]. "Daniel Defoe (1660-1731)." In The Cambridge Bibliography of English Literature. Edited by F.W. Bateson. 4 vols. New York: Macmillan; Cambridge: University Press, 1941, 2:495-514.

Chalmers's Bibliography (1790) Chalmers, George. "A List of Writings . . . undoubtedly Defoe's" and "A List of Books . . . supposed to be Defoe's." In The Life and Strange Surprizing Adventures of Robinson Crusoe. 2 vols. London: John Stockdale, 1790, 2:441-56.

Chalmers's Life of Daniel De Foe Chalmers, George. The Life of Daniel De Foe. London: John Stockdale, 1785; 1786; 1790; 1841.

Critical Heritage Defoe: The Critical Heritage. Edited by Pat Rogers. London and Boston: Routledge & Kegan Paul, 1972.

Defoe's Library (1970) The Libraries of Daniel Defoe and Phillips Farewell. Edited by Helmut Heidenreich. Berlin: Freie Universität Berlin, 1970.

DNB The Dictionary of National Biography. Edited by Sir Leslie Stephen and Sir Sidney Lee. Reprint. 66 vols. London: Oxford University Press, 1963-1965.

Dottin's Daniel De Foe et ses romans Dottin, Paul. Daniel De Foe et ses romans. 3 vols. Paris: Les Presses Universitaires de France; London: Oxford University Press, 1924.

Filmographic Dictionary of World Literature Thiery, Herman [Johan Daisne]. Dictionnaire filmographic de la littérature mondiale. Filmographic Dictionary of World Literature. Filmographisches Lexicon der Weltliteratur. Filmografisch lexicon der wereldliteratur. 2 vols. Gent: E. Storyscientia, 1971-1975. Supplements, 1977, 1978.

Gove

Gove, Philip Babcock. The Imaginary Voyage in Prose Fiction. New York: Columbia University Press, 1941. Reprint. London: Holland Press, 1961.

Hammerschmidt

Hammerschmidt, Hildegard. "Daniel Defoe: Articles in Periodicals (1950-1980)." Bulletin of Bibliography 40, no. 2 (June 1983):90-102.

Hazlitt's Works
of Daniel De Foe
(1840-1843)

The Works of Daniel De Foe. Edited by William Hazlitt [the younger]. 3 vols. London: John Clements, 1840-1843.

Healey

The Letters of Daniel Defoe. Edited by George Harris Healey. Oxford: Clarendon Press, 1955.

Heidenreich and
Heidenreich

Daniel Defoe: Schriften zum Erzählwerk. Edited by Regina Heidenreich and Helmut Heidenreich. Wege der Forschung, vol. 339. Darmstadt: Wissenschaftliche Buchgesellschaft, 1982.

Howell's Life
. . . of Selkirk
(1829)

Howell, John. The Life and Adventures of Alexander Selkirk; Containing the Real Incidents upon Which the Romance of Robinson Crusoe is Founded. Edinburgh: Oliver & Boyd; London: Geo. B. Whittaker, 1829.

Hutchins's "Robinson Crusoe"
and Its Printing
(1925)

Hutchins, Henry Clinton. "Robinson Crusoe" and Its Printing 1719-1731: A Bibliographical Study. New York: Columbia University Press, 1925.

Lee's Defoe
(1869)

Lee, William. Daniel Defoe: His Life, and Recently Discovered Writings: Extending from 1716 to 1729. 3 vols. London: John Camden Hotten, 1869.

London Stage
1660-1800

The London Stage 1660-1800 . . . Part 5 (1776-1800). Edited by Charles Beecher Hogan. 4 vols. Carbondale: Southern Illinois University Press, 1968.

Mann

Mann, William Edward. Robinson Crusoé en France: Étude sur l'influence de cette oeuvre dans la littérature francaise. Paris: Typographie A. Davis, 1916.

Maynadier's Works
of Daniel Defoe

The Works of Daniel Defoe. Edited by G.H. Maynadier. 16 vols. New York: Thomas Y. Crowell, 1902-1904.

Minto's <u>Defoe</u>
(1879)

Minto, William. <u>Daniel Defoe</u>. English Men of Letters. London: Macmillan & Co., 1879.

Moore's <u>Checklist</u>

Moore, John Robert. <u>A Checklist of the Writings of Daniel Defoe</u>. 2d ed. Hamden, Conn.: Archon Books, 1971.

Moore's <u>Daniel Defoe</u> (1958)

Moore, John Robert. <u>Daniel Defoe: Citizen of the Modern World</u>. Chicago: University of Chicago Press, 1958.

Moore's <u>Defoe in the Pillory</u> (1939)

Moore, John Robert. <u>Defoe in the Pillory and Other Studies</u>. Indiana University Publications, Humanities Series, no. 1. Bloomington: Indiana University Press, 1939.

Morley's <u>Earlier Life</u> (1889)

<u>The Earlier Life and the Chief Earlier Works of Daniel De Foe</u>. Edited by Henry Morley. The Carisbrooke Library, 3. London: George Routledge & Sons, 1889.

Nangle (1934)

Nangle, Benjamin Christie. <u>The Monthly Review, First Series, 1749–1789</u>. Oxford: Clarendon Press, 1934.

Nangle (1955)

Nangle, Benjamin Christie. <u>The Monthly Review, Second Series, 1790–1815</u>. Oxford: Clarendon Press, 1955.

<u>National Union Catalog</u>

<u>The National Union Catalog: Pre-1956 Imprints</u>. London: Mansell Foundation Publishing; Chicago: American Library Association, 1971.

<u>New CBEL</u> (1971)

N[ovak], M[aximillian] E. "Daniel Defoe." In <u>The New Cambridge Bibliography of English Literature</u>. 5 vols. Edited by George Watson. Cambridge: University Press, 1971, 2:cols.880–917.

<u>Nichols File of "The Gentleman's Magazine"</u>

Kuist, James M. <u>The Nichols File of "The Gentleman's Magazine": Attributions of Authorship and Other Documentation in Editorial Papers at the Folger Library</u>. Madison: University of Wisconsin Press, 1982.

<u>Nouvelle Biographie générale</u>

<u>Nouvelle Biographie générale depuis les temps les plus reculés jusqu'a nos jours</u>. 46 vols. Paris: Firmin Didot Frères, Fils & Co., 1857–1886. Reprint. Copenhagen: Rosenkilde & Bagger, 1963–1969.

Novak's Biblio-
graphical Guide
(1974)

Novak, M[aximillian] E. "Defoe." In The
English Novel: Select Bibliographical Guides.
Edited by A.E. Dyson. London: Oxford Univer-
sity Press, 1974, pp. 16-35.

Payne's "Anno-
tated Bibliog-
raphy" (1975)

Payne, William L. "An Annotated Bibliography
of Works about Daniel Defoe, 1719-1974": Parts
1-3. Bulletin of Bibliography 32, no. 1:3-14,
27, 32; no. 2:63-75, 87; no. 3:89-100, 132.

Poole's Index

Poole, William Frederick, et al. Poole's Index
to Periodical Literature [1802-1907]. Rev. ed.
6 vols. Gloucester, Mass.: Peter Smith, 1963.

Rogers's Robin-
son Crusoe (1979)

Rogers, Pat. Robinson Crusoe. London: George
Allen & Unwin, 1979.

Scott's criti-
cism (1827)

Scott, Sir Walter. "Daniel De Foe." In Miscellaneous Prose Works. Vol. 4, Biographical
Memoirs. Edinburgh: Cadell & Co.; London:
Longman, Rees, Orme, Brown, & Green, 1827,
pp. 280-321.

Scott's Novels
of Daniel De Foe
(1809-1810)

The Novels of Daniel De Foe. Edited by Sir
Walter Scott. 12 vols. Edinburgh: John
Ballantyne & Co. and Brown and Crombie; London:
Longman, Hurst, Rees, & Orme, 1809-1810.

Secord (1924)

Secord, Arthur Wellesley. Studies in the
Narrative Method of Defoe. University of Illi-
nois Studies in Language and Literature, 9.
Urbana: University of Illinois Press, 1924.

Shakespeare Head
Edition of the
Novels

The Shakespeare Head Edition of the Novels and
Selected Writings of Daniel Defoe. 14 vols.
Oxford: Basil Blackwell, 1927-1928.

Shiels's Life
of Defoe (1753)

Cibber, Theophilus, and Shiels, Robert.
"Daniel De Foe." The Lives of the Poets of
Great Britain and Ireland. 4 vols. London:
R. Griffiths, 1753, 4:313-25.

Stoler's Bibliog-
raphy

Stoler, John A. Daniel Defoe: An Annotated
Bibliography of Modern Criticism, 1900-1980.
New York and London: Garland Publishing Co.,
1984.

Sutherland's
Defoe

Sutherland, James. Defoe. 2d ed. London:
Methuen & Co., 1950.

References Abbreviated in the Text

Trent

Trent, William P. "Defoe--The Newspaper and the Novel." In Cambridge History of English Literature. Edited by A.W. Ward and A.R. Waller. 14 vols. New York: G.P. Putnam's Sons; Cambridge: University Press, 191 , 9:1-28, 463-82.

Ullrich's Robinson und Robinsonaden

Ullrich, Hermann. Robinson und Robinsonaden. Bibliographie, Geschichte, Kritik. Ein Beitrag zur vergleichenden Litteraturgeschichte, im Besonderen zur Geschichte des Romans und zur Geschichte der Jugendlitteratur. Teil 1. Bibliographie. Litterarhistorische Forschungen, 7. Weimar: Emil Felber, 1898.

Ullrich's Supplement/Bibliographie (1907-1908)

Ullrich, Hermann. "Zur Bibliographie der Robinsonaden. Nachträge und Ergänzungen zu meiner Robinson-Bibliographie." Zeitschrift für Bücherfreunde 11 (1907-1908):444-56, 489-98.

Watt's Rise of the Novel

Watt, Ian. The Rise of the Novel: Studies in Defoe, Richardson and Fielding. London: Chatto & Windus, 1957.

Wellesley Index

The Wellesley Index to Victorian Periodicals 1824-1900. Edited by Walter E. Houghton. 3 vols. Toronto: University of Toronto Press; London: Routledge & Kegan Paul, 1966-1979.

Wilson's Memoirs of Defoe (1830)

Wilson, Walter. Memoirs of the Life and Times of Daniel De Foe. 3 vols. London: Hurst, Chance & Co., 1830.

Works (1840-1841)

The Novels and Miscellaneous Works of Daniel De Foe. 20 vols. Oxford and London: Thomas Tegg, 1840-1841.

Wright (1894)

Wright, Thomas. The Life of Daniel De Foe. London, Paris, and Melbourne: Cassell & Co., 1894.

Wright (1931)

Wright, Thomas. The Life of Daniel Defoe. Bi-Centenary Edition. London: C.J. Farncombe & Sons, 1931.

Writings about Daniel Defoe, 1731-1924

1731

1   BAVIUS SENIOR TO BAVIUS JUNIOR. Grub-street Journal, no. 90
     (23 September):1.
         Presents a witty epistle "from the Elysian Fields" on the
admission of "that universal Genius Mr. D– F-e, lately arrived,"
into our regular Grubean Society among the poets. He frequently
entertains us with accounts of how he wrote simultaneously "two
celebrated Papers, one on the Whig, and the other on the Tory
side," and pleased both parties; and of how booksellers put off
their authors. See James T. Hillhouse, The Grub-Street Journal
(Durham, N.C.: Duke University Press, 1928), pp. 48–49. Reprinted: Gentleman's Magazine 1, no. 9 (September, 1731):386–87.

2   "Deaths and Promotions in April, 1731." Gentleman's Magazine
     1, no. 4 (April):174.
         Under "Deaths": "Mr. Daniel De Foe, sen. eminent for his
many Writings."

3   "Domestic News." Grub-street Journal, no. 69 (29 April):3.
         Under the date, Wednesday, 28 April, D.J. gives a favorable
estimate of Defoe, who died a few days ago, referring to his "natural genius" and championship of "civil and religious liberty."
C. gives the date as the previous Monday [26 April], and the
place as Rope Makers Alley in Moorfields. The obituary concludes
with mordant irony about the Shortest-Way with the Dissenters.
See James T. Hillhouse, The Grub-Street Journal (Durham, N.C.:
Duke University Press, 1928), p. 48.

4   "From the PEGASUS in Grub-street." Grub-street Journal,
     no. 69 (29 April):3.
         Immediately after the notice of Defoe's death appears the
story of how afflicted the members were "at the news of the death
of that ornament of our Society" that they adjourned, but only
after the Epigram was read, which some thought to be "the last
Work of the Great Author deceas'd" and in line with his principles. The eleven-line Epigram is quoted. See James T. Hillhouse, The Grub-Street Journal (Durham, N.C.: Duke University
Press, 1928), pp. 48–49.

5   "Librorum ex Bibliothecis Philippi Farewell, D.D. & Danielis De Foe, Gen. Catalogus." [London] Daily Advertiser, nos. 244-46 (13, 15, 16 November).

       Reproduces the title page of the Olive Payne catalogue announcing the sale of the combined libraries of the "learned" Philips Farewell and the "ingenious Daniel De Foe, Gent. lately deceas'd," and listing the broad classifications of the books and manuscripts. For the catalogue itself, see 1731.7 and Defoe's Library (1970).

*6   Obituary of Defoe's death. Read's Weekly Journal, 1 May.

       Quoted in Notes and Queries 160 (2 May 1931):308. Brief, positive estimate: "He had a great natural Genius; . . . in the main, he was in the Interest of Civil and Religious Liberty, in behalf of which he appear'd on several remarkable Occasions."

7   PAYNE, OLIVE. Librorum ex Bibliothecis Philippi Farewell, D.D. et Danielis De Foe, Gen. Catalogus: or a Catalogue of the Libraries of the Reverend and Learned Philips Farewell, D.D. Late Fellow of Trinity-College, Cambridge; and of the Ingenious Daniel De Foe, Gent. lately Deceas'd. [London: . Olive Payne], 53 pp.

       Only since Aitken unearthed the unique copy of the British Museum (1895.3) has the sales catalogue of Defoe's and Farewell's libraries begun to be used in the search for Defoe's sources. Describes on the title page the different classes of books which Payne offered for sale, beginning on 15 November, and "the very good conditions" of the books. Catalogues the books confusingly in order of format size and at times cryptically, with essential information lacking or inaccurate, so that exact identifications are difficult. For the complete sales catalogue in usable form, with introduction (35 pp.), full identification of items, and indexes, see Defoe's Library (1970).

8   SCHNABEL, JOHANN GOTTFRIED [Gisander]. Foreword to Wunderliche Fata einiger See-Fahrer, absonderlich Alberti Julii. 4 vols. Nordhausen: Johann Heinrich Gross, 1731-1743. Reprint. Edited by Peter Gugisch. Munich: Herbig, 1966, pp. 7-14.

       This important work, commonly known as Die Insel Felsenburg, uses the term "Robinsonaden" for the first time (Gove, p. 286). Contains ironic reference to the many Robinsonades, almost numberless, for almost every nation. Realizing that some readers take it amiss that the writers of these tales claim them to be true, he allows that a writer should be free to write what he wants to in this regard, so long as it does nobody any harm, no matter how far-fetched the material.   (P.E.C.)

1732

1   BIBLIOPOLA [pseud.]. Letter to Mr. Bavius. Grub-street Journal, no. 150 (9 November). Reprint (with changes).

"Mercenary Authors characteriz'd." <u>Gentleman's Magazine</u> 2, no. 23 (November 1732):1050-51.

Corrects Mr. Bavius's explication of an "emblematical Picture" that appeared in an earlier issue by noticing the favored treatment given to authors and the biases against booksellers. Explains, in reference to authors represented by Janus, that the face of the Janus is more like "a Mask than a natural Countenance, to shew, hireling Authors generally write under a Disguise, which they can change at Pleasure." The Janus also points to the genuine successors of Defoe "who is believed to have had a Hand at the same Time in a Whig and a Tory Paper." The reprint is much less severe with Defoe.

2   [OLDMIXON, JOHN.] <u>Mr. Oldmixon's Reply to the Late Bishop Atterbury's Vindication of Bishop Smallridge, Dr. Aldrich, and Himself. . . .</u> London: J. Pemberton; T. Cox, R. Ford & R. Hett; & J. Roberts, p. 7.

Refers to "a Book suppos'd to be written by Daniel Foe, by Direction, or Encouragement of the Quondam Treasurer Har[le]y who could not but be well acquainted with the Subject thus describ'd." Continues with a long quotation from the book, <u>Mesnager</u>, with page 76 cited in the text and the identification given in a marginal note. The quotation describes Laurence Hyde, first Earl of Rochester..

*3   SAVAGE, RICHARD [Iscariot Hackney]. <u>An Author to Be Lett</u> (1729), p. 4. In <u>A Collection of Pieces in Verse and Prose, Which have been publish'd on the Occasion of the Dunciad.</u> London: Lawton Gilliver.

Savage claims to be "deeply read in all Pieces of Scandal, Obscenity, and Profaneness" in a number of writers whom he names, including "D'Foe." Admirably reveals the subculture satirized by Pope in the <u>Dunciad</u>. The <u>Collection</u> reprints the Savage piece with some revisions. The 1729 publication is reprinted in the Augustan Reprint Society, no. 84 (Los Angeles: William Andrews Clark Memorial Library, 1960).

<u>1733</u>

1   "The <u>Daily Courant</u>, Jan. 18." <u>Gentleman's Magazine</u> 3, no. 25 (January):19-20.

Writer in the <u>Courant</u> questions the fairness and honesty of those opposed to the Administration's Excise Tax. Mr. D'anvers is like Defoe who "would write an Answer to Books before they were published; and . . . once he writ an Answer to a Book that was never published"; D'anvers followed the example of "so mercenary a Writer, for whom he takes every Occasion to express so great a Contempt."

1734

1 LENGLET-DUFRESNOY, N[ICOLAS] [C. Gordon De Percel]. Biblio-
theque des romans. In De l'usage des romans. 2 vols. Amsterdam: De Poilras, 2:341. Reprint. Geneva: Slatkine
Reprints, 1970.
    Makes a strong defense of novels and their usefulness; and
lists (among the French novels in a miscellaneous classification)
La Vie & les avantures surprenantes de Robinson Crusoë, le tout
écrit par lui-même, 4 vols. (Amsterdam, 1720) by Thémiseul de
Saint-Hyacinthe, without any mention of Defoe.

1735

1 Corn-Cutter's Journal, nos. 74-76 (25 February; 4 and 11
March):[7 pp.].
    With a one-paragraph introduction, reprints the Argument
shewing, That a Standing Army, with Consent of Parliament, is not
inconsistent with a free Government, &c. Identifies Defoe as the
author, and observes that since "the Number of Forces now to be
raised for the Nation's Security, is the present universal Topick
of Discourse," the essay deserves to be reprinted. About Defoe,
the editor adds: "I know not whether to say of famous or infam-
ous Memory, for I think, before his Fall into Jacobitism, he as
fairly merited the former Epithet, as he afterwards justly deserved the latter." Describes the piece as written "with great
Strength of Argument, as well as Sprightliness of Stile." The
reference survives in Stace, 1829.4.

2 OLDMIXON, MR. [JOHN]. The History of England. London:
Thomas Cox, Richard Ford & Richard Hett, pp. 37, 235, 301,
456, 519, 536.
    Narrates events, generally in a hostile tone, about Daniel
Foe: (1) the City of London's celebration on Lord Mayor's day,
29 October 1689, with a banquet at Guildhall, to which William
III and Mary were escorted by leading citizens, including Daniel
Foe among the Dissenters; (2) the incident of the Kentish Petition at Maidstone, Kent, on 29 April 1701, with emphasis upon the
leader, Daniel Foe, "at that time a zealous Revolutioner and Dissenter," whose "daring dauntless Temper" was infused into the
Memorial he gave to the Speaker, Harley, on behalf of the people;
(3) the prosecution of Defoe following upon the Shortest-Way with
the Dissenters, with examination of the irony and the means for
persuading High Church to betray its true sentiments; (4) Oldmixon's conversation with Arthur Maynwaring about Michaelmas,
1710, in which Maynwaring mentioned Defoe's betrayal of Harley in
favor of Godolphin; (5) the first publication in 1713 of the
British Merchant, with important biographical comments on Defoe's
"genius" compared with Harley's; (6) Defoe's protection from
prosecution in writing pamphlets apparently favoring the Pretender in 1713, being then "in the Earl of Oxford's pay, as he said
himself to me and many more."

3   [SWIFT, JONATHAN.] <u>A Letter from a Member of the House of</u>
     <u>Commons in Ireland, to a Member of the House of Commons in</u>
     <u>England, Concerning the Sacramental Test</u> (1709). Reprint.
     In <u>The Works of J.S., D.D., D.S.P.D.</u> 4 vols. Dublin: George
     Faulkner, 4:4.
          Wearing the mask of a House of Commons member in Ireland
     writing a letter to a House of Commons member in England, publish-
     ed in 1709, turns vehemently upon "those weekly Libellers" who
     argue for the repeal of the Sacramental Test in both England and
     Ireland. Intended to reach "the Understandings of a great Num-
     ber," these papers have become "a necessary Part in Coffee house
     Furniture, and some Time or other happen to be read by Customers
     of all Ranks. . . . One of these Authors (the Fellow that was
     *<u>pilloryed</u>, I have forgot his Name) is indeed so grave, senten-
     tious, dogmatical a Rogue, that there is no enduring him; the
     <u>Observator</u> is much the brisker of the two; and, I think, farther
     gone of late in Lies and Impudence than his <u>Presbyterian</u> Bro-
     ther." The marginal notation gives the identification as "<u>Daniel</u>
     <u>Defoe</u>." See also 1752.1; 1755.1. Reprinted, in part: <u>Critical</u>
     <u>Heritage</u>.

1737

1   BAKER, HENRY [Henry Stonecastle]. "From my Chambers,
     Lincoln's Inn." <u>Universal Spectator, and Weekly Journal</u>,
     no. 466 (10 September).
          Comments on the popularity of voyages and travels, "for
     which Reason several fictitious Adventures and Voyages have been
     publish'd, and been received with as much Satisfaction as if
     every Page bore the strongest Testimony of Truth. For instance,
     the Life and Adventures of <u>Robinson Crusoe</u> has been read over the
     Whole Kingdom, and pass'd as many Editions as, perhaps any Book
     now extant." Though Crusoe's daily tasks are trifling, yet they
     are natural. But of the "fictitious Voyages," the most excellent
     is <u>Gulliver's Travels</u> both for "the romantic Air of the Travel-
     ler" and "the fine Strokes of the Satyrist."

1738

1   CHECKLEY, JOHN. <u>The Speech of Mr. John Checkley, upon His Try-</u>
     <u>al, At Boston in New England</u>. 2d ed. London: J. Applebee,
     p. 11.
          Checkley was tried for publishing a seditious libel Charles
     Leslie's <u>Short and Easy Method with the Deists</u> (1723), convicted,
     and sentenced on 27 November 1724. Cites Defoe as an example of
     the Deists, "their <u>Veteran Mercenary</u>, their Oracle"; mistakenly
     quotes three lines from Dryden's <u>Conquest of Granada</u> as if they
     were Defoe's (noted in 1897.8), and concludes: "This is their
     <u>Wild Notion</u> of an <u>independent State of Nature</u>." Reprinted:
     1831; 1897.8; Louisville, Ky.: Lost Cause Press, 1979.

2   A Letter to the Society of Booksellers, or the Method of Form-
     ing a True Judgment of the Manuscripts of Authors. London:
     J. Millan, pp. 13, 31.
          In this controversy between booksellers and authors, offers
     probably the first printed account of the famous anecdote:
     "Robinson Crusoe's Manuscript also run thro' the whole Trade, nor
     would any one print it, tho' the Writer D. Defoe was in good
     Repute with them, as an Author; until one of their Body (at last)
     of a forward and bustling Genius [William Taylor], sufficiently
     known, who had not, or, at least, is not thought to have had the
     best Choice of Copies, engag'd in the Publication; and it turned
     to such Account, that he gained no less than a thousand Guineas
     thereby, and 'tis believed, as much more has been acquired by it
     since that Time." In explaining such misjudgments by booksellers
     of a manuscript, the anonymous writer observes later that the
     sale of a book depends on "the Universality of the Subject, and
     that the most excellent do not meet with the greatest Success;
     and accordingly we find, that Robinson Crusoe sells quicker than
     Locke on Human Understanding. . . ." See also Hutchins's "Robin-
     son Crusoe" and Its Printing (1925), pp. 45-46 (n.7).

                                    1740

1   HILLIAR, ANTHONY. A Brief and Merry History of Great Britain.
     London: J. Roberts et al., pp. 18, 49.
          Pretends to be a translation by Hilliar from the Arabic of
     Ali Mohammed Hadji. Continues the tradition of Robinson Crusoe
     as containing "agreeable Lyes." Cheats in Physick are best regu-
     lated in England by "Tinctura Nervosa Cardiaca, or the Cordial
     Tincture, both which will enliven an Author, and cause him to
     write on either Side, in a most Nervous manner, recommended to
     the Publick, by the famous Mr. De Foe." The date of publication
     is given in the National Union Catalog as "[1730?]," but there is
     no evidence available for the early date.

                                    1741

*1   [DE BROSSES, CHARLES.] Histoire des navigations aux terres
     australes. 2 vols. Paris: Durand.
          This edition listed in National Union Catalog incorrectly
     at the Hispanic Society of America Library. See the earliest
     located edition, 1756.2.

2   "On Some of Our Moderns." London Magazine 10:97.
          A verse epigram of eight lines, closing with "Down in the
     kitchen, honest Dick and Doll, / Are studying Colonel Jack and
     Flanders Moll."

*3   The Secret History of Betty Ireland. London: Printed in the
     Year M.DCC.XLI, 35 pp.

                                    6

Although it first appeared with Colonel Jack, the work has
no known connection with Defoe. In the undated reprint [1750?]
published by S. Lee, the title page gives the quotation:

> Read Flanders Moll, the German Princess scan,
> Then Match our Irish Betty if you can;
> In Wit and Vice she did 'em both excel,
> And may be justly call'd a NONPAREIL.

Donald A. Stauffer, The Art of Biography in Eighteenth Century
England. Bibliographical Supplement (Princeton University Press,
1941), p. 130, describes the fifth and ninth editions as not
dated, and characterizes the work as "simple salacity."

1743

1   Catalogus Bibliothecae Harleianae. 5 vols. London: Thomas
    Osborne, 1:466; 2:922; 3:291; 4:824, 848.
        Useful to Chalmers's Life of Daniel De Foe (1790) in the
    early efforts to establish the canon of Defoe's works. Rodney
    M. Baine points out that although there were numerous Defoe items
    not identified as his, only five were "conservatively" assigned
    to Defoe by the compiler, Oldys or Dr. Johnson ("Chalmers' First
    Bibliography of Daniel Defoe," Texas Studies in Literature and
    Language 10, no. 4, Winter, 1969:563).

2   DE MONCRIF, FRANÇOIS AUGUSTIN PARADIS. "Réflexions sur quel-
    ques ouvrages faussement appellés: ouvrages d'Imagination."
    In Oeuvres mêlées, tant en prose qu'en vers. Reprint. Oeu-
    vres de Moncrif. New ed. 2 vols. Paris: Maràdan, 1791, 1:
    306-17.
        In an address first given before the Academy in 1741,
    argues categorically that novels of the marvellous and the super-
    natural, imaginary voyages, and fairy tales are not works of the
    imagination. Finds in Robinson Crusoe (as in Gulliver's Travels)
    the second of four sources or methods which make it unnecessary
    for authors to use the imagination, namely, that as in the
    Persian tales, one or more characters, such as Robinson Crusoe on
    a desert island, are placed in extraordinary and embarrassing
    situations.

1744

1   HARRIS, JOHN. Navigantium atque itinerantium Bibliotheca.
    Or, A Complete Collection of Voyages and Travels. 2 vols.
    London: T. Woodward et al., 1:150-84.
        In section 13 of Captain Woodes Rogers's narrative, tells
    the story of Alexander Selkirk's abandonment on the island of
    Juan Fernandez, and anticipates the later legend (1757.1) in the
    title, which ends with the words, "on which the Story of Robinson
    Crusoe was founded."

2   MEAD, RICHARD. A Discourse on the Plague. 9th ed. London:
    A. Millar & J. Brindley, pp. 105-6. Reprint. New York: AMS
    Press, 1978.
        Graphically describes the effects of "shutting up" persons
    infected with the plague: breaking out of "prison" through win-
    dows, "bribing the Watchmen at their Doors," sometimes even mur-
    dering them, the "hideous Shrieks of Horror and Despair"; flights
    into the country to live with friends, build huts or tents in the
    open fields, get on board ships lying in the river. Closes with a
    footnote reference to the Journal of the Plague Year as if it
    were an authentic historical document, but with no mention of
    Defoe as the author. Mead's first edition of his Short Discourse
    Concerning Pestilential Contagion was published in 1720, and
    could therefore not have taken information from Defoe's Journal.
    Mead's ninth edition, however, has been "corrected and enlarged,"
    and does include additional material from the Journal. Nine-
    teenth-century commentators became accustomed to noting that the
    eminent Dr. Richard Mead had accepted the Journal as an histori-
    cal source for the Plague of 1665.

                                1745

1   "Providence Displayed: Or, a Very Surprising Account of one
    Mr. Alexander Selkirk. . . ." In The Harleian Miscellany.
    Edited by William Oldys. Vol. 5. London: T. Osborne,
    pp. 402-6.
        This anonymous early account of Selkirk's experience on
    Juan Fernandez, as we learn from the notes to the reprint
    (1810.5), was mainly borrowed from Captain Woodes Rogers's Cruis-
    ing Voyage Round the World (1712). Includes the graphic descrip-
    tions of Selkirk when found, "a Man cloathed in Goat Skins, who
    seemed as wild as the Goats themselves"; his experience on the
    island for over four years; and "An Account of the Island of Juan
    Fernandez." Makes no mention of Defoe or Robinson Crusoe. See
    also 1806.1; 1810.5.

                                1746

1   RALPH, JAMES [A Lover of Truth and Liberty]. The History of
    England: During the Reigns of K. William, Q. Anne, and K.
    George I. 2 vols. London: F. Cogan & T. Waller, 2:998-99.
        Specifically, and in a hostile tone, mentions Defoe by name
    in describing the conflict (1701) between the House of Commons
    and the Kentish Petitioners. Sums up "the celebrated Tract,
    call'd, Jura populi Anglicani" as opposed to the Commons because
    it presumed to commit the Kentish Petitioners. Assigns to Defoe
    The Original Power of the Collective Body of the People of En-
    gland (1701), and identifies him ["Foe"] as "the Legion-Letter-
    Writer and author of The Present State of Jacobitism Considered
    (1701), and describes "the Aim of this Proteus of an Author" with
    respect to Jacobites.

1747

1 HOGARTH, WILLIAM. Plate 1, "The Fellow 'Prentices at Their
Looms." Industry and Idleness. Reproduced in Ronald Paulson,
Emblem and Expression: Meaning in English Art of the Eigh-
teenth Century. London: Thames & Hudson, 1975, p. 59.
    Shows the two apprentices, Francis Goodchild and Tom Idle,
as they appear in the twelve plates of Hogarth's Industry and
Idleness. In plate 1, focusses upon the two typically at work.
Clearly posted over Idle's head, to the left side of the plate,
"the ballad of Moll Flanders" stands out as his favorite. For
Goodchild, posted to the right side, are his favorite ballads, of
Dick Whittington and The London Prentice. See Paulson's discussion of the Hogarth tradition (pp. 58-78).

1748

1 Caledonia: A Poem in Honour of Scotland, and the People of
that Nation. London: W. Owen, 58 pp.
    Reprints Defoe's poem (1706), published with the preface
to Parliament and dedication to the Duke of Queensberry both
over his name. In this edition, completely effaces any sign of
Defoe's authorship, dedicates the poem to the Duke of Argyll, and
substantially alters the text to make the praises of Scotland
suitable to the mid-century.

2 "The Fate of the Mouse. A Tragick-comick Poem." London Magazine 17:329.
    Four lines of doggerel on tastes of readers in Defoe,
Bunyan, Fox's Lives.

3 [SMOLLETT, TOBIAS.] The Adventures of Roderick Random.
2 vols. London: J. Osborn, 2:283. Reprint. Edited by Paul-
Gabriel Boucé. Oxford English Novels. Oxford: Oxford University Press, 1979, p. 383.
    In telling Roderick about his efforts to have his tragedy
published (chap. 61 in first edition), Mr. Melopoyn has his poems
rejected by a third bookseller, and is asked if he has "never a
piece of secret history, thrown into a series of letters, or a
volume of adventures, such as those of Robinson Crusoe, and Colonel Jack, or a collection of conundrums, wherewith to entertain
the plantations."

1749

1 FIELDING, HENRY. The History of Tom Jones: A Foundling.
Edited by Martin C. Battestin and Fredson Bowers. Wesleyan
Edition. 2 vols. Oxford: Clarendon Press, 1974, 1:401, 422.
    Fielding's narrator (8, i), commenting upon "that Species
of Writing which is called the Marvellous," urges placing the

"memorable Story of the Ghost of George Villiers" in Drelincourt to keep "the Ghost of Mrs. Veale Company, at the Head of his Discourse upon Death," rather than in the Earl of Clarendon's history of the Rebellion. A few chapters later (8, v), Benjamin the Barber offers Tom Jones, after they have been drinking heartily, "several of the best books" to read in English, including Robinson Crusoe, and in fairly distinguished company. Fielding makes two earlier references to Robinson Crusoe (Champion, 20 March 1740; Jacobite's Journal, 27 February 1748), but curiously never refers to Defoe by name.

1750

1   [GRIFFITHS, RALPH.] Review of Robert Paltock's The Life and Adventures of Peter Wilkins, A Cornish Man. Monthly Review 4 (December):157.
      Author identified in Nangle (1934). Describes this "very strange performance" as "the illegitimate offspring of no very natural conjunction betwixt Gulliver's travels and Robinson Crusoe; but much inferior to the meaner of these two performances, either as to entertainment or utility." The comparison of the three works continues briefly in much the same vein.

[ca.1750]

1   LISTER, JAMES. "The Publisher of this Second Edition, to the Reader." In Memoirs of a Cavalier: or A Military Journal of the Wars in Germany, and the Wars in England. Leeds: James Lister et al., pp. iii-v.
      Asks who is the author of these "Historical Memoirs," and rejects any possibility of its being a romance: "if it be, 'tis a Romance the likest to Truth that I ever read." On the basis of the content, proposes Andrew Newport, Esq., second son to Richard Newport, of High Ercoll, Esq. So firmly entrenched did this identification of the Cavalier become as a tradition, which even affects the text, it reappears today in unexpected places. No mention of Defoe's name is made anywhere in the Leeds edition. The date around 1750 is given in the Boston Public Library Catalog, nos. 484, 485.

1752

1   BOYLE, JOHN, FIFTH EARL OF CORK AND ORRERY. Remarks on the Life and Writings of Dr. Jonathan Swift, Dean of St. Patrick's, Dublin. London: A. Millar, pp. 191-95.
      Examines Swift's Letter . . . Concerning the Sacramental Test, Written in the Year 1708. Points to "one particular piece of satyr, that is entirely in Swift's own style and manner," and quotes his anonymous attack: "One of these authors (the fellow that was pilloried, I have forgot his name). . . ." Identifies

"the fellow" as Daniel Defoe, and insists that Swift knew the
name well and remembered it, but that here he shows "great art in
the nicest touches of satyr," which he later describes as being
"like the bite of a rattle snake . . . more venemously dangerous
than the wounds of a common serpent."

1753

1   CIBBER, [THEOPHILUS], and [SHIELS, ROBERT]. "Daniel De Foe."
    In The Lives of the Poets of Great Britain and Ireland.
    4 vols. London: R. Griffiths, 4:313-25.
        With Robert Shiels generally regarded as the main author,
    introduces certain themes which become more pronounced in later
    biographies, such as Defoe's devotion to the principles of the
    Revolution, his "very true notion of civil liberty," his under-
    standing "as well as any man, the civil constitution of the king-
    dom, which indeed was his chief study," the tendency to view him
    as a popular hero for his fortitude during the punishment in the
    pillory. Even though "poetry was far from being the talent of
    De Foe," places an inordinate emphasis on the verse satires: the
    True-Born Englishman, Reformation of Manners, More Reformation,
    and Hymn to the Pillory. Admires the "perspicuity and strength"
    of the prose works, the Original Power of the Collective Body of
    the People of England, Examined and Asserted (1702) and the
    Shortest-Way with the Dissenters. Among Defoe's "many works of
    fancy," assigns a special status to Robinson Crusoe as emerging
    from an imagination "fertile, strong, and lively," written in "so
    natural a manner, and with so many probable incidents, that, for
    some time after its publication, it was judged by most people to
    be a true story." In the list of thirteen "principal perfor-
    mances," includes (aside from Robinson Crusoe) "Memoirs of the
    Plague, published in 1665," "History of Colonel Jack," and "Cleve-
    land's Memoirs, &c. . . . ." Excludes: Memoirs of a Cavalier,
    Captain Singleton, Moll Flanders, and Roxana. In opposition to
    Pope's attack in the Dunciad, generally assesses Defoe as "a man
    of the strongest natural powers, a lively imagination, and solid
    judgment, which, joined with an unshaken probity in his moral
    conduct, and an invincible integrity in his political sphere,
    ought not only to screen him from the petulant attacks of satire,
    but transmit his name with some degree of applause to posterity."
    See also 1787.12, which unabashedly borrows this "life," and
    reproduces it with a few minor changes over the name of William
    Shiells, as an introduction to one of Francis Noble's publica-
    tions. Reprinted: Anglistica & Americana 17, Hildesheim: Georg
    Olms, 1968; in part, Critical Heritage.

1755

1   SWIFT, JONATHAN. A Letter from a Member of the House of
    Commons in Ireland, to a Member of the House of Commons in

England, Concerning the Sacramental Test. In The Works of
Jonathan Swift, D.D. Edited by John Hawkesworth. 6 vols.
London: C. Bathurst, 2:120-38.

In annotating Swift's parenthetical comment, "the fellow
that was pilloried (I have *forgot his name)," Hawkesworth quotes
Orrery, explaining the asterisk, that the fellow was Daniel Defoe, "whose name Swift well knew and remembered, but the circumstance of the pillory was to be introduced, and the manner of
introducing shews great art in the nicest touches of satire, and
carries all the marks of ridicule, indignation, and contempt."
For other reprintings of Swift's Works, see the listing in the
New CBEL, 2:1054. See also 1735.3; 1752.1.

1756

*1   BARROW, JEAN. Abrégé chronologique ou histoire des découvér-
     tes faites par les Européens dans les différentes parties du
     monde. Translated by M. [Jean Baptiste] Targe. Paris:
     Saillant et al.
         Fréron, reviewing the 1765 [i.e., 1766] enlarged edition of
     the Abrégé chronologique in L'Année littéraire, 1767.2, noted
     that Targe formed the design of translating the work, and brought
     it out, in 1756; and later brought out an augmented edition in
     1766. See 1765.1; 1766.2.

2   [DE BROSSES, CHARLES.] "XXXIX. Woodes Roggers [sic], En
     Polynèsie & en Australasie." In Histoire des navigations aux
     terres australes. 2 vols. Paris: Durand. Reprint. Biblio-
     theca Australiana, no. 1. Amsterdam: N. Israel; New York:
     Da Capo Press, 1967, 2:185.
         While narrating the accounts of navigations to south sea
     lands, turns to the adventures of Alexander Selkirk and the Mos-
     quito Indian, both abandoned at different times on Juan Fernan-
     dez. Writing from personal impressions, observes that the two
     became the subject of the English novel, Robinson Crusoe, which
     "the singularity of the event made us read eagerly in our youth."
     Recalls the impression one had then for this book "composed by
     Daniel de Foë," namely, that "there is some truth to the fabulous
     history of the pretended Robinson." Summarizes also the informa-
     tion about the Mosquito Indian, in 1681, on Juan Fernandez—drawn
     from Ringrose, Captain Sharp, and Dampier. See also 1741.1.

3   [PARFAICT, FRANÇOISE and CLAUDE.] "Robinson." In Diction-
     naire des Théâtres de Paris. 7 vols. Paris: Lambert,
     4:504-5.
         Refers briefly to a lost one-act piece of Lesage and
     Orneval, performed successfully at Saint-Germain market in 1721
     while the novel was still popular.

1757

1   ENTICK, JOHN. A New Naval History: or, Compleat View of the
     British Marine. London: R. Manby, W. Reeve, W. Bizet,
     P. Davey, B. Law, & J. Scott, pp. 670-71.
         Starts the legend of Defoe's receiving notes from Selkirk
     on his adventures, and of unscrupulously turning them into the
     immensely successful Robinson Crusoe. Concludes Woodes Rogers's
     account with the legend full-blown. See an anticipation by
     Harris, 1744.1.

1762

1   Annales typographiques, ou notice du progrès des connoissances
     humaines 2 (November):428.
         Under "Belles-Lettres," lists the new edition of La Vie et
     les aventures surprenantes de Robinson Crusoe. 3 vols. (Paris:
     Cailleau & Bauche, 1761). Briefly mentions that "this allegor-
     ical novel" has been known for a long time in France, and its
     third volume includes "the reflections of the author." Makes no
     reference to Defoe.

2   ROUSSEAU, J[EAN]-J[ACQUES]. Émile: ou de l'Éducation.
     2 vols. Frankfurt: [n.p.], 2:41-48.
         First hints at his famous interpretation of Robinson Crusoe
     in an apparently casual reference, in book 2, to a desert island
     as among the places we might raise a child without any feelings;
     and again, more pointedly, at the beginning of book 3, where Jean-
     Jacques is concerned with the third stage of Émile's childhood,
     and he wants to illustrate how preoccupied human beings should be
     with nature rather than with books about nature. Refers to a phi-
     losopher on a desert island with instruments and books, but one
     who will not look at a single book, preferring instead to look
     directly at every corner of his island. Although he hates books,
     Jean-Jacques offers a single gift of a book for Émile, Robinson
     Crusoe--"the happiest treatise on natural education." He will
     make this the first book his pupil will read, and for some time
     it will be his entire library. So thoroughly will Émile absorb
     himself in the book, he will think himself, and even become, Rob-
     inson Crusoe--totally self-efficient. Jean-Jacques does not see
     this relationship of Émile to nature as being anything permanent.
     Soon the passions will take over; soon it will be the turn of
     "social man." But for now the lesson of Robinson Crusoe is the
     essential means for Émile to measure the relative value of
     things--to see himself "in the place of an isolated man, and to
     judge everything as this man himself ought to judge of it with
     regard to its own utility." So close should be Émile's identifi-
     cation with Robinson Crusoe, to bring about this state of mind,
     he must even see himself dressed like him in all respects,
     "except for the parasol, which he will not need." From this imi-
     tation, too, Émile will learn "the practice of the natural arts"

which suffices for "solitaries" or "savages." The physical needs
of the individual are soon followed by those of society, and so
Émile must turn next to men working together. Jean-Jacque enun-
ciates here the concept of "the division and distribution of
labor." For studies of the influence, reprintings and translations, see the CBEL (1941) and the New CBEL (1971); see also the
translations by Rogers, in Critical Heritage; and the introduction and translation, in Allan Bloom, Émile or On Education (New
York: Basic Books, 1979).

1762-1764

1   Zhizn' i prikliucheniia Robinzona Kruza prirodnago angli-
    chanina [The life and adventures of Robinson Crusoe, trueborn
    Englishman]. 2 vols. Translated from the French by Y[akov]
    T[rusov]. St. Petersburg: Imperial Academy of Sciences.
       In Russian. Translation only: vol. 1, 1762; vol. 2, 1764.
    The third edition was published in 1787; fourth edition, 1797.
                                                       (A.L.S.R.)

1764

1   BAKER, DAVID ERSKINE. The Companion to the Play-house: or,
    An Historical Account of all the Dramatic Writers (and their
    Works) that have appeared in Great Britain and Ireland.
    London: [publisher?], vol. 1, s.v. The Careless Husband.
       Colley Cibber's comedy The Careless Husband, wrongly dated
    1700, attributed also to the Duke of Argyle, to whom it was ded-
    icated; and to Defoe and Manwaring. The date was corrected to
    1704 in the reprints. Reprinted, with additions and changes:
    1782.1 and 1812.2.

2   FOOTE, SAMUEL. The Patron, A Comedy, in Three Acts, As Per-
    formed at the Theatre-Royal, Haymarket. In The Works of
    Samuel Foote, Esq. with Remarks on Each Play, and an Essay on
    the Life, Genius and Writings of the Author. By Jon Bee, Esq.
    3 vols. London: Sherwood, Gilbert & Piper, 1830, 2:239-90.
       Basing the comedy on one of Marmontel's Contes Moraux,
    models the main satirical character, Sir Thomas Lofty, on George
    Bubb Doddington, and works out the comical effects in having him
    egotistically write a play on Robinson Crusoe which he will have
    his niece's suitor, Richard Bever, present to an audience, and
    claim if it is a failure and assign to Sir Thomas if it is a
    success. In an early dialogue, introduces the character Puff
    speaking about authors whose ears have been "cropped" or who have
    been showered with eggs as they mount the pillory; and the char-
    acter, Dactyl, who lists "the Life of Moll Flanders, with cuts"
    as being part of Puff's trade. Turns attention to Sir Thomas's
    "chef d'oeuvre": his boasting of "the whole fable [as] finely
    conducted, and the character of Friday, qualis ab incepto, nobly
    supported throughout"; Bever's reading from the manuscript about

14

"some savages, dancing a saraband"; finally the audience's reac-
tion against the play, including a quarrel "between the gentry
and a black-a-moor man." See also Simon Trefman, Sam. Foote, Comedian, 1720-1777 (New York University Press, 1971), pp. 143-45.

1765

1   BARROW, JOHN. A Collection of Authentic, Useful, and Enter-
    taining Voyages and Discoveries, Digested in a Chronological
    Series. London: J. Knox, 2:97.
        Briefly interrupts the account of Alexander Selkirk as told
    from Captain Woodes Rogers's narrative: "This account gave
    Daniel Defoe, to whom Selkirk sent his papers in order to their
    being prepared for the press, the hint of writing his ingenious
    romance of Robinson Crusoe." See the expanded version of this
    statement in 1766.2.

1766

1   "Advertisements" in [Defoe's] A Military History of Germany
    and of England. Edinburgh: Ebenezer Wilson, pp. iii-iv.
        Nowhere in the entire book does Defoe's name appear as the
    author. Explains that three editions bear the title Memoirs of a
    Cavalier in Germany and England: the first published in London,
    1720; the second at Leeds "a considerable time afterwards"; the
    third at Edinburgh, 1759; and now the fourth, since the others
    are out of print. Omits the first part of the old title because
    the word "Cavalier" has both an English and a French meaning, and
    "conveys an idea of the book, very different from that which
    every reader will acquire from the perusal of it"; it has served
    to reduce the number of readers and lessen the "general esteem"
    of the book. Supports the view that the Military History is not
    a romance, and reprints "The Preface of the First Publishers" and
    "Preface to the Second Edition" (pp. v-xv).

2   BARROW, JEAN. Abrégé chronologique ou histoire des découver-
    tes faites par les Européens dans les différentes parties du
    monde. Translated by [Jean Baptiste] Targe. Paris:
    Saillant, et al., 10:158-68.
        Summarizes the discovery on Juan Fernandez, in February
    1709, of Alexander Selkirk by men from Captain Woodes Rogers's
    ships--the castaway abandoned on the desert island for more than
    four years--the story told in memorable details by the Captain
    himself. Interrupts the narrative flow to express a strongly
    held view: "When Selkirk returned to England, he gave his mem-
    oirs to Daniel Defoe who was since pilloried, in order that he
    edit them [or: write them up] to make them public: but this
    honest writer appropriated them, and composed the novel of Rob-
    inson Crusoe; and when he returned Mr. Selkirk's papers, the voy-
    ager was almost deprived, by this fraud, of any benefit that he
    might have derived from them." See also 1756.1; 1765.1; 1767.2.

3   FEUTRY, AIMÉ AMBROISE JOSEPH. Preface to <u>Robinson Crusoé,</u>
     <u>nouvelle imitation de l'Anglois</u>. 2 vols. Amsterdam and
     Paris: Charles J. Panckoucke, pp. i-iv.
         Assigns the authorship of <u>Robinson Crusoe</u> to Richard
     Steele, "one of the writers of the <u>Spectator</u>." Explains his
     reasons for writing this adaptation: Rousseau's choice of <u>Robin-</u>
     <u>son Crusoe</u> for Émile, an interest in pedagogy and new systems of
     education. Finds that the situation of <u>Crusoe</u> is "much better
     described here than our philosophers could do it, at least . . .
     with more truth and simplicity." Admits that the book can be
     pruned, without the least alteration of the character which
     distinguishes it from other novels. See also 1769.4; 1775.2-3;
     Mann.

4   FRÉRON, [ÉLIE CATHERINE]. Review of Feutry's <u>Robinson Crusoé.</u>
     <u>Nouvelle imitation de l'Anglois</u>, 1766. In <u>L'Année littéraire</u>.
     Amsterdam; Paris: Lacombe, 3:133-40.
         While the attention is directed to the "new imitation,"
     provides information on the status in France of Defoe's <u>Robinson</u>
     <u>Crusoe</u>. Notes that the early translation [1720] had rendered it
     "common" and generally liked; and corrects Feutry's error of
     attributing <u>Robinson Crusoe</u> to Richard Steele. Stresses certain
     philosophical differences which Feutry introduced for his
     "recasting" of the original, namely, in making the castaway find
     strength and resources in his reason and his trust in God. Clos-
     es the review curiously with an expression of thanks to Feutry
     for (among other things) "extricating this novel from the jumble
     [or rubbish] of the old translation."

5   GOLDSMITH, OLIVER. <u>The Vicar of Wakefield</u>. Salisbury:
     F. Newberry. Reprint. <u>Collected Works of Oliver Goldsmith</u>.
     Edited by Arthur Friedman. Oxford: Clarendon Press, 1966,
     4:45, 83.
         In chap. 7, Olivia (so named because her mother had been
     reading romances during pregnancy) insists that she has skill
     enough in controversy to convert the apparently free-thinking
     Thornhill. To Vicar Primrose, she says she has read "the dis-
     putes between Thwackum and Square; the controversy between
     Robinson Crusoe and Friday the savage, and I am now employed in
     reading the controversy in Religious courtship." In the very
     next chapter, the Primroses arrange to have a "large historical
     family piece" drawn by a limner. When the picture is finished,
     they are dismayed: "One compared it to Robinson Crusoe's long-
     boat, too large to be removed."

6   [OLDYS, WILLIAM.] "Arbuthnot, John." In <u>Biographia Britanni-</u>
     <u>ca: or, the Lives of the Most Eminent Persons . . . To which</u>
     <u>are added, A Supplement and Appendix</u>. 6 vols. London: J.
     Walthoe et al., vol. 6, pt. 2, note [N].
         Extended footnote comment about Arbuthnot's having "several
     brats illegitimately fathered upon him, among which the famous
     romance of <u>Robinson Crusoe</u> is worth mentioning." The note as-

signs the work to Defoe, and repeats biographical information and
critical judgments which were known since Shiels's Life of Defoe
(1753). In the second edition of Biographia Britannica (1788),
the content of note [N] is removed. See also 1770.1. Reprinted:
Hildesheim, West Germany: Georg Olms, 1969.

1767

1   The Female American; or, the Adventures of Unca Eliza Wink-
     field. Compiled by Herself. 2 vols. London: Francis Noble
     & John Noble. Reprint. New York and London: Garland Publish-
     ing, 1974, 2:15-16.
         As the female narrator continues her next lengthy escapade,
     her abandonment on an uninhabited island, she interrupts with a
     digression. Her experiences have taken on Crusoe-like coloring.
     Now, since her story is set in the time of James I, she suddenly
     predicts that such events, as here, will be famous throughout
     Europe, "in different languages, and in succeeding ages, . . .
     the delight of the ingenious and inquisitive." She foresees
     "some future bold adventurer's imagination, lighted up by my
     torch, will form a fictitious story of one of his own sex, the
     solitary inhabitant of a desolate island.*" In the note she
     identified Robinson Crusoe, by name, "which is inferior to her
     own, as fiction is to truth." See Tremaine McDowell, "An Ameri-
     can Robinson Crusoe," American Literature 1, no. 3 (November,
     1929):307-9.

2   FRÉRON, [ÉLIE CATHERINE]. "Lettre I. Abrégé chronologique ou
     histoire des découvertes faites par les Européens dans les dif-
     ferentes parties du monde." In L'Année littéraire. Amster-
     dam; Paris: Lacombe, 1:3-30.
         Reviews the enlarged edition of Abrégé chronologique which
     was extracted by Jean Barrow and translated from English into
     French by Jean Baptiste Targe, and probably first published in
     1756 and again in 1765 [1766]. Places Alexander Selkirk's "dis-
     coveries" in Juan Fernandez chronologically by retelling the
     story of Captain Woodes Rogers's voyage around the world--curi-
     ously, in the year 1717--coming upon Selkirk, in a voyage that
     started from the Amazon River and went to the desert isle, Juan
     Fernandez. Quotes the source directly that "[Selkirk] gave his
     Memoirs to Daniel de Foe . . . to write them up to make them
     public," but that Defoe misappropriated the papers, created the
     novel Robinson Crusoe from them, and by this fraud ["tromperie"]
     deprived Selkirk of any benefits. See also 1756.1; 1765.1;
     1766.2.

3   HARTE, WALTER. The History of the Life of Gustavus Adolphus,
     King of Sweden, Surnamed the Great. 2d ed. rev. 2 vols.
     London: J. Hinton & R. Baldwin, W. Johnston; Bath: W. Freder-
     ick, 1:xxxiii; 2:198.

In the first edition (1759), Harte noted that the Swedish King's forces had difficulties in constructing a bridge over the River Lech, and he declined to tell the story, "having some doubts concerning the authenticity of the narration" (p. 139). At this point, in a footnote to the second edition, Harte adds the information that identifies the narrative as "Memoirs of a Cavalier, 8vo, Printed at Leeds, in Yorkshire, about the year 1740," and includes it in a list of 117 books "made use of in composing The Life of Gustavus Adolphus"--but nowhere mentions Defoe as the author. Reprinted: 1777; 1807.

1768

1   FRÉRON, [ÉLIE CATHERINE]. Review of Montreille's L'Isle de Robinson Crusoé, extraite de l'Anglois, 1767. In L'Année littéraire. Amsterdam; Paris: Lacombe, 2:235-39.
        Observes that since Rousseau's Émile (1762), abridgers have been trying to prune Robinson Crusoe. Sums up how Montreille wished to "paint Robinson," and thus suggests what might have been his interpretation. At the close of the review, strikingly identifies Defoe by name as the "man of letters" who took the memoirs of a castaway "Englishman" and deprived him of "the fruits" which he could expect from his misfortunes--a not so clear reference to Selkirk.

2   [GOUGH, RICHARD.] Anecdotes of British Topography. Or, an Historical Account of What Has Been Done for Illustrating the Topographical Antiquities of Great Britain and Ireland. London: T. Payne & W. Brown, p. 299.
        In the section on "London," lists the first edition of Journal of the Plague Year, and unequivocally assigns the authorship to Defoe. Cites also the edition published in 1754 under the title The History of the Great Plague in London 1665. Reprinted, in enlarged edition: 1780.1.

3   MORANT, PHILIP. The History and Antiquities of the County of Essex. 2 vols. London: T. Osborne, J. Whiston, S. Baker, L. Davis & C. Reymers, B. White, 1:134-35.
        Refers to "the most considerable estate" in the parish of Mile-end, within the liberties of Colchester, as being leased to Defoe on 6 August 1722 at the yearly rent of £120 and a fine of £500, formerly known as Kings-wood Heath.

1769

1   "A Catalogue of New Publications." Gentleman's Magazine 39 (July):356.
        Briefly reviews the Original Power of the Collective Body of the People of England, 1769.5, referring to it as "a tract written with old de Foe's usual freedom and spirit."

18

*2   [DEFOE, DANIEL.] The History of the Great Plague in London,
      in the Year 1665; containing Observations and Memorials of the
      most remarkable Occurrences, both public and private, that
      happened during that dreadful period. By a Citizen, who lived
      the whole time in London.
          No copy of this work has been located. All the information
      about it derives from 1822.2.

3   D[UNCOMB], W[ILLIAM]. Letter to Mr. Urban. Gentleman's Maga-
      zine 39 (April):171-72.
          Discusses the manuscript journal written by the seaman John
      Benbow, eldest son of the vice-admiral bearing the same name.
      When the son died in 1708, he left the journal with his brother
      William who, in 1713, "read it over" to Duncombe and others. The
      manuscript, unfortunately destroyed by fire in 1714, told of Ben-
      bow's having served on the East-Indiaman Degrave, his being ship-
      wrecked on the coast of Madagascar, his capture with Drury, and
      subsequent escape, the massacre of the entire crew, with the ex-
      ception of four boys. The accounts given here "exactly tallied"
      with Madagascar (1729) written by Robin Drury, one of the four
      boys who escaped from the massacre. So convinced is Duncombe of
      the genuineness of Drury's Journal, and so oblivious to any au-
      thorial or editorial role for Defoe, he judges the true narrative
      to be "as entertaining as Gulliver or Crusoe." For differing
      viewpoints on Duncombe's contribution, see John Robert Moore, De-
      foe's Source for Robert Drury's Journal, Indiana University Publi-
      cations, Humanities Series, no. 9 (Bloomington, Ind., 1943) and
      Arthur W. Secord, Robert Drury's Journal and Other Critical Stud-
      ies (Urbana: Illinois University Press, 1961). See also 1772.1.

4   FEUTRY, AIMÉ AMBROISE JOSEPH. Préface to Les Avantures, ou,
      la vie et les voyage de Robinson Crusoë, traduction libre de
      cet ouvrage anglois attribué au célébre Richard Steele.
      2 vols. Frankfurt and Leipzig: La Compagnie, 1:5-8.
          On the title page and again in a note, attributes Robinson
      Crusoe to Richard Steele. Quotes Rousseau, and adds that there
      is more truth and simplicity here than the philosophers could
      give it. The dedicatory epistle is signed by Feutry. See
      1766.3; 1775.2.

5   A LIVERYMAN OF THE CITY OF LONDON [pseud.]. "To the Gentle-
      men, Clergy, and Freeholders of the County of Middlesex and
      the Liverymen of the City of London." In The Original Power
      of the Collective Body of the People of England. Examined and
      Asserted. By Daniel De Foe. To Which Are Added, by the Same
      Author, Some Distinguishing Characters of a Parliament-Man.
      London: R. Baldwin, pp. iii-iv.
          According to the Dedication, this "excellent Tract . . .
      wrote by the celebrated Daniel De Foe, was being reprinted to
      support the persons petitioned in their direct address to the
      King upon the failure of petitions to the Commons and the Lords.
      Defoe, mentioned as an authority on "the civil constitution of

the kingdom," provided the theoretical background in the Original Power which was first published in 1701. The tract was a reminder that power resides in "the Persons represented" and not in "the representing," the Commons. The review in the London Magazine (1769.7) hints at the current relevance of the work. Although elected three times to be parliamentary member for Middlesex, John Wilkes was expelled from the House of Commons. Ultimately he did gain his seat. The second reprint, first published in 1701 as the Six Distinguishing Characters of a Parliament Man, also had current relevance. Wilson records a third edition with a different dedication.

6   Preface to A Tour Through the Whole Island of Great Britain.
     . . . Originally Begun by the Celebrated Daniel De Foe, Continued by the Late Mr. Richardson, Author of "Clarissa," and brought down to the present Time by a Gentleman of Eminence in the Literary World. 7th ed. 4 vols. London: J. & F. Rivington et al., 1:iii-vi.
        On the title page, states that there are "very great Additions, Improvements; and Corrections," although the preface continues to describe the Tour as containing the original author's own observations and as not being dependent upon the observations of other men. Quotes the first edition that the author lived in Scotland and travelled over a great part of the country; describes the "improvements." See also Godfrey Davies, "Daniel Defoe's A Tour Thro' the Whole Island of Great Britain," Modern Philology 48 (August, 1950):21-36.

7   Review of The Original Power of the Collective Body of the People of England Examined and Asserted. By Daniel de Foe. To Which Are Added by the Same Author, Some Distinguishing Characters of a Parliament-Man, 1769. London Magazine 38 (July): 376.
        Briefly reviews new combined reprintings with Defoe's name on the title page; refers to him as "well known in this country" and to his writings as "remarkable for an extraordinary portion both of intelligence and severity." Praises the current reprints as "calculated for the meridian of the present hour"—a reference to the John Wilkes controversy.

                              1770

1   "Memoirs of the Life of Dr. John Arbuthnot." In Miscellaneous Works of the Late Dr. Arbuthnot. New ed. 2 vols. London: W. Richardson & L. Urquart, & J. Knox, 1:xiv-xv.
        Near the end of the Life, observes that Arbuthnot, like Pope and Swift, had "several Brats illegitimately fathered upon him, among which the famous Romance of Robinson Crusoe is worth mentioning." Explains in an extensive footnote that the romance, written in "so natural a Manner, and with so many Incidents," was thought "for sometime to be a true Story." Assigns the work to

Defoe, "a Writer famous in his Generation for Politics and Poetry, expecially the former"; and proceeds to repeat the usual
vituperations leveled at him, including Pope's famous distich in
the Dunciad. See also 1766.6.

1771

1 "Chronicle." The Annual Register, or a View of the History,
   Politics, and Literature, for the Year 1771. 3d ed. London:
   J. Dodsley, 1779, 14:65.
      John Joseph Defoe, among three convicts executed at Tyburn
   for robbing, "said to be grandson to the celebrated Daniel Defoe,
   who wrote the True-born Englishman, Robinson Crusoe, Col. Jack,
   and other ingenious pieces."

1772

1 [DUNCOMBE, JOHN], ed. Letters, by Several Eminent Persons
   Deceased. Including the Correspondence of John Hughes, Esq.
   . . . and Several of His Friends. 2 vols. London: J. Johnson, 2:254-62.
      Letter 141 reprints the description of Madagascar by
   W. Hirst, chaplain of the Lenox, written in 1759; and annotates
   the details by comparisons with "the best and most authentic account ever given of Madagascar . . . published in 1729 by Robert
   Drury." Accepts Drury as "a downright honest man" and the authorship of his narrative in Madagascar, on the grounds of evidence
   given in 1769.3, a reference which is not cited in the letter.

1775

1 DEFOE, DANIEL. "Proper for the Reader to be Acquainted with."
   The History of Mademoiselle de Beleau; or, the New Roxana,
   the Fortunate Mistress . . . Published by Mr. Daniel De Foe.
   And from Papers found, Since his decease, It appears was greatly altered by Himself; and From the said Papers, the Present
   Work is produced. London: F. Noble & T. Lowndes, pp. 3-9.
      Develops the publishers' hoax of a new edition based on
   papers discovered at the time of the author's death--in the preliminaries, "Proper for the Reader to be Acquainted with," which
   appeared along with the revised preface of the first edition, now
   signed for the first time by Defoe and dated from "Islington,
   August 9, 1730." Defoe is represented as giving a copy of The
   Fortunate Mistress "to my old friend and acquaintance Mr. Thomas
   Southerne, author of the Tragedy of Oroonoko," and as receiving
   criticism in a thoroughly sentimental vein which motivated him to
   recast the novel completely into "the New Roxana." Not one bit
   of this story can be substantiated. So altered was Defoe's original text that critics generally referred to it as "mutilated."
   See the reviews 1775.4-5.

2   FEUTRY, AIMÉ AMBROISE JOSEPH.   Préface to Robinson Crusoë,
    nouvelle imitation de l'Anglois. 2d ed., revised and correct-
    ed. Lille: J.B. Henry, pp. xv–xx.
         Although Robinson Crusoe had been attributed to Richard
    Steele (1769.4), Daniel Defoe was the author, his name given
    here, as it was not in the first edition, 1766.3. A long foot-
    note, providing information from Shiels's Life of Defoe (1753),
    contains a few obvious errors which keep cropping up, as in the
    later Mme. Panckoucke editions. Shows how the canon of Defoe
    might be regarded in France at this time. See 1775.3.

3   Review of Feutry's Robinson Crusoé, nouvelle imitation de
    l'Anglois, 2d ed., 1775. Journal Encyclopédique 5, pt. 2
    (July):353–54.
         Describes Feutry's aim of purging Robinson Crusoe from "the
    absurd system of fatalism," reflections of which appear on almost
    every page of the old Robinson, and his deliberate removal of the
    tedious prolixities in the original. Notes that the mistaken
    attribution of authorship to Richard Steele has been continued in
    the Preface; and that Feutry's style is especially suitable to
    the subject. See also 1766.3; 1775.2.

4   Review of the History of Mademoiselle de Beleau; or, the New
    Roxana, the Fortunate Mistress, 1775. London Magazine 44:
    371.
         Comments: "This Mademoiselle is good for little. . . ."

5   Review of the History of Mademoiselle de Beleau; or, the New
    Roxana, the Fortunate Mistress, 1775. Monthly Review 52,
    no. 3 (March):274.
         Calls "the story of the Lewd Roxana" immoral, Noble's edi-
    tion a genuine production, and Defoe the forerunner of the ordi-
    nary intrigue-novel. Scathing: "but the breed of De Foes has so
    much increased, of late years, that hundreds of them are to be
    found in the garrets of Grubstreet, where they draw nutrition,
    propagate, and rot: and nobody minds them."

6   WATSON, JOHN. "Foe, Daniel De." In The History and Antiq-
    uities of the Parish of Halifax, in Yorkshire. London:
    T. Lowndes, pp. 298–99, 470–71, 496–98.
         Establishes the tradition that Defoe had been forced to
    abscond because of his political writings [no dates given], and
    that he had lived at Halifax "in the Back-lane, at the sign of
    the Rose and Crown," and had written there Jure Divino and Robin-
    son Crusoe, the story of which Defoe had taken from Selkirk.
    Mentions that Defoe was "known" to the physician, Dr. Thomas
    Nettleton, and the Dissenting minister, Nathaniel Priestly, both
    of whom appear in the History.

1776

1   DEFOE, DANIEL. "The Introduction, Which the reader may, or
    may not peruse." In The History of Laetitia Atkins, Vulgarly
    called Moll Flanders. Published by Mr. Daniel DeFoe. And
    from Papers found since his Decease, it appears greatly alter-
    ed by himself; And from the said Papers, the Present Work is
    produced. London: F. Noble & T. Lowndes, pp. iii-vii.
        The introduction, dated from Islington, 20 December 1730,
    completely fabricates a new edition by the enterprising Francis
    Noble, which is intended for the booksellers' stalls and the cir-
    culating libraries. Laetitia Atkins, as Moll is now named, has
    had a liberal education, but she still needs the services of an
    editor. Upon reading the book after its first printing, and upon
    maturer reflection, Defoe realized he had mistakenly allowed
    "many circumstances to appear in print," and was now altering
    "many parts of it, to give it the better reading, as I some lit-
    tle time before had done by Roxana; or the Fortunate Mistress."
    Not only did Noble regard the History of Laetitia Atkins and the
    History of Mademoiselle de Beleau as companion novels, he also
    published an edition of Captain Singleton, and so concentrated on
    Defoe's crime novels. Except for Colonel Jack, he produced edi-
    tions of Defoe's major novels. More than any single person, for
    good or ill, he was responsible for Defoe's standing as a novel-
    ist in the latter half of the eighteenth century. Mrs. Anna
    Letitia Barbauld is sometimes cited as the editor of this work,
    but the evidence for this attribution has not been found.

1778

1   "The True History of Robinson Crusoe." Universal Magazine,
    August, pp. 63-64.
        Presents a brief composite account of Alexander Selkirk.
    States flatly that on Selkirk's return to England, he placed his
    papers in Defoe's hands "who ungenerously formed his History of
    Robinson Crusoe from these materials and his own invention, and
    returned Selkirk his papers again, as too trifling to deserve
    attention. A cruel fraud, for which, in an humane view, the
    distinguished merit of that romance can never atone."

1779

1   "Avanture qui a servi de fond au roman intitulé: Robinson
    Crusoe; traduite de l'Universal magazine du mois d'Août 1778."
    Journal Encyclopédique 47, no. 1 (January):125-28. Reprint.
    Geneva: Slatkine Reprints; Nendeln, Liechtenstein: Kraus
    Reprint, 1967, 47:38.
        Identifies "the adventure" on which Robinson Crusoe is
    based as Alexander Selkirk's, summarized mainly from Woodes
    Rogers's Cruising Voyage round the World (1712). Adds, then,

without giving any source, that Selkirk wrote down his adventures, and asked the famous Defoe to retouch his memoirs and put
them into shape for publication. "But [Defoe] returned the manuscript to Selkirk, refused to consent to its printing, under the
pretext that the historical base was not interesting enough; but
he kept the materials for himself in order to write his Robinson
Crusoe, a disgraceful fraud and one which will always be a blem-
ish on this writer's life."

1779-1780

1   CAMPE, JOACHIM HEINRICH. Robinson der Jüngere, zur angenehmen
und nützlichen Unterhaltung für Kinder. 2 pts. Hamburg: Carl
Ernst Bohn, 288 pp., 366 pp.
     Makes no reference to Defoe, but uses Robinson Crusoe as
the base for changes in the narrative which would permit Campe to
advance a completely different pedagogical purpose. Explains his
dissatisfactions with "old Robinson's history": he intends to
entertain young readers; to add "elemental knowledge" to the narrative; to replace the fictions "with which the original history
of Robinson is crammed" with "true objects, true productions and
phenomena of nature"; to alter and, when necessary, create "the
circumstances and adventures so as to be productive of many moral
remarks, and natural occasions for pious and religious sensa-
tions, adapted to the understanding and hearts of children." Perhaps most important, states his strong opposition to "that fatal
sentimental fever"; wants his work to be "an antipode to the
over-affected sentimental books of our times." Starts a major
controversy by disagreeing with Rousseau about Robinson Crusoe's
not needing any assistance from art: "In this Mr. Rousseau is
mistaken. Old Robinson had saved a number of tools from the
wreck, whereas our younger Robinson had nothing but his hands and
his head, to procure himself subsistence." Finds this feature of
the original most disadvantageous: the old Robinson is given
"all the necessary European instruments to procure him many of
those conveniencies, which social life affords among civilized
people." By deviating from the original, presents a truer picture of the solitary man's needs and society's blessings. Struc-
tures the Island experience into three periods: man alone, the
benefits of a companion, the arrival of a ship. See the translations into English: Robinson the Younger (Hamburg: C.E. Bohn,
1781-1782) and The New Robinson Crusoe (London: John Stockdale,
1789). For the numerous editions and translations of Campe's
work, see Ullrich's Robinson und Robinsonaden, pp. 67-84; and the
recent edition by Alwin Binder and Heinrich Richartz (Stuttgart:
Philipp Reclam Jun, 1981), 427 pp.

1780

1   [GOUGH, RICHARD.] British Topography. Or, An Historical
Account of What Has Been Done for Illustrating the Topograph-

ical Antiquities of Great Britain and Ireland. 2 vols.
London: T. Payne & Son, & J. Nichols, 1:39, 699; 2:574.
    In an enlarged edition of Anecdotes of British Topography
(1768.2), makes use of Defoe's Tour, with an awareness of additions made to the editions of 1738, 1748, 1753, 1761, 1769.
Repeats the assignment of authorship for the Journal of the
Plague Year to Defoe. Includes Defoe's poem, Caledonia (1707)
in a listing within the chapter "General Geography of Scotland."

1781

*1   BECKET, THOMAS. A Short Account of the Situations and Inci-
     dents Exhibited in the Pantomime of Robinson Crusoe at the
     Theatre-Royal, Drury-Lane. (Taken from the Original Story).
     London: T. Becket, 20 pp.
         An extremely rare pamphlet, a copy of which has been found
     and is discussed in Nettleton (reference below). The invaluable
     scenario of the Crusoe portions of the pantomime is reprinted
     here, except for the lengthy quotations from Robinson Crusoe.
     See also 1781.4. Reprinted: 1789; 1797; in summary, George H.
     Nettleton, "Robinson Crusoe: Sheridan's Drury Lane Pantomime"--
     I and II, TLS, no. 1186 (25 December 1943):624 and no. 2187 (1
     January 1944):12; and "Sheridan's Robinson Crusoe," TLS, no. 2202
     (15 April 1944):192.

2   DEPERTHES, JEAN LOUIS HUBERT SIMON, ed. "Délaissement d'un
     Matelot Ecossois, nommé Alexandre Selkirk. . . ." In Rela-
     tions d'infortunes sur mer. 3 pts. Rheims. Reprint. His-
     toire des naufrages, ou recueil des relations les plus intéres-
     santes des naufrages, hivernemens, délaissemens, incendies,
     famines, & autres evénemens funeste sur mer. 3 vols. Paris:
     Née de la Rochelle, 1789, 3:105-24; Maradan & Lettelier, 1790,
     3:105-24.
         Information on the 1781 edition appears in Gove (p. 27n).
     The Histoire des naufrages was also published uniformly as a Sup-
     plément, vols. 37-39 of Garnier's Voyages imaginaires (1787-
     1789). In the "Délaissement," retells the stories of Selkirk
     from Edward Cooke, Robert Lade, and Woodes Rogers; and of Will,
     the Mosquito Indian, from Dampier. States specifically that
     their adventures became the subject of Robinson Crusoe, eagerly
     read particularly by young people, and that Defoe was the author.
     Asks that we recall here, in Rogers's account, "what was true in
     the history of the pretended Robinson." Reprinted: Maradan &
     Lettelier, 1790; Cuchet, [1795].

3   The Novelist's Magazine. Vol. 4, Daniel Defoe. The Life
     and Adventures of Robinson Crusoe. London: Harrison & Co.,
     291 pp.
         Begins publication of favorite novels in 1780 without any
     general introduction. Includes in vol. 4 Lesage's Gil Blas, and
     follows with the two parts of Robinson Crusoe, each with the orig-
     inal single-page preface, but now signed "Daniel Defoe."

*4   [SHERIDAN, RICHARD BRINSLEY.] Robinson Crusoe; or, Harlequin
      Friday.
           A new pantomime performed for the first time on 29 January
      at the Theatre Royal, Drury Lane. Although the pantomime is well
      known from the extensive reviews of the first performance in con-
      temporary periodicals and from Becket (1781.1), no edition dated
      1781 has survived; a Newcastle-upon-Tyne edition does exist for
      1791. According to Nettleton (1943-1944) the pantomime was first
      performed at the Theatre Royal in Drury Lane on 29 January 1781
      as an after-piece to The Winter's Tale, and had an immensely suc-
      cessful run of forty recorded performances during the first four
      months of the first season and twenty-eight performances in the
      1781-82 season. Between 1781 and 1800, the Crusoe pantomime was
      performed 123 times (London Stage 1660-1800, 1:clxxiii); there
      were three London editions of Becket's Short Account including
      the scenario: 1781, 1789, 1797. Horace Walpole, in a letter to
      Lady Ossory, 3 November 1782 (Correspondence 33:361-62), judged
      a performance to be less witty and coherent than the earlier pan-
      tomimes of John Rich. Only the first of the three parts of the
      pantomime is concerned with Robinson Crusoe in twelve elaborately
      set and costumed scenes, taken (according to Nettleton) with
      "scrupulous deference to the precise authority of Defoe's text."
      In Becket's Short Account, not only are the scenes transcribed,
      seriously and credibly, but the appropriate passages from Robin-
      son Crusoe are quoted. The other two parts show, in Becket's
      words, "that Friday being invested with the power of Harlequin,
      after many fanciful distresses, and the usual pantomimical revo-
      lutions, receives his final reward in the hand of Columbine."
      Although there has been some questioning of Sheridan's authorship
      of the pantomime (e.g., 1914.2), the current view favors Sheri-
      dan. According to one theatre tradition he is even thought to
      have acted in the role of Harlequin Friday. See also R. Crompton
      Rhodes, ed., "Robinson Crusoe (1781)," in The Plays & Poems of
      Richard Brinsley Sheridan (New York: Macmillan Co., 1929), 3:
      337-41; George H. Nettleton's articles cited in 1781.1; and The
      Dramatic Work of Richard Brinsley Sheridan, ed. Cecil Price
      (Oxford: Clarendon Press, 1973), 2:784-87.

                                  1782

1   BAKER, DAVID ERSKINE. Biographica Dramatica, or, A Companion
      to the Playhouse. New ed. 2 vols. London: Rivington
      et al., 2:44.
           Corrects 1764.1 with respect to the date of Cibber's The
      Careless Husband, 1704. Continuation to 1782 is by Isaac Reed.
      See also 1812.2.

2   COWPER, WILLIAM. "Verses, Supposed to be written by Alexander
      Selkirk, during his solitary Abode in the Island of Juan Fer-
      nandez." In Poems. London: J. Johnson. Reprint. A Scolar
      Press Facsimile. Yorkshire and London: Scolar Press, 1973,
      pp. 305-10.

Cowper's popular poem "I am monarch of all I survey" was
frequently reprinted, at times the lines assigned to Selkirk as
the author (1787.3). Although written in the first person and
from Selkirk's point of view, the piece has the title "Robinson
Crusoe" in Cowper's record of his poems at the Henry E. Huntington Library--The Poems of William Cowper, ed. John D. Baird and
Charles Ryskamp (Oxford: Clarendon Press, 1980), p. 403. The
verses were actually given the title in print, "Robinson on His
Island," in an adaptation Robinson Crusoe for Boys and Girls,
1904.3.

3   SPENCE, THOMAS. A Supplement to the History of Robinson
     Crusoe, Being the History of Crusonia, or Robinson Crusoe's
     Island, Down to the Present Time. New ed. Newcastle:
     T. Saint, pp. 5-35.
         Captain Wish-it of the Good-Intent, writing to "an intel-
ligent friend" in England, ingeniously continues "the History of
Crusonia" as a Robinsonade ostensibly "on the Government, Religion, and Customs of this famous Island, as they are at present,"
but actually to advance favorite ideas on land tenure which, as
early as 1775, Thomas Spence had promulgated in a paper "The Real
Rights of Man" (DNB). In considerable detail the Captain describes "the Parish System," its key features being the elimination of landlords and rents, and the consequent benefits to
Crusonian life. Near the end of his letter, he resolves never to
return to "poor wrangling Britannia, once so dear to me, till I
be certain this Paradisiacal System has taken Place in it."

4   STAVELEY, E. "The Editor's Preface." In The History of the
     Civil Wars in Germany, from the Year 1630 to 1635: Also,
     Genuine Memoirs of the Wars of England, in the Unhappy Reign
     of Charles the First. . . . Written by a Shropshire Gentle-
     man. Newark: Printed by James Tomlinson for the Publisher,
     pp. v-vii.
         Expresses thanks to the subscribers to this publication,
Memoirs of a Cavalier; but makes no acknowledgement of any earlier printings, as if the work were now being published directly
from manuscript, the author of which was the unnamed Cavalier.
Since the author/Cavalier had been a major participant in the
actions of the two wars, the narrative must be "genuine and in-
controvertible... candid, ingenuous, and impartial." See also
ca.1750.1; 1857.3, 6.

                              1783

1   BEATTIE, JAMES. "On Fable and Romance." Dissertations Moral
     and Critical. London: W. Strahan, T. Cadell; Edinburgh:
     W. Creech, pp. 518, 565-67.
         In an influential essay, makes an important advance for
novel-writers in the recognition that they make their inventions
"probable," but "do not even pretend that they are true." These

"fabulous narratives" Beattie then places in his own personal
system. His chief subject, "the modern serious romance," falls
within the larger category of "Modern Prose Fable"; it can be
either allegorical (historical or moral), on the one hand, or
"poetical" (serious or comic). Robinson Crusoe is definitely not
allegorical: "when I read Robinson Crusoe or Tom Jones, I attend
simply to the narrative; and no key is necessary to make me com-
prehend the author's meaning." But Robinson Crusoe follows an
"historical arrangement," and thus differs from the modern serious romances which are "poetical," that is, they begin in medias
res (e.g., Richardson's Sir Charles Grandison and Clarissa
Harlow). On Robinson Crusoe, disagrees with "the late French
writer" who said that Selkirk wanted to remain a savage; appears
to accept the tradition that Defoe used materials taken from the
illiterate Selkirk as "the groundwork of Robinson Crusoe," and
made considerable money on the publication; stresses the moral
"profit" obtainable from the novel in its "spirit of piety and
benevolence" and its stress on "the importance of the mechanic
arts" and "the horrors of solitude" and "the sweets of social
life." Reprinted: see New CBEL, 2:640; Critical Heritage.

2   BLAIR, HUGH. "Lecture XXXVII." In Lectures on Rhetoric and
      Belles Lettres. London: W. Strahan & T. Cadell; Edinburgh:
      W. Creech. Reprint. Carbondale and Edwardsville: Southern
      Illinois University Press, 1965, 2:308-9.
         Expresses the same attitude of caution toward "fictitious
history" as Beattie (1783.1) does toward romances. Again like
Beattie, sets up a system in which he differentiates the earlier
romances based on chivalry and the "less marvellous" romances of
D'Urfé, Scuderi, and Sir Philip Sidney from the more recent
"Familiar Novel" which mainly imitates ordinary life and character. English writers in this mode are inferior to the French,
with one exception: "No fiction, in any language, was ever
better supported than the Adventures of Robinson Crusoe." Without any reference to Defoe as author (whereas Fielding and
Richardson are named), praises Robinson Crusoe for its capacity
to hold the imagination of all readers and instruct them "by
showing how much the native powers of men may be exerted for sur-
mounting the difficulties of any external situation." Reprinted:
see New CBEL, 2:2061; Critical Heritage.

3   S. Letter to Mr. Urban. Gentleman's Magazine 53, pt. 1
     (May):409.
        Recognizes Defoe as the author of the Tour. As originally
written, the book is "an entertaining and useful book, describing
faithfully the face of the country as it appeared about the year
1725; but the last edition is the strangest jumble and unconnected hodge-podge that ever was put together." The Tour should deal
with the present, and avoid antiquities.

<u>1784</u>

1   [BADCOCK, SAMUEL.] Review of <u>Memoirs, Travels, and Adventures</u>
    <u>of a Cavalier</u>, 1784. <u>Monthly Review</u> 70 (May):382.
         Authorship identified in Nangle (1934). Briefly notes why
    the work has interest: the author places you where he wishes.
    "You are only afraid of coming to your journey's end too soon."
    See 1784.3.

2   "De Foe (Daniel)." In <u>A New and General Biographical Dic-</u>
    <u>tionary; Containing an Historical and Critical Account of the</u>
    <u>Lives and Writings of the Most Eminent Persons in Every</u>
    <u>Nation</u>. 12 vols. London: W. Strahan et al., 4:348-50.
         Borrows from 1753.1, with a final comment upon the natu-
    ralness of <u>Robinson Crusoe</u>.

3   DEFOE, DANIEL. <u>Memoirs, Travels, and Adventures of a Cava-</u>
    <u>lier</u>. 2d ed. 3 vols. London: Francis Noble, 1:iii-viii,
    232 pp.; 2:236 pp.; 3:234 pp.
         Unusual among the seven editions of the <u>Memoirs of a Cava-</u>
    <u>lier</u> published in the eighteenth century: for the first time
    Defoe's name appears prominently as the editor. The title page
    reads: "First published from the original manuscript, By the
    late Mr. Daniel DeFoe, Author of the Adventures of Robinson
    Crusoe, and many other Books of Entertainment." Defoe's name
    appears at the end of the preface which is now entitled "Preface,
    By the Editor, To the First Edition." On the last page of the
    preface, right after Defoe's name, are advertised as "lately pub-
    lished, new Editions of the following entertaining Books, written
    by the Editor of the present Work, viz. <u>Roxana; or, the Fortunate</u>
    <u>Mistress</u>; <u>Laetitia Atkins, vulgarly called Moll Flanders</u>; and <u>Ad-</u>
    <u>ventures of Captain Singleton</u>." At the end of vol. 3, 133 novels
    are listed as "Books Printed for F. Noble, in Holborn" available
    to "any dealer, <u>paying ready money</u>." All four books, in addition
    to the <u>History of the Plague</u>, appear on the list at three shil-
    lings per volume.

4   GRIVEL, GUILLAUME. "Copie d'une lettre." In <u>L'Ile inconnue,</u>
    <u>ou mémoires du Chevalier des Gastines</u>. New ed. Paris:
    Moutard, 1:xx-xxxii.
         Answers the question that has arisen with the enormous popu-
    larity of Grivel's <u>L'Isle inconnue</u> (1783). Is the book an imita-
    tion of <u>Robinson Crusoe</u>? Addressing his comments in a letter to
    C., admits that between the two works there are some striking
    "traits of resemblance," but rejects the publisher's explanation
    in his preface (1784.6) that <u>Robinson Crusoe</u> is "a defective
    work," and argues simply that <u>Robinson Crusoe</u> and <u>L'Isle inconnue</u>
    resemble one another because they return to Alexander Selkirk as
    a common source. Argues also that whereas the idea of <u>Robinson</u>
    <u>Crusoe</u> is contained in "The History of Selkirk," and does not pro-
    gress much farther, <u>L'Isle inconnue</u> endeavors to execute "a very
    vast design . . . the History of the Civilization of peoples, or

of the foundation of empires." Comments on the central significance of a hero Robinson's having a male companion named Friday,
and a hero Gastines's having a female companion named Eléonore.
See also 1784.7-8; 1787.5.

5   "Obituary of considerable Persons; with Biographical Anec-
     dotes." <u>Gentleman's Magazine</u> 54, no. 3 (March):238.
       Obituary of Mrs. Sophia Standerwick, wife of James, late of
Cornhill. She was the daughter of "Mr. Daniel Defoe, who died in
North America some years since, and was son of the ingenious
Daniel Defoe, of <u>exalted</u> memory, formerly of Stoke Newington, to
which parish, on Easter Monday, being April 10, 1721, he paid £10
to be excused serving parish offices."

6   Preface to <u>L'Isle inconnu, ou mémoires du Chevalier des</u>
     <u>Gastines</u>. New ed. Paris: Moutard, 1:i-xix.
       Here, in responding to the criticisms which <u>L'Isle inconnue</u>
(1783) has received, the publisher takes up the second: "The subject is not new; it is Robinson Crusoe on his island." He agrees
wholeheartedly with this criticism, noting only that "Robinson
was no other than the Scotsman Alexander Selkirk, abandoned on
the desert island of Juan Fernandez." Both Robinson and Gastines, says the publisher, are cast on desert islands: "there's
the resemblance; all the rest is difference. I ask the pardon of
Rousseau and of so many other panegyrists of the English novel,
but <u>Robinson Crusoe</u> is a defective work, expressive of small
views, small means, small effects. Right from the outset, the
idea is false. . . ." He continues in the same vein, slashingly,
finding it preferable for one of the two castaways to be as in
<u>L'Isle inconnue</u>, "a tender companion." On Grivel's disagreement
concerning <u>Robinson Crusoe</u>, see 1784.4.

7   Review of Guillaume Grivel's <u>L'Isle inconnue</u>, 1783. <u>L'Année</u>
     <u>littéraire</u>. Année M.DCC.LXXXIV 4:273-78.
       Insists on making a comparison of Grivel's <u>L'Isle inconnue</u>
and Defoe's <u>Robinson Crusoe</u>, sensing deep similarities in the
very "soul" of the two works and a single important dissimilar-
ity. Notes that only in respect to the Chevalier des Gastines's
constant companion Eléonore, do the two pieces differ significantly: <u>Robinson Crusoe</u> lacks the "sweet sensibility" which the
reviewer finds in <u>L'Isle inconnue</u>.

8   Review of Guillaume Grivel's <u>L'Isle inconnue</u>, 1783. <u>Journal</u>
     <u>des sçavans</u> (May):283.
       Focuses the review on the contrast between Robinson and the
Chevalier des Gastines, a castaway on a desert island, who differs from his model in having "a dear companion" and therefore entirely additional needs that affect his industry and resources--
differs also in having numerous children and raising them, and
thus puts into practice useful views on education that Grivel
discussed in his <u>Théorie de l'education</u> (1776).

1785

1   CHALMERS, GEORGE. The Life of Daniel De Foe. London: John
    Stockdale, 24 pp.
        As a prospectus for Stockdale's edition of Defoe's History
    of the Union (1786.1), these preliminary sheets were issued anon-
    ymously, and constitute the first formal biography of Defoe which
    utilizes sound techniques of research. Although rising at times
    to a Johnsonian eloquence, Chalmers more characteristically pre-
    sents information gleaned from the writings of Defoe's enemies,
    records at Doctors Commons, prefaces or autobiographical pieces
    in his True Collection, surviving anecdotes, and especially the
    Appeal to Honour and Justice. From only a handful of pamphlets
    in the Defoe canon, he writes with considerable respect for Defoe
    as the staunch advocate of English liberty and trade. For the
    Original Power of the Collective Body of the People of England
    (1701), he ranks him with Locke. In the Shortest-Way with the
    Dissenters, "a piece of exquisite irony," he finds evidence that
    might have shown "considerate men, how much the Author had been
    in jest." He has high praise for the narrative in the History of
    the Union as a drama which alone would have preserved his name,
    even if his Crusoe entertained us less. On many of Defoe's other
    works, especially the major novels, Chalmers has nothing to say
    at this date. Reprinted: 1786.1; in part, Critical Heritage.

2   LANGBOURNIENSIS [pseud.]. Gentleman's Magazine 55, pt. 2,
    no. 12 (December):953.
        Replies to Philobiblios, 1785.3. Mentions a recent obit-
    uary in Gentleman's Magazine (1784.5) for Defoe's granddaughter,
    Mrs. James Standerwick, and discusses "Memoirs of the Plague
    Year" as "a Romance of a very peculiar kind, but which is very
    strongly marked with his character, minute pathetic descriptions
    . . . ." Although regarded as fiction, it is one founded "on
    truth, and a tradition he received from his mother, or some near
    relation, who survived the plague in London." Defoe also wrote
    the "History of Colonel Jack, a work excellent in its kind,
    though little known; it contains much manner of low life, and
    much nature: this author appears never to have attempted any
    scene in high life, with which doubtless he was unacquainted, but
    his rank is very exalted as a writer of original genius." See
    reply, 1789.1. Reprinted, in part: Critical Heritage.

3   PHILOBIBLIOS [pseud.]. Gentleman's Magazine 55, pt. 2, no. 11
    (November):881-83.
        Expresses curiosity about the authorship of Robinson
    Crusoe, "a book scarcely less known than Don Quixote." Defoe
    generally regarded as the author, but "particulars" of his life
    are not known, or what other works he wrote. Dr. Swift appears
    to be "superficial" when compared with Defoe. "The Dr. was an
    able satirist, Defoe might have founded a colony." Despairs of
    learning who was the author of "that singular book, Memoirs of a
    Cavalier." See replies, 1785.2; 1787.7. Reprinted, in part:
    Critical Heritage.

4   REEVE, CLARA. <u>The Progress of Romance</u>. Colchester: W. Key-
     mer; London: G.G.J. and J. Robinson. Reprint. 2 vols. in
     1. Series I, Literature and Language, vol. 4. New York:
     Facsimile Text Society, 1930, 1:122-27.
       In the discussion between Hortensius, Sophronia, and Euphra-
sia, Euphrasia (who speaks for Clara Reeve) centers the discussion upon novels which are "originals" and specifically "one of
the <u>old</u> <u>Novels</u>," on the life of Cleveland, the natural son of Oliver Cromwell. Thought to have "uncommon merit" for that time, it
was, says Hortensius, "ascribed to <u>Daniel</u> <u>de</u> <u>Foe</u>, who as 'I think
was also the Author of <u>Robinson Crusoe</u>." This statement leads to
Euphrasia's clear acceptance of the charges of theft and plagiarism against Defoe with respect to Selkirk and her comparison of
<u>Robinson Crusoe</u> and <u>Gaudentio di Lucca</u> (1725) as accounts of
"unknown or rather of <u>Ideal</u> countries," witten in a natural and
credible manner, and intended "to promote the cause of religion
and virtue." The speakers generally agree that <u>Robinson Crusoe</u>
should be read by adults, being a book which can be placed "too
soon into the hands of children." But if read, it should be in
"the old Edition of <u>Crusoe</u>," as Sophronia points out, because
"<u>Fanaticism</u> has laid her paw" upon the book, and has added the
<u>Visions of the Angelical World</u>.

5   SCHWABE, JOHANN JOACHIM. <u>Catalogus Bibliothecae Selectae</u>.
     2 vols. Leipzig: Breitkopf. Reprint. Munich: Omnia-Mikro-
     film-Technik, 1977, 1:118, 119, 121, 123, 125.
       In the Latin preface "To the Reader," I.G.E. Breitkopf
describes Schwabe's collecting for forty years. In the section
"English and Italian literature," lists five works by Defoe, only
the <u>Hymn to the Pillory</u> identified as his. The other four: <u>Tour</u>
(1724), <u>Capt. George Carleton</u> (1728), <u>Consolidator</u> (1705), <u>Essays</u>
<u>upon Several Projects</u> [sic] (1702).

1786

1   CHALMERS, GEORGE. "The Life of De Foe." In <u>The History of</u>
     <u>the Union between England and Scotland, by Daniel De-Foe</u>.
     London: John Stockdale, pp. i-xxiv.
       Reprint of 1785.1. See the anonymous review, 1787.9.
Reprinted: (extracts) 1787.9; with additions, 1790.1; 1793.1;
1804; 1841.2.

2   FORSTER, JOHN RHEINHOLD. <u>History of the Voyages and Discover-</u>
     <u>ies Made in the North. Translated from the German</u>. London:
     G.G. and J. Robinson, pp. 453-55.
       In book 3 "Discoveries Made in the North in Modern Times,"
includes chap. 4 on the discoveries of the Spaniards, with
section 8 on the "very famous expedition" of Admiral Bartholomeo
de Fonte exploring a northwest passage from the Pacific to the
Atlantic Ocean. Refers to the controversy started by the first
published account of this voyage in [<u>Monthly Miscellany: or,</u>]

Memoirs for the Curious, April and June 1708. Rejects vigorously
a northwest passage as impossible--the "reverie of de Fonte" or
"the production of some idle visionary." Claims that these
dreams "would make much such a figure in this work as an extract
of 20 pages from the well-known Daniel de Foe's New Voyage round
the World, by a course never sailed before, would, when blended
with the genuine materials for history gathered from state-
papers, or with a collection of authentic records." See also
1787.4. On de Fonte's letter, see Percy G. Adams, Travelers and
Travel Liars (Berkeley: University of California Press, 1962),
pp. 64-72.

3 PIOZZI, HESTER LYNCH. Anecdotes of the Late Samuel Johnson,
   L.L.D. during the Last Twenty Years of His Life. London:
   T. Cadell, p. 281.
      Dr. Johnson, commenting upon the difficulties in reading
   books to the last page: "Was there ever yet any thing written
   by mere man that was wished longer by its readers, excepting
   Don Quixote, Robinson Crusoe, and the Pilgrim's Progress?"
   Reprinted: Johnsonian Miscellanies, ed. George Birkbeck Hill
   (Oxford: Clarendon Press, 1897); (London: Constable & Co.,
   1966), 1:332-33.

                              1787

1 [ANDERSON, JAMES.] Review of J[ean] L[ouis] de Lolme's An
   Essay . . . Being an Introduction to De Foe's "History of the
   Union." Monthly Review 77 (December):501-502.
      Author identified in Nangle (1934). Explains that De Lolme
   wrote the first part, a history of "the relative state of England
   and Scotland" from Edward I to Queen Anne, as an introduction to
   Defoe's History of the Union which was edited by George Chalmers
   and published by John Stockdale in 1786. The second part is by
   De Lolme and "another hand," relating "the political situation"
   of Ireland and presenting the case for "an incorporating union
   between Great Britain and Ireland."

*2 ARNOULD, JEAN FRANÇOIS MUSSOT [d'Arnould]. Robinson Crusoé
    dans son ile. Comédie en un acte. Amsterdam.
       No copy of this comedy, mentioned by Mann (p. 100), has
    been located.

3 EDINBURGENSIS [pseud.]. "A Poem by Alexander Selkirk, Robinson Crusoe." Scots Magazine 49 (November):528.
      Assigns to Alexander Selkirk the authorship of William
   Cowper's "Verses, Supposed to be Written by Alexander Selkirk,
   during his Solitary Abode in the Island of Juan Fernandez," and
   reprints a version of the poem. Selkirk, as "the original Robinson Crusoe," had formed "the various wonderful incidents of his
   life" into a history, and "applied to Daniel De Foe for embel-
   lishments." The merits of the Robinson Crusoe story are thus
   "falsely" given to Defoe. See 1782.2.

                              33

4   THE EDITOR. Note to William Shiells's "The Life of Mr. Daniel
     De Foe," 1787. In Daniel De Foe's Voyage Round the World, by
     a Course Never Sailed Before. 3 vols. London: F[rancis]
     Noble, 1:28.
         Contends that while up to now Defoe's "inventions" were
     generally believed to be "founded upon real truths," William
     Shiells has confirmed the New Voyage Round The World to be a
     fiction, by revealing that "the ingenious Mr. [Johann Reinhold]
     Forster," in his Voyages and Discoveries in the North (1786.2),
     describes "a pretended discovery" of the Spanish Admiral, Bar-
     tholomew de Fonte, as comparable to a twenty-page extract "from
     the well-known Daniel de Foe's New Voyage round the World, by a
     course never sailed before." In a postscript advertises another
     book Memoirs of a Cavalier, said to be "discovered" by William
     Shiells and Paul Whitehead--lately published in three vols. by
     F. Noble, 1784.3.

5   GARNIER, C[HARLES] G[EORGES] T[HOMAS], ed. "Avertissement.
     de l'Éditeur." In Voyages imaginaires, songes, visions, et
     romans cabalistiques. Vol. 7, Guillaume Grivel, L'Ile incon-
     nue, ou mémoires du Chevalier des Gastines. Amsterdam and
     Paris: Rue et Hôtel Serpentes, pp. vii-xii.
         Amidst a most favorable reception given to Grivel's L'Isle
     inconnue since 1783, vigorously defends the book from charges of
     plagiarism. Argues that as an imitation of Robinson Crusoe it
     has its own distinct purpose and progress of narrative events.
     Sets up a comparison and contrast between Robinson Crusoe, "sepa-
     rated from all society, overwhelmed with all his needs, and strug-
     gling against necessity," who finds the resources within himself,
     and Gastines whose creator seeks to depict "the origin and the
     formation of society, to present the history of the civilization
     of peoples, or the foundation of empires." Finds the goals of
     the two authors to be "absolutely contrary" and the effects on
     their readers to be sharply different. See also 1784.4, 7-8.

6   [GILBERT, THOMAS], ed. A Collection of Pamphlets Concerning
     the Poor: with Abstracts of the Poor's Rates; Expenses of Dif-
     ferent Houses of Industry, &c. and Observations of the Editor.
     London: C. Elliott, T. Kay & Co., pp. 3, 65-86.
         Explains in the advertisement that the pamphlets on the
     poor are here being reprinted while "revisal of the Poor's laws"
     is under active consideration, and the rates are increasing to
     alarming levels. Recognizing Defoe as the author, reprints
     Giving Alms No Charity (1704), "addressed to the Parliament of
     England" and "first printed in 1704."

7   HARFORD, JOSEPH [A Subscriber]. Gentleman's Magazine 57,
     pt. 2, Supp. (December):1155.
         A "Subscriber," now identified as Joseph Harford, replies
     to Philobiblios (1785.3), noting that Defoe was "the reputed
     author of Robinson Crusoe." The truth, however, was not to his
     credit. He then tells "the real history" of Selkirk's turning to

Defoe for help to prepare his "diary" for publication. Defoe "swelled" the simple story into the book, told him it would not sell, and "deprived him of all the profit." See replies by 1788.1, 3; 1909.9.

8 HARWOOD, ED., JUN. Letter to Mr. Urban. Gentleman's Magazine 57, pt. 2, no. 6 (December):1088.
As a surgeon on one of His Majesty's ships, the writer talked with a sailor named "Daniel Defoe" who claimed "his grandfather had written Robinson Crusoe, The True-born Englishman, &c." The sailor's name was "so familiar to me."

9 HIRONS, JABÉZ. Review of George Chalmers's edition of The History of the Union, 1786. Monthly Review 77 (December):459-61.
Author identified in Nangle (1934). Reviews very favorably both Chalmers's Life of Daniel De Foe and the History of the Union, to which the former is prefixed. Stresses the "difficulties and ill-treatment" which Defoe received from his own party as well as the party he opposed as being "really honourable to him." Sees him "a sincere friend . . . to the cause of liberty, civil and religious," not always able to agree with those who pursued the same designs. Although his memory is preserved by the seventeen editions and many translations of Robinson Crusoe, for which he is mainly known, his "distinguished sphere, or that to which he principally applied himself, appears to have been policy and trade." In line with this judgment, urges that the lovers of liberty and trade must wish to see his political and commercial tracts accurately republished. Summarizes contents of the History; praises the style as different from that prevailing, "but by no means unpleasant." Reprinted, in part: Critical Heritage.

10 [MATY, P.M.; HARPER, S.; and AYSCOUGH, S.]. Librorum Impressorum Qui in Museo Brittanico Adservantur Catalogus. 2 vols. London: [British Museum, Department of Printed Books], s.v. "Foe (Daniel De).
Lists surprisingly few books: Works, New Voyage Round the World (1725), Memoirs of a Cavalier (Leedes), True-born Englishman (1701), Essays upon Several Projects (1702), Jure Divino (1706), Caledonia (London, 1707), The Family Instructor (1710, sic), Appeal to Honour and Justice.

11 Review of La Vie et les aventures surprenantes de Robinson Crusoé, Contenant son retour dans son île, ses autres nouveaux voyages, & ses réflexions, 1768. In Bibliothèque universelle des romans 2 (July):3-146. Reprint. 28 vols. Geneva: Slatkine Reprints, 1969, 25:63-99.
So important is this "collection" (1775-1789) as a barometer of pre-Revolutionary French interest in serious fiction that it has been called (1910.2) "a sort of 'Encyclopedie' of the world's prose fiction." Intersperses critical comments on all three parts of Robinson Crusoe in this lengthy condensation.

12   SHIELLS, WILLIAM. "The Life of Mr. Daniel De Foe." In <u>Daniel
     De Foe's Voyage Round the World, by a Course Never Sailed
     Before</u>. 3 vols. London: F. Noble, 1:1-27.
            Cribbed entirely from 1753.1, the primary author of which
     is generally thought to be Robert Shiels. In place of the thir-
     teen works listed as Defoe's in 1753.1, includes twelve that are
     "now well known" to be his. Narratives cited here, but absent
     from 1753.1: <u>New Voyage Round the World</u>, <u>Captain Singleton</u>, <u>Rox-
     ana</u>, and <u>Life of Laetitia Atkins; or, Moll Flanders</u>.

13   "Some Account of De Foe." In <u>New Annual Register for the Year
     1786</u> 7:27-34.
            Extracts from Chalmers's <u>Life of Daniel De Foe</u> prefixed to
     the <u>History of the Union</u> (1786).

                              1787-1789

1   GARNIER, C[HARLES] G[EORGE] T[HOMAS], ed. <u>Voyages imagin-
     aires, songes, visions, et romans cabalistiques</u>. 39 vols.
     Amsterdam and Paris: Rue et Hôtel Serpentes.
            Garnier's plan was to divide the narratives into three
     main "classes": "Voyages imaginaires," "Songes et visions," and
     "Romans cabalistiques." Within the first class, he established
     four "divisions": "Romanesques," "Merveilleux," "Allégoriques,"
     and "Amusans, comiques & critiques." The first division, <u>Voyages
     imaginaires romanesques</u>, he exemplified in twelve volumes, begin-
     ning with <u>La vie et les aventures surprenantes de Robinson Cru-
     soe</u>, translated by Thémiseul de Saint- Hyacinthe and Justus Van
     Effen, in three volumes, Amsterdam, 1720-21, and in two volumes,
     with a slightly different title, in 1720. Garnier does not men-
     tion Justus Van Effen, although it is well known that most of the
     translating was his work. Scattered throughout the three vol-
     umes are important critical comments. In his "Avertissement de
     l'éditeur" (1:1-10) Garnier claims <u>L'Histoire de Robinson</u>, known
     all over the world, holds the first rank in the genre of the
     novel. From its first appearance, the book was regarded as a
     masterpiece. The idea was new, one of the happiest. The citizen
     of Geneva had exempted <u>Robinson Crusoe</u> from the general proscrip-
     tion of books for Émile. Garnier then follows, curiously, with a
     series of mistakes: for example, Richard Steele was thought by
     some to be the author of <u>Robinson Crusoe</u>; two other novels by
     Defoe are the <u>History of Colonel Sack</u> [sic] and the <u>Memoirs of
     Cleveland</u>; Defoe died "à Plingron en 1731." For an explanation
     of these mistakes, see Mann. Each of the three reprinted pref-
     aces of the 1720 translation is replete with unusually sensitive
     comments of a tone and emphasis not found in any criticism
     published in England (1:11- 16; 2:1-12; 3:1-14). Along with
     <u>Robinson Crusoe</u>, and still within the "romanesque" division, are
     found translations into French of such related works as Longue-
     ville's <u>Hermit: or, the Unparallel'd Sufferings . . . of Philip
     Quarll</u> (vol. 4) and Chetwood's <u>Voyages of Captain Robert Boyle</u>

(vols. 10–11); and in the division of the "Merveilleux," Swift's
Gulliver's Travels (vol. 14) and Paltock's Life and Adventures of
Peter Wilkins (vol. 22). See 1812.6; Gove.

1788

1   D., H. Gentleman's Magazine 58, pt. 1, no. 3 (March):206–8.
        Reacts to the inaccuracies of Subscriber (1787.7) by inves-
tigating the "original narratives" about Alexander Selkirk, and
providing a convenient summary. His conclusions about Defoe's
integrity are, nevertheless, devastating. Not only did Defoe
steal the basic idea from Selkirk's papers, he "very dishonestly
defrauded the original proprietor of the profits."

*2   [DAY, THOMAS.] The History of Little Jack. By the Author of
"Sanford and Merton." London: John Stockdale, 113 pp.
        Published the same year in Stockdale's Children's Miscel-
lany and known from frequent reprintings as in A Storehouse of
Stories, ed. Charlotte M. Yonge, 1st ser. (London: Macmillan,
1872), and E.V. Lucas, 1905.4. Little Jack's experiences appear
to be a blend of Émile's and Robinson Crusoe's, although there is
no specific reference to either one. See also Sylvia W. Patter-
son, Rousseau's Émile and Early Children's Literature (Metuchen,
N.J.: Scarecrow Press, 1971), p. 75.

3   W., W. Gentleman's Magazine 58, pt. 1, no. 3 (March):208.
        Writing Mr. Urban from Dublin, sums up a conversation as
a complete non-sequitur to the Defoe/Selkirk issue. A nobleman
"of the first consequence and information in this kingdom" had
reported that according to Mr. Benjamin Holloway, Robinson Crusoe
had been written by Robert Harley, Earl of Oxford, when his lord-
ship was imprisoned in the Tower, and that the manuscript had
been given to Defoe on one of his frequent visits to Harley.
Defoe had added the second volume of Robinson Crusoe, and published the entire work as his own. "This anecdote, I would not
venture to send to your valuable Magazine if I did not think my
information good. . . ." See also 1785.3; 1805.2; 1814.1;
1826.4; 1903.12–13.

1789

1   BOREALIS [pseud.]. Gentleman's Magazine 59, pt. 2, no. 5
     (November):992.
        Replies to Langbourniensis, 1785.2. Notes the shortcomings
of Chalmers's Life of Daniel De Foe, prefixed to the republica-
tion of the History of the Union (1786). No information, for example, will be found there on "the . . . Histories of the Plague,
and of Colonel Jack." The "editor" Chalmers did not know that
Defoe also wrote a New Voyage Round the World, the History of
Roxana, Memoirs of a Cavalier, the History of Moll Flanders, and

37

Religious Courtship (now advertised in its 21st edition). "All
his productions of the romantic species, particularly the last-
mentioned, are much in vogue amongst country readers." Defoe's
moral and religious "tendency" went counter to "the pernicious
effects" of modern novels. Smollett, in Roderick Random, treated
Robinson Crusoe and Colonel Jack "with great contempt" for political and religious reasons. In a P.S., Borealis passes on the
rare guess as to authorship that Norton Defoe wrote the Political
History of the Devil and a System of Magick, "both in the style
and manner of his father." See the reply, 1789.2. Reprinted, in
part: Critical Heritage.

2   A FRIEND TO BRITISH TRAVEL [pseud.]. Gentleman's Magazine 59,
     pt. 2 , Supp. (7 December):1202.
          Replies to 1789.1. Tour, originally written by Defoe
     "(I have heard say in his closet)," about to be reprinted. Owes
     its original plan to Defoe, "and, as such, may claim the assis-
     tance of the admirers of that very ingenious author."

                                  1790

1   CHALMERS, GEORGE. "The Life of Daniel De Foe." In The Life
     and Strange Surprizing Adventures of Robinson Crusoe, of York,
     Mariner. 2 vols. London: John Stockdale, 2:367-456.
          The earlier Life (1785.1) has now evolved into a recogniz-
     able, full-scale biography with a uniqueness of its own. Chalm-
     ers pursued his inquiries until they produced a considerable
     amount of new information. He organized the material skillfully
     into new unities, at times with a Johnsonian eloquence, and
     gained the preeminence of having the Life included in the Works
     (1840-1841). The significant additions take the form, first, of
     biographical data which had not been known before or, if known,
     had been interspersed--from primary documents or records, from
     contemporaries such as Dunton and Oldmixon, or from Defoe's own
     Mercator or Appeal to Honour and Justice. The additions, second-
     ly, are drawn from Chalmers's close knowledge of the expanding
     Defoe canon. In his "List of Writings, which are considered as
     undoubtedly De Foe's" (14 pp.), he included eighty-one items; and
     in his "List of Books which are supposed to be De Foe's" (3 pp.)
     he added twenty more. He described his search of "the Register
     of Books" entered at Stationers Hall, and his surprise and dis-
     appointment at finding "so few of De Foe's writings entered as
     property, and his name never mentioned as an author or a man."
     From the corroborated writings, Chalmers analyzed the contents of
     works which had hitherto not been known to be Defoe's, and so had
     more extensive biographical knowledge than any of his predeces-
     sors. Although he now adds a new section on Defoe's books pub-
     lished after the death of Queen Anne in 1714, he still holds to
     the belief that Defoe ended his political life in 1715. More
     pronounced here than in 1786.1 are Chalmers's convictions: the
     superiority of his own time over Defoe's in civility and freedom,

the opposition to slanders brought against Defoe by Gay, Pope,
and Savage; the firm rejection of rumors being circulated that
Defoe misappropriated the papers of Alexander Selkirk. At the
end of the Life, Chalmers based his final assessment on five cri-
teria for admitting Defoe to the "pre-eminence" of being acknowledged "one of the ablest, as he is one of the most captivating
writers, of which this island can boast": as a poet, novelist,
polemick, commercial writer, and historian. Only in the qualifi-
cations of novelist and commercial writer does Defoe emerge "fore-
most" with hardly any reservation. For the view "that Chalmers'
assignment of any particular item to Defoe constitutes in itself
no evidence that Defoe wrote it," see Rodney M. Baine, "Chalmers'
First Bibliography of Daniel Defoe," Texas Studies in Literature
and Language 10, no. 4 (Winter, 1969):547-68. Reprinted: in The
History of the Union (London: John Stockdale, 1790), pp. 1-86;
1793.1 (condensed, with a few minor additions); 1804; in part,
1823.1; 1841; 1970.

2   E. Gentleman's Magazine 60, pt. 2 (August):681.
        Calls attention to Chalmers's catalogue, at the end of his
Life, of the writings of "that versatile genius Daniel Defoe."
See 1790.1, 4.

3   GOUGH, RICHARD [D.H., pseud.]. Gentleman's Magazine 60,
    pt. 2, Supp.:1189-90.
        Authorship identified in The Nichols File of "The Gentle-
man's Magazine." Replies to 1790.7, that he could not find the
account of cutting steaks from the living animal, in the 1729
edition of the "History of Madagascar"; gives biographical background for Robert Drury, "a Leicestershire man," who after returning from fifteen years captivity, went to Loughborough. He was
authentic--not "another, but earlier, Robinson Crusoe." Drury's
father left him the reversion of a house in Stoke Newington.

4   INDEX INDICATORIUS [pseud.]. Gentleman's Magazine 60, pt. 2
    (July): 647.
        Adds to works of Defoe already mentioned: "Memoirs of the
Life and Piracies of Capt. Singleton," lately republished with
"more of Defoe's" by Noble. See 1790.1.

5   NOORTHOUCK, JOHN [N., pseud.]. Review of Chalmers's Life of
    Daniel De Foe (1790). Monthly Review, 2d ser. 3 (December):
    471.
        Author identified in Nangle (1955). Praises "the ingenious
and well-informed Daniel De Foe" as well as his biographer Chalmers, who has generously claimed the full merit of his subject.
Chalmers has set Defoe's "character and conduct in a true light."
In particular, he has "satisfactorily vindicated his Robinson
Crusoe from being a piracy of Alexander Selkirk's papers." Reprinted, in part: Critical Heritage.

6 Preface to The Life and Adventures of Robinson Crusoe.
2 vols. London: W. Lane 1:i-ii.
Names Defoe as the author. His book read avidly by readers
of all ages: "the circumstances it contains engage the mind, and
its principles of instruction are founded on Virtue and Religion;
yet they are conveyed in such a pleasing manner, that you are
imperceptibly led through a wonderful history to a system of
morality." Reprinted: 1813.

7 W. Gentleman's Magazine 60, pt. 2, no. 6 (December):1075.
Refers to a custom "circumstantially described" in Robert
Drury's "History of Madagascar, published about forty years ago,"
of cutting steaks from the living animal. See 1790.3.

8 WALTER, JOHN, ed. A Selection from the Works of Daniel
De Foe. 3 vols.; London: Logographic Press.
In the "Advertisement by the Publisher" (1:1-2), Mr. Wil-
liam Coombe singles out Defoe as a writer most barbarously treat-
ed by the "abridgers," particularly "his most celebrated work,"
Robinson Crusoe. It has appeared "in a garb more worthy of a
Grub-street production, than a work on which Rousseau has bestow-
ed the highest encomiums. . . ." In a handsome format, vols. 1
and 2 present the complete Robinson Crusoe; vol. 3 reprints the
Serious Reflections, the True-Born Englishman, and the Original
Power of the Collective Body of the People of England.

1791

1 BOSWELL, JAMES. The Life of Samuel Johnson, LL.D. 2 vols.
London: Charles Dilly, 1:362-63; 2:212, 524. Reprint. Edited by George Birkbeck Hill and L.F. Powell. 6 vols. Oxford:
Clarendon Press, 1934-1950, 2:163; 3:267-68; 4:333-34.
To Boswell's question, 28 March 1772, about "any well-
attested stories of the appearance of ghosts," referring to the
Mrs. Veal story, Dr. Johnson replied: "I believe, Sir, that is
given up. I believe the woman declared upon her death-bed that
it was a lie." On 10 April 1778, Boswell reports Dr. Johnson as
telling us he gave Mrs. [Elizabeth] Montague "a catalogue of all
Daniel Defoe's works of imagination; most, if not all of which,
as well as of his other works, he now enumerated, allowing a considerable share of merit to a man, who, bred a silversmith [sic],
had written so variously and so well. Indeed, his 'Robinson Crusoe' is enough of itself to establish his reputation." For the
date 27 June 1784, Boswell records the conversation of Dr. Johnson with Edward Lord Eliot, a member of the Literary Club, regarding the Capt. George Carleton. Dr. Johnson knew nothing of this
book. In the conversation he endeavored to draw "particulars"
about the Earl of Peterborough from Lord Eliot whose family had
shared the same tutor with the Peterborough family, Dr. Walter
Harte. Lord Eliot sent Dr. Johnson "Captain Carleton's Memoir,"
the best account of the Earl of Peterborough. When the Memoirs

arrived, Dr. Johnson was going to bed, but "sate up till he had
read it through." He found there "such an air of truth, that he
could not doubt of its authenticity." Reprinted: 1807; 1821;
1826; 1831; Critical Heritage.

2   FRANKLIN, BENJAMIN. Mémoires de la vie privée de Benjamin
    Franklin. Translated by Jacques Buisson. Paris: Buisson,
    pp. 20-21, 43-44.
       In the preface, the editor, probably Buisson, explains that
    the Mémoires is translated from the original English manuscript
    and that this publication presents only the first period of the
    young Franklin's life (including the year 1771) and preserves
    anecdotes and humble details out of a fear that future editions
    may be "truncated." On two occasions, movingly describes the in-
    fluence of Defoe: first, after having read most of the books "on
    polemic and practical theology" in his father's small library,
    discovers an Essay upon Projects, "from which I took, perhaps,
    impressions which afterwards influenced some of the principal
    events of my life." Second, during a storm in Franklin's passage
    to Amboy, in the rescue of the drunken Dutchman with an elegant
    edition of Bunyan's Pilgrim's Progress in his pocket, praises
    "Honest John" for being the first to mix narration and dialogue,
    "a manner of writing very engaging for the reader, who in the
    most interesting passages, is found, so to speak, admitted into
    the company and present in the conversation." Argues that Defoe
    successfully imitated Bunyan in Robinson Crusoe and Molly Flan-
    ders [sic]; and Richardson, in Pamela, etc. See also 1817.5; The
    Autobiography of Benjamin Franklin, ed. Leonard W. Labaree, Ralph
    L. Ketcham, Helen C. Boatfield, and Helene H. Fineman (New Haven
    and London: Yale University Press, 1964), pp. 58, 72.

3   NOORTHOUCK, JOHN. Review of A Selection from the Works of
    Daniel Defoe. 3 vols. London: Logographic Press. Monthly
    Review, 2d ser. 6 (December):466.
       Published by J. Walter. Vols. 1 and 2 include The Life and
    Adventures of Robinson Crusoe; vol. 3, Serious Reflections of Rob-
    inson Crusoe, the True-Born Englishman, the Original Power of the
    Collective Body of the People of England, Examined and Asserted.

4   Review of Chalmers's Life of Daniel De Foe (1790). In Gentle-
    man's Magazine 61, pt. 1, no. 4 (April):346-48.
       Summarizes Chalmers's Life of Daniel De Foe, with very few
    additions. Life had been prefixed without author's name to Stock-
    dale's edition of De Foe's History of the Union (1786). "It is
    now prefixed, with the author's name, to the splendid edition of
    Robinson Crusoe, and also published separately."

5   Robinson Crusoe; or Harlequin Friday. A Grand Pantomime in
    Two Acts, As Performed at the Theatre-Royal, Newcastle-upon-
    Tyne. Newcastle: Hall & Elliot, 27 pp.
       Adaptation of Sheridan's pantomime, 1781.4.

1792

1   Memoirs of the Honourable Col. Andrew Newport, a Shropshire
    Gentleman. New ed. London: Edward Jeffery & R. Faulder,
    439 pp.
        This reprinting of Memoirs of a Cavalier scrupulously
    avoids any hint of Defoe's authorship. It does not have a pref-
    ace or introduction. On the title page, advertises itself as a
    complete military history of the middle of the seventeenth cen-
    tury; the frontispiece is a portrait of the Earl of Essex, "Com-
    mander of the First Army formed by the Parliament against the
    King."

2   SOMERVILLE, THOMAS. The History of Political Transactions,
    and of Parties, from the Restoration of King Charles the
    Second, to the Death of King William. London: A. Strahan &
    T. Cadell, pp. 472-74, 497-500.
        In chap. 18, narrates in graphic details the story of the
    Glenco massacre, beginning with Lieutenant Lindsay's shooting of
    Glenco at his home on 13 February 1692, followed by the massacre,
    the plunder, burning of houses and villages. Amasses the evi-
    dence, in appendix 2, that the massacre was not so much owing to
    any cruelty in William III's disposition as it was to the deliber-
    ate machinations of his advisers. Cites among his three refer-
    ences: Defoe's History [of the Union, 1786], p. 70, which gives
    a similar explanation of the Glenco massacre.

1793

1   "Memoirs of the Life and Writings of Daniel De Foe: With a
    Fine Portrait of that celebrated Author." In the Universal
    Magazine of Knowledge and Pleasure 92 (January):16-23; (Febru-
    ary):102-9.
        The portrait, "from an Engraving by Gucht." A comprehen-
    sive view of Defoe's life, but mainly a pastiche of quotations
    from Chalmers's Life of Daniel De Foe (1790), with some minor
    additions. See Critical Heritage, p. 15.

2   PERCIVAL, THOMAS. "Robinson Crusoe." In A Father's Instruc-
    tions; Consisting of Moral Tales, Fables, and Reflections.
    8th ed. London: J. Johnson, pp. 322-26.
        In the preface, explains the pedagogy for the collection as
    refining "the feelings of the heart" and inspiring the mind with
    "love of moral excellence," attending to "the truth of nature,"
    and promoting "a more early acquaintance with the use of words
    and idioms." In the commentary on Robinson Crusoe, after a sum-
    mary of the Selkirk story, asserts that Selkirk told his adven-
    tures to Defoe "who founded upon them the History of Robinson
    Crusoe, the best and most entertaining moral romance now extant."
    Maintains that Robinson Crusoe shows the important benefits to
    man arising from manual exertion, the mechanic arts, division of

labour, and especially society. Such "improving lessons" Percival finds "admirably enforced" in Cowper's poem, quoted here in
its entirety.

3   T[OWERS, JOSEPH]. "De Foe (Daniel)." In <u>Biographia Brittan-</u>
     <u>ica: or, the Lives of the Most Eminent Persons Who Have Flour-</u>
     <u>ished in Great Britain and Ireland</u>. 2d ed. 5 vols. Edited
     by Andrew Kippis. London: T. Longman et al., 5:45-74. Re-
     print. Anglistica & Americana 69. Hildesheim and New York:
     Georg Olms, 1974.
          K [Andrew Kippis] gives addenda to Towers's account of
     Defoe (5:74-75). An entry on Defoe did not appear in the first
     edition (London: W. Innys, 1750, vol. 3). A supplement to the
     1766 edition did include an entry for John Arbuthnot, and a
     passing reference to <u>Robinson Crusoe</u> as Defoe's, not Arbuthnot's
     (see 1766.6). Follows the broad biographical outlines of George
     Chalmers, but quotes extensively, and thus influentially, from
     Defoe's writings. Also introduces information from contemporary
     periodical literature. Towers's article was probably not so
     inconsequential as in the judgment of the <u>Critical Heritage</u>.

1795

1   EDWARDS, R., ed. "To the Right Honourable Lord Berwick" and
     "Address to the Reader." In <u>A Collection of Scarce and Inter-</u>
     <u>esting Tracts, Tending to Elucidate Detached Parts of the His-</u>
     <u>tory of Great Britain; Selected from the Sommers-Collections</u>.
     London: R. Edwards, pp. iv-ix.
          While making no reference to Defoe by name, here or later
     in the reprint of <u>The History of the Kentish Petition</u>, explains
     the principles for selecting tracts from the prestigious <u>Sommers</u>
     <u>Collections</u> published between 1748 and 1751. Seeks to produce a
     more organized compendium, like the <u>Harleian Miscellany</u>; has a
     curious error of the date "1740" in the table of contents and on
     the first page.

1796

1   MAVOR, WILLIAM FORDYCE. <u>Historical Account of the Most Cele-</u>
     <u>brated Voyages, Travels, and Discoveries, from the Time of Col-</u>
     <u>umbus to the Present Period</u>. 20 vols. London: E. Newbery,
     3:183-94.
          Retells the Alexander Selkirk story as it appeared in
     Captain Woodes Rogers's <u>A Cruising Voyage round the World</u> (1712),
     focusing upon details similar to those in <u>Robinson Crusoe</u> and
     praising Selkirk as a person "who will ever be distinguished in
     historical romance." Later interrupts the flow of the Woodes
     Rogers summary with the charge: "what indeed few are ignorant
     of, that when Selkirk came to England, he was advised to put his
     papers into the hands of the celebrated Daniel Defoe, to arrange

for publication; but that ingenious literary pirate, converting
the original materials, by the aid of a luxuriant fancy, into the
well known romance of Robinson Crusoe, defrauded Selkirk of the
emolument, which it was reasonable to suppose he might have reap-
ed, from an unaffected narrative of his solitary occupations and
thoughts." Assigns all the distinction for the romance, "while
the English language lasts," to Selkirk.

2   MELMOTH, WILLIAM, [Jr.]. Letter from William Melmoth [senior]
    to Defoe [November, 1706?]. In Memoirs of a Late Eminent
    Advocate. London: T. Cadell, Jun. & W. Davies, pp. 55-57.
        Reprints a part of a letter from Melmoth [senior] which
    urges Defoe to continue his opposition to the stage and the
    players, in the Review. The original manuscript letter has not
    survived. In a footnote to the Review, refers to "the well-known
    and very informing Daniel Defoe." Reprinted: Healey.

                              1797

1   [CUSSANS, JACK.] Oh, Poor Robinson Crusoe. London:
    E. Bates.
        All the information on Mr. Cussans who wrote the popular
    comic chant, "Oh, poor Robinson Crusoe," and sang it at the Royal
    Circus and Sadler's Wells, derives from 1869.7. The ten stanzas
    of the chant were reprinted as a broadside (New York: H. de Mar-
    san, [n.d.]) and in The Universal Songster (Fairburn, 1825) as
    well as in the London edition (3 vols. London: Jones & Co.,
    [1832], 1:54), and inserted into Samuel Foote's farce The Mayor
    of Garratt (1820.7) and into Irish Girl (1820?.1). See also
    1850.10; 1864.3; 1880.11.

2   [MONTMORENCY-LAVAL, MADAME DE], trans. "Avertisement." In
    La Vie et tres surprenantes aventures de Robinson Crusoe.
    2 vols. [Paris]: A. Dampierre, 1:iii-iv.
        Describes her experience in developing an interlinear meth-
    od for teaching students to read French. Modifies the method
    used by Dumarsais for Latin and Luneau de Boisjermain for En-
    glish, and applies it to Robinson Crusoe. See also Mann, p. 46.

                              1799

1   LA HARPE, J[EAN] F[RANÇOIS DE]. "Romans." In Lycée ou cours
    de littérature ancienne et moderne. Reprint. 16 vols.
    Paris: Depelafol, 1825, 14:253-54.
        Turns from the French to the English novelists, and com-
    ments at length on Richardson's Clarissa and Fielding's Tom Jones
    ("for me, the first novel in the world"). After Prévost, pauses
    to say that "we know little beyond Robinson," and summarizes Rous-
    seau's view, without any mention of Defoe by name, that "civil
    man has too many comforts around him to be aware of his strengths
    and know all his resources, but that left alone to himself, like

                              44

Robinson, he is indebted only to misfortune for the education
which he received in the savage state from nature." Argues that
the novel should have ended with Robinson's leaving the island,
but the English always seem to lack moderation. Reprinted:
Paris: Firmin Didot Frères, Sons & Co., 3:189-90.

2   "The New Robinson Crusoe." Walpoliana. 2d ed. 2 vols.
     London: R. Phillips, 2:131-32.
        One of Horace Walpole's anecdotes tells of the whimsical
Sir T. Robinson who went about "in his hunting dress, a postil-
lion's cap, a tight green jacket and buckskin breeches." Quite
suddenly he visited his married sister who lived in Paris, and
arrived during an elaborate dinner party. To everyone's amaze-
ment, he was announced as "M. Robinson." A French abbé present
could no longer restrain his curiosity: "Excuse me, Sir, Are you
the famous Robinson Crusoe so remarkable in history?"

[179-]

1   "To the Reader" and Preface. In The Exploits of Robinson
     Crusoe, Mariner, of York. . . . Written originally by Himself,
     and Now first Abridged from the Genuine Original Copy, Present-
     ed to the Editor by a Descendant of the Family. Illustrated
     with Cuts. To Which Is Prefixed, Some Account of the Editor
     of the First Edition, pp. [viii], ix-xii.
        All the preliminaries are a complete fabrication. The "pre-
sent editor" corrects the first editor, Mr. Defoe, by expunging
the latter's interpolations. Although Defoe (says the preface)
was "a man universally acquainted with nature, manners and mankind, and of a liberal mind and understanding," he did not know
"the ways of gain, or getting money by his writing." The preface
compounds error upon error. Confusing the True-Born Englishman
with the Shortest-Way with the Dissenters, the new editor says
the poem was condemned as a libel by the Houses of Lords and
Commons, and "to be burnt by the hands of the common-hangman."
Defoe was sentenced to stand on the pillory at Charing-cross as a
libeller, but he is rescued by "chimney-sweepers boys" who, on a
pre-arranged signal, "plied the populace so effectually with
soot, that they soon dispersed, and left poor Daniel to the protection of his sable attendants." The preface ends problemati-
cally, deftly weaving in compliments if it were regarded as "mere
fiction," interpolations and all. As it is, however, the work is
"restored to the truth of history." The Exploits drastically
abridges Parts One and Two of Robinson Crusoe and the Serious
Reflections. Reprinted: [Liverpool? ca.1810].

1800

1   FOE, E. Preface [by the Author of the Review] to the Reader.
     In Thomas De Laune's A Plea for the Non Conformists. Balls-
     ton, N.Y.: William Child, pp. xxiii-xxxvi.

No explanation can be offered for the garbled state of
Defoe's name, "E. Foe," which generally appeared as "D. Foe" in
editions for 1706, 1709, 1720. The "Preface to the Ballston
Edition" was signed by Elias Lee.

2   JAMES, ISAAC. Providence Displayed: or, the Remarkable Adven-
     tures of Alexander Selkirk, of Largo, in Scotland . . . And on
     Whose Adventures was Founded the Celebrated Novel of Robinson
     Crusoe. Bristol: I. James et al., 204 pp.
         Gathers information for Alexander Selkirk's history because
     it is "universally allowed to be the Ground-work of Robinson
     Crusoe." Although the design is "to relate nothing but absolute
     Facts," the situation being an "affecting" one in itself, one
     must also consider "the lively Fancy of De Foe." Describes the
     topography of Juan Fernandez, and narrates the experiences of Sel-
     kirk and other isolated mariners shipwrecked on islands. At one
     point, admits that if Defoe were impious enough to forge the Mrs.
     Veal story to sell copies of Drelincourt's Consolations against
     the Fears of Death, he would not hesitate to mistreat Selkirk, as
     "universal Tradition" said he did. Supports this view by refer-
     ring to the preface of Serious Reflections where Defoe seems to
     be claiming the existence of a real Selkirk; lists other persons
     (e.g., Dr. Arbuthnot, Lord Oxford) said to be the author of Robin-
     son Crusoe.

3   LABAUME, A. G[RIFFET]. "Vie de Daniel Defoe." In La Vie et
     les aventures de Robinson Crusoë, par Daniel Defoe. 3 vols.
     Paris: H. Verdière, 1:xxv-c.
         Criticizes Chalmers in a note, to the effect that his Life
     of Daniel De Foe (1790) had to be rewritten for French readers,
     since it is confusing and too local and even lacks interest.
     Taking the information directly from Chalmers, rewrites the biog-
     raphy of Defoe popularly, makes him heroic and thus appealing to
     French readers. Includes Chalmers's account of the beginnings of
     interest in an accurate canon. Earlier than Philarète Chasles
     (1833.2), not without help from Chalmers: one of the best early
     accounts of Defoe published and read in France. Reprinted:
     1816, 1821.

4   MONTLINOT, C[HARLES ANTOINE LECLERC DE]. Preface to La Vie et
     les aventures de Robinson Crusoë, par Daniel Defoe. 3 vols.
     Paris: H. Verdière, 1:i-viii.
         This impressive edition, referred to as Mme. Panckoucke's
     by Mann, assigns the authorship to Defoe on the title page, and
     explicitly rejects Richard Steele as the author in one of the
     preliminary "Advertissements." The translation into French used
     the text of the Stockdale edition (1790) as the base. Among the
     preliminaries were Saint-Hyacinthe's preface, part of the "Ad-
     vertissement" in Garnier's collection of Voyage imaginaires, and
     A. Griffet Labaume's "Vie de Daniel De Foe" which expanded Chalm-
     ers's Life of Daniel De Foe in the Stockdale edition. Distin-
     guishes significantly between English and French or continental

views of Robinson Crusoe, emphatically preferring the former--the
depiction of isolated man--as opposed to the latter--the "improvements" of the Robinsonades that show "man as a social being and
the central interest in the family." Of particular note here:
Montlinot's distinction between the French and English physiog-
nomies in this "political novel" and the principal traits that
give Robinson Crusoe "the English and popular physiognomy."

1801

1   EDGEWORTH, MARIA. "Forester." In Moral Tales for Young
    People. 5 vols. London: J. Johnson. Reprint. With an
    Introduction by Gina Luria. 3 vols. New York and London:
    Garland Publishing Co., 1974, 1:1, 30.
        Characterizes Forester as a person having "some singulari-
    ties of opinion," including a love of independence so extreme
    that he preferred Crusoe's life on his desert island to any other
    in cultivated society, and in particular he had contempt for
    "self indolence," which he associated with gentlemen. Describes
    Forester's habit of losing himself at critical moments "in the
    history of a man, who had been cast away some hundred years ago
    upon a desert island." Reprinted: in Tales and Novels: The
    Longford Edition (1893), Anglistica & Americana, 31, vol. 1
    (Hildesheim: Georg Olms, 1969).

1802

1   Introduction and "Avant Propos" to Histoire de Sudmer; ou
    Robinson Crusoé rétabli dans son intégrité. 3 vols. in 1.
    Londres [Augsburg, Doll], pp. 3-20, 21-32.
        Advancing the thesis that Robinson Crusoe holds no interest
    after he leaves the island, the anonymous narrator presents here
    a manuscript which, he claims, tells the true story of Lewis
    Balseil--the Crusoe who, in fact, never left the island, and who
    populated and cultivated it. Elaborates upon this fiction in the
    introduction. The narrator also critiques Robinson Crusoe, with-
    out any mention of Defoe: "The author, in an amusing form, gives
    some healthy lessons of religion and morality. . . ." Limits the
    action to the island in order to stress Crusoe's courage, indus-
    try, and especially his trust in the Lord.

1804

1   LAHARPE, J[EAN] F[RANÇOISE DE]. "Romans." In Lycee, ou cours
    de litterature ancienne et moderne. 16 vols. Paris: H.
    Agasse, 14:254-56.
        Provides a panoramic view of the French novel (including
    English novels translated into French) which becomes leisurely
    criticism for such works as Marivaux's Mariane, Prévost's Manon

Lescaut, Richardson's Clarissa, and Fielding's Tom Jones. Inter-
rupts the apparently chronological presentation to describe the
effects of Rousseau's Émile (1762) on changing the interpretation
given to Robinson Crusoe, which up to then was scarcely known.
Makes a special point of declaring Part One of Robinson Crusoe to
be "a truly original work."

2   TRIMMER, MRS. SARAH. Review of [Joachim Heinrich] Campe's New
     Robinson Crusoe. Stockdale, 1789. Guardian of Education
     3:356–60.
        Comments only incidentally on Robinson Crusoe as "the plain
simple narrative of a sea-faring man" which Campe, under the in-
spiration of Rousseau, converted to "a Treatise of Natural Education." Observes that the religion which Mr. Billingsley teaches
his children in the New Robinson Crusoe, and in which Robinson
Crusoe instructs Friday, is Deism or "natural, and not revealed
Religion"; and thus favors the original work.

3   _____. Review of Robinson Crusoe. Guardian of Education
     3:297–300.
        Holds Robinson Crusoe in high esteem: "in respect to its
general merits we believe it to be the universal opinion, that it
is one of the most interesting and entertaining books that was
ever written." Argues the book strikingly demonstrates the power
of the human mind "to relieve the wants of the body; and to sus-
tain the evils of life with fortitude and resignation under the
most distressing circumstances." Answers the question with a
firm negative: whether such a book should be placed in the hands
of all boys indiscriminately. Accepts Alexander Selkirk as the
source, and at the end inserts "the verses by the late Mr. Cowper" supposed to have been written by Selkirk on Juan Fernandez.

                                    1805

1   "Advertisement." In The Life and Adventures of Robinson
     Crusoe, Originally Written by Daniel Defoe. London: Tabart
     & Co., pp. iii–iv.
        Explains that while this narrative was not written for
young people and must therefore be abridged, no other book "lays
such strong hold on the curiosity of Youth" as a "lively picture"
of man in a state of nature. Makes early use of color in the
sixteen copper plates.

2   CLARKE, JAMES STANIER. Naufragia or Historical Memoirs of
     Shipwrecks and of the Providential Deliverance of Vessels.
     2 vols. London: J. Mawman, 1:1–25.
        Since this book deals with true shipwrecks, makes the case,
in section 1 ("Dissertation on Alexander Selkirk and on the real
author of Robinson Crusoe"), that the person who experienced the
shipwreck was known "under the real name of 'Alexander Selkirk,'
or the fictitious one of 'Robinson Crusoe.'" Even though Robin-

son Crusoe surpasses Gil Blas in "universal suffrage," Selkirk
and Defoe must divide the honors while "a specious Frenchman"
receives the full credit alone. Selkirk gave Defoe the outlines
for the narrative, but "it does not follow, nor can it be proved,
that Defoe made an improper or unfair use of the papers of Selkirk." Makes the defense for Defoe that the Selkirk story was
known for seven years before Robinson Crusoe was written. Among
the early criticisms received by the book there was never any
accusation of plagiarism or theft, but (on the contrary) of the
story's being "feigned." As an after-thought, feels obliged to
produce the latest "report" (1788.3) that the author of the first
part of Robinson Crusoe was not Defoe, but Lord Oxford. Although
he cannot accept the report, agrees personally that there is "a
falling off" between the two parts as if they were the work of
different writers. Reproduces the early accounts of Selkirk by
Captain Woodes Rogers and Sir Richard Steele. In section 2, mainly about the island Juan Fernandez, quotes Dampier's "anecdote"
about "this early and interesting Crusoe" [meaning Selkirk], but
it is really about the Mosquito Indian, later named "Will," who
has been abandoned at Juan Fernandez in 1681 by Captain Watlin's
bucanneers. When the Indian was rescued some three years later,
he was joyously received by another Mosquito Indian named
"Robin."

3   DRAKE, NATHAN. Essays, Biographical, Critical, and Histori-
    cal, Illustrative of the Tatler, Spectator, and Guardian.
    3 vols. London: John Sharpe, 1:23-24.
        Recognizes, in the preface, that Steele and Addison were
    "the fathers and founders of Periodical Writing," and mentions
    Defoe's Review in connection with the "Rehearsals" of Charles
    Lesley. Admits the Review was "of a kind far superior to any
    thing which had hitherto appeared" and Defoe, "a man of undoubted
    genius . . . who, deviating from the accustomed route, had chalk-
    ed out a new path for himself." Yet because of the ephemeral
    quality of its subjects, the Review "appears . . . to have soon
    sunk into oblivion." Notes that a complete set of the Review is
    probably no longer in existence.

4   NAUTICUS [pseud.]. "Anecdotes of Alexander Selkirk, the origi-
    nal Robinson Crusoe." Scots Magazine, and Edinburgh Literary
    Miscellany 67 (September):670-74.
        Agrees with George Chalmers that since Selkirk did not have
    pen, ink, or journal, Defoe could not have stolen any papers.
    He did adopt "the fundamental incident of Selkirk's adventures,"
    and produced a work that "at once fixed the attention of the
    reading world by its various events, engaging style, and useful
    moralities." Provides little biographical information aside from
    the accounts by Captain Woodes Rogers and Captain Edward Cooke,
    the power of attorney and will (both reproduced) in favor of his
    "loving friend" Sophia Bruce, and the legal suit brought by
    Frances Hall to secure all Selkirk's property after his death.

5   PIXERÉCOURT, R[ENÉ] C[HARLES] GUILBERT de. Robinson Crusoé,
    mélodrame en trois actes, à grand spectacle. Paris: Barba,
    79 pp.
        Provides the text of the "melodrama," an adaptation of Rob-
    inson Crusoe, as it was first performed in Paris at the theatre
    Porte Saint Martin on 2 October 1805. Pixerécourt, author or
    co-author of many melodramas, wrote the words, and directed the
    performance. Alexander Piccini and Gerardin Lacour composed the
    music, and M. Aumer arranged the ballets. Introduces new action
    as well as new characters, such as D. Diego, Robinson's brother-
    in-law; Emma, wife of Robinson and sister of Diego; Isidor, son
    of Robinson and Emma; Iglou, Friday's Father and chief of the
    Caribs; Parouba, chief of a Carib tribe and enemy of Iglou; and
    others. As an urgent note explains, Iglou, Friday, and the other
    Caribs are not to be portrayed as being black, but olive-hued or
    lightly tawny. Stages the entire melodrama "in a desert island,
    situated near the mouth of the Orinoco"; act 1 in the part of the
    island which Robinson calls his "metairie"; act 2 in "the inter-
    ior of Robinson's grotto; and act 3 on "the beach where Robinson
    had been cast by the storm." Reprinted: 1841.9.

                              1805-1808

1   HAKEN, JOHANN C[HRISTIAN] L[UDWIG], ed. Prefaces to Biblio-
    thek der Robinsone. In zweckmässigen Auszügen von Verfasser
    der grauen Mappe. 5 vols. Berlin: Johann Friedrich Unger,
    1:i-xix; 2:i-ii; 3:i-iv; 4:i-ii; 5:i-ii.
        Endeavors to do for "Robinsonades" what Garnier had done
    for the "imaginary voyages" (1787-1789.1), namely, define and
    classify the type, and illustrate it with "suitable" abridge-
    ments, adaptations, and summaries. Altogether, according to Gove
    (p. 128), Bibliothek der Robinsone deals with some thirty-four
    works: Robinson Crusoe and Insel Felsenburg, extensively; and
    twenty-five Robinsonades and seven adaptations, much less exten-
    sively. Of these, twenty-six are German originals, and the rest
    translations from the French (2), English (2), Italian (2), and
    Dutch (1). In the very important preface (19 pp.) to the "li-
    brary of Robinsons," states "the objective, plan and limits," of
    the project. Eloquently defines the significance of Robinson
    Crusoe as a seminal work both in itself and German Romanticism.
    Maintains that Robinson Crusoe "set things in action; for several
    decades of the past century it rained countless Robinsons." Des-
    cribes the movement as "an awakening" for both the British and
    the Germans, the emergence of "a new poetic art," and "the dawn
    of an improved taste." Observes that while these Robinsons are
    now ignored in libraries and "in the dusty corners of the book-
    seller and the cheese-grocer," they deserve at least to have
    their existences recorded. Asks why these Robinsons "once pleas-
    ed and entertained two generations of our country people," and
    had "a certain not inappreciable influence on their education or
    bad training." Why did this poetic art win so much affection?

To this central question, responds: "Robinson's history is the
history of mankind and its progressive culture in miniature";
proceeds, insightfully, to analyze isolated man's relationship to
"omnipotent necessity." Urges that we are always in complete
sympathy with "our islander." Identifies the relationship of man
with necessity as the "given theme" of Robinson Crusoe and the
numerous Robinsonades written both before and after 1719. As
part of the systematization with which he hopes to introduce
order, identifies six main classes of Robinsonades: (1) actual
Robinsons; (2) works with "Robinson" in their titles, such as
the French Gil Blas curiously re-titled "the Spanish Robinson";
(3) German works (e.g., Insel Felsenburg, 1731) that expressed or
went beyond "Defoe's basic [social] idea"; (4) a vaguely defined
class of narratives concerned with bringing "situations and institutions (political as well as civic) of people lost in a dream"
into "paintings" expressive of specific values; (5) a special
artistic class in which the island experience is less essential
to the "plan" than such motifs as "sea-voyages, freebootery,
Turkish slavery, Romance banditry"; and (6) some "cross-breeds"
consisting of eight Robinsons on "an attractive theme, the psychological development during the gradual spiritual development
from the earliest child's age to [the emergence of] society."
Insists that with all six classes, and some 150 titles, the editor has been guided less by his "schema" than by chronology, and
more by "the relationship of their ideas." In the prefaces to
vols. 2-5, explains the adjustments being made to the reprinting
of the Robinsonades; comments more about their qualities than
about Robinson Crusoe.

1806

1   "Account of Selkirk." Scots Magazine; and Edinburgh Literary
    Miscellany 68 (January):18-20; (March):169-72.
        Extracts from Providence Displayed: Or, a Very Surprizing
    Account of One Mr. Alexander Selkirk, published in the Harleian
    Miscellany, 1745.1.

2   NOBLE, MARK. "Daniel De Foe." In A Biographical History of
    England, from the Revolution to the End of George I's Reign;
    Being a Continuation of the Rev. J. Granger's Work. London:
    W. Richardson, Darton & Harvey, & W. Baynes, 2:305-7.
        Lists four portraits, of which the one engraved by W. Skel-
    ton and prefixed to the History of the Union (1786) is of Ned
    Ward; describes the "curious print," a medley by George Bickham
    entitled "The [Three] False Brethren," showing in the upper por-
    tion Defoe's "Deformed Head in the Pillory" grossly caricatured,
    and in the lower portion Defoe "in his actual state, seated in
    his study." On the bottom left of the print appears a card with
    the inscription "G.B. ingraver, MDCCXII." See E.H.W. Meyerstein,
    "Daniel, the Pope and the Devil: A Caricaturist's Portrait of
    the True Defoe," TLS, no. 1776 (15 February 1936):134.

51

<u>1807</u>

1   GODWIN, WILLIAM. Preface to <u>Faulkener: A Tragedy. As It Is</u>
    <u>Performed at the Theatre Royal, Drury Lane</u>. London: Richard
    Phillips, pp. v-vi.
       On the dubious assumption that Defoe left traces of his
    handiwork in the sequel published as part of the 1745 edition,
    <u>Roxana, or the Fortunate Mistress</u>, early nineteenth-century
    critics--Godwin, Charles Lamb, Walter Wilson, and William Hazlitt
    the younger--insisted upon the 1745 publication as being the only
    "perfect edition." Of the seventeen different editions of the
    novel through the year 1776, nine of them containing sequels,
    only the 1745 has ever been thought to have any merit. Godwin
    and Lamb never quite penetrated the textual maze of <u>Roxana</u> edi-
    tions, but they were always enthusiastic about the depiction of
    guilt and pursuit which they thought were strictly in the 1745
    sequel. Their intense interest, indeed, helped the novel to
    shake off the Francis Noble crudities (1775.1, 4-5) and make some
    textual improvements in the two comprehensive editions of 1840.
    Godwin planned <u>Faulkener</u> in 1801, wrote it in 1804, and presented
    it at Drury Lane Theater for a run of six nights. Holcroft's
    revisions of the play before the production occasioned a quarrel
    between Godwin and himself. Coleridge also saw the play before
    it was produced. In the preface, Godwin admits the apocryphal
    character of the sequel, but he makes clear why the novel was
    always somewhat a favorite with him as a boy: "The terrors of a
    guilty mind, haunted with mysterious fears of retribution, have
    seldom been more powerfully delineated." Lamb's prologue is
    essentially an encomium to Defoe; the first six lines were quoted
    on the title page of Hazlitt's <u>Works of Daniel De Foe</u> (1840).
    The influence of Godwin and Lamb was transmitted primarily
    through Wilson's <u>Memoirs</u> of Defoe (1830). See also Lamb, 1807.2.

2   LAMB, CHARLES. "Prologue" to William Godwin's <u>Faulkener:</u>
    <u>A Tragedy</u>. London: Richard Phillips, p. vii.
       Because Godwin's play was based on Defoe's <u>The Fortunate</u>
    <u>Mistress</u>, Lamb's prologue reminds older readers of the pensive
    Crusoe's story, of Defoe's genius "skill'd by native pathos to
    prevail," of his "various pen" ("Nov'list, historian, poet, pam-
    phleteer"). In the novel, Defoe "drew a striking sketch from
    private life, . . . A real story of domestic woe" that trusts "to
    truth, to nature, and <u>Defoe</u>." For the two letters in which Lamb
    gives advice to Godwin about <u>Faulkener</u>, 9 and 17 September 1801,
    see 1886.12, and see also <u>The Letters of Charles and Mary Lamb</u>,
    ed. Edwin W. Marrs (Ithaca and London: Cornell University Press,
    1976), 2:17-20, 23-25; and 1807.1; Wilson's <u>Memoirs</u> of Defoe
    (1830); 1848.4. Reprinted: 1903.4; <u>The Letters of Charles Lamb</u>,
    ed. E.V. Lucas (London: J.M. Dent & Sons; Methuen & Co., 1935),
    1:268-70, 275-77.

1808

1   "Life of the Author." In <u>The Life and Adventures of Robinson
      Crusoe</u>. London: J. Walker et al., pp. iii-vi.
           Errs in the few biographical details given, e.g., that
      Defoe became a political writer <u>before</u> he engaged in business as
      a hosier and then as a pantile-maker. Started writing with the
      <u>True-Born Englishman</u> and <u>Reformation of Manners</u>, but ran into
      trouble with the irony of the <u>Shortest-Way with the Dissenters</u>.
      Began the <u>Review</u> while he was in Newgate. Wrote the "History of
      Addresses." Relinquished politics altogether in 1715, and turned
      to "subjects of morals and manners" in the <u>Family Instructor</u>,
      <u>Religious Courtship</u>, and the novels. "The morality of some of
      these has been justly questioned, but they have all the fascina-
      tion of simplicity of style and probability of adventure, and
      all enjoyed a considerable share of popularity." Reprinted, in
      part: 1812.

2   NICHOLS, JOHN, ed. <u>The Works of the Rev. Jonathan Swift, D.D.</u>
      Edited by Thomas Sheridan; corrected and rev. by John Nichols.
      19 vols. London: J. Johnson et al., 3:133-34; 4:29-33;
      17:460-61.
           Reprints the <u>Letter . . . concerning the Sacramental Test</u>
      (1709), including Swift's contemptuous aside "(the fellow that
      was pilloried, I have forgot his name*)" and the note identify-
      ing Defoe, as in earlier entries 1735.3; 1752.1; 1755.1. Pro-
      vides the text for the <u>Examiner</u>, no. 16 (16 November 1710) which
      finds fault with "two stupid illiterate scribblers, both of them
      fanaticks by profession, I mean the Review, and Observator," and
      compares "the mock authoritative manner of the one, and the in-
      sipid mirth of the other," but makes no mention of their authors
      by name. Before the reprint of <u>The Present State of Wit</u> (1711),
      claims "great reason" for assigning the pamphlet to John Gay. In
      giving "the histories and characters of all our periodical pa-
      pers," annotates the references to "the poor Review" and to Defoe
      as a fellow having "excellent natural parts," but little learn-
      ing, with a paragraph-long account which is, on the whole, favor-
      able. Mentions that among all his writings Defoe is perhaps best
      known for <u>Robinson Crusoe</u>.

3   SCOTT, SIR WALTER. Preface to <u>Memoirs of Capt. George Carle-
      ton, an English Officer . . . Written by Himself</u>. Edinburgh:
      A. Constable & Co.; London: J. Murray, pp. i-xxiii.
           Assigns the authorship to Captain George Carleton, with no
      mention of Defoe. Places the emphasis on the principal subject
      of the <u>Memoirs</u>, Charles Mordaunt, afterwards 3d Earl of Peter-
      borough; discusses the author and his style briefly. Reprinted:
      <u>Memoirs of Captain Carleton</u>, ed. Cyril Hughes Hartmann (New York:
      E.P. Dutton & Co., 1929), pp. 1-10.

1809

1 [BALLANTYNE, JOHN.] "A Biographical Memoir of Daniel De Foe."
   In The Life and Adventures of Robinson Crusoe . . . Embellished with Wooden Cuts. 3 vols. Edinburgh: John Ballantyne &
   Co.; London: John Murray, 1:i-xxxii.
         Shows negligible advance in biographical knowledge over
   Chalmers's Life of Daniel De Foe (1790). Most of the biographical information derives from a small number of documents and the
   few frequently repeated, autobiographical statements in Defoe's
   writings. Even such basic information as the time and place of
   Defoe's early education is missing. Large gaps of time appear in
   the narrative. Events in Defoe's life rise to a crisis in 1715,
   with him "struck with apoplexy" and his Appeal to Honour and Justice left unfinished and published by friends. Thereafter, "his
   mind had changed its tone. . . ." About half a page more covers
   such works only as Serious Reflections . . . of Robinson Crusoe,
   Captain Singleton, Dumb Philosopher, Duncan Campbell, Colonel
   Jack, Roxana, and New Voyage Round the World. Although Ballantyne will not attempt "a critical analysis of Robinson Crusoe" or
   an assessment of character, he closes with strong praise for
   Defoe as a writer, "a man of powerful intellect and lively imagination," and as a person. Ballantyne's "Biographical Memoir"
   appeared also in the first collected edition of Defoe's narratives, in vol. 1 of Robinson Crusoe, in Scott's Novels of Daniel
   De Foe (1809-1810), as well as in the more visible and far more
   prestigious Oxford Works (1840-1841). Defoe's influence on
   Scott, and more important Scott's influence on Defoe's literary
   reputation, are summarized in John Robert Moore, "Defoe and
   Scott," PMLA 56, no. 2 (1941):710-35; and Scott's relationships
   with the printer James Ballantyne and his younger brother, the
   publisher and bookseller John Ballantyne, are described in Edgar
   Johnson, Sir Walter Scott: The Great Unknown (New York: Macmillan, 1970), 1:263, 308, 362, 416. Ballantyne's authorship of
   the "Biographical Memoir" was generously acknowledged in Works
   (1840-1841). Reprinted: 1809-1810.1; 1810; 1812; 1827.2; 1830
   (Paris); 1840-1841.1; 1861; 1864; 1865; 1867; 1868; 1878; 1882;
   1903. With Scott's criticism: 1827.2; 1834; 1836; 1865; 1877.

2 LONDINENSIS [pseud.]. Letter to Mr. Urban. Gentleman's Magazine 79 (12 December):1126-27.
         Expresses surprise that a periodical, the Beauties of En-
   gland (1810.3), had published on the first of the month Defoe's
   celebrated History of the Plague in London as "a genuine piece of
   History." The History is well known to be "as much a work of
   imagination as his Robinson Crusoe, except as to the circumstance
   of there having been a plague in the year 1665." See also
   1810.2-3.

3 Review of James Stanier Clarke's Naufragia, 1805. Monthly
   Review, 2d ser. 60 (October):219-20.

Calls attention to the section on Selkirk and <u>Robinson Crusoe</u>, and to Clarke's inclining to "an opinion which has been started, that Daniel Defoe was not in fact the author of that popular book." Transcribes the letter by W.W. to the same point, published in the <u>Gentleman's Magazine</u>, 1788.3. Thinks the matter should be decided "as a piece of literary history."

1809-1810

1   <u>The Novels of Daniel De Foe</u>. Edited by Sir Walter Scott.
    12 vols. Edinburgh: John Ballantyne & Co. & Brown & Crombie;
    London: Longman, Hurst, Rees, & Orme.
        Publishes here, for the first time, the largest number of
    works by Defoe in a collected edition, including six novels,
    John Ballantyne's "Biographical Memoir of Daniel De Foe" (33
    pp.), which had already appeared (1809.1) and would frequently
    be reprinted separately and combined with Sir Walter Scott's
    continuation. The idea was Scott's--to publish, with biogra-
    phies, uniform editions of such novelists as Defoe, Richardson,
    Fielding, and Smollett. Only the <u>Memoirs of a Cavalier</u>, vols. 4
    and 5, has the date 1809 on the title page while all the others
    have the date 1810, including <u>The Life and Adventures of Robin-
    son Crusoe</u>, vols. 1-3; <u>The Life of Colonel Jack</u>, vols. 6-7; <u>The
    Adventures of Captain Singleton</u>, vols. 8-9; <u>The True-Born English-
    man. A Satire</u>, also in vol. 9; <u>A New Voyage Round the World</u>,
    vols. 10-11; and <u>The History of the Plague in London, in 1665</u>,
    in vol. 12. Especially important as an early effort to fix the
    canon of Defoe's writing was Scott's "List of De Foe's Writings,
    As Far As They have Been Ascertained" (12:271-88), only a few of
    which have since been rejected. The "Advertisement to the
    Present Edition" of the <u>Memoirs of a Cavalier</u> briefly discusses
    the authenticity of the memoirs, without reaching any conclusion.
    The notes to this work in vols. 4 (5 pp.) and 5 (8 pp.) are
    mainly extracts from such periodicals of the time as the <u>Swedish
    Intelligencer</u>, contemporary memoirs, and histories.

1810

1   BARBAULD, ANNA LETITIA. "De Foe." <u>The Life and Surprising
    Adventures of Robinson Crusoe</u>. 2 vols. In <u>The British
    Novelists; with an Essay and Prefaces, Biographical and
    Critical</u>. London: F.C. & J. Rivington et al., 16:i-viii.
        Places <u>Robinson Crusoe</u> among the novels because "it yields
    to few in the truth of its description and its power of interest-
    ing the mind." Compares Swift and Defoe in the use of "grave
    irony" and "minute circumstances." When the Whigs returned to
    power in 1715, Defoe was not rewarded with an office: "he had
    given offence by some publications which were at least ambiguous,
    and laid him open to the censure of writing on both sides." He
    left politics, and turned to the works which made his name "best

55

known to posterity." Among the novels, falls short of praising
the Journal of the Plague Year; it had deceived readers like
Dr. Mead into believing in its authenticity. Has nothing to say
about the other novels. In discussing both parts of Robinson
Crusoe, focusses upon the positive implications, the capacity of
solitary man to overcome obstacles, and upon circumstances "which
strongly affect the feelings." Recognizes Alexander Selkirk as a
real castaway, but at the same time firmly rejects any "unacknowl-
edged" use of Selkirk's papers.

2   BRAYLEY, E[DWARD] W[EDLAKE]. Letter to Mr. Urban. Gentle-
     man's Magazine 80, pt. 1 (March):215-17.
         Of the three objections raised by Londinensis (1809.2):
     acknowledges the error of referring to Defoe as "the author" of
     the Journal of the Plague Year rather than "the Editor only," and
     admits the mistake of identifying him with one of the Examiners.
     Does not agree that the Journal of the Plague Year is "as much a
     work of imagination as his Robinson Crusoe." Stresses major
     differences between Withers's Britain's Remembrancer and Defoe's
     Journal of the Plague Year. See also 1810.3.

3   _____. London and Middlesex; or, an Historical, Commercial,
     & Descriptive Survey, vol. 1. In his Beauties of England and
     Wales 10, pt. 1:374-403.
         Parallels an account in the main text of the plague with
     long extracts in the footnotes, primarily from Journal of the
     Plague Year. In a brief introduction, states that Defoe was "the
     Author," and that he had stayed in London during the plague and
     on occasion had served as one of the "Examiners." See the objec-
     tions to this item raised by Londinensis, 1809.2; and the reply
     by Brayley, 1810.2.

4   DUMOULIN, F[RANÇOIS] A[IMÉ] L[OUIS]. Collection de cent-cin-
     quante gravures représentant et formant une suite non inter-
     rompue des voyages et aventures surprenantes de Robinson
     Crusoé, desinées et gravées par F.A.L. Dumoulin. Vevey:
     Loertscher et fils, 6 pp., 148 plates.
         Graphically interprets the widely varied scenes in Robinson
     Crusoe through 148 of the 150 plates announced in the title. In
     the advertisement (4 pp.), describes these plates as etchings
     ("gravures à l'eau forte et retouchées au burin"), and refers to
     himself as a self-taught apprentice working without the help of a
     master. Praises Robinson Crusoe and its characters generously as
     having, from the engraver's childhood, shaped his taste in read-
     ing, sketching, the study of nature, and the desire to travel.
     Explains that in order to make you feel his etchings are "a faith-
     ful copy of what I have seen and observed," he has to describe
     the influences upon him, including his own "studies" of the land
     and the sea and his use of specific books. Tells of his life
     from 1773 to 1782, experiencing "a frightful tempest" that lasted
     four days and wrecked sixty ships; visiting the islands of Grena-
     da, Trinidad, Tobago, the mouth of the Orinoco River; and final-

ly, returning home and doing the engravings for his favorite
novel, Robinson Crusoe: "imagination was joined with memory."
For the publication date 1810, see Paul Morand, Monsieur Dumoulin
à l'isle de la Grenade (Paudex, Switzerland: Editions de Fon-
tainemore, 1976), p. 7.

5   "Providence Displayed: Or a Very Surprising Account of One
     Mr. Alexander Selkirk. . . ." In The Harleian Miscellany.
     Edited by William Oldys and Thomas Park. Vol. 5. London:
     White & Co., John Murray, John Harding, pp. 429-33.
         Reprints 1745.1, and gives information in the notes that
"Providence Displayed" was taken "nearly verbatim" from Captain
Woodes Rogers's account of Selkirk in his Cruising Voyage Round
the World (1712) and that Defoe was charged with "surreptitiously
appropriating the papers of Selkirk" for his Robinson Crusoe, but
the charge was without any basis.

6   SELCHRIG, SOPHIA. Petition to Mr. Say for Relief. Monthly
     Repository 5 (November):531.
         The editor, referring to her as "the widow of Alexander
Selkirk, Defoe's Robinson Crusoe," quotes her petition to Mr. Say
which describes her as "much reduced to want."

                                1811

1   BOLL, F.C. "Der erste Robinson." Morgenblatt für gebildete
     Stände 5, no. 155 (29 June):617-19.
         Gives a brief account of the Robinsonade extending back to
Sophocles' Philoctetes. Among such stories in Germany inspired
by the English classic, he cites the list of a manuscript in the
second part of Heinrich A.O. Reichard's Bibliothek der Romane
(1782). Mentions further Reichard's contention that Defoe betrayed Selkirk's trust, but sides with Johann Beckmann (Litteratur
der älteren Reisebeschreibungen, 1807) who found the charge uncon-
vincing. Leaves the question undecided. Surmises Defoe may have
known of the earlier Robinsonade, the story of Serrano shipwrecked on an island off the Mexican coast, in Garcilaso de la Vega's
Geschichte der Yncas.   (P.E.C.)

2   LAMB, CHARLES [L.B., pseud.]. "The Good Clerk, a Character;
     with Some Account of The Complete English Tradesman." Reflec-
     tor 2, no. 4:432-37.
         Offers an idealized "character" of the good clerk, and then
demonstrates that it is not "a creature of fancy," but it fits
"those frugal and economical maxims" that were instilled into
"London apprentices" during the early part of the last century,
"(England's meanest period)"--as illustrated in Defoe's Complete
English Tradesman. Vigorously attacks the meanness of the book,
with its "hundreds of anecdotes, dialogues (in Defoe's liveliest
manner) interspersed, all tending to the same amiable purpose,
namely, the sacrificing of every honest emotion of the soul to

what he calls the main chance." Insists that he does not know if
Defoe is in jest or earnest. Defoe's possible hypocrisy seems
more dangerous than anything in Mandeville's Fable of the Bees.
Was "this Philosopher of Meanness" seriously recommending "the
meanest, vilest, wretchedest degradations of the human character," or was he laughing in his sleeve? Reprinted: 1864.2;
William Hone, The Table Book (London: William Hone, 1827), reprinted, London and New York: Ward, Lock & Co., 1891, pp. 282–
84; 1903.4.

1812

1   "Anecdotes of Literati, Collectors, &c." Gentleman's Magazine
    82, pt. 1 (March):206.
        Henry Baker (d.1774) married the daughter of "the famous
Daniel Defoe," had two sons who died before him.

2   BAKER, DAVID ERSKINE. Biographia Dramatica; or a Companion to
    the Playhouse. 3 vols. London: Longman, Hurst, Rees, Orme,
    & Brown et al., 2:83.
        As in the reprint, 1782.1, assigns the revised date 1704 to
Colley Cibber's The Careless Husband, but continues to mention
"Mr. Defoe" as one of three possible authors to whom the play has
been attributed. Stephen Jones has made the considerable addi-
tions and improvements in the Biographia Dramatica to the end of
November, 1811.

3   BIGLAND, JOHN. Beauties of England and Wales 16:765–66.
        Briefly tells of Defoe's living in Halifax where he wrote
"De Jure Divino" [i.e., Jure Divino] and Robinson Crusoe, and of
his defrauding Selkirk.

4   GREEN, M. Letter to Mr. Urban. Gentleman's Magazine 82,
    pt. 1 (June):529–30.
        Defoe's facsimile autograph from a bond dated 5 April 1729,
in which £500 is to be paid as the marriage portion of his daughter Sophia, to Henry Baker.

5   "The Life of Daniel De Foe." In The Life and Adventures of
    Robinson Crusoe. 2 vols. London: Chiswick Press, 1:v–xvi.
        Differs here and there from the common run of biographical
prefaces, as in the rewards given by King William to Defoe, not
only a pension but an appointment, "as his opponents denominated
it, "pamphlet-writer general to the court." Places emphasis on
Robinson Crusoe as the book recommended by Rousseau to promote
natural education. Mentions only one other work, the Tour, "a
performance of very inferior merit, but De Foe was now the garru-
lous old man. . . ." Coleridge's famous marginalia on Robinson
Crusoe were written in Henry Gillman's copy of this edition. See
also 1902.19; F.D.Klingender, "Correspondence: Coleridge on Robinson Crusoe," TLS, no. 1774 (1 February 1936):96; Coleridge's

Miscellaneous Criticism, ed. Thomas Middleton Raysor (Cambridge, Mass.: Harvard University Press, 1936). Reprinted: 1836; 1839; 1843; 1845; 1853; 1859.

6   WEBER, HENRY WILLIAM. Introduction to Popular Romances: Consisting of Imaginary Voyages and Travels. Edinburgh: John Ballantyne et al. London: Longman et al., pp. xvii-xliii.
        Important as an early English attempt to define the term "imaginary voyages," derived from the French. Refers to the "extensive collection of these classes of romantic voyages" published at Amsterdam in thirty-five volumes (1787.5), reprinted since, and now a standard work. Makes important critical connections and distinctions between Gulliver's Travels and Robinson Crusoe. Claims that all European countries, and most German provinces, have "their own Robinson." The "rage" for imitation seems "ludicrous." In addition to the two parts of Robinson Crusoe, reprints Gulliver's Travels, A Journey to the World Under Ground, R.S.'s The Life and Adventures of Peter Wilkins, and The History of Automathes. Quotes extensively Defoe's "borrowings" from the Selkirk incidents in the Voyage of Captain Woodes Rogers (1712).

1812-1813

1   WYSS, JOHANN RUDOLF, ed. Preface to Der schweizerische Robinson, oder der schiffbrüchige Schweizer-Prediger und seine Familie. 2 vols. Zurich: Orell, Füssli & Co., 1:3-12. Translated by William Godwin as The Family Robinson Crusoe: or, Journal of a Father Shipwrecked, with His Wife and Children, on an Uninhabited Island. 2 vols. London: M.J. Godwin & Co., at the Juvenile Library, 1814, 1:vii-xix.
        Placed among the "true Robinsonades" rather than the "false" (1898.16), the influential Swiss Family Robinson arose more in response to the philosophical and moral debate started by Rousseau than out of a desire to retell a mariner's story. Its main purpose was "to be of use to children and the friend of children" and, more specifically, "to fashion the character of four sons" by the pedagogical device of the father (Johann David Wyss) holding evening conversations, and with one of the four sons (Johann Rudolf Wyss) serving as the editor. Accepts Rousseau's idea that no book had been "more universally read and approved, for the opening of the infant mind, than The Adventures of Robinson Crusoe," and that every child imagined Crusoe as "existing with no aids but those of his own industry, and carrying on, single-handed, the tremendous battle which man, wherever he lives alone, must have to fight with nature." Continues with an interpretation of Crusoe as representing "human nature in its origin," as benefiting in its weakness from his "reflection and labours," and as "feelingly" dependent upon "the social state." In common with its model: shipwreck, desert island, resources from the ship. Different from its model: instruction in the sciences, especially the natural history of countries and climates; "painting the family scene"; father's care for instructing the children.

1813

1   CHALMERS, ALEXANDER, ed. "De Foe (Daniel)." In The General
    Biographical Dictionary. New ed., rev. and enlarged.
    32 vols. London: J. Nichols & Son et al., 11:391-406.
         Contains standard biographical information drawn, without
    acknowledgement, from the "Memoirs" of Defoe published in the
    Universal Magazine of Knowledge and Pleasure, 1793.1, which in
    turn borrowed heavily, with partial acknowledgement, from Chal-
    mers's Life of Daniel De Foe (1790). Rejects the story of De-
    foe's "surreptitiously obtaining the papers of Alexander Selkirk"
    even more strongly than does his source, and argues from "inter-
    nal evidence" strongly for Defoe's originality. As in 1793.1,
    surveys quickly Captain Singleton, New Voyage Round the World,
    Duncan Campbell. About the morality of Moll Flanders, Colonel
    Jack, and Roxana, restates a deep concern. Introduces one new
    sentence, making the Journal of the Plague Year, like the Memoirs
    of a Cavalier, "a pure fiction." The final long paragraph, which
    does not appear in 1793.1, asserts that Defoe's lasting fame must
    rest on his writings which were "entirely the offspring of inven-
    tion," and of these Robinson Crusoe "rises superior to every
    thing of the kind." Agrees with Andrew Kippis (1793.3): Defoe
    passed on to Richardson "that mode of delineating characters, and
    carrying on dialogues, and that minute discrimination of the cir-
    cumstances of events"; in turn he learned "simplicity of style"
    from Bunyan. See also 1784.2.

1813-1814

1   SCOTT, WALTER, ed. A Collection of Scarce and Valuable
    Tracts, on the Most Interesting and Entertaining Subjects:
    But Chiefly Such as Relate to the History and Constitution of
    These Kingdoms. Selected from . . . Libraries; Particularly
    That of the Late Lord Somers. 2d ed., rev. 13 vols. London:
    T. Cadell & W. Davies et al., 9:569-80; 11:242-75.
         Briefly introduces, with historical background and comments
    on authorship, reprintings of five political works by Defoe.
    Identifies the author of A New Test of the Church of England's
    Loyalty, which is dated 1700 rather than 1702: "The defence of
    Whiggish loyalty seems to have been written by the celebrated
    Daniel De Foe, a conjecture which is strengthened by the frequent
    reference to his poem of the True-born Englishman." For the His-
    tory of the Kentish Petition, curiously dated 1740, gives a brief
    sketch of the Whig activity in 1701 which led to the Kentish
    petition and the arrest of the petitioners, but makes no mention
    of Defoe. On the authorship of the reprinted "Address" [Legion's
    Memorial, 1701], claims that it was "written, it is said, by the
    celebrated Daniel de Foe," and repeats the now-discredited myth
    that Defoe, in disguise as a woman, presented the petition to the
    Speaker, Robert Harley. In a quotation of James Ralph's History
    of England (1746.1), implies that "the same brazen author," name-

ly, Defoe, also wrote <u>Legion's New Paper</u> (1702), reprinted later.
Without any mention of Defoe as author, reprints <u>Ye True-Born En-</u>
<u>glishmen Proceed</u> (1701) and <u>Legion's Humble Address to the Lords</u>
(1704).

1814

1   DAVIS, WILLIAM. <u>An Olio of Bibliographical and Literary Anec-</u>
    <u>dotes and Memoranda, Original and Selected</u>. London: J. Rod-
    well, pp. 38-47.
        Attributes <u>Robinson Crusoe</u> to the Earl of Oxford on the
    authority of Benjamin Holloway (1788.3); summarizes as "the most
    generally received opinion" the story of Selkirk's giving his
    papers to Defoe.

2   DUNLOP, JOHN [COLIN]. <u>The History of Fiction: Being a Criti-</u>
    <u>cal Account of the Most Celebrated Prose Works of Fiction,</u>
    <u>from the Earliest Greek Romances to the Novels of the Present</u>
    <u>Age</u>. 3 vols. London: Longman, Hurst, Rees, Orme, & Brown,
    3:398-402.
        Examines English prose fictions under the broad divisions
    of "The Serious, Comic, and Romantic novels." Judges that En-
    gland excells all other European countries in "Voyages imagin-
    aires," with <u>Robinson Crusoe</u>, <u>Gulliver's Travels</u>, and <u>Gaudentio</u>
    <u>di Lucca</u>. Compares Defoe and Swift in "the unaffected simplicity
    of their narratives" and the circumstantial manner in which the
    incidents are related. Notes sharp differences in the moral
    effect of their works: we rise from <u>Robinson Crusoe</u> "exulting in
    our nature"; but from <u>Gulliver's Travels</u>, "giddy, and selfish,
    and discontented, and, from some parts, I may almost say bruti-
    fied." Reprinted, with additions: 1816.3.

3   Preface to <u>The Life and Adventures of Robinson Crusoe</u>. <u>Faith-</u>
    <u>fully Epitomized from the Three Volumes</u>. Dublin: William
    Jones, pp. v-vi.
        Does not believe the "exceptions" taken to the story
    deserve any comment. Even if it were "mere fiction," persons
    having "any taste for the metaphorical way of writing" must
    regard this as "a masterpiece . . . the first and best of the
    kind that ever appeared in the English language."

4   SCOTT, SIR WALTER, ed. "Memoirs of Jonathan Swift" and Appen-
    dix to <u>Gulliver's Travels</u>. In <u>Works of Jonathan Swift, D.D.</u>
    19 vols. Edinburgh: Archibald Constable & Co.; London:
    White, Cochrane, & Co., & Gale, Curtis, & Fenner; Dublin:
    John Cumming, 1:340, 494-96; 12:5-6.
        (1) Compares Gulliver with Crusoe as a strictly English ima-
    ginary traveller who sails through distant seas "without losing a
    single English prejudice." (2) Observes that Swift or Defoe has
    the discrimination to "select, in a fictitious narrative, such an
    enumeration of minute incidents as might strike the beholder of a

real fact"; and applies John Dunlop's comment on Crusoe's use of "circumstantial detail" to Gulliver. Generalizes that Defoe's "capacity of fictitious invention," his "disguises," were limited to only a few characters: a sailor, a Cavalier, a lowly sharper. (3) Draws the distinction between real narrative, which uses "petty particulars" of interest only to the narrator, and fictitious narrative, which uses incidents of interest only to the reader. By writing narratives of the first kind, Defoe "carried the air of authenticity to the highest pitch of perfection" in Robinson Crusoe and Memoirs of a Cavalier. In this respect he was imitated by Swift. Reprinted: Sir Walter Scott: On Novelists and Fiction, ed. Ioan Williams (New York: Barnes & Noble, 1968), pp. 151, 154-55, 157-58.

1815

1   HYDROGRAPHER OF THE NAVAL CHRONICLE [pseud.]. Preface to Robinson Crusoe . . . A New Edition Revised and Corrected for the Advancement of Nautical Education. Illustrated by Technical and Geographical Annotation and Embellished with Maps and Engravings. London: Joseph Mawman. pp. iii-xvi; 497-579 (Appendix).
     Stands out uniquely for the stated objective of reversing Crusoe's aim to avoid "technical descriptions" in the annotations, and sees all previous editions defective in this respect. Intends this Robinson Crusoe as an educational work for youthful readers: to instruct in geography, hydrography, topography, and botany, while at the same time to please with a narrative which has the reality of any true "naufrage" or shipwreck story. Lavishly overannotates both general and nautical details, and supplies a ponderous appendix in the most heavily researched edition to date. Who was the Hydrographer of the Naval Chronicle? No one seems to know, although traces of him are in the early volumes of the Naval Chronicle. Reviewed very favorably in the Naval Chronicle for 1817 37:155-58.

2   _____. "To the Readers of the Naval Chronicle." Naval Chronicle 34 (July- December):153-54.
     Announces a new edition of "a favorite book," Robinson Crusoe, for which he will use the kind of technical information contributed for years to the hydrographic section of the Naval Chronicle. Special features of the edition: annotations which are "scientific and technical," a Mercator's chart tracing Crusoe's travels over the world, hydrographic details for the China coast, some forty other subjects engraved on wood and an index.

3   MACKINTOSH, JAMES. Review of William Godwin's Lives of Edward and John Philips, Nephews and Pupils of John Milton. Edinburgh Review 25, no. 50 (October):487-88.
     Authorship is given in Wellesley Index. Esteems Godwin's Caleb Williams as "probably the finest novel produced by a man--

at least since the <u>Vicar of Wakefield</u>." Caleb's "disguises and
escapes in London . . . have a frightful reality, perhaps nowhere
paralleled in our language, unless it be in some paintings of
Daniel De Foe, with whom it is a distinction to bear comparison."
Finds "somewhat similar scenes" in <u>Colonel Jack</u>, which is second
only to <u>Robinson Crusoe</u>, popular in all countries and read by
everyone "from the philosopher to the child." Like Defoe's
novels, <u>Caleb Williams</u> "rejects the agency of women and the power
of love." Reprinted: <u>The Miscellaneous Works of the Right Honourable Sir James Mackintosh</u>, 3 vols. (London: Longman, Brown,
Green, & Longmans, 1846), 2:495-97.

4   [WILLIAMS, WILLIAM.] <u>The Journal of Llewellyn Penrose, A Sea-
    man</u>. 4 vols. London: John Murray; Edinburgh: William Black-
    wood. Reprint. <u>Mr. Penrose: The Journal of Penrose, Seaman</u>.
    Edited by David Howard Dickason. Bloomington and London:
    Indiana University Press, 1969, 384 pp.
        Presents a castaway narrative, in a posthumous edition, by
    William Williams (1727-1791). The comparison with <u>Robinson Cru-
    soe</u> was not made in the <u>Journal</u>, but even before publication, in
    James Stanier Clarke's preface to <u>Naufragia, or Historical Mem-
    oirs of Shipwrecks and of the Providential Deliverance of Vessels</u>
    (1805-1806); in the anonymous review, 1816.6; and in the title of
    the pirated German translation, <u>Der Neue Robinson, oder, Tagebuch
    Llewellin Penroses, eines Marosen</u> (1817). For a complete and
    accurate edition of the original manuscript at the Lilly Library,
    see the publication by Dickason. Reprinted: London: Taylor &
    Hessey, 1825.

                                1816

1   BURNEY, JAMES. <u>A Chronological History of the Discoveries in
    the South Seas</u>. 5 vols. London: G. & W. Nicol et al.,
    4:461-67.
        Examines all the evidence on the charges against Defoe for
    the theft and plagiarism of Selkirk's papers in the writing of
    <u>Robinson Crusoe</u>. States fully the rumors and innuendos, probes
    into the amount of time elapsing between the publication of early
    accounts of Selkirk and of <u>Robinson Crusoe</u>, tries to understand
    Defoe's state of mind as he suffers illness and quits politics
    around 1715. The verdict—an unqualified rejection of the
    charges: "There appears . . . no solid ground for disputing the
    legitimacy of De Foe's <u>Crusoe</u>."

2   CAREY, JOHN. <u>Practical English Prosody and Versification</u>.
    New and improved ed. London: Baldwin, Cradock, & Joy,
    pp. 232-33.
        Annotates Cowper's poem which begins "I am a monarch of all
    I survey" (1782.2) by explaining that the fictitious <u>Robinson
    Crusoe</u> was "built on the real story" of Selkirk, and stolen from
    papers entrusted to Defoe.

3 DUNLOP, JOHN [COLIN]. The History of Fiction: Being a Critical Account of the Most Celebrated Prose Works of Fiction,
   from the Earliest Greek Romances to the Novels of the Present
   Age. 2d ed. 3 vols. Edinburgh: Longman, Hurst, Rees, Orme,
   & Brown, 3:487-94.
       Reprint of 1814.2, with additions. Aside from the brief
   note on Gabriel Foigny's style as being like Swift's and Defoe's
   in the use of details, adds commentary (2 pp.) on the imitations
   of Robinson Crusoe, including "the best . . . the Voyage of Peter
   Wilkins" (1750).

4 [JEFFREY, FRANCIS.] Review of John Wilson's The City of the
   Plague, and Other Poems. Edinburgh Review 26, no. 52 (June):
   458-76 passim.
       For Jeffrey's authorship, see the Wellesley Index. In
   general, offers considerable praise of Wilson's genius, of "a
   certain pastoral purity, joined with deeper feelings." Specifically, on the Journal of the Plague Year, Jeffrey makes clear
   that the anonymity which once surrounded the book has now been
   removed, and that its character as history is better understood:
   "a work in which fabulous incidents and circumstances are combined with authentic narratives, with an art and a verisimilitude
   which no other writer has ever been able to communicate to
   fiction." From this source Wilson has drawn a good part of his
   materials and "most of the ground colour." See also 1816.9.

5 "Memoir of Daniel De Foe" and "To the Reader." In The Life
   and Adventures of Robinson Crusoe . . . By Daniel De Foe.
   Manchester: J. Gleave, pp. iii-xvi, iii-vi.
       "Memoir" rearranges materials taken directly and sequen-
   tially from the frequently reprinted "Life of De Foe" by George
   Chalmers into an impressively smooth narrative, but without any
   acknowledgment. Omits portions of the biographical narrative and
   all of Chalmers's critical comments on novels other than Robinson
   Crusoe. Repeats Chalmers's explanation of the charges against
   Defoe for "surreptitiously" appropriating Selkirk's papers to his
   own use, as the work of Defoe's enemies. "To the Reader" gives
   perfunctory high praise of Robinson Crusoe as a didactic work
   "calculated to produce the most powerful and salutary impressions, especially upon juvenile minds."

6 Review of [William Williams's] The Journal of Llewellyn Penrose, A Seaman, 1815. Eclectic Review, n.s. 5 (April):395-98.
       Insistently compares Robinson Crusoe with Penrose, a man
   "thrown on an uninhabited shore" for twenty-eight years, but not
   left in solitude and otherwise only on the surface "a real and
   true" Crusoe. Claims, however, that while the Journal has all
   the internal marks of being authentic, it fails completely in
   "external evidence," and can only be regarded as "an interesting
   story" especially to children, "of the same romantic cast as in
   Robinson Crusoe," although not a copy.

7   "Robinson Crusoe." <u>Naval Chronicle</u> 35 (January–June):460.
     Preserves an early version of the priceless anecdote about
Madame Talleyrand's mistaking "Denon's Travels" for <u>Robinson</u>
<u>Crusoe</u>, based on an incident which took place seven years prior.
The anecdote appears somewhat differently in <u>Bookman</u>, 1902.2.

8   S[UAR]D, [JEAN BAPTISTE ANTOINE]. "Foé (Daniel de)." In
     <u>Biographie universelle, ancienne et moderne</u>. Paris: L.G.
     Michaud, 15:115–21.
     A comprehensive and favorable entry, up-to-date on both
accurate and inaccurate information for the biography and canon.
Enumerates the novels other than <u>Robinson Crusoe</u>; persists in
using the title <u>Molly Flanders</u>. Has an occasional broad generalization: "[Defoe] reunited the talent of the writer with that
of the man of affairs; firmness, courage and activity, with a
quiet taste for literature." Emphasizes current French and continental perspectives, such as the lack of knowledge in France
about any writings by Defoe other than <u>Robinson Crusoe</u>; Charles
Panckoucke's reprinting in 1800 of the corrected translation by
Saint-Hyacinthe and Van Effen; Madame de Montmorency-Laval's
interlinear translation (1797); Montreille's "boring" abridgement
(1768); Campe's German adaptation for children; Rousseau's high
praise for <u>Robinson Crusoe</u> in <u>Émile</u>; James Beattie's acceptance
of the charge that Defoe misused Selkirk's manuscript memoirs;
and the growing evidence pointing to Lord Oxford's authorship of
the first volume of <u>Robinson Crusoe</u>.

9   WILSON, JOHN. <u>The City of the Plague, and Other Poems</u>. Edin-
     burgh: Archibald Constable & Co.; Glasgow: John Smith & Son;
     London: Longman, Hurst, Rees, Orme, & Brown. Reprint. Gar-
     land Publishing, 1979, pp. 1–167.
     Casts Defoe's <u>Journal of the Plague Year</u> into a dramatic
poem—three acts, dramatic scenes, and new characters, such as
Frankfort and Wilmot (two young naval officers who have returned
to London during the plague), Frankfort's mother and younger
brother William, and the heroine "the holy Magdalene." See the
review by Jeffrey, 1816.4.

                                  <u>1817</u>

1   BRAZIER, [NICOLAS]; ARTOIS, [FRANÇOIS VICTOR ARMAND D'];
     [LURIEU, GABRIEL DE]; and BALISSON DE ROUGEMONT, M[ICHEL]
     N[ICHOLAS]. <u>Robinson dans son isle, comédie en un acte, mêlée</u>
     <u>de couplets et a spectacle</u>. Paris: J.N. Barba, 34 pp.
     Drastically alters the original significance of the desert
island experience and especially the conceptions of Robinson and
Friday. Limits the action to Friday, the savage Caribs and a
few new characters in minor roles (e.g., the sailors Sabord and
Misaine); but ventures into a bold new direction by creating the
female role of Zilia, daughter of the Caribs' cruel enemy and
thus creating (with Friday and Robinson) a love triangle and per-

mitting such theatrical effects as the lively Ritornello and the
heavy use throughout of the French equivalent of the broken
English spoken by the natives. Announces the first performance
on the title page as being on 24 January 1817 at the Théâtre de
la Porte Saint-Martin.

2   COLERIDGE, SAMUEL TAYLOR. Biographia Literaria; or Biographi-
     cal Sketches of My Literary Life and Opinions. 2 vols. Lon-
     don: Rest Fenner, 2:147.
         In chap. 22, argues against Wordsworth's theory that poets
were more readily formed by humbler life. To illustrate his
point about misdirected Poetic Genius, posits the author who
chose to make his poet and philosopher into a chimney-sweeper,
and then invented "an account of his birth, parentage and education." This could only be done in a biography. If it were
to be done in a novel, "it must be one in the manner of De Foe's,
that were meant to pass for histories, not in the manner of
Fielding's: in The Life of Moll Flanders, or Colonel Jack, not
in a Tom Jones, or even a Joseph Andrews." Reprinted: ed. J.
Shawcross (Oxford: Clarendon Press, 1907); The Collected Works
of Samuel Taylor Coleridge, vol. 7, ed. James Engell and W.
Jackson Bate, Bollingen Ser., 75 (London: Routledge & Kegan
Paul; Princeton, N.J.: Princeton University Press, 1983).

3   "Compendium of the History of Durham." Gentleman's Magazine
     87, pt. 1 (March):212.
         At Gateshead Defoe composed Robinson Crusoe. See also
1826.1.

4   D'ISRAELI, ISAAC. "Robinson Crusoe." In Curiosities of Lit-
     erature. 3 vols. London: John Murray, 3:285-90.
         Among the frequently reprinted volumes of the Curiosities
of Literature appears this brief essay on Robinson Crusoe which,
while it acknowledges a debt to "Crusoe's prototype," Alexander
Selkirk, at the same time gives ample recognition to Defoe's
originality. As a part of this originality, stresses the "comparative state of solitude" in both Defoe and Selkirk which,
along with "a vivifying hint" from Steele, led to Robinson
Crusoe. Translated into French: 1819.2. Reprinted: Works,
ed. Benjamin Disraeli (London, 1881); (Hildesheim and New York:
Georg Olms Verlag, 1969), 3:274-77.

5   FRANKLIN, BENJAMIN. Memoirs of the Life and Writings of Ben-
     jamin Franklin . . . Written by Himself to a Late Period, and
     Continued to the Time of His Death by His Grandson, William
     Temple Franklin. 3d ed. 6 vols. London: Henry Colburn,
     1818, 1:31-32.
         Compared with Buisson, 1791.2, omits Franklin's account of
Defoe's influence from an Essay upon Projects, but includes the
anecdote of the drunken Dutchman and Franklin's interest in the
mixing of narration and dialogue by Bunyan, Defoe, and Richardson. In the text of the Autobiography, ed. Leonard W. Labarree,

Ralph L. Ketcham, Helen C. Boatfield, and Helene H. Fineman (New
Haven and London: Yale University Press, 1964), pp. 58, 72, the
reference to the Essay upon Projects is included, but substantive-
ly altered in meaning by the insertion of the words (after citing
the Essay upon Projects) "and another of Dr. [Cotton] Mather's,
call'd Essays to do Good which perhaps gave me a Turn of Thinking
that had an influence on some of the principal future Events of
my Life." In the reference to the mixing of narration and dialogue, this text (1964) names specific additional works having
the mixture: Religious Courtship and Family Instructor. Reprinted: The Life of Benjamin Franklin, ed. Jared Sparks (Boston:
Tappan & Dennet, 1844), p. 30.

6   LOCKHART, GEORGE. The Lockhart Papers. Edited by Anthony
    Aufrere. 2 vols. London: William Anderson, 1:164-68.
      Includes the "Memoirs and Commentaries upon the Affairs of
Scotland from 1702 to 1715," which reproduces Lockhart's Memoirs
Concerning the Affairs of Scotland, the manuscript first published in 1714 against the author's wishes. Remains an invaluable,
although biased (Jacobite), source of information about the persons and events involved in the Union, as witnessed by one of the
Queen's commissioners. While "the Key to the Memoirs" identified
the characters in appendices to the second and third editions
(1714), now provides the full names directly in the text. Severely castigates (by his full name in all editions) "that vile Monster and wretch Daniel De Foe" and "other mercenary tools [1714
eds.: Fools] and trumpeters of rebellion" for refusing to accept
the numerous "addresses" which strongly opposed the Union.

7   POCOCK, I[SAAC]. Robinson Crusoe; or, The Bold Bucaniers:
    A Romantic Melo-drama. London: John Miller, 48 pp.
      According to the title page: produced for the first time
at the Theatre-Royal in Covent-Garden on Easter Monday. Aside
from some scenic reminders and a few characters, bears little
resemblance to the original, but see the "Remarks" by George
Daniel [?] as well as the reprint, 1831.3.

8   [SCOTT, SIR WALTER.] Review of Tales of My Landlord, 1817.
    Quarterly Review 16, no. 32 (17 January):454-55.
      Interrupts a review of the story, after transcribing a
scene which "seems to have been sketched with considerable attention to the manners," in order to point out the original in
Defoe's Memoirs of the Church of Scotland (1717). Anecdotes concerning "this unhappy period" (the Union) interested "a man of
his liveliness of imagination, who excelled all others in drama-
tizing a story, and presenting it as if in actual speech and
action before the reader." Dialogue of the Soldier and Country
Man includes Scotticisms. For the relationship between Defoe's
Memoirs of the Church of Scotland and Scott's Tales of My Landlord, see also Lockhart, 1820.4. Reprinted: The Miscellaneous
Prose Works of Sir Walter Scott, Bart., vol. 3, Periodical Criticism (Edinburgh: Robert Cadell; London: Whitaker & Co., 1835),

19:40–43; <u>Sir Walter Scott: On Novelists and Fiction</u>, ed. Ioan Williams (New York: Barnes & Noble, 1968), pp. 248–50.

1818

1   BERNARDIN DE SAINT-PIERRE, JACQUES HENRI. <u>Harmonies de la na-ture</u>, vol. 3. In <u>Oeuvres complètes de Jacques-Henri-Bernardin de Saint-Pierre, mises en ordre et précédées de la vie de l'auteur</u>. Edited by L[ouis] Aimé-Martin. 12 vols. Paris: Méquignon-Marvis, 1818, 10:279.

     While never once referring directly to his Robinsonade, <u>Paul et Virginie</u> (1787), states here, in "Conjugal Harmony" (Book 8), that he has wished more than once for a novel like <u>Robinson Crusoe</u> "where a man and woman, on a desert island, might contribute to the happy life--the one preoccupied with labors requiring strength, the other with those which resort to pleasure." He once sketched the subject, placing it in Siberia and basing the story on "some very happy marriages that I had seen in poor Finland."

2   HAZLITT, WILLIAM. "Lecture I. Introductory: On Poetry in General." In <u>Lectures on the English Poets</u>. London: Taylor & Hessey. Reprint. In <u>The Collected Works of William Hazlitt</u>. Edited by A.R. Waller and Arnold Glover. London: J.M. Dent & Co.; New York: McClure, Phillips & Co., 1902, 5:13.

     Names as "poetry in kind" <u>Pilgrim's Progress</u>, <u>Robinson Cru-soe</u>, and the tales of Boccaccio. Movingly compares Philoctetes confined in his island of Lemnos, as in Sophocles's tragedy, to Robinson Crusoe, and praises Defoe "the relator" as having "the true genius of a poet." Reprinted: <u>The Complete Works of William Hazlitt</u>, ed. P.P. Howe, Centenary Edition (Toronto: J.M. Dent & Sons, 1933), 5:13.

3   N[ICHOLS], J[OHN] B[OWYER], ed. <u>The Life and Errors of John Dunton, Citizen of London . . . To Which Are Added, Dunton's Conversation in Ireland; Selections from His Other Genuine Works; and a Faithful Portrait of the Author</u>. 2 vols. London: J. Nichols, Son & Bentley, pp. xxviii, 180–81, 191–92, 423–26, 438, 453–54, 461, 472, 474, 757.

     Reprints two pieces by a contemporary, John Dunton, who knew Defoe at firsthand. In his <u>Life and Errors</u> (1705), Dunton characterizes Defoe as "a man of good parts, and very clear sense," praises his conversation as "ingenious and brisk enough," but faults him in "prudence" for the <u>Shortest-Way with the Dissenters</u>. Dunton judges that he would have deserved applause, had he written only the <u>True-Born Englishman</u> and "spared some particular Characters that are too vicious for the very Originals." In <u>The Whipping-Post</u> (1706), although he introduces minor improprieties against Defoe (e.g., his borrowing the "Question-Project" for the <u>Review</u>), Dunton presents him first for a "Panegyrick"--on his mastery of the English tongue, facility in rhyming verses, integrity, loyalty to the Queen, and courage.

4   SCOTT, SIR WALTER. Introduction to Rob Roy. Edinburgh: A.
     Constable & Co. Reprint. The Waverley Novels by Sir Walter
     Scott Bart. New York and London: Harper & Brothers, [n.d.],
     5:xl.
        Mentions that as the fame of Rob Roy spread beyond Scot-
     land, "a pretended history" was published during his lifetime
     under the title of The Highland Rogue [1723]. The "catch-penny
     publication" has on occasion been attributed to Defoe [e.g.,
     Boston Public Library Catalog, p. 50]. Scott states that the
     pamphlet is mainly fictitious: "It is great pity so excellent a
     theme for a narrative of the kind had not fallen into the hands
     of De Foe, who was engaged at the time on subjects somewhat simi-
     lar, though inferior in dignity and interest."

                                 1819

1   "De Foe on Apparitions." Blackwood's Edinburgh Magazine 6,
     no. 32 (November):201-7.
        Writes attractively about the "odd matter" in Defoe's
     "curious volume," An Essay on the History and Reality of Appari-
     tions, (1727), giving his "ideas about the devil" and other
     assorted apparitions. Mainly in a facetious tone, summarizes a
     short chapter "on the appearance of the devil in human shape";
     retells stories about phantoms from the land of Nowhere, as for
     instance, the fascinating ones about Owke Mouraski or the appar-
     itional "grave ancient man" who frustrated the robbery of a rich
     man's house by turning into "the most horrid monster that ever
     was seen"; discusses the question debated in the chapter on
     "Apparitions in Dreams . . ." whether a person complying with the
     devil's temptation in a dream is "as guilty of the fact as if he
     had been awake."

2   [D'ISRAELI, ISAAC.] "Naufrage et aventures véritables d'après
     lesquelles a été composé le roman de Robinson Crusoé." In
     Annales maritimes et coloniales. Edited by [Louis Marie]
     Bajot and M. Poirré. Paris: Imprimerie royale, 2:101-5.
        Translates D'Israeli's essay on "Robinson Crusoe" which
     first appeared in the third volume of Curiosities of Literature
     (not Curiosities of Nature, as given here), 1817.4.

3   [LEAKE, WILLIAM MARTIN], ed. "Memoirs on the Life and Travels
     of John Lewis Burckhardt." In Travels in Nubia. London:
     John Murray, pp. xxviii, xxxvi.
        Quotes two letters from Burckhardt, probably addressed to
     an official of the African Association, from Aleppo. The first
     letter of 2 July 1810 describes his "application to Arabic liter-
     ature" and his efforts to learn Arabic by translating "the well-
     known novel of Robinson Crusoe into an Arabian tale, adapted to
     Eastern taste and manners." He calls the translation "this
     travestied Robinson or . . . in Arabic, Dur el Bahur, the Pearl
     of the sea." The second letter, of 15 August 1810, states that

he had completed the "Arabic imitation," and sent it with his
July letter.

4   MASON, WILLIAM MONCK. The History and Antiquities of the
    Collegiate and Cathedral Church of St. Patrick, near Dublin.
    Dublin: Printed for the Author, p. 355n.
        Finds resemblances between Gulliver's Travels and Robinson
    Crusoe, such as "unaffected simplicity," variety of incidents,
    and especially "the air of truth." Admires Scott's view of Defoe
    who at times, like Shakespeare, violated the unities in order to
    achieve genius. Reprinted: Swift: The Critical Heritage, ed.
    Kathleen Williams (New York: Barnes & Noble, 1970), pp. 339-40.

                              1820

1   BARBAULD, ANNA LETITIA. "De Foe." The Life and Surprising
    Adventures of Robinson Crusoe, 2 vols. In The British Novel-
    ists; with an Essay, and Prefaces Biographical and Critical.
    New ed. London: F.C. & J. Rivington et al., 16:i-viii.
        Reprint of 1810.1.

2   BARTON, BERNARD. "Introductory Verses to Maria Hack." In
    Poems. London: Harvey & Darton, pp. iii-viii.
        Builds "this poor monument" of eleven Spenserian stanzas
    to Maria Hack on the recollection of "the debt my early childhood
    seems to owe." If the Quaker poet, friend of Lamb and Southey,
    invoked a blessing "On them who first excited rapture's glow /
    'T would fall on Barbauld, Berquin, Bunyan, Day, Defoe." See
    also 1831.1; 1845.1. Reprinted: 1821; 1822; 1825.

3   The History of Alexander Selkirk, the Real Robinson Crusoe.
    New Haven, Conn.: J. Babcock & Son, 30 pp.
        Brigham (1957): No. 98. Near the close of this miniature
    book for children, states that "the public curiosity being excit-
    ed respecting [Selkirk], he was induced to put his papers into
    the hands of Defoe to arrange and form them into a regular narra-
    tive." Charges Defoe not only with taking the idea for Robinson
    Crusoe, but of defrauding "the original proprietor of his share
    of the profits."

4   [LOCKHART, JOHN GIBSON.] "Preface to the Present Edition."
    In The Life and Adventures of Robinson Crusoe. 2 vols.
    London: T. Cadell & W. Davies; Edinburgh: W. Blackwood,
    1:i-lxxxii.
        Lockhart's authorship of this lengthy biographical and cri-
    tical preface, probably the best assessment since Chalmers's Life
    of Daniel De Foe (1786), has been established by M.A. Hassan
    ("Lockhart's 'Life' of Defoe," Notes and Queries, n.s. 20, no. 8
    [August, 1973]:294- 95). At the end of the preface there appears
    "A List of De Foe's Writings, As Far As They Have Been Ascertain-
    ed" (16 pp.) which is identical to the list in vol. 12 of Scott's

Novels of Daniel De Foe (1809-1810). Among the 100 items contained in the two lists are at least six which are not accepted
today as part of the Defoe canon. Freshly reexamines the known
biographical information, but also introduces new material, such
as the explanation from Richard Savage's Author to Be Let (1729)
of the "piece of scandal," about Defoe's "son of love by a lady
who vended oysters"; and introduces the new comment that Swift
took hints from Defoe's Consolidator and developed them in the
Laputa section of Gulliver's Travels. Contributes to Defoe's
achievements a much greater recognition of his Scottish accom-
plishments and writings. Notes "the cockney prejudices" in Defoe's lack of appreciation for certain "romantic beauties" of
Scotland in the Tour. Regrets that the Scotland volume of the
Tour and the Memoirs of the Church of Scotland were never published in Scotland. Like Scott before him, compares favorably
the Memoirs of the Church of Scotland with Tales of My Landlord
(1817.8). Turns to "a few general remarks on the peculiar character of Defoe as a writer" (12 pp.). Compares him with other
authors: for instance, "the unequalled intense reality which
[Defoe] throws around every part of his fiction"; his skill in
the way "the chief personage is made to tell his own story"; and
the differences, on the one hand, between Fielding, Smollett,
Le Sage, and Scott in the descriptions of "persons and attire,"
and on the other hand, Defoe. Makes comparisons between other
writers as "more or less painters of the ideal of human life" and
Defoe as depicting, simultaneously, "the minute items of human
life" as well as "its whole scope and tenour." Explains the
biographical and literary effects of Defoe's "intensely natural
mode of writing," the insights his writings provide into "the
characters and manners of the middle classes." Of all writers,
Defoe is most perfectly a "national writer."

5   ROBINSON, WILLIAM. The History and Antiquities of the Parish
     of Stoke Newington. London: John Nichols & Son, pp. 84-87.
         Aside from references to Defoe as one of Stoke Newington's
     "eminent inhabitants" who received his education at Newington
     Green and resided in the parish about the year 1710, offers sur-
     prisingly no other connections. Rehearses general information
     including details now known to be erroneous; mentions Robinson
     Crusoe and its "supposed" basis in the Selkirk story, the Journal
     of the Plague Year, and Religious Courtship. Reprinted: 1842.

6   SINGER, SAMUEL WELLER, ed. Anecdotes, Observations, and
     Characters of Books and Men. Collected from the Conversation
     of Mr. Pope, and Other Eminent Persons of His Time by the
     Reverend Joseph Spence. London: W.H. Carpenter; Edinburgh:
     Archibald Constable & Co., pp. 258-59, 340.
         Pope comments in 1742-43: "The first part of Robinson Cru-
     soe is very good.--De Foe wrote a vast many things; and none bad,
     though none excellent, except this. There is something good in
     all he has written." A certain Mr. H. is quoted without date on
     the sales of the first two volumes of Robinson Crusoe and on the

general feeling among booksellers that the first part would have
been much more saleable without the second part. For different
readings of Spence's manuscript, see the edition by James M.
Osborn (2 vols. Oxford: Clarendon Press, 1966), 1:213, 391.
Reprinted: ed. Bonamy Dobrée (Carbondale, Ill.: Southern Illinois University Press, 1964), p. 168.

7   "Song. / When I was a lad . . ." In Samuel Foote's The Mayor
of Garratt. A Farce. Oxberry's Edition. London: W. Simpkin
& R. Marshall, pp. 9-11.
     Without much relevance to what had already become Foote's
most popular farce, substitutes the "Song" which begins "When I
was a lad" and which became better known separately, even in America, as "Oh, poor Robinson Crusoe," for [John Gay's] song which
is given to the character Jerry Sneak, "An old woman cloathed in
grey" in the first performance (1763), in all the early editions
of The Mayor of Garratt, and in The Works of Samuel Foote, Esq.
(London: Sherwood, Gilbert, & Piper, 1830, vol. 2). Since the
text of the ten stanzas is fairly close to Jack Cussan's (1797),
as the latter survives in The Universal Songster (1832), the
adaptation of the Song to the 1820 acting version of the farce
was probably the work of the comedian William Oxberry, as the
title page suggests. In a comparison of the "Song" and the Irish
Girl (1820?.1), the differences seem to indicate that each work
returns to Cussan's text independently. See also 1864.3.

8   VITRUVIUS [pseud.]. "The Bag-Piper in Tottenham Court Road."
London Magazine 1, no. 4 (April):389-90.
     Summarizes an alternative version of the anecdote about the
Scottish bagpiper almost buried alive during the Plague--which
H.F. [Defoe], in Journal of the Plague Year, mentions as reject-
ing in favor of the version told by John Hayward. Makes no
mention of Defoe.

1820?

1   "Robinson Crusoe." In Irish Girl, To which are added, Robinson Crusoe, the Tempest, and the Young Man's Dream. [Phila-
delphia, Pa.]: Patents-Office, pp. 3-4.
     Reprint of 1820.7. A comparison of the two texts suggests
that the version in the Oxberry Edition of Samuel Foote's The
Mayor of Garratt was probably the earlier one. Foote himself
probably had nothing to do with the composition of the verses.
Reprinted, with additions: 1850.10.

1821

1   [BARKER, C.] Review of Memoirs of the Honourable Col. Andrew
Newport, 1792. Retrospective Review 3, pt. 2:354-79.
     Authorship given in Poole's Index. In the first of two

parts, takes up "the singular genius" of Defoe, "with a view of
proposing our own doubts and difficulties on a subject that seems
to set criticism at defiance." Defoe had no followers with
respect to his genius. Lacking all the talents of other writers,
he created fictions which are "not so much counterfeit of something existing as they are themselves the originals." Identifies
"the grand secret of [Defoe's] art" as "an instinct," consisting
"in the astonishing minuteness of the details, and the circumstantial particularity with which everything is laid before us."
Asserts further that certain details could be captured only by
the eye-witness, and not by the writer of fiction. Defoe's "singular merit" was "to have overcome this difficulty, and to have
communicated to his fictitious narratives every characteristic
mark by which we distinguish between real and pretended adventures." Writes about "this marvellous faculty" with a full command of mature critical language, and illustrates by comparing
Defoe and Smollett in their strikingly different representations
of a sailor's life, Defoe's Colonel Jack and Fielding's Jonathan
Wild, Defoe's Cavalier and Scott's Captain Dalgetty. At one
point, appears to be discussing novels such as Moll Flanders, but
does not name them; refers to Defoe as "a painter after the Flemish fashion," caring little "what the thing represented was; or
if he had any predilection, it was for objects that were coarse,
vulgar, and indelicate." In the second part of the review, analyzes Defoe's Memoirs of the Honourable Col. Andrew Newport,
regrettably making few or no direct connections with the earlier
general assessment. Quotes from the Memoirs lengthily and sensi-
tively. At one point, does appear to refer to the general comments on Defoe's "singular genius" when he notes how perfectly
the fictitious and historical parts are blended together, and how
effectively "a dull gazette, like the Swedish Intelligencer (the
rude mine from which De Foe seems to have derived his materials)
is quickened with life. . . ."

2   HAZLITT, WILLIAM. "Character of Cobbett." In Table Talk; or,
    Original Essays. London: John Warren. Reprint. In The
    Collected Works of William Hazlitt. Edited by A.R. Waller and
    Arnold Glover. London: J.M. Dent & Co.; New York: McClure,
    Phillips & Co., 1903, 4:334.
        Claims that Cobbett had "the clearness of Swift, the nat-
    uralness of Defoe, and the picturesque satirical description of
    Mandeville. . . ." Reprinted: "Mr. Cobbett," in The Spirit of
    the Age: or Contemporary Portraits (London: Henry Colburn,
    1825); The Complete Works of William Hazlitt, ed. P.P. Howe,
    Centenary ed. (Toronto: J.M. Dent & Sons, 1931), 8:50.

3   [HONE, WILLIAM.] The Right Divine of Kings to Govern Wrong!
    3d ed. London: William Hone, 60 pp. passim.
        Illustrates well the early nineteenth-century view of Defoe
    as the champion of the people's rights and liberties. Adapts his
    Jure Divino (1706)--separating "the gold from the dross"--to a
    vigorous attack upon the "priestcraft" and "kingcraft" of the

day. Argues that Defoe's long satire is as apropos now as an
exposé of passive obedience and non-resistance as it was on its
first appearance. For Hone, Defoe was "the ablest politician of
his day, an energetic writer, and, better than all, an honest
man; but not much of a poet." Proceeds to rewrite Jure Divino
into three books "improving" the frequently harsh rhythms, and
replacing the topical allusions of the original poem with current
political illustrations which more adequately meet the needs of
his satire. See also 1912.9.

4   [WHATELY, RICHARD.] Review of Jane Austen's Northanger Abbey
      and Persuasion. Quarterly Review 24, no. 48 (January):360-62.
        Among writers participating in "a new style of novel" which
arose in the past fifteen or twenty years, and which is character-
ized by "the art of copying from nature as she really exists in
the common walks of life," Austen writes faultless fables in the
third-person. Compares her method with "the two other methods of
conducting a ficticious story, viz. either by narrative in the
first person, when the hero is made to tell his own tale, or by a
series of letters." Argues that first-person narratives, other
things being equal, approach nearest to "a deception," and cites
Defoe's novels, Memoirs of a Cavalier and Journal of the Plague
Year, as "having been oftener mistaken for true narratives than
any fictions that ever were composed." Offers as a reason the
distinction between the kind of details given by the writer who
goes beyond the material and the kind used by the real historian
or autobiographer. Defoe produced the latter kind of details.
Reprinted: 1861.9; Jane Austen: The Critical Heritage, ed. B.C.
Southam (London: Routledge & Kegan Paul; New York: Barnes &
Noble, 1968), pp. 96-97.

5   Y., X. "Sonnet. To Robinson Crusoe." Blackwood's Magazine
      8, no. 48 (March):632.
        As "a simple child," shares easily the joy or woe of
Crusoe's adventures.

1822

1   FORTESCUE, F. Robinson Crusoe; or, the Island of Juan Fernan-
      dez, An Operatic Drama, in Three Acts. Boston: Jackson,
      79 pp.
        Focusses upon a few principal scenes drawn from the origi-
nal, using characters such as Atkins, Ben, Captain Bowling, Friday, and developing themes more fully, such as Crusoe's industry.

2   [SOUTHERN, HENRY.] Review of The History of the Great Plague
      in London, in the Year 1665, 1769. Retrospective Review 6,
      pt. 1:1-20.
        Authorship given in Poole's Index. Opens with the argument
that the fictions of the historical novelist are not "entirely
innocent" because they can tamper with truth, but never turns the

argument against Defoe. Particularly, in his <u>History of the
Great Plague in London</u>, are there evident the "marks of genuine-
ness" which the reviewer has been describing. Extracts follow,
plentifully from Defoe's <u>History,</u> a few from the <u>Loimologia</u> of
Nathaniel Hodges, M.D. Of all the pamphlets and publications consulted, only Defoe's work "attempts to give any picture of London
as it appeared at the time to a spectator." Still, neither Defoe
nor Hodges have the striking eye-witness quality one finds in
Thucydides. See also "Writers on the Plague," <u>Retrospective Re-
view</u> 7, pt. 2 (1823):219-39, concerned with poems on the plague;
the article continues the earlier one, but makes no reference to
Defoe. Reprinted: 1849.8.

<u>1823</u>

1   "The Life of Defoe." In <u>The Life and Adventures of Robinson
    Crusoe</u>. London: R. Walwyn, pp. 296-320.
         Borrows, without acknowledgement, most of Chalmers's <u>Life
    of Daniel De Foe</u> (1790). Omits the footnotes in which Chalmers
    identified his sources, and gave a considerable amount of addi-
    tional information.

2   Review of <u>Bishop Burnet's History of His Own Time</u>. <u>Quarterly
    Review</u> 29, no. 57 (April):180-81.
         Interrupts account of Charles II's reign to show the misfor-
    tunes "of marriage between persons of opposite persuasions in
    religion." Illustrates the point through Defoe's <u>Religious Court-
    ship</u>, "one of those books which were printed on coarse paper for
    popular sale, and to be found at fairs and country shops with
    Pomfret's Poems, Harvey's Meditations, and the Death of Abel."
    Defoe could also have used the "ill-omened marriage of Charles I"
    as an example.

3   Review of Robert Paltock's <u>The Life and Adventures of Peter
    Wilkins, A Cornish Man</u>, 1784. <u>Retrospective Review</u> 7, pt. 1:
    123, 125.
         Explains why this imitation of <u>Robinson Crusoe</u>, first
    published in 1751 by Paltock, did not succeed. Not only are
    imitations rarely popular, when they follow in "the track of the
    author of <u>Robinson Crusoe</u>" they especially fail: "that celebrat-
    ed production having, like the unnatural father of heathen mythol-
    ogy, devoured its own progeny, and its brethren to boot, born of
    the same pen, and conceived in the same brain with itself."

4   [SCOTT, SIR WALTER.] "Prefatory Memoir to Clara Reeve." In
    <u>The Novels of Sterne, Goldsmith, Dr. Johnson, Mackenzie,
    Horace Walpole, and Clara Reeve</u>. Ballantyne's Novelist's
    Library. London: Hurst, Robinson, & Co., 5:lxxxvi.
         Compares Reeve's use of "prolix, minute, and unnecessary
    details" in her <u>Old English Baron</u> with Defoe's art of circumstan-
    tiating his fictions so that they appear to be true. Reprinted:

Miscellaneous Prose Works (Edinburgh: Cadell & Co.; London: Longman, Rees, Orme, Brown, & Green, 1827), 3:399-400; Sir Walter Scott: On Novelists and Fiction, ed. Ioan Williams (New York: Barnes & Noble, 1968), p. 100.

1824

1   DIBDIN, T[HOMAS] F[ROGNALL]. The Library Companion. 2 vols. London: Harding, Triphook, Lepard, & J. Major, 2:205-8.
     Defoe's readers came from "almost every class." Singles out the historical writings for praise, Journal of the Plague Year and Memoirs of a Cavalier, as having "all the apparent fidelity of an eye-witness," and the History of the Union as placing him "among the soundest historians of his day." Mistakenly believes that Robinson Crusoe was first published in a periodical, the Original London Post, or Heathcote's Intelligence. Robinson Crusoe delights, but Moll Flanders and Colonel Jack are "such low-bred productions, as to induce us to put an instantaneous negative on their admission into our Cabinets." Reprinted: 1825.

2   KERR, ROBERT. A General History and Collection of Voyages and Travels. Edinburgh: William Blackwood; London: T. Cadell, pp. 348-56.
     Woodes Rogers's account of Alexander Selkirk's rescue from Juan Fernandez in February, 1709; no reference to Robinson Crusoe.

3   WATT, ROBERT. "Foe, Daniel De." In Bibliotheca Britannica; or A General Index to British and Foreign Literature. 4 vols. Edinburgh: Archibald Constable & Co.; London: Longman, Hurst, Rees, Orme, Brown, & Green, 1:374-75.
     Lists a total of fifty-six items by Defoe, including [mistakenly] History of Addresses.

1825

1   [HAZLITT, WILLIAM.] "Mr. Wordsworth." In The Spirit of the Age: or, Contemporary Portraits. London: Henry Colburn. Reprint. In The Collected Works of William Hazlitt. Edited by A.R. Waller and Arnold Glover. London: J.M. Dent & Co.; New York: McClure, Phillips & Co., 1902, 4:277.
     Among the comments on Wordsworth's reading: "He also likes books of voyages and travels, and Robinson Crusoe." Reprinted: The Complete Works of William Hazlitt, ed. P.P. Howe, Centenary ed. (Toronto: J.M. Dent & Sons, 1932), 11:93.

2   LAMB, CHARLES. "Ode to the Tread Mill." New Times, 24 October, [page numbers not given].
     From letters to Walter Wilson, dated 28 May and 15 November 1829, it is clear that Lamb had offered him the "Pindaric Ode"

for the Memoirs of Defoe (1830), and was somewhat disappointed
when it was omitted. With deliberate echoes of Defoe's Hymn to
the Pillory, he mocks the current mode of prison discipline in a
comparison of the ineffectual pillory to the "Great Mill" which
grinds "the Human will," and makes "men's consciences . . . clean
and sweet." More than half of the verses are devoted to Defoe's
novels, in particular the novels of crime. Here, as in his
better-known "Estimate of [Defoe's] Secondary Novels" (1830.4),
he lavishes praise on the novels, "second" only to Robinson Crusoe, and on their main characters: "Rogue-harlot-thief that live
to future ages." Specifically: "pirate Singleton," "pilfering
Jack," "Flandrian Moll," and "Vice-script Roxana" whom he and
Godwin knew in the 1745 edition, the only "perfect" or "complete"
edition, containing the sequel [which we now know Defoe could not
possibly have written]. Reprinted, in part: 1830.5; 1903.4.

3   _____. "Reflections in the Pillory." London Magazine, n.s.
     no. 3 (March):368-70.
        In this whimsically ironic piece of prose, addresses the
pillory as Defoe did in his Hymn to the Pillory (1703), both
echoing his master and adding new dimensions of satire: "Shades
of Bastwick and of Prynne hover over thee--Defoe is there, and
more greatly daring Shebbeare--from their (little more elevated)
stations they look down with recognitions." See also 1825.2.
Reprinted: 1864.2; 1903.4.

4   L-C-S, W. Letter to Mr. Urban, 4 May. Gentleman's Magazine
     95, pt. 1 (June):502.
        Replies to 1825.8. Describes the anonymous extracts from
Defoe's Due Preparations for the Plague as "the Fabius-like
caution and firmness exhibited by a London Citizen during the
dreadful visitation which was permitted to waste this city."
Notes the current interest in sanitary laws and "received opinion
on contagion and infection."

5   [OWEN, HUGH, and BLAKEWAY, JOHN BRICKDALE.] A History of
     Shrewsbury. 2 vols. London: Harding, Lepard, & Co., 1:419,
     n.4.
        Notes a contradiction as to Charles I's activities on 19
September 1642 with one of Defoe's "amusing romances . . . entitled 'Memoirs of Col. Andrew Newport,' and purporting to be a
production of the second son of Sir Richard Newport." Observes
that "no circumstantial narrative, if fabulous, can abide a
minute scrutiny."

*6   [REID, WILLIAM HAMILTON.] Extracts from Due Preparations for
     the Plague. Youth's Magazine; or, Evangelical Miscellany,
     n.s. 10 (July):307-.
        Reprint of 1825.7-8. Information from Britannicus, "The
Great Plague and Fire of London," Youth's Magazine; or, Evangel-
ical Miscellany, n.s. 10 (August):383.

7   ____. Letter to Mr. Urban, London, 14 July. <u>Gentleman's</u>
       <u>Magazine</u> 95, pt. 2 (July):14-17.
           Continues to publish extracts from the second part of <u>Due</u>
       <u>Preparations for the Plague</u>, the authorship of which at this time
       was not known to be Defoe's. Carries the title here <u>Account of</u>
       <u>a Family preserved on Shipboard in the Thames during the Great</u>
       <u>Plague in 1665</u>. Omits most of the dialogue. See 1825.4, 8.
       Reprinted: 1825.6.

8   ____ [An Occasional Correspondent, and Searcher after Antiq-
       uities]. Letter to Mr. Urban. <u>Gentleman's Magazine</u> 95, pt. 1
       (April): 311-16.
           Authorship identified in the <u>Nichols File of "The Gentle-</u>
       <u>man's Magazine</u>." Without any awareness of Defoe's authorship,
       publishes extracts from the first part of <u>Due Preparations for</u>
       <u>the Plague As well for the Soul as Body</u> (1722) under the title
       <u>Account of a Grocer in Wood Street, Cheapside, who preserved him-</u>
       <u>self and Family from Infection during the great Plague in 1665</u>.
       For the second part, see 1825.7. For a reply, see 1825.4. Re-
       printed: 1825.6.

*9   <u>Robinson cru Zoé ou la méprise sans resemblance</u>.
           Described as "a vaudeville piece of foolery in one act, mix-
       ed with couplets, 1825, by an anonymous author: vaudeville scene
       and other scenes of Robinsonades of the nineteenth century"--in
       Alaine Buisine, "Repères, Marques, Gisements: A propos de la Rob-
       insonnade Vernienne," <u>La Revue des lettres modernes</u>, nos. 523-29
       (1978):113, 134n.

                                  1826

1   "Compendium of County History--W. Riding of Yorkshire."
       <u>Gentleman's Magazine</u> 96, pt. 2, Supp.:599.
           At Halifax: "the celebrated Daniel De Foe here wrote his
       'Robinson Crusoe,' 'De Jure Divino,' &c." See also 1817.3.

2   "Editor's Preface." In <u>The Pleasant and Surprizing Adventures</u>
       <u>of Robert Drury</u>. London: Hunt & Clarke, pp. v-vi.
           Makes a special point that these adventures are autobio-
       graphical and have therefore the attractions of being "faithfully
       related by the person" to whom they occurred, and that the "plain
       and unpretending manner" of the narrative, in a writer of Drury's
       class, contributes to its credibility. Notes that the account is
       corroborated by the journal of Mr. Benbow, son of the famous ad-
       miral and first mate of the <u>Degrave</u>. Reproduces also the Preface
       of the 1743 edition.

3   [LOCKHART, JOHN GIBSON.] Review of <u>The Subaltern. The Adven-</u>
       <u>tures of a Young Rifleman</u>, and <u>The Adventures of a French</u>
       <u>Serjeant</u>. <u>Quarterly Review</u> 34, no. 68 (September):407.
           Brief passing reference to the "happy use" of military ma-
       terials made by persons "who never dreamt of authorship," such as

Defoe in <u>Memoirs of a Cavalier</u>, and Swift in his <u>Memoirs of Captain Chrichton</u>. "But what," exclaims the reviewer, "would we not give to have the great civil war of England, or even the contests in which Chrichton had a part, painted by an eye-witness . . .!"

4   PLUMPTRE, JAMES. Introduction to <u>The Life and Surprising Adventures of Robinson Crusoe</u>. New ed., rev. and corrected. London: C. & J. Rivington, pp. iii-xx.
      To demonstrate the popularity of <u>Robinson Crusoe</u> as well as its "power of interesting," quotes the usual authorities, Dr. Johnson and Dr. Blair, but also introduces new ones, Mrs. Trimmer, "in her Guardian of Education," and Dr. Percival, "in his Father's Instructions." Apparently, from Mrs. Trimmer's book, learns the objections to <u>Robinson Crusoe</u>, which he finds justified, namely, that "it favoured the doctrine of predestination, or fatalism, as Robinson Crusoe represented himself as born to be his own destruction, and urged on by a <u>fate</u> which he could not resist." Presents a brief biographical account of Defoe but with original speculations, such as the exemption of tallow-chandlers and butchers from the Plague because they used olive oil. Rejects any suggestion of fraud by Defoe against Selkirk; repeats the story mainly from Captain Woodes Rogers. On Lord Oxford as author of <u>Robinson Crusoe</u>, introduces new hearsay evidence in favor of Lord Oxford's authorship: in the autumn of 1811, when Plumptre was in Epsom, he was told by the late Miss Hamilton that "her father, the late Captain Hamilton, used to say, that 'Robinson Crusoe was written by Lord Oxford, while a prisoner in the Tower, and was fathered by Daniel Defoe.'" Observes that "the internal evidence" does not oppose Lord Oxford's authorship, and that "the general cast of the work is such as was not unlikely to proceed from the solitude of a prison"; and points to chapter 56, dealing with "the exiled nobles of Muscovy," as savouring "much of the writing, or at least the suggestion, of the impeached statesman." The rapid publication of the <u>Farther Adventures</u> can be more readily explained in terms of two authors. Believes that Cowper's "Verses Supposed to be written by Alexander Selkirk" were suggested by his reading <u>Robinson Crusoe</u>, and therefore should be reprinted in every edition, as here. In the Postscript (2 pp.), buttresses the case for Lord Oxford's authorship by quoting W.W.'s letter in the <u>Gentleman's Magazine</u>, 1788.3, and Clarke's preface to the second volume of his <u>Naufragia</u>, 1805.2. Reprinted: Society for Promoting Christian Knowledge, 1837.

5   SHELLEY, MARY. <u>The Last Man</u>. 3 vols. London: Henry Colburn. Reprint. Edited by Hugh J. Luke, Jr. Lincoln: University of Nebraska Press, 1965, 342 pp. passim.
      As the author explains in her introduction, during the year 1818 she and her "companion" (Shelley) visited Sibyl's cave in Naples, and found the "Sibylline leaves" containing the "prophecies" which she "translated" into the ensuing narrative. Writing in the first person, Lionel Verney tells his story which reaches its climax in the year 2097, about characters who have real-life counterparts: Adrian (Shelley), Lionel's father (William God-

win), Lord Raymond (Lord Byron), Lionel Verney (Mary Shelley),
and others identified in Luke's introduction. As the story moves
toward the extinction through plague, of the entire human race
except for Verney, deliberate echoes are introduced of Defoe's
Journal of the Plague Year, as well as Charles Brocken Brown's
Arthur Mervyn. Again, when the narrator has been cast on an
empty shore, he reflects: "For a moment I compared myself to
that monarch of the waste--Robinson Crusoe." The contrast continues: "desolate island" for Crusoe, "desolate world" for the
narrator; need of necessities for Crusoe, "Sybarite enjoyments"
which the narrator could command. Crusoe's terror at seeing the
human footprint contrasts with the narrator's: "it cannot be I
shall never behold a fellow being more!--never!--never!--not in
the course of years!" Uses Defoe's works to create the vision of
England's desolation and depopulation.

6   [SMITH, HORATIO.] Brambletye House; or Cavaliers and round-
     heads. A Novel. 3 vols. London: Henry Colburn, 3:52-89.
        Tells a story which takes place at the end of Cromwell's
     protectorate about a character named Jocelyn, the only son of
     a Cavalier, Sir John Compton, fighting against the Roundheads.
     Among his adventures, Jocelyn returns to London which has been
     struck by the Plague--graphically described by words, phrases,
     and images taken without acknowledgement from the Journal of
     the Plague Year. Sir Walter Scott, in his Memoirs (1837) for
     18 October 1826, complained about this open theft by Mr. Smith.

                                   1827

1   HAZLITT, WILLIAM. "On the Want of Money." Monthly Magazine
     n.s. 3, no. 13 (January):39.
        Turns from the experience of lacking money in real life to
     literary examples, recalling the "striking picture" in Colonel
     Jack of the "young beggarly hero" for the first time eating at an
     ordinary, relishing the soup, and delighted by the waiter's
     repeated response "coming, gentlemen, coming"; and of the other
     instance of new-found wealth. Reprinted: 1902- 1904.1; The
     Complete Works of William Hazlitt, ed. P.P. Howe, Centenary ed.
     (Toronto: J.M. Dent & Sons, 1933), 17:181.

2   SCOTT, SIR WALTER. "Daniel De Foe." In Miscellaneous Prose
     Works. Vol. 4, Biographical Memoirs. Edinburgh: Cadell &
     Co.; London: Longman, Rees, Orme, Brown, & Green, pp. 280-
     321, 322-38 (Appendix no. 1-2).
        A full-scale, early piece of comprehensive criticism, with
     strong praise from a fellow novelist. Arranges the critical
     assessment of Defoe's narratives around five "species of compo-
     sition": (1) about "water-thieves," pirates, and buccaneers;
     (2) about "land thieves," rogues and criminals; (3) about "great
     national convulsions," war, pestilence, storm; (4) about "theur-
     gy, magic, ghost-seeing, witchcraft, and the occult sciences";

and (5) about the economy of life, history, and other descriptive
subjects. Bridging literatures in discussing the second species,
alludes to the style "termed by the Spaniards Gusto Picaresco, of
which no man was ever a greater master." Integrating the arts,
discovers resemblances between "the strange and blackguard
scenes" of Defoe and "the gipsy-boys" of the seventeenth-century
Spanish painter, Murillo. Nevertheless, although selections
might be amusing, these "picaresque romances" must be passed by,
"as we would persons" unfit for good society. Again, in illustrating the third species with the History of the Great Plague,
raises an idea about art which runs through the entire essay,
namely, that works can be admired "however low and loathsome the
originals from which they are taken." The subjects may be "dis-
gusting," on low life or disease; yet the admiration for Colonel
Jack or the History of the Great Plague is undeniably strong.
Later, re-states the idea, and compares admiration for writing
"with all the plausibility of truth" and for "the paintings of
some Flemish artists." In painting, finds "a double source of
pleasure, both in the art of the painter, and in the interest
which we take in the subject represented." Calls this "the style
of probability with which De Foe invested his narratives," and
[in a surprising contradiction] finds it "ill bestowed or rather
wasted" on Colonel Jack or Moll Flanders, but it is "the same talent [which] throws an air of truth about the delightful history
of Robinson Crusoe." Explains the "general charm" of Defoe's
romances by resorting to the broad generalization of the practitioner in the novel. It is due "chiefly" to "the unequalled dex-
terity with which our author has given an appearance of reality
to the incidents which he narrates." All of Defoe's lacks in
style, language, or art make the case for him "as one who speaks
the truth." Illustrates this simple principle, which contains a
paradox, by a practitioner's "reference to common life." Gives
current examples of Defoe's "peculiar style of narrative" to show
how an author assumes an "imaginary personage." Differences between Scott's contemporaries and Defoe lie in the naturalness of
the latter--for example, in his Cavalier's language, as compared
with Crusoe's or Defoe's. Proceeds to a lengthy commentary "on
what may be called the plausible style of composition," in Mrs.
Veal. Writes casually, hastily, at times erroneously, especially
on the titles of works. Mistakenly attributes certain pieces to
Defoe, such as the History of Addresses. But for insights into
Defoe's narrative art--invaluable. Reprinted: Sir Walter Scott:
On Novelists and Fiction, ed. Ioan Williams (New York: Barnes &
Noble, 1968), pp. 164-83; in part, Critical Heritage; with John
Ballantyne's biography: 1834; 1836; 1865; 1877.

1828

1   [CARLYLE, THOMAS.] Review of John Gibson Lockhart's The Life
    of Robert Burns. Edinburgh Review 48, no. 96 (December):280.

No poet is "more graphic" than Burns. Regards "this clearness of sight" as a basic talent; it is "capable of being united
indifferently with the strongest, or ordinary power." Compares
Homer, Richardson, and Defoe with regard to "clearness" and the
"great garrulity" with which it is combined: Homer has "fire"
occasionally, which is lacking in Defoe and Richardson. Reprinted: "Burns," in The Works of Thomas Carlyle, ed. H.D. Traill,
Centenary ed. (London: Chapman & Hall, [1899]), 26:276-77; in
part, Critical Heritage.

2   HONE, WILLIAM. "April 26." In The Table Book. London:
    William Hone. Reprint. London and New York: Ward, Lock,
    Bowden & Co., 1892, p. 253.
       For the anniversary date of Defoe's burial, quotes the
reflections in Wilson's Memoirs of Defoe (1830).

3   _____. "Defoeana. No. 11. Mixed Breeds; or, Education
    Thrown Away." In The Table Book. London: William Hone.
    Reprint. London and New York: Ward, Lock, Bowden & Co.,
    1892, pp. 313-14.
       Quotes an unidentified account in which "a black Mulatto-
looking man," in a public house, describes the discriminations he
suffers, being "a true born Englishman," who has had a good
education but can use it to no purpose.

4   [MACAULAY, THOMAS BABINGTON.] Review of The Poetical Works of
    John Dryden, 1826. Edinburgh Review 47, no. 93 (January):7-8.
       Compares the change in an individual from infancy to matur-
ity, with the change in a nation from barbarism to civilization.
At first, one reads Robinson Crusoe with full enjoyment, but without being able to appreciate "the power of the writer." Now he
understands better, and appreciates less. Shows a close remem-
brance of the usual Robinson Crusoe favorites: "Xury, and Friday, and pretty Poll, the boat with the shoulder-of-mutton sail,
and the canoe which could not be brought down to the water edge,
the tent with its hedge and ladders, the preserve of kids, and
the den where the old goat died, can never again be to him the
realities which they were." Then the [Wordsworthian] climax:
"Such is the law of our nature. Our judgment ripens; our imagination decays." Continues with an illustration from Fielding's
Tom Jones: Partridge's behavior at the theatre. Reprinted:
1880.10.

5   [SOUTHEY, ROBERT.] Review of Reports of the Select Committee
    on Emigration from the United Kingdom. Quarterly Review 37,
    no. 74 (March):541-44.
       Authorship given in Wellesley Index. In a discussion of
issues such as "an overgrown trade" and "a redundant population,"
uses the views held by Defoe on the poor-laws, manufactures, and
"circulation of trade" to contrast the England of a hundred years
ago with the present. Finds that "few men have been more accurate observers of life and manners and of the mechanism of soci-

ety than Defoe"; yet he comprehended intermittently how "changes in the human system" disturb the inland trade. Gives as example the effects on trade resulting from the arrival of the French cloth-weavers into provincial towns such as Norwich, the introduction of machines like the stocking-frame, and the transfer of certain manufactures almost exclusively to London. Reprinted: 1832.4.

1829

*1 DEFOE, DANIEL, attributed author. Dissectio Mentis Humanæ. London: Whitmore and Fenn.
    Mistakenly thinking this piece to be Defoe's, the publishers Whitmore and Fenn advertise 100 copies, and propose another re-printing when these are subscribed for (1829.4). Bezaleel Morrice is generally identified as the author of the poem Dissectio Mentis: Or a Satyrical Display of the Faults and Errors of Human Nature (1731).

2 HOBHOUSE, JOHN CAM. Speech during debate on the "Regulation of Parish Vestries." In Hansard's Parliamentary Debates. New Series. London: Baldwin & Cradock et al., 21:898-99, 906.
    On 28 April, advocated a reform of "select vestries" based on the principle "that representation and taxation should go hand in hand," and drew upon a much-esteemed author of "one of the most current books in the English language--he meant De Foe, the author of Robinson Crusoe." For "a very strong picture drawn of the evils which were produced by select vestries," referred to Defoe's Parochial Tyranny [1727], "a tract not, perhaps, so much known by hon. members as Robinson Crusoe." Hobhouse then went on to quote Defoe on the nature of the abuse.

3 HOWELL, JOHN. The Life and Adventures of Alexander Selkirk; Containing the Real Incidents upon Which the Romance of Robinson Crusoe is Founded: In which also the Events of His Life, Drawn from Authentic Sources, are traced from his birth, in 1676, till his Death in 1723. With an Appendix, Comprising a Description of the Island of Juan Fernandez, and Some Curious Information Relating to His Shipmates, &c. Edinburgh: Oliver & Boyd; London: Geo. B. Whittaker, 196 pp.
    The introduction (16 pp.) is mainly responsible for a frequently stated view that although Defoe drew his main idea for Robinson Crusoe from "the singular circumstances of Selkirk's residence on the solitary and uninhabited island of Juan Fernandez, he is himself responsible for "all the incidents, details, and descriptions . . . in that beautiful fiction." He has been charged with theft, and denied "the reputation of being in any sense the author of Crusoe." By writing the biography of Selkirk, Howell intended to vindicate Defoe. Reprinted: Henry William Weber, Popular Romances: Consisting of Imaginary Voyages and Travels, 2d ed., 2 vols. (Edinburgh: W. & R. Chambers et

al., 1838); editions of Robinson Crusoe including 1836; 1837; 1844; 1847; 1850(5); 1872.

4 [STACE, MACHELL.] An Alphabetical Catalogue of an Extensive Collection of the Writings of Daniel De Foe and of the Different Publications for and against That Very Extraordinary Writer. London: Whitmore & Fenn, 47 pp.
    For Walter Wilson's high regard for Stace's collection, see his Memoirs of Defoe (1830), 2:xx-xxi. The sales catalogue lists some 278 assorted items, mainly by Defoe, but also several written against him. Included are later editions of the novels, pamphlets relating to the "standing army controversy," and twenty tracts relating to Dissenters.

1830

1 [FARRAR, ELIZA WARE ROTCH.] "Address to Parents." The Children's Robinson Crusoe: or the Remarkable Adventures of an Englishman. Boston: Hilliard, Gray, Little, & Wilkins, pp. v-viii.
    Describes the purposes of this "original narrative" (Brigham [1957], no. 123). Defoe's naturalness, his great merit, makes the book "unfit for the perusal of children"; and so the language was revised as well as the incidents altered. Enlists Defoe's hero "on the side of industry, perseverance, resignation to the will of God, and numerous other good qualities of which he might be supposed an example." Takes anecdotes and description of the Island's scenery from "The Life and Adventures of Alexander Selkirk, lately published from authentic sources" [Howell, 1829.3]. Friday becomes a native of the Sandwich Islands. Only those religious sentiments are allowed which are common to all Christian creeds.

2 HAZLITT, WILLIAM. Conversations of James Northcote, Esq., R.A. London: Henry Colburn & Richard Bentley. Reprint. In The Collected Works of William Hazlitt. Edited by A.R. Waller and Arnold Glover. London: J.M. Dent & Co.; New York: McClure, Phillips & Co., 1903, 6:413, 430.
    Notes that children from six to twelve read Pilgrim's Progress, Robinson Crusoe, Fielding's novels, and Don Quixote. Later, also, presents N. telling the anecdote to H. that no one read Drelincourt on Death until "Defoe put a ghost-story into it, and it has been a stock-book ever since." Reprinted: The Complete Works of William Hazlitt, ed. P.P. Howe, Centenary ed. (London and Toronto: J.M. Dent & Sons, 1932), 11:267, 284.

3 _____. Review of Wilson's Memoirs of Defoe (1830). Edinburgh Review 50, no. 100 (January):397-425.
    Authorship identified in 1902-1904.1. Summarizes the tiresomely long biographical parts of Walter Wilson's Memoirs; catches fire when he begins to argue for the complete separation

of biography and fiction through Defoe's "world of abstraction"
particularly in <u>Robinson Crusoe</u>. In this interpretation of Defoe
as an author and his relationship to the writings, gives a highly
individualized reading of the novels. Represents Defoe, in 1715,
retiring to Stoke Newington, not only turning "his thoughts into
a new channel" and writing romances, but in <u>The Family Instructor</u>
letting his pen fly "for relief to the details and incidents of
private life." While <u>Robinson Crusoe</u> was the best, the other
fictions were (relatively speaking) not read because they were
"not fit to be read." Argues forcefully that Defoe, "brought up
and trammelled all his life in the strictest notions of religion
and morality, and looking at the world, and all that was ordinar-
ily passing in it, as little better than a contamination, is, <u>a
priori</u>, [not] the properest person to write novels." Finds in
Defoe "overstrained Puritannical notions," with choices only between "God or the Devil--Sinners and Saints--the Methodist meeting or the Brothel--the school of the press-yard of Newgate, or
attendance on the refreshing ministry of some learned and pious
dissenting Divine." While his characters are "of the worst and
lowest description," they do not have "an <u>immoral</u> tendency" since
(as in <u>Moll Flanders</u> and <u>Roxana</u>) the author has neutralized the
question. Applies this criticism to males as well as to females,
and also to <u>Captain Singleton</u> and <u>Colonel Jack</u>. Concludes the
critical estimate of the novels by placing the <u>Journal of the
Plague Year</u> after <u>Robinson Crusoe</u> as "the finest of all his
works." Reprinted: 1902-1904.1; <u>The Complete Works of William
Hazlitt</u>, ed. P.P. Howe, Centenary ed. (Toronto: J.M. Dent &
Sons, 1933), 16:364-93, 440-42; in part, <u>Critical Heritage</u>.

4   LAMB, CHARLES. "Estimate of [Defoe's] Secondary Novels." In
     Walter Wilson, <u>Memoirs of the Life and Times of Daniel De Foe</u>.
     3 vols. London: Hurst, Chance, & Co., 3:636-39.
          Reinforces and adds momentum to the interest in the "sec-
ondary novels" as "all genuine offspring of the same father."
Discovers in <u>Roxana</u>, <u>Captain Singleton</u>, <u>Moll Flanders</u>, and
<u>Colonel Jack</u> certain similarities of subject (solitude and human
loneliness) and of manner (e.g., "naturalness," "the air of true
stories," "homeliness" of style). Regards the four narrators as
"startling ingredients in the bill of fare of modern literary
delicacies." Nowhere else in fiction has he found "guilt and
delinquency made less seductive, or the suffering made more
closely to follow the commission, or the penitence more earnest
or more bleeding. . . ." Reprinted: 1864.2; 1903.4; in part,
<u>Daniel Defoe: Moll Flanders</u>, ed. J. Paul Hunter, Crowell Criti-
cal Library (New York: Thomas Y. Crowell Co., 1970), pp. 271-
72; <u>Lamb As Critic</u>, ed. Roy Park (Lincoln: University of Nebraska Press, 1980), pp. 280-82.

5   ____. "Pindaric Ode to the Tread Mill." In <u>Album Verses,
     With a Few Others</u>. London: Edward Moxon, pp. 69-74.
          Lamb substantially altered the "Pindaric Ode," removing
what he later described as "silly lines" from the first printing

of 1825.2. For the changes made in the 1830 version, see Lucas's
notes, 1903.4, pp. 317-18. Lamb wrote the verses for Wilson's
Memoirs of Defoe (1830), and had them published in the New Times,
1825.2. The "Pindaric Ode" was not included in Wilson's Memoirs,
but certain of its ideas were incorporated into Lamb's "Estimate
of [Defoe's] Secondary Novels," which did appear there.

6   _____. Remarks on Defoe's "works of genius." In Walter Wil-
     son, Memoirs of the Life and Times of Daniel De Foe. 3 vols.
     London: Hurst, Chance, & Co., 3:428-29.
        The first of two critical "estimates," which Lamb contri-
buted to Wilson's Memoirs of Defoe (1830), was sent as part of a
letter dated 16 December 1822. He could offer only "a slight
general character of what I remember" of the novels, which Wilson
inserted verbatim as being "original" from his "highly esteemed
friend." Defoe's narrative qualities are summed up in comments
on the "perfect illusion" of the novels, the reader's belief in
the narrator, "the minute detail of a log-book," the story-
teller's repetitions, the style "every where beautiful, but plain
and homely." Lamb ranks his favorites among the novels: the
first part of Colonel Jack, Crusoe, Roxana [the 1745 edition].
For Lamb's letter to Wilson clarifying these comments (24 February 1823), see 1848.4; 1886.12; and The Letters of Charles Lamb,
ed. E.V. Lucas (London: J.M. Dent & Sons; Methuen & Co., 1935),
2:371-72. Reprinted: 1903.4.

7   LINGARD, JOHN. A History of England from the First Invasion
     by the Romans. 2d ed. London: Baldwin & Cradock; & B. Fel-
     lowes, 12:125-35.
        Narrating vividly the events of the London plague in 1665,
follows closely and borrows heavily from Defoe's "History of the
Plague in London," and gives credit to this and other sources.
Mentions specifically in a note: "Though De Foe, for dramatic
effect, wrote as an eye witness, which he could not be, yet his
narrative, as to the substance of the facts, is confirmed by all
the other authorities."

8   AN OLD MEMBER [pseud.]. "Christian-Knowledge Society's Cata-
     logue. To the Editor of the Christian Observer." Christian
     Observer & Advocate (London) 30:759-60.
        Objects generally to the mixing of fact and fiction, and
specifically to the first volume on the supplemental list published by the Society for Promoting Christian Knowledge, "De Foe's
fictitious account of the Great Plague, with Evelyn's sober
History of the Great Fire." Robinson Crusoe does not deceive;
Journal of the Plague Year and the Mrs. Veal were intended to
deceive. The ability to make "fiction pass for truth" appears in
a "fabulous" history (which is not named, but is clearly Memoirs
of a Cavalier) and the Shortest-Way with the Dissenters. A religious society should not encourage "literary frauds."

9   WILSON, WALTER. <u>Memoirs of the Life and Times of Daniel</u>
    <u>De Foe</u>. 3 vols. London: Hurst, Chance, & Co., 1:542 pp.;
    2:542 pp.; 3:700 pp.
       Surpassing all previous biographers in depth and scope,
    explores the life and career sympathetically--a biographer who,
    like his author, is "a cordial friend to civil and religious
    liberty." Covers the entire span of Defoe's life unevenly, since
    Wilson writes before the great exposé (1864.16), and therefore
    fixes upon 1715 as the pivotal year of Defoe's "retirement" from
    politics, devoting four to seven chapters to a single year (e.g.,
    1701, 1704), but only single chapters to 1715-1719 and 1726-1730.
    Parallels his narrative through 1713 with long accounts taken
    from the <u>Review</u>, now scrutinized for the first time to reveal a
    wealth of information both about the life and writings. Intro-
    duces a host of new names and personalities. Culls numerous pam-
    phlets, histories, periodicals by hostile contemporaries such as
    John Oldmixon, Abel Boyer, Charles Leslie to throw light on old
    controversies or respond to intricate questions of authorship.
    Specifically, on biography, takes a major step forward since
    Chalmers's: uses autobiographical statements in works by Defoe,
    or interprets the charges made by enemies, to add new information
    about Defoe's travels to the continent, his secret journeys to
    the southwest of England, his three different missions to Scot-
    land. While laying certain tenacious myths to rest (e.g., De-
    foe's theft of Selkirk's diary), revives others, such as his con-
    cealment in Bristol as the "Sunday gentleman" in 1692 or his two
    marriages. Draws discriminatingly from histories (Somerville,
    MacPherson, Cunningham), biographies (Chalmers), and criticism
    (Lamb, Scott, Lockhart). On the canon, makes relatively conser-
    vative judgments. In comparison with Chalmers's eighty-one works
    listed as "undoubtedly De Foe's" and twenty more "supposed to be
    his" (1790.1), offers a "Catalogue of Defoe's Works" (25 pp.) in
    vol. 1, listing 210 items, four of which are marked "doubtful":
    only twenty-four have not withstood the test of time, in that
    they do not appear in Moore's <u>Checklist</u>. Confirms the remaining
    186 items as Defoe's on the basis of explicitly stated criteria.
    Not revealed in the "Catalogue" is the careful weighing of evi-
    dence for authorship that went into individual judgments. Admits
    honestly that for certain works he was unable to locate copies.
    For others, states that the "common report" assigns them to
    Defoe, but such evidence is not adequate, and proceeds with his
    own analysis. Eliminates works that had long cluttered the Defoe
    canon: <u>The Free State of Noland</u> (1701) or Ned Ward's <u>Mars Strip-</u>
    <u>ped of His Armour</u> (1709). Makes significant suggestions for a
    few additions which he does not place in the "Catalogue." Identi-
    fies certain political tracts as the work of Defoe <u>after</u> 1715,
    and with a sense of self-contradiction feels obligated to include
    them. Most disappointing, however, is Wilson's critical assess-
    ment of the imaginary works, including <u>The Storm</u> (1704) and <u>Mrs.</u>
    <u>Veal</u>, and the novels (vol. 3, chaps. 17-22; about 143 pp.). For
    the first time, assigns <u>Capt. George Carleton</u> to Defoe, admitting
    that the hero is "in all likelihood, a fictitious character,"

but the book itself has been generally read "as an authentic work," like the Journal of the Plague Year and Memoirs of a Cavalier. Insists upon the apparent authenticity of both these lighter historical works, and their qualities as eye-witness narratives. Focuses attention on the two pieces of literary criticism by his friend Charles Lamb (1830.4, 6); accepts the "secondary novels"--Roxana, Captain Singleton, Moll Flanders, Colonel Jack-- as being (aside from their situations) the equals of Robinson Crusoe. In addition to a pronounced Victorian bias, offers criticism independent of Lamb's: for instance, on Defoe's "great skill as a mental physiognomist" in Colonel Jack and Moll Flanders, or the superiority of Roxana, especially in "original-ity of invention," over the other novels. See also the review: 1830.3. Reprinted: (New York: AMS Press, 1973); in part, Critical Heritage.

1831

1   BARTON, BERNARD. "Introductory Verses, or A Poet's Memorial of Robinson Crusoe." In The Life and Adventures of Robinson Crusoe. 2 vols. London: John Major, 1:i-xv.
    For the beginnings of these twenty-eight Spenserian stan-zas, see 1820.2, with its heartfelt tribute to Defoe for affect-ing "my early Child-hood." Now structures an entirely new poem based on the vivid scenes of Robinson Crusoe, probably those il-lustrated with engravings from drawings by George Cruikshank, and occasionally directed toward ideas, such as the anti-slavery one in stanza 8, which were close to the Quaker poet. J[ohn] M[ajor] explains in the preface that several years ago Barton had prefix-ed, "to a Volume of his own, some Verses inscribed to a Friend and Relative," Maria Hack, in which he alluded to Defoe, along with other writers for children. Subsequently, Wilson closed the preface to his Memoirs of Defoe (1830) with a fourteen-line En-glish sonnet by Barton. Struck with the beauty of the verses, Major requested Barton "to amplify them so as to form a full and appropriate Introduction." In the "Introductory Verses," printed here, the lines of the sonnet have now become the latter half of stanza 4 and all of a slightly revised stanza 5. Except for the change in title to "A Poet's Memorial of Robinson Crusoe," the verses are the same in the edition published by J. Chidley, 1836. In Barton's Household Verses, 1845.1 and 1849, the poem has stanzas 3, 4, 5, and 23 omitted.

2   "Biographical Sketch of Daniel Defoe." In The Life and Sur-prising Adventures of Robinson Crusoe. London: Baldwin & Cradock, pp. ix-xxiv.
    Written freshly for this edition, the "Biographical Sketch" reappears frequently, including the Bohn's Library Editions. Com-pares Defoe with Shakespeare and Cervantes: "it is not the skill of the artist that enchants us, but the perfect naturalness of the picture, which is such that we mistake it for a mirror; so that every reader persuades himself that he could write as well,

perhaps better, were he but furnished with the materials for an equally interesting narrative." Accepts as definite Defoe's travels to Spain and Germany, as well as his experience of shipwreck. On the novels, explains the swift succession of works which entitle Defoe to a place among "the Worthies of English literature" as "an extraordinary instance of rejuvenescency of mind in the decline of years." This edition, including the "Biographical Sketch," was pirated in 1835 by the New York publishers, Harper & Brothers, and reviewed by Edgar Allan Poe in the Southern Literary Messenger (1836.10). For the influence of the "Biographical Sketch" upon Poe's concept of verisimilitude, see Burton R. Pollin, "Poe and Daniel Defoe: A Significant Relationship," Topic: 30 16 (1976):3-22. Reprinted: 1835.2; 1839; 1844; 1846; [184-]; 1852; 1854(2); 1855; 1856(2); 1858; 1859; [185-?]; 1860; 1863; 1865; [186-?]; 1871(3); 1873; 1874(2); 1875; 1876(2); [187-?]; [188-]; [191-].

3   D[ANIEL], G[EORGE]. "Remarks" before Isaac Pocock's Robinson Crusoe; or, the Bold Buccaniers: A Romantic Drama, In Three Acts. London: John Cumberland, [n.d.], 41 pp. In Cumberland's British Theatre. London: [n.p.], 28, no. 9:5-8.
    Neither the date 1831 nor the author George Daniel are given with any certainty. The "Remarks" lead up to the statement that Pocock's "romantic drama" was first performed at Covent Garden on Easter Monday, 1817. Reflect nostalgically on the original Robinson Crusoe as a favorite for its instruction and delight, providential meaning, and popularity. Defend Defoe from any charge of theft from Selkirk; note the name Timothy Crusoe had appeared in Dunton's Life and Errors. Criticize Pope for including in the Dunciad "this honest, well-intentioned, laborious, persecuted, and happy genius." On the romantic drama itself, offer a rationale for the adaptation of a well-known story, and particularly praise Mr. Pocock for "launching Robinson Crusoe on the dramatic ocean."

4   ROSCOE, THOMAS, ed. "Biographical Sketch of De Foe." In The Life and Adventures of Robinson Crusoe. 2 vols. The Novelist's Library. London: Cochrane & Pickersgill, & J. Andrews, 1:i-lxiv.
    Roscoe's authorship is not conclusive. In the advertisement of "The Novelist's Library" series, which precedes the title page, Cochrane and Pickersgill announce the sale of "classical novels," one volume per month at five shillings a bound volume. Deliberately aim at being international by offering "cheap editions of the Works of those great painters of life and manners who reflect lustre on their respective countries, comprehending only such novels and romances as have been unequivocally stamped with popular regard, and which, from their long admitted superiority over all competitors of their class, and their translation into various languages, are for ever associated with the literature of the world." The series, "uniform with the Waverley Novels," began with Robinson Crusoe, and included Smollett, Goldsmith,

Fielding, and Sterne. Before and during this venture, Roscoe had similar publications for the Italian, German, and Spanish novelists. Recognizes the fame of Robinson Crusoe as extending not only over "the whole of polished Europe, but even to the sandy plains of Arabia" through Burckhardt's translation (1819.3). Interest in Robinson Crusoe leads to biographical curiosity about the author. Not since Lockhart's biographical preface (1820.4) have there been such a high quality and such a detailed, accurate presentation, owing in part to the close paralleling of Wilson's Memoirs of Defoe (1830). Follows sequentially Wilson's three-volume biography, occasionally lifts sentences and whole paragraphs, and even borrows critical viewpoints (e.g., four-page analysis of rhetorical strategy in the Shortest-Way with the Dissenters). Acknowledges Wilson's most "perfect catalogue" of Defoe's works, and shares his interest in the canon which now stands at "two hundred acknowledged publications, besides anonymous ones." In spite of the occasional borrowings from Wilson, remains an important account, frequently expresses independent critical judgments, movingly describes Defoe's afflictions—when pilloried, when imprisoned for ironical pamphlets, and when betrayed at the end of his life by an ungrateful son.

1832

1   GENT, THOMAS. The Life of Mr. Thomas Gent, Printer, of York. London: Thomas Thorpe, pp. 121-24.

In his autobiography written in 1746, Gent tells an incident in which he is awakened by the King's messenger at night, searched, arrested and brought to a public-house where he is kept under guard. Information has been "lodged at the Secretary's office, before Mr. De la Faye, about some lines concerning the imprisoned Bishop of Rochester, that had given offence. . . ." What makes the incident bizarre is that when "my master," the bookseller Mr. [Edward] Midwinter is brought in as a prisoner, Gent says, "What, sir, . . . have they made me appear greater than you, by placing me first in the warrant for our apprehension? me, who am but your servant, and, you know, has wrote nothing for you this long time, except an abridgement of three volumes of 'Crusoe' into one, or being otherwise employed in the affairs of printing only?" A strong case has been made that Gent's abridgement is identical with Midwinter's dated 1722; see Hutchins's "Robinson Crusoe" and Its Printing (1925), pp. 135-39; and 1865.3.

2   Preface to The History of the Great Plague in London, in the Year 1665. New ed. London: Renshaw & Rush, & James Gilbert, pp. iii-vii.

The History takes its place among the medical publications of Renshaw and Rush. Stresses the lack of any resemblance between the cholera of 1831 and the Plague of 1665. Places emphasis on the feelings: plague harrows up the feelings, "carries us into the bosoms of families"; miseries strike "a responsive chord in every breast." The History must not be taken as altogether authentic: "Defoe has embellished his melancholy narrative with imaginary facts, and heightened the picture of wretchedness and misery. . . ."

3 SCOTT, JOHN. Narratives of Two Families Exposed to the Great Plague of London A.D. 1665; with Conversations on Religious Preparation for Pestilence. Republished with Notes and Observations. 2d ed. London: R.B. Seeley & W. Burnside, 186 pp.
      Abridges and adapts Defoe's Due Preparations for the Plague (1722), referring frequently to "our author," but never identifying him. Takes special interest in reprinting about half of Defoe's book, "the best picture I have seen of the state of London at that awful period." Believes that the book should be particularly relevant to young readers who at a time when cholera threatens should always be spiritually prepared, as were the sister and younger brother in Defoe's narratives. In a number of footnotes, stresses theological differences with the unnamed author.

4 SOUTHEY, ROBERT. "Essay X. On Emigration." In Essays, Moral and Political. 2 vols. London: John Murray, 2:211-17.
      Reprint of 1828.5.

1832?

1 STEBBING, H., ed. Introduction to De Foe's History of the Plague. London: Scott & Webster, pp. v-xxxii.
      Shows how the human mind preoccupies itself in a safe contemplation of "danger and misfortune" by an historical listing of Biblical and classical accounts of pestilence. Includes Thucydides's powerful description of the plague at Athens. Recognizes that Boccaccio, "as well as De Foe, drew his impressive details from the narratives of others." Lengthily (11 pp.), describes the Plague at Marseilles in 1720, and asserts that although the evil had a "natural origin," such an explanation did not interfere with "the doctrine which assigns its ravages to Divine appointment." Reprinted: 1839; Philadelphia, [n.p., n.d.].

1833

1 "Biographic Sketches. Daniel Defoe, The Author of Robinson Crusoe." Chambers's Edinburgh Journal 2, no. 65 (27 April): 100-1.
      Borrows from William Hazlitt, senior, 1830.3, the well-established biographical information and certain critical attitudes, but also expresses its own views. Starts the sketch with a quotation from Hazlitt which nostalgically associates a "world of abstraction" with Robinson Crusoe. Continues in the same vein

with another reviewer's greater "sympathy" for Crusoe's situation
than for his character. Claims with this reviewer that while
Moll Flanders, Captain Singleton, Colonel Jack, and the other
romances do not have the same merit as Robinson Crusoe, nevertheless "they show, equally with Crusoe, that first-rate sign of
genius, the power of imagining a character within a certain range
of existence, and throwing into it the breath of life and indivi-
dualization, which was a pre-eminent mental characteristic of
De Foe." Includes among the veritable histories and biographies,
which have this genius, "the Citizen's Account of the Great
Plague of London in 1665" and "the Memoirs of Captain Carleton."

2   CHASLES, PHILARÈTE. "Daniel De Foe, Auteur de Robinson Cru-
     soe." Revue de Paris 55 (October):150-70, 206-20; 56 Supp.
     (November):17-25, 84-105.
        Probably the most sympathetic biographical and critical
account to appear in both France and England, reveals instantly
a new, attractive perspective on Defoe. Deliberately takes issue
with the dulness of Wilson's Memoirs of Defoe (1830). Follows
a dramatic rather than chronological order of events, brings a
poetic enthusiasm to the narrative (considerably diminished in
1846.2), draws parallels between Defoe and "Socrate . . . Don
Quichotte" (epigraph from Lord Byron). Using biographical information (sometimes incorrect), stresses the poverty (alleged at
the time of his death), and the imprisonments (states at one
point Defoe was in prison for four years!). Reaches a climax in
section 10, "The End of His Political Life," with the powerful
quotation on Socrates's mission, from his Apology. Makes comparisons with Don Quijote or Cervantes: Defoe emerges an idealist,
hopelessly fighting for significant lost causes. At the age of
fifty-eight, turning to Robinson Crusoe, he was "like Cervantes"
in the range of his hapless experiences. When Charles Gildon
attacked Defoe for the "Don Quixotism" in Robinson Crusoe, Defoe
replied that "this criticism was the greatest of panegyrics."
Near the end of the article, likens Defoe to "Don Quijote of
justice," beaten by all the political parties which live in iniq-
uity. Introduces from an unidentified source the story of the
Ohio colonist who drew his courage from this "divine volume" of
Robinson Crusoe. Still more important in giving an urgent tone
to the writing, relates Defoe to writers such as Locke, Rousseau,
Franklin, Voltaire, Junius, and Burke. Identifies certain of
Defoe's ideas on "social ameliorations" in An Essay upon Projects
(1697) and The Poor Man's Plea (1697) as having the currency and
vitality of the French Revolution. See also Chasles, 1844.2.
Reprinted: 1845.6; 1846.2.

3   "Daniel De Foe." In The Life and Surprising Adventures of
     Robinson Crusoe. London: J. Limbird, pp. v-viii.
        Contains the inaccuracies expected for the date, but dif-
fers from the ordinary run of prefaces in that the author has
freshly reexamined the information available. Makes Defoe's
travel to Spain and his experience of shipwreck definite rather
than speculative; refers to him as "the Father of the English

Essayists." Rejects "the imputation" that <u>Robinson Crusoe</u> was
founded upon Alexander Selkirk's papers. Devotes only a few
sentences to the "other lives and adventures in character."
Starts the account with an unidentified quotation of five lines
of verse referring ostensibly to Defoe ("spider-like, out of his
self-drawing web, he gives us note"); and preserves the anecdote
of how the young Napoleon, the Duke of Reichstadt, who greatly
abhorred fiction, was nevertheless educated by <u>Robinson Crusoe</u>
through "its powerful resemblance to truth." Reprinted:
[186-?].

4   "Daniel Defoe." <u>Penny Magazine</u> 2, no. 67 (20 April):151-52.
       Offers a sympathetic biographical account in this magazine
published by the Office of the Society for the Diffusion of Useful Knowledge; recognizes the anniversary of the death of "this
greater writer." Although known to readers generally for his
<u>Robinson Crusoe</u>, Defoe does not yet have "in the general estima-
tion that share of fame and that rank in English literature to
which he is justly entitled." Traces his career from failure as
a tradesman to preoccupation with political writing and natural
affairs. Stresses his disinterestedness, independence, adherence
to principles, and courage. Regards 1715 as the turning point,
when he abandoned politics and took up "less ungrateful themes."
His subsequent achievements earned him a fame as extensive and as
lasting as the language itself. Mentions briefly the productions
other than <u>Robinson Crusoe</u>. Includes <u>Colonel Jack</u> with <u>Journal
of the Plague Year</u> and <u>Memoirs of a Cavalier</u> as "mere fabrications of the writer's invention," but "distinguished by an air of
nature and truth, which it is impossible during the perusal not
to take for genuine."

5   "Defoe." In <u>Gallery of Portraits</u>. Society for the Diffusion
of Useful Knowledge, vol. 7, no. 43. London: Charles Knight,
pp. 112-20.
       Relies heavily upon Chalmers's <u>Life of Daniel De Foe</u> (both
the 1786 and 1790) and perhaps Wilson's <u>Memoirs</u> of Defoe (1830)
for biographical information and for the listing of a relatively
small number of major works (curiously omitting <u>Roxana</u>). Selects
the <u>Journal of the Plague Year</u>, <u>Memoirs of a Cavalier</u>, and <u>Robin-
son Crusoe</u> as "the best known and most deserving." Praises Defoe
and Bunyan as authors who wrote without "the trammels of a learned education . . . for and to the people," and closes with Dunlop's notes on the resemblances between Swift and Defoe (1814.2
or 1816.3).

6   "England. Daniel Defoe." <u>Magazin für die Literatur des Aus-
landes</u>, No. 71 (14 June):284.
       Compactly, sums up the life of Defoe "to whom adequate
recognition has yet not been given." Mentions the <u>Essay upon
Projects</u>, <u>Review</u>, <u>Jure Divino</u>, and the Union (both history and
event). Of the novels, lists only <u>Robinson Crusoe</u> (of European
fame), the "true histories" of the <u>Journal of the Plague Year</u> and
<u>Memoirs of a Cavalier</u>, and <u>Colonel Jack</u>.

7   [SCROPE, G. POULETT.] "Miss Martineau's Monthly Novels."
     Quarterly Review 49, no. 97 (April):137.
        Finds that Harriet Martineau's Illustrations of Political
     Economy, appearing in twelve numbers during 1832-1833, has been
     itself "illustrated" long ago and much more amusingly by Robinson
     Crusoe, which makes readers aware of the value of civilization
     without "such unintelligible and fantastical refinements" as are
     found in Martineau.

                                1834

1   LOWNDES, WILLIAM THOMAS. "Defoe, Daniel." In The Bibliog-
     rapher's Manual of English Literature. 4 vols. London:
     William Pickering, 2:560-65.
        For some 103 entries of Defoe's "works," does not dis-
     tinguish between hostile pamphlets attacking Defoe and those
     actually written by him; includes also items which are no longer
     assigned to him. Annotates selected works, at times with quali-
     tative judgments, such as on the superiority of the Review to
     "any thing which had hitherto appeared" or on the Memoirs of a
     Cavalier as "well known to have been frequently cited as a his-
     torical authority." See also 1858.2.

2   MÉZIÈRES, L[OUIS]. "De Foe." In Histoire critique de la
     littérature Anglaise, depuis Bacon jusqu'au commencement du
     dix-neuvième siècle. 3 vols. Paris: Baudry, 1:217-42.
        Thoughtfully reexamines the broad question of the origins
     of Robinson Crusoe. Deals exclusively with Robinson Crusoe as
     Defoe's most popular success. Makes the point that almost from
     the start there was lively controversy: at first most readers
     saw only "an amusing fiction," and none of "the philosophy hidden
     under the charm of the fable." Reviews Defoe's alleged miscon-
     duct toward Selkirk and "the more injurious supposition" made by
     Dr. Beattie (1783.1) that Defoe misappropriated profits from the
     Scottish mariner. Rejects completely the slanderous allegations,
     and makes a strong artistic case for Defoe, analyzing the mind of
     Selkirk as revealed in his interview with Richard Steele, publish-
     ed in the Englishman, and juxtaposing the traits revealed there
     with the quite different ones revealed in the mind of Robinson
     Crusoe. Argues, for instance, that Defoe's conception of his
     character started with Steele's "moral observation," his interest
     in "the different impressions of the mind in solitude," and that
     Defoe ruled out of his character "the profound indifference to
     the world and the perfect resignation of Selkirk." Accepts
     D'Israeli's account (1817.4) of Defoe's turning from his own per-
     sonal "bitterness of fortune" and finding inspiration directly in
     Selkirk and "the moving tableau of Steele" to write a narrative
     showing "what man can do for himself, and what man can do for
     man--the courage of piety." Proceeds to analyze the central
     theme of "self-preservation," the brilliantly fitting style, an
     excellence in depicting sailors (here, sharing with Swift and

Smollett "something conforming to national genius"), and Defoe's perfect identification with his character's isolation through his own imprisonment in Newgate for bad debts. While being one of the first critics to use "Visions of the Angelic World" in Serious Reflections, nevertheless severely criticizes certain incidents, such as Crusoe's destroying the idol of the Tartars. Stands out, refreshingly, for its strongly critical convictions: for instance, on Robinson Crusoe as "a sort of popular Odyssey"; on the language of "the true narrator" ("This grave and sententious tone befits well an old solitary"); on "the strong and picturesque words" describing the young girl dying of hunger, a tableau with "some of the sombre energy of Dante." Concludes by placing Defoe in "the glorious triumvirate of Richardson, Fielding and Smollett." If "the palm of genius" is withheld from him, he still has "an equally universal success--and not one of those can equal him in popularity."

1835

1   "Advertisement" and "Biographical Notice of Daniel Defoe." In
      The Life and Adventures of Robinson Crusoe, from the Original
      Work, by Daniel Defoe. New ed., Carefully Adapted to Youth.
      New York: C. Wells, pp. [i], 331-35.
           Advertises the purity of thought and expression here; and
      explains the charges against Defoe for having stolen Selkirk's
      papers as due to his enemies. Rejects the accusation as "totally
      false."

2   "Biographical Sketch of Daniel Defoe." In The Life and Sur-
      prising Adventures of Robinson Crusoe. New York: Harper &
      Brothers, pp. ix-xxiii.
           Reprinting of 1831.2. This pirated edition was reviewed by
      Edgar Allan Poe when he first joined the staff of the Southern
      Literary Messenger, 1836.10. Reprinted: [184-].

3   "Book-Puffing a Century Ago." Chambers's Edinburgh Journal
      4:52-53.
           Through summary and extensive quotation, illustrates Sir
      Walter Scott's concept of Defoe's "plausible style of composi-
      tion." Retells Scott's ingenious account of Defoe's publishing
      hoax for stimulating the sales of Drelincourt's Consolation
      Against the Fears of Death through the ghost's recommendation of
      the book in Mrs. Veal. Mistakenly assigns the borrowed material
      to John Ballantyne rather than Scott and claims to take them from
      "the Life of Daniel De Foe, connected with Ballantyne's Novel-
      ist's Library." Ballantyne's biography and Scott's criticism,
      the latter including the publishing hoax, were combined in
      1827.2, and reprinted in 1834. Even though Scott's criticism
      was being planned for the Ballantyne's Novelist's Library, the
      "Defoe" was never included in the series.

4   BRAYLEY, EDWARD WEDLAKE. "Introductory Observations." A
     Journal of the Plague Year . . . By Daniel De Foe. The Family
     Library, no. 52. London: Thomas Tegg & Son, pp. iii-xviii.
         Considers the Journal's "genuineness and accuracy"; reiter-
     ates and develops further his position in 1810.2, that the Jour-
     nal is "not a fiction, nor is it based upon fiction." Explores
     the possibility of Defoe's having used "some diary, or manuscript
     observations," like William Boghurst's, quoted at length in appen-
     dix 1. Assesses the "printed sources": the Bills of Mortality
     for 1665 in London's Dreadful Visitation, Hodges's Loimologia,
     and Vincent's God's Terrible Voice in the City. Quotes Walter
     Wilson's fine judgments on the Journal in his recent biography
     (1830), and offers his own strong appraisal of the Journal as be-
     ing "paralleled" only by Thucydides's account of the Plague in
     Athens. So strong was the impression on Defoe's mind made by the
     subject, "it imparted a high moral character to his work." Pro-
     vides extensive "historical notes" and six appendices which repro-
     duce documents relating to the Plague. Reprinted: 1839; 1848.

5   COLERIDGE, SAMUEL TAYLOR. Specimens of the Table Talk. Edit-
     ed by Henry Nelson Coleridge. 2 vols. London: John Murray;
     New York: Harper & Brothers. Reprint. Complete Works. Edit-
     ed by Professor [William Greenough Thayer] Shedd. 7 vols.
     New York: Harper & Brothers, 1853, 6:521.
         Entry: 5 July 1834. Admires Peter Wilkins as "a work of
     uncommon beauty." Praises the "exquisite image" of "Peter's Glum
     fluttering over the ship, and trying her strength in lifting the
     stores!" Believes that Robinson Crusoe and Peter Wilkins "could
     only have been written by islanders." No French or German author
     could entirely understand the "'desert island' feeling." If Cole-
     ridge were to attempt something similar, he would prefer "the mar-
     vellous line of Peter Wilkins" to "the real fiction of Robinson
     Crusoe."

6   DICKENS, CHARLES [Boz]. "Sketches of London.--No. XII."
     Evening Chronicle, 19 May. Reprint. Sketches by Boz. Oxford
     Illustrated Dickens. London: Oxford University Press, 1957,
     p. 11.
         In the parish, among the old lady's neighbors, lives the
     naval captain on half-pay whose "bluff and unceremonious behav-
     iour disturbs the old lady's domestic economy, not a little." He
     is described as "a bit of a Jack of all trades, or to use his own
     words, 'a regular Robinson Crusoe.'" He performs well-intention-
     ed tasks for the old lady, without permission, which turn out
     badly for her.

7   REYBAUD, LOUIS. "Notice sur Daniel De Foé." In Aventures de
     Robinson Crusoé. Translated by Mme. Amable Tastu. Edition de
     grand luxe. 2 vols. Paris: Moutardier, 2:371-84.
         Robinson Crusoe has so completely dominated its author that
     very little seems to be known about Daniel Defoe. Challenges
     anyone to compare his achievements with Addison's, Steele's, or

Swift's. Includes biographical errors, such as Defoe's marriage
to a woman named Suzanne in 1687, or his meeting with Selkirk in
Bristol. Tells the anecdote of the Robinson Crusoe manuscript being refused by all the London booksellers until purchased by William Taylor for £10 sterling. Of the two sources for the novel--
Selkirk or Pedro Serrano--prefers the former. Defoe's other
major fictions do not have "the power and significance" of Robinson Crusoe; they do have originality and verve, Defoe's two great
qualities. Notes that Defoe anticipated the ideas of Rousseau,
Tourgot, Franklin, and Condorcet. Reprinted: 2 vols. (Paris:
Didier, 1837); 2d ed., rev. and corr. (Paris: Didier, 1839).

8   TASTU, [SABINE CASIMIRE] AMABLE, transl. Aventures de Rob-
     inson Crusoé. Edition de grand luxe. 2 vols. Paris:
     Moutardier, 1:396 pp.; 2:384 pp.
         The "Avis de l'éditeur" (3 pp.) explains that the transla-
tion was first assigned to Louis Reybaud (1835.7) and then to
Madame Tastu. A well-known children's author, she undertook to
rehabilitate Robinson from the stylistic vagaries of earlier
translators. Not until the fourteenth number of this publication
was Madame Tastu identified as the translator. Among her innovations, she sought advice from an old sea-officer to translate
faithfully scenes of the sea. Engravings were commissioned from
the distinguished artist, M. de Sainson, who had traveled over
the places described. For the literary quarrel between Madame
Tastu and Pétrus Borel, see chap. 2 and appendix B in Mann. See
also 1836.3; 1845.6.

1836

1   [BALLANTYNE, JOHN.] "The Life of Daniel De Foe [with contin-
     uation by Sir Walter Scott]." In The Life and Adventures of
     Robinson Crusoe. Collection of Ancient and Modern English Au-
     thors, vol. 141. Paris: Baudry's European Library, pp. i-xl.
         Ballantyne's "Life" first appeared in the Robinson Crusoe
edition which launched the publication of Scott's Novels of Daniel De Foe, in twelve volumes; it was reprinted on occasion
during the century (1809.1; 1809-1810.1). Scott continued the
work of his "late regretted friend" with some of the finest early
criticism of Defoe as a novelist for his Miscellaneous Prose
Works (1827.2). The combined biographical and critical accounts
were frequently published together in editions of Robinson Crusoe. Included here also as appendices: John Howell's "Some
Account of Alexander Selkirk" (4 pp.) and Mrs. Veal (6 pp.).

2   "Biography of Daniel Defoe." In The True-Born Englishman:
     A Satire. With a Copious Memoir of the Author. Leeds: Alice
     Mann, pp. 3-7.
         In one long unbroken paragraph, summarizes the biographical
information with emphasis on Defoe's "personal courage and fortitude." Makes the common mistakes of assigning his birth to 1663

and beginning the Review in Newgate. Introduces the interesting
biographical error of identifying "the unfeeling child" who
caused Defoe trouble in his last years as a daughter rather than
a son. Wrongly assigns the History of Addresses (1709) to Defoe;
omits completely any mention of novels such as Moll Flanders or
Roxana; recognizes Robinson Crusoe, Journal of the Plague Year,
Family Instructor, and Religious Courtship.

3   BOREL, PETRUS, transl. Robinson Crusoë, par Daniel de Foë.
    Traduction de Petrus Borel. Enrichi de la vie de Daniel De
    Foë, par Philarète Chasles; de notices sur le matelot Selkirk,
    sur Saint-Hyacinthe, sur L'isle de Juan Fernandez, sur les
    Caraïbes et Puelches, par Ferdinand Denis; et d'une disserta-
    tion religeuse, par la Abbé La Bouderie, Vicaire-générale
    d'Avignon. 2 vols. Paris: Francisque Borel & Alexandre
    Varenne, 1:424 pp.; 2:507 pp.
        In the elaborate edition, which seems to be the work of the
    translator Borel and includes 250 engravings on wood, a full-
    length frontispiece of Defoe, and all the items promised in the
    title except Chasles's "Life" of Defoe which had already appeared
    in the Revue de Paris, 1833.2, and would appear again in Mme.
    Tastu's rival translation of 1845.6. On Saint-Hyacinthe, the
    first translator of Robinson Crusoe and his immediate predeces-
    sor, holds strong, severely critical views which he expresses in
    the preface (2 pp.). In contrast to Saint-Hyacinthe and Justus
    van Effen, describes himself translating as a poet "seized by a
    beautiful passion and courage." Castigates the mediocrity of the
    old translation as being so bad that no bookseller has dared to
    reprint it for sixty years. Argues that not only is the old
    translation inaccurate, it even substitutes "a wan verbosity" for
    Defoe's "simple, nervous, accented narrative"; claims for his own
    translation "exactitude and conscience." In the translation
    itself, adds occasional notes signed "P.B." which at times praise
    the author Defoe, (for instance) as "a man of taste and good
    service," or identify a particular mistranslation or an outright
    error by his predecessor. For Borel's rivalry in translation
    with Mme. Tastu, see also 1835.8; 1845.6; his translations were
    also published in 1878 and 1920.

4   COLERIDGE, SAMUEL TAYLOR. "Lecture XI. Asiatic and Greek
    Mythologies—Robinson Crusoe—Use of Works of Imagination in
    Education." In The Literary Remains of Samuel Taylor Cole-
    ridge. Edited by Henry Nelson Coleridge. 4 vols., London:
    William Pickering, 1:189-97.
        In Lecture XI (1818), includes a paragraph on "the charm of
    De Foe's works, especially of Robinson Crusoe," which appears to
    have little connection with the subject of the lecture. Briefly
    develops the view of Crusoe as "merely a representative of human-
    ity in general." Mistakenly incorporates here, in a separate sec-
    tion "Notes on Robinson Crusoe," Coleridge's marginalia "written
    . . . in Mr. Gillman's copy of Robinson Crusoe, in the summer of
    1830." Altogether, there were nineteen notes, some omitted by

H.N. Coleridge, and some garbled. H.B. Wheatley took his text
directly from the marginalia (1902.19), and Raysor reprinted the
1902 text, but based the Defoe texts on both the 1836 and the
1902, "but with some slight variations resulting from a collation
of the two and from a study of internal evidence." Includes some
of Coleridge's most famous pronouncements on Robinson Crusoe. On
the comparison of "the contemptuous Swift with the contemned De
Foe" and the superiority of the latter: [H.N. Coleridge's garbled text] "De Foe's excellence it is, to make me forget my specific class, character, and circumstances, and to raise me while I
read him, into the universal man." On the passage "Worthy of
Shakespeare!" Coleridge's insight hinges upon a semicolon in Crusoe's words ("'O drug!' . . . I took it away;"); and his meaning
becomes blunted by the lack of the full text, the editor's unwarranted change to Italic letter, and the liberties taken with
marks of punctuation. On Crusoe's and Friday's "discourse" about
the devil: Coleridge finds this conception of the devil more
according to Milton's Paradise Lost than the Bible. On Defoe's
avoidance of the periodic style: Coleridge finds it conflicting
with "the every-day matter-of-fact realness, which forms the
charm and the character of all his romances." Makes a final comment on Defoe's restraint in, for example, not giving Crusoe a
turn for natural history. This he could have done, but at great
sacrifice: "Crusoe would have ceased to be the universal representative, the person for whom every reader could substitute himself." Reprinted: Miscellanies, Aesthetic and Literary, ed.
T. Ashe (London: George Bell & Sons, 1885), pp. 154-60; 1902.19;
Coleridge's Miscellaneous Criticism, ed. Thomas Middleton Raysor
(Cambridge, Mass.: Harvard University Press, 1936), pp. 292-300;
in part, Critical Heritage.

5   DENIS, FERDINAND. "Notice." In Robinson Crusoé, par Daniel
     De Foe. Traduction de Petrus Borel. 2 vols. Paris: Fran-
     cisque Borel & Alexandre Varenne, 2:i-xv.
         Writes exuberantly on Robinson Crusoe, Selkirk, Juan Fer-
nandez, the Caribs, and the Puelches. Admires Defoe's work as
having influenced all nations--"among the number of those books
which increase thought and which initiate young minds to the most
elevated moral truths." Discusses at length the geographical
details of the two islands comprising Juan Fernandez, explaining
the name "Island of Despair" given by Robinson Crusoe to his
solitude as appropriate to the severe weather. Traces the two
castaways who arrived at Juan Fernandez, one before 1680 in
Ringrose's narrative, and the other (the Mosquito Indian) whom
Captain Sharp left there in 1680. Comments uniquely on Alexander
Selkirk's personality as it relates to Defoe's creative process,
noting in the Scotsman's temperament a reflective spirit and a
somewhat melancholic seriousness, but also a lack of industry.
Defoe himself "felt" these attributes in Selkirk, and created
them in the character of Robinson Crusoe. Argues that "with some
perseverance, a child will become like that; it is what makes
[Robinson Crusoe] so dear to children." Continues to compare
Selkirk and Robinson Crusoe with the emphasis on what was or was

not Defoe's invention, particularly the effects of the solitude
on the man himself. On Juan Fernandez: demonstrates that
Defoe's "independent fantasy" did not submit to the exigencies
of geography. Points out such "errors" as the fact that the
Puelches and Araucans were not cannibals and that Defoe invented
the religious ideas and religious words. Compares the Caribs
with Friday. Reprinted: 1845.6; 1861.4.

6   DICKENS, CHARLES. The Posthumous Papers of the Pickwick Club
     . . . Edited by "Boz." Reprint. Oxford Illustrated Dickens.
     London: Oxford University Press, 1948, p. 83.
         In chap. 7, Mr. Pickwick meets his host Mr. Wardle "carry-
     ing both guns like a second Robinson Crusoe," as the latter waits
     in the garden for Mr. Winkle to go out "rook-shooting before
     breakfast."

7   LABOUDERIE, [JEAN]. "Dissertation religeuse." In Robinson
     Crusoé, par Daniel de Foe. Traduction de Petrus Borel.
     2 vols. Paris: Francisque Borel & Alexandre Varenne, 2:
     xvi-xxviii.
         Writing as the vicar-general of Avignon, expresses a deep
     admiration of Robinson Crusoe, at first in general terms, for its
     "profound knowledge of the human heart, a painting so natural of
     the events of life that all ages recognize them . . .; it exhales
     a perfume of religion smooth and soft that it ought to appear
     agreeable to all souls sensible of, and penetrated with respect
     for revelation." For the "Dissertation religeuse," in order to
     gather "noble inspirations" from Robinson Crusoe for the imita-
     tion of young people, analyzes closely the "religious sentiments"
     from a Catholic point of view. Offers insights into repentance
     and return to religion, and into Providence, by repeatedly com-
     paring Robinson Crusoe with Silvio Pellico whose memoirs of im-
     prisonment were published in Italian (1832) and in English (My
     Prisons, 1834) and with whom quite often there was found a "per-
     fect resemblance." Contrasts Crusoe also with Job whose fate was
     the opposite, namely, to face Providence dispensing good and evil
     indiscriminately. Makes a special analysis of the Benedictine in
     the last part of Robinson Crusoe, and finds the character to be
     literally beautiful as Papist, priest, and Frenchman: "The times
     have advanced, and so has sociability." Finds Robinson Crusoe
     most expressive of this greatly increased tolerance for Catholi-
     cism. Reprinted: 1845.6.

8   "The Life of Daniel De Foe." In The Life and Adventures of
     Robinson Crusoe. Halifax: W. Milner, pp. v-vi.
         In a brief and hasty account, admits that Defoe may have
     inspected Selkirk's journal, but states firmly that "[Defoe's]
     character of general integrity" should reject any suspicion of
     fraud or injustice. Reprinted: London, [185-].

9   POE, EDGAR ALLAN. Review of The Confessions of Emilia Har-
     rington, by Lambert A. Wilmer. Southern Literary Messenger 2,
     no. 3 (February):191-92.

Describes his excitement in reading works "in which the author utterly loses sight of himself in his theme, and, for the time, identifies his own thoughts and feelings with the thoughts and feelings of fictitious existences." Values "the power of accomplishing this perfect identification" as the mark of genius. "It is the spell of Defoe." One finds it also in Boccaccio, the Arabian Tales, Scott, Shakespeare. Repeats part of the second paragraph in his review (1836.10) of the Robinson Crusoe edition published by Harper & Brothers. See also Burton R. Pollin, "Poe and Daniel Defoe: A Significant Relationship," Topic: 30 16 (1976):16. Reprinted: 1902.11.

10   ____. Review of The Life and Surprising Adventures of Robinson Crusoe . . . with a Biographical Account of Defoe. New York: Harper & Brothers, 1835. Southern Literary Messenger 2, no. 2 (January):127-28.

In a four-paragraph review focussing upon the anonymous "Biographical Sketch," mixes together well-known information taken from the source (some misstated) with a personal appreciation of Robinson Crusoe and a few original observations on Defoe as a writer. In one special instance, starts with an idea from the "Biographical Sketch," namely, that Robinson Crusoe does not draw attention to its author, and then continues: "All this is effected by the potent magic of verisimilitude. Indeed, the author of Crusoe must have possessed, above all other faculties, what has been termed the faculty of identification--that dominion exercised by volition over imagination which enables the mind to lose its own, in a fictitious individuality. This includes, in a very great degree, the power of abstraction; and with these keys we may partially unlock the mystery of that spell which has so long invested the book before us." For the connection of observations like these with Poe's critical thought generally, see Burton R. Pollin, "Poe and Daniel Defoe: A Significant Relationship," Topic: 30 16 (1976):3-22; and for an effort to link Poe's "faculty of identification" with Coleridge and Hazlitt, see Robert D. Jacobs, Poe: Journalist & Critic (Baton Rouge, La.: Louisiana State University Press, 1969), pp. 120-21. Reprinted: 1902.11.

1837

1   CHAMPAGNAC, JEAN BAPTISTE JOSEPH DE [C.H. dè Mirval]. "Avant-Propos." Le Robinson des sables du désert, voyage d'un jeune naufragé sur les côtes et dans l'intérieur de l'Afrique, offrant le tableau résumé des curiosités naturelles, des moeurs, usages, et coutumes de ces contrées peu connues. Brussells: La Société Nationale, 1:v-ix.

While setting out the objectives of this new Robinson Crusoe imitation, describes also the characteristics of the genre initiated by Foe--"a book of natural education." Presents to young readers "the industrious efforts of a young castaway, but [comments] as much on the shores and interior of Africa as on the manners, usages, and customs of little known countries." Claims a precedent in that Daniel Foe's Robinson is not entirely an imaginary character, his actions having their basis in real-life voyagers. Notes particularly that Selkirk was Foe's model; "some have even asserted that Foe had only to arrange, in his own manner, the adventures of the Scottish mariner." Reprinted: 5th ed., 1853; 1865; 1874.

2   [COLERIDGE, HENRY NELSON.] Review of his Literary Remains of Samuel Taylor Coleridge and Joseph Cottle's Early Recollections; Chiefly Relating to the Late S.T. Coleridge. Quarterly Review 59, no. 117 (July):10-11.
      According to the Wellesley Index, the editor ot The Literary Remains was also the author of this review. Refers to the remarks on Milton and Defoe, "two writers . . . of whom Coleridge was an almost life-long student," Summarizes Coleridge's appreciation of Defoe from the marginalia (1836.4).

3   Female Robinson Crusoe, A Tale of the American Wilderness. New York: Jared W. Bell, 286 pp. passim.
      As the preface makes clear, this first-person narrative—one of many about children lost in the woods, in states beyond the Alleghany mountains—identifies itself as an imitation of Robinson Crusoe. Claims to gain its title through "its analogy to the circumstances attending the long residence of Alexander Selkirk upon an island, of which he was for a considerable period the only inhabitant." Among her adventures, Lucy Ford procures fire from lightning striking a tree, recalling "the incident in the celebrated Robinson Crusoe," read to her "with great delight" by her older brother.

4   [FORSTER, JOHN.] Review of Dickens's The Pickwick Papers, no. 15. Examiner, no. 1535 (2 July):421-22.
      Judges this issue number describing Fleet prison to be Dickens's masterpiece: "Over all there is a dreadful restlessness, a terrible and undefined restlessness, which is pictured throughout with the minute reality of a Defoe."

5   HOGUET, M[ICHAEL FRANÇOIS]. Robinson. Pantomimisches Ballet in 3 Abtheilungen. Berlin: [n.p.], 29 pp.
      While using the characters Robinson and Friday and the settings of the "mainland of South America" and the island itself, takes the story in the direction of Pixerécourt's "melodrama" (1805.5) rather than that of the original. Continues with Pixerécourt's characters—Iglou, Parouba, Don Diego, Emma (Robinson's wife), Isidor (Robinson's son)—and introduces a few new ones. In the preface, calls attention to the difficulty of introducing ballet-dances with women.

6   [LOCKHART, JOHN GIBSON.] Memoirs of the Life of Sir Walter Scott, Bart. 7 vols. Edinburgh: Robert Cadell; London: John Murray & Whitaker & Co., 2:172, 173; 3:58; 6:357.
      Comments on Scott's interest in republishing Capt. George Carleton, and expresses in a note the general belief "that

Carleton's Memoirs were among the numberless fabrications of
Defoe," but he argues that here, as with the <u>Memoirs of a Cava-
lier</u>, "[Defoe] no doubt had before him the rude journal of some
officer who had really served in the campaign described with such
an inimitable air of truth." Describes the work with Murray as
the projector, on "a General Edition of British Novelists, beginning with De Foe and reaching to the end of the last century."
Quotes the entry of 18 October 1826 in Scott's diary on the
compulsion of his contemporaries to steal too openly, as did
Horatio Smith in <u>Brambletye House</u> (1826.6) "from De Foe's 'Fire
and Plague of London.'" Itemizes purchases by Constable on 18
May 1813: "an edition of Defoe's novels, in twelve volumes."

7   [MAIDMENT, JAMES], ed. <u>Analecta Scotica: Collections Illus-
    trative of the Civil, Ecclesiastical, and Literary History of
    Scotland</u>. 2d ser. Edinburgh: Thomas G. Stevenson, pp. 79-
    80.
        Prints for the first time the letter from Joseph Button to
Defoe in Edinburgh, 1710, which was preserved in the Advocates'
Library with no. 65 of the <u>Newcastle Gazette, or the Northern
Courant</u> for the date 23-25 December 1710. Represents Button
[incorrectly assigning the first name William in the signature]
as the publisher of the <u>Newcastle Gazette</u> expressing a number of
publishing and personal concerns, some of which cannot be understood today because of the tears in the letter and inadequate
identification. Throws light on Defoe's activities in the north
of England and Edinburgh. See also Healey, pp. 304-5.

8   TALFOURD, THOMAS NOON. "House of Commons, 18 May 1837." In
    <u>Hansard's Parliamentary Debates</u>. 3d ser. London: Thomas
    Curson Hansard et al., 38:col. 876.
        Pleads eloquently for extending the copyright protection
period; uses the examples of Burns, Scott, and later Wordsworth
to illustrate authors who have been hurt by the old copyright
law. Elaborates on Defoe: "a man of genius and integrity, who
has received all the insult and injury from his contemporaries,
and obtains nothing from posterity but a name. Look at Daniel
De Foe; recollect him pilloried, bankrupt, wearing away his life
to pay his creditors in full, and dying in the struggle!--and his
works live, imitated, corrupted, yet casting off the stains, not
by protection of law, but by their own pure essence." Reprinted:
<u>Critical and Miscellaneous Writings of T. Noon Talfourd</u>, 2d Amer-
ican ed. (Philadelphia: Carey & Hart, 1848), p. 163.

                              1838

1   C[OCHRANE], J[OHN] G[EORGE]. <u>Catalogue of the Library at
    Abbotsford</u>. Edinburgh: Bannatyne Club, 464 pp. passim.
        Lists works attributed to Defoe, in Sir Walter Scott's
library, accessible through the main index entry--64 items having
Defoe's name.

2   CROSSLEY, JAMES. Letter to Mr. Urban, from Manchester,
     14 July. Gentleman's Magazine 10 (November):370-71.
          Makes the first public identification of Defoe as the au-
     thor of Due Preparations for the Plague. Notes the perfect resem-
     blances "in style and manner" of Due Preparations to the earlier
     Journal of the Plague Year. See the reply by John Scott, 1838.6.

3   ELLIS, WILLIAM. History of Madagascar. 2 vols. London:
     Fisher, Son, & Co.; Paris: Quai de l'École, 2:34-44.
          Gives lengthy extracts and comments from Madagascar without
     any reference to Defoe as author or editor.

4   KELLY, T.W. "Sonnet Stanzas: On the Recollection of Reading
     Robinson Crusoe, when Six Years of Age." In The Surprising
     Adventures of Robinson Crusoe. London: Scott, Webster &
     Geary, p. vi.
          Identifies himself as the author of Myrtle Leaves, and
     produces here two matching English sonnets. Reprinted, in part:
     1847.3; 185-.

5   [MALDEN, HENRY.] "Defoe." In Distinguished Men of Modern
     Times. 4 vols. London: C. Knight. Reprint. New York:
     Harper & Brothers, 1842, 2:87-100.
          Aside from placing Defoe in special company, presents the
     well-known biographical facts, guesses, and errors, relying heavi-
     ly on quotations from Chalmers's Life of Daniel De Foe. Empha-
     sizes The Original Power of the Collective Body of the People of
     England, Examined and Asserted; The Freeholder's Plea; "The
     Legion Letter;" and the Shortest-Way with the Dissenters--works
     which show Defoe a champion of liberty and the people's cause.
     Describes him after 1715 "discountenanced and neglected," turning
     away from controversial subjects and toward "works of a more
     popular and lucrative kind." Among the fictions, recognizes that
     certain of Defoe's subjects are vulgar, and the style coarse.
     Names all the well-known novels except Roxana; praises the Jour-
     nal of the Plague Year for "a homely pathos, a minute and scrupu-
     lous adherence to verisimilitude," the "Memoirs of a Cavalier for
     "the same air of truth," and Robinson Crusoe for its "universal
     acceptation." Repeats the accusations against Defoe regarding
     his unfair use of Selkirk's papers, and vigorously rejects them.
     Closes with quotations from Dunlop's History of Fiction on the
     comparison between Defoe and Swift, the moral of Robinson Crusoe,
     the scenes there which "fill us with alarm and terror."

6   SCOTT, JOHN. Letter to Mr. Urban, from Hull, 6 October.
     Gentleman's Magazine, n.s. 10 (November):458.
          Replies to 1838.2, first, by noting that extracts from
     Due Preparations had appeared anonymously in the April and July
     issues, 1825, of the Gentleman's Magazine, and from there in the
     Youth's Magazine. Second, although there was no reference to
     Defoe as the author, the late Reverend John Scott of Hull publish-
     ed "the larger and by far the more interesting portion" of Due

Preparations as Narratives of Two Families Exposed to the Great
Plague of London, A.D. 1665 in two editions (1832).

7   STEBBING, H.   "Memoir."   In The Surprising Adventures of Robinson Crusoe.   London: Scott, Webster & Geary, pp. i-v.
Reprinted: 1860; 1867.

1840

1   "De Foe's Works."   Tait's Edinburgh Magazine 7, no. 74 (February):132.
Announces a cheap edition of "this popular favorite," beginning with Colonel Jack: ". . . the author is well worthy of
entire preservation.   Besides being sound in his opinions, he is
genuinely and racily English."

2   "A Memoir of the Author and an Essay on His Writings."   In
The Life and Adventures of Robinson Crusoe by Daniel De Foe.
London: Robert Tyas, pp. v-xviii.
Presents an account of Defoe which is both accurate and com-
prehensive for its time.   Borrows heavily from Wilson's Memoirs
of Defoe (1830), but diverges occasionally to offer independent
judgments: Defoe's being disguised as a woman to present the
Speaker of the House of Commons with his "Legion Paper"; the admiration for the preface to the 1712 volume of the Review ("the
beauty of its simplicity"); the final eloquent paragraph on
Defoe's writing "in the simplest style," comparing him with
Cobbett.   Reprinted: 1844; 1850; 1852; 1853; 1855; 1858; 1859;
1860; 1861(2); 1864; 1868; 1873; [1875]; [1877]; [188-](3).

3   "Prefatory Notice."   The Life, Adventures, and Pyracies of
the Famous Captain Singleton.   In The Novels and Miscellaneous
Works of Daniel De Foe.   20 vols.   Oxford: Thomas Tegg, 3:ix-
xiv.
Characterizes the work by a long quotation (5 pp.) from
Wilson's Memoirs of Defoe (1830); comments on Singleton's journey
across central Africa, the geographical features of which have
been "wonderfully verified in our days"; and notes evidence of
haste in this publication.

4   "Prefatory Notice."   The Life and Adventures of Robinson Crusoe, vol. 2.   In The Novels and Miscellaneous Works of Daniel
De Foe.   20 vols.   Oxford: Thomas Tegg, 2:[9-14].
Heaps praises on Robinson Crusoe.   Identifies the interest
which Defoe, like Shakespeare and "other followers of nature,"
created in his work, as dependent "not on any age or nation, or
time, or circumstance, but on its general adaptation to the
feelings and passions which belong to the whole family of man."
Finds in Robinson Crusoe both pleasure and profit, both "a spirit
of piety" and a benevolence.   Quotes Beattie on "the importance

of the mechanic arts" (1783.1) and Scott on "the artless and plain language" (1827.2). Stresses Friday as being like a character in modern melodrama.

1840-1841

1   <u>The Novels and Miscellaneous Works of Daniel De Foe. With a Biographical Memoir of the Author, Literary Prefaces to the Various Pieces, Illustrative Notes, etc., Including All Contained in the Edition Attributed to the Late Sir Walter Scott.</u> 20 vols. Oxford and London: Thomas Tegg.

     Competes with Hazlitt's <u>Works of Daniel De Foe</u> (1840-1843) for the honor of being the most complete collected edition produced in the nineteenth century. Reprints Ballantyne's "Biographical Memoir of Daniel De Foe" (1809.1) in vol. 1 and Chalmers's <u>Life of Daniel De Foe</u> (1790.1) in vol. 20, the latter with considerable additions in the notes (1841.2). Published also all the major novels in 1809-1810.1, the edition "attributed to the late Sir Walter Scott," including his notes as in the <u>Memoirs of a Cavalier</u>, here vol. 6. Adds <u>Moll Flanders</u> and <u>Roxana</u>, both silently excluded in 1809-1810.1, now appearing in vols. 4 and 11, respectively, the latter adding the 1745 continuation from the Hazlitt edition (1840). In vol. 5, <u>Mrs. Veal</u> follows <u>Colonel Jack</u>, with an appendix "To the Reader" which reprints Scott's account of the story's origin, 1827.2. Assigns <u>Capt. George Carleton</u> to Defoe as the author, and reprints the work in vol. 8 from Scott's edition published in Edinburgh, 1809, with his preface clearly leaning toward Carleton himself as the author. Also, in vol. 8, includes <u>The Life and Adventures of Mrs. Christian Davies</u>, for which there has never been any substantial evidence to support Defoe's authorship. In vol. 9, quotes under the heading "Advertissement" the important paragraph from 1827.2 on the <u>Journal of the Plague Year</u> as "one of that particular class of compositions which hovers between romance and history." Reprints other works: <u>Consolidator</u> (vol. 9); <u>Political History of the Devil</u> (vol. 10); <u>System of Magick</u> (vol. 12); <u>[An Essay on] The History and Reality of Apparitions</u> (vol. 13); <u>Religious Courtship</u> (vol. 14); <u>Family Instructor</u> (vols. 15 and 16); <u>Complete English Tradesman</u> (1745 ed.), <u>An Humble Proposal to the People of England</u>, <u>Augusta Triumphans</u>, and <u>Second Thoughts Are Best</u> (vols. 17 and 18); <u>Duncan Campbell</u>, including in the appendix <u>A Remarkable Passage of an Apparition, 1665</u>, <u>The Dumb Philosopher</u>, and <u>Everybody's Business Is Nobody's Business</u> (vol. 19); and "A List of De Foe's Works" (174 numbered items, plus the manuscript owned by Dawson Turner on the "Conduct of a Gentleman"), <u>An Appeal to Honour and Justice</u>, and six more reprinted pieces (vol. 20). See also the reviews, 1854.12; 1861.2; 1882.7. Reprinted: AMS Press, Inc., 1973.

1840-1843

1   HAZLITT, WILLIAM [the younger], ed. The Works of Daniel
    De Foe, with a Memoir of His Life and Writings. 3 vols. Lon-
    don: John Clements, 759, 659, 568 pp.
        More functional, but less elegant, than the Works (1840-
    1841) was the rival three-volume edition published by the younger
    Hazlitt, crammed with reprints of the rarest pamphlets and tracts
    and all the major novels. Suddenly, through these two editions,
    both reliable enough to be still in active use, were fresh new
    resources to undergird interpretations of the life, career, and
    art of Defoe. Impressive as a cohesive biographical unit was the
    first part of vol. 1, separately printed in 1840, made up of a
    frontispiece portrait engraved by H. Barnett; dedication to Wal-
    ter Wilson (who made his library available, including "the first
    and only complete collection of the writings of Daniel De Foe");
    preface (expressing the aim of furnishing the world with "an
    entire collection of these works"); "Life of Daniel De Foe" (158
    pp.), which borrows heavily from Wilson's Memoirs, and quotes,
    generously, Chalmers, Hazlitt (senior), the Retrospective Review
    (1821.1) on Memoirs of a Cavalier, the "Biographical Preface" to
    Cadell's edition of Robinson Crusoe (1820.4), and Scott's criti-
    cism; Appeal to Honour and Justice; and the chronological lists
    of works assigned to Defoe (183 items) and "attributed" (52
    items), which served as the basis for the single list in Works
    (1840-1841). Reprinted in the rest of vol. 1: Colonel Jack,
    Moll Flanders (with one page of critical appendix), Memoirs of a
    Cavalier (with the "Advertisement," 1809-1810.1, and prefaces to
    the first and second editions), Roxana (with a preface [4 pp.]
    strongly defending Defoe's fidelity to human nature, and the
    presumably apocryphal "continuation of Roxana's life . . . first
    printed in 1745"), and New Voyage Round the World. Reprinted in
    vol. 2: Duncan Campbell (2d ed., corr., including "A Remarkable
    Passage of an Apparition . . . 1665"), The Dumb Philosopher
    (1719), Journal of the Plague Year (with "Notes," 2 pp.), Capt.
    George Carleton, three parts of Robinson Crusoe (with a compre-
    hensive introduction, 12 pp., on publishing history, survey of
    critical comments, the Selkirk problem, imitations), and Captain
    Singleton. Reprinted in vol. 3 (dedicated to James Crossley):
    twenty-three pamphlets and tracts, ranging from those readily
    available, like the True-Born Englishman or the Shortest-Way with
    the Dissenters, to others extremely rare, like the Original Power
    of the Collective Body of the People of England (1702) or Jure
    Divino. A Satyr (1706)--altogether, a windfall of powerful non-
    fictional writing by Defoe. See also the review, with Works
    (1840-1841), by Forster, 1845.4.

[1840-1857]

1   [DUGDALE, WILLIAM (Henry Smith).] Peeping Tom, Wit, Fun and
    Facetia. London: H[enry] Smith, nos. 1-8, 11-51.

For the general dating of this item and the identification
of the publisher Henry Smith with the pornographer William Dug-
dale, I am indebted to Mr. David Warrington, The Lilly Library,
Indiana University. See also Henry Spencer Ashbee [Pisanus
Praxi], Index Librorum Prohibitorum (London: Privately Printed,
1877), pp. 127, 135, 192; and William B. Todd, A Directory of
Printers . . . London and Vicinity, 1800-1840 (London: Printing
Historical Society, 1972), p. 178. In an extremely rare serial
at the Lilly Library, Peeping Tom introduces "The History of Moll
Flanders," without referring to Defoe as the author, and continues the installments, off and on, through no. 51. A "notice"
appears in no. 52: "The next number of this publication will
appear in a quarto shape, under the title of Peeping Tom: or,
the Mirror of the age." Earlier, in "Peeping Tom to His Readers"
(no. 1), he claimed to be "the original Peeping Tom of Coventry"
and to peep for the benefit of society.

1841

1   AINSWORTH, WILLIAM HARRISON. Old Saint Paul's: A Tale of the
    Plague and the Fire. 3 vols. London: Hugh Cunningham. Re-
    print. London: George Routledge & Sons, [1897?], 426 pp.
       In the "Advertisement" (1 p.) of this historical romance,
    claims that he drew the part of his story relating to the grocer
    Stephen Bloundel and his family from Due Preparations, at the
    suggestion of James Crossley. Asserts that the author was Defoe
    (see 1838.2): "I venture to pronounce it his masterpiece."
    Combines respectable middle-class characters such as the grocer,
    his daughter Amabel, and his apprentice Leonard Holt, with lurid-
    ly licentious court villains such as the Earl of Rochester, Sir
    George Etherege, and even Charles II. Creates strong quasi-his-
    torical settings (1665-1666) of the Plague (books 1-5) and the
    Great Fire (book 6). Takes from Due Preparations the details of
    how the grocer closed up his house during the Plague; and from
    the Journal of the Plague Year (among other things) the masterful
    character of the half-crazed Solomon Eagle. Reprinted: 1841;
    1846; 1847; 1855.

2   CHALMERS, GEORGE. The Life of Daniel De Foe and "A List of
    De Foe's Works, Arranged Chronologically." In The Novels and
    Miscellaneous Works of Daniel De Foe. 20 vols. Oxford:
    Thomas Tegg, 20:1-118, 119-57.
       Reprints the text of the Life of Daniel De Foe, 1790.1,
    without change, but adds considerable new information through the
    many notes which summarize the contents of works previously men-
    tioned only by title, or introduce new works assigned to Defoe,
    or correct information given inaccurately before. Frequently
    quoted in the notes is a new source of information, Wilson's Mem-
    oirs of Defoe (1830). Compared with Chalmers's Life of Daniel De
    Foe, 1786.1 or 1790.1, the revised Life has the effect almost of
    a new biography inasmuch as it is based on a thoroughly revised

listing of Defoe's works. The advances made in comprehending the problems in the Defoe canon may be judged by comparing the 174 separate items listed here with the 81 items described as "undoubtedly" Defoe's and the 20 described as "supposed" to be his, in 1790.1.

3   DE QUINCEY, THOMAS. "Homer and the Homeridae. Part III. Verdict on the Homeric Questions." Blackwood's Edinburgh Magazine 50, no. 314 (December):754-55.
     Explains the "circumstantiality" of the Iliad as "now a well known artifice of novelists," but only once has it been "successfully applied to regular history." Defoe alone has "so plausibly circumstantiated his false historical records, as to make them pass for genuine, even with literary men and critics." Cites Memoirs of a Cavalier, and refers to (but does not name), Memoirs of an English Officer as illustrations. Reprinted, with slight revision: 1890.8; Critical Heritage.

4   FREELING, ARTHUR. "The Life of De Foe." In The Plague: A Fiction Founded upon Fact. London: George Routledge, pp. iii-xxxii.
     Depends heavily upon Hazlitt's Life of Daniel De Foe (1840-1843) from which both epigraphs (admiring the Journal of the Plague Year) are taken as well as the biographical facts and judgments. Pushes the thesis that Defoe always collected "nutriment even from the most poisonous ingredients," such as adversities, criminal environs, low fortunes; predicts the maturing of his fame as "one of the greatest political and ethical writers of his age." Hardly more than a few lines are given to quick mentions of Robinson Crusoe and "other" fictional works written after his retirement from politics in 1715--but with the omission of Roxana. No date appears anywhere on the title page of Freeling's publication, but it was probably published in 1841 since it refers to the Hazlitt edition of Defoe's works which is "now publishing."

5   [GOODRICH, SAMUEL G.] The Story of Alexander Selkirk. With Engravings. Peter Parley's Little Library. Philadelphia: Henry F. Anners, 200 pp.
     Starts with the premise that Robinson Crusoe is not a true story, but one made up by the famous Defoe from the adventures of Selkirk. Appropriately brings together eight chapters on Selkirk, reaching a climax with the well-known rescue of the castaway from Juan Fernandez; and the "Life of De Foe" (60 pp.). In the latter, traces "the painful history" of Defoe's imprisonments, persecution by enemies, and illness, as recorded in his Appeal to Honour and Justice; and describes Defoe, by chance, reading "the history of Selkirk" and finding there "the idea of writing Robinson Crusoe." Summarizes "the romantic part of our story" [Part One]. Mentions generally works that show Defoe to be "a man of genius and imagination," but refers only to Captain Singleton.

6   KÄSTNER, ABRAHAM GOTTHELF. "Ob Robinson Crusoe auch Robinson
     I. ist?" In <u>Gesammelte poetische und prosaische schönwissen-
     schaftliche Werke</u>, vol. 1, pt. 2. Berlin. Reprint. Frank-
     furt: Athenäum, 1971, pp. 135-38.
         Pointing to a few curious similarities, Kästner bemusedly
     suggests that Grimmelshausen's <u>Simplicissimus</u> (1669) should be
     considered an earlier forerunner of <u>Robinson Crusoe</u> than was the
     Selkirk narrative. Or rather, one might call Defoe's novel a
     latter-day English <u>Simplicissimus</u>.   (P.E.C.)

7   MARRYAT, FREDERICK. Preface to <u>Masterman Ready; or, the Wreck
     of the Pacific. Written for Young People</u>. 3 vols. London:
     Longman, Orme, Brown, Green, & Longmans, 1:v-viii.
         Tells the story of a family stranded on an island more in
     reaction to <u>Swiss Family Robinson</u> than to <u>Robinson Crusoe</u>. Ex-
     presses his reasons for turning against <u>Swiss Family Robinson</u> as
     a model (e.g., lack of adherence to probability or possibility).
     Critics, such as R. Brimley Johnson, <u>The Novels of Captain Marry-
     at</u> (London: Phoenix Book Co., 1929), 17:xxxiv, find in Marryat
     "the lying precision of detail with which Defoe achieved realism
     by deception."

8   NODIER, CHARLES. Introduction to <u>Le Robinson suisse. Traduit
     de l'Allemand de Wyss par Mme. Élise Voiart</u>. Paris: Lavigne,
     pp. i-vi.
         Isolating the central philosophical differences between
     <u>Robinson suisse</u> [1812-1813.1] and the English <u>Robinson</u>, sets up a
     broad interpretation in which Defoe is seen as failing to depict
     the third of the duties man owes as an intelligent creature, name-
     ly, his obligations to others. Builds up to an eloquent analysis
     of Robinson as lacking humanity, the reader as having a very
     limited sympathy, and the novel impressing one as a masterpiece--
     but "a cold masterpiece." Asks if, in the final analysis, Robin-
     son is not "just a singular and striking individuality, separated
     from all connections, all obligations, all affections of ordinary
     life." Judges that <u>Robinson Crusoe</u> (aside from the episodic role
     of Friday) completely misses the cry of Terence's old man, "I
     am human; I think nothing human alien to me." Wyss's <u>Robinson
     suisse</u>, in contrast, embodies all the human needs and concerns
     that are absent in its model; merits "perhaps the first place
     among all works of imagination intended for the education of chil-
     dren and men."

9   PICCINI, ALEXANDER. "Lettre . . . à M. de Pixerécourt";
     GEOFFROY, [JULIEN LOUIS]. "Notice sur Robinson Crusoé";
     LEPEN; BABIÉ; DUSAULCHOY; COLNET; and BEAUMONT. "Judgements
     des journaux." In <u>Théatre choisi de G. de Pixerécourt</u>.
     Edited by Charles Nodier. 2 vols. Paris: Tresse; Nancy:
     l'Auteur, 2:169-73, 174-78, 179-87.
         In addition to reprinting Pixerécourt's melodrama (1805.5),
     the principals involved in the production and its reception recap-
     ture full details about the motives for selecting Defoe's novel

as the base, the nature of "melodrama" as interpreted in Parisian theater around 1805, the controversy over whether or not any drama were possible in the dramatization of man alone on a desert island. The critic Geoffroy refers to such sceptics as "dawdlers," and ridicules the notion that this melodrama was "a new kind of spectacle," called "monodrama," which the journals boasted as having been created. Geoffroy stresses the importance of surprises and comments further that the objective of the novel was to make the necessity felt for society and its advantages; his interpretation of both the novel and the melodrama opposes not only Rousseau but apparently the French Revolution. The journals reviewing the early performances are Courrier des spectacles, Journal d'indications, Journal de Paris, Gazette de France, and Journal du soir. Lengthy quotations suggest what aspects of Defoe's Robinson Crusoe continued to have appeal to large popular audiences.

10   POE, EDGAR ALLAN. Review of Edward Lytton Bulwer's Night and Morning: A Novel. Graham's Magazine (April). Reprint. The Complete Works of Edgar Allan Poe. Edited by James A. Harrison. Croxley Edition. New York: Society of French and English Literature, 1902, 10:120-21.
     "Interest of plot" in a novel has been neglected in "some of the finest fictions in the world," including Gil Blas, Pilgrim's Progress, and Robinson Crusoe. Since it is not essential, "no merit of a higher class"--such as one "founded in nature"-- should be sacrificed to it.

11   _____. Review of William Harrison Ainsworth, Guy Fawkes; or the Gunpowder Treason. An Historical Romance. Graham's Magazine (November). Reprint. The Complete Works of Edgar Allan Poe. Edited by James A. Harrison. Croxley Edition. New York: Society of French and English Literature, 1902, 10:218.
     Severely criticizes books like Guy Fawkes which are totally lacking in autorial comment, and cites Robinson Crusoe and Godwin's Caleb Williams as having the "juste milieu," the right balance.

                                    1842

1   BARBIERI, GAETANO. "Il Tradutore" [The translator]. In Avventure di Robinson Crusoe di Daniele De Foe. Naples: Gaetano Nobile, pp. v-vii.
     In Italian. The translator praises "the naturalness of the images" and "the inventiveness of the descriptions" in Robinson Crusoe. Asserts that in this novel we feel it is Robinson whom we come to know rather than Defoe himself, as a personality with historical reality. Warns of the excesses and inconsistencies that result from a too-literal translation from English into Italian. Attributes these defects in craftsmanship to the cul-

tural limitations and education of Defoe. Claims to have preserved both "the clarity of the text and possibly the force of
the ideas."   (R.F.)

2   ELLMS, CHARLES. Robinson Crusoe's Own Book; or, The Voice of
     Adventure, from the Civilized Man Cut Off from His Fellows, by
     Force, Accident, or Inclination, and from the Wanderer in
     Strange Seas and Lands. Boston: William C. Perry, 431 pp.
         The preface (4 pp.) states the purpose of the book as the
     celebration of encountering danger and wandering. "Mankind are
     all more or less imbued with the spirit of Robinson Crusoe; and
     we daily see those whose incurable restlessness strikingly assim-
     ilates their real characters to the ideal one, of that universal
     favorite, in his goat-skin breeches, with his man Friday, dancing
     cats, and parrot." The Crusoe-like narratives are true ones,
     "simple, unpretending, and artless," ranging from "A Memoir of
     Jean Bart, the daring Frenchman" (1697) to "Incidents of Adven-
     ture during a Ramble from the Pacific to the Atlantic Ocean"
     (1834). The introduction (4 pp.) waxes mystically on the praises
     of mountain, desert, forest, and prairie.

                                  1843

1   DICKENS, CHARLES. A Christmas Carol in Prose Being a Ghost
     Story of Christmas. Reprint. Christmas Books. Oxford
     Illustrated Dickens. London: Oxford University Press, 1954,
     pp. 27-28.
         As Scrooge watches his younger self reading "near a feeble
     fire" in the "melancholy" schoolroom, the Ghost of Christmas Past
     brings before him Ali Baba, then Crusoe's Parrot, Crusoe himself,
     and Friday. Scrooge's change begins at that point.

2   ELLIS, SIR HENRY. Original Letters of Eminent Literary Men of
     the Sixteenth, Seventeenth, and Eighteenth Centuries. London:
     Camden Society, pp. 320-24.
         Reprints from British Museum manuscripts two letters by De-
     foe to Charles Montagu, first Earl of Halifax, dated 5 April 1705
     and [early summer, 1705?]; and Thomas Warton's anecdote concern-
     ing Robert Harley's authorship of the first volume of Robinson
     Crusoe. In this memorandum, dated 10 July 1774, Warton records
     that the Rev. Mr. Benjamin Holloway, as chaplain to Lord Sunder-
     land, had often heard Sunderland say Lord Oxford wrote "the first
     volume of the History of Robinson Crusoe, merely as an amusement
     under confinement; and gave it to Daniel De Foe, who frequently
     visited Lord Oxford in the Tower, and was one of his Pamphlet
     writers. That De Foe, by Lord Oxford's permission, printed it as
     his own. . . ." See also 1788.3; 1805.2; 1814.1; 1826.4; 1843.7;
     1903.12-13; James Means, "Lord Oxford and the Authorship of Rob-
     inson Crusoe," Scriblerian 9, no. 2 (Spring 1977):139-40; J.A.
     Downie, "Letter to the Editor," Scriblerian 10, no. 1 (Autumn
     1977):62.

                                  112

*3   KORSAKOV, P.A., trans. Robinson Crusoe.
        In Russian. See the brief reference to Korsakov's commen-
tary to his translation of Robinson Crusoe, in A.G. Cross, "Don't
Shoot Your Russianists; or, Defoe and Adam Brand," British Journal for Eighteenth-Century Studies 3 (1980):230-33. A copy of
Korsakov's translation has not been located.

4   [LAURENT, JEAN.] Preface to Le Robinson industrieux, his-
        toire semée de details sur la botanique; sur la physique, la
        géographie, les arts industriels, l'histoire naturelle, etc.
        Reprint. Paris, Limoges: Martial Ardant Frères, 1846,
        pp. v-xiv.
        Adapts Robinson Crusoe (Part One) to a school text which
shows the strong influence of Campe, but avoids the objectionable
features of "the old Robinson." Turns especially critical, without mentioning Defoe, of the original Crusoe's gaining the benefits of civilization, and of his constant complaining and revealing weaknesses. Believing that children's books should also
instruct, introduces accurate information on plants and animals
appropriate to the region. Reprinted: 1859; 1861; 1862.

5   POE, EDGAR ALLAN. Review of James Fenimore Cooper's Wyan-
        dotté, or the Hutted Knoll. Graham's Magazine (November).
        Reprint. The Complete Works of Edgar Allan Poe. Edited by
        James A. Harrison. Croxley Edition. New York: Society of
        French and English Literature, 1902, 11:205.
        Finds Cooper to be "regardless, or incapable" of plot, but
dependent upon theme, "a Robinson-Crusoe-like detail in its management," and the depiction of "the half-civilized Indian."

6   SAINT-MARC GIRARDIN, FRANÇOIS AUGUSTE. "Comment les Anciens
        et les modernes ont peint la lutte de l'homme contre le dan-
        ger.--Le Naufrage d'Ulysse dans Homère, et de Robinson dans le
        roman de ce nom." In Cours de littérature dramatique, ou de
        l'usage des passions dans le drame. Reprint. 2d ed. Paris:
        Charpentier, 1845, 1:50-74.
        To illustrate the theme of man's struggle against dangers,
makes grand poetic comparisons, including the major one of
Homer's shipwrecked Ulysses and Defoe's Robinson. Starts the comparison noting that "the famous English novelist" was "inspired
by Homer," the traits of resemblance going beyond anything ex-
plainable by chance. Observes a significant difference, namely,
that "the ancients try especially to depict; the moderns, to
explain. The ancients address the imagination; the moderns, the
reason." Continues the comparison of Ulysses and Robinson
through parallel incidents and passages. Culminates the lofty
rhetoric in a "mythic" view of Robinson Crusoe, without using
that term: "each of [Robinson's] efforts represents . . . one of
the phases of human society, which has suffered also and travail-
ed to invent the arts." Extends the mythic reading into specific
interpretations of the Bible/Friday sequences, summing up the
reason for the book's immortality, namely, the character of Robinson. Reprinted: New ed., 1868; see also National Union Catalog.

7   [SUTCLIFFE, THOMAS.] <u>Crusoniana; or, Truth versus Fiction,</u>
      <u>Elucidated in a History of the Islands of Juan Fernandez.</u> By
      <u>the Retired Governor of that Colony.</u> Manchester: [Author],
      pp. i, vi, 12, 50-52.
         Describes the fascination for many visitors of Juan Fernan-
dez, long associated with Alexander Selkirk and <u>Robinson Crusoe.</u>
States in chap. 1, more accurately, that Selkirk's adventures,
"ascribed to the fictitious character Robinson Crusoe, and painted by the masterly hand of a man of genius," were "the groundwork" of Defoe's fiction. In chap. 2, relying almost exclusively
upon Isaac James's <u>Providence Displayed</u> (1800), faces the two
apparently unrelated charges levelled against Defoe: first, that
he used Selkirk's narrative, "mingling the products of his own
lively fancy with the real adventures of Selkirk," and returned
the papers to Selkirk, "telling him his history would not sell";
and second, that the Earl of Oxford was the real author of Part
One of <u>Robinson Crusoe.</u> Presents or cites the secondary evidence, but offers no new information, and emphatically agrees
with the complete rejection of both charges.

1844

1   [BAYLEY, FREDERICK WILLIAM NAYLOR.] <u>Robinson Crusoe: with</u>
      <u>Thirty Illustrations.</u> London: Wm. S. Orr & Co., 39 pp.
         Author given in John Mackay Shaw, <u>Childhood in Poetry</u>
(Detroit, Mich.: Gale Research Co., 1967), 1:153. Transforms
Crusoe's adventures into humorous verses and illustrations. Not
infrequently, strains at a contemporary reference. Example: on
Crusoe's inability to populate the island, "Which he sure would
have thought the most pleasing of facts, / Had he only read
Malthus' and Martineau's tracts."

2   CHASLES, PHILARÉTE. "Les pseudonymes anglais au dix-huitième
      siècle." <u>Revue de deux mondes</u>, 5th ser. 6, pt. 2 (June):453-
      59.
         Interprets the novels as pseudonymous and anonymous writ-
ings with considerable originality. Asks why there should be,
exclusively in England, between 1688 and 1800, a "bizarre group"
of "English pseudonyms" which included Defoe, Psalmanazar,
Lauder, Macpherson, Chatterton, Ireland. Specifically recognizes
Defoe as appearing here "under a new face"; appraises his motives
as "honorable and innocent"--the pseudonyms necessary for revealing "the truth to which he was devoted." Makes the important distinction that in works like <u>Memoirs of a Cavalier</u> or <u>Mrs. Veal,</u>
the question becomes, not what are the merits of the narrative,
but what do the significant details attest to its truth. Ranges
widely in illustrating the point: <u>Mesnager</u>, <u>Dickory Cronke</u>, <u>Dun-</u>
<u>can Campbell</u>, <u>Captain Singleton</u> [wrongly dated, 1717], <u>Molly Flan-</u>
<u>ders</u> [wrongly dated, 1729], <u>Colonel Jack</u>, <u>Journal of the Plague</u>
<u>Year</u>, <u>Roxana</u>, and <u>Capt. George Carleton</u>. Reiterates a concept
which became familiar later in the century: "Defoe lied in the

name of the truth; he lied resolutely and heroically." Persists
in the conclusion to regard Defoe as "the Don Quijote of morality," writing his Robinson Crusoe as "the memoirs of a man facing
his God, returned to the primitive life and discovering God in
the desert." See also 1833.2. Reprinted: 1845.6; 1846.2.

3   [EASTLAKE, ELIZABETH.] "Children's Books." Quarterly Review
    74, no. 147 (June):16-17, 21.
        Authorship identified in Wellesley Index. Finds that the
    true secret of a child's book lies not "in its being less dry and
    less difficult, but more rich in interest--more true to nature--
    more exquisite in art--more abundant in every quality that re-
    plies to childhood's keener and fresher perceptions"; and that
    such books are more apt to be in the libraries of adults than of
    juveniles and more apt to please both sets of readers. Offers
    different examples: Robinson Crusoe, "the standing favorite of
    above a century," was not intended for children, and yet the
    taste for it continues into "Columbus's discoveries, Anson's
    voyages, and Belzoni's travels."

4   [POE, EDGAR ALLAN.] Review of Ned Myers; or, A Life Before
    the Mast, 1843. Graham's Magazine 24 (January):46. Reprint.
    Burton R. Pollin. Discoveries in Poe. Notre Dame, Ind., and
    London: University of Notre Dame Press, 1970, pp. 136-37.
        Notes that J. Fenimore Cooper, said to be the "editor" of
    the book, can be suspected of being the author. Cites similar
    cases, such as "the Narrative of Sir Edward Seaward, edited by
    Miss Porter--a work of deeper interest, and of a far more vrai-
    semblant character than even Robinson Crusoe, upon which it is
    modeled." Points to his own Arthur Gordon Pym as "purporting to
    be edited only by Mr. Poe, was in reality his own composition."

5   VINET, A[LEXANDRE]. "Robinson." Revue suisse 7 (January):
    10-29.
        Prefers unequivocally "the old Robinson"--the one known by
    children and adults, and the one envisioned by Defoe--to earlier
    and later variations. In a highly impressionistic reading, clar-
    ifies the central idea as being the diminishing or restriction of
    man's power when he is "uprooted" from society, and carefully dis-
    criminates this "Robinson" from the potentially dull Robinson fac-
    ed with complete solitude (Sophocles's Philoctetes), or the less
    philosophical or human Robinson stripped entirely of any benefits
    of civilization (Campe), or the Robinson invented by "our genera-
    tion" faced with "involuntary solitude." To Vinet the old Robin-
    son could have emerged only at the time it did. Describes the
    old Robinson's appeal to all people and all countries as "any man
    whatsoever"--not "a man but man"--and having only average traits,
    participating in "a bourgeois epic," more "a vagabond" than an
    adventurer. Comments on "what makes Robinson what it is" in its
    use of details, the narrator's naiveté, the author's objectivity
    "felt on every page"--on the book as a "conversion" story much
    like Don Quijote.

6   WILSON, WILLIAM. "Editor's Preface" and "Notes by the Editor." In <u>Memoirs of the Church of Scotland, in Four Periods</u>. Perth: James Dewar; Glasgow: W. Whyte & Co. et al.; Dundee: William Middletown, pp. iii-viii, 365-72.

Sums up the evidence for the authorship of the <u>Memoirs</u> as by Defoe, including the traits of style which it shares with <u>Robinson Crusoe</u>: "the same lively and vigorous style, the same captivating interest, the same inimitable art of simplicity, which has made <u>Robinson Crusoe</u> one of the most fascinating and popular books of any age or country." Argues that the strongest evidence is Defoe's interest in his theme, "his passionate admiration of the Church of Scotland," which gives shape and meaning to such biographical events as the pillory and the ruinous fines and to his lifelong hatred of the Stuarts. Explains also why the <u>Memoirs</u> have been left in "comparative oblivion." In the "Notes," annotates little-known events and persons mentioned in the text, with now and then a comparison of Defoe's account with one from another source (e.g., Wodrow's).

1844-1845

1   CRAIK, GEORGE LILLIE. <u>Sketches of the History of Literature and Learning in England</u>. 6 vols. in 3. London: Charles Knight & Co., 5:123-27.

With his fictions Defoe began "a new life of authorship"; reached "the highest rank" with certain popular books flowing readily from his fertile imagination. He excelled in "the air of reality which he throws over the creations of his fancy" and the "illusion" by which his fiction appears "like a matter of fact." The style of his fictions, as distinct from that of his tracts, had "a simplicity and plainness . . . a homeliness approaching to rusticity." With respect to "the truthful air" of these fictions, the <u>Memoirs of a Cavalier</u>, <u>Journal of the Plague Year</u>, and <u>Capt. George Carleton</u> were received to a degree, like Swift's <u>Gulliver's Travels</u> as authentic narratives. Reprinted: <u>Compendious History of English Literature, and of the English Language</u>, 2 vols. (New York: Charles Scribner, 1863 and 1869).

1845

1   BARTON, BERNARD. "A Poet's Memorial of Robinson Crusoe." In <u>Household Verses</u>. London: George Virtue. Reprint. Philadelphia: J.W. Moore, 1849, pp. 170-82.

In this reprint of 1836, omits stanzas 3, 4, 5, and 23. See also 1831.1.

2   "De Foe (Daniel)." In <u>The London Encyclopaedia, or Universal Dictionary of Science, Art, Literature, and Practical Mechanics, Comprising a Popular View of the Present State of Knowledge</u>. 22 vols. London: Thomas Tegg; Boston: Charles C.

Little & James Brown; Philadelphia: Thomas Cowperthwaite &
Co., 2:114.
   Introduces a rare anecdote about Selkirk's telling his
adventures in a London coffee-house, "where money was frequently
given him by the company, and where De Foe so often heard them,
that out of them he formed the above mentioned history. De Foe's
malignant enemies have misrepresented this to his disadvantage."

3   [FORSTER, JOHN.] Review of <u>Works</u> (1840-1841), and Hazlitt's
    <u>Works of Daniel De Foe</u> (1840-1843). <u>Eclectic Magazine</u> 6,
    no. 4 (December):465-94.
       Reprint of 1845.4.

4   _____. Review of <u>Works</u> (1840-1841), and Hazlitt's <u>Works of</u>
    <u>Daniel De Foe</u> (1840-1843). <u>Edinburgh Review</u> 82, no. 166
    (October):480-532.
       Reviews the two most comprehensive editions of Defoe's
    works prepared to date, each containing also an expanded "life"
    and a chronological listing of the writings; and, on this basis,
    provides a considerably advanced assessment, biographical and
    critical. The review was substantively revised and expanded,
    particularly in the footnotes, as a book, 1855.3, which in turn
    was much less extensively increased in 1858.6 and still less in
    1860.5. Forster's additions from 1845 to 1860 do not represent
    any essential change in view; they simply add information which
    new discoveries provided. As James A. Davies points out ("Striv-
    ing for Honesty: An Approach to Forster's Life," <u>Dickens Studies</u>
    <u>Annual</u> 7, 1978:34), in Dryden, Churchill, Foote, Steele, and
    Swift--as well as Defoe and Dickens--Forster selects subjects
    which permit "the idealization of writers and a concern for the
    dignity of literature." His biographical facts come from George
    Chalmers, William Hazlitt the younger, and especially Walter Wil-
    son, as he generously acknowledges. Certain emphases, which had
    not been encountered before, are emerging here that do not yet
    have the solidity of themes: for example, the relative isolation
    of Defoe from "the reigning wits of his time." Forster sounds
    this note in the opening sentence, and repeats it later in such
    variations as the reasons for Pope's or Swift's hostility toward
    Defoe. He plods through the chronology of complicated events or
    through complex political controversy, always exercising his
    individual judgment. Now and then, he allows for humor and wit,
    for example, on Defoe's aloofness from his contemporaries: "His
    life, to be fairly written, should be written as the 'Life and
    Strange Surprising Adventures of Daniel De Foe, who lived above
    Seventy Years all alone, in the Island of Great Britain.'" Into
    the historical panorama, he introduces contemporary historical
    personages as part of the background; weaves in such anecdotes as
    the one [from the <u>Review</u>, 4:531] about six Frenchmen having stol-
    en the Monument during the Popish Plot, and about some "unbeliev-
    ers" who, in a Public House, are told by Defoe "to satisfy their
    doubts by going to the spot, 'where they'd see the workmen em-
    ployed in making all fast again,'" and who "'swallowed the joke,

and departed quite satisfied.'" Forster has taken certain liberties with the text; specifically, it was not Defoe but "another
Person" who makes the proposal, and it was not "unbelievers," but
only one "unbeliever." But the biographer bows to the critic
here, and has reasons for making these unwarranted changes;
closes the anecdote by adding whimsically: "The touch of reality
sent it down. A genius for homely fiction had strolled into the
tavern, and found its first victims. They deserved a ripe old
age, and the reading of Robinson Crusoe." Errors of previous
biographers are transmitted: for instance, Defoe as the author
of Speculum Crape-Gownorum (1682) as in Hazlitt's "Chronological
Catalogue"; but in 1855.3 Forster has begun to doubt Defoe's
authorship. On the young Defoe's participation in the Monmouth
Rebellion, repeats the familiar account, and states definitely
that Foe escaped abroad, and returned--something new--with the
name "De Foe." Forster never corrected the common mistake of
giving Defoe two wives, Mary and Susannah. Also perpetuates the
legend of Defoe, the "Sunday Gentleman," living in Bristol in the
1690's to escape his creditors; in 1855.3, adds information from
Walter Wilson on Mark Watkins's observing Selkirk and Defoe in
Bristol. As in other biographies before 1864, moves to an expected sharp transition, around 1715, from politics to a "new life"--
"the life by which he became immortal." Forster rises to a
degree of eloquence, as he emphasizes his special view of Defoe:

> De Foe is our only famous politician and man of letters,
> who represented, in its inflexible constancy, sturdy resolu-
> tion, unwearied perseverance, and obstinate contempt of danger
> and of tyranny, the great Middle-class English Character . . .
> And when he now retreated from the world Without to the world
> Within, in the solitariness of his unrewarded service and in-
> tegrity, he had assuredly earned the right to challenge the
> higher recognition of posterity. He was walking toward His-
> tory with steady feet; and might look up into her awful face
> with a brow unabashed and undismayed.

These words remained in all the subsequent reprintings suggesting
that Forster held a single, unswerving view of Defoe which provided the structure for the developing biography from the outset.
In the years of retirement, Defoe produced the popular Family
Instructor, Religious Courtship, Political History of the Devil,
his "most remarkable" Complete English Tradesman, and other
works. Altogether, no more than two pages are given to the fictions. For the "Masterpieces," Robinson Crusoe and the History
of the Plague, Forster finds "the secret" of the fascination in
each to be its "reality." He also praises the latter "for the
grandeur of the theme, and the profoundly affecting familiarity
of its treatment," as "one of the noblest prose epics of the language." Moll Flanders, Colonel Jack, and Roxana, while objectionable "on another score," are judged "not less decisive examples
of a wonderful genius." In their day they were not harmful, but
reviving them today might be questionable wisdom. "As models of
fictitious narrative, in common with all the writings of De Foe,

they are supreme; the art of natural story-telling has had no
such astonishing illustrations." Authorities are cited who accepted Defoe's fictions as real or historical narratives. Unsurpassed by "the highest masters of prose fiction" are the "particular scenes": "those of the Prison in Moll Flanders, of Susannah
in Roxana, and of the Boyhood in Colonel Jack." For Forster, "it
will remain the chief distinction of De Foe, in these minor tales
of English life, to have been the father of the illustrious family of the English Novel." The succession to Defoe is then named:
Swift, Richardson, Fielding, Smollett, Goldsmith, Godwin, Scott,
and Dickens. While "unapproached in his two great masterpieces,"
Defoe has been surpassed "in his minor works by these his successors." The critical assessment closes with Forster at his best:

> His language is as easy and copious, but less elegant and har-
> monious; his insight into character is as penetrating, but not
> so penetrating into the heart; his wit and irony are as play-
> ful, but his humour is less genial and expansive; and he wants
> the delicate fancy, the richness of imagery, the sympathy, the
> pathos, which will keep the later Masters of our English Novel
> the delightful companions, the gentle monitors, the welcome
> instructors, of future generations. So true it is, that every
> great writer promotes the next great writer one step; and in
> some cases gets himself superseded by him.

Reprinted: 1845.3, 5.

5   _____. Review of Works (1840-1841), and Hazlitt's Works of
       Daniel De Foe (1840-1843). Littell's Living Age 7, no. 79
       (15 November):299-319.
          Reprint of 1845.4.

6   TASTU, [SABINE CASIMIRE] AMABLE, Transl. Aventures de Robin-
     son Crusoé par Daniel De Foë . . . précedées d'une notice sur
     De Foe, par M. Philarète Chasles et suiviés d'une notice sur
     le matelot Selkirk et sur les Caraibes par F. Denis et d'une
     dissertation religeuse par l'abbé Labouderie. New ed. 2
     vols. Paris: Didier, 1:299 pp.; 2:343 pp.
          Madame Tastu's rival translation replaced Pétrus Borel's
     with a different publisher, 1836.3. While the biography of Defoe
     by Philarète Chasles had been advertised on Borel's title page,
     it was not included in the text; it does appear here, taken from
     1833.2 and 1844.2. The "Notice" by Ferdinand Denis and the "Dis-
     sertation religeuse" by Jean Labouderie are reprints of 1836.3;
     the "Notice" is also reprinted, 1861.4.

7   The Travels of Daniel De Foe in the Counties of Northumberland
     and Durham. In Reprints of Rare Tracts & Imprints of Antient
     Manuscripts. Miscellaneous. Newcastle: M.A. Richardson,
     1849, 30 pp.
          In the "Advertisement," states that Tour is attributed to
     Defoe "on sufficient grounds," and reprints extracts on these two
     counties.

1846

1   BASTIAT, [CLAUDE] FREDERIC. "Something Else." In Sophismes
économiques. Translated by Patrick James Stirling. New York:
G.P. Putnam's Sons, 1922, pp. 198-208 passim.
       Exposes the sophism of a protectionist economic policy by
using the simplest illustration of Robinson Crusoe alone (having
to make a plank without a saw) and then more complicated illustrations of "division of labor," when Crusoe is joined by Friday
and the foreigner who offers to exchange four baskets of game for
two of vegetables. Reprinted: (French) 1846; 1847; 1848; 1851;
1863. (English) 1848; 1854; 1869; 1870; 1871; 1873; 1874; 1877;
1878; 1882; 1886; 1888; 1893.

2   CHASLES, PHILARÊTE. "Daniel De Foe et ses contemporains." In
Le dix-huitième siècle en Angleterre. 2 vols. Paris: Libraire D'Amyot, 2:139-211, 213-25.
       Reprints of 1833.2 and 1844.2 combined. Makes primarily
stylistic changes. Among the few substantive changes: reduces
the references to Don Quijote and Socrates.

3   "The Life and Adventures of Miss Robinson Crusoe." Littell's
Living Age 10, no. 117 (8 August):294-95; no. 119 (22 August):
383-85; no. 121 (5 September):468-70; no. 124 (26 September):
601-4; 11, no. 125 (3 October):55-56; no. 130 (7 November):
285-87; no. 132 (21 November):367.
       Reprint of 1846.4.

4   "The Life and Adventures of Miss Robinson Crusoe." Punch 11
(July-December):9-10, 13, 29, 33, 49-50, 53, 66, 75-76, 85,
101, 121, 128, 135, 153.
       Parodies, without mention of Defoe, the characters and
actions of Robinson Crusoe; directs the heavy-handed humour and
satire mainly against the foibles of women. Transforms Robinson
himself into Miss Robinson Crusoe, who starts out on her travels
to India in the search for a husband, and in the passage suffers
shipwreck and is cast on a desert island. Presents the young
lady as fashionably educated, having a passion for elegant
clothes and a deep fear of celibacy, to which she is now doomed
on the island. Throughout the adaptation occur ingenious trans-
formations: the "shot-silk parasol," her dress of rabbit skins,
her illness and dream of endless marriages, her rescue of the
negress (subsequently named Friday) from the Amazons. Novel, and
appropriate to the theme, are the repeated references to celibacy. Revealing about the times, Miss Crusoe's exclamation: "I
always had a horror of a black skin, whereas there is something
romantic in the true olive." Reprinted: 1846.3.

5   Review of Melville's Typee, 1846. John Bull 26, no. 1317
(7 March):156.
       Starts the review enthusiastically by comparing the reading
of Melville's "bewitching" Typee with a first reading of Robinson

Crusoe. Suspects that if Melville were a real person, he employed "a Daniel Defoe to describe his adventures, or is himself both a Defoe and an Alexander Selkirk." Reprinted: <u>Melville: The Critical Heritage</u>, ed. Watson G. Branch (London and Boston: Routledge & Kegan Paul, 1974), pp. 64-65.

1847

1 [COOPER, JAMES FENIMORE.] <u>The Crater; or, Vulcan's Peak. A Tale of the Pacific</u>. 2 vols. New York: Burgess, Stringer & Co., vol. 1, chaps. 5, 6, 8.
    Through specific references to <u>Robinson Crusoe</u>, raises comparisons of Mark Woolston's and Bob Betts's adventures on their reef in the Pacific with Crusoe's experiences on his island. Creates for Bob who was "a good deal of a philosopher by nature" a fondness for locutions such as "'to Robinson Crusoe it'"; and for Mark, a habit like Crusoe's of balancing his advantages and disadvantages. Gove (p. 124n) points out that in Cooper's <u>Oeuvres complètes</u> (Paris, 1851-54) the title of <u>The Crater</u> was given as <u>Le Robinson américain</u>. See also W.B. Gates, "A Note on Cooper and <u>Robinson Crusoe</u>," <u>Modern Language Notes</u> 67, no. 6 (June, 1952):421-22; Thomas Philbrick's Introduction to Cooper's <u>The Crater or Vulcan's Peak</u>, John Harvard Library (Cambridge, Mass: Belknap Press of Harvard University Press, 1962), pp. vii-xxix.

2 JONES, W. ALFRED. "<u>The Life and Adventures of Philip Quarll</u>." In <u>Literary Studies: A Collection of Miscellaneous Essays</u>. 2 vols. New York: Edward Walker, 1:91-104.
    Strongly admires the <u>Life and Adventures of Philip Quarll</u>, which has only recently been republished. On the basis of close similarities between <u>Philip Quarll</u> and <u>Robinson Crusoe</u>, argues the highly probable supposition that Defoe was the author of the former. Reprinted: <u>Characters and Criticisms</u>, 2 vols. (New York: I.Y. Westervelt, 1857), 1:82-95.

3 R[USSELL], J.F. Preface to <u>The Life and Surprising Adventures of Robinson Crusoe</u>. Select Library Edition. London: James Burns, pp. v-x.
    Authorship given in Kelly, 1862.8. Concerns itself exclusively with Alexander Selkirk to show that <u>Robinson Crusoe</u> was "not altogether fictitious." Quotes lengthy extracts from the unpublished manuscript diary (1825- 1829) of William Harris, "a very intelligent seaman," as provided by T.W. Kelly, author of the sonnet "To Robinson Crusoe" on the very last page. Comments on the differences in style between Parts One and Two of <u>Robinson Crusoe</u> and on the editorial revisions which were necessary; shows awareness of "glaring instances of tautology" and prolixity; makes use of chapter divisions. Reprinted: 185-.

1848

1   COOKE, P[HILIP] PENDLETON. "Edgar A. Poe." Southern Literary
    Messenger 14, no. 1 (January):36-37. Reprint. The Complete
    Works of Edgar Allan Poe. Edited by James A. Harrison. Crox-
    ley Edition. New York: Society of English and French Litera-
    ture, 1902, 1:383-92.
        In this sequel to James Russell Lowell's "Memoir" of Poe,
    offers "a few hurried observations upon [Poe's] writings and
    genius." On the story, "The Facts in the Case of M. Valdemar,"
    identifies Poe's "most distinguishing power" in making fiction
    "sound like truth." Observes that Poe has "De Foe's peculiar tal-
    ent for filling up his pictures with minute life-like touches--
    for giving an air of remarkable naturalness and truth to whatever
    he paints." The same talent gave us Robinson Crusoe, but with
    Poe, it adds "the presence of a singularly adventurous, very
    wild, and thoroughly poetic imagination." Defoe stayed with "the
    homely" and the real. The "cheerful and delightful story of his
    colonist of the desert isle" does not have "strangeness enough in
    its proportions for Mr. Poe's imagination."

2   DUGUÉ, FERDINAND. L'Ile déserte ou le meilleur des mondes
    comedie en trois actes, en vers.
        See 1891.6.

3   FELLER, FRANÇOIS XAVIER DE. "Foé (Daniel)." In Biographie
    universelle: ou, Dictionnaire historique des hommes qui se
    sont fait un nom par leur génie, leurs talents, leurs vertus,
    leurs erreurs ou leurs crimes. Paris: J. Leroux, Jouby,
    3:564.
        Shows that certain misconceptions about "Foe" are still
    strong enough to require attention: for instance, the attribu-
    tion of Robinson Crusoe to Richard Steele; Feutry's efforts, in
    the 1783 abridgement, to reduce the anti-Catholic sentiments.

4   LAMB, CHARLES. Letter to Walter Wilson, 24 February 1823.
    In Thomas Noon Talfourd. Final Memorials of Charles Lamb;
    Consisting Chiefly of His Letters Not Before Published, with
    Sketches of Some of His Companions. 2 vols. London: Edward
    Moxon, 2:38-40.
        In reply to Lamb's letter of 16 December 1822, Walter Wil-
    son must have requested some clarifications; and Lamb responded
    on 24 February 1823. His comments are based not on any Defoe
    edition, but (unknown to him) on Francis Noble's preface to the
    drastically altered version of Roxana (1775.1). Other clarifi-
    cations include observations on the similar actions of Roxana's
    daughter and Richard Savage, and Godwin's possible borrowing from
    Dr. Johnson's Life of Savage for his play Faulkner (1807.1);
    Lamb's prologue (1807.2) to the play Faulkner; his correct rank-
    ing of the novels (Robinson Crusoe and Roxana over Colonel Jack);
    the difficulty in finding "any good character of DeFoe"; the
    authorship of the Robinsonade, The Hermit; Steele's fine account

of Selkirk in the <u>Englishman</u>; Captain Carleton's authorship of
his <u>Memoirs</u>. Reprinted: 1886.12; <u>The Letters of Charles Lamb</u>,
ed. E.V. Lucas (London: J.M. Dent & Sons; Methuen & Co., 1935),
2:371-72.

1849

1 [DUYCKINCK, EVERT.] "Passages from New Books." <u>Literary
World</u>, no. 145 (10 November):395.
Anticipates the publication of Melville's <u>Redburn</u> by
Harpers through offering passages in advance, calling the work
"a piece of fresh natural composition of the ocean life. . . ."
Closes: "Mr. Melville proves himself in this work the De Foe of
the Ocean." See also 1849.2.

2 _____. Review of Melville's <u>Redburn</u>, 1849. <u>Literary World</u>,
no. 146 (17 November):418-20.
Praises Melville as "the De Foe of the Ocean" for "the
life-like portraiture of his characters at sea, the strong rel-
ishing style in which his observations are conveyed, the fidelity
to nature, and, in the combination of all these, the thorough
impression and conviction of reality. The book belongs to the
great school of nature." Thinks occasionally of Defoe when he
encounters "one of those touches of nature" in <u>Redburn</u>. See also
1849.1. Reprinted: Watson G. Branch, <u>Melville: The Critical
Heritage</u> (London and Boston: Routledge & Kegan Paul, 1974),
pp. 201-2.

3 FRANCIS, JOHN. <u>Chronicles and Characters of the Stock Ex-
change</u>. London: Willoughby & Co., pp. 359-83.
Reprints Defoe's <u>The Anatomy of Exchange Alley; or, A System of Stock Jobbing</u> (1719), but makes no mention of the author.

4 [GREENE, CHARLES GORDON.] Review of Melville's <u>Redburn</u>, 1849.
Boston <u>Post</u> (20 November).
Follows up on his earlier praise of <u>Typee</u> (1846) and <u>Omoo</u>
(1847) for "their Crusoe-like naturalness" by offering now "the
highest praising." In "character-painting" <u>Robinson Crusoe</u> has
nothing comparable to that in Melville's novels; and "in truthfulness and vividness of detail" is just slightly superior. Then
comes the statement: "<u>Redburn</u> is a Robinson Crusoe <u>modernised</u>--
it has a breadth, purpose, elevation, of which Defoe, by the
nature of things, could never have dreamed . . ."; and continues
with an important recognition of Melville's continuity in the
representation of human nature. Reprinted: Watson G. Branch,
<u>Melville: The Critical Heritage</u> (London and Boston: Routledge &
Kegan Paul, 1974), pp. 203-4.

5 HUNT, LEIGH. <u>A Book for a Corner; or Selections in Prose and
Verse</u>. 2 vols. London: Chapman & Hall, 1:14, 46-67, 68-92.

Lists the five points of Crusoe's history, and illustrates
by selections: loneliness, means of living, footprint, first
sight of savages, Friday. Suggests that the "Selkirk adventure"
was an injury as well as a benefit to Defoe since "the world
would probably have had the fiction, whether the fact had existed
or not." Makes the observation that Defoe succeeded in creating
one person (himself), and not a multitude, "in the same intense
spirit of self-reference." Of his other invented characters none
was "greater than himself." In addition, whether in "the Ghost
of Mrs. Veal" or "the History of the Plague," he elaborated upon
a lie. Limits Defoe's love of truth to something like "a work-
man's love for his tools"--to "a masterly use of it, and a con-
sciousness of the mastery." Refuses to draw any connection
between this kind of lie and "his veracity between man and man,"
but hints at "the singularly material and mechanical nature" of
his genius, at "something vulgar" adhering to our idea of the
author of Moll Flanders, the Complete English Tradesman, and even
of Robinson Crusoe. He has no music, no thorough style, no accom-
plishments, no love; but he can make wonderful shift without them
all. . . ." The introduction makes reference to Robinson Crusoes
in the moral world which parallel those in the physical world;
one other selection briefly describes The Life and Adventures of
Peter Wilkins and Philip Quarll as imitations of Robinson Crusoe.
Reprinted: 1852; 1858.

6   "Iron Manufactures of Sussex." Notes and Queries, 1st ser. 1,
     no. 6 (8 December):87-88.
     Makes two extracts from "a once popular, but now forgotten
work," the Tour (1724), but does not mention the author by name,
to illustrate Sussex as the "main seat" for iron manufacture
within the last hundred years.

7   "Notes on Books--Catalogues, Sales, Etc." Notes and Queries,
     1st ser. 1, no. 5 (1 December):78.
     Sale by Puttick and Simpson of 154 volumes of Defoe's works
collected by the late Walter Wilson. Forty additional pieces
were added to the sale. See also Notes and Queries, 1st ser. 1,
no. 7 (15 December 1849):110.

8   [SOUTHERN, HENRY.] Review of The History of the Great Plague
     in London in the Year 1665, 1769. Littell's Living Age 22,
     no. 272 (4 August): 224-32.
     Reprint of 1822.2.

1849-1850

1   DICKENS, CHARLES. The Personal History of David Copperfield.
     Reprint. Oxford Illustrated Dickens. London: Oxford Univer-
     sity Press, 1948, p. 72.
     In this situation, David sees himself "more solitary than
Robinson Crusoe, who had nobody to look at him and see that he

was solitary." Mr. Peggotty, as observed by G.W. Kennedy in "The Uses of Solitude: Dickens and Robinson Crusoe," Victorian Newsletter, no. 52 (Fall, 1977):26, is one of a number of other Dickens characters who participate in the motif of "the stranded sailor, figuratively shipwrecked on the land," and thus brings into the novel a larger significance to solitude. See also Stanley Friedman, "Dickens' Mid-Victorian Theodicy: David Copperfield," Dickens Studies Annual 7 (1978):142-43.

1850

1   "Alexander Selkirk, the Original Robinson Crusoe." Eclectic Magazine 19, no. 2 (February):164-70.
        Reprint of 1850.2.

2   "Alexander Selkirk, the Original Robinson Crusoe." Hogg's Instructor, n.s. 4:131-34.
        Summarizes Selkirk's story mainly from Howell, 1829.3; accepts Selkirk without question as "the real prototype of that most interesting of all imaginary personages"--Robinson Crusoe. Reprinted: 1850.1.

3   ALPHA [pseud.]. "Gravesend Boats." Notes and Queries, 1st ser. 2, no. 44 (31 August):209-10.
        To illustrate the chances taken by watermen on the Thames, quotes from Defoe's Great Law of Subordination Consider'd (1724) a graphic description of an incident in which the steersman of a passage-boat between London and Gravesend caused the drowning of fifty-three people; and of still another incident in which Defoe was the only passenger in a boat from London to Gravesend. See reply, 1850.7.

4   B., L. "Duncan Campbell." Notes and Queries, 1st ser. 1, no. 12 (19 January):186.
        Queries whether Duncan Campbell was a real or imaginary person. See 1851.10.

5   B., N. "Couplet in De Foe." Notes and Queries, 1st ser. 2, no. 50 (12 October):310.
        Queries the source of the couplet at the end of the second letter in Defoe's Great Law of Subordination Consider'd (1724): "Restraint from ill. . . ." See 1851.8.

6   BASTIAT, [CLAUDE] FREDERIC. Harmonies économiques. Translated by Patrick James Stirling. 2 vols. London: John Murray, 1860, 1:74-75, 167-68, 205, 209.
        In the chapter "Exchange," distinguishes Crusoe deprived of all aids to survival and Crusoe benefited by such "social treasure" as "his ideas, his recollections, his experience, above all, his language." Later, in the chapter on "Capital," takes Crusoe as a paradigm of the man living in a state of isolation

who measures his labor and capital (tools, materials, provisions) in terms of the "satisfactions" desired or achieved, as contrasted with the man living in a social state who can also render services, and thus draw upon "the mechanism of exchange, for equivalent services." Reprinted: (French) 1851; 1855; 1860; 1864; 1870; 1879; 1893. (English) 1880; 1944-1945.

7   CRAFTER, W. "Daniel De Foe." Notes and Queries, 1st ser. 2, no. 54 (9 November):395.
        Replies to 1850.3. Notes that the incidents about the Gravesend passage-boats could have been "'a plain relation of matter of fact,'" and stresses Defoe's connection with the pantile works at Tilbury.

8   S., D. "Defoe's Tour through Great Britain." Notes and Queries, 1st ser. 1, no. 13 (26 January):205.
        Replies to 1850.13 for the identification of the Tour. Praises as worthy of Mr. Macaulay's attention the account in volume one of "Irish night," the skirmish at Reading between forces of the Prince of Orange and those of James II. "The whole work will well repay a perusal, and what is there of Defoe's writing which will not?"

9   Southey's Common-Place Book. Third Series. Edited by John Wood Warter. London: Longman, Brown, Green, & Longmans, pp. 160, 642.
        Notes from his reading that the name "Foe" was his father's and that the syllable was prefixed "to give it greater dignity"; at the time Defoe wrote Robinson Crusoe, he lived in Gateshead, Halifax.

10   Stories About Poor Old Robinson Crusoe. Portland, Me: S.H. Colesworthy, 9 pp.
        Reprint of 1820?.1. The ten stanzas of doggerel verses in the 1820? text are increased to fifteen.

11   WALKER, PETER. "Memoir of the Author." In The Life and Adventures of Robinson Crusoe. By Daniel De Foe with an Autobiographical Memoir of the Author, and a Life of Alexander Selkirk, by Whose Residence on the Island of Juan Fernandez the Work Was Suggested. Philadelphia: Journeymen Printers' Union, pp. ix-xxx.
        Claims to be a new biography "from original sources," although he also admits to have selected materials for his memoir "chiefly" from Walter Wilson; reprints Howell's "Life and Adventures of Alexander Selkirk" (1829.3) as an appendix. Repeats certain familiar statements now known to be errors, such as Defoe's authorship of Speculum Crape-Gownorum (1682), his concealment in Bristol after bankruptcy in 1692, his Mrs. Veal story as a publisher's hoax to sell Drelincourt "on Death." At the same time, has the merit of being at least partially interpretative. Devotes no more than half a page to the fictions other than Rob-

inson Crusoe. Reprinted: Philadelphia: Willis P. Hazard, [1850] and 1858; Philadelphia: W.G. Perry & Erety, 1853.

12   Y., D.S. "Daniel De Foe and His Ghost Stories." Notes and Queries, 1st ser. 1, no. 16 (16 February):241-42.
       Notes with surprise that the ghost story taken by Mrs. [Anna Eliza] Bray from [Charles Sandoe] Gilbert's History of Cornwall and adapted to her novel Trelawny of Trelawne was substantially identical with "A Remarkable Passage of an Apparition, 1665," published as an appendix in Defoe's Works (1840-1841), vol. 19. While ready to accept the "Remarkable Passage" as fiction much like Mrs. Veal, Mrs. Bray was informed by F.V.T. Arundell that he had lent the manuscript to Gilbert, which contained the story and which was in the "hand" of [Reverend John] Ruddell of Launceston. Insists the "doubt remains" that Defoe may be the author of the ghost story. See 1866.5 and 1895.32.

13   _____. "Defoe's Tour through Great Britain." Notes and Queries, 1st ser. 1, no. 10 (5 January):158.
       Quotes an earlier reference to the Tour (1724) as a "once popular, but now forgotten work." Asks also if the 1753 edition can be attributed to Defoe.

1851

1   ANATOL [pseud.]. "Defoe's Anticipations." Notes and Queries, 1st ser. 3, no. 78 (26 April):338.
       Adds information to 1851.20, about the great inland lake in Africa and some hints about the lake in Captain Singleton, which Defoe may have gotten from Father Dos Santos's Ethiopia Oriental in Purchas's Pilgrimes (1544 ed.).

2   BLANCHARD, SIDNEY LAMAN. "A Visit to Robinson Crusoe." Household Words 3, no. 69 (19 July):397-400.
       Two miles beyond the park at Sceaux, outside of Paris may be found "Robinson Crusoe": ". . . the spot is the most romantic--the most picturesque--and was the most desolate within so short a distance of Paris; and it has been called 'Robinson' as a tribute at once to these united charms, and to the merits of a work which is as popular in France as in its native country." As the English visitors soon discover, "Robinson Crusoe" is a restaurant with many lavish reminders of the Crusoe story everywhere. In the writer's mind, Robinson Crusoe's Island can only be Juan Fernandez.

3   BORROW, GEORGE. Lavengro; The Scholar--the Gypsy--the Priest. New York: G.P. Putnam, pp. 19-20, 185, 221-25, 236, 241-49.
       Early in this blend of autobiography and fiction Lavengro tells of a family friend's presenting him at the age of six with an illustrated Robinson Crusoe and of its awesome effects upon his mind. Now looking back, he gauges the influence of Robinson

Crusoe on "the minds of Englishmen . . . certainly greater than
any other of modern times"; on himself: "in this manner . . . I
first took to the paths of knowledge." Just as influential was
Moll Flanders, as Lavengro recalls in chaps. 31, 40, 44, 46, and
77: his readings of the "greasy black leather" volume at the
stall of the old appleseller on London Bridge; his dialogues with
the old woman who defends stealing on the authority of the "blessed Mary Flanders"; her change of heart as she becomes troubled by
the voices saying, "Thou shalt not steal"; his adventures in trying to replace Moll Flanders with the Bible; and (much later) the
spiritual transformation he works upon the sin-conscious Peter
Williams by recalling a passage in the appleseller's book, The
Blessed Mary Flanders. See also 1857.2; Michael Collie, George
Borrow Eccentric (Cambridge University Press, 1982), pp. 16-18,
21, 33, 42, 61, 76, 186, 191, 194, 205. Reprinted: Everyman's
Library (London and Toronto: J.M. Dent & Sons; New York: E.P.
Dutton & Co., 1906 [to 1925]; The Works of George Borrow, ed.
Clement Shorter, Norwich ed. (London: Constable & Co.; New York:
Gabriel Wells, 1923), 3:26-33, 324-26, 401-5, 423-44; in part,
Critical Heritage.

4   BRAY, MRS. [ANNA ELIZA]. Life of Thomas Stothard, R.A. with
     Personal Reminiscences. London: John Murray, pp. 19, 50,
     121, 229, 240.
        Comments briefly on Thomas Stothard, painter, exhibiting
"his exquisite design of Robinson Crusoe making his Long Boat,"
in 1808; and on his illustrations of Robinson Crusoe for the
Novelist's Magazine.

5   [BUTLER, WILLIAM A.] Review of Herman Melville's Moby-Dick,
     1851. Daily National Intelligencer 34 (16 December).
        Questions the authenticity of Typee (1846) and Omoo (1847),
and makes the comparison with Robinson Crusoe. Finds the resemblances to Defoe's "inimitable" novel to be "neither few nor
difficult to be traced." Compares the greater "naturalness and
vraisemblance" of Robinson Crusoe with the greater "fancy or invention" of Typee; a Friday who is more a favorite to youthful
readers with a Kory-Kory more appreciated by mature readers. But
Melville is not necessarily the greater artist. For in using
language so as "to make us forget the narrator in the interests
of his subject"--there lies "the charm of Robinson Crusoe--a book
which every boy reads and no man forgets; the perfect naturalness
of the narrative, and the transparent diction in which it is
told, have never been equalled by an subsequent writer, nor is it
likely that they will be in an age fond of point and pungency."
Reprinted: Watson G. Branch, Melville: The Critical Heritage
(London and Boston: Routledge & Kegan Paul, 1974), pp. 282-83.

6   CAMPKIN, HENRY. "Engraved Portrait." Notes and Queries,
     1st ser. 4, no. 110 (6 December):443-44.
        Asks for the identification of an engraved head in a
copper-plate print owned by him and for the conclusion of some
verses beneath the head. See 1851.15.

7   CROSSLEY, JAMES. "Anticipations of Modern Ideas by Defoe."
     Notes and Queries, 1st ser. 3, no. 71 (8 March):195.
          In reply to 1851.16, points out that Augusta Triumphans
     (1728) and Second Thoughts are Best (1729) are to be found in
     Works (1840-1841). Also on street-robberies, by Defoe, and never
     assigned to him: An Effectual Scheme for the Immediate Prevent-
     ing of Street Robberies (1731) and Street-Robberies, Consider'd
     (1726; corrected to 1728).

8   _____. "Couplet in De Foe." Notes and Queries, 1st ser. 3,
     no. 64 (18 January):45.
          Replies to 1850.5. Traces the couplet in the second letter
     of Defoe's Great Law of Subordination Consider'd (1724) to his
     True-Born Englishman, with important variants.

9   _____. "Daniel Defoe and the Mercator." Notes and Queries,
     1st ser. 4, no. 105 (1 November):338.
          Sums up the inaccurate information about the rare Mercator
     from Chalmers and Wilson, and explains Defoe's connection with
     this government paper, conceived by Harley, to support the
     proposed Treaty of Commerce with France. Maintains that while
     Defoe was not in control of the paper, he nevertheless did most
     of the writing. Compared with its opposite number, the British
     Merchant, the Mercator had too few copies to make a powerful
     impression on readers favoring free trade.

10   _____. "Duncan Campbell." Notes and Queries, 1st ser. 3,
     no. 74 (29 March):248-49.
          Replies to 1850.4 that Duncan Campbell was, without any
     doubt, a real person; lists the different accounts given of him
     and the evidence of his being authentic.

11   _____. "The Right divine of Kings to govern wrong." Notes
     and Queries, 1st ser. 4, no. 94 (16 August):125-26.
          Responding to a general query (S. Wmson, Notes and Queries
     3 [21 June 1851]:494), argues that Pope used this line reflecting
     the idea in, but not quoting from, Defoe's poem, Jure Divino
     (1706).

12   "Daniel De Foe." Chambers's Papers for the People 7,
     no. 56:1-32.
          Serves as a model for representing mid-nineteenth century
     attitudes toward Defoe. Works with some 200 items in the canon,
     but shows a close knowledge of certain non-fictional tracts, es-
     pecially those connected with dramatic events such as the trial
     and pillorying following upon the publication of the Shortest-Way
     with the Dissenters. Introduces harsh judgments of contempora-
     ries like Oldmixon and Leslie, and the balanced assessments of
     Chalmers and Wilson. Builds up a consistent image of Defoe as a
     person of absolute integrity and concern for the public welfare--
     a greater man than Cobbett. Moves abruptly from Defoe's public
     events of 1713 to his entertainments "as a popular author for all
     time," beginning with Robinson Crusoe, in 1719. Offers the

common praise of Robinson Crusoe: matter-of-factness, "air of
plausibility," diversity, pathos; then singles out as its "grand
peculiarity" the rare quality of being "imbued with a philosophy
of experience." In the other so-called minor fictions, finds
"the same significant sign of genius--the power of imagining a
character within a certain natural range of action and existence,
and of investing the conception with that breath of life and
individuality which it is the privilege of genius alone to give."
Commends Mrs. Veal for its "air of credibility," although he mistakenly believes in Scott's account of the bookseller's hoax, and
especially the Journal of the Plague Year as "the most beautiful
and interesting of these popular compositions." Reprinted:
1851.13.

13   "Daniel De Foe." Littell's Living Age 29, no. 360 (12 April):
      49-64.
          Reprint of 1851.12.

14   DICKENS, CHARLES (with W.H. Wills). "Plate Glass." Household
      Words 2, no. 45 (1 February): 433-37.
          During a visit to the Thames Plate Glass Company on 16 De-
      cember 1850, a certain Mr. Bossle describes the process of making
      plate glass to visitors W.H. Wills, Augustus Egg, and Dickens.
      The account concludes with a reference to "the narrow passages or
      caves underneath the furnaces." That was where "the boys employ-
      ed in the works love to hide and sleep, on cold nights." Then
      follows the non-sequitur, Dickens's recollection of his reading:
      "So slept De Foe's hero, Colonel Jack, among the ashes of the
      glass-house where he worked. And that, and the river together,
      made us think of Robinson Crusoe the whole way home, and wonder
      what all the English boys who have been since his time, and who
      are yet to be, would have done without him and his desert Is-
      land." Reprinted: Charles Dickens' Uncollected Writings from
      Household Words 1850-59, ed. Harry Stone (Bloomington and London:
      Indiana University Press, 1968), 1:205-15.

15   DREDGE, JOHN I. "Engraved Portrait." Notes and Queries, 1st
      ser. 4, no. 112 (20 December):491.
          In reply to 1851.6, identifies the portrait as Defoe's,
      engraved by W. Sherwin; completes the fourth line of verse, as
      in Joseph Ames's The Catalogue of English Heads.

16   H., R.D. "Anticipations of Modern Ideas or Inventions."
      Notes and Queries, 1st ser. 3, no. 69 (22 February):137.
          Cites two works by Defoe from Wilson's Memoirs of Defoe
      (1830) as "anticipations of modern ideas": Augusta Triumphans
      and Second Thoughts are Best. See reply, 1851.7.

17   M. "Defoe's House at Stoke Newington." Notes and Queries,
      1st ser. 4, no. 103 (18 October):299-300.
          Replies to 1851.22 by identifying the house as the one on
      the south side of Church Street occupied by the late William
      Frend, and giving additional details.

18   RUSKIN, JOHN. Notes on the Construction of Sheepfolds. Lon-
     don: Smith, Elder & Co. Reprint. The Works of John Ruskin.
     Edited by E.T. Cook and Alexander Wedderburn. London: George
     Allen; New York: Longmans, Green, & Co., 1904, 12:536.
         Asks what should be the offices of the clergy, and replies
     that they should be as various as necessities require: "Robinson
     Crusoe, in his island, wants no Bishop, and makes a thunderstorm
     do for an Evangelist."

19   SAINTINE, JOSEPH XAVIER BONIFACE. The Solitary of Juan Fernan-
     dez; or, the Real Robinson Crusoe. By the Author of Picciola.
     Translated by Anne T. Wilbur. Boston: Ticknor, Reed, &
     Fields, 141 pp. passim.
         Romanticizes the narrative of Selkirk's adventures leading
     to his being abandoned on the island of Juan Fernandez. Almost
     at the conclusion, relates that Selkirk returned to England in
     1712, and that among the accounts of his captivity appearing in
     the papers, Defoe published Robinson Crusoe in 1717 [i.e., 1719].
     Observes that while Robinson Crusoe is the "same personage" as
     Selkirk, the island is "peopled with savage Caribs; Marimonda
     is transformed into the simple Friday; history is turned into
     romance, but this romance is elevated to all the dignity of a
     philosophical treatise." Recognizes and credits Defoe with the
     complete change he has wrought upon his model--not isolated man,
     but "the European developing the resources of his industry, to
     contend at once with an unproductive land and the dangers created
     by his enemies." Continues the comparison of Selkirk and Robin-
     son Crusoe with respect to solitude and society.

20   SMITH, T.C. "Anticipations of Modern Ideas by Defoe." Notes
     and Queries, 1st ser. 3, no. 76 (12 April):287.
         Replies to 1851.7, 16, noting the recent discovery by
     Murray and Oswell of "a great inland lake in the South of
     Africa," located not very far from the "great lake of water" in
     Captain Singleton.

21   Southey's Common-Place Book. Fourth Series. Edited by John
     Wood Warter. London: Longman, Brown, Green, & Longmans,
     p. 688.
         Quotes four memorable extracts from unidentified works by
     Defoe.

22   SPERIEND [pseud.]. "De Foe's House at Stoke Newington."
     Notes and Queries, 1st ser. 4, no. 101 (4 October):256.
         Asks about the "large and handsome house" Defoe built for
     his own residence around 1722. See reply, 1851.17.

23   STEVENS, DAVID. "Defoe's Project for Purifying the English
     Language." Notes and Queries, 1st ser. 3, no. 79 (3 May):350.
         Editorializes that Defoe's scheme, in Essay upon Projects,
     for starting an academy or society for "correcting, purifying,
     and establishing the English language" is still most urgently
     needed.

24   Ts [pseud.]. "Coleridge's Opinion of Defoe." <u>Notes and</u>
     <u>Queries</u>, 1st ser. 3, no. 69 (22 February):136.
          Quotes Wilson's <u>Memoirs</u> of Defoe (1830), 2:205, to the
     effect that Coleridge wrote in the margin of a copy of Cadell's
     edition of <u>Robinson Crusoe</u> a sharp disagreement with the editor
     that there can be no doubt that Defoe lacked "many of those qual-
     ities, both of mind and manner, which fitted Steele and Addison
     to be the inimitable <u>arbitri elegantiarum</u> of English society."
     Coleridge: "I doubt this, particularly in respect to Addison,
     and think I could select from Defoe's writings a volume equal in
     size to Addison's collected papers, little inferior in wit and
     humour, and greatly superior in vigor of style and thought."

                                   1852

1   CROSSLEY, JAMES. "Daniel De Foe." <u>Notes and Queries</u>, 1st
     ser. 5, no. 133 (15 May):476-77.
          Replies to 1852.7, by citing Wilson's <u>Memoirs</u> of Defoe
     (1830) on the descendants John Joseph Defoe and the other who
     lived in or near Hungerford Market. Makes the correction that
     Defoe could not have used <u>Madagascar</u> to write <u>Robinson Crusoe</u>.

2   ____. "Defoe's Pamphlet on the Septennial Bill." <u>Notes and</u>
     <u>Queries</u>, 1st ser. 5, no. 138 (19 June):577-79.
          Criticizes Chalmers and Wilson most damagingly for lack of
     research. Illustrates his point by the solid case for the rejec-
     tion of Abel Boyer's claim of <u>The Triennial Bill Impartially</u>
     <u>Stated</u> (1716) as Defoe's work. Quotes a letter by Defoe in the
     public prints, 1717, where Defoe gives the mistaken impression
     that the pamphlet which Boyer praised, and the one Defoe says
     that he wrote, was <u>Arguments about the Alteration of Triennial</u>
     <u>Elections of Parliament</u>. Hypothesizes that Defoe confused this
     pamphlet with another which had never before been attributed to
     Defoe and does fit the description given by Boyer, with the title
     <u>Some Considerations on a Law for Triennial Parliaments</u> (1716).

3   HAWTHORNE, NATHANIEL. <u>The Blithedale Romance and Fanshawe</u>.
     Reprint. Columbus, Ohio: Ohio State University Press, 1964,
     p. 98.
          In chap.12, "Coverdale's Hermitage," a description of
     narrator's "little hermitage": "Far aloft, around the stem of
     the central pine, behold a perfect nest for Robinson Crusoe or
     King Charles!"

4   O., J. "Robert Drury." <u>Notes and Queries</u>, 1st ser. 5,
     no. 136 (5 June):533-34.
          Was <u>Robert Drury's Journal</u> [i.e., <u>Madagascar</u>] "what it
     pretends to be, or the speculation of some clever writer, envious
     of the fame and profit derived by Defoe from the publication of
     a similar work"? Cites from the <u>Journal</u> the assertion that Drury
     was "every day to be spoken with at Old Tom's Coffee House in

Birchin Lane" as evidence that he was the author. See also
1853.16-17.

5   Review of Jeanne-Marie Le Prince de Beaumont [Madame Le
     Prince], Le Robinson Chrétien. Paris, 1851. Eclectic Review,
     n.s. 4 (September):279-93.
         Lengthily summarizes and analyzes Le Robinson Chrétien, a
     French work intentionally taking the form of a Robinsonade [which
     may have been written much earlier than 1780, if it is indeed the
     work of Jeanne-Marie Le Prince de Beaumont since she died in that
     year]. Notes that Robinson's early scepticism and lack of belief
     were accompanied by a love of solitude and independence acquired
     from a reading of Robinson Crusoe: "Hence the popularity which
     has ever attended works of this description; and numerous are
     those which have appeared in emulation of the great original."
     Shows Robinson as a castaway on an island in the Arctic Sea under-
     going experiences similar to Crusoe's, yet strikingly different
     in religious and even mystical terms.

6   "Robinson-Crusoeism of Common Life." Chambers' Edinburgh Jour-
     nal, n.s. 18, no. 457 (2 October):209-11.
         Finds a special meaning in Robinson Crusoe through seeking
     there "the mystical sympathy" with struggle that makes the book
     "the most universally popular of all works of fiction." Identi-
     fies Crusoe experiences in common life, such as emigration or any
     rejection of conventionalism as when certain industries decay.
     Argues for reading Robinson Crusoe, but not as a romance: "Look
     upon it as a mirror of human life, in which the fortunes of men--
     in which your own possible fortunes are figured with photographic
     truth; and learn from it how to meet, how to resist, how to sub-
     due them."

7   WILTONIENSIS [pseud.]. "Daniel de Foe." Notes and Queries,
     1st ser. 5, no. 130 (24 April):392.
         Quotes brief extracts from old Wiltshire [news]papers on
     two different descendants, a criminal named John Joseph Defoe
     executed in 1777 at Tyburn for a robbery; and the other, living
     in Hungerford Market around 1836, "a creditable tradesman" with
     the same name as his famous ancestor.

                              1853

*1   BROWN, HUGH STOWELL. "Daniel De Foe." Lectures on Protestant
     Nonconformists. London: [n.p.].
         Listed in the National Union Catalog: copies not avail-
     able.

2   BURTON, JOHN HILL. History of Scotland, from the Revolution
     to the Extinction of the Last Jacobite Insurrection (1689-
     1748). 2 vols. London: Longman, Brown, Green, & Longmans,
     1:404-76; 2:9, 13, 16, 19-20, 34-35, 380.

Uses Defoe's History of the Union as a primary authority on the manner in which the proposed Union was received, including most graphic descriptions of mobs in Edinburgh (23 October 1706) and Glasgow (7 September 1706). Even though Defoe was at times the only source of information or the person given credit for solving a complex problem related to an article of Union, he is nevertheless treated patronizingly here--charged, for instance, with exaggerating the dangers in order "to laud the prudence of the ministry in suppressing [this affair]" and ridiculed for his "garrulity." Reprinted: The History of Scotland from Agricola's Invasion to the Extinction of the Last Jacobite Insurrection, 2d ed., 8 vols. (Edinburgh and London: William Blackwood & Sons, 1874), 8:142-73, 204, 207, 209.

3   CORNEY, BOLTON. "Robert Drury." Notes and Queries, 1st ser. 8, no. 199 (20 August):181.
     Uses the statement by "John Duncombe, M.A., one of the six preachers in Christ Church, Canterbury, 1773" to vouch for Robert Drury as a real person and as one having "the character of a downright honest man" and thus to argue that his Madagascar is "genuine." Refers also to Mr. Duncombe's statements quoted from Drury which coincide with those of Reverend William Hirst who had been at Madagascar in 1759. See 1852.4; 1853.16-17.

4   CROSSLEY, JAMES. "Inquiry into the State of the Union, by the Wednesday Club in Friday Street." Notes and Queries, 1st ser. 7, no. 189 (11 June):576.
     Replies to 1853.5, 19. Assigns three pamphlets which use the invented form of the Wednesday's club in Friday Street to William Paterson, but claims for Defoe's authorship, on external and internal evidence, a related work Fair payment No Spunge (1717), which is now assigned to him for the first time.

5   DAVIES, JAMES A. "Enquiry into the State of the Union." Notes and Queries, 1st ser. 7, no. 182 (23 April):409.
     Asks if "the Wednesday's Club in Friday Street," cited as the author of the Enquiry into the State of the Union of Great Britain, was a real or fictitious club. See reply, 1853.4.

6   DICKENS, CHARLES. "Covering a Multitude of Sins." In Bleak House. London: Chapman & Hall. Reprint. Oxford Illustrated Dickens. London: Oxford University Press, 1948, p. 108.
     Of "the little book" which Mrs. Pardiggle left behind for the edification of the brickmaker, Esther Summerson reports that "Mr. Jarndyce said he doubted if Robinson Crusoe could have read it, though he had had no other on his desolate island."

7   [DICKENS, CHARLES.] "Frauds on the Fairies." Household Words 8, no. 184 (1 October):97-100.
     Author identified in Anne Lohrli, Household Words: A Weekly Journal 1850-1859 Conducted by Charles Dickens (Toronto and Buffalo: University of Toronto Press, 1973), p. 115. Urges that

fairy tales, those "nurseries of fancy," should be preserved as
they are. Observes lately, "with pain, the intrusion of a Whole
Hog of unwieldy dimensions into the fairy flower garden." His
friend, Mr. George Cruikshank, has taken to "editing" his opinions into illustrations on such matters as Total Abstinence, Pro-
hibition, Free Trade, and Popular Education. Objects strongly to
this practice; asks the reader to imagine "a Total abstinence edition of Robinson Crusoe, with the rum left out. . . . a Peace edition, with the gunpowder left out, and the rum left in. Imagine
a Vegetarian edition. . . . a Kentucky edition. . . . an Abori-
gines Protection Society edition. . . ." Recasts the Cinderella
story with such editings made in the text--as an illustration.

8   _____. "Where We Stopped Growing." Household Words 6,
     no. 145 (1 January):361-63.
     Expresses thankfulnesses "to have stopped in our growth at
so many points," the first being the many great imaginative
moments in Robinson Crusoe: "We have never grown the thousandth
part of an inch out of Robinson Crusoe." We have never grown out
of his parrot, dog, fouling-piece, goat, rusty money, cap, umbrel-
la. Not just things, but persons and actions. Lavishly accumu-
lates the details from Robinson Crusoe, attesting to his fond-
ness. Our growth stopped also when similar effects were experienced through other books involving Haroun Alraschid, Blue Beard,
Don Quixote, Gil Blas, "real original roaring giants," "real
people and places," and so on. Reprinted: Miscellaneous Papers,
in The Works of Charles Dickens, National Library ed. (New York:
Bigelow, Brown & Co., [n.d.]), 18:337-43.

9   [EDWARDS, HENRY SUTHERLAND.] "Balzac and His Writings."
     Eclectic Magazine 30, no. 1 (September):29-37 passim.
     Reprint of 1853.10.

10   _____. "Balzac and His Writings." Westminster Review, n.s. 4
     (July):199-214 passim.
     Authorship given in Wellesley Index. In an important early
discussion of the "realist school" headed by Balzac, includes a
comparison of his Physiologie du Mariage (1829) and Defoe's "Marriage Bed" [Conjugal Lewdness, 1727], described here as unread-
able because of its coarse treatment of the subject. Analyzes
Balzac's ability "to invest the most ordinary occurrences with
interest," which he shares with Richardson as well as Defoe, by a
"system of details" which adds "reality to the characters"; illustrates by quoting from the beginning of Robinson Crusoe. Argues
forcefully that such details do not point to "the decay of an
art" but rather its enhancement. Reprinted: 1853.9.

11   GRUBE, H.A.W., ed. Foreword to [Thomas] Mayne Reid's Der
     Robinson der Wildniss. Erlebnisse und abenteuer einer in den
     Prairien des fernen Westens verirrten englischen Auswanderer-
     familie. Stuttgart: J.B. Müller's Verlagshandlung, pp. iii-
     iv.

Explains why he was drawn to adapt freely Mayne Reid's <u>De-</u>
<u>sert Home</u> (1851) for the enrichment of youthful German readers.
Describes himself entranced and excited by the English original,
"a companion of equal rank to Defoe's and Campe's <u>Robinsons</u>."
Notes that the author Mayne Reid, fairly well known in Germany,
now enters "a new province of literature" in which he uses the
framework of a tiny Robinsonade to describe the natural world.

12   JARDINE, D. "Rapping no Novelty." <u>Notes and Queries</u>, 1st
      ser. 8, no. 213 (26 November):512-13.
         Quotes a letter by Sir Thomas Tresham written about the
      year 1584 concerning spiritual knocking, with no reference to
      Defoe, but see the replies, 1853.18; 1854.1, 6.

13   JONES, EDWIN OWEN. "Daniel Defoe." <u>Eminent Characters of the</u>
      <u>English Revolutionary Period</u>. London: Saunders & Otley,
      pp. 201-35.
         Endeavors to describe the characteristics of the English
      Revolution, starting with a sweepingly general "Introduction" on
      British history from the fall of the Roman Empire, and continuing
      with independently written chapters on Oliver Cromwell, Sir
      Matthew Hale, John Milton, John Bunyan, and Daniel Defoe. Subor-
      dinates the few biographical details to a depiction of Defoe as
      in Wilson's <u>Memoirs</u> (1830): a person of heroic proportions, a
      champion of dissent and non-conformity, who had no flaws or im-
      perfection of character. Devotes much of the space to his bank-
      ruptcies, imprisonments, support of William III through the publi-
      cation of the <u>True-Born Englishman</u>, opposition to the occasional
      conformity of Dissenters, daring confrontation with the High
      Church in the <u>Shortest-Way with the Dissenters</u>, and suffering in
      the pillory--only the early events. Mentions Defoe's authorship
      of <u>Robinson Crusoe</u> glowingly, but quickly passes over the other
      novels as "open to the objection which generally attaches to
      popular works of fiction--the minute delineation of vice." Defoe
      was "unquestionably the father of the English novel"; his succes-
      sors from Richardson to Dickens were "to some extent his imita-
      tors." Names only the "History of the Plague" by title.

14   [MANNING, ANNE.] <u>Cherry & Violet, A Tale of the Great Plague</u>.
      London: Arthur Hall, Virtue, & Co., 311 pp.
         Narrates in the first person the fictionalized lives of the
      main character (Cherry) and the tradesmen (e.g., Mark Bleckinsop)
      who had shops on London Bridge, set against such historical
      events as the Civil War, parliamentary rule, and the Restoration.
      Of particular interest are the completely unacknowledged borrow-
      ings from the <u>Journal of the Plague Year</u> to create the historical
      background for the plague in chaps. 7 through 9. Makes similar
      cribs from Pepys's diary in the descriptions of Oliver Cromwell's
      guilt over his daughter's death and the Great Fire of London.
      See also James C. Simmons, "A Victorian Plagiarism of Defoe,"
      <u>American Notes and Queries</u> 10, no. 3 (November, 1971): 36-37.

15   Memoirs, Journal, and Correspondence of Thomas Moore. Edited
     by Lord John Russell. London: Longman, Brown, Green & Long-
     mans, 3:230.
          In the entry for 9 May 1821, tells the anecdote of Madame
     Talleyrand and Denon, but includes certain interesting changes.
     For example, Talleyrand forgets to leave Denon's book on the
     study table, and Madame instead finds Robinson Crusoe. Also, at
     dinner, her words that puzzle Denon are, "Ah then, this dear
     Friday!" Moore reports the incident as an instance of her
     "niaserie" [foolishness]. See also 1816.7; 1854.9; 1870.24;
     1902.2.

16   O., J. "Robert Drury." Notes and Queries, 1st ser. 8,
     no. 196 (30 July):104-5.
          Amasses evidence that Robert Drury is a real character, and
     his Madagascar "a true narrative of his shipwreck, sufferings,
     and captivity." See also 1852.4; 1853.17.

17   PINKERTON, W. "Robert Drury." Notes and Queries, 1st ser. 7,
     no. 185 (14 May):485-86.
          Rejects "credit attachable to Drury's Madagascar," and
     cites the examples of Mrs. Veal and The Four Years Voyages of
     Capt. George Roberts (1726). Of the latter, which he mistakenly
     entitles The Ten Years' Voyages . . ., maintains that it is "uni-
     versally . . . considered fictitious, and ascribed to Defoe"; yet
     it ends with a testimonial as to authorship not very different
     from the one in Drury's Madagascar. See also 1852.4; 1853.16.

18   R., R.I. "Rapping no Novelty." Notes and Queries, 1st ser.
     8, no. 217 (24 December):632.
          Replies to 1853.12 by quoting a story of a spirit knocking,
     from Baxter's History of Apparitions, which appears in Defoe's
     "veracious" Duncan Campbell (2d ed.). See also 1854.1, 6.

19   REED, CHARLES. "The Wednesday Club." Notes and Queries, 1st
     ser. 7, no. 176 (12 March):261.
          Query for information on the Wednesday Club. See 1853.5
     and reply, 1853.4.

                              1854

1   'ΑΛΙΕΫ́Σ [pseud]. "Defoe's Quotation from Baxter on Appari-
     tions." Notes and Queries, 1st ser. 9, no. 221 (21 January):
     62-63.
          Replies to 1854.6. Identifies the quotation in Duncan
     Campbell on spiritual knocking as from Richard Baxter's The
     Certainty of the Worlds of Spirits fully evinced by the unques-
     tionable Histories of Apparitions (1691). Finds little definite
     information on Dr. Beaumont, author of Treatise of Spirits.

2   C., H.B. "Robinson Crusoe." Notes and Queries, 1st ser. 10,
     no. 266 (2 December):448-49.

In reply to 1854.10, provides information on the Rev. Benjamin Holloway, and relates an anecdote showing him to have been "somewhat credulous."

3   DAVIS, A.W. "Robinson Crusoe." Notes and Queries, 1st ser.
     10, no. 266 (2 December):449.
        In reply to 1854.10, gives the present location of Selkirk's sea-chest and musket.

4   HETTNER, HERMANN. Robinson und die Robinsonaden. Berlin,
     [n.p.], 42 pp.
        Became in 1865 a part of his Literaturgeschichte des achtzehnten Jahrhunderts and thereafter a standard reference work.
     For a discussion of Hettner's two groups of Robinsonades, see
     Gove; and for Gotthard Erler's revised third edition of the part
     entitled Geschichte der deutschen Literatur im achtzehnten Jahrhundert, the last under Hettner's care, see 1879.3 in Hermann
     Hettner, "Die Robinsonaden und die Insel Felsenburg," in Geschichte der deutschen Literatur in achtzehnten Jahrhundert, ed.
     Gotthard Erler, 2 vols. (Berlin: Aufbau, 1961), 1:241-50, 561.
                                                              (P.E.C.)

5   JARLTZBERG. "High Church and Low Church." Notes and Queries,
     1st ser. 10, no. 257 (30 September):260-62; no. 258 (7 October):278-82.
        Recognizes at firsthand the important contributions of
     Defoe toward defining the meanings of "High Church" and "Low
     Church." Deals directly with the writings of Defoe's antagonists, such as the anonymous A Caveat against the Whigs (1711-
     1712) and The Fox with His Firebrand Unkennelled and Ensnared
     (1703), or of Sacheverell, Charles Leslie, James Owen, and the
     writers of the periodical press in Queen Anne's time.

6   MAITLAND, S.R. "Rapping no Novelty." Notes and Queries, 1st
     ser. 9, no. 219 (7 January):12-13.
        Replies to 1853.12, 18. Expresses distrust that Defoe
     really quoted Baxter on spiritual knocking, and quotes the
     passage from Duncan Campbell (2d ed.) to determine if it has the
     sanction of Baxter. Raises further questions about Dr. Beaumont,
     whom Defoe claims to know "personally," but who gives the same
     story in his book; and about Duncan Campbell. See also 1854.1.

7   N., G. "Robinson Crusoe." Notes and Queries, 1st ser. 10,
     no. 266 (2 December):448.
        Replies to the query, 1854.10, by referring to Isaac
     James's Providence Displayed, 1800.2, that includes six different
     "authorities," who show "that even De Foe has not always been
     thought the author of Crusoe." Notes that while James makes no
     judgement on authorship, he finds the "preponderance of evidence"
     favoring Defoe as author of Robinson Crusoe.

8   OLIPHANT, MARGARET. "Evelyn and Pepys." Blackwood's Edinburgh Magazine 76, no. 465 (July):35-52.

Authorship identified in <u>Wellesley Index</u>. In recreating
the times of Evelyn and Pepys, comes close to including "that
person of real flesh and blood, the citizen of London who indites
the true history of the Great Plague; and but that scoffers say
he is no more to be relied upon than the redoubtable Crusoe,
his brother and kinsman, no bit of individual story throws more
light upon the time than does his." Proceeds to rule out "Master
Defoe," on the one hand, and Clarendon, on the other.

9   R[OSENWA]LD, [VICTOR]. "Talleyrand (Charles-Maurice de)."
     In <u>Biographie universelle, ancienne et moderne</u>. Edited by
     J[oseph] F[rançois] Michaud. New ed. Reprint. Graz, Aus-
     tria: Akademische Druck- und Verlagsanstalt, 1969, 40:612.
     Tells briefly the incident that took place at an official
dinner in Paris around 1806, when citizen Madame de Talleyrand
mistook the famous "traveller," M. Denon, for Robinson Crusoe,
and asked him for news "about Friday and his parrot." Relates
the anecdote to indicate how slight the opposition was in Saint-
Germain to Talleyrand's marriage. For other accounts of the
anecdote, see 1816.7; 1853.15; 1870.24; 1902.2.

10   SCOTT, JAMES J. "<u>Robinson Crusoe</u>--Who Wrote It?" <u>Notes and
     Queries</u>, 1st ser. 10, no. 261 (28 October):345.
     Quotes from 1843.2, the story of Lord Sunderland's saying
to the Rev. Benjamin Holloway that "Lord <u>Oxford</u>, while prisoner
in the Tower of London, <u>wrote the first volume of the History of
Robinson Crusoe</u> . . ."; continues with the anecdote attributed to
Thomas Wharton. Queries whether or not there is any solid evidence to support Lord Oxford's authorship, and whether anyone
knows the whereabouts of Selkirk's chest and musket.

11   [THOMAS, ALEXANDRE.] Review "History of French Protestant
     Refugees." <u>Edinburgh Review</u> 99, no. 202 (April):454-93.
     Authorship identified in <u>Wellesley Index</u>. Reviews four
books on the French Protestants or Huguenots. Weaves in the
story told in the <u>Appeal to Honour and Justice</u> (1715) of the
<u>True-Born Englishman</u> as Defoe's defence of William III against
Tutchin's charges of the King's being a foreigner.

12   [TUCKERMAN, HENRY THEODORE.] Review of <u>Works</u> (1840-1841).
     <u>North American Review</u> 78, no. 163 (April):265-83.
     Authorship given in <u>Research Keys to the American Renais-
     sance</u>, ed. Kenneth Walter Cameron (Hartford: Transcendental
Books, 1967). Reflects the view of Defoe in America arising from
<u>Works</u> (1840-1841), in an edition dated 1848. Provides an essen-
tially romantic image of him throughout, but especially in his
turning to the novel, "like a brave soldier" returning home after
many a campaign, and yielding himself to the peace of fiction-
writing. Contrasts repeatedly the fashionable wits given to
frivolous pursuits--Swift, Steele, Addison, Bolingbroke--with the
neglected Defoe "wrestling for truth in Cripplegate." Describes
his political pamphlets (some 133 in the time of Queen Anne and

George I) as "like guerilla parties," always committed on "the
side of popular right and religious liberty"; or a treatise like
The Original Power of the Collective Body of the People of
England (1702) as a bold document in behalf of constitutional
freedom. Claims that Defoe anticipated every forward-looking
idea or improvement. In particular, with respect to "the modern
novel": the attributes of a matter-of-fact style, probability,
and verisimilitude still valid today as when Robinson Crusoe
first appeared. Emphasizes that in the contrast with his fashionable contemporaries, Defoe's moral "earnestness" stands out
strikingly. Even though the novels are in the main "devoted to
low life," and may even repel the reader, they nevertheless de-
serve attention as "the genuine precursors of the modern English
novel." Stresses in Robinson Crusoe the "thoroughly English"
qualities of the romance, and finds the hero "the moral ideal
and exemplar of his nation and class"--an interpretation made
possible because Defoe's life was itself "a moral solitude."
Reprinted: 1857.10.

1854-1865

1   The Novels and Miscellaneous Works of Daniel De Foe with
     Prefaces and Notes, Including Those Attributed to Sir Walter
     Scott. 7 vols. Bohn's British Classics. London: Henry G.
     Bohn.
          Reprints selections from Works (1840-1841), and thus
     strengthens the claim for Defoe's authorship where it was still
     problematical: for example, in vol. 2 by reprinting Sir Walter
     Scott's preface and edition (1809) of Capt. George Carleton; or
     where such claims were negligible, in vol. 4, the Life and
     Adventures of Mrs. Christian Davis, Commonly Called Mother Ross
     (1740) and Defoe's supposed continuation of Roxana in the 1745
     edition. Reprinted: London: George Bell & Sons, 1880; Bohn's
     Standard Library, London: George Bell & Sons, 1856-1884.

1855

1   CHAMBERS, ROBERT. "Daniel Defoe." In Cyclopaedia of English
     Literature: A Selection of the Choicest Productions of En-
     glish Authors, from the Earliest to the Present Time, Connect-
     ed by a Critical and Biographical History. 2 vols. Boston:
     Gould & Lincoln, 1:617-24.
          Presents Defoe first among the "miscellaneous writers" of
     the period 1689-1727. Interrupts the standard biographical in-
     formation to list the fictitious narratives beginning with Robin-
     son Crusoe (1719); while he includes Moll Flanders, curiously
     omits Roxana. In Defoe's total of 210 books and pamphlets, finds
     that the political writings have already sunk into oblivion, but
     the fictions "still charm by their air of truth, and the simple
     natural beauty of their style," although he deplores Defoe's not

infrequent choice of a disgustingly low subject. Regards Defoe
the novelist as "the father of Richardson, and partly of Fielding"; and contrasts Swift and Defoe in tone, including the manner
described by Dunlop (1814.2). Reprints the entire Mrs. Veal and
short extracts from the Journal of the Plague Year, Colonel Jack,
and Robinson Crusoe.

2   "Daniel Defoe." Boy's Own Magazine 1:257-60.
        The publisher Samuel O. Beeton subtitles his magazine "An
Illustrated Journal of Fact, Fiction, History, and Adventure."
Borrows heavily from Hazlitt, 1830.3, without acknowledgement.
Diverges briefly in omitting Hazlitt's fine critical distinction
concerning Robinson Crusoe as fiction, a "world of abstraction,"
completely separated from Defoe's life, and in substituting the
more conventional view of its being "truthful." Repeats the
judgments on the "other" novels as well as on the non-fictional
writings, often in the unquoted words of the original.

3   FORSTER, JOHN. "Daniel De Foe." In Daniel De Foe and Charles
    Churchill. London: Longman, Brown, Green, & Longmans, pp. 1-
    149.
        Reprint, with additions, of 1845.4. "Masterpieces of fresh
and spirited writing" was how the Athenaeum of 5 May described
Forster's two pieces. Now in five chapters, the Defoe biography
falls naturally into five divisions, according to the reigning
monarch. The additions contribute substance enough to transform
a review into a biography of prime importance: colorful phrases,
specific details, new anecdotes, comments expanded to stress
certain themes, lengthened quotations (or new ones) from Defoe's
works. Specifically, materials are added to give greater empha-
ses to certain events of Defoe's life: his lifelong admiration
of William III, advocacy of the Scottish people, estrangement
from genteel contemporaries, love of liberty. Techniques which
served admirably in Forster's other biographies function here
also. To illustrate the popularity of Religious Courtship, he
mentions that Goldsmith's "lively Livy Primrose" is "as thoroughly acquainted with the dialogue in Religious Courtship, as she is
with the argument of Man Friday and his Master in Robinson Crusoe, and the disputes of Thwackum and Square in Tom Jones." The
important additions are in the notes, taken from a fresh reading
of the scarce Review, Defoe's own writings (such as the little
known, Dyet of Poland), the vitriolic comments of enemies (such
as Oldmixon), or contemporary newspapers. The anecdotes proliferate mostly in the notes. At times they supply a personal note to
the narrative as when Forster defends Defoe against the "unfair"
strictures of Pope, or when he ends a partly mistaken note on
Drelincourt with comment on the Mrs. Veal story, Defoe's own belief in the possibility of communication between spirits and the
visible world, and the Devil, by saying: "I venture to commend
these sentences to the admiration of my friend Mr. Carlyle." At
times, the anecdote can be memorable: De Foe paid by Harley more
than Swift for services to the party because, according to Old-

mixon's "reckless assertion," he had "the shrewder head of the
two for business." In the notes, too, Forster went beyond his
predecessors, using (for example) James Crossley's copy of the
scarce Mercator which had not been available even to Walter Wilson. Not only does the biographer continue to assemble new information from a variety of sources, he also strengthens the unity
of his subject. Reprinted: The Traveller's Library, vol. 16,
1856; 1858.6; 1860.5; in part, Critical Heritage.

4   [GREG, W.R.] Review "The Newspaper Press." Edinburgh Review
    102, no. 208 (October):476.
        Authorship identified in the Wellesley Index. Compares
    Defoe's punishment in 1702, by gaol, pillory, and fine, with
    printer Twyn's in 1663--to demonstrate the decreasing severity of
    the law against treason.

5   LANDOR, WALTER SAVAGE. "A Descendant of Defoe to the Editor
    of the Times." Times (London), 1 November, p. 7.
        Eloquently pleads for contributions to aid the aging James
    William Defoe of Kennington. Cites his ancestor's achievements
    in the novel and history, his being "the earliest teacher of
    political economy, the first propounder of free trade . . . the
    most far-sighted of our statesmen." Concludes: "Achilles and
    Homer will be forgotten before Crusoe and Defoe."

6   Preface to Religious Courtship, or Marriage on Christian
    Principles; Being a Guide in the Selection of a Companion for
    Life. By Daniel Defoe. Cincinnati, Ohio: Applegate & Co.,
    pp. i-ii.
        Argues for the strong impression made by "historical
    dialogues," and defends the propriety of the woman's examining
    her lover on questions of harmony in religion. Claims Religious
    Courtship to be "scarcely less esteemed by the British public"
    than Robinson Crusoe; now offers it for the first time to Ameri-
    can readers.

7   SENIOR, N[ASSAU], and DAVIS, J.C.B. Review "Slavery in the
    United States." Edinburgh Review 101, no. 206 (April):297.
        Mentions briefly the treatment of slavery in Colonel Jack.
    Reprinted: Nassau W. Senior [collaborator omitted], "Harriet
    Beecher Stowe," in Essays on Fiction (London: Longman, Green,
    Longman, Roberts, & Green, 1864), p. 403.

8   S[TEPHEN], F[ITZJAMES]. "The Relation of Novels to Life." In
    Cambridge Essays, Contributed by Members of the University.
    London: John W. Parker & Son, pp. 148-92 passim.
        Defines the novel, in order to distinguish it from drama,
    as "a fictitious biography"; and illustrates with examples from
    French and English novelists, but only Memoirs of a Cavalier and
    Robinson Crusoe from Defoe. Constantly draws parallels to
    "modern novels" as, for example, in "the descriptions of nature"
    where such "machines" are said to be "never obtrusive or over

elaborate" in Gil Blas, Defoe ("the Cavalier's wanderings in Yorkshire"), Fielding, and Smollett. In a distinction between two
kinds of plots (drawn from the stage and life), argues for "the
wonderful superiority" of Swift and Defoe over successors, in
never having confused the two--drawing exclusively from life.
Illustrates this point vividly in a twofold comparison of Robinson Crusoe, which appears to be "almost faultless" in minimizing
the "disturbing forces" intruding upon the novel: first, with
Dickens's Bleak House; second, with Dickens's David Copperfield.
Emphasizes Defoe's superiority in representing the main character, closeness to life, pathos--in the novel as fictitious
biography. Reprinted: Notorious Literary Attacks, ed. Albert
Mordell (New York: Bond & Liveright, 1926), pp. 126-70.

1856

1   [BURTON, J.H.] "The Scot Abroad: The Man of the Sword."
     Blackwood's Edinburgh Magazine 79, no. 487 (May):583-85.
          Authorship identified in the Wellesley Index. Illustrates
     the greatness of Scottish troops in battle by describing their
     victories under Gustavus Adolphus in Memoirs of a Cavalier,
     "attributed in the critical world by a sort of acclamation to
     De Foe." Argues that if the book were "printed off from the
     actual diary or memorandum-book of an English gentleman volun-
     teer," who could better have done the perfecting or revising than
     Defoe? Offers this theory to explain the cavalier's attitude
     toward the Scots.

2   D., H.G. "Daniel De Foe." Notes and Queries, 2d ser. 1,
     no. 18 (3 May):356.
          In editor's reply to H.G.D.'s query, uses Wilson's Memoirs
     of Defoe (1830) to verify the date of his death, as given by
     Forster: 24 April 1731.

3   [JEAFFRESON, JOHN CORDY.] "Daniel De Foe." Dublin University
     Magazine 48, no. 283 (July):57-71.
          Authorship identified in 1858.8. Brings sympathy to the
     biographical portion, siding with Defoe against the Scriblerian
     wits and judging Defoe's heroism as having arrived too soon to be
     properly understood. Traces the well-known events, with new
     information probably drawn from Forster, 1855.3. Praises the
     Shortest-Way with the Dissenters as "perhaps his most brilliant
     political pamphlet," the irony here and elsewhere surpassing that
     of Gulliver's Travels. Locates the transition for this "lion-
     hearted man" in 1715, as he [supposedly] enters into retirement.
     With even greater sympathy, assesses the fiction: Colonel Jack
     for its Dickensian vision of childhood; Robinson Crusoe as "a
     great religious poem . . . the drama of solitude." Explains the
     paradox of a writer like Defoe who rigorously denounces immoral-
     ity, and yet lavishly indulges in obscene stories, as motivated
     by money which he needs to care for expensive tastes and specu-

lations. Estimates that besides the Review, Defoe wrote 183
separate works, with 52 more "attributed." Concludes with a
number of observations, a shrewd one being that Defoe was totally
deficient in any conception of plot. See the review, 1858.10.
Reprinted: 1856.4-5; 1858.8; in part, Critical Heritage; in
part, Daniel Defoe: Moll Flanders, ed. Edward Kelly (New York:
W.W. Norton & Co., 1973), pp. 329-30.

4   _____. "Daniel De Foe." Eclectic Magazine 39, no. 1 (Septem-
     ber): 18-30.
        Reprint of 1856.3.

5   _____. "Daniel De Foe." Littell's Living Age 50, no. 640
     (30 August):513-26.
        Reprint of 1856.3. Reprinted: in part, Daniel Defoe:
     Moll Flanders, ed. J. Paul Hunter, Crowell Critical Library (New
     York: Thomas Y. Crowell Co., [1970]), p. 273.

6   LETHREDIENSIS [pseud.]. "Defoe Queries." Notes and Queries,
     2d ser. 2, no. 52 (27 December):508.
        Raises two queries relating to Jure Divino (1706): (1) In
     the dedication to Lady Reason, why is she said to be "'governess
     of the fifteen provinces of speech'"? (2) In the preface, what
     is meant by "Salisbury" in the unexplained comment "'Salisbury
     for that, I'll not venture you'"?

7   M., S.N. "Stray Notes on Edmund Curll, His Life, and Publica-
     tions." Notes and Queries, 2d ser. 2, no. 48 (29 November):
     421-24.
        Among the severe denunciations of the disreputable book-
     seller Edmund Curll, includes one on the "sin of Curlicism," by
     "H," in Mist's Weekly Journal, or Saturday Post for 5 April 1718.
     Makes no identification of Defoe as the author of the piece; Lee
     would do this in Defoe (1869), 2:32-33.

8   O., J. "Defoe's Autobiography." Notes and Queries, 2d ser.
     1, no. 17 (26 April):333-34.
        Rejects Defoe's authorship of An Abstract of the Remarkable
     Passages in the Life of a Private Gentleman (1715), the work
     being only a reduced version of An Account of Some Remarkable
     Passages in the Life, &c. (2d ed., 1711); it should also not be
     confused with Some Remarkable Passages in the Holy Life and Death
     of Gervase Disney, Esq. (1692).

9   [ROSCOE, WILLIAM CALDWELL.] "De Foe as a Novelist." National
     Review 3 (October):380-410.
        For the high regard in which this essay is held, see Criti-
     cal Heritage; for the correct assignment of authorship to W.C.
     Roscoe, see Wellesley Index. Holds to the strong philosophical
     conviction, which shapes the entire criticism, that the modern
     novel has become "the characteristic literature of modern times"
     and that because of an increase in human personal liberty, it

preoccupies itself with characterization. Argues next, surprisingly, that "modern taste," searching for characters, "finds little to gratify it in the novels of De Foe." Since the reigns of William III and Queen Anne were not "adapted for the unhampered growth and quiet contemplation of character," but given to petty actions, asks what were the consequences for Defoe's novels. Follows up with acute observations: first, Defoe was interested only in "human existence," but due to the times, he "busied himself rather with what men were doing than with what they were." In his "proper novels," the "pure fictions"--<u>Roxana</u>, <u>Moll Flanders</u>, <u>Colonel Jack</u>, and <u>Robinson Crusoe</u> (Part I)--identifies "their reality, their life-likeness," as the unique feature. Compares Defoe's imagination here, at once so vivid and so limited, as the reverse of Shakespeare's "universal solvent." Defoe has "an enormous reconstructive and a very narrow creative imagination." But his limitations are his genius. Because he lacks the capacity to project the larger vision, he gives only what the lesser genius can give, namely, vividness or distinctness due to details and minutiae. Urges that Defoe's power does not lie in the handling of minute circumstance, but "in the constant and distinct presence before his own mind of the conception that controls and guides his minutiae." Hypothesizes how Defoe might have handled "the domestic life of his period," and compares him to Jane Austen who is similar "in some of the main aspects of her genius, though as much his superior in handling character as she is inferior in knowledge and vigour." After comments on Austen's well-defined limits in the novel, concludes the comparison: "De Foe goes down the ragged lanes, tramps through gorse and heather, sits by the side of the duckpond, and studies the aspect of the dunghill." Pursues the point that among Defoe's "<u>dramatis personae</u>," with the possible exception of the <u>Journal of the Plague Year</u>, he never drew "a respectable man"; elaborates upon the class from which he drew "his heroes and heroines" in terms of eighteenth-century social structure and with help from contrasts with Dickens's and Scott's characters. Turns to the second order of observations based on the kind of person Defoe was as a novelist. Among comments on his characters, strikes out with profoundly deep psychological observations relating the novelist to his characters. Describes a core of commonality in both the characters and their creator as "the innermost part of his nature which a man can least shake off in his writings." In an interpretation not previously encountered, asserts that Defoe's loneliness was one "which comes from a want of warmth in the emotions, from an incapacity for strong individual attachments." In his writings, Defoe rarely deals with normal human relations, such as the "simple love" of man and wife; quotes the long passage in <u>Moll Flanders</u> where Moll meets her son born to her in the marriage with her brother: "This is intense, if not refined, pathos." The novelist remains silent "on the more voluntary affections." The characters show complete "depravity of selfishness" and, like their creator, "insufficient affections." Offers another "glimpse into the interior of the writer" by noting the "passion"

for property in the novels. The characters themselves have "a
certain squareness and solidity; they are all of hardy and stubborn materials. They put you in mind of timber; they have no
sensibility, no pliancy." As with the characters, so with the
author: "He worked and lived, not like a winged Pegasus tramp-
ling the air, but like a serious laborious ox, dragging the slow
plough through the long furrows, and rolling round a patient
reproachful eye in answer to injury." Interprets Defoe the novelist as a man having the personal traits, intellect, instincts,
thoughts and ideas, even the dullness—of his characters. Defoe's imagination was so strong "its facts seem to him of equal
weight with those of memory or knowledge"; and his characters go
further. "They lie, to suit their purposes, at every turn, and
without scruple or remorse." Similarly, Defoe's religion projects into his characters, in the way they repent or become over-
whelmed with a sense of their crimes. Defends the frankness with
which Defoe's novels are written; regards them as "wholesome,"
compared with Richardson's "varnished prurience," Swift's "dis-
gusting filth," or Fielding's "somewhat too indulgent and sympa-
thising warmth." Argues finally that the novels have "a deeper
moral, not the less important because the writer was unconscious
of its existence," namely, the ease with which crime and sin are
confused, and the similarities of Defoe's thieves and harlots to
"human beings just like ourselves." Reprinted: 1860.9; in part
[not assigned to Roscoe], Critical Heritage.

10   RUST, J. CYPRIAN. "Fransham of Norwich." Notes and Queries,
      2d ser. 2, no. 50 (13 December):467–68.
          Seeks information on Isaac Fransham of Norwich who died
      7 May 1743. See 1874.5; 1875.3.

11   WEBSTER, DANIEL. Letter to John Brazer, Boston, 10 November
      1828. In The Private Correspondence of Daniel Webster.
      Edited by Fletcher Webster. 2 vols. Boston: Little, Brown &
      Co., 1:463–65.
          Comments on Richard Whately's Elementary Rhetoric (1828) as
      embodying certain ideas on style with which he agreed, but which
      had never before appeared in print. On the "particularization"
      of detail, states: "This minute statement of place as well as of
      time gives great notedness to narrative composition." Regards
      Homer and Defoe as "the greatest masters of this part of their
      art—always excepting the Scriptures." Also illustrates when
      particularization can have a "feeble" effect. Reprinted: The
      Papers of Daniel Webster. Correspondence, Volume 2: 1825–1829,
      ed. Charles M. Wiltse (Hanover, N.H.: University Press of New
      England for Dartmouth College, 1976), pp. 378–79.

                                1857

1   [ANGELL, JAMES BURRILL.] "Influence of the English Literature
      on the German." North American Review 84, no. 175 (April):
      328–33.

Authorship identified in Poole's Index. Reviewing literary histories by G.G. Gervinus, Wolfgang Menzel, and A.F.C. Vilnaar, recognizes Robinson Crusoe especially as the English novel being read by Germans and as starting "a new era" from 1722 to 1755. Observes that more than forty Robinson-like tales were being published in German as well as many other similar stories of the Aventuriers, and that these produced such effects to prepare readers for Rousseau's writings.

2   BORROW, GEORGE. "A Word for Lavengro." In Appendix to The Romany Rye: A Sequel to "Lavengro." Reprint. The Works of George Borrow. Edited by Clement Shorter. Norwich Edition. London: Constable & Co.; New York: Gabriel Wells, 6:196-99.
        Comments on "the hand of Providence" evident in Lavengro's giving a "balm" to cure the "ulcerated mind" of Peter Williams; quotes from memory a passage in the Life of Blessed Mary Flanders, which has a miraculous effect on the preacher. Pointedly observes that no such effect could have been produced from books like Rasselas or "other exceptionable works to be found in the library of Albemarle Street." See also 1851.3.

3   CRESWELL, S.F. "History of the Civil Wars." Notes and Queries, 2d ser. 4, no. 95 (24 October):331.
        Without any reference to Defoe as the author, describes the contents of Memoirs of a Cavalier as reprinted by James Tomlinson, for the Publisher, Newark, 1782. Gives a mistaken answer, which was subsequently corrected, 1857.6.

4   CROYDON, E.H. "De Foe." Notes and Queries, 2d ser. 3, no. 78 (27 June):510.
        To the query on the best authenticated life of Defoe, the editor replies: Wilson's Memoirs of Defoe (1830) and Forster's Life of De Foe (Travellers' Library, vol. 16, 1856).

5   "Defoe's Novels." Gentleman's Magazine, n.s. 3 (September): 235-42.
        Reviewing the Bohn Edition (1856), takes a not uncommon view of Defoe as "a stern and staunch defender of the principles of civil and religious liberty," but influenced by Scott's criticism, asserts an uncommonly strong preference for fictional narratives structured on facts or "important national events": Journal of the Plague Year, Memoirs of a Cavalier, and Capt. Carleton's Memoirs. Makes a special point that all three works have been found "authentic," and illustrates with a comment on "the eloquent eye-witness" in the Journal of the Plague Year; finds the narrators "all real persons--all, Defoe himself in a succession of assumed parts." For Colonel Jack, Moll Flanders, Roxana, even the apocryphal Mother Ross: withholds "unqualified approbation," but places these novels in the first rank.

6   Editor's reply to S.F. Creswell. Notes and Queries, 2d ser. 4, no. 96 (31 October):358.

In reply to query 1857.3, identifies the History of the Civil Wars as a reprinting in Newark of James Tomlinson, 1782, of "De Foe's Memoirs of a Cavalier (Col. Andrew Newport), 1722, with a new title page."

7   HANNAY, JAMES. Review "English Political Satires" of Thomas Wright's The Political Songs of England and four other books. Quarterly Review 101, no. 202 (April):410.
    Briefly refers to Defoe as "the greatest man who wrote political satires in the interval which divides Dryden and Marvell from Addison and Swift," but who "does not rank among writers of satire as he will ever rank among writers of fiction." Finds the invective of his True-Born Englishman "coarse," and the versification "bad"; and the irony of the Shortest-Way with the Dissenters, "though strong, is neither very subtle nor very delicate." Reprinted: Essays from "The Quarterly Review" (London: Hurst & Blackett, 1861), p. 98.

8   LUTTRELL, NARCISSUS. A Brief Historical Relation of State Affairs from September 1678 to April 1714. 6 vols. Oxford: University Press, 5:469; 6:98, 215, 216, 224.
    Publishes the entries on Defoe in Luttrell's manuscript diary, preserved in seventeen octavo volumes at All Souls' College library. Reveals important biographical information from a reliable source: on Defoe's being ordered into custody for reflecting on Admiral Rooke (26 September 1704); on his being carried before Lord Chief Justice Holt for inserting a pretended speech on the Union in his Review, and his being bound over (15 October 1706); on his troubles with the Swedish envoy for reflecting on the Swedish king (23 September 1707) and with the Muscovite ambassador for certain bold expressions used in the Review (18 October 1707).

9   ROSE, HUGH JAMES. "De Foe, (Daniel)." In A New General Biographical Dictionary. 12 vols. London: T. Fellowes et al., 7:44-45.
    Summarizes the biographical information including some errors (such as the year of birth) which have long since been corrected. Praises Robinson Crusoe as "the most lasting monument" of his literary fame, but only lists the other novels.

10 TUCKERMAN, HENRY T. "The Writer for the People. Daniel De Foe." In Essays Biographical and Critical: Studies of a Character. Boston: Phillips, Sampson, & Co., pp. 285-303. Reprint of 1854.12.

1858

1   ALLIBONE, S. AUSTIN. "De Foe, Daniel, 1661-1731." In A Critical Dictionary of English Literature, and British and American Authors. Philadelphia: Childs & Peterson, 1:488-90.

Quotes a wide variety of critical opinion on Defoe and his works, which number at least 210.

2   BOHN, HENRY G. "De Foe's (Daniel) Works." In The Bibliogra-
     pher's Manual of English Literature . . . by William Thomas
     Lowndes. New ed., rev., corr. and enlarged. 4 vols. London:
     George Bell & Sons, 1:612-22.
         Revises 1834.1, by increasing the list of works assigned to
     Defoe as author to 202, some of which are designated with a "?"
     indicating "doubtful." Also, assigns the appropriate black
     letter capitals to indicate works republished in any of four
     "modern" collections. In the annotations, states specifically
     the corrections of 1834.1. Reprinted: London: Henry G. Bohn,
     1858; 1864; 1883; Bell & Daldy, 1865.

3   _____. "Notice to the Third Part." In The Bibliographer's
     Manual of English Literature . . . by William Thomas Lowndes.
     New ed., rev., corr. and enlarged. 4 vols. London: George
     Bell & Sons, 1:xiii-iv.
         Takes the occasion of his revised entry for Defoe in
     Lowndes (1858.2) to call attention to the relatively complete
     list of his writings and to defend the slowness of his publishing
     "the works of Defoe." Observes that "although Defoe ranks as a
     Classic, and is a household word with the English public," only
     his Robinson Crusoe is read: "all the rest find but a slow and
     unrequiting sale."

4   ß [pseud.]. "Carleton's Memoirs of an English Officer."
     Notes and Queries, 2d ser. 6, no. 150 (13 November):392-94.
         Reviews the established ideas of authorship for Capt.
     George Carleton, including George Carleton, Swift, and Defoe; and
     then argues for the Rev. Lancelot Carleton, A.M., rector of Pad-
     worth, as the author. See also 1859.9.

5   FOA, EUGÉNIE [RODRIGUES-GRADIS]. "Daniel Foé." In Les Petits
     Poètes et littérateurs, contes historiques dediés à la jeun-
     esse. Paris: Bédelet, pp. 113-38.
         A fictionalized story of Defoe's childhood.

6   FORSTER, JOHN. "Daniel De Foe." In Historical and Biographi-
     cal Essays. 2 vols. London: John Murray, 2:1-103.
         Differs slightly from 1855.3 (which had introduced the
     major changes into 1845.4. Unlike 1855.3, does not have a five-
     chapter division; in two places, uses the recently published
     diary of Narcissus Luttrell (1857); strengthens the appreciation
     of the novels by inserting (p. 96) an unidentified quotation from
     the Gentleman's Magazine. Reprinted: 1860.5; Gregg Internation-
     al Publishers, 1972.

7   JAYDEE [pseud.]. "'Pepys's Diary': De Foe." Notes and Que-
     ries, 2d ser. 6, no. 139 (28 August):164.
         Queries what has become of the original printing from which
     the portrait of Defoe is engraved in the new edition of Pepys's

<u>Diary</u> [4 vols., ed. Richard Lord Braybrook, Bohn's Historical Library]. Is it the same portrait as the one at the beginning of the <u>True Collection</u>?

8   JEAFFRESON, J[OHN] CORDY. "Daniel De Foe." In <u>Novels and Novelists, from Elizabeth to Victoria</u>. 2 vols. London: Hurst & Blackett, 1:65-84.
       Reprint of 1856.3, as a chapter coming after "Mrs. Behn" and before "Mrs. Manley." Omits the nine-column extract from <u>Colonel Jack</u>--about which Jeaffreson says in the original: "Who has read this extract without having the vision of Charles Dickens rise before his eyes?" See also the review, 1858.10.

9   "The Real Robinson Crusoe." <u>Boy's Own Magazine</u> 4, no. 1:1-8; no. 2:33-38; no. 3:78-83; no. 4:97-100; no. 5:129-34; no. 6: 161-66; no. 7:193-99; no. 8:225-30; no. 9:257-62.
       With Alexander Selkirk as the central character, narrates a series of apparently imaginary adventures framing the famous castaway experience on Juan Fernandez island. Supplies the motivation for Selkirk's abandonment in his persistent rivalry with Captain Stradling for the affections of "pretty Kitty" Felton, hostess of the Royal Salmon inn at St. Andrew. Creates a completely fictional backdrop which includes not only William Dampier, but even Marimonda the monkey, Selkirk's companion. Leans heavily on the theme that only "a deceitful philosophy" glorifies "the power of the solitary man" and that such a man can survive, only "by means which civilization and society have furnished." Connects the Selkirk story with <u>Robinson Crusoe</u> in the conclusion, noting such differences in "Defoe's version": the savage Caribs, Friday's replacing Marimonda, and the elevation of the romance "to all the dignity of a philosophical treatise." Stresses the crucial difference in that Selkirk desperately needs society and becomes "brutified" without it, and Crusoe is "improved and perfected" by solitude.

10   Review of J. Cordy Jeaffreson's <u>Novels and Novelists, from Elizabeth to Victoria</u>, 1858. <u>New Quarterly Review</u> 7, no. 25 (February):259-64.
       Comments severely on the book in general, and particularly on Jeafreson's favorable treatment of Defoe as a champion of liberty. See also 1858.8.

11   "Selkirk in Town. (A Song of September, by a middle-aged Guardsman, picked up in Rotten Row)." <u>Living Age</u> 59, no. 753 (30 October):479.
       Reprint of 1858.12.

12   "Selkirk in Town. (A Song of September, by a middle-aged Guardsman, picked up in Rotten Row)." <u>Punch</u> 35 (11 September):103.
       Anonymous parody of William Cowper's "Verses, Supposed to be written by Alexander Selkirk," 1782.2. Reprinted: 1858.11.

13   THOMPSON, PISHEY. "J.J. Defoe." Notes and Queries, 2d ser.
      6, no. 140 (4 September):191.
           Query and reply concerning John Joseph Defoe, executed on
      2 January 1771, a great grandson of the celebrated writer.

14   [WINDSOR, ARTHUR LLOYD.] Review of The Works of De Foe.
      Bohn, 1856. British Quarterly Review 27, no. 53 (January):
      85-105.
           Authorship identified in 1860.10. Views Defoe as the man
      whose career illustrates best "the class of whom he was among the
      foremost." Exuberantly describes him as the writer whose imagin-
      ation amused people for over a century and a half, but who is
      himself unknown. Places Defoe clearly on certain sides of con-
      troversial issues, and strongly supports the position with sharp
      details, for instance: his long admiration of, early acquaint-
      ance with, and resemblance to William III, and the tracts he
      wrote in his behalf. Using comparisons, first, with Bunyan:
      argues that as in Robinson Crusoe, "the powers of man are bent on
      the attainment of earthly objects" and observes appropriately
      that Defoe's "characters are least fictitious." Secondly, with
      Swift: finds the style and language in all Defoe's works to be
      "Herodoteanly simple," and illustrates the point effectively by
      comparing an Essay upon Projects with Swift's Directions to
      Servants [1745]. While the reviewer gives general praise of "an
      argosy of fiction," mentions specifically Memoirs of a Cavalier,
      "the History of the Plague," and Captain Singleton, but only to
      focus upon their "present neglect." Reprinted, in part:
      1860.10; Critical Heritage.

1859

1   A., M. "De Foe's Descendants." Notes and Queries, 2d ser. 8,
      no. 197 (8 October):299.
           Replies to 1859.6. Since the family of Defoe is now
      extinct and six descendants are living in the Baker lines, names
      the present representative as the Rev. H. De Foe Baker, Thruxton,
      Hants.

2   BESLY, JOHN. "Carleton's Memoirs." Notes and Queries, 2d
      ser. 7, no. 161 (29 January):93-94.
           Replies to 1858.4; 1859.9. Lists some of the evidence
      confirming the authenticity of Capt. George Carleton and opposing
      Defoe's authorship. Guesses that Dr. Johnson's designation of
      George Carleton, in Boswell's Life, should be corrected to read
      "One who had distinguished himself at the siege of Denia," in
      place of the reference to "Derry."

3   ß [pseud.]. "Carleton's Memoirs." Notes and Queries, 2d
      ser. 7, no. 164 (19 February):150.
           Replies to 1859.5, 10. Notes that the title of Capt.
      George Carleton differs from the one given in Wilson's Memoirs

of Defoe (1830), and cites internal evidence that the work was written between 1726 and 1728.

4   CHADWICK, WILLIAM. The Life and Times of Daniel De Foe. London: John Russell Smith, 464 pp.
        Describing himself as a tile-maker "about as successful as De Foe" and a person inexperienced in scholarship, produces the principal biography between Wilson's Memoirs (1830) and Lee's Defoe (1869). Sets his objective, "to elucidate the character and times of Daniel De Foe," in his own words rather than from gossip or anecdotes. Admits openly a large indebtedness to Wilson, to the point of saying that he avoided "scores of minor events" in order not to give the appearance of "copying" his work. Concentrates on a small number of events in Defoe's life (up to 1715), with very little pure biography (a gap of five to seven years, from 1680 on), and selects events as reflected in his works or in the large number of attacks by enemies such as Oldmixon, Leslie, and others. Gives disproportionate emphases to the Kentish petition, Queen Anne's "church in danger" politics, the controversy over occasional conformity, Defoe's missions for Harley, Sacheverell's trial of 1710. Persists in introducing current issues [1858] that are parallel to Defoe's (e.g., free trade or government interference with education) and identifying controversial figures (Richard Cobden or John Bright) with predecessors. Indulges his own biases and views, and distorts historical perspective. Claims, for instance, that the Complete English Tradesman, "perhaps one of the best books ever printed," formed the character of Benjamin Franklin. Chief among the villains here are Harley, "a tricky quirking man," and Queen Anne, "a very narrow-minded weak woman, the daughter of a narrow-minded, bigotted father"; and among the saints, William III; the bishops who opposed "the tackers" in the House of Commons; Sarah Duchess of Marlborough, "one of the greatest women England ever knew." Credits the dissenters with having considerable power, during the crisis over occasional conformity, through their control of the "moneyed interests." Detects the machinations of Harley in bringing down the Earl of Nottingham through Defoe's Shortest-Way with the Dissenters, and the Earl of Godolphin through Harley's own pamphlet, The Secret History of Arlus and Adolphus (1710). Adds [incorrectly] the Groans of Europe (1713) to Wilson's list of Defoe's works, reenforces errors in the canon by ascribing Union Proverb (1708) to Defoe, and is mainly conspicuous for the many works (especially of fiction), about which there is absolute silence. Broaches, now and then, larger significant themes, but for the most part pursues a random and unscholarly course. Aside from a perfunctory allusion or two to Robinson Crusoe and Captain Singleton, contributes almost nothing to literary criticism of the novels. See the review in Tait's Edinburgh Magazine, n.s. 26 (1859):389-98.

5   LETHREDIENSIS [pseud.]. "Carleton's Memoirs." Notes and Queries, 2d ser. 7, no. 159 (15 January):54.

Replies to 1859.9 by correcting the title of the first edition.

6   M., C. "De Foe's Descendants." <u>Notes and Queries</u>, 2d ser. 8, no. 185 (16 July):51.
On the Rev. Henry De Foe Baker who sold the manuscript of "The Compleat Gentleman" and the correspondence of Henry Baker to Mr. Dawson Turner, and was living in 1830; and on James De Foe, who received a subscription raised by Dickens and others, and died in May, 1857. Queries if there are any known descendants now living. See 1859.1.

7   MCCULLOCH, JOHN RAMSAY, ed. Preface to <u>A Select Collection of Scarce and Valuable Economical Tracts</u>. London: Lord Overstone, pp. viii-xi.
As background to the thirty-three page reprint of the rare tract, <u>Giving Alms No Charity</u> (1704), gives the arguments on both sides: Defoe's opposition, on principle, to the Sir Humphrey Mackworth Bill authorizing "the levy of a parochial rate for the carrying on of manufactures in workhouses," as contrasted with "the advantage of new and cheaper markets and of new and improved methods of production." Finds the observations on both poverty and charity to be "alike able and discriminating" as well as relevant to the present. Reprinted: New York: Augustus M. Kelley, 1966.

8   _____, ed, Preface to <u>A Select Collection of Scarce and Valuable Tracts on Commerce</u>. London: Lord Overstone, pp. vii-viii.
Offers a forty-page extract from <u>A Plan of the English Commerce</u> (2d ed., 1730). Assigns the work to Defoe as author: "desultory," but well written. Criticizes the public taste for neglecting Defoe entirely while giving considerable popularity to Gee's "inferior work." Reprinted: New York: Augustus M. Kelley, 1966; New York: Burt Franklin, 1972.

9   MARKLAND, J.H. "Carleton's Memoirs." <u>Notes and Queries</u>, 2d ser. 7, no. 157 (1 January):11-12.
Replies to 1858.4. Claims the authorship of <u>Capt. George Carleton</u> entirely for George Carleton, and cites evidence that the Rev. Lancelot Carleton, M.A., Rector of Padworth, could not possibly be the same person as the author. Refers to correspondence with the present Lord Stanhope, acknowledging that Defoe's share was "simply in the arrangement of Carleton's papers," and to General Stanhope's papers, which confirm both the authenticity of the <u>Memoirs</u> and the identity of George Carleton.

10   _____. "Carleton's Memoirs." <u>Notes and Queries</u>, 2d ser. 7, no. 160 (22 January):74.
Compares the title of the first edition as given in Wilson's <u>Memoirs</u> of Defoe (1830) with that in 1859.5. Asks if a second title-page could have been substituted, giving prominence

to the name George Carleton. Concludes also that Capt. George
Carleton must not have been widely available.

11   MASSON, DAVID. "British Novelists of the Eighteenth Century."
     In British Novelists and Their Styles: Being a Critical
     Sketch of the History of British Prose Fiction. Cambridge,
     Mass.: Macmillan & Co., pp. 79-98.
        Delivered first as one of four lectures to the Philosophi-
     cal Institution of Edinburgh in March and April, 1858, expresses
     the commonplace view of the eighteenth century as beginning with
     the Revolution of 1688 and closing with the French Revolution of
     1789, and as being "a prosaic age"--but certainly of outstanding
     prose. Starts "Modern British Fiction" with Defoe and Swift, and
     makes broad comparisons between the two writers relative to age,
     status, and Whig politics. Places Defoe's canon at 210 works.
     Contrasts Swift in his fictions as "the British satirist of his
     age" with Defoe, in his fictions, as the age's "chronicler or
     newspaper-reporter." Defoe, as a journalist, wrote novels which
     were "plain narrations": "it was his own robust sense of reality
     that led him to his style." His strength lay in the power of his
     imagination to fill in the minute circumstances when once he had
     the initial conception. Praises Memoirs of a Cavalier and the
     Journal of the Plague Year. For Robinson Crusoe, has the highest
     praise: "his genius in matter of fact necessarily produced the
     effect of a poem." Reprinted: Boston, Mass.: Willard Small,
     1889, pp. 87-106.

12   RIX, JOSEPH. "Carleton's Memoirs." Notes and Queries. 2d
     ser. 7, no. 164 (19 February):151.
        Replies to 1859.5, 10. Identifies the Edinburgh octavo
     edition, 1808, of Capt. George Carleton as the third edition.
     Queries if Walter Scott was the editor of this edition.

13   "Robinson Crusoe." Living Age 63, no. 610 (3 December): 610-
     13.
        Reprint of 1859.14.

14   "Robinson Crusoe." Saturday Review 8, no. 205 (1 October):
     394-96.
        Uses the occasion of a new reprint (Routledge) to place
     Robinson Crusoe among the "classics" and to define a classic as
     "etymologically a class-book," and explain why the book is a true
     classic. Among the qualities which a classic possesses: it must
     express "the broad average sentiments . . . in which the mass of
     mankind can sympathize"; it cannot be original in style or sympa-
     thetic to a particular point of view. As a true classic, Robin-
     son Crusoe has "the great peculiarity of being intensely origin-
     al, and at the same time very commonplace." Places emphasis on
     the special character of the book as arising from the author's
     temperament reflected in Crusoe. Of the two moral "impossibili-
     ties" kept from the reader, one is "the psychological side of the
     story"; the other, the account of Friday. Reprinted: 1859.13.

15   S., H. "De Foe's Descendants." <u>Notes and Queries</u>, 2d ser. 8,
     no. 192 (3 September):197.
          Replies to 1859.17. On the descendants of Defoe through
     the Henry Baker line: David Erskine Baker died without children;
     Henry Baker had one child, the Rev. William Baker, rector of
     Lyndon, co. Rutland, who died in 1828 and had three children--the
     Rev. Henry De Foe Baker (d.1845), William Baker, M.D. (d.1850),
     and Mary Baker. The Rev. Baker left two children: the Rev. Hen-
     ry De Foe Baker and Harriet Elizabeth Baker; and Dr. Baker had
     four children: the Rev. William De Foe Baker, Charles Bernard
     Baker, Sophia Baker (d.1853), and Emily Dallas Baker.

16   S., T.G. "Carleton's Memoirs." <u>Notes and Queries</u>, 2d ser. 7,
     no. 167 (12 March):223.
          Replies to 1859.3. Gives the title of Sir Walter Scott's
     edition published by Archibald Constable & Co. at Edinburgh,
     1808, as it was first announced. Identifies the 1809 edition as
     the 1808 with a new title page.

17   ST., W. "De Foe's Descendants." <u>Notes and Queries</u>, 2d ser.
     8, no. 187 (30 July):94.
          Replies to 1859.6. Gives detailed information from the
     fly-leaf of a pocket-Bible on the descendants of Henry Baker and
     Sophia De Foe, married 30 April 1729: David Erskine Baker, born
     30 January 1730; and Henry Baker, born 10 February 1734. From a
     note in the <u>New England Genealogical Register</u>, July 1858: James
     De Foe was the father of eight children, of whom James and
     Priscilla survive.

18   Y., J. "Carleton's Memoirs." <u>Notes and Queries</u>, 2d ser. 7,
     no. 164 (19 February):150–51.
          Replies to 1859.5, 10. Quotes the advertisement of <u>Capt.
     George Carleton</u> from the <u>Evening Post</u>, 25–27 July 1728. Notes
     that it corresponds exactly with the title as given in Wilson's
     <u>Memoirs</u> of Defoe (1830).

[<u>185–</u>]

1   "Biographical Memoir of Daniel De Foe." In <u>The Life and
     Adventures of Robinson Crusoe</u>. London: Willoughby & Co.,
     pp. v–xxii.
          Concerns itself almost exclusively with biography, includ-
     ing such long-standing errors as Defoe's first production, <u>Specu-
     lum Crape Gownorum</u> (1682), or his writing the <u>Review</u> while in
     Newgate. On the novels: accepts Sir Walter Scott's judgment
     that Defoe's fame will rest upon his "popular narratives," and
     not his political works. Briefly discusses the novels borrowing
     the classification into "three kinds" from Scott as well as the
     misinformation about Defoe's residence in Limehouse. To give
     proof of Defoe's independence of Selkirk, quotes Woodes Rogers's
     account (1712). Reprinted, in part: 1850.

<u>1860</u>

1   BYRON, HENRY JAMES. <u>Robinson Crusoe; or, Harlequin Friday</u>
    <u>and the King of the Caribbee Islands</u>. <u>A Grotesque Pantomime</u>
    <u>Opening</u>. Reprint. <u>English Plays of the Nineteenth Century</u>.
    Vol. 5, <u>Pantomimes, Extravaganzas and Burlesques</u>. Edited by
    Michael R. Booth. Oxford: Clarendon Press, 1976, pp. 247-85.
        First performed at the Princess's Theatre, 26 December
    1860. Frames the action of Crusoe shipwrecked, "riding on a
    raft" to the island, later surrounded by his animals while the
    air "Oh, poor Robinson Crusoe" is played. When Crusoe discovers
    his beloved Jenny Pigtail, he asks, "How do I find you here?"
    Jenny replies, "Oh, I don't know. / There's nothing about me,
    dear, / in Defoe." And Crusoe: "But talking of <u>de foe</u>, where is
    de enemy?" See also <u>Plays by H.J. Byron</u>, ed. Jim Davis (Cam-
    bridge University Press, 1984), p. 216.

2   [DICKENS, CHARLES.] "The Uncommercial Traveller." <u>All the</u>
    <u>Year Round</u>, n.s. 3, no. 72 (8 September):517-21.
        The table of contents for <u>All the Year Round</u> (1860) gives
    the title "Nursery Stories"; the title "Nurse's Stories" seems to
    appear first in the reprints. In a series of autobiographical
    recollections, starts by telling of places which, "in an idle
    mood," I [Dickens] would like to revisit. The first, "Robinson
    Crusoe's Island": "I frequently return there." Vivid details,
    which are recalled in connection with specific incidents of
    <u>Robinson Crusoe</u>, impressed him as a boy. Reprinted: "Nurse's
    Stories," in <u>The Uncommercial Traveller and Reprinted Pieces</u>, New
    Oxford Illustrated Dickens (London: Oxford University Press,
    1958), pp. 148-49.

3   [ESPINASSE, FRANCIS.] "Histories of Publishing Houses.
    No. II--The House of Longman. Chapter I.--Thomas Longman, the
    Founder. Lombard-street and Pater-noster-row, 1716-55."
    <u>Critic</u> 20, no. 507 (24 March):366-72 passim.
        Author identified in Hutchins's <u>"Robinson Crusoe" and Its</u>
    <u>Printing</u> (1925), p. 43. Traces history of the current publishing
    firm, Longmans, Green, and Co., to William Taylor, stationer and
    bookseller at the sign of the Ship. Describes Taylor's publica-
    tions prior to <u>Robinson Crusoe</u> and his purchase of the Black Swan
    from the Churchill brothers next door. Repeats the established
    traditions of Defoe's seeking a publisher throughout the trade
    and Taylor's making a profit of £1,000. For an assessment of
    Espinasse's accuracy, see Hutchins, pp. 43-51.

4   EVANS, MARY ANN [George Eliot]. "Mr. Riley Gives His Advice
    Concerning a School for Tom." In <u>The Mill on the Floss</u>.
    3 vols. Edinburgh and London: William Blackwood & Sons.
    Reprint. Edited by Gordon S. Haight. Oxford: Clarendon
    Press, 1980, pp. 14-17.
        In chap. 3, the child Maggie Tulliver drops the "heavy
    book," which she has been admiring for its pictures; it turns

out to be Defoe's "The History of the Devil" (1726). She tells
of one "dreadful picture," a woman being tested by water to see
if she is a witch; and of another, a blacksmith, one of the
shapes taken by the devil. Reprinted (partial list): 1860;
1862; 1867; 1869; 1870; 1877; 1878.

5   FORSTER, JOHN. "Daniel De Foe." In Oliver Cromwell. Daniel
    De Foe. Sir Richard Steele. Charles Churchill. Samuel
    Foote. Biographical Essays. 3d ed.; London: John Murray,
    pp. iii-vi, ix-xiv, 57-158.
        Reprint, with additions, of 1855.3 and 1858.6. Shows the
    same biographical and critical techniques described in these en-
    tries and 1845.4. Evidences the same scrupulousness with docu-
    ments and sources; takes care, in the notes, to identify recent
    information by appending the date "1860." Most important, Fors-
    ter shows himself here not only as a person who collects manu-
    scripts, but one who uses them effectively. In the preface,
    states that he has added information from Defoe's family papers
    "obtained by me since the last edition appeared, and one letter,
    hitherto unprinted, written by De Foe himself." Prints two let-
    ters in their entirety, and calls attention to the specific inci-
    dent of his biography to which they relate. From a manuscript,
    "now in my possession," tells the full story of Henry Baker's
    five-year courtship of Sophia Defoe and the dowry negotiations--
    for the first time ever, almost fully, in Baker's own words. The
    additions set in greater relief the Defoe letter concerning the
    troubles with his second son, which Forster had already published
    earlier and which he had described as "one of the most affecting
    that the English language contains." Reprinted: Folcroft, 1973.

6   O., J. "Robinson Crusoe Abridged." Notes and Queries,
    2d ser. 9, no. 219 (10 March):178.
        Identifies Thomas Gent, printer of York, as the person who
    abridged Robinson Crusoe "into a twelve-penny book" for his mas-
    ter, Edward Midwinter (Gent's autobiography, 1832.1). Gives the
    title of this favorite undated abridgement, The Wonderful Life
    and most surprising Adventures of R. Crusoe, of York, Mariner
    (n.d.). See also 1860.11.

7   READE, CHARLES. The Eighth Commandment. Boston: Ticknor &
    Fields, pp. 274-75.
        Argues that English drama declines and French drama rises
    because "talent follows the market with the utmost fidelity." In-
    cludes among the examples Bunyan and Defoe as writers of fiction
    that was not brought "unbaptized into the market," but claims
    that Defoe was an exception to the general truth about talent; he
    "lied like a tooth-drawer, to keep out of so low a market as un-
    theatrical fiction." Cites the prefaces to Mrs. Veal, Robinson
    Crusoe, and New Voyage Round the World.

8   RIX, S.W. "Theophilus Gay, M.D.: William Gay, M.D." Notes
    and Queries, 2d ser. 10, no. 244 (1 September):169.

In a query for information about the two men named Gay, mentions a portrait (by Thomas Foster) and an engraving of the Rev. Timothy Cruso, whose surname Defoe borrowed.

9   ROSCOE, WILLIAM CALDWELL. Poems and Essays. Edited by Richard Holt Hutton. 2 vols. London: Chapman & Hall, 2:222-63, 271, 433-34.

     Reprints the highly regarded essay "Defoe as a Novelist," first published in the National Review, 1856.9. While the editor Hutton assigns the authorship to Roscoe, as does the Wellesley Index, Pat Rogers suggests, in Critical Heritage (p. 21), that Walter Bagehot may have written the essay. The reprint shows only minor changes in paragraphing and punctuation; but more important, entitles the essay "Unideal Fiction: De Foe," and places it for balance just after the essay "Unideal Poetry: Crabbe." In other critical essays, draws comparisons between writers: Thackeray's more complicated mode of creating "an impression of reality" and Defoe's; a comment on "the De-Foe school of mind" which will not be satisfied with partial beliefs—springing from a contrast of Catherine Crowe and Defoe as narrators who deal with ghosts of the imagination.

10   WINDSOR, ARTHUR LLOYD. "De Foe and the Rise of Pamphleteering." In Ethica: or, Characteristics of Men, Manners, and Books. London: Smith, Elder & Co., pp. 178-214.

     Reprinted from 1858.14. Inserts new material in appropriate places on contemporary pamphlet-writers, the early reign of Queen Anne, and the "New Robinson Crusoe."

11   WOODWARD, B.B. "A Penny Robinson Crusoe." Notes and Queries, 2d ser. 9, no. 223 (7 April):276.

     Replies to 1860.6, citing "a twelvepenny pamphlet" abridging Robinson Crusoe, printed by Marsden, at Chelmsford, purchased some forty years ago.

1861

1   CHAMBERS, ROBERT. Domestic Annals of Scotland from the Revolution to the Rebellion of 1745. Edinburgh and London: W. & R. Chambers, pp. 322-37, 351.

     Relies heavily upon a close reading of Caledonia (1707) and especially the History of the Union (1709) for explaining events related to the incorporating the Union and such intricate financial issues as "the Equivalent Money." Describes Defoe's participation (1706-1707) as dangerous, and his role even heroic. Includes mention of a few other activities after the Union.

2   [CHEEVER, D.W.] Review of Works (1840-1841). Christian Examiner 71, 5th ser. 9, no. 3 (November):340-53.

     Authorship given in Research Keys to the American Renaissance, ed. Kenneth Walter Cameron (Hartford: Transcendental

Books, 1967). Stays close to the interpretations found in the
Works (1840-1841), allowing emphasis on Christian or religious
matters. Tends to read Defoe literally; for example, the Appeal
to Honour and Justice as a straightforward autobiography; Colonel
Jack and Moll Flanders, as his "pure mind" confronting "the most
degraded criminals." Follows a standard classification of the
writings, judging "his merits as a poet, novelist, polemic, or
commercial writer,--as an historian, a moralist, and a man."
Places the four other novels on a par with Robinson Crusoe, while
admitting their infelicitous subjects.

3   CROMPTON, SARAH. The Life of Robinson Crusoe in Short Words.
     London: James Hogg & Sons, 124 pp.
         Drastically alters the original by using only short words.
Changes Crusoe's home town to Exeter, and omits entirely the
scenes of "the cannibal savages" as unfit for "early" readers.
Concludes with a final chapter on a visit in 1859 to Crusoe's
island, Juan Fernandez.

4   DENIS, FERDINAND. "Notice sur le matelot Selkirk, sur l'ile
     de Juan-Fernandez, sur les Caraibes et les Puelches." In
     Aventures de Robinson Crusoé par Daniel De Foë. Paris:
     Morizot, pp. 407-32.
         Reprint of 1836.5; 1845.6. Although Denis has already
published his "Notice" in the Petrus Borel and Madame Tastu translations, for the first time appears alone in a French edition
elegantly illustrated by Gavarni (pseudonym for Sulpice Guillaume
Chevalier).

5   FORTUNA NON MUTAT GENUS [pseud.]. "Descendants of Daniel
     De Foe." Notes and Queries, 2d ser. 9, no. 277 (20 April):
     303-4.
         Quotes from the Times (London), 25 March 1861, on the death
of Defoe's great grandson in 1857, and the "memorial" sent to the
prime minister, Lord Palmerston, to obtain a small grant of £100
from the Queen's Bounty to aid the two distressed great-great-
granddaughters of "one of the most remarkable writers of
England."

6   PATON, A[NDREW] A[RCHIBALD]. Researches on the Danube and the
     Adriatic. 2 vols. Leipzig: F.A. Brockhaus, 1:105.
         Records the author's visit to a monastery at Manasia in Ser-
via, and the toast by one of the monks complimenting the author
as a traveller: "The greatest traveller of your country that we
know of was that wonderful navigator, Robinson Crusoe, of York,
who, poor man, met with many and great difficulties, but at
length, by the blessing of God, was restored to his native country, his family, and his friends." See also Quarterly Review 117
(January, 1865):99. Reprinted: London: Trübner, 1862.

7   "Robinson Crusoe's Island." All the Year Round 5, no. 103 (13
     April):64-67.

Disputes the constant association in the popular mind for
over more than a hundred years, of the name Robinson Crusoe and
the island of Juan Fernandez because of the Selkirk story. Demonstrates the significant differences between the Selkirk and the
Crusoe stories, especially in the geographical locations of their
respective island. Offers the more likely "conjecture" that the
narrative of the Spanish sailor Peter Serrano, as it appeared in
the translation of Sir Paul Rycant [Rycaut], provided Defoe with
the main incidents for Robinson Crusoe. Serrano's island, now
called the Serrano Keys, lies "about midway between Cuba and the
Isthmus of Panama," only two degrees farther south and eighteen
degrees farther east than the location of Crusoe's Island given
by Defoe. Quotes extensively from Rycaut's translation of Garcilaso de la Vega's "Royal Commentaries of the Yncas" (1688), written originally in Spanish, to demonstrate the resemblances to the
Crusoe story.

8   WHATELY, RICHARD. "Lecture II. On the Origin of Civiliza-
     tion." In Miscellaneous Lectures and Reviews. London:
     Parker, Son, & Bourn, pp. 38-39.
        Uses Friday and the other savages to illustrate the mis-
     take, shared by Defoe's readers, of representing savages as being
     far more docile and intelligent than they actually are. Such
     savages are depicted "as wanting merely the knowledge that is
     possessed by civilised [sic] man, and as not deficient in the
     civilised character."

9   _____. Review of Jane Austen's Northanger Abbey and Per-
     suasion. In Miscellaneous Lectures and Reviews. London:
     Parker, Son, & Bourn, pp. 293-94.
        Reprint of 1821.4.

                              1862

1   COLLIER, WILLIAM FRANCIS. A History of English Literature, in
     a Series of Biographical Sketches. London: T. Nelson & Sons,
     pp. v, 252.
        In a history of English literature which divides writers
     into "Ten Eras," each developed around a principal author, ex-
     presses regret for assigning Defoe to a secondary place in the
     Fifth Era; in a short paragraph barely mentions Robinson Crusoe
     ("No English writer has ever excelled him in his power of paint-
     ing fictitious events in the colours of truth") and Mrs. Veal.
     Reprinted: Toronto: James Campbell & Son, 1872.

2   "Daniel De Foe." In The Adventures of Robinson Crusoe.
     London: Bickers & Bush, pp. xiii-xxxi.
        Presents mainly a well-informed biographical summary.
     Speculates at the outset on whether or not biographical details
     of Defoe would matter to the many boy readers of Robinson Crusoe.
     Nine-tenths of those readers believe that the hero Crusoe did

exist "in the flesh" and that his story was "narrated to" Defoe.
It comes as a blow to the reader to discover that Crusoe is fictitious and his creator has a reality of his own. Indulges in
only a few speculations: Defoe was "the sort of boy, in fact,
who runs away to sea"; while in Newgate, during 1704, he pro-
jected novels and pamphlets. Barely mentions the novels (2 pp.)
other than Robinson Crusoe. Reprinted: 1864.

3   DAVIES, J. ALEXANDER. "Robinson Crusoe." Notes and Queries,
    3d ser. 1, no. 16 (19 April):308.
        Accepts the ambiguity in the words "a just history of
facts" which the Editor uses to describe Robinson Crusoe in the
preface to Part One, but rejects ambiguity in a similar passage
of the preface to Part Two.

4   GALLOWAY, WILLIAM. "The Scottish Aceldama." Notes and
    Queries, 3d ser. 2, no. 52 (27 December):510.
        Continues an inquiry started by Chessborough (4 October)
and Sholto Macduff (18 October). Traces the account of "the
murder of 18,000 Presbyterians by 'black prelacy'" to Defoe's
Memoirs of the Church of Scotland (1717), and cites as source
beyond this book "Oral Tradition" or "Living Witnesses."

5   GREEN, T[HOMAS] H[ILL]. "An Estimate of the Value and Influ-
    ence of Works of Fiction in Modern Times." In Works of Thomas
    Hill Green. 3 vols. London: Longmans, Green, & Co., 3:28,
    36, 42-43.
        Describes a view of the novel as a form taken by the imagin-
ation, creative rather than passive, like the art of the painter
rather than the photographer. Selects the time of Addison as one
in which all the elements of the novel existed, but separately:
in Defoe's fictitious biographies, "a life-like reality which has
never since been equalled"; in the popular drama, plots; adventures that reveal character as in Addison, instead of being external as in Defoe. Observes later that the novelist must omit
or pass over quickly important human experiences; Defoe surpasses
other writers, but only through his inartistic "agglomeration of
details." Sums up Defoe as a social reformer by contrasting the
"vulgar" moral given in his preface to Moll Flanders (vice punish-
ed, virtue rewarded) with the "'harsh grating' cry of suffering
humanity," which he inserts into the histories of his thieves and
harlots.

6   H., C., and COOPER, THOMPSON. "Dr. Joseph Browne." Notes and
    Queries, 3d ser. 2, no. 27 (5 July):13-14.
        Of the seventeen works Browne wrote or edited, A Vindica-
tion of His Translation of Horace refers to Defoe in the full
title.

7   HAZLITT, W. CAREW. "Lowndes Bibliographer's Manual. Notes on
    the New Edition No. V." Notes and Queries, 3d ser. 2, no. 40
    (4 October):268-69.

Briefly comments on four Defoe items, two of which are
printed in Hazlitt's Works of Daniel De Foe (1840-1843): Christian Conversation (1720), "most probably from Defoe's pen"; Narrative of the Proceedings in France (1724), "possibly not by
Defoe."

8   KELLY, T[HOMAS] W. "Metrical Leaves, from Robinson Crusoe."
    In Night Among the Fairies; St. Agnes' Fountain, or the
    Enshrined Heart; the Peri's Charm; and Other Poems. Reprint.
    London: The Author, pp. 194-213.
        The date on the title page is 1842; the date at the end of
    the dedication, 1862. Reprints nine poems versifying memorable
    scenes from Robinson Crusoe or eulogizing Defoe, Selkirk, and
    Juan Fernandez. Includes an enthusiastic introduction made up of
    quotations, and has notes expanding upon natural history. Iden-
    tifies "Stanzas" as having already appeared in the Rev. H. Steb-
    bing's edition (1832); and "Crusoe's Solitude," in the Rev. J.F.
    Russell's edition (1847.3).

9   MERTIAN, H. "Le Robinson de la légende." Études religieuses,
    philosophiques et historiques, 3d ser. 1:372-85 passim.
        Begins the discussion of the Bollandists' life of St. Ma-
    caire, canonized in Greece since the tenth century, by referring
    briefly to P.V. de Buck's rejection of the saint as being no more
    a real person than "Robinson Crusoe among the English and Don
    Quijotte among the Spanish."

10 NEWMAN, F[RANCIS] W[ILLIAM]. "Modern Latin as a Basis of
    Instruction." Museum 1, no. 4 (January):409-21.
        Calls for "a Latin novel or romance . . . a pleasing tale
    of fiction" which would contain numerous Latin words not avail-
    able in poetry, history, or philosophy; and recommends "an imita-
    tion of the story of Robinson Crusoe," with its many references
    to special occupations, written in the simple style of Terence.
    For Newman's Rebilius Cruso: Robinson Crusoe, in Latin, see
    1884.7.

11 Preface to Robinson Crusoe. London: Bell & Daldy, pp. iii-
    viii.
        Avoids any biography, and concentrates wholly on an inform-
    ed assessment. Ranks Robinson Crusoe with Shakespeare, Pilgrim's
    Progress, and Holy Scripture. Describes the book's freshness,
    "plain and homely" style, accessibility to all classes. Parades
    the testimonials of Marmontel, Sir Walter Scott, Dr. Johnson,
    Blair, and Beattie. Staunchly defends Defoe against any charge
    of impropriety with respect to Selkirk. Admits that Selkirk's
    adventures made "a strong impression" on Defoe, but provided no
    more than "the slight fabric" of his romance. Aside from Robin-
    son Crusoe, only the Journal of the Plague Year receives mention
    by title.

12   SLOCOMBE, RD. "Quotation." <u>Notes and Queries</u>, 3d ser. 2,
      no. 35 (30 August):166.
          Without mentioning Defoe's <u>Robinson Crusoe</u>, Part One,
      queries the author of the verse: "For sudden joys, like grief,
      confound at first."

13   TOLSTOY, LEV N[IKOLAEVICH]. "The School at Yásnaya Polyána."
      <u>Yásnaya Polyána</u> (February). Reprint. [<u>Works</u>.] Translated
      and edited by Leo Wiener. Illustrated Sterling Edition.
      Boston: Dana Estes & Co., 1904, 4:262, 270.
          Describes the difficulties that his Russian pupils had
      during the summer of 1862 at Yásnaya Polyána school in trying
      to use <u>Robinson Crusoe</u> as graded reading to gain "knowledge of
      the literary language." So complete was the "vexation" of some
      boys that they wept and became angry. With Tolstoy's telling
      the story in his own words, they soon believed in "the possi-
      bility of grasping that wisdom, made out of the meaning of it."

14   WERL, ADOLPH. <u>Robinson's Stammbaum: eine Skizze der Robin-
      son-Jugendliteratur: nebst einer Abfertigung der Herren
      Julius Petzholdt und Emil Hallier</u>. 3d ed. Leipzig: Verlag
      der Expedition des Camp'schen Robinson, 17 pp.
          Includes a fold-out chart showing the various German-
      language adaptations for "children" of the Robinson story, and
      presents a sharp, taunting critique of some incompetent scholar-
      ship by Petzholdt and Hallier, who had evidently attempted to
      "defend" the "originality" of J.H. Campe's <u>Robinson der Jüngere</u>
      (1779- 1782 and later) against the "mimicry" of the "upstart,"
      Friedrich Campe's <u>Robinson Crusoe der Ältere</u> (1810 or 1812? and
      later).
                                                        (P.E.C.)

                              1862-1865

1   KJER, J., tr. "Robinsonimik nukardlermik" [a translation of
      Defoe's <u>Robinson Crusoe</u>]. <u>Atuagagdliutit</u>, nos. 8-12 (16
      October-15 December 1862); nos. 30-36 (10 October-3 December
      1864); nos. 39-41 (30 December 1864-13 January 1865).
          In Eskimo. Translates <u>Robinson Crusoe</u> into Eskimo for the
      first time, with a few plates lithographed in color by Lars
      Møller. See also Nathan Van Patten, "An Eskimo Translation of
      Defoe's <u>Robinson Crusoe</u>, Godthaab, Greenland, 1862-1865," <u>Papers
      of the Bibliographical Society of America</u> 36 (1942):56-58.

                               1863

1   B. "Alexander Selkirk's Cup and Chest." <u>Notes and Queries</u>,
      3d ser. 4, no. 96 (31 October):348.
          Includes an extract stating that the cup and chest of
      Alexander Selkirk, "the world-famed Robinson Crusoe of Defoe,"
      now the property of Mr. James Hutchinson, London.

2   DENIS, FERDINAND, and CHAUVIN, VICTOR. <u>Les Vrais Robinsons:</u>
    <u>Naufrages, solitude, voyages</u>. Paris: Librairie du Magasin
    Pittoresque, pp. 1-17, 133-43, 358-59, 370-73.
        Announce in the preface a strong preference for authentic
    rather than fictional narratives of "solitaires." Firmly set up
    <u>Robinson Crusoe</u> as the prototype, created by "the ingenious
    father of so numerous a posterity," and argue forcefully that
    "Daniel De Foe must have originally resorted to authentic narra-
    tives, real adventures, expression of sentiments which eternally
    stir the fibers of the heart, because they are true." Urge fur-
    ther that Defoe's "true merit" rises from the power of his imagin-
    ation and that those who believe in only a part of <u>Robinson Cru-</u>
    <u>soe</u> are mistaken. Give selections here that are not "imaginary
    Robinsons" but "Robinsons of necessity." In the lengthy survey
    of solitaires, call them "Robinsons" throughout, starting with "a
    mythological Robinson," going through "fantastic Robinsons" and
    concluding with true Robinsons. Includes a chapter on Selkirk,
    "the acknowledged model of <u>Robinson Crusoe</u>" (10 pp.) and notes on
    the island Juan Fernandez (3 pp.), taken partly from 1861.4. See
    also 1865.2.

3   G., J.A. "The Storm of 1703." <u>Notes and Queries</u>, 3d ser. 3,
    no. 61 (28 February):168.
        Refers to <u>The Storm</u> (1704) without recognizing the author
    to be Defoe, and specifically to a manuscript note there about
    performances of <u>Macbeth</u> and <u>The Tempest</u> at the very same time as
    the storm and about "the amusement and mockery" created. See
    replies, 1863.6-7; 1864.12; 1865.10.

4   "Notices to Correspondents." <u>Notes and Queries</u>, 3d ser. 3,
    no. 70 (2 May):360.
        Replies to 1864.17: no copy of Clarke's <u>Naufragia</u> (1805)
    listed in the British Museum or Bodleian catalogue; strong rejec-
    tion of Harley, Earl of Oxford, as author of <u>Robinson Crusoe</u>,
    given in Wilson's <u>Memoirs</u> of Defoe (1830).

5   TAINE, H[IPPOLYTE]. "Les romanciers." In <u>Histoire de la lit-</u>
    <u>térature anglaise</u>. Paris: Librairie Hachette. Translated by
    H[enri] Van Laun. Reprint. Edinburgh: Edmonston & Douglas,
    [1880], 3, 257-70, 329.
        Turns to the novelists of "the classic age" in book 3,
    chap. 6; starts with Defoe. Links the biographical information
    concerning Defoe (some of which is inaccurate) to a view of the
    fiction as joyless: "like a Presbyterian and a plebeian, with
    low subjects and moral aims, to treat of the adventures, and
    reform the conduct of thieves and prostitutes, workmen and sail-
    ors." Finds Defoe always under the compulsion to carry out this
    duty. Argues that his imagination was a business man's, and not
    an artist's, "crammed and, as it were, jammed down with facts."
    Describes the sense of the real in the fictions which he mentions
    (omits <u>Roxana</u>), and employs the paradox (details are so dull and
    tedious that they must be true) to explain the illusion. On the

apparition in <u>Mrs. Veal</u>, invites a comparison in a footnote with
Poe's "The Facts in the Case of M. Waldemar": "The American is a
suffering artist; De Foe is a citizen, who has common sense."
Consistently views <u>Robinson Crusoe</u> as a work whose art reveals it
to be both moral and English. Discerns in Crusoe a will and an
enthusiasm which formerly produced sea-kings in England, and now
produce emigrants and squatters in Australia or America. Reprinted: (French) frequently; (translation) 1871, 1873, etc.;
<u>Critical Heritage</u>.

6   WYLIE, CHARLES. "The Storm of 1703." <u>Notes and Queries</u>,
     3d ser. 3, no. 62 (7 March):197-98; no. 66 (4 April):273-74.
        Replies to 1863.3. On the storm of 1703: quotes lines
from Addison's <u>The Campaign</u> [1705] as well as the Lord Treasurer
Godolphin's approval, in Tickell's preface to the <u>Works</u> of
Addison (1721). Presents lengthy extracts also from the <u>Monthly
Mercury</u>, vol. 14 for 1703.

7   X., X.A. "The Storm of 1703." <u>Notes and Queries</u>, 3d ser. 3,
     no. 68 (18 April):319.
        Replies to 1863.3, 6. Notes that if the storm of 1703 was
treated with "amusement and mockery" by theatre groups, there
were also those who found "religious admonition and improvement"
in the event.

                              1864

1   "Advertisement" and "Memoir of De Foe." In <u>The Life and Adven-
     tures of Robinson Crusoe</u>. London: Routledge, Warne, & Rout-
     ledge, pp. v-vi, xiii-xx.
        Offers the highest praise of Defoe, one of a cluster of
men--Shakespeare, Bacon, Milton, Bunyan, and Newton--whose influence on mankind is only less than that of Scripture. Conveys
biographical information accurate for its time. Notes that Defoe, while in Newgate, "stored his mind with those facts relative
to the habits and pursuits of the prisoners, which he has detailed with so much truth to nature, as well as interest." Aside
from comments on <u>Robinson Crusoe</u>, devotes only a brief paragraph
to the other novels, but makes no mention at all of <u>Roxana</u>.
Among the positive qualities described in a final summary paragraph: he had "an unforced power" that on occasion rises to the
sublime. Reprinted ("Memoir"): 1869; 1872; 1879; [1884];
[190-]; [19--].

2   B[ABSON], J[OSEPH] E[DWARD], ed. <u>Eliana: Being the Hitherto
     Uncollected Writings of Charles Lamb</u>. New York: Hurd & Hough-
     ton; Boston: W. Veazie. Reprint. New York: W.J. Widdleton,
     1866, pp. v-ix, 59-67, 114-17, 167-71.
        In the preface, describes his manner of searching for uncol-
lected writings of Lamb in out-of-the-way books and periodicals--
and the sheer joy of his discoveries. Reprints as by Lamb "The

Good Clerk, A Character," which in the Reflector (1811) is said
to be written by L.B.; "Estimate of De Foe's Secondary Novels"
(1830); and "Reflections in the Pillory" (1825).

3   BROWNE, J. ROSS. Crusoe's Island: A Ramble in the Footsteps
    of Alexander Selkirk. With Sketches of Adventure in Califor-
    nia and Washoe. New York: Harper & Brothers, 165 pp.
        Shows the author's deep admiration for the seafaring life
    from his early reading of Robinson Crusoe, his later visits to
    Juan Fernandez, and his "glowing day-dreams of Robinson Crusoe"
    there among the relics of Alexander Selkirk. Recalls his fa-
    ther's gift of an illustrated volume, his childhood fantasies,
    and his desire "to become as wonderful a man as Robinson Cru-
    soe." Now, at Juan Fernandez, realizes that Crusoe may be no
    more than "the simple mariner Alexander Selkirk." In chap. 16,
    tells of the author and a few characters who sit drinking tea and
    listening to Abraham sing nine stanzas of ballad-like verses,
    "Poor Robinson Crusoe," which "it has been customary to introduce
    . . . in the character of Jerry Sneak in Foote's celebrated
    farce, the Mayor of Garratt." Notes that the verses came into
    existence because of the book's popularity. See also 1820.7.

4   C., B.S. "A Shropshire Inscription." Notes and Queries,
    3d ser. 6, no. 149 (5 November):370.
        Replies to 1864.6. Quotes an inscription read in front
    of a school-house in Shropshire, having only a remote connection
    with the first two lines of the True-Born Englishman.

5   C., H. "De Foe and Dr. Livingstone." Notes and Queries,
    3d ser. 5, no. 118 (2 April):281.
        Having read Captain Singleton and the "late travels" of
    Dr. [David] Livingstone, notes that Defoe must have known some
    African traveler. Raises a query about a book he remembers with
    an old map showing the route of a Portuguese traveler through the
    southern part of Africa. See 1864.20.

6   CYRIL. "Plagiarisms." Notes and Queries, 3d ser. 6, no. 142
    (17 September):231.
        Queries whether the first two lines of the True-Born
    Englishman may not be plagiarized from George Herbert's Jacula
    Prudentum, and the editor suggests that they might be "a well-
    known expression, or popular saying at the time." See replies,
    1864.4, 15, 19.

7   "Daniel Defoe, Author of Robinson Crusoe, As Exhibited in His
    Own Correspondence, Now First Published." London Review of
    Politics, Society, Literature, Art, and Science 8 (4 and 11
    June):590-91, 617-18.
        Announces anonymously--and the news received with shock--
    the discovery in the State Paper Office of five letters, written
    26 April through 13 June 1718, from Defoe to Charles De la Faye,
    Under-secretary in the office of the Secretary of State for the

Northern Department. Not only were the actual letters printed,
and Defoe revealed to have been working for leading Tory journals, he had also been secretly in the employ of the Whig Ministry for the express purpose of enervating and disabling the
opposition Tory papers. Beginning with disappointment that the
author of Robinson Crusoe could have descended to "the baseness
and dishonesty revealed in his own correspondence," becomes
vitriolic in its condemnation of Defoe's "dirty and disreputable
work." Levels scurrilous charges against him including the
authorship of the Memoirs Concerning the Affairs of Scotland
(1714) which, as Lee rightly pointed out, was not only well known
to be the work of George Lockhart, it even contained a severe
attack on "that vile Monster and Wretch Daniel De Foe." See also
the June 18 and 25 issues of the London Review for the continuation of the controversy, and the expansion to a larger audience
with the publication by L.O. of the original five letters and
another letter, in Notes and Queries (1864.16), in order to have
them "readily available for future use" and to stimulate from
"Defoe's admirers" a defence of his conduct. In 1865.5, 7, and
9, William Lee gave the spirited defence. In vols. 2 and 3 of
his Defoe (1869), Lee reprinted Defoe's contributions to the
journals that are identified in the letters as being the ones
managed by Defoe. For a reprinting of the letters, see Healey.

8   DE MORGAN, A[UGUSTUS]. "Cheap Repository Tracts." Notes and
     Queries, 3d ser. 6, no. 143 (24 September):243.
         Lists the title only of a Cheap Repository Tract, "Plague
in London, with suitable Thoughts," in the subscription plan of
the Religious Tract Society. See 1864.11.

9   HETZEL, PIERRE JULES [P.J. Stahl]. Preface to Le Robinson
     suisse. Translated by E[ugène] Muller. Reprint. 6th ed.
     Paris: Bibliothèque d'Éducation et de Récréation; J. Hetzel
     & Co., [1876], pp. iii-xii.
         Recognizes, briefly, that Rudolph Wyss does not matter in
letters compared with Defoe, who does not prevent Robinson suisse
from being "in its own right, for its small public, the happy
rival of Robinson Crusoe."

10   JUVERNA. "Carleton's Memoirs." Notes and Queries, 3d ser. 6,
     no. 152 (26 November):445.
         Replies to 1864.17. Refers to a letter appearing some
years ago in the Naval and Military Gazette, "signed, I think,
G.L.S.," in which Carleton was shown to be a real person and to
have served in the fifth and twenty-seventh regiments of
infantry.

11   LEE, W[ILLIAM]. "Cheap Repository Tracts." Notes and Que-
     ries, 3d ser. 6, no. 145 (8 October):291-94.
         Replies to 1864.8. Lists among the Cheap Repository Tracts
the "History of the Plague in London" as published before 1 June
1795, and identifies it as an abridgement of Journal of the
Plague Year.

12   ____. "The Storm of 1703." <u>Notes and Queries</u>, 3d ser. 5,
        no. 129 (18 June):504-5.
           Replies to 1863.3, 6-7. Locates possible sources for the
        information given in the manuscript note, on the performances of
        <u>Macbeth</u> and <u>The Tempest</u> during the storm of 1703, but gives the
        wrong reference and must make a correction in 1865.10. Contri-
        butes also a full reference to the literature on the storm, <u>A
        Warning from the Winds</u> (1704).

13   MACQUEEN, JAMES. "Captain Speke's Discovery of the Source of
        the Nile. A Review." In Richard F. Burton, <u>The Nile Basin</u>.
        London: Tinsley Brothers. Reprint. Introduction by Robert
        O. Collins. New York: Da Capo Press, 1967, pp. v-xxxvii,
        184-85.
           In the mid-nineteenth century dispute over the source of
        the White Nile, Burton argued that it was Lake Tanganyika; and
        Captain John Henning Speke, that it was Lake Ukarewe, renamed
        Lake Victoria. While the controversy became increasingly bitter
        between these two leaders, in 1863 Speke brought out his <u>Journal
        of the Discovery of the Source of the Nile</u>. On 15 September
        1864, at a debate scheduled in Bath before the British Associa-
        tion for the Advancement of Science, Speke did not appear, having
        been accidentally killed in a hunting accident. In late 1864
        Burton published his address along with James Macqueen's review
        of Speke's book in the <u>Morning Advertiser</u>. In his conclusion,
        Macqueen referred to a book which he had not himself read, but
        whose author, Defoe in 1720, was "another claimant for the honour
        of the discovery of the sources of the White Nile." From ex-
        tracts of <u>Captain Singleton</u> (Edinburgh, 1810) Macqueen was able
        to trace Singleton's journey across Africa, particularly around
        the area of "what must have been Lake Tanganyika, near its south
        end, as they struck it in 6·22° S. lat."

14   MEISSNER, FRIEDRICH. <u>Daniel Defoe, der Verfasser des Robinson
        Crusoe</u>. Basel: [n.p.], 38 pp.
           Celebrates the honest, virtuous Defoe, almost forgotten,
        yet who did more for the good of mankind than all the famous
        philanthropists, moralists, and literati of the eighteenth cen-
        tury taken together. Describes his heroic struggle for truth,
        justice, and common sense against a backdrop of church and state
        politics. Analyzes the popularity of <u>Robinson Crusoe</u>, especially
        among youth. Quotes Hettner (1854.4) on the value of this novel
        in mirroring mankind's development and presenting a philosophy of
        history. Discusses adaptations, especially that of Campe in Ger-
        many (in its forty-third edition by 1853), where the material
        retains its magnetism even in watered-down form. Sees value in
        poor imitations of <u>Robinson Crusoe</u> as documents of cultural his-
        tory. Credits the work for introducing to European literature a
        "modern," sentimental feeling for nature, particularly effective
        because of Defoe's great talent for combining simplicity and
        thoroughness.   (P.E.C.)

15   MIDDLETON, A.B. "Plagiarism." <u>Notes and Queries</u>, 3d ser. 6,
     no. 147 (22 October):337.
          Replies to 1864.6. Argues for "a more literal plagiarism"
     in the first two lines of the <u>True-Born Englishman</u> from Charles
     Aleyn's poem, <u>Historie of that Wise and Fortunate Prince Henrie
     of that name the Seventh</u> (1638).

16   O., L. "Letters of Daniel De Foe." <u>Notes and Queries</u>,
     3d ser. 6, no. 157 (31 December):527-30.
          Reprints the five shocking letters from Defoe to Charles
     De la Faye, Under-secretary in the Secretary of State's Office,
     Northern Department, discovered earlier in 1864, in the Public
     Record Office, and published anonymously in the <u>London Review</u>
     (1864.7), and adds a sixth letter which was found when the other
     five were collated with the originals. Assigns dates to the
     letters in 1718 on 12 and 26 April, 10 May, 23 May, 4 June, and
     13 June. Transcribes and briefly annotates the letters. See
     William Lee's vigorous defences of Defoe's conduct against the
     biased presentation in the <u>London Review</u> and his replies to L.O.,
     1865.5, 7.

17   R., M.S. "Carleton's Memoirs." <u>Notes and Queries</u>, 3d ser. 6,
     no. 149 (5 November):375.
          Replies to 1858.4; 1859.2-3, 9-10, 12, 18. Quotes a
     warrant (20 February 1705) found in the British Museum which
     authenticates an important detail of <u>Capt. George Carleton</u>:
     his being on half-pay with the army in Ireland.

18   RUSSELL, W[ILLIAM]. "Daniel De Foe." In <u>Eccentric Person-
     ages</u>. 2 vols. London: John Maxwell & Co., 1:255-76.
          Praises Defoe as one of the world's "chief benefactors" for
     his "History of the Plague" and "Robinson Crusoe," yet sees the
     course of his life as due to "eccentricity," defined here most
     favorably as the achievements of "an odd wrong-headed man."
     Offers an unusual perspective of Defoe as "an altogether wayward
     man [who] suffered the penalty which all incur who persist in
     knocking their heads against the orthodox granite walls by which
     'Society' is bounded and enclosed." Contains typical mid-nine-
     teenth-century misconceptions, such as Defoe's authorship of <u>Spec-
     ulum Crape-Gownorum</u> (1682); offers also new views: for instance,
     the change of name from Foe to De Foe when he did not wish it
     known "that his father, James Foe, was a butcher long established
     in London." Preserves an anecdote never encountered before, as
     "true or not," about Defoe's escaping from the Monmouth defeat in
     1685 by disguising himself as a ploughman and even making merry
     with the soldiers of Colonel "Kirke's Lambs." Makes the expected
     quick transition to Defoe's "romance writing." Accepts the idea
     of <u>Robinson Crusoe</u> as coming from "Selkirk's story," but "the
     treatment of the narrative" as "incomparably striking and origin-
     al." The other romances "have fallen out of the current litera-
     ture, are practically dead and buried. <u>Moll Flanders</u>, <u>Colonel
     Jack</u>, <u>Captain Singleton</u>, have disappeared, though they were not

without much merit." Defoe's "pre-eminent quality . . . as a
writer of fiction": "his power of realization." Reprinted: New
York: American News Co., 1866, pp. 174-88.

19   SHORTHOUSE, J. HENRY. "Defoe and George Herbert." Notes and
     Queries, 3d ser. 6, no. 147 (22 October):331.
          Replies to 1864.6. Shows that the first two lines of the
     True-Born Englishman echo a passage in a translation of Paracel-
     sus's Of the Nature of Things (1650, 1674), a work on magic and
     the occult, of the kind Defoe was familiar with.

20   VIATOR [pseud.]. "De Foe and Dr. Livingstone." Notes and
     Queries, 3d ser. 5, no. 122 (30 April):366.
          Replies to 1864.5. Reports that it is "not uncommon" for
     persons to make the journey across southern Africa, and cites the
     example of the Portuguese merchant, Silva Perto, two years before
     Dr. Livingstone. Argues that for Captain Singleton's adventures
     in Africa, Defoe based his story on some facts, and that "it is
     extremely likely" he drew his natural descriptions from informa-
     tion arriving in England from Portuguese settlers, 1710-1720.

                                   1865

1   BIRDWOOD, DR. "On Recent Discovery in Eastern Africa and the
     Adventures of Captain Singleton (DeFoe)." Journal of the
     Bombay Branch of the Royal Asiatic Society 7, no. 22:xlix-lxv.
          As part of a continuing controversy over the still-myste-
     rious geography of Africa, and in particular the source of the
     River Nile as it relates to the Victoria Nyanza and Lake Tangan-
     yika, draws attention (in a paper read before the Asiatic Society
     of Bombay on 13 August 1863) to selected passages in Captain
     Singleton describing the journey across Africa of Captain Single-
     ton and his party, the topographical features of which bear a re-
     markable resemblance to the geography in such Portuguese sources
     as Pigafetta's edition of Lopez's Relations del Reame di Congo
     (1599), and in such recent discoveries as those reported by the
     African explorer John Henning Speke in 1859 and 1863. Specif-
     ically, on the Portuguese source: "DeFoe could have had no bet-
     ter book than Pigafetta." On the narrative method in general:
     "I believe the story of this African journey must have been taken
     from one who had made it."

2   CHAUVIN, VICTOR. "Les vrais Robinson." Revue Bleue: Poli-
     tique Litteraire 2 (1 April):294-96.
          Summarizes the history of Robinsons as given in the book
     written with Ferdinand Denis, 1861.2. Makes no mention of Defoe,
     but regards Robinson Crusoe as "a masterpiece." Refers to the
     histories of Selkirk and the Mosquito Indian of Juan Fernandez as
     "the acknowledged types of Robinson Crusoe and Friday."

3   KNIGHT, CHARLES. "Thomas Gent, Printer, of York." In <u>Shadows of the Old Booksellers</u>. London: Bell & Daldy, pp. 76-99.
      Sketches an account of Thomas Gent from the autobiography, written in 1746 and published by Thomas Thorpe in 1832. Among Gent's Grub Street activities, records that he dishonestly abridged all three volumes of <u>Robinson Crusoe</u> into one volume.

4   LAROUSSE, PIERRE. "Foe (Daniel de)." In <u>Grande dictionnaire universel</u>. 15 vols. Paris: Administration du Grand Diction-naire Universel, 8:520.
      While the date of Defoe's birth is given [erroneously] as 1663, and the view of him as a champion of liberty persists, the titles of his "works of the imagination" are given as the <u>History of Molly Flanders</u>, <u>Memoirs of Captain Carleton</u>, <u>Life of Roxane</u>, and <u>Memoirs of a Cavalier</u>. Gives most of the entry to the suc-cess of <u>Robinson Crusoe</u> and particularly Rousseau's praise.

5   LEE, W[ILLIAM]. "Daniel Defoe and <u>The London Review</u>." <u>Notes and Queries</u>, 3d ser. 7, no. 160 (21 January):58-61.
      Replies politely to L.O., 1864.16, and severely to the anon-ymous <u>London Review</u>, 1864.7, both of which had published the re-cently discovered letters written by Defoe (12 April to 13 June, 1718) to Charles De la Faye, exposing himself as a Whig in the act of undermining Tory journals. The reprinting of the letters created considerable shock among the Defoe faithful. The letters disprove the view that Defoe ended his political activities in 1715, and call for "an entirely new chapter" of Defoe biography. In opposing the "objectionable manner" of the <u>London Reviewer</u>, Lee gives a reasonable explanation of Defoe's actual conduct under Lord Townshend in 1718, and promises a discussion later of the morality of this conduct.

6   _____. "Daniel Defoe on Assassination of Rulers." <u>Notes and Queries</u>, 3d ser. 8, no. 184 (8 July):21-23; no. 188 (5 August):101-3.
      Claims that Defoe wrote four "introductory letters" on the assassination of rulers against Cato's letters appearing in the <u>London Journal</u>, and published them in Applebee's <u>Original Weekly Journal</u> in four weekly installments beginning 16 December 1721--at a time when he was extremely busy with other newspapers, novels, and <u>Religious Courtship</u>. Reprints the items which, in turn, are reprinted: Lee's <u>Defoe</u> (1869).

7   _____. "Daniel Defoe, the News Writer." <u>Notes and Queries</u>, 3d ser. 6, no. 169 (25 March):244-46.
      Turns to the question of the morality of Defoe's conduct, as promised (1865.5) in his continuing response to L.O., 1864.16, and the <u>London Review</u>, 1864.7. Defends Defoe, first, by attempt-ing to place him in the midst of the circumstances surrounding him in 1718; and, second, by tracking down the publications identified in the "recently discovered" letters and analyzing Defoe's contributions and his techniques for disabling and ener-

vating the Tory journals. Examines the publications Mercurius
Politicus, Dormer's News-Letter, and Mist's Journal; concludes
Defoe "unwisely" agreed to Lord Townshend's proposal to write as
if he were "under the displeasure of the Government, and separated from the Whigs." Argues that once engaged in the questionable role, he conducted himself with integrity.

8   _____. "Daniel Defoe the News-Writer." Notes and Queries,
      3d ser. 7, no. 174 (29 April):343-44.
         With Defoe's partial departure from Mist's Journal in the
      middle of 1720, Mist was soon in trouble because of his Jacobit-
      ism. His severe sentence was announced in the Post Boy for 14-16
      February 1721. Reprints the editorial leading article in Apple-
      bee's Original Weekly Journal for 18 February, signed "Solomon
      Waryman" [Defoe], giving sound advice on how printers and public
      writers can survive. Reprinted: Lee's Defoe (1869).

9   _____. "A Moral Satire by Daniel Defoe." Notes and Queries,
      3d ser. 7, no. 179 (3 June):431.
         Offers still another piece (Applebee's Weekly Journal, 28
      October 1721) which he assigns to Defoe's authorship as included
      in the Tory journals identified in the "recently discovered"
      letters from Defoe to Charles De la Faye. Deals ingeniously with
      the question: ". . . what Religion are you Journal Writers of?"

10   _____. "The Storm of 1703." Notes and Queries, 3d ser. 7,
      no. 172 (15 April):302.
         Replies to 1863.3, 6-7; 1864.12. Cites two additional
      works on the storm of 1703 by Defoe: An Elegy on the Author of
      the True-Born-Englishman. With an Essay on the late Storm
      (1704). Corroborates, also, the manuscript note about the
      performances of Macbeth and The Tempest by quoting from Mr.
      Collier's Disuasive from the Play-House (1703).

11   S., J.F. "Defoe's House." Notes and Queries, 3d ser. 8,
      no. 204 (25 November):436.
         Seeks a view of Defoe's house in Church Street, Stoke
      Newington, pulled down last summer.

12   WHATELY, RICHARD. "Robinson Crusoe." In Miscellaneous
      Remains from the Commonplace Book of Richard Whately, D.D.
      Edited by E.J. Whately. New edition, with additions. London:
      Longman, Green, Longman, Roberts & Green, pp. 332-42.
         Offers disconnected observations: (1) two of "the most
      interesting tales ever written"--Robinson Crusoe and Uncle Tom's
      Cabin--do not have a love-story; (2) Gulliver's Travels contrasts
      strikingly with Robinson Crusoe in differing designs; (3) the
      omission of two incidents central to the Selkirk story from Robin-
      son Crusoe makes it unlikely that the history of the one was
      taken from the other; and (4) eight ingenious examples of "improb-
      abilities" in Robinson Crusoe are listed here as suggestive more
      of life than fiction: for instance, Crusoe's many failures and
      blunders.

1866

1   BOURNE, H[ENRY] R[ICHARD] FOX. English Merchants: Memoirs
    in Illustration of the Progress of British Commerce. London:
    R. Bentley. Reprint. London: Chatto & Windus, 1886,
    pp. 206-7, 281.
        Selects Defoe, in addition to Addison, as a spokesman for
    the benefits of trade in A Plan of the English Commerce (1728),
    just before the mid-century prosperity. Reprinted: 1898.

2   D., W. "Defoe on Maypoles." Notes and Queries, 3d ser. 10,
    no. 242 (18 August):124.
        Quotes Wilson's Memoirs of Defoe (1830) on the revival of
    maypoles after the Restoration.

3   HILLEBRAND, KARL. "Robinson Crusoé." Revue des cours littér-
    aires de la France et de l'étranger 3, no. 39 (26 August):640-
    47.
        Delves into the one peculiarity which separates Robinson
    Crusoe from the countless other imaginary voyages produced earli-
    er and later, namely, it was inspired by "a general idea." On
    these grounds, explains the unique phenomenon that everyone knows
    Robinson Crusoe, but no one knows its author or his very real
    achievements (thus the biographical summary, 3 pp.). On Robinson
    Crusoe, observes that the language and style are "selftaught" and
    enclose "sentiment of form" (which women acquire naturally, and
    men with difficulty); and that there is a general lack of "compo-
    sition." Makes the characterization of Robinson--particularly,
    the psychological change that comes over him when he is isolated
    on the island--central to an analysis of "the general idea."
    Elucidates a significant parallel between Robinson and all the
    "bold pioneers of civilization in the new world," and traces him
    as the "true type of the intrepid Anglo-Saxon." Presses even
    farther: "Each age has its philosophy of history; if Bossuet has
    given that of the XVIIth century; Hegel that of the XIXth; it is
    in Robinson that one will find that of the XVIIIth century."
    Ultimately, perceives Robinson as going through stages of "moral
    civilization" and natural religion.

4   LEE, WILLIAM. "Forgotten Periodical Publications." Notes and
    Queries, 3d ser. 9, no. 212 (20 January):53-54; "Periodical
    Publications during the Twenty Years 1712 to 1732." Notes and
    Queries, 3d ser. 9, no. 213 (27 January):72-75; no. 214
    (3 February):92-95.
        In an inquiry "collateral" to his search for "the hitherto
    unknown writings of Defoe," finds no titles associated with Defoe
    among the thirty-five early eighteenth-century periodicals in the
    folio volume at the British Museum, Harleian Catalogue 5958.
    Among the 277 periodicals published 1712 to 1732, going beyond
    the tables of Nathan Drake (1809) and John Nichols (1812), identi-
    fies six periodicals written or edited by Defoe, or including his
    work: Review (1712), Mercator (1713), The Flying Post, and Med-

ley (1714), <u>Mercurius Politicus</u> (1716), <u>Whitehall Evening Post</u> (1718), <u>Fogg's Weekly Journal</u> (1728).

5   <u>   </u>. "'Passage of an Apparition,' Defoe's <u>Life of Duncan Campbell</u>, Gilbert's <u>History of Cornwall</u>, Mrs. Bray's <u>Trelawny of Trelawne</u>." <u>Notes and Queries</u>, 3d ser. 10, no. 256 (24 November):417-18.
    Replies to 1850.12, noting that "A Remarkable Passage of an Apparition, 1665" was first published as the third section of <u>Mr. Campbell's Pacquet</u> (1720) and that it was, without any question, the work of Defoe. Offers the ingenious explanation that the manuscript notes in Dr. Ruddell's commonplace book were a transcription of Defoe's publication of the "Remarkable Passage."

6   <u>   </u>. "Servitude: A Poem." <u>Notes and Queries</u>, 3d ser. 9, no. 216 (17 February):141-43.
    Replies to 1866.9. Argues from internal evidence that Defoe wrote the title of <u>Servitude: A Poem</u>, the introduction, and postscript; and revised the poem itself. Admittedly, makes up the account of the young footman, Robert Dodsley, visiting the aged Defoe in his study at Stoke Newington and gaining his help on the poem. Mentions for the first time the catalogue of Defoe's library, quoting from the <u>Daily Advertiser</u>, 13 November 1731.

7   M., G. "Daniel Defoe in Edinburgh." <u>Notes and Queries</u>, 3d ser. 9, no. 213 (27 January):77.
    On two documents in the Scottish Record Office, Edinburgh: contract dated 13 December 1710 to print and publish a newspaper, <u>The Postman</u>; and "factory" empowering Hannah Goodale to act for Defoe in his absence, 7 August 1711.

8   M., J. "Plague in Newcastle, 1710: Daniel De Foe." <u>Notes and Queries</u>, 3d ser. 9, no. 226 (28 April):347.
    Reports a single number of the <u>Newcastle Gazette</u> for 23-25 December 1710 in the Advocate's Library, along with a letter from the publisher, [Joseph] Button to Defoe, printed by Maidment, 1837.7. Quotes also a notice from the <u>Scots Postman</u>, 29 July to 1 August 1710, for subscribers to Defoe's <u>Review</u>.

9   RIGGALL, EDWARD. "An Author in Livery." <u>Notes and Queries</u>, 3d ser. 9, no. 212 (20 January):60-61.
    Queries the authorship of <u>Servitude: A Poem</u> (undated) which has a postscript described as "a pithy reply" to Defoe's <u>Every-Body's Business, Is No-Body's Business</u>. Gives the Editor's reply that Robert Dodsley published <u>Servitude</u> about the year 1725, and the Postscript replied to Squire Moreton's [Defoe's] pamphlet. See also 1866.6.

10   RUSKIN, JOHN. "The Cestus of Aglaia." <u>Art-Journal</u>, n.s. 5 (January):9-10.
    Compares his own early experience in poring over the rude woodcut illustrations of the <u>Robinson Crusoe</u> published by the

Chiswick Press in 1812 and what might have been "the effect on my mind" of J.D. Watson's illustrations (1864). Maintains that he then received "more real sensation of sympathetic terror" from the woodcut representing Crusoe escaping from the wreck than he could have felt from Watson's "higher art." Tries to imagine what the benefits might be on the minds of children from "such lovely and expressive work as that of Watson." Yet he argues that the imagination ought not to be made "indolent" and that there should be an economy of line as with Holbein or Dürer. Reprinted: On the Old Road, 1885; 2d ed., 1899; The Works of John Ruskin, ed. E.T. Cook and Alexander Wedderburn (London: George Allen; New York: Longmans, Green, & Co., 1905), 19:138-40.

11   WHEELER, WILLIAM A. A Dictionary of the Noted Names of
      Fiction. London: Bell & Daldy, pp. 88, 134.
         In the brief entry for Robinson Crusoe, de-emphasizes any
debt to Selkirk. Reprinted: 1882, 1889, 1966.

1867

1   BYRON, HENRY J[AMES]; GILBERT, W.S.; HOOD, T.; LEIGH, H.S.;
     SKETCHLEY, A.; and THE AUTHOR OF "NICHOLAS." Robinson Crusoe;
     or, the Injun Bride & the Injured Wife. A Burlesque. London:
     "Fun" Office, 24 pp.
        First performed at the Theatre Royal, Haymarket, on 6 July
1867. Introduces familiar characters Crusoe and Friday, but also
new ones, Hunkey Dorum ("constitutional monarch of the Cannibal
Isles"), Pocahontas ("a dark fair, a colourable imitation of the
Africaine"), and others. Not infrequently, builds the action
around racial (or racist) humor, particularly in the songs. Par-
odies the original story, as in Crusoe's discovery of the single
human footprint, and ends with the chorus singing: "Our version
so differs from D. Defoe, / Who wouldn't know our Crusoe." See
also English Plays of the Nineteenth Century, vol. 5, Pantomimes,
Extravaganzas and Burlesques, ed. Michael R. Booth (Oxford: Clarendon Press, 1976), pp. 249-53; and Plays by H.J. Byron, ed. Jim
Davis (Cambridge University Press, 1984), p. 218.

2   CLARRY. "De Foe: The True Born Englishman: Banks." Notes
     and Queries, 3d ser. 11, no. 277 (20 April):315.
        Observes that in The Villainy of Stock-Jobbers Detected,
included in Defoe's True Collection (2d ed., 1705), are to be
found the same arguments for keeping banks solvent which are in
Mr. Leeman's current Parliament bill. Asks for the date of the
pamphlet's first publication, and is informed by the editor,
1701. See also 1867.5.

3   CORMON, E[UGÈNE]; CRÉMIEUX, HECTOR; and OFFENBACH, J[ACQUES]
     (musique). Robinson Crusoé, opera comique en trois actes
     (cinq tableaux). Paris: G. Brandus & S. Dufour, 326 pp.

4   "Cruso Pedigree." In Miscellanea Genealogica et Heraldica.
     London: Hamilton, Adams & Co., 1:229.
          Reproduces the arms ("Virtus nobilitat") of the Cruso fami-
     ly, and shows Timothy Cruso, the eldest son and heir of Timothy
     Cruso of London and his wife Katherine.

5   LEE, W[ILLIAM]. "Defoe." Notes and Queries, 3d ser. 11,
     no. 279 (4 May):364.
          Replies to 1867.2. Notes that within two days of each
     other Notes and Queries and the Pall Mall Gazette drew attention
     to an eminent solicitor's recently using the same arguments in
     Parliament, as contained in Defoe's The Villainy of Stock-Jobbers
     Detected. Provides more specific information on the publishing
     date (11 February 1701) of the pamphlet so that newspapers can be
     examined for the prices of stocks; and demonstrates the popular-
     ity of Defoe's pamphlet (at least four editions, by 1705).

6   MARX, KARL. Das Kapital: Kritik der politischen Oekonomie.
     Hamburg: Otto Meissner; New York: L.W. Schmidt. Capital:
     A Critique of Political Economy. Translated by Samuel Moore
     and Edward Aveling. Edited by Frederick Engels. Chicago:
     Charles H. Kerr & Co., 1926, 1:88-91.
          Observing that Robinson Crusoe on his island has been "a
     favorite theme with political economists," offers his famous para-
     digm of Crusoe as independent modern man (in contrast to depen-
     dent man of the middle ages), relying upon his own "different
     modes of human labour" and determining "value" on the basis of
     his relation to the objects of wealth that he creates. Argues
     further that in modern society "labour and its products" take on
     a social form as "services in kind and payments in kinds."
     Defines the unique "labour-power" emerging from a society that
     attends to both consumption and distribution of goods. Reprint-
     ed: Twentieth Century Interpretations of Robinson Crusoe, ed.
     Frank H. Ellis (Englewood Cliffs, N.J.: Prentice-Hall, Inc.,
     1969), pp. 90-92; in part, Critical Heritage.

7   THOMAS, RALPH. "Robinson Crusoe." Notes and Queries, 3d ser.
     11, no. 280 (11 May):374.
          Refers to a note in the Miscellaneous Remains of Archbishop
     Whately, 1865: on Robinson Crusoe, "this pseudonymous narra-
     tive," pointing out that "it is fictitious, and not founded on
     A. Selkirk's adventures."

                                   1868

1   AIKIN, LUCY [Mary Godolphin]. Robinson Crusoe in Words of One
     Syllable. London and New York: George Routledge & Sons.
     Reprint. New York: McLoughlin Brothers, 1882, 93 pp.
          Adapts the language to words of one syllable except for
     names and titles in illustrations; does not omit the grim scenes
     such as the cannibals' feasting.

2   AXON, WILLIAM E.A. "Daniel Defoe and John Dove, D.D." <u>Notes</u>
    <u>and Queries</u>, 4th ser. 2, no. 36 (5 September):232.
         Replies to 1868.10. Since the phrase "<u>Wherever God</u>
    <u>buildeth a Church, there Satan erecteth a Chappell</u>" has the
    status of a proverb, and since Defoe's first two lines were
    designated "an English proverb" in the first edition of his
    <u>True-Born Englishman</u>, charge of plagiarism cannot be directed
    against him.

3   BEDE, CUTHBERT. "Robinson Crusoe." <u>Notes and Queries</u>,
    4th ser. 1, no. 14 (4 April):320.
         Replies to Henry Kingsley's inquiry in the <u>Gentleman's Mag-</u>
    <u>azine</u> (January) on the Family of Faux living now in Yaxley and on
    a Mr. Creuso living at Fotheringhay in Queen Elizabeth's time.

4   BYRON, HENRY J[AMES]. <u>Robinson Crusoe; or, Friday and the</u>
    <u>Fairies! A Pantomime</u>. London: Hopwood & Carew, 20 pp.
         Performances were announced in the <u>Times</u> (London), 24
    December 1868, for this Grand Christmas Pantomime at the Theatre
    Royal, Covent Garden, on 26 and 30 December 1868, and for chil-
    dren on every Wednesday and Saturday thereafter. Mixes together
    characters like the Sedate Fairy of the Virgin Island (who
    dislikes men), the Elf ("who is smart enough to take care of
    his-<u>elf</u>"), Hokypokywankyfum (the King of the Cannibal Islands),
    with the shrewish Mrs. Crusoe and Robinson Crusoe. As in 1867.1,
    includes a parody of Crusoe's finding the "human footprint." See
    also <u>English Plays of the Nineteenth Century</u>, vol. 5, <u>Pantomimes,</u>
    <u>Extravaganzas and Burlesques</u>, ed. Michael R. Booth (Oxford: Clar-
    endon Press, 1976), pp. 249-53; and <u>Plays by H.J. Byron</u>, ed. Jim
    Davis (Cambridge University Press, 1984), p. 218.

5   CHASLES, PHILARÈTE. "Robinson Crusoe." <u>Notes and Queries</u>,
    4th ser. 1, no. 10 (7 March):227-28.
         Replies to 1868.14, on the French trisyllabic pronunciation
    of "Crusoe" and "De Foe" which requires the spelling "De Fo" and
    "Crusó." See the reply, 1868.15.

6   CLARKE, HYDE. "Robinson Crusoe." <u>Notes and Queries</u>, 4th ser.
    1, no. 14 (4 April):321.
         Disagrees entirely with Chasles (1868.5) and the other
    correspondents on the name "Foe"; offers suggestions for further
    research to trace the family of Foe in Elton, Northamptonshire,
    including the use of the <u>Post Office Directory</u> for a number of
    cities.

7   COLLINS, WILKIE. <u>The Moonstone: A Romance</u>. Serialized in
    <u>All the Year Round</u>, 4 Janaury-8 August 1868. Reprint. Univer-
    sity Edition. Chicago: Hooper, Clarke & Co., [n.d.], 512 pp.
         Introduces Gabriel Betteredge, the supremely commonsensical
    Englishman, into the oriental exoticism of this famous "sensation
    novel." In a story where by design the author attempts "to trace
    the influence of character on circumstance" (preface), Collins
    makes Betteredge, house-steward to Lady Verinder, the narrator

for the "first period" and again for the eighth and final narrative. Characterizes him as being motivated entirely by idolatry
of Robinson Crusoe. Shows him fortified by "a whiff of tobacco"
and "a drop of drink," persistently consulting his Robinson Crusoe as if it were his Bible, before making a decision, and repeatedly expressing admiration for Crusoe's wisdom. For the view
that Betteredge loves Robinson Crusoe because "it squares with
his 'English ideas'" and "parallels his understandings of race,"
and he is therefore (like current critics) oblivious to the
racism of Robinson Crusoe, see Abby Arthur Johnson, "Old Bones
Uncovered: A Reconsideration of Robinson Crusoe," College Language Association Journal 17, no. 2 (December, 1973):271-78.

8   "De Foe in the Pillory." Art Journal 30:28.
     Describes briefly the painting by E[yre] Crowe, "De Foe in
the Pillory," now in the collection of J.L. Newall, Esq., Forest
Hill, Ongar, and illustrated here (opposite p. 27) by J.C. Army-
tage, engraver. Claims that Crowe drew the exciting scene at
Temple Bar from Wilson's Memoirs (1830) where Defoe appears
mounted in the pillory: the name "De Foe" visibly lettered over
his head, the mob drinking his health, the "machine" adorned with
garlands.

9   FITZHOPKINS. "Daniel Defoe and John Dove, D.D." Notes and
     Queries, 4th ser. 2, no. 38 (19 September):284.
     Replies to 1868.2, 10-11, 23. Finds the thought of the
first two lines in Defoe's True-Born Englishman also in Franz
Horn's Die Poesie und Beredsamkeit der Deutschen (1822) where it
is associated with Erasmus.

10   GROSART, ALEXANDER B. "Daniel Defoe and John Dove, D.D."
     Notes and Queries, 4th ser. 2, no. 34 (22 August):177.
     The first two lines of Defoe's True-Born Englishman: finds
the same idea in almost the same words--in Dr. John Dove's The
Conversion of Salomon (1613).

11   _____. "Daniel Defoe and John Dove, D.D." Notes and Queries,
     4th ser. 2, no. 36 (5 September):232.
     Gives the page reference to Dove's book, which he had over-
looked in 1868.10.

12   _____. "Daniel Defoe and John Dove, D.D." Notes and Queries,
     4th ser. 2, no. 38 (19 September):284.
     Replies to 1868.2. Denies making any charge of plagiarism
against Defoe in 1868.10; offers still another example of the
proverb, this time, from William Roe's Christian Liberty rightly
stated and enlarged (1662).

13   H., A. "Robinson Crusoe." Notes and Queries, 4th ser. 1,
     no. 10 (7 March):227.
     Replies to 1868.14, on "Foe" as possibly an old French or
Dutch patronymic; on "Robinson" as in the title Swiss Family

Robinson; and on "Crusoe" as meaning a <u>settler</u>. See also reply, 1868.15.

14 JAYDEE [pseud.]. "Robinson Crusoe." <u>Notes and Queries</u>, 4th ser. 1, no. 7 (15 February):145.
    On three-syllable pronunciations of the French: "Crusoë or Crusoé," and even "De Foë"; and on French, German, and Swiss references to Defoe's hero indifferently as "Crusoe" or as "Robinson." See replies: 1868.3, 5-6, 13, 15, 24-25.

15 _____. "Robinson Crusoe." <u>Notes and Queries</u>, 4th ser. 1, no. 14 (4 April):320-21.
    Raises disagreements with Chasles's explanation (1868.5) of the French trisyllabic pronunciation and writing of "De Foë" and "Crusoé"; and with A.H. (1868.13) on "De Fooe" as having "a Dutch look" and on <u>Kreutzner</u> as being German for <u>Cruiser</u>. Points out that Cruso or Crusoe is "a real English surname."

16 KINGSLEY, HENRY. "Biographical Introduction." <u>Robinson Crusoe. Edited after the Original Editions</u>. Globe Edition. London: Macmillan, pp. vii-xxxi.
    Strongly admires Wilson's <u>Memoirs</u> of Defoe (1830), and uses Chalmers's <u>Life of Daniel De Foe</u> and Chadwick's <u>Life and Times of Daniel De Foe</u> (1859), yet expresses a fresh enthusiasm for <u>Robinson Crusoe</u> and its author. While he has not done any original research for the biography, rehearses the well-known facts about Defoe, including the information now known to be incorrect, such as his authorship of <u>Speculum Crape-Gownorum</u> (1682). In a curious passage, waxes melodramatic as the effects of the <u>Shortest-Way with the Dissenters</u> are anticipated: "A dark night of misery and disgrace, such as none of us could bear now and live, was coming on rapidly. To us, in these days, such a phase in our lives would be unbearable: the author of <u>Moll Flanders</u>, tougher in mental fibre than we are, the author of <u>Robinson Crusoe</u>, tenderer in mental fibre than we are, lived through it, and wrote <u>Robinson Crusoe</u>, almost the tenderest, gentlest, purest book in the language afterwards." Claims Defoe's pillorying jarred Kingsley's sense of respectability. Specifically, interprets <u>Robinson Crusoe</u> as "no romance at all, but a merely allegorical account of Defoe's own life for twenty-eight years"--not so much exact relationships between events in Defoe's life and Crusoe's as broad and general representations: "The worn-out, sensitive nature of the man threw itself in his Protestant Utopia, where everything was perfectly ordered, and where there was peace, alone, with God. Crusoe is merely an ideal Protestant monk, a man who has got himself out of the turmoils of the world, with regulated order all around him, and his God face to face with him,--the Bible, in this case, standing for the priest. . . . Crusoe's life is, I think, Defoe's life, as he would have had it at nearly sixty years of age." Continues in this vein with illuminating comments on Defoe's deep knowledge of travel, voyages, and geography, and his use of such knowledge (Hackluyt, Purchas, "probably

Ramusio," Robert Everard) in his "romances"; argues that he drew
the knowledge not only from his reading, but "very probably from
talking to the Portuguese merchants and sailors." Seriously
objects to the confusing of Crusoe's island with Selkirk's Juan
Fernandez, noting that what preserves the Crusoe story is the
"well-ordered decorous protestantism [brought] out of the disorder of nature." Offers little criticism for Defoe's other novels: high praise for Captain Singleton although "it has fallen
dead"; Chatham's belief in the reality of the Memoirs of a Cavalier; the rest better forgotten. Reprinted: 1873; 1882; 1905.

17   MIDDLETON, A.B. "Daniel Defoe A Plagiarist." Notes and Que-
      ries, 4th ser. 2, no. 43 (24 October):403.
         Replies to 1868.12. Insists on the charge of plagiarism
against Defoe because of "surely something more than mere coincidence" between the opening couplet of his True-Born Englishman
and the similar verses found in Charles Aleyn's Historie of that
Wise and Fortunate Prince Henrie of that name the Seventh (1638).
Notes also that Samuel Richardson [in Clarissa, 1747-1748] was
wrong in thinking that Defoe was the first to versify a well-
known proverb in the first two lines of the True-Born Englishman;
Charles Aleyn had already done this much earlier. See also
1864.15; 1868.23.

18   "Monument to Alexander Selkirk." Notes and Queries, 4th ser.
      2, no. 48 (28 November):503-4.
         Lists accounts of castaways living on Juan Fernandez, from
Captain William Dampier's New Voyage round the World (1699) to
the extract from the Panama Star and Herald, 6 October, on the
monument with a special inscription to the memory of Alexander
Selkirk at Juan Fernandez.

19   RIGGALL, EDWARD. "Portraits of Daniel De Foe." Notes and
      Queries, 4th ser. 2, no. 46 (14 November):465.
         Asks why there were no portraits of Defoe in the two most
recent National Portrait Exhibitions at South Kensington, and
where were the originals of the engravings in the first volume of
the True Collection (1703), Jure Divino (1706), History of the
Union (1709), and Wilson's Memoirs of Defoe (1830). Was the
portrait in Wilson's Memoirs (1830) authentic?

20   [STEPHEN, LESLIE.] "De Foe's Novels." Cornhill Magazine 17,
      no. 99 (March):293-316.
         Turns critical attention to the "secondary" novels--Roxana,
Captain Singleton, Moll Flanders, and Colonel Jack--as well as
the Journal of the Plague Year, Memoirs of a Cavalier, Capt.
George Carleton, and Robinson Crusoe. Identifies Defoe's "peculiar power," his verisimilitude, as "the most amazing talent on
record for telling lies." Demonstrates that the same narrative
devices, which Scott had found in Mrs. Veal, were also present in
the prefaces and narratives of the novels. Probes more deeply into the concept of Defoe as a liar by relating "his peculiar cast

of talent" to the habit of "mystification" which appears in his
political writings and actions, and also his novels. Compares
Defoe's objectivity, his equanimity, and his lack of emotion, col-
or, or perspective with the photographer's art, as distinct from
the painter's. Comments on "the singular calmness with which he
describes his villains," and finds them much inferior to Thackeray's in Barry Lyndon. Asserts here, and again with Robinson
Crusoe: "All which goes by the name of psychological analysis in
modern fiction is totally alien to his art." While acknowledging
that Defoe has complete "objectivity" and "veracity," observes
that such powers may not be enough, and so he has Defoe compensat-
ing by introducing "mystery," as in the Xury incident of Robinson
Crusoe or the daughter's pursuit in "the original conclusion of
Roxana." Traces the attraction to Defoe of "the mysterious,"
both in the non-fictional works on the supernatural and in certain novels. Explains emphatically why he ranks Defoe very high
as a writer, but not as a novelist: he can tell stories or spin
yarns; he can never produce a "novel of sentiment or passion or
character"--now and then, only "powerful fragments" of novels.
Picks out some "genuine De Foe" in Capt. George Carleton and Memoirs of a Cavalier. Extolls the Journal of the Plague Year for
its superior artistry ("next in merit to Robinson Crusoe"); compares its images of horror with "certain ghastly photographs
published during the American [Civil] war." Finally, on Robinson
Crusoe, insists that it stands above all Defoe's other writings
because it has the "freshness" of a first work of art and "something of the autobiographical element which makes a man speak
from greater depths of feeling than in a purely imaginary story."
Judges that while Robinson Crusoe is not a work of the first
order, it still holds a special place in having pleased "all the
boys in Europe for near a hundred and fifty years." Reprinted:
1868.21-22; with revisions, 1874.8; 1877; 1892.17; 1894; 1904;
1917.

21   ____. "De Foe's Novels." Every Saturday 5 (11 April):453-
      64.
           Reprint of 1868.20.

22   ____. "De Foe's Novels." Littell's Living Age 97, no. 1247
      (25 April):195-210.
           Reprint of 1868.20.

23   T. "Daniel Defoe and John Dove, D.D." Notes and Queries, 4th
      ser. 2, no. 36 (5 September):232.
           Replies to 1868.10. Quotes from Richardson's Clarissa
      (1747-48) on "Mr. Daniel Defoe (an ingenious man though a
      Dissenter)" who was probably the first to versify a well-known
      proverb, in the opening lines of the True-Born Englishman.

24   TIEDEMAN, H. "Robinson Crusoe." Notes and Queries, 4th ser.
      1, no. 20 (16 May):469.
           In reply to 1868.14 and others, quotes an entry of a book
      by J. Cruso, written in 1642.

25   W., E. "Robinson Crusoe." <u>Notes and Queries</u>, 4th ser. 1,
     no. 14 (4 April):319-20.
          Replies to 1868.13-14, with a summary of information on the
     Reverend Timothy Cruso, Defoe's schoolfellow at the nonconformist
     academy in Stoke Newington. The name was Flemish.

26   WATSON, J. "Daniel De Foe." <u>Notes and Queries</u>, 4th ser. 2,
     no. 42 (17 October):373.
          To a query for evidence that Defoe wrote <u>Robinson Crusoe</u> in
     Halifax, the editor cannot offer help. While he mainly corrects
     Watson's <u>History of Halifax</u> (1775.6), he accepts the fact that
     Defoe resided at the Rose and Crown, Back Lane, probably in 1712;
     and may have written there <u>A Seasonable [Warning and] Caution</u>
     <u>against the Insinuations of Papists</u> and <u>Hannibal at the Gates</u>.

1869

1   CALLIN, F. "Neues über Daniel Defoe." <u>Archiv für das Studium</u>
     <u>der neueren Sprachen und Literaturen</u> 24, no. 45:313-20.
          Reviews Lee's <u>Defoe</u> (1869).

2   CONWAY, M[ONCURE] D. "Concerning Hawthorne and Brook Farm."
     <u>Every Saturday</u> 7 (2 January):13-18. Reprint. <u>Hawthorne Among</u>
     <u>His Contemporaries</u>. Edited by Kenneth Walter Cameron. Hart-
     ford, Conn.: Transcendental Books, 1966, p. 482.
          Describes the effects of the Civil War on Hawthorne. On an
     evening at the house of his publisher, Mr. Fields, he was much
     dejected, and escaped to his room. When he appeared at breakfast
     the next day, he explained "that he had become lost the night
     before in Defoe's Ghost Stories, until it was too late to make
     his appearance in the company." Guesses that Hawthorne must have
     been "contemplating some phantasmal production at that time": he
     asked many questions about "the ghost beliefs of the negroes
     among whom I had passed my early life." Reprinted: 1904.2.

3   CROSSLEY, JA[ME]S. "Defoe: <u>Mercurius Politicus</u>: Mesnager's
     <u>Negociations</u>." <u>Notes and Queries</u>, 4th ser. 3, no. 76
     (12 June):548-49.
          Quotes the entire letter by D.F. published in the July num-
     ber of <u>Mercurius Politicus</u>, 1717, in which Defoe clearly denies
     the authorship of <u>Minutes of the Negotiations of Monsr. Mesnager</u>
     (1717), as asserted by Abel Boyer in <u>The Political State of Great</u>
     <u>Britain</u>. Presents Defoe's letter in its entirety since Lee's
     <u>Defoe</u> (1869) listed <u>Mesnager</u> among Defoe's works without having
     had access to the letter in <u>Mercurius Politicus</u>. In addition, on
     the basis of the same letter, admits that Defoe probably wrote
     <u>Advice to the People of Great Britain</u> (1714), and had "some hand"
     in the three parts of <u>The Secret History of the White Staff</u>
     (1714-1715), <u>Mercurius Politicus</u>, and <u>The Mercator</u>. Acknowledges
     also the existence of a contemporary who, as in <u>Mesnager</u>, success-
     fully imitated Defoe's style and manner. See also 1870.6, 11-12.

4   . "Defoe's Due Preparations for the Plague." Notes and
Queries, 4th ser. 3, no. 70 (1 May):402-3.
    While applauding Lee's Defoe (1869) for its listing of the
works, including the addition of sixty-four new pieces, claims
that at least fifty more can be "confidently" ascribed to him.
Adds to the canon Due Preparations, "one of the most striking
narratives that even the genius of Defoe ever constructed," and
finer than Journal of the Plague Year. States that he first
announced the work to be Defoe's in the Gentleman's Magazine,
1838.2, and subsequently lent his rare copy to William Harrison
Ainsworth who based his Old St. Paul's (1841) on it.

5   . "Defoe's Letter to Keimer." Notes and Queries, 4th
ser. 3, no. 71 (8 May):422.
    From Samuel Keimer's tract A Brand Pluck'd from the Burning
(1718), describes the situation vividly and reprints Defoe's
letter [1717?]. Shows Defoe's deep compassion for his friend
committed to the Gatehouse by the warrant of Lord Townshend,
including "a sincere prayer put up to heaven, tho' in verse."
The letter has been reprinted in Healey. See also 1869.9.

6 DAVIES, EDWARD C. "Robinson Crusoe's Island." Notes and
Queries, 4th ser. 4, no. 89 (11 September):214.
    Quotes a report from the San Francisco News about Juan Fer-
nandez, "where once upon a time Alexander Selkirk . . . gathered
the material for Defoe's Robinson Crusoe," as being colonized in
December, 1868, by Robert Wehrhan and his society of from sixty
to seventy individuals from Saxony, Germany.

7 DEFOE [pseud.]. "Robinson Crusoe." Notes and Queries, 4th
ser. 3, no. 60 (20 February):175.
    In reply to the query made by "Defoe," responds that
Mr. Cussans wrote and sang the popular comic chant, "Oh, poor
Robinson Crusoe," at the Royal Circus and Sadler's Wells, which
was published by E. Bates, Blackfriars Road, in 1797; the words
reprinted in The Universal Songster (1825) and editions of Samuel
Foote's farce, The Mayor of Garratt (1820.7).

8 THE EDITOR OF DEBRETT. "Alexander Selkirk." Notes and Queries, 4th ser. 3, no. 55 (16 January):69.
    Quotes a letter in the Times (London), 24 December 1868,
from Thomas Selcraig, Edinburgh, expressing the thanks of Selkirk's lineal descendants for the honor being done by Commodore
Powell and his officers in their erecting on Juan Fernandez a
monument to Selkirk, "whose history is popularly believed to have
afforded Defoe the materials of his attractive story. . . ."

9 EPICTETUS [pseud.]. "Affliction." Notes and Queries, 4th
ser. 3, no. 74 (29 May):501.
    Replies to 1869.5. Describes the "poetical lines" in
Defoe's letter to Keimer as "a Christian paraphrase" of a letter
by Pliny (Epistles, vii, 26).

10   FORSTER, JOHN. Walter Savage Landor, A Biography. 2 vols.
     London: Chapman & Hall, 2:360–61.
         Recalls an evening, 1836–1837, in which he and Dickens
     visited Landor to celebrate his birthday. Upon Landor's mention-
     ing the many tears he had shed over David Copperfield, Dickens
     asked, "'But is it not yet more wonderful that one of the most
     popular books on earth has absolutely nothing in it to cause any-
     one either to laugh or to cry?'" He affirmed "with confidence"
     that such was Defoe's masterpiece, Robinson Crusoe, and gave the
     example of Friday's death as "one of the least tender, and, in
     the true sense, least sentimental things ever written." Assigns
     the strong effect on numerous readers to "its mere homely force
     and intensity of truth." For Dickens's judgment on Robinson
     Crusoe, see his letters in 1856 to Forster, 1872–1874.1, and
     Landor, 1880.4.

11   "A Gentleman of the Press." All the Year Round, n.s. 2,
     no. 32 (10 July):132–37; no. 33 (17 July):156–61.
         Reviews Lee's Defoe (1869), places the same emphasis on
     Defoe as a staunch defender of liberty, defends him against the
     one "spot [that] has been discovered on his hitherto unsullied
     name." Selects activities in his life which show him aggressive
     in support of liberty, such as his participation in the Monmouth
     Rebellion, support for the Prince of Orange, personal sacrifice
     on account of the Shortest-Way with the Dissenters, the mission
     to Scotland, and his ideas on free trade conforming exactly with
     those of Mr. Gladstone or Mr. Bright in the year 1869. Turns
     finally to the "spot" which sullied Defoe's name, and refers to
     "the accidental discovery in 1864, in the State Paper Office, of
     six previously unknown letters of Defoe, in his own handwriting,
     and undoubtedly genuine, addressed to Charles De la Faye, Esq.,
     . . . confidential secretary to the Secretary of State in 1713."
     See 1864.7, 16. Forthrightly admits that Defoe really sold "the
     birthright of his personal honour for a mess of very dirty pot-
     tage," but does not seem to have lessened his esteem for Defoe.
     Does not accept all of Lee's "recently discovered writings" as
     genuinely Defoe's, but finds that "these waifs and strays of a
     bygone time form a valuable seed-ground of history. . . ." Does
     accept Lee's identification of Mist with the "enemy" mentioned in
     Defoe's final letter to his son-in-law, Henry Baker. Closes the
     essay with a plea for "the great Daniel Defoe: who sinned a
     little, but suffered much, and left behind him a name as a states-
     man, a patriot, a philosopher, and a novelist, that shall last as
     long as the English language."

12   HALL, ARTHUR. "Dates of Entry and First Publication of Works
     by Daniel Defoe." Notes and Queries, 4th ser. 4, no. 101
     (4 December):477.
         Cites information from Stationers Hall on the entry for
     Moll Flanders. Lee gives the publication date 27 January 1722
     by W. Chetwood whereas the Stationers Hall entry is 12 January
     1722/3, in the name of Thos. Edlin. The explanation may be that

Edlin issued an edition not known to Lee; he may have obtained
the copyright from Defoe and assigned his right in succession to
other publishers; or he may have been the printer. The Family
Instructor was entered 31 March 1715, in the name of Eman. Matthews for the whole copyright. The first part of Robinson Crusoe
was entered on 23 April 1719, in the name of Wm. Taylor for the
whole copyright--two days before publication. The second part
was entered on 17 August 1719--three days before publication; and
the third part, on 3 August 1720--three days before publication.
Nowhere in the books of the Stationers Company is the name of Defoe to be found. See also Lee's Defoe (1869); 1870.7, 9-10, 19.

13   KELTIE, JOHN S., ed. The Works of Daniel Defoe Carefully
     Selected from the Most Authentic Sources. Edinburgh: William
     P. Nimmo. Reprint. 1872, pp. v, vii-xi, 1-30, 31-35, 209,
     303-4, 386, 450-52, 522, 528-29, 548, 591, 604.
         Appearing in the same year as Lee's biography (which was
     accompanied by two volumes of "recently discovered writings"),
     declares his objective to be the traditional one of anthologizing
     standard works to "form a notion of what manner of man he was":
     Robinson Crusoe (two parts), Colonel Jack, Memoirs of a Cavalier,
     Duncan Campbell, Journal of the Plague Year, Everybody's Business
     Is Nobody's Business, Mrs. Veal, Shortest-Way with the Dissent-
     ers, Giving Alms No Charity, Complete English Tradesman (ex-
     tracts), True-Born Englishman, and Hymn to the Pillory. In the
     Preface (1 p.), describes Defoe as one of the most prolific
     writers, with a canon of 250 works and additional journal contri-
     butions just now reprinted by Lee, but without any effect on the
     current anthology. Similarly, in the "Note on the Recently
     Discovered Facts Concerning Defoe" (5 pp.), assesses the impact
     as minimal on Defoe's reputation, from Lee's discovery in 1864 of
     the notorious letters found in the State Paper Office which
     directly linked Defoe with both Tory and Whig newspapers. To
     Chalmers's "Life of Daniel De Foe" (30 pp.), adds heavy annota-
     tions from Wilson's Memoirs of Defoe (1830), Lee's Defoe (1869),
     and other sources. Introduces each of the twelve anthologized
     pieces with a commentary (consisting usually of borrowed quota-
     tions). Reprinted: 1875; Brooklyn and New York: Wm. W. Swayne,
     [n.d.]; 1903.

14   L., R.C. "Defoe's History of the Devil." Notes and Queries,
     4th ser. 4, no. 98 (13 November):409.
         Sets up a query for identifying the characters referred to
     by nicknames or asterisks in the Political History of the Devil
     (1726). Argues that whereas Pope's dunces are immortalized by
     name, Defoe's are not, and he is "by far the sharper satirist of
     the two." See also 1869.28.

15   "The Later Life of De Foe." British Quarterly Review 50, no.
     100 (1 October):483-519.
         Reconsiders the later life by reviewing Lee's Defoe (1869)
     and challenging certain main points. Acknowledges that the six

incriminating letters do attest to Defoe's employment by a Whig
ministry to play a Tory role, but such work was "akin to previous
political engagements" and therefore not dishonorable; they show
him not so much a spy as "a secret literary censor"--one who
compromised both character and reputation, and gave in to "a life
of deception." With Lee's expanding the canon so rapidly, expresses a vigorous skepticism about Defoe's authorship, for
example, of certain works not admissible because of statements in
the Appeal to Honour and Justice. Questions why the contributions to the journals had to be written ones? On what evidence
can the majority of the 350 "newly discovered writings" be
claimed as Defoe's? Reprinted, in part: Critical Heritage.

16   LEE, WILLIAM. Daniel Defoe: His Life, and Recently Discov-
      ered Writings: Extending from 1716 to 1729. 3 vols. London:
      John Camden Hotten, 1:535 pp.; 2:535 pp.; 3:485 pp.
      As the first truly important biography since Wilson's
Memoirs of Defoe (1830), reexamines the entire field of biography
and canon, and introduces more than 350 "newly discovered writings" culled from six contemporary periodicals. Represents a
careful, at times pedestrian, scholarship that would have a revo-
lutionary effect on Defoe studies even to the present day. In
the "Chronological Catalogue" (29 pp.), sums up the investigation
of the canon and publication dates, and builds the biography in
the nineteen chapters of the first volume around the authentic
writings, and reprints the "selected" pieces (1716-1729) in the
second and third volumes. Disagrees philosophically with Wilson's presentation of Defoe as "a Sectarian bigot," but takes the
initial impulse for his biography from the six incriminating
letters (1864.16) that show, beyond any doubt, that Defoe did not
"retire" into general literature in 1715, as everyone supposed,
but in fact entered into the most frenetic activity imaginable
during the last sixteen years of his life, writing and managing
certain Tory and Jacobite journals and newspapers (at times,
simultaneously) while, in truth, he served Whig ministers as
"Censor of the Journals." Draws important new biographical information also from the writings of enemies (e.g., Charles Lesley,
John Oldmixon, Abel Boyer), numerous letters of Defoe now published for the first time, and especially contemporary newspapers.
Takes the biography into new directions; holds the premise that
Robinson Crusoe is an "emblem" of autobiography, and investigates
tenaciously the principal events of Defoe's life--for instance,
discovering a new role for Defoe in Monmouth's rebellion, according to the Consolidator; rejecting Wilson's account of Defoe in
Bristol during 1692; rating the quality high of the pantiles made
at Tilbury; ferreting out bits of information about William III
and the Partition Treaty; establishing Defoe's loyalty to Harley
right after the Queen's death. Amasses the evidence painstakingly that Defoe's "retirement" from politics never took place.
Then, using veiled references in articles signed T. Experience,
Solomon Waryman, and Sir Timothy Caution, narrates for the first
time Defoe's uncomfortable relationship with Nathaniel Mist--

estrangement, rupture, duel, dire threats--the "wicked, perjur'd, and contemptible Enemy" mentioned in Defoe's last letter to Henry Baker. No less significant is Lee's work on the canon. Of the 254 items listed in the "Chronological Catalogue," sixty-four distinct works are added for the first time, marked with an asterisk; sixty are rejected from Lowndes, thirty from Wilson, and twelve from Hazlitt. Lee states, "modestly, but with strong assurance," that Defoe was the author of these works and no others. All except eleven items still survive in Moore's Check-list. So well has Lee determined the dates of first publication from contemporary newspapers that Moore accepts the dates, more often than not, as given by Lee. Among his more unusual additions, which no longer seem valid are The Union Proverb (1708), A Short Narrative of the Life and Death of John Rhinholdt Count Patkul (1717), Mr. Campbell's Pacquet (1720, including "A Remarkable Passage of an Apparition, 1665"), The Life and Actions of Lewis Dominique Cartouche (1722), and The Highland Rogue (1723). Lee, in turn, rejects Capt. George Carleton and Madagascar, and inadvertently omits Due Preparations. He characterizes the 350 uncollected new pieces as "Essays and Letters, moral and religious--imaginative,--humourous,--amatory,--ironical, and miscellaneous," but offers only internal evidence (unspecified) for Defoe's authorship. In chaps. 13-15 of vol. 1 (73 pp.), intermittently discusses the novels and works of the imagination: "the simple truthfulness" of Memoirs of a Cavalier, "so convincing" that the work can hardly be taken as anything other than "a purely historical account"; Captain Singleton, in no way inferior to the other literary works; Moll Flanders, "the apparently artless story . . . [that] continually appears more like the gushing of a fountain, than, as it really is, the flowing of a polluted stream"; Journal of the Plague Year, the authentic perfectly blended with the imaginary; Colonel Jack, using its "wonderful power" in good causes, yet a work not to be trusted with children; and Roxana, surpassing the other two novels of crime "in originality of invention and perfection of delineation." Recognizes continually that Defoe's subjects were, in general, "offensive to modern notions of delicacy"; yet persists in reading the works for their moral instruction. See also reviews, 1869.1, 11, 15, 20, 22-25; 1870.1, 15; 1882.7. Reprinted: Hildesheim: Georg Olms, 1968; New York: Burt Franklin, 1969; in part, Critical Heritage.

17   . "Daniel Defoe's First Publication." Notes and Queries, 4th ser. 4, no. 91 (25 September):252-53.
        Corrects his listing of the first published work in his De Foe (1869) as A Letter, containing some Reflections on His Majesty's Declaration for Liberty of Conscience. Now admits this work to be by Gilbert Burnet. See also 1869.21.

18   . "Defoe's Due Preparations for the Plague." Notes and Queries, 4th ser. 3, no. 71 (8 May):442.
        Replies to 1869.4. Admits to forgetfulness in omitting Due Preparations from his listing in Defoe (1869).

19   _____. "Introduction to the Present Edition." In The Life
        and Adventures of Robinson Crusoe, Now First Correctly
        Reprinted from the Original Edition of 1719. London and New
        York: Frederick Warne & Co., pp. v-xvi.
            Balances a consideration of Alexander Selkirk as "the
        historic original of Robinson Crusoe" with a consideration of
        Robinson Crusoe as the "Emblematic Original" of events in Defoe's
        life. Supports the latter interpretation with the well-known
        passage in the preface to Serious Reflections; expresses the
        caution that the parallels in the life of Defoe may now be "ob-
        scure, if not consigned to entire oblivion." Rejects the rival
        claimants (Arbuthnot, Lord Oxford) to the authorship of Robinson
        Crusoe. Of the five locations vying to be the place where Defoe
        (presumably in disfavor with the government) wrote Robinson Cru-
        soe, selects and defends Stoke Newington. Because of special
        efforts to make the edition accurate, claims "to represent the
        only perfect text of Defoe's narrative since the time of its
        Author."

20   [MACKAY, CHARLES.] "A Great Whig Journalist." Blackwood's
        Edinburgh Magazine 106 [American ed., 69], no. 648 (October):
        457-87.
            Authorship identified in Wellesley Index. In a review of
        Lee's Defoe (1869), summarizes the journalistic contributions to
        the Whig party, including the "newly discovered" surreptitious
        pieces. Explains (with Lee) that Defoe must have regarded such
        services as his patriotic duty. Claims that Defoe's plain style
        is like the speeches of Cobden or Bright, and certain of his
        ideas (e.g., in an Essay upon Projects) anticipate John Stuart
        Mill. Praises Robinson Crusoe and Journal of the Plague Year as
        unrivalled for their "simple naturalness"; judges other works to
        be "dead books" that have little interest for anybody, or are
        offensive in our time (Roxana, Moll Flanders, Colonel Jack).
        Reprinted, in part: Critical Heritage.

21   MAYER, S.R. TOWNSHEND. "Daniel Defoe's First Publication."
        Notes and Queries, 4th ser. 4, no. 93 (9 October):307.
            Confirms Lee, 1869.17, by providing the reference in
        Gilbert Burnet's bibliography to the pamphlet wrongly assigned
        to Defoe.

22   [PEARSON, C.H.] Review of Lee's Defoe (1869). North British
        Review 51, no. 101 (October):249-51.
            Authorship identified in Wellesley Index. Refuses to
        accept Lee's favorable estimate of the blatant contradictions
        revealed in Defoe's career, his political manoeuvres as well as
        his writing Moll Flanders and Roxana.

23   Review of Lee's Defoe (1869). Athenaeum, no. 2166 (1 May):
        597-98.
            Complains about Lee's admiration for Defoe even after the
        revelation of the "unseemly work" he performed for the Whig

government in 1718 and later. Expresses also doubt about the
internal evidence used to determine Defoe's authorship of the
reprinted pieces.

24   Review of Lee's Defoe (1869). Notes and Queries, 4th ser. 3,
      no. 69 (24 April):397.
          Praises Lee's research and even his "hero worship," and
      predicts the new pieces reprinted in vols. 2 and 3 will have a
      value equal to that of the biography.

25   Review of Lee's Defoe (1869). Saturday Review of Politics,
      Literature, Science, and Art 27, no. 707 (15 May):651-52.
          Explains the significance of the six letters discovered in
      1864 and investigated by Lee, and assesses their effect on
      Defoe's reputation as "little less than a revolution." Analyzes
      and accepts Lee's biographical findings: the relationship of
      Defoe and Nathaniel Mist, the growing estrangement of the two
      men, the identification of Mist with Defoe's implacable enemy
      mentioned in the letter to Henry Baker.

26   ROBINSON, HENRY CRABB. Diary, Reminiscences, and Correspon-
      dence. Edited by Thomas Sadler. 2 vols. in one. Boston:
      Houghton, Mifflin & Company, [n.d.], 1:8, 209; 2:371.
          Makes use of Defoe's Family Instructor; offers comments on
      Colonel Jack; imagines an anecdotic letter from Defoe to Bunyan
      about Milton.

27   W., A.E. "Nathaniel Johnston, M.D.: De Foe." Notes and
      Queries, 4th ser. 3, no. 63 (13 March):244-45.
          Mentions vaguely an advertisement relating to the bank-
      ruptcy of Daniel Foe, merchant, in the London Gazette, at about
      issue no. 4317, 24-27 March 1707.

28   W., J.W. "Defoe's History of the Devil." Notes and Queries,
      4th ser. 4, no. 103 (18 December):545.
          Replies to 1869.14. Questions the grounds for calling
      Defoe's Political History of the Devil (1726) his chef-d'oeuvre--
      over his Robinson Crusoe.

                                 1870

1   BLERZY, H. "Un Publiciste du dix-huitième siècle: Daniel De-
      foe, sa vie et ses écrits." Revue des duex Mondes 86:685-708.
          While reviewing Lee's Defoe (1869), independently assesses
      the new findings here, and reaches less sympathetic conclusions,
      regarding Defoe as a publicist, particularly in the light of "the
      ambiguous role" he played after 1715 in connection with the Tory
      journals. Analyzes carefully Lee's numerous revelations "that
      add nothing certainly to the glory of Defoe, but show the un-
      stable character of this man whom age and adversity could not
      beat down." Makes a special point of relating the anonymity and

duplicity of these later pieces for Mist's and Applebee's journals. Demonstrates also how his work for Applebee led to the
sensational accounts of thieves and pirates. Places a special
emphasis on Defoe's geographical knowledge evident in the first
two parts of Robinson Crusoe, the account of Avery [The King of
Pirates, 1720], and Captain Singleton. See also Critical Heritage, pp. 24-25.

2   BRIDGMAN, CUNNINGHAM V. Ridiculous Robinson Crusoe. London:
Dean & Son, 17 pp.
    A child's colored-picture book, with somewhat silly verses
telling the story, Friday speaking in pidgin English.

3   C. "Daniel De Foe and Sir Walter Scott." Notes and Queries,
4th ser. 5, no. 127 (4 June):533.
    Claims a contradiction in Lee's listing The Highland Rogue
(1723) as Defoe's, and Scott's statement in his introduction to
Rob Roy [1818] that Defoe had no interest in any narrative about
Rob Roy. See 1870.8.

4   CURWEN, J.S. "Defoe's 'Hymn to the Pillory.'" Notes and
Queries, 4th ser. 5, no. 117 (26 March):318.
    Calls attention to the significant textual differences in
the last stanza of Hymn to the Pillory as given in Nimmo's Works
of Daniel Defoe (1869), compared with the so-called "old version." Includes the explanation by the journal editor that
Nimmo's text is, in fact, from the first edition, as Defoe wrote
it on the day he stood in the pillory, while the other text is
the "improved" later one from the corrected "third edition" and
Defoe's collected Second Volume (1705).

5   "The Defoe Monument." Saturday Review 30, no. 778 (24 September):391-92.
    Criticizes severely some implications in the addresses by
James Clarke, editor of the Christian World, and Charles Reed,
M.P.--particularly with regard to Defoe as double-dealing in his
service as a spy or as designating the author of Moll Flanders
and Roxana "a Christian hero." Finds Defoe to be "an untruthful
man" for certain writings that are fictions, but "written as, and
intended to be taken for, real and genuine books." Sums up his
life as illustrating "the nothingness of gifts without graces."
See also 1870.17; 1871.10.

6   H., A. "Defoe: Mercurius Politicus: Mesnager's Negotiations." Notes and Queries, 4th ser. 5, no. 120 (16 April):
393.
    Replies to 1869.3; 1870.11. Asks if Defoe's double might
not have been his own son.

7   HALL, ARTHUR. "Date of Entry and First Publication of Works
by Daniel Defoe." Notes and Queries, 4th ser. 5, no. 110 (5
February):155.

Argues vigorously against Lee's <u>Defoe</u> (1869) that the date
in "the Books of Entry at Stationers' <u>Hall</u>" for the first edition
<u>Moll Flanders</u> copyright is 1722/3, <u>not</u> 1721/2; quotes the entry
verbatim. See also 1869.12; 1870.9-10, 19.

8   LEE, W[ILLIAM]. "Daniel Defoe and Sir Walter Scott." <u>Notes
    and Queries</u>, 4th ser. 5, no. 130 (25 June):604.
       In reply to 1870.3, notes that as in the case of <u>Capt.
    George Carleton</u>, he has not always agreed with Scott. So, here,
    while admitting that <u>The Highland Rogue</u> (1723) may be only "a
    pretended history" or "a catch-penny publication," as Scott
    observed, still argues forcefully that Defoe was the author.

9   _____. "Date of Entry and First Publication of Works by
    Daniel Defoe." <u>Notes and Queries</u>, 4th ser. 5, no. 105
    (1 January):21-22.
       Replies to Arthur Hall's claim (1869.12) that too much time
    has elapsed between the first publication of <u>Moll Flanders</u> by
    W. Chetwood, on 27 January 1722, and the date of entry for the
    book in Stationers Hall on 12 January 1722/3. Hypothesizes that
    this entry at Stationers Hall is for Thomas Edlin's third edition
    or an unknown fourth edition. Confirms that the dates of all
    Defoe's other works entered into Stationers Hall register agree
    with his publication dates as given in <u>Defoe</u> (1869). See also
    1870.7.

10 _____. "Date of Entry and First Publication of Works by
    Daniel Defoe." <u>Notes and Queries</u>, 4th ser. 5, no. 111
    (12 February):183-84.
       Sharply disagrees with Arthur Hall (1869.12; 1870.7) that
    the one entry for <u>Moll Flanders</u> in Stationers Hall, dated 12
    January 1722/3, cannot possibly refer to the first edition.
    Cites the title page of John Brotherton's "second edition" which
    is dated 1722. See also 1870.19.

11 _____. "Defoe: <u>Mercurius Politicus</u>: Mesnager's <u>Negotia-
    tions</u>." <u>Notes and Queries</u>, 4th ser. 5, no. 111 (12 February):
    177-79; and no. 112 (19 February):202-5.
       Replies to 1869.3. Admits the contradiction between
    his own claim of Defoe's authorship for <u>Mesnager</u> and Defoe's
    disclaimer in the July number of <u>Mercurius Politicus</u>, 1717.
    Analyzes the full complexity of Defoe as the author, under six
    heads relating to <u>Mesnager</u>: I. Its genuineness ("a forgery").
    II. Its authenticity (a fictional presentation of conversations
    between Mesnager and Mr. St. John, incorrectly referred to as
    "my Lord--"). III. Its object (a hastily written defence of
    Lord Oxford, published long after Mesnager's death). IV. Its
    author (undeniably Defoe, on the external evidence: the faith-
    ful friend to Lord Oxford, the author of the <u>Appeal to Honour
    and Justice</u>, 1715; on internal evidence: Defoe's highly char-
    acteristic style). V. Defoe's disclaimer (still mysterious).
    VI. If Defoe did not write <u>Mesnager</u>, who did? (rejects the
    possibility of Defoe's having a "double" or an imitator).

12   _____. "Defoe: Mercurius Politicus: Mesnager's Negotia-
        tions." Notes and Queries, 4th ser. 6, no. 131 (2 July):15.
            Replies to 1870.6. States that Benjamin Norton Defoe,
        while "not without some smartness of style," did not have his
        father's genius, and could not have written "the quasi Defoe
        productions."

13   _____. "Rob Roy and His Descendants." Notes and Queries,
        4th ser. 6, no. 132 (9 July):30-31.
            Replies to 1870.14. Since Lee was the first to believe The
        Highland Rogue (1723) to be by Defoe, and since he was challenged
        on this point by C., 1870.3, argues here that Defoe knew far more
        than Sir Walter Scott about Rob Roy. Makes important correc-
        tions, and adds new information about Robert MacGregor, commonly
        called Rob Roy, and his family connections, and about each of his
        five sons.

14   LLOYD, M. "Rob Roy." Notes and Queries, 4th ser. 5, no. 127
        (4 June):534.
            Asks for information on living descendants of "the celebrat-
        ed Rob Roy," and provides unconfirmed or hearsay information on
        persons named MacGregor. Replies to this query, given by Isabel-
        la Drummond Swifte, née Ross, and Sp. (no. 130, 25 June:607-8),
        make no mention of Defoe. See 1870.13.

15   MAYER, S.R. TOWNSHEND. "Mr. William Lee's 'Life and Newly
        Discovered Writings of Daniel Defoe.'" Notes and Queries,
        4th ser. 6, no. 148 (29 October):363-64.
            For a future edition of Lee's Defoe (1869), offers six
        possible revisions: the first three calling for corrections of
        dates due to the more ample evidence available from Luttrell's
        Brief Historical Relation of State Affairs (1857). Argues con-
        vincingly, for instance, that Defoe must have been in London on
        17 October 1706, and not in Edinburgh, and that Lee will have
        to reconsider Defoe's return to London in late September 1707.
        Makes new suggestions for investigating the travels "abroad" on
        any secret mission.

16   Memorial to Daniel Defoe. Notes and Queries, 4th ser. 5,
        no. 116 (19 March):307.
            On the restoring of Defoe's grave in Bunhill Fields; a
        brief record of his father, butcher in Fore Street, Cripplegate.

17   "Memorial to Daniel De Foe." Times (London), 17 September:11.
            Describes the unveiling of the monument on 16 September,
        with Mr. J. Clarke speaking of the contributions mainly from the
        boys and girls of England, and with Mr. Charles Reed, M.P., speak-
        ing in "honour to the memory of a neglected man" who wrote sixty-
        four public works, besides many other pieces," but was being
        commemorated now for his Robinson Crusoe. Quotes the inscription
        on the monument [erroneously for the year of death, 1781]. Re-
        printed: 1871.10.

18　MERIVALE, HERMAN. Review of Philip Henry Stanhope, 5th Earl,
　　History of England, comprising the Reign of Anne until the
　　Peace of Utrecht, 1870. Edinburgh Review 132, no. 270
　　(October):548-53.
　　　　Authorship identified in Wellesley Index. Sets up a con-
　　text of writers in the nineteenth century, such as Sir Walter
　　Scott, who killed themselves by over-excessive work; then turns
　　to Defoe as "the prototype of the prolific, versatile, indefati-
　　gable class of slaves to the press whom modern facilities of
　　production have created." Critically considers Lord Stanhope's
　　assessment of Defoe as a literary and political figure, vis-à-vis
　　Oldmixon, Steele and Prior, but can find his equal only in Swift.
　　Clearly influenced by Blerzy's critique (1870.1) of Lee's biog-
　　raphy, baldly states the idea of Defoe's moral degeneracy: "the
　　honest if vehement partisan in youth degenerated into a mere mer-
　　cenary in advanced life." Reproduces Defoe's letter to General
　　Stanhope, to argue against Lee, by showing its author's actual
　　vengeful feelings toward Sacheverell; and disagrees again with
　　Lee on Defoe's last years remaining still a mystery. Regards the
　　novels--aside from Robinson Crusoe, which "stands alone"--ade-
　　quate to secure for him a high place in fiction, but claims that
　　Defoe is like Rétif de la Bretonne who, because of his ability to
　　evoke "homely interest by lifelike incident," was called "the
　　Rousseau of the gutter." See also 1870.21. Reprinted, in part:
　　Critical Heritage.

19　PEACOCK, EDWARD. "Date of Entry and First Publication of
　　Works by Daniel Defoe." Notes and Queries, 4th ser. 5,
　　no. 111 (12 February):184.
　　　　Replies to 1870.7. On the publication date of Moll Flan-
　　ders: insists that Arthur Hall cannot read the date 3 December
　　1722 in the transcripts of the Stationers Hall as if it were
　　3 December 1721/2.

20　"Restoration of Bunhill Fields Burial-ground." Notes and
　　Queries, 4th ser. 6, no. 142 (17 September):246.
　　　　On the obelisk erected over Defoe's grave with funds con-
　　tributed by the boys and girls of England, uncovered 16 September
　　1870.

21　STANHOPE, PHILIP HENRY, 5th EARL. History of England Com-
　　prising the Reign of Queen Anne Until the Peace of Utrecht.
　　London: John Murray, pp. 549-51.
　　　　Publishes for the first time Defoe's letter to Lieutenant-
　　General James Stanhope, dated 8 March 1710 and preserved among
　　Lord Stanhope's Chevening MSS. The letter gives unsolicited
　　advice on the character of Henry Sacheverell at a time when the
　　General was one of the managers appointed by the Commons to
　　conduct the prosecution of Sacheverell. Although the historian
　　Stanhope recognizes Defoe's "genius and power of writing," he
　　faults him for "party rancour" and endeavoring to turn the trial
　　into "a prying and inquisitorial process of the lowest kind."

See also 1870.18. Defoe's letter is reprinted in George Macaulay
Trevelyan, England under Queen Anne: The Peace and the Protes-
tant Succession (London, New York, Toronto: Longmans, Green &
Co., 1934), pp. 332- 33; Healey.

22   "Who Wrote Robinson Crusoe?" Eclectic Magazine 74 (March):
     366-71.
          Reprint of 1870.24.

23   "Who Wrote Robinson Crusoe?" Littell's Living Age 104,
     no. 1339 (29 January):301-4.
          Reprint of 1870.24.

24   "Who Wrote Robinson Crusoe?" London Society 17, no. 47
     (January):67-71.
          Assembles the evidence on the question of the authorship of
     Robinson Crusoe, and sifts through the claims of Alexander Sel-
     kirk and the charge that Defoe "took the idea of writing a more
     extensive work, 'The Romance of Robinson Crusoe,' and very dishon-
     estly defrauded the original proprietor of his share." Rejects
     also the claims of authorship by John Arbuthnot and especially
     Lord Oxford. Surveys the places where Robinson Crusoe might have
     been written, and reaffirms Stoke Newington. To illustrate the
     book's essential truthfulness, repeats different versions of anec-
     dotes, such as the one about Madame de Talleyrand [see 1816.7;
     1853.15; 1854.9] and the one about Sir Thomas Robinson of Rokeby
     Park [see 1799.2]. Reprinted: 1870.22-23.

                              1870-1871

1   STRICKER, W. "Ueber Robinsonaden und fingirte Reisen."
     Jahresbericht des Frankfurter Vereins für Geographie und
     Statistik 35:29-38.
          Presents a rambling recounting of various Robinsonades and
     other fictional travel tales, without any original contribution.
                                                            (P.E.C.)

                                1871

1   A[DAMS], W[ILLIAM] H[ENRY] D[AVENPORT]. "Daniel De Foe: A
     Biography." In The Life and Strange Surprizing Adventures of
     Robinson Crusoe, of York, Mariner. The Household Robinson
     Crusoe. London, Edinburgh, and New York: Thomas Nelson &
     Sons, pp. 9-48.
          Advances the thesis that while a general parallelism exists
     between Robinson Crusoe and Defoe's biography, it should not be
     pushed too far, and that the "pretended allegory" is more an
     after-thought. Aims at demonstrating that Defoe was himself "a
     greater, a braver, and a more self-controlled man than Robinson
     Crusoe." Using evidence from Forster, describes Defoe as one of

the most liberal and tolerant spirits of his time. In chap. 3,
"De Foe As a Writer of Fiction" (16 pp.), quotes from Scott,
Rousseau, Stephen, Forster, and Lamb, but also introduces the
important distinction between "inventiveness," which appears
almost exclusively in Robinson Crusoe, and imagination, which may
be found rarely, as in the incident of Crusoe's discovering the
footprint in the sand. For chap. 4, "Last Years and Death,"
relies completely upon Lee's Defoe (1869). See also 1886.2.
Reprinted: 1876, 187-.

2   AXON, WILLIAM E.A. "Defoe and Manchester." Notes and Que-
     ries, 4th ser. 7, no. 159 (14 January):34.
         Queries any family connection between the novelist and the
widow Mercey Defoe, buried 1743, according to the Manchester
Cathedral registers.

3   "Books Written in Prison." All the Year Round, n.s. 7,
     no. 158 (9 December):32.
         Comments upon the many "prison books," including those of
Bunyan's contemporary--Daniel Defoe who was "often in trouble,
and on one occasion suffered the pillory as well as imprisonment." He wrote "Hymn to the Pillory" while in prison, and
started "a political periodical" there, but did not write "his
immortal Robinson Crusoe" in prison.

4   [DENNIS, JOHN.] "Daniel Defoe." Cornhill Magazine 23
     (March):310-20.
         Author identified in Wellesley Index. Explains why, except
for the fame from Robinson Crusoe, Defoe was little known in his
own time and almost entirely neglected by literary and political
historians. What slight reputation he held, since it consisted
of enemies' comments, tended to be negative. Wilson's bulky volumes of biography were dull; Lee's defense of Defoe's character
was not very successful against the damaging revelations of the
six letters found in the Public Record Office. Argues for Defoe's integrity as a politician and journalist on the grounds of
his moral superiority to such contemporaries as Swift or Walpole,
and his anticipations of certain social and political reforms.
On Robinson Crusoe and "the minor fictions," makes a strong case
for an even greater recognition of Defoe: "in his staid Dutch
fashion a consummate literary artist," unsurpassed in producing
fine effects out of "the accumulation of prosaic details," his
inventive faculty strongest in Robinson Crusoe," a capacity to
identify with all his characters. Compared with the other
novels, Robinson Crusoe stands out "like a noble mountain amidst
a range of stunted hillocks." It is a companion to the Faerie
Queene and Pilgrim's Progress. Now where do you place Roxana and
Moll Flanders, Colonel Jack and Captain Singleton? "Not certainly with books in which splendid powers are perverted to evil, and
vice is tricked out to wear the semblance of virtue; but among
books that display, with the fidelity of a photographer, human
nature at its worst, vice in all its grossness, and the low aims

of low people in all their vulgarity." Continues with Defoe's
limitations in representing love and women; reinforces Wilson and
Lee on the minor fiction as not fit "for universal perusal."
Reprinted: 1871.5-6; in part, Daniel Defoe: Moll Flanders, ed.
J. Paul Hunter (New York: Thomas Y. Crowell Co., 1970); Critical
Heritage; revised with changes, 1876.3.

5   ____. "Daniel Defoe." Eclectic Magazine, n.s. 13, no. 5
       (May):580-88.
         Reprint of 1871.4.

6   ____. "Daniel Defoe." Littell's Living Age, 4th ser. 21
       (1 April):56-62.
         Reprint of 1871.4.

7   EIRIONNACH. "Quotations in Robinson Crusoe." Notes and Que-
    ries, 4th ser. 7, no. 177 (20 May):426-27.
         Verse quoted in Robinson Crusoe, "For sudden joys, like
    griefs, confound at first": searches for the source. See also
    1862.12. Quotes also the verses near the beginning of Part Two:
    "Free from vices, free from care, / Age has no pain, and youth no
    snare." Repeats the anonymous poem "The Country LIfe" containing
    the two lines, from an undated song book of the previous century,
    The British Musical Miscellany, or the Delightful Grove.

8   FORSYTH, WILLIAM. The Novels and Novelists of the Eighteenth
    Century, in Illustration of the Manners and Morals of the Age.
    New York: D. Appleton & Co., pp. 11, 22-23, 213, 263.
         Inasmuch as the author states his general aim is to dis-
    cover "the habits and manners and social life of our ancestors"
    reflected in their novels, he finds these stories to be "deplor-
    ably dull"; the narrative "insipid," and the dialogue "stupid."
    Dismisses Defoe completely (and surprisingly) because his works
    "throw little or no light upon the social manners of the age" and
    because his heroes and heroines (Singleton, Roxana, Moll Flan-
    ders, and Colonel Jack) pose such insurmountable difficulties
    even to discuss them.

9   GRANT, JAMES. The Newspaper Press: Its Origin, Progress, and
    Present Position. 2 vols. London: Tinsley Brothers, 1:92-
    94.
         Concerns the Review (1704-1713), its brief history and
    demise due to the tax imposed on newspapers.

10 HORNER, SAMUEL. Introduction to A Brief Account of the inter-
    esting Ceremony of Unveiling the Monument erected by the Boys
    and Girls of England to the Memory of Daniel Defoe, author of
    "Robinson Crusoe," in Bunhill Fields Cemetery, September 16th,
    1870. Southampton: Hampshire Independent, pp. 1-15.
         In this compilation by the sculptor of the monument, brief-
    ly introduces the ceremony of the unveiling of the monument, and
    compiles accounts of the event taken from three leading news-
    papers published the day after, 17 September 1870. Aside from

general references to his "works of imagination" and especially
<u>Robinson Crusoe</u>, makes no mention of the other novels, but typi-
cally quotes James Clarke, editor of the <u>Christian World</u>, on
Defoe as "one of England's moral and intellectual nobles, who
helped greatly to make us the people that we are . . ."; and
closes with "Sonnet on the Defoe Monument," by John Askham, on
the same theme. Of special biographical interest: reports the
unearthing of Defoe's coffin and Horner's description of the
framework of the body "as that of a man about five feet four
inches high with a peculiarly massive under-jaw."

11   PALIN, WILLIAM. <u>Stifford and Its Neighbourhood, Past and Pres-</u>
      <u>ent</u>. [London: Printed for Private Circulation], pp. 92-93.
      Notes the entry in the registers of Chadwell, St. Mary, of
the marriage on 12 February 1621 of Robert Smith to Katherine
Foe, daughter of Edmund Foe, deceased, and his wife Lucie. Comments also that the "Foes" had property here, and that biographers such as Forster are wrong in locating Defoe's tile-factory
and house in West Tilbury rather than Chadwell. Although the
author apparently made his own inquiries, he has not been able to
identify the locations.

12   READE, CHARLES. "To the Editor of <u>The Daily Globe</u>, Toronto:
      A Reply to Criticism" [pamphlet]. Reprint. In <u>Readiana:</u>
      <u>Comments on Current Events</u>. London: Chatto & Windus, 1883,
      pp. 279-94 passim.
      Replies vigorously to Mr. Godwin Smith's "malicious and de-
famatory libel" attacking his novel <u>A Terrible Temptation</u> (1871).
Against the charges of the "criticaster," whom he refers to as
"an anonymuncule," defends his method of documentation in novels
by citing the use of facts by "the chiefs of fiction"--Shake-
speare, Scott, and Defoe. Argues that in <u>Mrs. Veal</u>, Defoe wrote
"a narrative on the plan that the anonymuncule praises," and
therefore told lies; and that in <u>Robinson Crusoe</u>, he wrote "on
the method I have adopted," gathering facts from Selkirk himself
and the accounts of Woodes Rogers and William Dampier, and therefore told truths.

13   RUSKIN, JOHN. <u>Fors Clavigera: Letters to the Workmen and</u>
      <u>Labourers of Great Britain</u>, vol. 1. London: Printed for the
      Author. Reprint. <u>The Works of John Ruskin</u>. Edited by E.T.
      Cook and Alexander Wedderburn. London: George Allen; New
      York: Longmans, Green, & Co., 1907, 27:167.
      Explains to readers of the monthly letter his background
as "a violent Tory of the old school (Walter Scott's School, that
is to say, and Homer's)." While reading only Scott's novels and
Pope's translation of the <u>Iliad</u> on weekdays, he reserved Sundays
for <u>Robinson Crusoe</u> and <u>Pilgrim's Progress</u> at the wish of his
mother who had it "deeply in her heart" he would become "an evan-
gelical clergyman." Writes that ultimately he "got all the noble
imaginative teaching of Defoe and Bunyan, and yet--am not an evan-
gelical clergyman." With only very minor change, this passage
appears in chap. 1, section one, of Ruskin's <u>Praeterita</u> (1885).

14 RUSSELL, W. CLARK. The Book of Authors. Chandos Classics.
    New ed. London: Frederick Warne & Co., pp. 91, 133-35.
        Under the heading "John Bunyan," quotes Benjamin Franklin
    on the mixing of narration and dialogue; and under "Daniel
    Defoe," collects well-known quotations from Dr. Johnson, Sir
    Walter Scott, newspaper advertisement (1703), Isaac D'Israeli,
    Edinburgh Review (1830), Pope, Swift, Cornhill Magazine.

15 [WOOD, HENRY H.] Review of G. Peignot, Dictionnaire critique,
    litteraire et bibliographique des principaux livres condamnés
    au feu, supprimés ou censures. Paris, 1806. Edinburgh Review
    134, no. 273 (July):191-92.
        Authorship identified in Wellesley Index. As an example of
    an English suppressed and censored book, offers the Shortest-Way
    with the Dissenters.

16 ____. "Suppressed and Censured Books." Edinburgh Review
    (American edition) 134, no. 273 (July):98.
        Authorship identified in Wellesley Index. Explains briefly
    the trouble Defoe encountered from both high and low churchmen
    because of "a satire of exquisite irony from beginning to end,"
    the Shortest-Way with the Dissenters. Among the severe penalties
    leveled against the author was the burning of the book by the
    hangman in New Palace Yard.

                              1872

1   BLANCHARD, ÉMILE. "L'Ile de Madagascar." Revue des deux
    mondes 100 (1 July):69-71.
        Surveying the early eighteenth-century history of Madagas-
    car, relies heavily upon The Pleasant and Surprising Adventures
    of Robert Drury during His Fifteen Years' Captivity on the Island
    of Madagascar (1729). While he accepts "the veracity of the
    narrator" as being confirmed, nevertheless proceeds to register
    a series of doubts, and thus at the same time that he makes no
    claim for Defoe's authorship he leaves the way open for S. Pas-
    field Oliver to make such a claim, 1890.15, 17.

2   MINTO, WILLIAM. "Daniel Defoe, 1661-1731." In A Manual of
    English Prose Literature: Biographical and Critical Designed
    Mainly to Show Characteristics of Style. Edinburgh and Lon-
    don: William Blackwood & Sons, pp. 397-414.
        In the brief biographical portion, makes the charge of
    dishonesty against Defoe which he would repeat and amplify later,
    1879.5. Concentrates the analysis of style on an examination of
    (1) "elements of style"--vocabulary, sentences and paragraphs,
    figures of speech--similitudes, contrast; (2) "qualities of
    style"--simplicity, clearness, strength, the ludicrous (including
    banter, humour, irony); and (3) "kinds of composition"--descrip-
    tion, narrative, and exposition. Reprinted: 1886; 1892.

3   UNEDA. "Defoe's <u>True-Born Englishman</u>." <u>Notes and Queries</u>,
      4th ser. 9, no. 230 (25 May):424.
          Corrects James Grant's statement in <u>The Newspaper Press</u>
      (1871) that the <u>True-Born Englishman</u> ridiculed foreigners, by
      quoting the more accurate account in 1787.12.

                              1872-1874

1   DICKENS, CHARLES. Letters to John Forster, in Forster's <u>Life</u>
      <u>of Charles Dickens (1872-74)</u>. Edited by J.W.T. Ley. New
      York: Doubleday, Doran & Co., 1928, pp. 96, 182, 320, 342,
      398, 611.
          3 November 1837: reads Defoe's <u>History of the Devil</u>.
      "What a capital thing it is!" 20 September 1840: compares Angus
      Fletcher's howl to that of a wolf. "The description of the
      wolves in <u>Robinson Crusoe</u> is the nearest thing. . . ." 21 Febru-
      ary 1844: shows concern over a cheque of £20 received from the
      Liverpool Institution, and thinks he should return it: "I am as
      much puzzled with the cheque as Colonel Jack was with his gold."
      6 October 1844: has been "deep in Voyages and Travels, and in
      De Foe." 8 July 1846: compares the fetal position taken by a
      ten-year-old girl born deaf, dumb, and blind when left alone and
      in fear, with the behavior of savages described in books of
      voyages and travels; finds "exactly the same attitude" among the
      savages described in <u>Robinson Crusoe</u>. In Paris, 1855-56, accord-
      ing to Forster's biography, Dickens was frequently entertained
      with dinners at Eugène Scribe's, meeting such guests as Lamartine
      and talking "of De Foe and Richardson, and of that wonderful
      genius for the minutest details in a narrative which has given
      them so much fame in France." Later in 1856, still at Paris,
      repeats to Forster (as he will again to Landor, 1869.10; 1880.4)
      that "<u>Robinson Crusoe</u> should be the only instance of an univer-
      sally popular book that could make no one laugh and could make no
      one cry." Has read the book again: ". . . I will venture to say
      that there is not in literature a more surprising instance of an
      utter want of tenderness and sentiment, than the death of Friday.
      It is as heartless as <u>Gil Blas</u>, in a very different and far more
      serious way." The second part of <u>Robinson Crusoe</u> is "perfectly
      contemptible," in the glaring defect that it exhibits the man who
      was 30 years on that desert island with no visible effect made on
      his character by that experience. De Foe's women too--Robinson
      Crusoe's wife for instance--are terrible dull commonplace fellows
      without breeches; and I have no doubt he was a precious dry and
      disagreeable article himself--I mean De Foe: not Robinson. Poor
      dear Goldsmith (I remember as I write) derived the same impres-
      sion." See other Dickens's letters: 1880.4; <u>The Letters of</u>
      <u>Charles Dickens</u>, ed. Madeline House and Graham Storey (Pilgrim
      Edition. Oxford: Clarendon Press, 1969), 2:235; <u>The Letters of</u>
      <u>Charles Dickens</u>, ed. Madeline House, Graham Storey, Kathleen Til-
      lotson (Pilgrim Edition. Oxford: Clarendon House, 1974), 3:183-
      84, 554-55. Reprinted: in vols. 1, 2, <u>The Letters of Charles</u>
      <u>Dickens</u>, ed. Walter Dexter (Bloomsbury: Nonesuch Press, 1938).

1873

1   B., J. "Memoirs of a Cavalier." Notes and Queries, 4th ser.
    11, no. 286 (21 June):509.
        Replies to 1873.4. From the viewpoint of a military man,
    protests strongly against assuming that the Memoirs of a Cavalier
    is a fictitious narrative; cites the description of Gustavus
    Adolphus's crossing the Lech as "probably the most scientific
    operation of military engineering ever performed"; finds similar
    internal evidence in Capt. George Carleton.

2   BATES, WILLIAM. "Philip Quarll." Notes and Queries, 4th ser.
    12, no. 297 (6 September):193.
        Summarizes the problem of authorship in The Hermit, an
    imitation of Robinson Crusoe: P.L. in the preface assigns the
    book to Edward Dorrington, two of whose narratives are drawn from
    Woodes Rogers's Cruising Voyage Round the World (1712).

3   KING, R.J. Review of A Handbook for Travellers in Devon and
    Cornwall, 8th ed., 1872. Edinburgh Review 138, no. 282
    (October):491-94.
        Authorship identified in Wellesley Index. Compares "the
    places and objects" which most attracted the Reverend James
    Brome, of Cheriton, Kent, in his unnamed work [CBEL: Travels
    over England, Scotland and Wales, 1700--not 1726], with Defoe's
    Tour; and finds much similarity. While Defoe's narrative is
    generally "prosaic and practical enough," quotes at length the
    natural description in the account of crossing Blackstone Edge
    which shows "at once the master hand." States surprisingly, with-
    out giving evidence, that Defoe wrote vol. one, only a part of
    vol. two, and supervised the rest.

4   LOBBAN, W. "Memoirs of a Cavalier." Notes and Queries,
    4th ser. 11, no. 271 (8 March):193.
        Raises the question of why, if the Memoirs of a Cavalier is
    "generally supposed" to be "purely imaginary," it is used as a
    historical reference--for instance, in [Walter] Harte's Life of
    Gustavus Adolphus [1759]. Claims that if the work were not
    autobiographical, as stated, it must certainly copy "authentic
    history" closely. The editor inserts a recommendation to the
    discussion in Lee's Defoe (1869). See 1873.1.

5   READE, CHARLES. "The Sham Sample Swindle." Once a Week
    (25 January-8 February). Reprint. In Readiana: Comments on
    Current Events. London: Chatto & Windus, 1883, pp. 302-11
    passim.
        Defends his Foul Play against charges that he plagiarized
    Le Portefuille rouge. Using the device of "The Sham Sample
    Swindle," contends that his contemporary, Samuel Warren, sur-
    passed Defoe as a novelist: "Now, Defoe wrote several stupid
    stories, and one masterpiece. . . ."

6   SABIN, JOSEPH. A Dictionary of Books Relating to America,
     from Its Discovery to the Present Time. New York: J. Sabin
     & Sons, 5:310-13.
         Under the entry "Defoe," lists eleven different items relat-
     ed to America, with brief comments on editions, dates, or impor-
     tance, such as for The Judgment of Whole Kingdoms and Nations
     (1710): "reprinted in America to justify the Revolution." See
     also 1888.19; 1891.16.

7   SOLLY, EDWARD. "Defoe's Essay on Projects." Notes and Que-
     ries, 4th ser. 11, no. 270 (1 March):175-76.
         Observes that the title-page of his Essay upon Projects
     differs from Lee's listing with respect to the printer's address,
     and then points out how rare it is for a printer's address to be
     given on a title page than a publisher's.

                                1874

1   BELJAME, ALEXANDRE. "Notice sur Daniel De Foe." In Vie et
     aventures de Robinson Crusoé. New ed. Paris: Librairie
     Hachette & Cie., pp. i-xv.
         Expresses an admiration for Defoe stronger and more com-
     plete than in his Le Public et les hommes de lettres, 1881.1.
     Here, in a school text in English, esteems him as "one of the
     most original and fecund minds." Sees him as the creator of a
     genre in which the English have produced masterpieces, "the novel
     of observation as well as adventures." Traces in Defoe (unlike
     Dryden) a close allegiance to "the ideas of liberty and tolerance
     to which he vowed his disinterested talent"; summarizes such advo-
     cacy in the True-Born Englishman, Shortest-Way with the Dissent-
     ers, Hymn to the Pillory, and Review. Accepts the view of his
     "retirement" into writing novels; rejects any imputations with
     regard to Selkirk. Mentions at least the "other" novels (except
     Roxana), and finds "the merit of a novelist" especially in the
     "authenticity" generally praised in Memoirs of a Cavalier and
     Journal of the Plague Year. Lavishes praise on Robinson Crusoe
     as a book read "with passion" by children, but also for reasons
     "more reflective." Unexpectedly, makes the point that Robinson
     Crusoe has merit for "the boldness of its subject" (man alone).
     Presses the thesis that Defoe started out in the early pages
     preaching "the duties of children toward their parents," but
     gradually dropped this interest for an entirely new "moral les-
     son"--one identified with Rousseau's Émile--the capacity of man
     alone, through his intelligence, perseverance, and energy, to
     triumph over difficulties. See also 1877.3.

2   "Defoe, Daniel." In The American Cyclopaedia: A Popular
     Dictionary of General Knowledge. Edited by George Ripley and
     Charles A. Dana. Vol. 5. Reprint. New York and London:
     D. Appleton & Co., 1883, pp. 762-64.
         Fairly accurate and comprehensive. Chooses Peter Serrano
     as "the most probable prototype" of Robinson Crusoe, and locates

the island in the Caribbean. Finds the main characteristic of
the fiction to be "the distinctness of reality" due to Defoe's
use of details.

3   EHRENTHAL, HEINRICH NICOLAUS. The English Novelists. Inau-
    gural dissertation, University of Rostock. Rostock: Adler's
    Erben, pp. 3-4.
        Hesitates to claim for Defoe the title of "father of the
English novel" because his Robinson Crusoe is not a real novel;
it does not describe the life and manners of a particular time,
and does not draw any characters.

4   A LITERARY IDLER [pseud.]. "First Sketch of English Litera-
    ture." Notes and Queries, 5th ser. 1, no. 4 (24
    January):66-67.
        Corrects Henry Morley's handbook (1873): Defoe fought in
Monmouth's insurrection at "Sedgmoor," not "Marston Moor"; according to Lee's Defoe (1869), he continued active in politics
during 1718 and long after.

5   NORGATE, FR. "Isaac (and John) Fransham." Notes and Queries,
    5th ser. 2, no. 28 (11 July):37.
        Replies to query, 1856.10. Identifies Isaac Fransham as
the older brother of John Fransham, linen-draper of Norwich and
friend of Daniel Defoe. Mentions for the first time that he
(Norgate) has "a parcel of [John Fransham's] note-books," containing copies of his verses contributed to the Gentleman's Journal
and his correspondence with Daniel Defoe, never before printed,
which he intends to publish in Notes and Queries, as soon as he
has the leisure to make transcriptions. See 1875.3.

6   RUSKIN, JOHN. Letter 46, October 1874. In Fors Clavigera:
    Letters to the Workmen and Labourers of Great Britain, vol. 4.
    London: Printed for the Author. Reprint. The Works of John
    Ruskin. Edited by E.T. Cook and Alexander Wedderburn. London:
    George Allen; New York: Longmans, Green, & Co., 1907, 28:170,
    199.
        Explains what he means by a house that is "fit" or "unfit";
turns to "the simplest idea of operation" for the reader who
claims he is a poor man, describes Crusoe's building of his cave,
and relates it to "the arts of the Greeks, Etruscans, Normans,
and Lombards, in their purest form, on the wholesome and true
threshold of all their arts. . . ."

7   SEDLEY, E. "Notice sur Daniel De Foë." In Les Aventures de
    Robinson Crusoé par Daniel De Foë. Édition classique. Paris:
    Jules Delalain & Son, pp. i-xvi.
        Surmises that at the end of his life, Defoe--poor, old,
harassed--would never have guessed that Robinson Crusoe was not
just the life of a man, but "the history of humanity and its progress." In recalling the main biographical events, casts Defoe
somewhat in the image of Milton, and holds on to old fictions,

such as his retiring from public life in 1715 and his resuming
the pen to earn his daily bread. Claims <u>Memoirs of a Cavalier</u> to
be an authentic narrative, cited even by Lord Clarendon; and
<u>Journal of the Plague Year</u>, to have a perfect realism employed by
"the imaginary chronicler." <u>Robinson Crusoe</u> he especially
admires for its "vivifying idea" of "the revolution in the soul
and character" of poor abandoned Crusoe. Believes with Taine
[1863.5]: "Never was art the instrument of a work more moral and
more English"; and with Girardin [1843.6]: in solitude, Crusoe
ultimately rediscovers his religion, and so becomes "all that man
can become while he is alone." Reprinted: 1880; 1902.

8   STEPHEN, LESLIE. "De Foe's Novels." In <u>Hours in a Library</u>.
     First Series. London: Smith, Elder, & Co., pp. 1-58.
        Revises 1868.20. Among the more substantive changes: adds
a brief passage that Richardson and Defoe "stumbled" on fiction
as lying; softens the statement on the posthumous "conclusion" of
<u>Roxana</u> being a forgery; introduces a lengthy critique of Lee's
<u>Defoe</u> (1869); provides the pungent phrase that the "secondary"
novels can claim no higher interest than that belonging to "the
ordinary police report." Reprinted: 1875; 2d ed., 1877; with
revisions, 1892.17; 1894; 1899; 1904; 1907; 1909; 1917.

9   VERNE, JULES. "L'Ile mystérieuse." <u>Magasin d'éducation et
     de récréation</u> 19 (1 January 1874)-22 (15 December 1875).
     Reprint. Paris: J. Hetzel, 1874-1875. In <u>Works of Jules
     Verne</u>. Edited by Charles F. Horne. New York and London:
     F. Tyler Daniels Co., 1911, 5:318-19, 366.
        Information on publications from Edward J. Gallagher, <u>Jules
Verne: A Primary and Secondary Bibliography</u> (Boston, Mass.:
G.K. Hall & Co., 1980), pp. 123-14. In this Robinsonade, tells
the story of five prisoners of war who escape from Richmond in a
balloon during the War of Secession and who drop down on an apparently uninhabited island, and of their ingenious efforts to
survive. Compares, on one occasion, these colonists and their
"absolute destitution" with "the imaginary heroes of Daniel De
Foe or of Wyss, as well as Selkirk and Reynal." Reprinted:
1874; 1875; 1876; 1918; 1958; 1959; 1970.

                              1875

1   DUMANOIT, J. <u>Les Aventures extraordinaires de Robinson
     Crusoe</u>. Paris: Bernardin Béchet, 104 pp.
        Robinson Crusoe "retold."

2   J., F.P. "Daniel Defoe." <u>Notes and Queries</u>, 5th ser. 4,
     no. 79 (3 July):9.
        Raises the question of the correct division of Defoe's name
into syllables. Believes [mistakenly] that the name was originally "Defoe," and so the correct division should be "Def-oe,"
suggesting Danish or Norse origin. See replies, 1875.4-5, 8-9.

3   NORGATE, FR. "Correspondence between De Foe and John
    Fransham, of Norwich (1704-1707)." Notes and Queries, 5th
    ser. 3, no. 66 (3 April):261-63; no. 67 (10 April):282-84.
         Publishes for the first time a part of the surviving eleven
    letters exchanged between John Fransham (six), linen-draper of
    Norwich, and Defoe (five) from October 1704(?) to 20 December
    1707. Shows Fransham a loyal friend, an admiring critic of such
    works as the Consolidator, and a trusted business associate and
    political agent in Norwich; and presents Defoe selling subscrip-
    tions to his Jure Divino and passing on explanations of the
    government's political strategies. Since some letters lack
    dates, they are here printed in the wrong chronological order.
    Reprinted: Healey.

4   P., E.A. "Daniel Defoe." Notes and Queries, 5th ser. 4,
    no. 90 (18 September):238.
         Replies to 1875.2, 5, 9. On Defoe's name: the preface to
    a 1712 edition of De Laune's Plea for the Non-Conformists (1706)
    is signed "D. Foe."

5   SOLLY, EDWARD. "Daniel Defoe." Notes and Queries, 5th ser.
    4, no. 85 (14 August):135.
         Replies to 1875.2. Presents the generally accepted explana-
    tion of how the original name "Daniel Foe," by accident or conven-
    ience, evolved into "De Foe" or "Defoe" around 1702-1703. Seems
    to favor the derivation of the name from the Old Norman "De Beau
    Foy." See also 1875.4, 8-9.

6   _____. "Defoe's English Commerce." Notes and Queries, 5th
    ser. 3, no. 63 (13 March):205.
         Rejects the view held by both Wilson and Lee that the Com-
    plete English Tradesman was published in only one edition, but in
    three issues and with three different title pages--for the years
    1728, 1730, and 1737. Points out the textual differences of the
    three issues.

7   TREVELYAN, GEORGE OTTO. The Life and Letters of Lord
    Macaulay. 2 vols. in one. New York and London: Harper &
    Brothers, 2:383-84.
         Quotes from Macaulay's journal a vitriolic critique which
    starts out "I can not understand the mania of some people about
    De Foe." Continues with increasing severity to call into ques-
    tion all of Defoe's achievements except for the first part of
    Robinson Crusoe. The History of the Plague and the Memoirs of
    a Cavalier are "wonderfully like true histories; but, considered
    as novels, which they are, there is not much in them." He had
    "a knack at making fiction look like truth." But why should
    this knack be admired? Is it anything more or less than "the
    knack of the painter who takes in the birds with his fruit?" How
    "immeasurably inferior" to Scott's novels! On Moll Flanders,
    Roxana, and Colonel Jack: "they are utterly wretched and nau-
    seous; in no respect, that I can see, beyond the reach of Afra

Behn." On some of his tracts: "worse than immoral; quite beast-
ly." A final comment: "Altogether I do not like him."

8   V., V.H.I.L.I.C.I. "Daniel Defoe." Notes and Queries,
     5th ser. 4, no. 90 (18 September):238.
          Replies to 1875.2, 5, 9. Quotes register of baptisms for
     the Octagon Chapel, Norwich, for Benjamin, son of Benjamin and
     Hannah D'Foe, 6 June 1719. Queries if this is Defoe's relative.

9   WARD, C.A. "Daniel Defoe." Notes and Queries, 5th ser. 4,
     no. 85 (14 August):135-36.
          Replies to 1875.2. On Defoe's name: calls attention to
     links of the family with Northamptonshire, a possible family con-
     nection with persecuted Spanish refugees from the Spanish Nether-
     lands in the reign of Elizabeth; or the change in the name as
     intended simply to avoid the name "Foe." See also 1875.4-5, 8.

                            1875-1876

1   HARDY, THOMAS. The Hand of Ethelberta. Serialized in Corn-
     hill Magazine 32-33, nos. 187-97 (July, 1875-May, 1876).
     Reprint. The Hand of Ethelberta: A Comedy in Chapters. The
     New Wessex Edition. London: Macmillan, 1975, pp. 93, 113-15,
     127-28.
          Continues the strong admiration of Defoe which Hardy first
     expressed in the "lost" novel The Poor Man and the Lady (1867),
     written in a "style having the affected simplicity of Defoe's,"
     and perhaps surviving in An Indiscretion in the Life of an Heir-
     ess (1878). In The Hand of Ethelberta, commissioned as a serial
     by Leslie Stephen, editor of the Cornhill Magazine, Hardy creates
     a character--Ethelberta or Mrs. Petherwin--who is herself an
     author, with a keen fascination in Defoe. Experimenting with
     "the point of view of the servants' Hall" (preface), Hardy has
     Mrs. Belmaine discuss with Ethelberta a topic of current interest
     in "some periodical of the time," namely, the improving of ser-
     vants' taste and morals, and thus making them dissatisfied. As
     the daughter of a butler, Ethelberta suggests that someone should
     write "a pamphlet 'The Shortest Way with Servants,' just as there
     was once written a terribly stinging one, 'The Shortest Way with
     the Dissenters,' which had a great effect." Later, during an
     interview with Christopher Julian, Ethelberta describes "a prose
     story" she had written upon request, "in the first person, and
     the style was modelled after De Foe's"; she differentiates
     between Defoe's style of telling from one of writing, "abounding
     as it does in colloquialisms that . . . have a wonderful power in
     making a narrative seem real." When she does give her first
     public reading, she is a "Professed Story-teller," practicing an
     ancient art, delivering "her pretended history and adventures"
     and relying wholly on her method--"the one pre-eminent merit of
     seeming like truth." She continues, "A modern critic has well
     observed of De Foe that he had the most amazing talent on record

for telling lies. . . ." Nowhere does the narrator identify the
critic; we are told: "Ethelberta, in wishing her fiction to
appear like a real narrative of personal adventure did wisely to
make De Foe her model." See also Florence Emily Hardy, The Early
Life of Thomas Hardy 1840–1891 (New York: Macmillan Co., 1928),
pp. 81–82, 125–38, 143.

1876

1   BROWN, FREDERICK. "History and Antiquities of Nailsea Court,
    Co. Somerset." Journal of the British Archaeological Associa-
    tion 32:381–82.
        Records briefly the name of Nathaniel Wade as being "rated"
    for an estate in Nailsea Court in the year 1698, and the names of
    Major Wade in 1704 and Mrs. Wade in 1717. Mentions also a corres-
    pondence appearing in Bristol papers (1851), in which reference
    is made to Alexander Selkirk "whose papers being put into the
    hands of Daniel Defoe were drawn out into the story of Robinson
    Crusoe."

2   CROSSLEY, JA[ME]S. "Lord Macaulay and Daniel Defoe." Notes
    and Queries, 5th ser. 5, no. 121 (22 April):327.
        Expresses sharp disagreement with Lord Macaulay's judgments
    on Defoe, and even considerable surprise, given his "genius and
    sufferings, his loyalty to William III . . ." (1875.7). Ques-
    tions particularly the statement that "some of [Defoe's] tracts
    are worse than immoral, quite beastly"; suggests that Macaulay
    has mistaken Ned Ward for Defoe.

3   [DENNIS, JOHN.] "Daniel Defoe." In Studies in English Litera-
    ture. London: Edward Stanford, pp. 77–108.
        Revision of 1871.4. The changes are not substantive, con-
    sisting mainly of excisions and additions. Biographical informa-
    tion has been added, here and there: a sentence or paragraph
    introduced to give a sense of fullness. An entire new section
    (4 pp.) describes the pamphlets written for William III after he
    became acquainted with Defoe through the True-Born Englishman.
    Except for the addition in a note of Lord Macaulay's strictures
    on the "minor" novels, none of the changes affects the criticism
    of the fiction.

4   DIBDIN, THOMAS FROGNALL. "Supplement." In Bibliomania; or
    Book-Madness; A Bibliographical Romance. New and improved ed.
    London: Chatto & Windus, p. 596.
        Lists an excessively rare edition of the Review in eight
    volumes: "the great desideratum of all the collectors of
    De Foe's works."

5   FORMAN, H. BUXTON. "Portraits of Defoe." Notes and Queries,
    5th ser. 6, no. 149 (4 November):377.
        Replies to 1876.6, 11. Corrects 1876.11 on the portrait of
    Defoe in the frontispiece to Jure Divino (1706): the spelling

M. Vander Gucht, not Gutch. Refers to another engraving by
"I. Taverner," probably the portrait painter Jeremiah Taverner.

6   FRANCIS, THO[MA]S. "Portraits of Defoe." Notes and Queries,
    5th ser. 6, no. 142 (16 September):229.
        Asks if there are many portraits, and where one can be
    seen. See replies, 1876.5, 11.

7   [IRELAND, MARY E.] "The Defoe Family in America." Scribner's
    Monthly 12, no. 1 (May):61-64.
        Tells the apocryphal story of an American branch of the
    family descended from Defoe's widowed sister, Elizabeth Maxwell,
    with whom he took refuge in London around 1705 and whose daughter
    Elizabeth came to the New World in 1718, was sold in Philadel-
    phia, was subsequently married to Thomas Job and became one of
    the Friends who lived within two miles of the Brick Meeting-
    House, Cecil County, Maryland. Records the tradition that Eliza-
    beth Job preserved all the letters from her famous uncle until
    her death in 1782, and she constantly reminisced about him.
    Observes that a chair from Defoe's study has been presented by
    James Trimble to the Historical Society of Delaware.

8   O., J. "Robinson Crusoe." Notes and Queries, 5th ser. 6,
    no. 154 (9 December):466.
        Notes that the first four editions of Robinson Crusoe (Part
    One) were not just "re-issues" to meet the demand, but they were
    also "re-set." Compares two personal copies of different edi-
    tions.

9   "Reminiscences of the Rev. R.P. Graves, M.A., Formerly of
    Windermere, Now of Dublin." In The Prose Works of William
    Wordsworth. Edited by Alexander B. Grosart. London: Edward
    Moxon, Son & Co., 3:468.
        Recalls Wordsworth as having thought that the charm of Rob-
    inson Crusoe did not arise from its "naturalness," but from "the
    extraordinary energy and resource of the hero under his difficult
    circumstances," beyond anything expected; and that the pleasure
    over Crusoe's "successes and good fortunes" did arise from "the
    peculiar source of these uncommon merits of his character." Re-
    printed: New York: AMS Press, 1967; Critical Heritage.

10 RUSKIN, JOHN. Letter 68 "Bags that Wax Old." In Fors Clavi-
    gera: Letters to the Workmen and Labourers of Great Britain,
    vol. 6. London: Printed for the Author. Reprint. The Works
    of John Ruskin. Edited by E.T. Cook and Alexander Wedderburn.
    London: George Allen; New York: Longmans, Green, & Co.,
    1907, 28:673-74.
        Describes it as an encouragement to some, "especially those
    evangelically bred," toward altering their belief in interest and
    capital, "to think of our old converted friend, Friday," and view
    themselves as falling short of being Christians. Argues that the
    gain by "the lender of capital" is matched by an equivalent loss

to the borrower. Even worse is the psychic damage to both borrower and lender.

11   WARD, C.A. "Portraits of Defoe." Notes and Queries, 5th ser.
      6, no. 146 (14 October):315.
            Replies to 1876.6. Lists portraits including two probably
      by the engraver Michael Vander Gutch [sic], one for Jure Divino
      (1706) and the other from a picture by Taverner; oval portraits
      by Medland and W. Skelton.

12   WELLS, DAVID A[MES]. Robinson Crusoe's Money; or, The Remark-
      able Financial Fortunes and Misfortunes of a Remote Island
      Community. New York: Harper & Brothers, 118 pp.
            Writing on behalf of "certain prominent friends of hard
      money" and taking his model from Washington Irving's Tales of a
      Traveller (1824), advances a somewhat heavy allegory of Robinson
      Crusoe's island community as progressing through the stages of
      barter, money, and currency, and experiencing fiscal crises not
      unlike those of the United States during the recent Civil War.
      Starts with the incident of Crusoe's finding the three bags of
      money, and develops the circumstances under which money gains
      utility and value, and becomes the standard for setting price.
      Simplifies complex economic principles into stories, for example,
      about Twist the tailor or Needum the baker, or about pretty
      shells called "cowries." Near the conclusion, in chap. 11, "The
      New Millenium," describes the "Friends of Humanity" as leading
      the attack on "poor old Robinson Crusoe," the advocate of the
      gold standard, and as creating the problems of an inflated
      currency and an enormous national debt. Reprinted: New York:
      Peter Smith, 1931.

13   WYON, FREDERICK WILLIAM. The History of Great Britain during
      the Reign of Queen Anne. London: Chapman & Hall, 1:139-42,
      352n, 473-74; 2:259, 394, 448, 470.
            Retells the familiar story of Defoe's persecution by the
      high-church Tories, but dwells upon his complete lack of vanity
      in the writings and his imprudence in opposing occasional con-
      formity and using irony in the Shortest-Way with the Dissenters.
      Comments further on Defoe's "composition" of the Capt. George
      Carleton; his work for the Scottish union; his writing of "a
      series of masterly treatises upon finance, some of which Harley
      condescended to publish to the world as his own composition"; his
      support for free trade; and his troubles with the Whigs over
      ironical pamphlets.

                                  1877

1   ADAMS, H[ENRY] C[ADWALLADER]. The Original Robinson Crusoe
      Being a Narrative of the Adventures of Alexander Selkirk and
      Others, on Which De Foe is Believed to Have Founded His Famous
      Romance. Every Boy's Library. London: George Routledge &
      Sons, 256 pp.

Working from "original records," such as those found in
Dampier, Funnell, Cook, Woodes Rogers, Steele, and John Howell,
and from still later accounts, sets up deliberately a sequential
personal narrative of Selkirk's adventures. Forthrightly dismisses the "groundless calumny" that Robinson Crusoe was "stolen"
from Selkirk by Defoe in the summer of 1711 or 1712. Raises the
altogether different question of the extent to which these adventures may have contributed to Robinson Crusoe. In the introductory chapter of biography, emphasizes Defoe's "enforced solitudes," his imprisonments, as isolating him from his fellow men.
In chaps. 2 through 13, allows Selkirk to tell his own story, in
the first person, to a group at a coffee-house, made up of Dick
Steele, Pope, Gay, and Addison, incorporating the latest information on himself from the sources listed in the preface. In the
appendix, brings together accounts of other castaways who resemble both Selkirk and Robinson Crusoe. Notes particularly how
many were stranded on Juan Fernandez, thus making the island, as
Captain Burney says, "the land of Robinson Crusoes."

2   BATTIER, W[ILLIAM]. "Étude sur Daniel De Foe." In Daniel
    De Foe. Étranges aventures de Robinson Crusoe: Traduction
    de l'édition princeps (1719) avec une étude sur l'auteur.
    Paris: Jules Bonnassies, pp. i-xx.
         Interprets Defoe's career as a novelist within an early
    nineteenth-century biographical framework. Accepts long-standing
    minor errors (e.g., date of birth as 1661), but also such substan-
    tive myths as Defoe's sharp break from politics in 1715, his sup-
    posed withdrawal from writing in periodicals, and his turning to
    novels. Significantly reverses Taine's view (1863.5) in arguing
    that Robinson Crusoe has only a single character ("personnage")
    and that it sustains interest by the diversity of the situation
    and the variety of the difficulties triumphed over. Identifies
    Robinson Crusoe as "the personification of the nation," summing
    up "the spirit of adventure, love of voyages, perseverance pushed
    to obstinacy, indomitable energy, untiring work, all the quali-
    ties of the Saxon race." Stresses that Crusoe is not "a perverse
    man regenerating himself by solitude," but by work, and voluntar-
    ily. Distinguishes Robinson Crusoe as "a novel of character"
    (concerned with the individual or the soul), as distinct from the
    "novels of adventures" (concerned with "external circumstances
    and details of action")--Colonel Jack, Moll Flanders, Captain
    Singleton, Duncan Campbell. Finds among the latter "the pica-
    resque novel," along with the low-life characters who were
    Defoe's favorites. Reserves a special place for Journal of the
    Plague Year, quoted at length to demonstrate how details can be
    accumulated to "the point of horror." Persists in making the
    point, repeatedly, that the personal experiences of Defoe or his
    friends are reflected directly, or indirectly, in the style of a
    novel.

3   BELJAME, ALEXANDRE. Review of Battier's study of Defoe, 1877.
    Revue critique d'histoire et de littérature 25 (23 June):
    395-98.

Balances the assessment with comments on the two genres which Defoe founded, the literary press and the English novel. Praises Battier's translation for giving French readers "the true Robinson," no longer treating Robinson Crusoe as a book for children and therefore readily subjected to revision or abridgement-- above all, providing a respectable text for a work so important from a literary and moral point of view. Regrets the absence of the work by Lee, Forster, Hettner, Masson, and Chasles; and advocates a stronger position on Defoe as the writer who introduced, in place of "romances, faded narratives of amorous adventures, novels, based on the observation of real life," and as such became the precursor of an illustrious series--Richardson, Fielding, and Smollett.

4   P., P. "Whately on Defoe." Notes and Queries, 5th ser. 8, no. 198 (13 October):296.
       Replies to 1877.6. Asks if Archbishop Whately would not have had better criticism in the lack of water for growing rice. See also 1865.12.

5   "Robinson Crusoe." Bow Bells 27, no. 682 [August?]:187.
       Claims to establish "the real existence of a hero of fiction heretofore regarded as a myth." Traces the name "Robinson Crusoe" to a tombstone in a graveyard at Lynn Regis and the Crusoe family of seafaring people still living there in 1835.

6   SOLLY, EDWARD. "Whately on Defoe." Notes and Queries, 5th ser. 8, no. 193 (8 September):185.
       Questions the soundness of Whately's criticism of the passage in Robinson Crusoe which describes the "culture of rice" here as "an absolute impossibility" (1865.12). Disagrees with Whately in that Defoe specifically refers to the rice as being in its husk and ready for feeding poultry. Concludes that the criticism has no basis whatsoever.

1878

1   GIBBS, MONTGOMERY [Gilbert Mortimer]. Six Hundred Robinson Crusoes, or, The Voyage of the Golden Fleece. A True Story for Old and Young. London: Sampson Low, Marston, Searle, & Rivington, 298 pp.
       Describes the shipwreck and rescue of 630 passengers and crew aboard the Golden Fleece during a voyage in the Caribbean. States in the preface that the incident, "a true one," was told in a way "rivalling in many of its details Defoe's romantic but imaginary history of the hermit of Juan Fernandez." Not infrequently, draws comparisons with, or themes from, Robinson Crusoe. See Gove (p. 124n) for the designation of the book as one of the "new Robinsons" appearing in the nineteenth century.

2   J[OUAUST], D[AMASE], ed. "Avertissement." In <u>Vie et aven-</u>
     <u>tures de Robinson Crusoé par Daniel De Foe.</u> Traduction de
     <u>Petrus Borel</u>. Edition Jouaust. 4 vols. Paris: Librairie
     des bibliophiles, 1:a-d.
        Insisting on accurate translations of foreign masterpieces,
     chooses the text of Petrus Borel over Saint-Hyacinthe's and Van
     Effen's or Madame Tastu's. Observes that Reynald's introduction
     (1878.8) presents "the philosophical side of <u>Robinson Crusoe</u>, which
     is generally ignored.

3   LECKY, WILLIAM EDWARD HARTPOLE. <u>A History of England in the</u>
     <u>Eighteenth Century</u>. 8 vols. New York: D. Appleton & Co.,
     1:58, 65-67, 471, 529-30, 608-10.
        In all but one of the citations, introduces Defoe as an his-
     torical witness, through Wilson's <u>Memoirs</u> of Defoe (1830), on
     such matters as women taking part in political agitations, the
     popularity of the <u>True-Born Englishman</u>, opposition to "the rotten
     boroughs" in the <u>Tour</u>, hostility to Englishmen abroad for plunder-
     ing shipwrecked vessels at home. But goes directly to <u>Giving</u>
     <u>Alms No Charity</u> (1704) to present data on weekly wages, the poor
     and the causes of poverty. Reprinted: 1892.

4   L'ESTRANGE, A.G. <u>History of English Humour</u>. Reprint.
     2 vols. in one. Research & Source Works Series 415. New
     York: Burt Franklin, 1970, 1:22-36.
        In a general study of the ludicrous, humour, laughter, wit,
     and other related terms, enters into "an almost untrodden and
     apparently barren region." Makes important definitions and dis-
     tinctions in "Preliminary Observations" and the early chapter
     "Origin of Humour," and in the last five chapters; proceeds
     historically through "Greek Humour," "Roman Humour," and "English
     Humour" through Dickens. In the selected non-fictional works of
     Defoe, finds sarcasm, irony, invective, amusement, and humour.
     Erroneously, assigns to Defoe the <u>Comical Pilgrim</u> and a coarsely
     humorous quotation on the audience of a theatre.

5   MINTO, WILLIAM. "'Through the Dark Continent' in 1720."
     <u>Macmillan's Magazine</u> 38, no. 228 (October):459-66.
        Describes the controversy which has arisen over the "antici-
     pations" of the recent discoveries about the geography of Central
     Africa, in Captain Singleton's trek from Zanzibar to the Gold
     Coast. Of particular interest are the sources of the rivers Nile
     and Congo, and the geographical locations and sizes of certain
     lakes. On a "first impression," so closely does Singleton's itin-
     erary conform to Central African geography, Defoe appears to be
     using the notes of a Portuguese trader. He actually follows "the
     best knowledge of his time," represented by seventeenth-century
     mapmakers, but falls short of the geographical discoveries made
     by Speke, Burton, Stanley, Livingstone. Hypothesizes that Single-
     ton may have sailed up the river Rufigi [Rufiji], probably the
     Quilloa of <u>Captain Singleton</u>; then travelled directly west for
     thirty miles to Lake Tanganyika, on recent maps or Lake Zafflan

on early maps. Contends that beyond this point Defoe had the
benefit of notes, for his "geography becomes indisputably wild
and fabulous." From the second huge lake, the rivers Nile and
the Congo issued—each in turn surprised Singleton and his men.
Asserts that only with considerable error can the second lake be
identified with the Victoria Nyanza, but easily with Lake Zaire
of the early maps. For an assessment and corrections of Minto's
errors, see 1924.20.

6   MITCHELL, DONALD G[RANT]. "Robinson Crusoe." In About Old
     Story-Tellers: Of How and When They Lived, and What Stories
     They Told. New York: Scribner, Armstrong, & Co., pp. 198-
     218.
        Popularizes in "this half-hour's talk" a few high points of
biography, particularly the troubles connected with the Shortest-
Way with the Dissenters; and chats about the earlier success of
the True-Born Englishman and about the satire [Good] Advice to
the Ladies (1702), later the editing of the Review while he was
still in prison, and the production of numerous other works, but
especially the memorable Robinson Crusoe. Rejects any notion
that Defoe stole the story from Selkirk, and identifies its chief
merit to be a certain plainness of style.

7   REYNALD, HERMILE. "La Société anglaise au temps de Daniel
     De Foe: Robinson Crusoé." Revue bleue, 2d ser. 15, no. 21
     (23 November):486-94.
        While the article appeared in print just before the elegant
Jouaust Edition of Robinson Crusoé, it was a considerably reduced
version of Reynald's "Notice sur Robinson Crusoé," and served to
introduce the new work. See also 1878.8.

8   _____. "Notice sur Robinson Crusoé" and "Notes." In Vie et
     aventures de Robinson Crusoé par Daniel De Foë. Traduction de
     Petrus Borel. Edition Jouaust. 4 vols. Paris: Librairie
     des bibliophiles, 1:i-xlvii, 257-60; 2:251-52; 3:265-67; 4:
     227-29.
        Aims at a high level of critical judgment and current schol-
arship by reprinting Borel's translation of the two-part Robinson
Crusoe and using Chasles's Life (1836) and Lee's Defoe (1869).
Adjusts the views of both biographers—severely disagreeing with
Chasles for his assumption that Defoe lived in poverty after
1715, and criticizing Lee for being "perhaps too complaisant" in
judging Defoe to be patriotic while he was undermining journals
such as Mist's. Directs his introduction to a philosophical
analysis of Robinson Crusoe, subordinating biography entirely to
this purpose. Recognizes Robinson Crusoe as having a strong
appeal to children and young men; sees it also as being like Don
Quijote, meaningful to adults. Asks how an author, generally
given to mediocre labors, could produce "a book which all humanity admires." Seeks an answer in political and religious terms,
describing "the old Robinson" as "an allegorical painting" and
finding there "an imprint of all the preoccupations which England

then experienced." Accepts the tradition of Defoe's meeting Selkirk in Bristol. Observes that the skills revealed in <u>Mrs. Veal</u>
or the "thought" found in the <u>Family Instructor</u> (1715; 1718)
would recur in <u>Robinson Crusoe</u>. Makes tenuous connections at
times as between Defoe's listening to the voice that urges him to
write to Lord Chief Justice Parker and Crusoe's return to religious sentiments, or between Dickory Cronke's isolation and Robinson Crusoe's. Comments on the immediate relevance of <u>Robinson
Crusoe</u>, permitting readers to rediscover "their own preoccupations, fears, hopes, prejudices" and confronting in the book a
reality which one would expect in an authentic document. Stresses "the moral and religious character by demonstrating Defoe's
preoccupation with the "paternal curse." Powerfully depicts Robinson Crusoe as "a true character of grandeur," and his history
one of rediscovery, showing a man abandoned to his own resources
and painfully recovering the benefits of civilization. Reprinted, in part: 1878.7.

9   SAINTSBURY, GEORGE. "Defoe, Daniel (1661-1731)." In <u>Encyclo-
    paedia Britannica</u>. 9th ed. New York: Charles Scribner's
    Sons, 7:26-31.
         Shows the biographical account of Defoe and the appraisal
    of his non-fictional works as yielding to lengthy criticism of
    the novels. In addition to <u>Robinson Crusoe</u>: <u>Memoirs of a Cava-
    lier</u>, <u>Captain Singleton</u> ("surprising anticipations" of recent
    discoveries in Africa), <u>Moll Flanders</u>, <u>Roxana</u>, <u>Colonel Jack</u>, and
    <u>Journal of the Plague Year</u>. Reserves special praise for <u>Moll
    Flanders</u>: "next to <u>Robinson Crusoe</u> in order of merit, or bracket-
    ted for that position with the somewhat similar <u>Roxana</u>." Sees
    the difference between these two works "much more one of morals
    than of manners." Claims also that no scene in all of English
    literature can equal or surpass the incident in <u>Colonel Jack</u>
    where the youthful pickpocket loses his ill-gotten gains. Pro-
    vides up-to-date references and analysis for biography, criti-
    cism, and canon. Reprinted: 1890; considerably revised in
    1910.18 and later.

                              1879

1   ARBER, EDWARD, ed. "Daniel Defoe. The Education of Women."
    In <u>An English Garner: Ingatherings from Our History and Liter-
    ature</u>. London: E. Arber, 2:265-68.
         Reprints the selection from <u>An Essay upon Projects</u>, "writ-
    ten about 1692." Reprinted: 1903.1.

2   GUEST, JOHN. "The Don Navigation." In <u>Historic Notices of
    Rotherham: Ecclesiastical, Collegiate, and Civil</u>. Worksop:
    Robert White, pp. 537-39, 659 (map).
         Traces the parliamentary proposal to make the River Don
    more effectively navigable, from 1721 to 1726; interrupts to
    present an important discovery just made by William Lee--Defoe's

letter in the Daily Post, 8 February 1723. Shows Defoe making
the argument that the improved navigation, as the cause of inun-
dating 30,000 acres, is "as mere Romance as the Life of Robinson
Crusoe." See also Dorothy Greene, "Daniel Defoe's Letters,"
Notes and Queries 187, no. 5 (26 August 1944):109.

3   HETTNER, HERMANN. Geschichte der deutschen Literatur im
     achtzehnten Jahrhundert, 3d ed. Reprint. Edited by Gotthard
     Erler. 2 vols. Berlin: Aufbau, 1961, 1:241-50, 561.
         Reprints Hettner's text, with minor corrections, of a
     portion of his Literaturgeschichte des achtzehnten Jahrhunderts--
     some of which was published as early as 1854. Robinson's name
     was attached to every kind of publication in Germany after 1719
     as a certain attention-getter. The tradition of the actual Rob-
     insonade, however, is seen to stem from mid-seventeenth-century
     adventure novels (in turn derived from Spanish picaresque nov-
     els), extending across Simplicissimus-style writings, to which
     the post-Defoe Robinsonades attach themselves. These form three
     main groups: (1) satirical-didactic (very bleak, pedantic
     stuff), (2) adventure tales (numerous exempla of the moral deprav-
     ity of the age), and (3) adventure-filled travel accounts (more
     closely Robinsonesque, yet equally depressing in their unpoetical
     sensationalism). In Germany, Robinson Crusoe was seminal in turn-
     ing popular novelists' tastes towards English models, away from
     picaresque influences. Only one work, Schnabel's Insel Felsen-
     burg (1731), stands out above the rest for its powerful poetic
     vision, differing from Defoe's novel, however, in depicting the
     lovingly nurtured island society as a utopian alternative to the
     deplorable state of affairs in Europe. The Marxist scholar Erler
     obviously shares Hettner's enthusiasm for Schnabel's "socialist
     communist experiment." Despite its many weaknesses, which place
     it far behind Robinson Crusoe in aesthetic value, this "Rousseau
     before Rousseau" was Germany's best offering among the Robinson-
     ades. See also 1854.4.   (P.E.C.)

4   KEER, W.B. "Robinson Crusoe's Island." Boy's Own Annual 1,
     no. 35 (13 September):558-59.
         On Juan Fernandez: nostalgic associations, factual infor-
     mation on topography, dull actual experience of Selkirk, Cowper's
     verses.

5   MINTO, WILLIAM. Daniel Defoe. English Men of Letters.
     London: Macmillan & Co., 179 pp.
         Most provocatively, Minto observes about Defoe: "He was a
     great, a truly great liar, perhaps the greatest liar that ever
     lived." The general effect of this influential "English Men of
     Letters" study has been to reduce the hero-worship with which
     earlier biographers had enveloped their subject and to diminish
     the reputation of both the man and the novelist. Devoting nine
     of his ten chapters to biography organized around topical head-
     ings, he gives, as he says in the preface, "a true appreciation
     of [Defoe's] main lines of thought and action." To his overall

interpretation he brings a thorough-going skepticism about Defoe's veracity concerning himself where the "facts" do not have
"independent confirmation"--and a determined readiness to believe
the worst about his subject. In chap. 9, "The Place of Defoe's
Fiction in His Life" (25 pp.), Minto offers a general interpretation of the novels, which had never been advanced before, yet
one which rises easily from his view of Defoe's mixed nature as
a man. The art of Defoe's novels he declares to be "simple,
unique, incommunicable." It is the relationship of the novels to
Defoe's life which Minto finds worth exploring. He explains the
relationship by theorizing that "the invention of plausible circumstances," the "great secret" which Defoe discovered in writing
Robinson Crusoe, was something he had practiced all his life. It
was the same "genius for 'lying like truth'" he displayed in his
early missions for Harley when he travelled the land "in assumed
characters and on factitious pretexts"; in his disguises in
Scotland when he worked on behalf of the Union; in "passages of
circumstantial invention" in the Review; in the threat of trans-
portation to the West Indies, which hung over him, as real in his
private life as in Moll Flanders, Colonel Jack, or Robinson
Crusoe. For the final step in developing the relationship of the
novels to Defoe's life, Minto turns to Serious Reflections; and
utilizing Defoe's conception of Robinson Crusoe as an allegory,
sharply differentiates such allegory from "talking falsely" or
"the minor vice of falsehood." For Defoe, "this supplying a
story by invention" can be described as "a sort of lying that
makes a great hole in the heart, in which by degrees a habit of
lying enters in." Not only Colonel Jack, Moll Flanders, and
Roxana, but even Robinson Crusoe are "inventions" and "lying like
truth." Minto takes the well-known passage in Serious Reflec-
tions--"Necessity makes an honest man a knave"--as "Defoe's excuse for his backslidings put into the mouth of Robinson Crusoe";
he argues that "it might be inscribed also on the threshold of
each of his fictitious biographies." As an integral part of his
method, Minto repeatedly blends together the experiences of Defoe
with those of his characters. That the method can be productive
of keen insights may be illustrated by the critique of Moll Flanders as failing because it lacks a "unique creative purpose" and
in the comparison of the heroes and heroines to "tradesmen who
have strayed into unlawful courses." See also 1882.7. Reprinted: 1879, 1885, 1887, 1902, 1907, 1909, 1968; in part, Critical
Heritage. Translated in condensed form in German, 1880.9.

6   "Robinson Crusoe." Boy's Own Annual 1, no. 2 (25 January):29.
        At the Museum of the Society of Antiquaries, Edinburgh:
the drinking cup and sea-chest of Alexander Selkirk "whose solitary exile . . . gave the idea of De Foe's world-famed romance."

7   SCOTT, SIR WALTER; WILSON, WALTER; and BRAYLEY, E[DWARD]
    W[EDLAKE]. Quotations before "Journal of the Plague in London
    by Daniel Defoe, Author of Robinson Crusoe, etc." Franklin
    Square Library, 46. New York: Harper & Brothers, 44 pp.

Quotes Scott's "Advertisement" (Works, 1840-1841), Wilson's Memoirs of Defoe (1830), and Brayley (1835.4)--seven paragraphs introducing this reprint of the Journal of the Plague Year.

8   TOURNEUX, MAURICE. Correspondance littéraire, philosophique et critique par Grimm, Diderot, Raynal, Meister, etc. 16 vols. Paris: Garnier Frères, 8:37.
    Comments briefly on the madness for abridging works as being so great that a certain M. de Montreille (pseudonym of M. Savin, professor of Humanities at Bordeaux) brought out Isle de Robinson Crusoë (London and Paris, 1768; reprinted Robinson dans son isle, 1774) which curtailed "the dangerous maxims" of the original.

                              1880

1   BURTON, JOHN HILL. A History of the Reign of Queen Anne. 3 vols. Edinburgh and London: William Blackwood & Sons, 1:69-70, 94-98, 314-17, 342-45; 2:42-43, 52-53, 170-78; 3:256-67.
    Stands apart from the usual recognition given to Defoe as an historical source. Recognizes him as the single most preeminent authority on such matters as the Union and the "Worcester" affair; and quotes his History of the Union and Review, respectfully, to describe events at firsthand. Now and then, hints at a bias, as when describing Defoe's weakening under Lord Nottingham's threats, observes that "scrupulosity as a public man" was not among his virtues. Makes effective use of materials, at times reaching original conclusions: the Shortest-Way with the Dissenters as "high rhetorical wit" and as such embodying a mimickry not unrelated to that of Robinson Crusoe; manuscript letters and a memorandum about Defoe; a firm rejection of Defoe's authorship of Capt. George Carleton on the grounds that the central character lacks the egotism which one finds readily in Captain Singleton or Memoirs of a Cavalier. See also 1853.2.

2   CONNOLLEY, GUS. Robinson Crusoe, or the Bad King, the Good Fairy and the Lucky Friday. Derby: J. Harwood, 29 pp.
    A pantomime, listed in the National Union Catalog, copy in the Theatre Collection of the Harvard University Library.

3   DEMOGEOT, J[ACQUES CLAUDE]. Histoire des littératures étrangères. Paris: Librairie Hachette & Co., pp. 126-28, 130-32.
    Discusses briefly the opening up by Defoe of double careers, first, in publishing the Review, among periodicals "a point of departure and a model"; and second, in producing fiction that was generally regarded as "authentic." On the novels, expresses the view that Defoe spent twenty years preaching "his rigid doctrine" of Puritanism, and twenty more in shoring up "pious falsehoods." Robinson Crusoe may thus be viewed as "the least of novels" or "a perfect illusion."

4   DICKENS, CHARLES. Letter to Walter Savage Landor. In The
    Letters of Charles Dickens. Edited by His Sister-in-Law and
    His Eldest Daughter. 2d ed. 2 vols. London: Chapman &
    Hall, 1:443.
        5 July 1856: repeats the comment to Walter Savage Landor
    which he wrote earlier to Forster (1872-1874.1) that "one of the
    most popular books on earth [Robinson Crusoe] has nothing in it
    to make any one laugh or cry." Friday's death seems "one of the
    least tender and (in the true sense) least sentimental things
    ever written. It is a book I read very much. . . ." See also
    1869.10. Reprinted: in vol. 2, The Letters of Charles Dickens,
    ed. Walter Dexter (Bloomsbury: Nonesuch Press, 1938).

5   FAMA. "Defoe's Review." Notes and Queries, 6th ser. 1,
    no. 11 (13 March):226.
        Replies to 1880.6. Reports that the Bodleian Library
    possesses only vols. 1-3 of the Review.

6   H., S. "Defoe's Review." Notes and Queries, 6th ser. 1,
    no. 9 (28 February):175.
        Endeavors to ascertain which sets of the Review are com-
    plete, observing that for "a work of such rarity and importance,"
    the information is most desirable. Maintains that an eight-
    volume set lacks the ninth volume or the first volume of the new
    series. Requests readers to examine sets in the British Museum
    and Bodleian Library, and report on their completeness. See
    reply, 1880.5.

7   HALE, E[DWARD] E[VERETT]. "Alexander Selkirk." In Stories
    of the Sea Told by Sailors. Boston: Roberts Brothers,
    pp. 107-18.
        Presents Uncle Fritz as explaining to the children that
    Robinson Crusoe was shipwrecked on an island in the mouth of the
    Orinoco River, and not on Juan Fernandez; and as summarizing
    Alexander Selkirk's story from Providence Displayed (1810) and
    Isaac Disraeli's Curiosities of Literature (1817). The children
    are quick to notice the discrepancies between Crusoe's behavior
    and Selkirk's.

8   _____. "Crusoe in New York" and Other Tales. Boston:
    Roberts Brothers, pp. 1-58.
        Narrates in the first person Robinson Crusoe's account of
    himself, born in New York in 1842. He builds a secret cottage on
    Ninth Avenue, which he calls his "castle" and where he and his
    mother live together happily and are finally joined by the Swed-
    ish girl, Frida, who has fled from the savage "toughs" and whom
    Crusoe marries. Constantly echoes the original story in words,
    ideas, and incidents. Reprinted: The American Short Story
    Series, vol. 19 (New York: Garrett Press, 1968).

9   KATSCHER, LEOPOLD, trans. Foreword to Daniel Defoe, der Ver-
    fasser von "Robinson Crusoe." Von William Minto. Zierden der
    englischen Literatur. Leipzig: E. Wartig, pp. vii-viii.

Discusses briefly the decision of the editor and translator
to condense William Minto's text [1879.5] and annotate the original for the benefit of German readers.   (P.E.C.)

10   MACAULAY, THOMAS BABINGTON. "John Dryden (January 1828)."
     The Miscellaneous Writings, Speeches and Poems. 4 vols.
     Longmans, Green, & Co., 1:12-13.
          Reprint of 1828.4.

11   "Robinson Crusoe Jap." Harper's Young People 1, no. 26
     (27 April):357.
          In four seven-line stanzas, offers a Japanese version of
     "Oh, poor Robinson Crusoe," a title appearing clearly in one of
     the illustrations surrounding the verses. Tells about Foo
     Chung's finding a footprint in the sand, and asks if it can be,
     "the savage Fee Gee / Is the race that inhabits this land?" In
     one illustration, clearly shows Defoe the author of Robinson
     Crusoe.

12   "Robinson Crusoe's Island." Harper's Young People 1, no. 37
     (13 July):527-30.
          While unfolding a travelogue account of lovely Juan Fer-
     nandez in close association with colorful history of Selkirk's
     abandonment (complete with illustrations), keeps up a running
     commentary on the absurdity of confusing this island with Cru-
     soe's island "near the mouth of the great river Orinoco" and of
     believing that Defoe had to read Selkirk's account of his adven-
     tures which suggested "the idea of inventing Robinson Crusoe."

13   RUSSELL, J. FULLER. "William Hone." Notes and Queries,
     6th ser. 1, no. 9 (28 February):171.
          During an interview in 1833, Hone recalls that he took
     the idea for his Every Day Book, in 1814, from Defoe's Time's
     Telescope.

                                1881

1   BELJAME, ALEXANDRE. Le Public et les hommes de lettres en
     Angleterre au diz-huitième siècle 1660-1740. Paris and Lon-
     don: Hachette & Co., pp. 231, 235, 255, 260, 270, 273-77,
     330, 337-38, 341, 343, 389, 439.
          In a seminal study of "John Dryden and the Theatre," "John
     Dryden and Politics," and "Joseph Addison," expresses strong con-
     victions about the narrow conception of literature and the low
     esteem of the writer in the time of Dryden; describes and defines
     new concepts of "the public" and "man of letters," emerging in
     the time of Addison, that allowed writers to make authoritative
     contributions to "a great revolution in manners and morals."
     Clearly assigns to Defoe a secondary role in this revolution: in
     the Jeremy Collier controversy; in the Review (anticipating Addi-
     son's Spectator); and in Robinson Crusoe (establishing the novel

of manners rather than the romance). Argues that in journalism,
his influence was limited because unlike Steele, he was not
"a man of the world," and his style was "straightforward" and
"without grace or art." See the edition with an introduction by
Bonamy Dobrée, translated by E.O. Lorimer (London: Kegan Paul,
Trench, Trubner & Co., 1948). Reprinted: 1897.

2   CHERBULIEZ, VICTOR [G. Valbert]. "Robinson Crusoé et la
    littérature électorale." Revue des deux mondes 47:214-26.
        Responding positively to Minto's Defoe (1879), takes the
    view of Defoe as "the greatest liar that ever lived," and elabo-
    rates it into a full critical understanding of Robinson Crusoe
    and the author's relationship to his work. Recognizes Defoe as,
    in literary history, "the rare example of the man who passed his
    life in the mire without satisfying his imagination, without los-
    ing the marvelous precision of his mind and the lucidity of his
    reason." Describes Robinson Crusoe as "a happy accident" and a
    "miracle": from a source so pure and limpid, soil "so muddy and
    contaminated." Posulates that there were "two Defoes": the one
    who grubbed in the corrupt politics of the time and became him-
    self corrupted; the other, the author of Robinson Crusoe, who
    wrested his narrative from psychological conflicts due to serving
    two different political parties. Describes the second Defoe as
    descending into his conscience and discovering there "a mine of
    virgin gold," and creating a hero from the figure who passed in
    and out of his dreams: "'It is me, he had been able to say, and
    yet it is not me.'" Throughout the literary discussion, uses
    Robinson Crusoe and its author to lambast the innovative liberal-
    ism of the day. Reprinted: Hommes et choses au temps présent
    (Paris: Hachette, 1883).

3   "Dr. Thomas Dover, of Bristol." Gloucestershire Notes and
    Queries 1, part 12 (October):435-36.
        On Dr. Dover as the first medical man to offer "gratuitous
    services" to the poor in 1696: he also later participated in the
    rescue of Selkirk. Repeats Wilson's opinion that when Defoe was
    living on Castle Street in Bristol, he met Captain Rogers or
    Selkirk and "so got the frame work of Robinson Crusoe."

4   HALE, EDWARD E[VERETT]. Stories of Adventure Told by Adventur-
    ers. Boston: Roberts Brothers, pp. 178-80, 185-86, 275-76.
        Retells lively narratives about an Indian woman taken pris-
    oner by the Athapuscow Indians in the summer of 1770, told under
    the running title "A Woman Robinson Crusoe"; about the travels of
    Alexander von Humboldt educated by "the stone-axe Robinson"
    (Campe's Robinson the Younger, 1779-1780.1); and about Siberia,
    China, and even slavery in The Farther Adventures of Robinson
    Crusoe.

5   HOOPER, JAMES. "The Vicar of Baddow." Notes and Queries,
    6th ser. 4, no. 104 (24 December):512.

Queries about a poem concerning the devil, of which three
stanzas are quoted, in "a very strange old book, called The
History of the Devil." Asks for the identity of the author and
also of "the Vicar of Baddow" alluded to in the verses. Of the
four replies two give the author as Defoe and the publication
date as 1726. See the replies 1882.2-3, 10 and the explanation
by Solly, 1882.9.

6   UNEDA. "Robinson Crusoe in Latin." Notes and Queries, 6th
    ser. 3, no. 78 (25 June):517.
        In 1821, an earlier edition of Goffaux's Latin text of Rob-
inson Crusoe was used in Philadelphia at James P. Espy's classical school. New words had to be invented for things unknown to
the Romans, such as guns (tormenta).

7   WALFORD, E. "Robinson Crusoe in Latin." Notes and Queries,
    6th ser. 3, no. 69 (23 April):326.
        Discusses briefly J.F. Goffaux's translation of Robinson
Crusoe into Latin (1823), its four editions on the continent.

1882

1   BOTT, THOMAS H. Preface to Robinson Crusoe in Verse. London:
    Simpkin Marshall & Co.; Birmingham: Midland Educational Co.,
    p. 12.
        Explains his purpose in heroic couplets: "Defoe's Immortal
work, so good and terse. / I felt should now be put in modern
verse." In Robinson Crusoe in Verse (161 pp.), follows the broad
outlines of the original closely and at times awkwardly.

2   BROWN, JAMES ROBERTS. "The Vicar of Baddow." Notes and Que-
    ries, 6th ser. 5, no. 111 (11 February):117.
        Replies to 1881.5. Identifies the book as a late edition
of Defoe's Political History of the Devil (1726), but cannot
identify "the Vicar of Baddow." See also 1882.9.

3   JONAS, ALFRED CHAS. "The Vicar of Baddow." Notes and Que-
    ries, 6th ser. 5, no. 111 (11 February):117.
        Replies to 1881.5, without identifying "the Vicar of
Baddow." See also 1882.9.

4   LAUD, J.C. "Portrait of Daniel De Foe by Sir Godfrey Knel-
    ler." Notes and Queries, 6th ser. 5, no. 129 (17 June):465.
        Describes a recently purchased portrait by Sir Godfrey
Kneller which shows the artist in his "very best style" and his
work "as delicate as a miniature, as powerful as one would wish."
Kneller's portrait depicts Defoe at "about thirty," quite different from Taverner's likeness of him at about forty-two. See
1910.19.

5   LOEWE, HEINRICH, ed. Foreword and "Defoe's Leben und Werke."
     In The Life and Surprising Adventures of Robinson Crusoe by
     Daniel Defoe. Für den Schul- und Privatgebrauch eingerichtet
     und erklärt. Halle: Hermann Gesenius, pp. iii-viii.
         Provides a brief introduction to Defoe's life and works for
     this school edition of Robinson Crusoe in English, with pronunci-
     ation guide and explanatory notes in German, and text based on
     Keltie's edition, 1880 [see 1869.13].   (P.E.C.)

6   MARSHALL, ED. "Defoe: Robinson Crusoe." Notes and Queries,
     6th ser. 5, no. 127 (3 June):428.
         Asks for the name of the reviser M.D***, of the Robinson
     Crusoe, 2d ed., Paris, 1783. See reply, 1882.8.

7   Review of Lee's Defoe (1869) and Minto's Defoe (1879), and
     Works (1840-1841). London Quarterly and Holborn Review 57,
     no. 114 (January):345-70.
         Ranges broadly over the biographies and editions, summar-
     izing extensively the life and works, focusing upon the ethical
     issues wich separate the viewpoints of Lee and Minto (e.g.,
     Defoe's "double part" revealed in the six letters discovered in
     1864). Confirms that by 1882 Defoe had a higher standing because
     of "his service to literature than to politics." On the novels:
     regards Robinson Crusoe as "pure and healthy"; Moll Flanders and
     Roxana, "indecent and vile"; Colonel Jack, "strongly tainted with
     foul infection"; Captain Singleton, neglected because of an
     unattractive hero. Turns to Minto's reasoning to explain certain
     of Defoe's distinctive qualities, such as "the peculiar air of
     truth," as necessitated by the unfamiliarity of English readers
     with "avowed fiction." Nevertheless, in the conclusion, reaf-
     firms the claims of "conscience" and "principle" upon Defoe, and
     rejects Minto's dictum: "He was a great, a truly great liar,
     perhaps the greatest liar that ever lived."

8   SMITH, HUBERT. "Defoe: Robinson Crusoe." Notes and Queries,
     6th ser. 6, no. 132 (8 July):39.
         Replies to 1882.6, by referring to still another edition of
     Robinson Crusoe--in Welsh, published at Gwrecsam (Wrexham), 1795.

9   SOLLY, EDWARD. "The Vicar of Baddow." Notes and Queries,
     6th ser. 5, no. 113 (25 February):159.
         Replies to 1881.5. In the stanzas concerning the devil,
     quoted anonymously in Defoe's Political History of the Devil
     (1726), notes that "the Vicar of Baddow" refers to Little Baddow
     in Essex, identifies the vicar in 1720 as John Gordon, explains
     the allusion as meaning the Vicar "had practically nothing to do,
     and was of questionable appointment." See also 1906.3.

10   TOLE, F.A. "The Vicar of Baddow." Notes and Queries, 6th
     ser. 5, no. 111 (11 February):117.
         Replies to 1881.5, noting that the "learned Dr. B--"
     mentioned in the paragraph following the one quoted may be "the
     Vicar of Baddow." See also 1882.9.

11   TUCKERMAN, BAYARD. A History of English Prose Fiction. New
     York & London: G.P. Putnam's Sons, pp. 183-93, 216-17.
          Endeavors to frame a hypothesis that offers a pattern for
     Defoe's fiction, namely, that he progressed from writing "the
     life of a well-known individual," to writing about a fictitious
     person in a historical setting, finally to writing about "a fic-
     titious person amidst fictitious scenes." Turns for the third
     phase to the other novels--Colonel Jack, Captain Singleton, Moll
     Flanders, Roxana--as fictions that "have been surpassed, and are
     neglected" while Robinson Crusoe remains "of its kind, perfect,
     and therefore enduring." Insists that the other novels have an
     uniquely historical, as well as literary, interest in that they
     deliberately, and accurately, study the lower classes and analyze
     crime, with the author in the role of reformer. Argues that
     Defoe, "thoroughly a man of his time," believed that he could
     place the coarsest narrative (e.g., Roxana) before the reader,
     and have him derive moral benefit. Reprinted, in part: Daniel
     Defoe: Moll Flanders, ed. J. Paul Hunter, Crowell Critical
     Library (New York: Thomas Y. Crowell Co., 1970), pp. 275-76.

12   VERNE, JULES. L'École des Robinsons. Magasin d'éducation
     et de récréation 35 (1 January)-36 (1 December). Reprint.
     Paris: J. Hetzel, 1882. In Works of Jules Verne. Edited by
     Charles F. Horne. Vol. 13, The Robinson Crusoe School. New
     York and London: F. Tyler Daniels Co., 1911, 146 pp. passim.
          Information on publications from Edward J. Gallagher, Jules
     Verne: A Primary and Secondary Bibliography (Boston, Mass.:
     G.K. Hall & Co., 1980), p. 20. Still preoccupied with the Robin-
     son Crusoe theme stemming from both Defoe's novel and Wyss's
     Swiss Family Robinson (1812-1813), Verne now offers a light jeu
     d'esprit which has little of the seriousness found in L'Île mys-
     térieuse (1874). Essentially an extended practical joke, The Rob-
     inson Crusoe School turns on a series of Crusoe-like experiences
     encountered by Godfrey Morgan and Professor Tartlet, who consis-
     tently identify themselves as "Crusoes," and by Carefinotu, who
     literally acts out the part of Friday. As the adventures build
     to a climax with the three heroes trapped in a fire within their
     cavernous sequoia tree home, they are suddenly rescued, and all
     their terrible escapades (except a few) are revealed to be fakes
     perpetrated by Godfrey Morgan's millionaire uncle. Explicit
     references to Defoe, Wyss, and "Crusoes" keep this slight piece
     from being just another Robinsonade. Reprinted: 1883; 1966.

                              1882-1883

1   COURTNEY, W.P. "Mr. James Crossley." Bibliographer 3:97-99.
          In Crossley's library were the 254 books which, as one of
     Defoe's biographers, he had claimed as the production of his
     hero, besides fifty-two tracts which he "attributed" to Defoe and
     "eight thick quarto volumes" of Henry Baker's correspondence.

2   WHITTAKER, ELIZABETH. "Robina Crusoe, and Her Lonely Island
     Home." <u>Girl's Own Paper</u> 4, nos. 156–86 (23 December 1882–
     21 July 1883):184–669 passim.
           Named after "the world-famed Robinson Crusoe," this in-
     domitable woman has her wish fulfilled of living on a deserted
     island, as narrated in a first-person imitation, through weekly
     installments, with illustrations and a reference now and then to
     the original. These adventures called forth other accounts of
     female Crusoes, such as the one from Mr. Hearne about the Indian
     woman captured in the summer of 1770 (4, no. 172, 14 April 1883:
     439) or another about an Indian woman alone on an island off the
     California coast for eighteen years (4, no. 185, 14 July 1883:
     646). See also Hale, 1881.4.

                              1882–1888

1   HALKETT, SAMUEL, and LAING, JOHN. <u>A Dictionary of the Anony-</u>
     <u>mous and Pseudonymous Literature of Great Britain</u>. 4 vols.
     Edinburgh: William Paterson, vols. 1–4 passim.
           Indexes the 252 anonymous and pseudonymous works assigned
     to Defoe in vol. 4, cols. cxcvii–cxcviii.

                              1883

1   ANDERSON, WM. "Daniel Defoe and His Church." <u>Catholic Presby-</u>
     <u>terian</u> 9 (February):102–8.
           On Defoe's religion, an evangelical Trinitarian Presbyteri-
     anism.

2   APPERSON, GEO. L. "A 'Robinson.'" <u>Notes and Queries</u>, 6th
     ser. 8, no. 187 (28 July):67.
           Asks why in Paris a "Robinson" is a "rustic garden party,"
     as in the days of Marie Antoinette. The editor adds that Robin-
     son is also an umbrella. See replies, 1883.4, 17.

3   ARBER, EDWARD, ed. "Daniel Defoe." In <u>An English Garner:</u>
     <u>Ingatherings from Our History and Literature</u>. 7 vols. Bir-
     mingham, England: E. Arber, 7:459, 460, 554, 586–88, 604.
           Annotates briefly, on occasion from autobiographical writ-
     ings, some of the seventeen rare reprinted works of Defoe, be-
     ginning with the <u>True-Born Englishman</u> and ending with the <u>Appeal</u>
     <u>to Honour and Justice</u>. Arranges the selections historically
     rather than in order of publication. Evaluates Defoe as "the
     least known," but probably the most influential and powerful, and
     artistically the best, of the four great prose writers of Queen
     Anne's reign—the other three being Swift, Steele, and Addison.
     Views Defoe as "the great native writer of the day," one who
     contributed far more than "a mere bagatelle" entitled <u>Robinson</u>
     <u>Crusoe</u>, through writings on behalf of English law and liberties.
     See also 1903.1.

4   B., E.S. "A 'Robinson.'" Notes and Queries, 6th ser. 8,
     no. 188 (4 August):95.
         Replies to 1883.2. "Robinson," meaning in French, "a
     garden party," is derived from the name of the restaurant in the
     Seine, "L'île de Robinson."

5   [BEZLEY, REV. WALTER.] "Robinson Crusoe." Bibliographer 3,
     no. 4 (March):113.
         Brief note on German translation published at Nurnberg,
     1728, and Frankfurt and Leipzig, 1731, in two volumes, with
     frontispieces and illustrations.

6   DOBSON, AUSTIN. Introduction to Robinson Crusoe. Being a
     Facsimile Reprint of the First Edition Published in 1719.
     London: Elliot Stock, pp. vii–xiv.
         Cites the catalogue of Defoe's works in Lee's biography
     (1869) to suggest the large amount of experience, but also the
     variety of writings represented in the 190 works which were pub-
     lished prior to Robinson Crusoe. Finds impressive the "sleepless
     activity and unwearied versatility of the author." He could
     report an event with stenographic fidelity, or invent a report,
     which was believable, if one were lacking. He had "a very pro-
     nounced mental bias towards circumstantial forgeries" such as
     Mesnager or Mrs. Veal. Here we have, "superficially speaking,
     the qualities which produced Robinson Crusoe." Defoe's mind was
     not of the highest creative order, as the Selkirk borrowing
     illustrates. See also 1883.14–15.

7   FOTH, K. Review of Heinrich Loewe's edition of The Life and
     Surprising Adventures of Robinson Crusoe by Daniel Defoe,
     1882. Englische Studien 6, no. 1:116–23.
         Reviews negatively a carelessly annotated school text in
     English, of Robinson Crusoe (1882.5), the first of its kind in
     Germany. See also Dorr, 1884.2.   (P.E.C.)

8   MÉZIÈRES, A[LFRED JEAN FRANÇOIS]. Hors de France: Italie--
     Espagne--Angleterre--Grèce moderne. Paris: Hachette & Co.,
     pp. 145-54, 179-80, 184.
         While retelling the story, in chap. 1, of "the beginnings
     of the liberty of the press in England," stresses the point that
     Defoe, when he was being severely punished in the pillory, was
     not succumbing to "the resentment of power" so much as to "a
     coalition of parties who composed the nation at that time." In
     chap. 3, "The English Novel in the Eighteenth Century," discusses
     only Robinson Crusoe among Defoe's novels--as a "popular legend,"
     generally interpreted as a "national epic" about the hero belong-
     ing to "the race [Anglo-Saxon] which has produced the boldest
     adventures of the modern world." Reprinted: 1887; 1907.

9   NICOLL, HENRY J. "Our First Great Novelists: Defoe; Rich-
     ardson; Fielding; Smollett; Sterne." In Landmarks of English
     Literature. New York: Appleton. Reprint. Haskell House
     Publishers, 1973, pp. 203-8.

Advocates a general plan for literary study which concen-
trates on only the very best literature. Tends to regard Defoe's
life as "shifty and intricate," and his statements about it as
untrustworthy. Only Robinson Crusoe receives extended discussion
as being "infinitely healthier in tone and superior also in literary skill." His works of fiction "for the most part" deal with
"characters from the lowest strata of society." Quotes Fitzjames
Stephen (1855.8) on Defoe's confident depiction of Crusoe's
situation on the island, a grief amounting to madness and then a
growing courage.

10   "Notice sur la vie et les ouvrages de Daniel De Foé." In
      Daniel De Foé. Robinson Crusoé. Paris: Firmin-Didot & Co.,
      pp. v-x.
          Unevenly accurate, summarizes the life and career, and
      assesses the writings from a typically French perspective. Con-
      tinues certain factual errors (e.g., year of birth 1663); mis-
      takenly assigns History of Addresses to Defoe; broadly general-
      izes that the True-Born Englishman distracted him from trade and
      thus contributed to his bankruptcy. On the novels, praises
      Robinson Crusoe as a solitary achievement. In listing the "other
      novels," shows some confusion: for instance, in not recognizing
      that Roxane and La Maîtresse fortunée are the same work. Gener-
      ally disparages the publications as uneven performances.

11   OGLE, JOHN J. "Robinson Crusoe, Arabic Edition." Bibliogra-
      pher 3, no. 6 (May):179.
          Briefly notes the extract of Burckhardt's letter in The
      Gate to the Hebrew, Arabic, and Syriac, Unlocked . . . (1828)
      about his Arabic translation of Robinson Crusoe under the title
      Dur el Baheer--"The Pearl of the Seas."

12   PELLISSIER, EUGÈNE. Introduction to Daniel Defoe: Robinson
      Crusoe. New ed. Paris: Ch. Delagrave, pp. v-lix.
          In an informative, biographical and critical summary, shows
      mature French scholarship benefitting especially from the dis-
      coveries of Lee's Defoe (1869), the insights of Minto's Defoe
      (1879), and to a less extent wide reading of Chalmers, Scott,
      Forster, Stephen, and Jeaffreson. Accepts Minto's view that
      Defoe deteriorated morally, and so calls attention repeatedly to
      his betrayal of principle. Starts the decline with Defoe's ac-
      cepting secret service work for Harley in 1704 in order to gain
      release from Newgate; finds the fallaciousness heavy in the
      Appeal to Honour and Justice. Enlarges upon a theory (begun by
      Minto) that Defoe brought the germ of novels like Moll Flanders
      and Colonel Jack into his periodicals to distract public atten-
      tion away from the current political polemics in which he was
      engaged. States independent critical judgments as when he ques-
      tions the existence of the manuscript behind the Memoirs of a
      Cavalier or the source of Defoe's knowledge of criminals as being
      his imprisonments. Veers away from Scott and Minto to argue that
      Defoe wrote on popular subjects for reasons that were not always

pecuniary. Reaffirms Jeaffreson (1858.8) that Defoe created the historical novel, and his <u>Memoirs of a Cavalier</u> and <u>Journal of the Plague Year</u> were "the precursors of the <u>Waverley Novels</u>." Claims that adventure stories like <u>Colonel Jack</u> have the same "simplicity of style and naturalness of characters" as does <u>Robinson Crusoe</u>, but they show a complete lack of artistic order. Curiously, makes no mention of <u>Roxana</u>. Devotes the last of the three sections entirely to <u>Robinson Crusoe</u> (14 pp.), its sources in the narratives of Woodes Rogers, Captain Edward Cooke, and Richard Steele, but also in Defoe's own life.

13 PERRY, THOMAS SERGEANT. <u>English Literature in the Eighteenth Century</u>. New York: Harper & Brothers, pp. 310-16.
  In locating Defoe's novels between <u>The English Rogue</u> and Richardson's <u>Pamela</u>, shifts the emphasis to the "secondary" novels. Follows, and extends Minto, in stressing novels such as <u>Colonel Jack</u> which represent "the lower stratum of literature." Argues that Defoe contributed to an already existent "realistic biographical novel" and that as a novelist he studied man in relation to society, a reformer--"a wonderful craftsman," but not a great artist. Finds the "moral" of <u>Robinson Crusoe</u> to be that if "a man in solitude," with such limited resources, can succeed, "what may we not expect of good people in England with abundance about them?" Quotes <u>Colonel Jack</u> at length to show how close in subject Defoe was to the Spanish picaresque and how much greater the influence was from the "other" novels.

14 Review of Austin Dobson's Introduction to <u>Robinson Crusoe</u>, 1883. <u>Athenaeum</u>, no. 2883 (27 January):117.
  Reinforces or qualifies Dobson's comments, 1883.6. Notes that although <u>Robinson Crusoe</u> and its author were not adequately recognized earlier, eminent writers of our time have discussed Defoe's life and writings. Has difficulty with Dobson's statement about Defoe's lack of creative talent. Still <u>Robinson Crusoe</u> will probably be read when the best of Dickens is forgotten.

15 "Robinson Crusoe." <u>Bibliographer</u> 3, no. 2 (January):33-36.
  Lists editions of <u>Robinson Crusoe</u> from 1719 to 1879, and translations. See also 1883.5.

16 S., J. "Scotch Newspaper of the Age of Queen Anne." <u>Notes and Queries</u>, 6th ser. 7, no. 177 (19 May):386.
  Reproduces notes concerning the <u>Edinburgh Courant</u>, the death of the proprietor Adam Boig on 27 January 1710, the ordinance of the Town Council authorizing Defoe to print the <u>Edinburgh Courant</u>, and his first number dated 20 March 1710.

17 THOMAS, MOY. "A 'Robinson.'" <u>Notes and Queries</u>, 6th ser. 8, no. 188 (4 August):95.
  Replies to 1883.2. Describes the "Robinson" which served Parisianers as a favorite vacation resort some forty years ago.

18 WOODS, JAS. C. "Robinson Crusoe. (III. 33.)." Bibliographer
4, no. 3 (August):88.
Adds to the listing, 1883.15, the sixteenth edition, containing "The Vision of the Angelic World," printed by T. Martin, 1792.

1884

1 BRAY, ANNA ELIZA. Autobiography. Edited by John A. Kempe.
London: Chapman & Hall, pp. 178-91 passim.
Describes in chap. 11 the formation of her taste and style as a novelist through reading that included Robinson Crusoe among "early favorites" and "the most celebrated of De Foe's [other] novels" at a later time. Comments generally on novelists that interested her, placing emphasis on Richardson and Clarissa; returns at the end of the chapter to Defoe's "other novels" which, "though not so fascinating as his Robinson Crusoe, are no less admirable." Finds that the Memoirs of a Cavalier borrows heavily from Clarendon and other contemporaries, and is therefore less appealing, and that Roxana, Moll Flanders, Colonel Jack, and Captain Singleton are faulty because "the action is carried on by the lowest creatures, and that the scenes and vices are of the lowest order." Exempts only the Journal of the Plague Year from the criticism of an exclusive concern with "the base and the depraved."

2 DÖRR, FRANZ. "Zu: Englische Studien VI, p. 122." Englische
Studien 7, no. 1:205-6.
Underscores Foth, 1883.7, in his critique of Loewe's school edition of Robinson Crusoe (1882.5) as pedagogically unsound and thoughtlessly thrown together. (P.E.C.)

3 FREELOVE, WM. "Robinson Crusoe." Notes and Queries, 6th ser.
9, no. 213 (26 January):69.
Claims [incorrectly] that the "Robinson Crusoe's Vision of the Angelic World," found in a Paris 1783 edition has never been seen in an English edition.

4 HAWTHORNE, JULIAN. "Literature for Children." North American
Review 138, no. 329 (April):394-95.
States the "literature proper to manhood is not proper to childhood, though the reverse is not--or, at least, never ought to be--true." Makes the argument that children do not have morality, and this element should not be present in their literature. Finds the "fascination" of Robinson Crusoe to reside in the subject: "the story of the struggle of man with wild and hostile nature." In particular, "the child reader" identifies completely with Robinson. Just the contrary are the effects of Robinson's "progeny," the deleterious moralizing in such works as Maria Edgeworth's "Frank" and "The Parent's Assistant." Reprinted: Confessions and Criticisms (Boston: Ticknor & Co., 1887), pp. 122-25.

5   JOY, FRED. W. "Autograph Letter of Daniel De Foe." Notes and
      Queries, 6th ser. 9, no. 213 (26 January):65.
         Reprints a letter from Defoe to an unidentified lord, dated
      from "Newington, May 29, 1711." The letter is reprinted and anno-
      tated in Healey (pp. 328-29). The lord addressed is identified
      as David Erskine, Earl of Buchan. The original letter, according
      to Healey, is now "untraced."

6   MORLEY, HENRY. Introduction to A Journal of the Plague Year.
      London: George Routledge & Sons, pp. v-viii.
         In a standard biographical summary, uses incorrectly the
      year of birth 1661, making Defoe four years old at the time of
      the Plague. Describes Defoe under George I seeking "quiet means
      of further provision for his family by spending his imagination
      upon story-books," producing among other works the "master-
      pieces," Robinson Crusoe and Journal of the Plague Year. Sug-
      gests a contrast in the designs of the two: the one, a tale of a
      man cast on a desert island relying on his own energies and trust
      in God; the other, the tale of "a city of men on whom a great
      plague falls, a community in which the bonds of fellowship are
      tried as by fire, and the imperishable part is separated from the
      flax and tow." Reprinted: 2d ed., 1886; 3d ed., 1888.

7   NEWMAN, FRANCIS WILLIAM. Preface to Rebilius Cruso: Robinson
      Crusoe, in Latin. London: Trübner & Co., pp. iii-v.
         Expresses his theories for translating into Latin this
      adaptation of Robinson Crusoe, completed in 1861. Holds the
      belief, for instance, that we should learn a language first and
      then its literature; that we should read large portions of the
      Latin rather than small ones to gain accuracy, in a style that is
      easy and with a content that is attractive. See also 1862.10.

8   PRESTON, M. ELLA. "Poor Robinson Crusoe." Saint Nicholas
      Magazine 11, no. 11 (September):849.
         Includes five lines of verse, beginning "Poor Robinson
      Crusoe! / What made the poor man do so?"

9   ROBBINS, ALFRED F[ARTHING]. Launceston, Past and Present:
      A Historical and Descriptive Sketch. Launceston: Cornish &
      Devon Printing Co., pp. 216-20.
         Quotes the account in Lee's Defoe (1869) of "A Remarkable
      Passage of an Apparition, 1665," first published in Mr. Camp-
      bell's Pacquet (1720); and seems to reaffirm the view that Defoe
      wrote it. At the same time, in tracing the story to the present,
      mentions the manuscript "in the handwriting of Ruddle himself"
      as the basis for the story given by the Rev. F. Jago-Arundell to
      C.S. Gilbert for his History of Cornwall (1817). Notes also that
      the place for exorcism is given either as Trebursye (e.g., De-
      foe's version) or Little Petherick (e.g., R.S. Hawker's, 1870).

10   SOLLY, EDWARD. "The Bibliography of Sacheverell." Bibliogra-
      pher 5, no. 3 (February):66-72.

On Henry Sacheverell's sermon <u>The Perils of False Brethren</u> (1709) and the impeachment trial of 1710: adds to Madan's bibliography a few listings which have Defoe in the titles; strongly recommends his articles on Sacheverell in the <u>Review</u>, vol. 7 for 1710.

11 _____. "The Story of Mrs. Veal." <u>Notes and Queries</u>, 6th ser. 10, no. 261 (27 December):521.
Replies to 1884.12. According to Lee's <u>Defoe</u> (1869) <u>Mrs. Veal</u> was reprinted with Drelincourt (4th ed.) as early as 1706 by Robinson and that the reprinting with Sherlock was to be expected. Calls attention also to the high cost of tea and the use of "trinkets" to mean "tea-cups or mugs."

12 WARREN, C.F.S. "The Story of Mrs. Veal." <u>Notes and Queries</u>, 6th ser. 10, no. 257 (29 November):426.
Notes that <u>Mrs. Veal</u> was actually published in editions of <u>Sherlock on Death</u>--for instance, in the 25th edition, 1747--and not just in editions of Drelincourt. Points out, also, a few textual differences in the <u>Mrs. Veal</u> as published with Sherlock and as in the Nimmo edition (1869). See reply, 1884.11.

<u>1885</u>

1 APPERSON, GEORGE L. "Robert Drury's <u>Journal</u>." <u>Notes and Queries</u>, 6th ser. 11, no. 285 (13 June):477.
Replies to 1885.5, with information on an abridgement as tract no. 36 in <u>Chambers's Miscellany</u>, 1869.

2 B., G.F.R. "Robert Drury's <u>Journal</u>." <u>Notes and Queries</u>, 6th ser. 11, no. 285 (13 June):477.
Replies to 1885.5. Gives information on the editions for 1743, 1748, 1808, and 1826; and on the authorship, in Chalmers's <u>Biographical Dictionary</u>.

3 CUSHING, WILLIAM. "Defoe, Daniel, 1661-1731." In <u>Initials and Pseudonyms: A Dictionary of Literary Disguises</u>. First series. New York: Thomas Y. Crowell & Co., p. 407.
Lists twenty-one different identifications. See also additional entries under "Crusoe, Robinson" and "Dodsley, Robert" (<u>A Footman</u>), pp. 72, 412, 1888.2, 4.

4 DE SAINT-HERAYE, B.H.G. "Notice sur Daniel Defoe." In <u>Lady Roxana; ou L'heureuse maitresse par Daniel Defoe, traduit de l'Anglais. Édition illustrée de magnifiques gravures hors texte par les meilleurs artistes</u>. Paris: LibrairE générale illustrée, pp. v-vii, 360.
<u>Lady Roxana</u> has all the fine qualities and defects of the author: a requisite negligence, prolixities, repetitions of ideas as well as expressions, an absence of art, finally, that can well be, in Defoe, the height of art. The novel ends as in

the first edition (1724); then follows a sixty-page continuation.
At the transition (p. 360) a note explains that the editor of the
continuation in the 1745 edition expressed the belief, in a long
preface, that the sequel was the posthumous work of the famous
writer. Nevertheless, one finds it full of contradictions with
the rest of the novel, in style and general tone, and is
therefore without any authenticity for us.

5   F., T. "Robert Drury's Journal." Notes and Queries, 6th
    ser. 11, no. 279 (2 May):348.
        Queries the reasons why this work has sometimes been attrib-
uted to Defoe, and asks if it has been recently reprinted. See
replies: 1885.1-2, 7.

6   HALE, EDWARD EVERETT. "Daniel De Foe and Thomas Shepard."
    Atlantic Monthly 56, no. 334 (July):85-87.
        Among Defoe's connections with North America, notes "some
striking resemblances in detail" between the descriptions of a
storm and shipwreck at Yarmouth Roads in the manuscript autobiography of Thomas Shepard and Robinson Crusoe. Theorizes that
Defoe had heard Shepard's account "from some one who was in the
ship . . . and that he was glad to work the detail into his
story."

7   LOVEDAY, JOHN E.T. "Robert Drury's Journal." Notes and
    Queries, 6th ser. 11, no. 285 (13 June):476-77.
        Replies to 1885.5, with information on Robin Drury as a
person and on Madagascar, from 1769.3; 1772.1; and 1790.3.

8   OLIVER, S. PASFIELD. "Robert Drury's Madagascar: Is It a
    Fiction?" Antananarivo Annual and Madagascar Magazine, no. 9
    (Christmas):17-26, 192-95.
        States the case, in fullest details to date, for doubting
the unaided authorship of Robert Drury and for accepting the
extensive role of Defoe as writer. Surveys the authorities on
Madagascar, and finds them (especially, the French) committed to
accepting Madagascar as "Gospel truth." Quotes the entire letter
of the Rev. Mr. Hirst, 1772.1, which confirms the authenticity of
Madagascar and the veracity of Drury. But despite this weighty
evidence, pushes beyond Lee, who ultimately rejected Madagascar
from Defoe's canon, and beyond Blanchard (1872.1) to the conclusion that Defoe or one of his contemporaries wrote Madagascar.
Cites such evidence as parallels between Robinson Crusoe and Madagascar, and the use of African sources, such as Flacourt's French
work on Madagascar (1661). See the adaption of this article and
its elaboration in the introduction to Oliver's edition of Madagascar, 1890.

9   Remarks and Collections of Thomas Hearne. Vol. 1 (July 4,
    1705-March 19, 1707). Edited by C.E. Doble. Oxford: Oxford
    Historical Society, pp. 164, 166, 238, 297.

Makes accessible, in the first volume of an eleven-volume series, the invaluable manuscript papers at the Bodleian Library of Hearne, the Nonjuror and antiquary. Provides here "the substance of thirteen only out of the 145 MS. volumes." Claims in the entry for 21 January 1706 that Defoe wrote a reply to [William] Stephens's "Letter in Answer to The Memorial of ye State of England" (1705). See Douglas Coombs's reference to Hearne's evidence that Defoe was the author of A Letter to the Author of the Memorial of the State of England, Answered, Paragraph by Paragraph (1706) in his article, Bulletin of the Institute of Historical Research 32, no. 85 (May, 1959):33n. In the entries for 30 April 1706 and 21 October 1706, reports other important public actions relating to Defoe. See also 1886.15.

10   RUSKIN, JOHN. Praeterita. Outlines of Scenes and Thoughts Perhaps Worthy of Memory in My Past Life. Reprint. The Works of John Ruskin. Edited by E.T. Cook and Alexander Wedderburn. London: George Allen; New York: Longmans, Green, & Co., 1908, 35:13.
       Opens with a revealing autobiographical paragraph which repeats the account of influences on him as given in Flors Clavigera, 1871.13.

11   S., T. "Robinson Crusoe." Notes and Queries, 6th ser. 11, no. 263 (10 January):26-27.
       Quotes from the manuscript collections of the Rev. John Rippon, D.D., in the British Museum, on the Robinson Crusoe manuscript circulating through "the whole trade" and not finding anyone who would print it, and on the bookseller's clearing one thousand guineas by printing it.

12   SKEAT, WALTER W. "Robinson Crusoe Anticipated." Notes and Queries, 6th ser. 12, no. 290 (18 July):48.
       Cites Dampier's story, in his Voyages (1699), of the Indian left at Juan Fernandez island in 1681, as preceding the account told about Alexander Selkirk.

13   ULLRICH, H[ERMANN]. "Daniel Defoe's Satire: The Shortest Way with the Dissenters. Zum erstenmal in das Deutsche übersetzt, als Probe einer Auswahl von Defoe's publizistischen Schriften." In Ernst Zeidler. Programm: Lehr- und Erziehungs-Anstalt für Knaben Realschule. Program number 512. Dresden: Lehmannsche Buchdruckerei, pp. 3-10.
       For this first translation into German, includes introductory footnote mainly biographical and a small number of glosses.

14   VENABLE, WILLIAM H. "Defoe in the Pillory." In Melodies of the Heart, Songs of Freedom and Other Poems. Cincinnati: Robert Clarke & Co., pp. 131-32.
       Offers verses saluting Defoe in the pillory, as spoken by the leader of the mob. Reprinted: Saga of the Oak and Other Poems (New York: Dodd, Mead & Co., 1904), pp. 44-45.

<u>1886</u>

1 A., G. "Robinson Cruso." <u>Notes and Queries</u>, 7th ser. 1,
no. 5 (30 January):89.
   Tells of a person who recently died at King's Lynn, named
"Robinson Crusoe," as were "father and son from time immemorial";
considers the possibility of Defoe's having passed through Lynn
and taking the name for his hero. See replies, 1886.3-4, 6, 10-
11, 17, 20; 1888.1, 3, 17, 21, 25.

2 ADAMS, W[ILLIAM] H[ENRY] DAVENPORT. "A Lonely Man Of Let-
ters--Daniel Defoe." In <u>Good Queen Anne; or, Men and Manners,
Life and Letters in England's Augustan Age</u>. 2 vols. London:
Remington & Co., 2:203-30.
   Revises 1871.1 to bring into sharp focus the parallelism
between Robinson Crusoe and his creator--to show Defoe "from
first to last, a lonely Man of Letters." Removes the tentative-
ness from the earlier version; absorbs borrowings from sources
such as Forster, Stephen, or Lee, into his own presentations; and
rewrites now with a more self-assured style. On the novels, re-
places lengthy extracts from Scott or Lamb with expanded critical
judgments: for instance, the fine distinction in <u>Robinson Crusoe</u>
between "inventiveness" and "imagination." Enters into a general
critique of the novels as related to the art of the photographer:
"the effect [the novel] produces depends very much upon the object treated." On these grounds, rates the <u>Journal of the Plague
Year</u> high; <u>Moll Flanders</u> and <u>Colonel Jack</u> low. Maintains that
the "minute realistic style" could be adapted only to "themes of
a low range and scope," and so Defoe could not treat "the higher
passions of humanity" any more than [Adriaen van] Ostade could
paint a "Transfiguration" or Jan Steen a "Madonna."

3 BEDE, CUTHBERT. "Robinson Cruso." <u>Notes and Queries</u>, 7th
ser. 1, no. 11 (13 March):215.
   Replies to 1886.1. Repeats information given earlier
(1868.3) on "Creuso" as a surname at Fotheringhay in 1573.

4 COWPER, J.M. "Robinson Cruso." <u>Notes and Queries</u>, 7th ser.
1, no. 8 (20 February):158.
   Replies to 1886.1. Cites surnames "Cruzo," "Defo," and
"Friday" in Canterbury registers.

5 DAWSON, GEORGE. "Daniel Defoe." In <u>Biographical Lectures</u>.
Edited by George St. Clair. London: Kegan Paul, Trench &
Co., pp. 125-40.
   In the form of a popular lecture, aims to show "what <u>charac-
ter</u> Defoe had." Rehearses biographical facts at times obsolete
or mistaken, in the light of Lee's researches (<u>Defoe</u>, 1869).
Espouses clearly the view that "the courtly historians" have
given a more favored treatment to Addison, Swift, and others than
to the Dissenter "who stood in the pillory, and who learned much
of his wisdom in the dark cells of Newgate." Generally, however,

does not inspire confidence in the critical judgments expressed: refers to a non-existent work "Reformation of English Morals" or to Mrs. Veal, "than which few things are more humorous." Describes Robinson Crusoe as "that sunshiny golden book" and (along with Memoirs of a Cavalier and Journal of the Plague Year) "a veritable narrative." On the "other" novels, takes a more cautious attitude; they emerged from his Newgate associations, are now out of date, and need not be read.

6 DEEDES, C. "Robinson Cruso." Notes and Queries, 7th ser. 1, no. 15 (10 April):295.
      Replies to 1886.1. Quotes some verses dated 1855 written by Rev. E. Adams in the appendix to unpublished verses on Shakespeare's birthplace. Includes a pun on "friend / Without a glimmer of Defoe."

7 "Defoe (Daniel)." In British Museum. Catalogue of Printed Books. London: William Clowes & Sons, 24 cols.
      Lists 197 separate works by Defoe, 238 additional copies or editions, eleven biographical items and thirteen "replies" to, or attacks on, Defoe. Assigns or attributes some twenty-three works that are not listed in Lee's Defoe (1869).

8 DOYLE, A[RTHUR] CONAN. "Cyprian Overbeck Wells. A Literary Mosaic." Reprint. The Captain of the Polestar and Other Tales. London: Longmans, Green, & Co., 1890, pp. 203-29.
      In an early short story (having nothing to do with Sherlock Holmes), presents literally "a literary mosaic" in which a number of eighteenth- and nineteenth-century writers are introduced, and their styles parodied, as they advise the narrator Smith how to tell his story. Presents Defoe first, participating in a dialogue with Lord Rochester and starting the story; and then continues with Swift, Smollett, Scott, and Bulwer Lytton. See also John Robert Moore, "Sherlock Holmes Borrows a Plot," Modern Language Quarterly 8, no. 1 (March, 1947):86-87; and Pierre Nordon, Conan Doyle: A Biography, trans. John Murray (New York: Holt, Rinehart & Winston, 1966), pp. 31, 205, 214, 225, 237, 292-93, 329-30.

9 FARNIE, HENRY BROUGHAM. Robinson Crusoe. [London: Swift & Co.], 25 pp.
      An Avenue Theatre performance, with the date 1886 not certain. The words are by Farnie and Reece, and the music by John Croo[letters torn away].

10 GRIFFINHOOFE, H.G. "Robinson Cruso." Notes and Queries, 7th ser. 1, no. 7 (13 February):137-38.
      Replies to 1886.1. Locates the reference in 1859.4 to Defoe's having been educated at Charles Morton's academy at Stoke Newington "at the same time" as Timothy Cruso. Was there a person named Robinson Cruso before 1719?

11   JAYDEE [pseud.]. "Robinson Cruso." Notes and Queries, 7th
      ser. 1, no. 11 (13 March):215.
           Replies to 1886.1. Finds "Cruso" and "Crusoe" in current
      Clergy List and London Post-Office Directory, and "Cruso" in
      Strype's Survey (1720).

12   LAMB, CHARLES. Letters of Charles Lamb . . . By the Late Sir
      Thomas Noon Talfourd, D.C.L. Edited by W. Carew Hazlitt. 2
      vols. Bohn's Standard Library. London: George Bell & Sons,
      1:305-9; 2:105-7, 330-32.
           In his letters to William Godwin, dated 9 and 17 September
      1801, Lamb gave his friend advice on the play Faulkner which was
      being planned and would be performed at Drury Lane Theatre in
      1807. He urged Godwin, in the earlier letter, to base the drama
      on the life of Richard Savage, but made no mention of Defoe's
      Roxana; in the later letter he recommended that "the story of
      Savage" be grafted upon Defoe. See also 1807.1-2. For Lamb's
      letters to Walter Wilson, dated 16 December 1822 and 24 February
      1823, see Wilson's Memoirs of Defoe (1830); and 1848.4, respec-
      tively. On 15 November 1829, upon receiving the three-volume
      set of the Memoirs of Defoe, Lamb wrote to Wilson: "De Foe was
      always my darling." He praised the biography enthusiastically.
      He regretted the absence of the "Pindaric Ode to the Treadmill,"
      and hoped readers will not be puzzled by his two pieces in the
      Memoirs "being so akin." Reprinted: The Letters of Charles
      Lamb, ed. E.V. Lucas (London: J.M. Dent & Sons; Methuen & Co,
      1935), 1:268-70, 275-77; 2:352- 53; 3:232-34.

13   MORLEY, HENRY. Introduction to Famous Pamphlets. London and
      New York: George Routledge & Sons, pp. 5-8.
           Brings together eloquent defences of freedom: Milton's
      Areopagitica (1644), Colonel Sexby's Killing No Murder (1657),
      Defoe's Shortest-Way with the Dissenters (1702), Steele's Crisis
      (1714), Richard Whately's Historic Doubts Respecting Napoleon
      Buonapart (1819), and Edward Copleston's Advice to a Young Review-
      er (1807). Notes a curious stylistic resemblance between the
      Shortest-Way with the Dissenters and Killing No Murder--the one
      a satiric "incitement to the assassination of a party" and the
      other a serious "incitement to the assassination of a man."

14   [PROTHERO, ROWLAND E.] "The Growth of the English Novel."
      Quarterly Review 163, no. 325 (July):34-64 passim.
           Authorship given in Wellesley Index. Limits the discus-
      sion of the novel's growth to the eighteenth century, the period
      "before the Wizard of the North laid his spell on a listening
      world." Identifies "realism" as the distinctive feature of both
      "modern civilization" and "the modern novel"--and Defoe as "the
      first of modern novelists." Defines realism as the treating of
      events "such as might occur in ordinary experience," starkly
      differentiated from the idealizations of the earlier romances.
      In Defoe's novels specifically, realism takes the form of "an
      appearance of veracity"; even introduces characters in the

secondary novels from "among the dregs of the population." Standing "in the baldest contrast" to romance-writers, Defoe minimizes
the effects of style, characterization, plot; finds his power "in
producing illusion, in giving an air of authenticity to fictitious narration."

15   Remarks and Collections of Thomas Hearne. Vol. 2 (March 20,
      1707–May 23, 1710). Edited by C.E. Doble. Oxford: Oxford
      Historical Society, pp. 14, 53.
            Continues 1885.9. Reports on 22 May 1707: Defoe received
      some money, apparently his pension, from "a certain Minister of
      State." On 27 September 1707: John Tutchin died last Tuesday
      and "his Brother Libeller Dan. de Foe" has been arrested for
      "abuse" of the Swedish king.

16   SAINTSBURY, GEORGE, ed. Specimens of English Prose Style.
      London: Kegan Paul, Trench & Co.; Chicago: Jansen, McClurg
      & Co., pp. 125–32.
            Selections, with brief commentary: "The Shipwreck" from
      Robinson Crusoe; "Signs and Wonders" from Journal of the Plague
      Year; "The Skirmish after Marston Moor" from Memoirs of a Cava-
      lier.

17   SAWYER, FREDERICK E. "Robinson Cruso." Notes and Queries,
      7th ser. 1, no. 20 (15 May):398.
            Replies to 1886.1 and others: on Aquila Cruso, B.D.,
      rector of Sussex, in West Sussex, 1634.

18   TOWNLEY, CHARLES [Geoffrey Thorn]. Robinson Crusoe, a Christ-
      mas Story of a Good Friday; or, Harlequin Pretty Polly Perkins
      and the Cruise of the "Saucy Sarah." [London: n.p.], 45 pp.
            See two other pantomimes by Townley: 1894.23; 1900.13.

19   WAGNER, H[ERMANN] F. Robinson in Oesterreich. Ein Beitrag
      zur Geschichte der deutschen Robinson-litteratur. Salzburg:
      Heinrich Dieter, 27 pp.
            Drawing on Hettner (1854.4), fills in background informa-
      tion on Robinson Crusoe and the Robinsonades. Recommends one
      Austrian Robinsonade as suitable for young readers: Zöhrer's
      Österreichischer Robinson, an 1885 adaptation of the anonymous
      Robinson, der Oberösterreicher (1802). Discusses at some length
      Karl Temlich's Österreichischer Robinson (1791), praised faintly
      by Haken in his Bibliothek der Robinsone, 1805-1808.1. Describes
      briefly other Austrian products, including Bohemian and Hungar-
      ian. Notes that a common feature of all the Austrian Robinson-
      ades is that Robinson has a female companion in place of Friday.
                                                              (P.E.C.)

20   WARD, C.A. "Robinson Cruso." Notes and Queries, 7th ser. 1,
      no. 7 (13 February):137.
            Replies to 1886.1: cannot locate the reference to Defoe's
      schoolfellow, Cruso, at Charles Morton's academy in Stoke Newing-
      ton.

1887

1 BOURNE, H.R. FOX. English Newspapers: Chapters in the History of Journalism. London: Chatto & Windus, pp. 63-69, 100-11.
    Taking full advantage of Lee's discovery of Defoe's continued political activity from 1715 to 1726, as told in his Defoe (1869), traces his revolutionizing of English journalism, beginning with the Review (1704) and continuing with the Mercator, the monthly Mercurius Politicus, Dormer's Newsletter, Mist's Weekly Journal, The Whitehall Evening Post, and The Daily Post (mistakenly says that the significant contribution here was "the original of Robinson Crusoe"). Shows Defoe's contributions to the publication of newspapers in relation to other events, for instance, Samuel Bulkeley's Daily Courant (1702-1714). Gives a balanced view in recognizing that Defoe was not able to maintain his high ideal in journalism and that during the ten years or so in which he produced Robinson Crusoe and other works, "he wrote much more anonymously, and, if with what he may have regarded as patriotic purpose, trickily and with lamentable lack of self-respect and honour from those around him." Ends on the strong note that he was, more often than not, statesman-like in his journalism; we see in him more clearly than in contemporaries such as Steele or Addison "the promise of 'society journalism.'"

2 CLOCK-HOUSE [pseud.]. "Moll Flanders." Notes and Queries, 7th ser. 4, no. 94 (15 October):307.
    Seeks information on Moll Flanders as a real person, beyond that given for Laetitia Atkins and Mary Patricksen in pirated or abridged editions.

3 "Defoe as a Story-Teller." Athenaeum, no. 3128 (8 October): 461-63.
    Reviewing Sparling's edition of Captain Singleton (1887.10), broadens the literary form voyages imaginaires to include narratives from the Odyssey or Sinbad the Sailor to Gaudentio di Lucca, Allan Gordon, Arthur Gordon Pym, Treasure Island, King Solomon's Mines. Finds less poetic charm in Captain Singleton than in Typee or Omoo, but more direct treasure-hunting than in Dumas, Poe, Stevenson, Haggard. Observes how much Defoe surpasses Scott, Dickens, and Thackeray in "general knowledge." Uses Arnold's "criticism of life" to demonstrate the important distinction between writing adventures "proferred as fictitious" and writing adventures "proferred as true": since Defoe wrote the latter, we (as readers) perform our own criticism of life, finding "an adequate raison d'être for his cumulative method." Offers other equally fascinating insights: Defoe's humour compared with Dickens's or the critique of Carlyle's "clearness of sight" in Homer, Richardson, and Defoe.

4 FORD, J. HERBERT, ed. The Life and Strange Surprising Adventures of Robinson Crusoe . . . Written in Pitman's Phonography. London: Isaac Pitman & Sons, 349 pp.

Turns the <u>Robinson Crusoe</u> text published by Cassell & Co.
into shorthand, with illustrations.

5   FREELOVE, WILLIAM. "Defoe and His Descendants." <u>Notes and</u>
<u>Queries</u>, 7th ser. 4, no. 88 (3 September):194.
        Replies to 1887.11. Claims that Defoe lived in Bury
St. Edmunds at a house known as the "old curiosity shop."

6   GOEDEKE, KARL. <u>Grundrisz zur Geschichte der deutschen Dich-</u>
<u>tung aus den Quellen</u>. 2d ed. Dresden: Ls. Ehlermann,
3:262-64.
        This bibliographical monument lists thirty-eight "Defoe
imitations" with "Robinson" in their titles, 1722-1756, and fourteen more adventure novels, 1724-1770, somehow reminiscent of
Defoe's masterpiece. Schnabel's <u>Insel Felsenburg</u>, in its several
editions is given a separate entry immediately following the
above. Altogether quite incomplete, with several inaccuracies.
See also Mildebrath, 1907.9.   (P.E.C.)

7   JUSSERAND, J.J. <u>Le Roman anglais et la réforme littéraire de</u>
<u>Daniel Defoe. Conférence faite à Bruxelles, le 16 Mars 1887</u>.
Brussels: Ferdinand Larcier, 35 pp.
        States forcefully and even eloquently Defoe's significance
in "the art of narrative in prose" as a "literary reform" which
he singlehandedly brought to England and the continent. Describes this phenomenon as the opening up suddenly of "a new literary world," which was greeted everywhere with enthusiasm and with
the instant familiarity one discovers in Fielding and Richardson
as compared to Shakespeare. Bases this principal achievement on
a definite sense of Defoe as a person given to dissimulation and
secrecy, "a double-faced hypocrite"; and as a writer, "perfectly
isolated." Argues that his immense literary influence arises not
from any devoted followers, but "entirely from the power of his
simple style." Traces the "magnificent simplicity" of style to
his journalistic experience and the experience gained there in
writing without artifice and "making himself credible," accomplishing his literary reform, as it were, unconsciously. Presents a well-defined conception of Robinson Crusoe as a character, and delineates it as being drastically different from any
Elizabethan predecessor--an authentic illusion of a real person.
Singles out in Crusoe "the spirit of enterprise, perseverance,
and pluck" as the most dominant quality--to reappear in Clarissa
and Jane Eyre. Identifies in him also "the qualities of the
race," the spirit and courage that would bring Englishmen to
empire. Praises <u>Memoirs of a Cavalier</u> and <u>Journal of the Plague</u>
<u>Year</u> as having "the simple style of Defoe and his sincere
accent." Compares the novels of manners--<u>Moll Flanders</u>, <u>Colonel</u>
<u>Jack</u>, and <u>Roxana</u>--with <u>Gil Blas</u>; and assesses them, in contrast,
as picaresque works that totally lack any sympathy for the main
characters. Sums up Defoe's literary reform, his elimination of
any visible trace of art, as being even more meritorious in that
it was accomplished, perhaps for the first time in English letters, when stylistic tendencies (Pope's, for example) went in the

opposite direction. While in <u>Moll Flanders</u>, <u>Colonel Jack</u>, and
<u>Roxana</u>, he cannot "compose" a novel or coordinate the parts, his
style remains inimitable: he imprisons the reader with his
"sincerity of accent, in the presence of this strange phenomenon,
of objects tangible in appearance and of characters constantly
living without any appeal to our imagination or our sensibility."
Describes Defoe's "fictive beings" as observed, not through the
multicolored stained-glass windows of the Middle Ages or Elizabethan times, but through the transparent window-panes which show
reality as it is, and which he invented and popularized. Illustrates the point by referring to "moving" scenes, such as Crusoe's discovering the wheat growing miraculously or Colonel
Jack's anguish (like Macbeth's) after his first theft; and the
scene of interpretative gesture, surpassing anything in Sterne,
when Crusoe comes upon the strange animal resembling a savage
cat. Calls Defoe's "the style of a clerk of court addressing a
legal action," and contrasts it with Marivaux's in <u>Surprising</u>
<u>Effects of Sympathy</u> (1713) or Bernardin de Saint-Pierre's in <u>Paul</u>
<u>and Virginia</u> (1788). His chief glory was to make common the use
of a perfectly sober prose and bring it to "an eqoch of matur-
ity." See also 1887.8.

8   . <u>Le Roman au temps de Shakespeare</u>. Paris: Librairie
    Ch. Delagrave, pp. 11, 109, 120, 136, 140, 142, 156, 167.
       Comments on anticipations of "the practical Defoe" and his
"great reform of the style" among such Elizabethan predecessors
as Thomas Nash. In terms of the novel, finds the later seventeenth century a waste; and the eighteenth century, a continuation of "the novel of real life" begun by Nash--his <u>Jack Wilton</u>,
"the worthy brother of <u>Roxana</u>, <u>Moll Flanders</u> and <u>Colonel Jack</u>."
See also 1887.7. Reprinted: Translated by Elizabeth Lee (Lon-
don: T.F. Unwin, 1890); (London: Ernest Benn; New York: Barnes
& Noble, 1966).

9 PLUMPTRE, E.H. "Workhouses." <u>Notes and Queries</u>, 7th ser. 4,
    no. 97 (5 November):369.
       On Defoe's rejection of the "workhouse" run on "philan-
thropic principles."

10 SPARLING, H. HALLIDAY. Introduction to <u>The Life, Adventures,</u>
    <u>and Piracies of the Famous Captain Singleton</u>. <u>By Daniel De-</u>
    <u>foe</u>. London: Walter Scott, pp. vii-xix.
       "Overshadowing greatness" of one work thrusts Defoe's other
productions into comparative oblivion. Before Defoe, there had
been "no fiction that painted men and manners as they were, and
wrote down the folk of its own time in their habit as they
lived." Places Defoe as a writer of fiction in the succession
from Behn and Bunyan to Richardson ("whom we know to have been an
admiring reader of his"), Fielding, and other followers who "added glory to the English tongue unequalled by all else." In the
biographical account, stresses Defoe's heavily productive journalistic and pamphleteering activities even while he was in
prison in 1704. Regards the <u>Review</u> as probably "the chief work

of his life." Devotes the last three pages to the fictions,
today "held [to be] of most importance." All of Defoe's fictions
are alike in telling the story for its own sake and avoiding
"meretricious adornment." On Defoe's characters: "Universal
man, the very central truth of him, Defoe felt, and it is this
that makes his creations appeal to all men of all times and
places and tongues. We know them as though we had lived with
them for years, not as though we had gone over them with scalpel
or microscope." Chooses Captain Singleton as "representative of
Defoe's style and method," and offers special praise for "the
trans-African journey." Lists a few of Defoe's principal works
and the biographical accounts; of the latter the best are Lee's
and Forster's. See also the review, 1887.3.

11 TALLACK, T.R. "Defoe and His Descendants." Notes and Que-
    ries, 7th ser. 3, no. 75 (4 June):450.
        Quotes the records at Norwich on Benjamin De Foe's marriage
    to Hannah Coates, 22 September 1718, and the baptism of a son
    Benjamin, 6 June 1719.

12 WOTTON, MABEL E. "Daniel De Foe." Word Portraits of Famous
    Writers. London: Richard Bentley & Son, pp. 83-86.
        Arranges sketches of celebrated men alphabetically. Dis-
    tinguishes between "personal details" actually seen from those
    responded by others. In the first category: the "Secretary of
    State's Proclamation" during the search for Defoe for writing the
    Shortest-Way with the Dissenters.

1887-1889

1   WINSOR, JUSTIN, ed. Narrative and Critical History of Amer-
    ica. 8 vols. Boston and New York: Houghton, Mifflin & Co.,
    5:284, 342; 8:205-7.
        Cites Colonel Jack as a fiction reference to Virginia; two
    pamphlets on religious controversy in South Carolina, Party-
    Tyranny: Or, An Occasional Bill in Miniature (1705) and The Case
    of Protestant Dissenters in Carolina (1706); and Alexander Sel-
    kirk on Juan Fernandez.

1888

1   BUCKLEY, W.E. "Robinson Cruso." Notes and Queries, 7th ser.
    6, no. 140 (1 September):174.
        Replies to 1888.25: information about Henry Edmund Tilsley
    Cruso.

2   CUSHING, WILLIAM. "Defoe, Daniel." Initials and Pseudonyms:
    A Dictionary of Literary Disguises. Second series. New York:
    Thomas Y. Crowell & Co., p. 206.
        Adds eight identifications (two repeated) to the earlier
    list, 1885.3. See also 1888.4

3   D., C.E. "Robinson Cruso." <u>Notes and Queries</u>, 7th ser. 6,
    no. 140 (1 September):174.
        Confirms 1888.21, on the two Bible clerks named "Robinson"
    and "Cruso," about 1861 or 1862 at Worcester College, Oxford.

4   DENHAM, EDWARD. "Additions." In William Cushing. <u>Initials
    and Pseudonyms: A Dictionary of Literary Disguises</u>. Second
    series. New York: Thomas Y. Crowell & Co., pp. 306-11.
        Lists 184 pseudonyms for Defoe, using the bibliography in
    Lee's <u>Defoe</u> (1869) as the base; briefly annotates each item. See
    also 1885.3; 1888.2.

5   "The First Edition of <u>Robinson Crusoe</u>." <u>Bookworm</u> 1:173-76.
        Sums up information on the early editions of <u>Robinson Cru-
    soe</u>, separating out myths from the facts. For instance, Taylor
    was not the last of the booksellers to have the manuscript
    offered to him, and he did make a fortune from the publication.
    Enters into detail concerning Taylor's suit in Chancery against
    T. Cox for the latter's alleged spurious abridgement.

6   G[ARNETT], R[ICHARD]. "Robert Drury (<u>fl</u>. 1729)." <u>Dictionary
    of National Biography</u>. Edited by Sir Leslie Stephen. Re-
    print. Oxford University Press 1909, 6:59-60.
        Accepts <u>Madagascar</u> as genuine, and Defoe's role of editor
    as "conjectured." Regards the editor's "natural religion" as
    strikingly different from Defoe's theological belief.

·7 HARRISON, FREDERIC. <u>The Choice of Books and Other Literary
    Pieces</u>. London and New York: Macmillan, p. 64.
        In the essay "The Choice of Books," briefly but forcefully
    views <u>Robinson Crusoe</u> as having an "extraordinary influence over
    the whole European mind": a fairy tale to the child, a book of
    adventures to the young, "a work of social philosophy" to the
    mature reader.

8   HIPWELL, DANIEL. "Daniel De Foe." <u>Notes and Queries</u>, 7th
    ser. 6, no. 137 (11 August):105.
        Quotes a record from Aske's Hospital, Hoxton, on the mar-
    riage of Daniel De Foe to Mary Webb, 29 March 1720; and queries
    whether it refers to the famous author or his eldest son. See
    reply, 1888.26.

9   LYNN, W.T. "Prototypes of Robinson Crusoe." <u>Notes and Que-
    ries</u>, 7th ser. 6, no. 146 (13 October):286.
        Balances Alexander Selkirk and Peter Serrano as prototypes
    of Robinson Crusoe; concludes that Defoe could have gotten few
    hints from either Captain Woodes Rogers's narrative about the
    former or from Sir Paul Rycaut's translation of Garcilasso's
    <u>History of Peru</u> about the latter. Makes one exception: from
    Rogers--the designation of Robinson Crusoe as "the governour."
    See reply, 1888.11.

10   M., H.   Introduction to From London To Land's End By Daniel
     Defoe. And Two Letters from the "Journey through England by
     a Gentleman." Cassell's National Library. New York: Cassell
     & Co., pp. 5-10.
         Refers confusingly to Defoe's Travels in England and the
     extract reprinted here "Journey from London to the Land's End,"
     but has in mind the Tour (1724) and letter 3 describing "the
     South Coasts of Hampshire, Wilts, Dorsetshire, Somersetshire,
     Devonshire, and Cornwall." To allow for a contrast of views,
     reprints also two letters (1722), not by Defoe, on Bath and the
     journey to Holyhead by way of Chester. Remarks upon some impor-
     tant points: the proposal advocated by Defoe to Godolphin [in
     1709] which, if successful, would have settled the Palatinate
     refugees in what is "now the most beautiful part of the New For-
     est, near Lyndhurst"; the dialect changes made by the young boy
     reading his Bible; the tales told about the Great Storm of 1703.
     Reprinted: London, Paris & Melbourne: Cassell & Co., 1892.

11   MARSHALL, ED. "Prototypes of Robinson Crusoe." Notes and
     Queries, 7th ser. 6, no. 155 (15 December):476.
         Replies to 1888.9 by citing H.C. Adams, 1877.1.

12   M[ORLEY], H[ENRY]. Introduction to London in 1731. By Don
     Manoel Gonzales. Cassell's National Library. London, Paris,
     New York & Melbourne: Cassell & Co., pp. 5-10.
         Takes this account of London (182 pp.) from John Pinker-
     ton's General Collection of the Best and the Most Interesting
     Voyages and Travels of the World (1808-1814), which in turn
     derives from the Harleian Collection (1745-1746). Attributes the
     work to Defoe, giving only general arguments for authorhsip, and
     dates the writing in 1731. See also Moore's Defoe in the Pillory
     (1939), pp. 72-103, and his Checklist, no. 517.

13   MULLER, EUGÈNE. "Daniel De Foë." In Lés Aventures de Robin-
     son Crusoé par Daniel De Foë. Voyages dans tous les mondes.
     Nouvelle bibliothèque historique et littéraire. Paris:
     Ch. Delagrave, pp. 5-17.
         Comments on the general lack of interest in Defoe after his
     death and the issues for which he struggled, and on the anonymity
     of authorship which enveloped Robinson Crusoe around the middle
     of the eighteenth-century in France. Describes the style as
     appropriately associated rather with the hero than with Defoe and
     as best captured in the translation of Thémiseul de Saint-Hya-
     cinthe (reprinted here). Tries to maintain this "particular
     physiognomy" of the text--the repetitions and anticipations, the
     reflections and digressions. States grandly that Robinson Crusoe
     demonstrates the old truth that "man, neglecting always to ap-
     preciate the good which he possesses, is ordinarily the artisan
     of his troubles. . . ." Insists that Robinson's situation of
     solitude was "absolutely new" at the time, and it made Defoe
     immortal, but it was only "the Robinson of the isle."

14   N., R.E. "Robinson Crusoe." Notes and Queries, 7th ser. 5,
      no. 120 (14 April):297.
            Replies to 1888.15. Quotes the Kirk Session records of
      Largo in Fifeshire, from the Edinburgh Magazine (July, 1818) on
      Selkirk's troubles with the church in 1695 and 1701.

15   P., I.M. "Robinson Crusoe." Notes and Queries, 7th ser. 5,
      no. 118 (31 March):245.
            Lists the numerous similarities between Grimmelshausen's
      Simplicissimus (1670) and Robinson Crusoe, and the single major
      difference in that the former deals with the supernatural. In
      treating the Thirty Years' War and "naval adventures," Simpli-
      cissimus reminds one also of Memoirs of a Cavalier and Captain
      Singleton. See reply, 1888.14.

16   PARNELL, ARTHUR. Appendix C "The Military Memoirs of Captain
      Carleton." In his The War of the Succession in Spain During
      the Reign of Queen Anne, 1702-1711. Based on Original Manu-
      scripts and Contemporary Records. London: George Bell &
      Sons, pp. 316-26.
            Admits in the preface that the literary part of this en-
      quiry, "relating purely to the question of authorship," has not
      yet been exhausted. In appendix C, investigates the authorship
      of Capt. George Carleton mainly because of interest in its au-
      thenticity. Makes the observation that every nineteenth-century
      English history of the War in Spain based itself on the Memoirs
      as having been authentically written by a soldier named Captain
      George Carleton and yet, in a striking contradiction, every
      edition of Defoe's works included the same Memoirs as among his
      fictions. Interjects here a third possible author who, in some
      respects, fits the puzzle better than Carleton or Defoe, namely,
      Jonathan Swift.

17   PICKFORD, JOHN. "Robinson Cruso." Notes and Queries, 7th
      ser. 6, no. 138 (18 August):138.
            Replies to 1886.1 and others. Reports the name inscribed
      on a gravestone in Cawston churchyard near Aylsham; the name used
      by a prominent family at Leek in Staffordshire, with motto "Sub
      Cruce." Reminds us that Crusoe, according to Robinson Crusoe,
      was born in York.

18   RUGE, SOPHUS. "Über einige vor-Defoe'sche Robinsonaden" and
      "Die ersten Einsiedler auf der Robinsonsinsel Juan Fernandez."
      In Abhandlungen und Vortrage zur Geschichte der Erdkunde.
      Dresden: G. Schonfeld's Verlagsbuchhandlung, pp. 71-101,
      102-14.
            In the first of the essays, discusses primarily geographi-
      cal, but also religious, philosophical and political dimensions
      of pre-Defoe Robinsonades, with particular emphasis on Sadeur
      (1676). In the second essay, compares the real, "geographically
      more interesting" Juan Fernandez castaways (the Mosquito Indian
      and Selkirk) with Defoe's synthetic hero.   (P.E.C.)

19   SABIN, JOSEPH. <u>A Dictionary of Books Relating to America,</u>
     <u>from Its Discovery to the Present Time</u>. New York: J. Sabin &
     Sons, 17:411-15.
          Includes the entry "<u>Robinson Crusoe</u>": a general listing of
     editions and abridgments, and twenty-two separate translations or
     imitations. See also 1873.6; 1891.16.

20   S[TEPHEN], L[ESLIE]. "Defoe, Daniel (1661?-1731)." In <u>Dic-</u>
     <u>tionary of National Biography</u>. Edited by Sir Leslie Stephen
     and Sir Sidney Lee. Reprint. London: Oxford University
     Press, 1963-1965, 5:730-43.
          Although the entry does contain errors, it should still be
     consulted, cautiously, for citations of Defoe's works and refer-
     ences by contemporaries or biographers, and for narrative of
     events in which he participated. Of particular interest is the
     canon, divided into classifications (the sum within parentheses
     being the number of items): "political tracts" (50), "verse"
     (16), "upon dissent and occasional conformity" (25), "economical
     and social tracts" (14), "didactic" (23), "narratives (real and
     fictitious)" (25), and "historical and biographical" (9). See
     also 1903.15. Reprinted: 1921-1922; 1937-1938; 1949-1950;
     1959-1960; 1963-1964.

21   TANCOCK, O.W. "Robinson Cruso." <u>Notes and Queries</u>, 7th ser.
     6, no. 133 (14 July):25-26.
          Replies to 1886.1 and others, on the surname "Cruso" among
     persons living in Norwich. Mentions also the names "Robinson"
     and "Cruso" as being held currently by Bible clerks at Worcester
     College, Oxford. See replies, 1888.1, 3, 22, 25.

22   _____. "Robinson Cruso." <u>Notes and Queries</u>, 7th ser. 6,
     no. 140 (1 September):174.
          Replies to 1888.25, who had disagreed with him on the two
     Bible clerks named "Robinson" and "Cruso" elected in 1860 and
     1862 for Worcester College, Oxford University.

23   TROLLOPE, T.A. "Marginalia by S.T. Coleridge." <u>Notes and</u>
     <u>Queries</u>, 7th ser. 6, no. 157 (29 December):501-2.
          Among the marginalia in Coleridge's hand and signed
     "S.T.C." in volume one of Thomas Fuller's <u>Worthies</u> (2 vols.,
     London, 1811): places "Shakespear! Milton! Fuller! Defoe!
     Hogarth!" all in the category of "uniques." See also the
     reprintings in <u>Coleridge's Miscellaneous Criticism</u>, ed. Thomas
     Middleton Raysor (Cambridge, Mass.: Harvard University Press,
     1936), pp. 272-73; and <u>Critical Heritage</u>, p. 85.

24   VERNE, JULES. "Deux Ans de vacances." <u>Magasin d'éducation</u>
     <u>et de récréation</u> 47 (1 January)-48 (15 December). Reprint.
     Paris: J. Hetzel, 1888. <u>Two Years' Holiday</u> (I <u>Adrift in the</u>
     <u>Pacific</u>. II <u>Second Year Ashore</u>). Edited by I.O. Evans.
     2 vols. London: Arco Publications, 1964, 1:36-37, 50, 56,
     68, 73, 131, 165, 168, 172; 2:60, 93, 102.

Information on publications from Edward J. Gallagher, Jules Verne: A Primary and Secondary Bibliography (Boston, Mass.: G.K. Hall & Co., 1980), p. 24. As a Robinsonade, blends together incidents modeled after Robinson Crusoe and the Swiss Family Robinson (1812-1813), which center in the character of the young schoolboy named Service who knew these books by heart. Reprinted: 1888; 1889; 1964; 1967.

25 WALFORD, E. "Robinson Cruso." Notes and Queries, 7th ser. 6, no. 138 (18 August):138.
    Disagrees with 1888.21, on the existence at Worcester College, Oxford, of Bible clerks named Robinson and Cruso about 1859 or 1860. See replies, 1888.1, 3, 22.

26 WALLIS, ALFRED. "Daniel De Foe." Notes and Queries, 7th ser. 6, no. 146 (13 October):294.
    Replies to 1888.8 that the marriage record is the younger Defoe's; gives information also on his losing the election for the position of secretary to the Million Bank, in 1736.

27 ZETTEL, JOSEF. World-Book-Fame Reasons. To Enumerate These Reasons Wherefore Defoe's Robinson Has Become Famous Throughout All Europe. Neustadt: J. Zettel, 28 pp.
    Lavishes praise on Robinson Crusoe as "a truly common book" having "universality" and "classic simplicity." Claims for the book a "European fame" as a classic for children, but also an interest for the elderly, learned, and literate, and therefore the designation of being "a world-book." Places most emphasis on its "principal fame" arising from the work as "a social romance." Uses the word "Defoeism" curiously as a philosophical concept.

1889

1 AITKEN, GEORGE A. "Defoe's Brick-Kilns." Athenaeum, no. 3207 (13 April):472-73.
    Summarizes new information about Defoe's financial losses in connection with the tile- and brick-kiln works at Tilbury, of which he was secretary and owner. In the single surviving Chancery document dated 3 July 1703, one week before the sentencing to the pillory, finds Defoe's answer to Paul Whitehurst's suit against him and a person named Chapman over payment for drink consumed by workmen at the tile-factory. Suggests that the charge made by Defoe's enemies, on his not paying employees, may be based on this incident.

2 ____. "Defoe's Consolidator." Notes and Queries, 7th ser. 7, no. 178 (25 May):409.
    Queries the identification of two persons in the Consolidator: (1) in the passage referring to Addison's holding out for £200 per annum to write the Campaign, who is the author "that writes for 'em for nothing, and he's labouring very hard to

obtain the title of blockhead, and be paid for it"? (2) in the passage on the "Cogitator," is "honest S......" an allusion to Steele?

3   ALONZO. "Questions." <u>Bizarre Notes and Queries</u> 6, no. 8
    (August):348.
        Were Selkirk and Crusoe the same person? Where does Defoe
    say, "Thirteen times I have been rich and poor"?

4   ALPHA [pseud.]. "Defoe's Dutchman." <u>Notes and Queries</u>, 7th
    ser. 8, no. 206 (7 December):448-49.
        Asks for the identification of the incident referred to in
    the <u>Shortest-Way with the Dissenters</u>: "like the Dutchman with
    his man and his bear." See his own reply, 1890.4.

5   BACKUS, TRUMAN J., and BROWN, HELEN DAWES. "Daniel Defoe
    (1661-1731)" and "Defoe" [selections]. In <u>The Great English
    Writers from Chaucer to George Eliot</u>. New York, Cincinnati,
    Chicago: American Book Co., pp. 133-39, 303-9.
        In this textbook for the schools, claims that prose narra-
    tive was developed in the eighteenth century by Defoe, Richard-
    son, Fielding, Smollett, and Sterne; but denies that Defoe's
    novels were studies of character or had elaborate plots or dealt
    with love. States that in <u>Robinson Crusoe</u>, "the most fascinating
    boys' book in the world's literature," Defoe brought to the situ-
    ation of an isolated man a special power of imagination which he
    calls "a marvelous power of invention," but also "this lower
    order of imaginative writing" ["lower" than Spenser's or Mil-
    ton's] and "'the most amazing talent on record for telling lies'"
    [Leslie Stephen].

6   CLARKE, WM. A. "<u>Robinson Crusoe</u>." <u>Notes and Queries</u>, 7th·
    ser. 7, no. 173 (20 April):306.
        Notes apparent textual discrepancies in the early editions
    of <u>Robinson Crusoe</u>, as indicated by the word "apply" spelled
    "apyly" in the preface to his copy of the first edition. Stock's
    "facsimile" edition (1883) does not reproduce this spelling, and
    differs from the first edition in the line-endings of the pref-
    ace. Seeks further communication. See also 1902.3.

7   "De Foe and Dunton." <u>Bookworm</u> 2 (December):6.
        Quotes Wilson's <u>Memoirs</u> of Defoe (1830) on the <u>Shortest-Way
    with the Dissenters</u> as probably the occasion for Dunton's <u>A Satyr
    upon King William</u> (2d ed., 1703).

8   ERMEL, ALEXANDER. <u>Eine Reise nach der Robinson-Crusoe-Insel</u>.
    Hamburg: L. Friederichsen & Co., 134 pp.
        A detailed, first-hand description of Selkirk's (hence,
    presumably, Robinson's) island and an account of its history.
    Makes a short comparison of parallel landmarks and features re-
    ported by Selkirk and Robinson. Offers as background material in
    support of his contention that Selkirk served as the main source

for Defoe (to be proven in a promised second volume), but also in an effort to attract more German settlers to Chile. Includes a map and eleven photographs.   (P.E.C.)

9   GOSSE, EDMUND. A History of Eighteenth Century Literature
    (1660-1780). London and New York: Macmillan & Co., pp. 160,
    176-85, 242, 245, 385.
        Places the main discussion in chap. 6 "Defoe and the
    Essayists" rather than chap. 8 "The Novelists," while admitting
    that Defoe's genius was the ploughshare "needed to break up the
    fertile but unready soil." On this one point, disagrees with
    Jusserand's otherwise invaluable criticism (1887.7). Now and
    then, in the biographical summary, shows Minto's bias: "[De-
    foe's] character exhibits, almost to excess, some of the least
    pleasing qualities of the eighteenth-century mind and morals."
    Declares that it is difficult to have any sympathy for his "per-
    sonal character"; finds him dishonest: "'perhaps the greatest
    liar that ever lived'" (Minto). In Robinson Crusoe, judges that
    "Selkirk's story formed much more than the germ of Robinson
    Crusoe." On the secondary novels, however, displays a close
    attention to the works themselves and some independent critical
    judgments: for example, the ranking of Roxana as "perhaps the
    best of his novels after Robinson Crusoe"; mistaken chronologies
    in both Roxana and Moll Flanders; the comparison of Defoe and
    Zola, of Moll Flanders with Prévost's Manon Lescaut. Believes
    strongly that "the darkest side of Defoe's character" is that he
    presented his novels as "histories," and not as works of the
    imagination. See the review, 1889.14. Reprinted: 1897.

10 HOWELLS, W[ILLIAM] D. A Hazard of New Fortunes. Harper's
    Weekly 33, no. 1712 (12 October):810.
        In part 5th, chap. 3, being asked to write something dif-
    ferent on the strike for the magazine Every Other Week, Fulkerson
    says to Basil March, the editor: "But you could treat it in the
    historical spirit--like something that happened several centuries
    ago; De Foe's Plague of London style. Heigh?" Reprinted: A
    Selected Edition of W.D. Howells, ed. David J. Nordloh et al.
    (Bloomington and Indiana: Indiana University Press, 1976), 16:
    409.

11 HUNT, WILLIAM. Bristol. Historic Towns. 3d ed. London and
    New York: Longmans, Green, & Co., pp. 172-76.
        Summarizes briefly Defoe's alleged connections with Bris-
    tol, such as his meeting Selkirk there and writing Robinson
    Crusoe from his papers.

12 MORLEY, HENRY, ed. The Earlier Life and the Chief Earlier
    Works of Daniel Defoe. Carisbrook Library, 3. London,
    Glasgow, Manchester, and New York: George Routledge & Sons,
    446 pp.
        Alternates five chapters of sketchy biography (1661-1706)
    with the complete texts of six major works, all increasingly rare

since their last publication in Works (1840–1841) or Hazlitt's
Works of Daniel De Foe (1840–1843): Essay upon Projects (1697),
True-Born Englishman (1701), Shortest-Way with the Dissenters
(1702), Hymn to the Pillory (1703), Consolidator (1705), and Mrs.
Veal (1706). Builds the biographical narrative around political
events that serve as background for the reprinted pieces, and
thus makes available definitions and explanations (e.g., "occasional conformity"), comparisons with contemporaries (e.g.,
Swift, Addison). Aside from a few allusions to the "well-pointed
satire" of the Consolidator (Defoe second only to Swift as a sat-
irist) or the "jeu d'esprit" of Mrs. Veal, contains very little
discussion of literature as such, and makes no mention of the
novels. Quotes generously from other exceedingly rare works—The
Character of the Late Dr. Samuel Annesley (1697) or The Poor
Man's Plea (1698)—and weaves in summaries of pamphlets. Annotates the texts sparsely and randomly. See also 1889.15. Reprinted: New York: Burt Franklin, 1970.

13   PARNELL, ARTHUR. "Defoe and the Memoirs of Captain Carleton."
     Athenaeum, no. 3201 (2 March):279–80.
          Argues more extensively than in the appendix to his history
     of the War of the Succession in Spain, 1888.16, that Defoe was
     not the author of Capt. George Carleton. Describes the two sides
     of the authorship controversy as, on the one hand, consisting of
     "the school of Carletonians" who assign the authorship of Memoirs
     of a Cavalier and Capt. George Carleton to the same person, name-
     ly, Defoe on the grounds of "general internal resemblance"; and,
     on the other hand, consisting of "Defoeists" who seek to elimin-
     ate altogether "the personality of Capt. Carleton." Sides with
     the Defoeists as being "infinitely nearer the truth; for my re-
     searches have made it absolutely certain that in point of history
     the 'Memoirs' of this officer are sheer fiction." But the fic-
     tion here is so bad, "it is distinctly derogatory to the memory
     of the creator of Robinson Crusoe." Bases the entire case for
     Capt. George Carleton as fiction—on Defoe's honesty and integ-
     rity, and sense of fair play with the reputations of contempora-
     ries. Begins here to state the case for Swift as author, as he
     will do fully in 1891.12. Editor's note rudely rejects Parnell's
     opinions on authorship: they take for granted "Defoe's honesty
     and independent nature."

14   Review of Edmund Gosse's A History of Eighteenth Century Lit-
     erature (1660-1780), 1889. Athenaeum, no. 3199 (16 February):
     206.
          Makes two points in regard to Defoe: (1) the treatment of
     subject in Swift's Argument . . . Abolishing Christianity (1711)
     was "clearly suggested" by Defoe's Shortest-Way with the Dissent-
     ers; and (2) the carelessness evident in Capt. George Carleton
     is further proof that the work is not authentic, but the work of
     Defoe.

15   Review of Henry Morley's <u>The Earlier Life and the Chief</u>
      <u>Earlier Works of Daniel Defoe</u>, 1889. <u>Athenaeum</u>, no. 3218
      (29 June):816–17.
          Aside from the favorable judgment that this book contains
      some of Defoe's best publications up to and including <u>Mrs. Veal</u>
      (1706), severely criticizes such defects as "a manifest bias"
      (smooths over religious inconsistencies), inadequate evidence for
      his command of foreign languages, and especially an unwillingness
      to face up to "disagreeable incidents in his career." Concludes
      that the <u>Earlier Life</u>, while attractive in its style, can be
      "neither a useful guide for students nor an important addition to
      the literature of the subject." See also 1889.12.

16   ROBINSON, E. FORBES. <u>Defoe in Stoke Newington</u>. London:
      W.L. Prewer, 14 pp.
          Traces Defoe's "footprints" in Stoke Newington where, at
      14, he went to school at Newington Green by a path which still
      exists, leading from Church Street; and where, at 58, he wrote
      <u>Robinson Crusoe</u>. Refers vaguely to Defoe's house, shows an illus-
      tration and says it "was pulled down some five and twenty years
      ago," and thus confuses it with another house in which Defoe
      lived earlier, mentioned in Nicholas Clarke's will, dated 9 March
      1709 and proved 5 May 1715, as "now or late in the tenure or
      occupation of Daniell Defoe." Quotes an extract from the minutes
      of the Stoke Newington vestry for 10 April 1721 which shows that
      Defoe was chosen for a parish office and required to pay a fine
      of £10 to avoid public service. Using Henry Baker's diary
      (1727), describes his courtship of Sophia, Defoe's youngest daugh-
      ter, with glimpses of the father in his handsome house at Stoke
      Newington. Closes with part of a letter from the Quaker, Thomas
      Webb, expressing gratitude to Defoe for his generosity.

17   WILDE, OSCAR. "The Decay of Lying." <u>Nineteenth Century</u> 25,
      no. 143 (January):35–56 passim.
          In his sprightly dialogue with Cyril, Vivian argues that
      fiction declines as it turns away from "lying" (the imaginary) to
      facts and realism. He includes "Defoe's <u>History of the Plague</u>"
      among works like Casanova's memoirs, Boswell's <u>Life of Johnson</u>,
      and Carlyle's <u>French Revolution</u> as instances where "facts are
      either kept in their proper subordinate position, or else entire-
      ly excluded on the general ground of dullness." Reprinted:
      <u>Essays by Oscar Wilde</u>, ed. Hesketh Pearson (London: Methuen &
      Co., 1952).

1890

1   AITKEN, G[EORGE] A. "Defoe's Birth and Marriage." <u>Athenaeum</u>
      2, no. 3278 (23 August):257.
          Establishes the date of Defoe's marriage to Mary Tuffley as
      1 January 1684 [New Style], and the year of his birth as "in the
      latter part of 1659 or early in 1660." See also 1890.2; 1909.9.

2 _____. "Defoe's Wife." Contemporary Review 57 (1 February):
    232-39.
        From firsthand documents, corrects the long-standing error
    that Defoe was married twice, to a first wife named Mary, and a
    second named Susannah. Provides a full account of the one and
    only wife, Mary Tuffley, drawn from her will and that of her
    brother Samuel Tuffley, as well as other information about the
    immediate family. See also 1890.1; 1909.9.

3 ALPHA [pseud.]. "Daniel Defoe." Notes and Queries, 7th ser.
    9, no. 220 (15 March):218.
        Replies to 1890.12, 27. Quotes William Stebbing's Peter-
    borough (1890) on problems in assigning the authorship of Capt.
    George Carleton to either Swift or Defoe. Prefers Stebbing's
    view that the book is "still one of the mysteries of literature."

4 _____. "Defoe's Dutchman." Notes and Queries, 7th ser. 9,
    no. 218 (1 March):173.
        Replies to his own query, 1889.4, by citing an incident in
    [Charles] Kingsley's Two Years Ago [1857] which is attributed to
    a Greek painter: "like the old Greek who wrote 'This is an ox'
    under his picture."

5 BUCKLEY, W.E. "Sir Peter Parravicini." Notes and Queries,
    7th ser. 9, no. 217 (22 February):152.
        Provides information on the Original London Post, or
    Heathcot's Intelligence, and corrects Dibdin (1824.1) on the date
    for the beginning of the serial publication (7 October 1719) of
    Robinson Crusoe. Locates the Granville copy now in the British
    Museum, and asks for information on the copy once owned by Dr.
    [Philip] Bliss.

6 BÜLBRING, KARL D., ed. Forewords to The Compleat English
    Gentleman. London: David Nutt, pp. ix-lxxxiv.
        Makes available in print, for the first time, the accurate
    text of the manuscript in Defoe's hand, "The Compleat English
    Gentleman." Prints the entire text (276 pp.) of British Museum,
    Add. MSS. 32,555, explanatory notes (9 pp.) including all the
    passages marked for deletion, and an index. At the beginning of
    the manuscript are proof-sheets of sixteen pages by the printer
    T. Watts in Wild Court, suggesting that the work had been "per-
    haps interrupted by the misfortune which darkened the end of
    [Defoe's] life." In the forewords, establishes the time of com-
    position as being from 1728 to early 1729; reproduces the first
    and third introductions, which the editor rejected in favor of
    the second introduction; describes the appearance of the manu-
    script, its peculiarities of spelling and abbreviations; and
    assesses Defoe's aims in writing a work defining the "gentleman"
    for his time. Stresses the importance to Defoe of a gentleman's
    possessing landed estate, and relates his views of the gentleman
    to earlier and later definitions in the two forewords "History of
    the Word Gentleman" (14 pp.) and "The Education of the Born

Gentleman" (40 pp.). See also reviews in Notes and Queries, 7th
ser. 9, no. 231 (31 May 1890):439; Spectator 49, no. 3231 (31 May
1890):766-67; Ullrich, 1890.26. Reprinted: Folcroft, Pa.:
Folcroft Library Editions, 1972.

7   CLARKE, HYDE. "Bell Alley: Defoe." Notes and Queries, 7th
    ser. 10, no. 245 (6 September):183-84.
        Traces current Telegraph Street and Copthall Avenue back to
the Bell Alley mentioned in Journal of the Plague Year. See also
the replies, without reference to Defoe, by Jaydee, no. 247 (20
September):234; T.R. Sleet, no. 252 (25 October):335; and Jaydee,
no. 258 (6 December):458.

8   DE QUINCEY, THOMAS. "Homer and the Homeridae." In The Col-
    lected Writings of Thomas De Quincey. Edited by David Masson.
    Edinburgh: Adam & Charles Black, 6:84-85.
        Reprint of 1841.3, with only one revision, the added words
in apposition to Memoirs of a Cavalier: "one of his poorest
forgeries."

9   DNARGEL. "Books Written in Prison." Notes and Queries, 7th
    ser. 9, no. 222 (29 March):256.
        Replies to query by J. Maskell, no. 217 (22 February):147:
among other books, [mistakenly] Defoe's Review.

10 FISCHER, HUGO. "Defoe's Leben." In Sociale Fragen vor zwei-
    hundert Jahren (An Essay on Projects) von Daniel Defoe 1697.
    Translated by Hugo Fischer. Leipzig: C.L. Hirschfeld, pp.
    v-x. Reprint. Daniel Defoe: Über Projektemacherei (An Essay
    on Projects). Edited by Harry Schmidtgall. Wiesbaden: B.
    Heymann Verlag, 1975.
        Introduces his translation into German of an Essay upon Pro-
jects with a biographical sketch that makes reference to Hettner,
Scott, and Minto. Commends modern German emperors for having
taken the initiative to enact a number of Defoe's ideas, whereas
the author's contemporaries and subsequent politicians had failed
to recognize their wisdom. See the review by Ullrich, 1890.25.
                                                            (P.E.C.)

11 GEORGE, MRS. L.T. "Robinson Crusoe--Alexander Selkirk--Daniel
    De Foe." Bizarre Notes and Queries 7, nos. 3-4 (March and
    April):65.
        In reply to queries from Alonzo (1898.3), defends Defoe on
the Selkirk matter, and cites the preface to the Review (1712) as
the place where Defoe says he had been "thirteen times . . . rich
and poor."

12 HOPE, HENRY GERALD. "Daniel Defoe." Notes and Queries, 7th
    ser. 9, no. 218 (1 March):173-74.
        Replies to 1890.27 by quoting John Forster's Biographical
Essays (1860) that neither Smollett nor Lord Mahon took any
notice of Defoe.

13 MITCHELL, DONALD G[RANT]. "A Pamphleteer." In English Lands
    Letters and Kings from Elizabeth to Anne. New York: Charles
    Scribner's Sons, 2:272-79.
       Deals with Defoe, under William III and Queen Anne, in such
    broad terms that "Advice to English Tradesmen" [i.e. The Complete
    English Tradesman] and Family Instructor pass for pamphlets, and
    are treated to chatty comments. Suggests that only one book need
    be read by "this bustling, bouncing, inconsistent, indefatigable,
    unsuccessful scold of a man"--Robinson Crusoe. Reprinted: 1893.

14 MURRAY, JAMES O. "The Author of Robinson Crusoe." Presbyter-
    ian and Reformed Review 1:403-24.
       While relying heavily upon Forster, Lee, and Minto, directs
    some criticism at their works; and concludes that a satisfactory
    biography has yet to be written. Divides his appraisal into
    accounts of Defoe's Dissenting religion; writings as a social
    reformer; journalism, praising especially the Review and Lee's
    "newly discovered writings"; political journalism, including the
    satirical verses, pamphlets, and the secret government work after
    1715 ("a blot on the fame of their author"); and the novels.
    Starts the assessment of the fiction with the Consolidator and
    Mrs. Veal, and discusses Robinson Crusoe. Classifies separately,
    as works of "pure invention," Moll Flanders, Colonel Jack, and
    Roxana, forerunners of the realistic school headed by Zola.
    Unhesitatingly labels such fiction as "morally bad," and claims:
    "It is a somewhat repulsive picture this, of an old man like
    Defoe writing such fictions, no matter with what intent."

15 OLIVER, [S.] PASFIELD. Introduction to Madagascar; or Robert
    Drury's Journal, During Fifteen Years' Captivity on That
    Island. London: T. Fisher Unwin. Reprint. New York: Negro
    Universities Press, 1969, pp. 9-27.
       For this important modern reprint of Madagascar, brings
    together the evidence first presented in Antananarivo Annual,
    1885.8. Expands the earlier statement to a more definitive
    account of Defoe's role as editor and his use of sources such as
    Flacourt. Rejects completely the view of Madagascar as "the
    unsophisticated story of the poor deserted cabin boy, Robin."
    Argues also that Drury was most likely himself a pirate and his
    narrative of fifteen-year captivity was a "trumped-up story" to
    cover up his consorting with pirates like Captain White.

16 _____. "Madagascar; or, Robert Drury's Journal (1729)."
    Notes and Queries, 7th ser. 9, no. 214 (1 February):88.
       Asks for the identification of the "Gentleman of undoubted
    integrity" and of his "curious Remarks," mentioned in the Tran-
    scriber's preface.

17 _____. "Robert Drury." Notes and Queries, 7th ser. 9,
    no. 216 (15 February):121-24.
       Makes the case emphatically against "the veracity of Robert
    Drury" and, for the first time, firmly in favor of Defoe's sub-

stantial contribution. Calls attention to similarities with works at least partly set in Madagascar, Robinson Crusoe and Captain Singleton; provides further evidence of the editor's "artifice."

18 _____. "Robert Drury." Notes and Queries, 7th ser. 9, no. 225 (19 April):315-16.
　　　Replies to 1890.28: on the different editions of Madagascar, Drury's possible death between 1743 and 1750, the testing of his Malagasy vocabulary and the influence of his Cockney accent on its written forms, frequent citation of his book in William Ellis's History of Madagascar (1838).

19 PEET, WILLIAM H. "Booksellers' Sales in the Eighteenth Century." Notes and Queries, 7th ser. 9, no. 225 (19 April): 301-2.
　　　Prints extracts from catalogues of sales (1704-1768) in the possession of Longmans & Co. In catalogue of William Taylor's sales in 1725, for Robinson Crusoe in two volumes, 8vo and 12mo, specifies the amounts to be paid to the author for the sale of a certain number of copies, and the amounts paid for the copyrights of Parts One and Two.

20 "Quotations and Sayings on the Devil." Bizarre Notes and Queries 7, nos. 7 and 8 (July-August):139-40.
　　　Includes the first two lines of the True-Born Englishman.

21 RANNIE, DAVID WATSON. Daniel Defoe. The Stanhope Essay, 1890. Oxford: B.H. Blackwell; London: Simpkin, Marshall, Kent, & Co., 57 pp.
　　　States forcefully "the historian's point of view" regarding Defoe's importance. Sees him as "one of the heroes of a new time" (generally judged unheroic), "the oracle" of certain "master-forces" imbued with the modern spirit, such as the Habeas Corpus Act, parliamentary independence, ministerial responsibility, government by parties. Through six chapters and a conclusion, using Defoe's works at firsthand, dwells mainly on his participation in, and contribution to, historical/political events up to 1719; claims that the last ten or twelve years were essentially "an appendix to his tale" and definitely of secondary interest. Commenting altogether very little on the novels, insists they do not throw light on him as a man; they were never made "the vehicle of his social and political ideas"; but Robinson Crusoe and Journal of the Plague Year, and the pamphlets, do have Defoe's principal "literary distinction," namely, "sympathy." Reprinted: Folcroft Library Editions, 1977.

22 RUSSELL, JOHN R. Preface to An Account of the Conduct and Proceedings of the Pirate Gow. Reprint. New York: Burt Franklin, 1970, pp. v-vii.
　　　Calls the period 1720 to 1730 "the Age of Crime," which produced Defoe's Account . . . of the Pirate Gow (1725) as well

as his criminal novels. His purpose was to show "the evil of
their ways to the wretched classes of whom his subjects were the
representatives." Reprints the Account.

23　STEBBING, WILLIAM. Peterborough. English Men of Action.
　　London and New York: Macmillan & Co., pp. 53-58.
　　　　Judges that few military campaigns were more remarkable
than the one led by Charles Mordaunt, Earl of Peterborough and
Monmouth, in 1705, during the War of the Succession in Spain; but
its history is rendered difficult, among other reasons, by the
rejection of any evidence drawn from Capt. George Carleton, la-
beled "still one of the mysteries of literature." Rejects Defoe
as editor or author, arguing [incorrectly] the book did not
appear in his lifetime; it was never attributed to him until a
hundred years after his death; and it does not reach Defoe's high
standard. Assigns it accordingly to "the limbo of historical
romance."

24　Two notes on Robinson Crusoe. Library 2:468.
　　　　Quotes the response to M. Jules Simon's complaint that
Robinson Crusoe is boring to the modern schoolboy, by the Daily
Graphic (24 October); and the further response to the Daily Gra-
phic, by the Public Librarian of Aberdeen, about how well nine
copies of Robinson Crusoe circulate.

25　ULLRICH, HERMANN. Review of Hugo Fischer, trans., Sociale
　　Fragen vor zweihunder Jahren (An Essay on Projects), 1890.
　　Literarisches Zentralblatt für Deutschland, no. 50:1740-41.
　　　　Judges the translation to be generally true to the origi-
nal, despite some difficult problems. Notes that the biographi-
cal introduction perpetuates outdated notions and cites Walter
Scott in statements which can only be attributed to him.
　　　　　　　　　　　　　　　　　　　　　　　　　　　　(P.E.C.)

26　ULLRICH, HERMANN. Review of K.D. Bülbring's edition of The
　　Compleat English Gentleman, 1890. Litteraturblatt für german-
　　ische und romanische Philologie 11, no. 11:404-9.
　　　　Praises the conscientious work of this continental scholar
in preparing an eminently scholarly annotated edition of the very
difficult manuscript that had been in the British Museum collection since 1885. Takes issue with the editor's reference to Defoe's frequently "unscrupulous and dishonest conduct," preferring
to see in his actions merely the unavoidable manoeuverings of the
political activist, far less compromising than those of a self-
serving Dryden or Swift. Closes with an account of the current
(anemic) state of Defoe research in Germany. Finds much work to
be done on translations, for example, not to mention the fact
that a decent German biography of Defoe has yet to be written.
　　　　　　　　　　　　　　　　　　　　　　　　　　　　(P.E.C.)

27　WELCH, J. CUTHBERT. "Daniel Defoe." Notes and Queries, 7th
　　ser. 9, no. 214 (1 February):90.

Seeks the reference for the doubts concerning Defoe's authorship of Capt. George Carleton expressed by Lord Mahon [Philip Henry Stanhope, fifth Earl], in History of the War of Succession in Spain (1832); and more information on the authorship of The Free State of Noland (1701), attributed to Defoe. See replies, 1890.3, 12.

28　WOODALL, W.O. "Robert Drury." Notes and Queries, 7th ser. 9, no. 218 (1 March):177.
　　　　Replies to 1890.17, with some hard questions on the authenticity of Madagascar, relating to Defoe as the editor and Drury as the author. Specifically: the long, unbroken narrative, the doubtful Malagasy vocabulary, Drury's inability to speak English.

1891

1　B., H.E.B. "Robinson Crusoe." Notes and Queries, 7th ser. 12, no. 312 (19 December):488.
　　　　Asks if Campe was the author of Robinson Crusoe. See replies, 1892.4, 11, 18.

*2　BONAR, J[AMES?]. Daniel Foe.
　　　　In spite of an extended search, no copy has been located.

3　BÜLBRING, KARL D. "Defoe and Mary Astell." Academy 39, no. 984 (14 March):259.
　　　　Identifies Mary Astell's A Serious Proposal to the Ladies (1694) as the book referred to by Defoe in Essay upon Projects, which influenced his view of education for women. In commenting upon her Essay in Defense of the Female Sex (1696), stresses that Astell has "the merit of priority to Defoe," and that his "reformatory ideas and schemes" were again borrowed from someone else. Refers to his forthcoming article, 1891.4. See also the reply, 1891.5.

4　_____. "Mary Astell, An Advocate of Women's Rights Two Hundred Years Ago." Journal of Education, n.s. 13, no. 261 (1 April):199-202, and no. 262 (1 May):240-44.
　　　　Asserts strongly the claim of the long-neglected Mary Astell as an advocate for the rights of women. Deals with the ideas, and also the tone and style of her three principal works. Identifies her Serious Proposal to the Ladies (1694) as the specific work that influenced Defoe's thinking on women's education in his Essay upon Projects, and may even have "caused" him to write the section, demonstrating again that he was less an originator than a promoter of another person's "reformatory ideas and schemes." Shows that in her sprightly Essay in Defense of the Female Sex (1696), Astell shares ideas also advocated in Defoe's Compleat English Gentleman, a work still in manuscript at the time of his death. Even more concerned with the relationships of men and women—love, women's subjection to men—is

Astell's third work, <u>Some Reflections upon Marriage</u> (1700); and
she appears to have become "bolder and more radical" in the long
preface added to later editions. See also 1891.3, 5.

5   CARRUTHERS, S.W. "Defoe and Mary Astell." <u>Academy</u> 39,
     no. 986 (28 March):305.
         Arguing that Mary Astell and Defoe advocated independently
     for two totally different educational schemes, disagrees strenu-
     ously with Bülbring's suggestion (1891.3) that Defoe in <u>An Essay</u>
     <u>upon Projects</u> was "a plagiarist."

6   DUGUÉ, FERDINAND. <u>L'Ile déserte ou le meilleur des mondes:</u>
     <u>Comédie en trois actes, en vers</u>. In <u>Théatre complet de Ferdi-</u>
     <u>nand Dugué</u>. Paris: Calmann Lévy, 1:393–460.
         In this comedy first acted in 1848, but not published then,
     characterizes the misanthrope Ariste, who lives the life of a
     savage on a deserted island, by having him denounce Robinson as
     "whimperer . . . glutton, whose greatest misfortune was not to
     have saved a cooking-pot from the shipwreck to make his soup."
     At the end of act 1, Ariste learns that his enemies are about to
     descend upon the island, and now admits that he slandered Robin-
     son Crusoe, "great man," who faced cannibals much less dangerous
     than his own "anthropophagi."

7   FIELD, E.M. [LOUISE FRANCES]. "Some Nursery Classics." In
     The Child and His Book: Some Account of the History and Pro-
     gress of Children's Literature in England. 2d ed. London:
     Wells Gardner, Darton & Co., 1892. Reprint. Detroit: Sing-
     ing Tree Press, 1968, pp. 229–42.
         Makes the point that <u>Robinson Crusoe</u> and <u>Gulliver's Travels</u>
     were, until the advent of cheap editions, "nursery classics" for
     only a small number of children, due to their expense and grown-
     up content (e.g., religious dialogues between Crusoe and Friday).

8   HALE, EDWARD E., ed. Preface to the <u>Life of Colonel Jack</u>. An-
     other Robinson Crusoe. By Daniel Defoe. Boston: J. Stilman
     & Co., pp. [vii-viii].
         Claims that <u>Colonel Jack</u>, now being published probably for
     the first time in the United States, was "thoroughly American,
     and its important movement . . . all in this country,"--the rest
     being "padded," and thus removed from this condensation (181
     pp.). Includes special recognition of <u>Colonel Jack</u> as being next
     to <u>Robinson Crusoe</u> in importance; of Defoe as "the greatest of
     novelists," a judgment given in 1863 by a "distinguished" Civil
     War general [who can be identified as Benjamin Franklin Butler];
     and of a bold public interest in contrasting forms of slavery,
     white slavery here and slaveholding in <u>Robinson Crusoe</u>.

9   HARRISON, HENRY. "Defoe's Political Career: Its Influence on
     English History." <u>Westminster Review</u> 135, no. 5 (May):512-23.
         Concentrates exclusively on biography and history as "col-
     lateral studies," and uses the example of Defoe's political life

to demonstrate how significant were his contributions in (for example) the defence of liberty and tolerance in his time, and how
completely neglected has been his political career. Divides the
subject into three parts: (1) <u>Literary</u>: in which Defoe is viewed as "political littérateur," producing the <u>True-Born Englishman</u>
and the <u>Shortest-Way with the Dissenters</u>, continuing with the
<u>Review</u>--definitely shaping public opinion: "a model of untiring
energy and industry, of erudition and wisdom, scarce surpassed by
a Napoleon or a Gladstone." (2) <u>Courtly</u>: makes the bold claim
that Defoe not only won the confidence and personal friendship of
William III, he also shaped the King's policy through interviews,
serving as "chosen cousellor" on at least two occasions--the war
with France, which Defoe proposed to finance by capturing the
Spanish West Indies, and the legislative Union with Scotland.
(3) <u>Official</u>: asserts that Defoe held a series of somewhat mysterious appointments, the most important being the quasi-ambassa-
dorial role in the negotiations leading to the Union and another
as "general advisor of the Ministry" in the amendment of the
Bankruptcy Acts. Constantly links all these activities with an
intensely energetic "temperament."

10   HUXLEY, THOMAS HENRY. Letter in the <u>Pall Mall Gazette</u>, 22
      October. In Leonard Huxley. <u>Life and Letters of Thomas Henry</u>
      <u>Huxley</u>. 2 vols. New York: D. Appleton & Co., 1900, 2:301-2.
         Rather than being preoccupied with Middle English philolo-
      gy, argues vigorously for the serious study of "our great English
      writers" through the new chair of English literature at Oxford.
      Insists that even his distinguished contemporaries might benefit
      in their style: from the study of Hobbes, dignity; Swift, conci-
      sion and clearness; and Goldsmith and Defoe, simplicity. Attest
      to the value of reading the masterpieces (<u>Robinson Crusoe</u>, <u>Vicar</u>
      <u>of Wakefield</u>, <u>Gulliver's Travels</u>) and of knowing the eighteenth
      century.

11   LIEBHABER, E[RIC LOUIS MARIE] DE, ed. Preface to Campe's <u>Le</u>
      <u>Nouveau Robinson (Robinson der Jüngere)</u>. Édition Classique.
      Paris: Belin Frères, pp. v-xviii.
         Describes the relationship of the old and new <u>Robinson</u> as
      part of a continuing interest in the reform of education, begin-
      ning with Locke and persisting through Rousseau. States categori-
      cally that he does not find in Defoe's <u>Robinson Crusoe</u> the "unity
      of views which marks great minds and which marks also men whose
      lives are passed in the pursuit of an idea." Recognizes no con-
      nection between <u>Robinson Crusoe</u> and Defoe's other works, but does
      find "an incontestably original mind" rambling across many differ-
      ent domains of thought.

12   PARNELL, ARTHUR. "Dean Swift and the <u>Memoirs of Captain Carle-</u>
      <u>ton</u>." <u>English Historical Review</u> 6, no. 21 (January):97-151.
         In the controversy over who wrote <u>Capt. George Carleton</u> the
      main issue is the credibility of a major source for the history
      of events in the War of the Succession in Spain. Amasses the

evidence that Carleton existed, but the events of his life bear
no resemblance to those narrated in Capt. George Carleton. Argues that of the two prime candidates for the authorship of the
fictional work, the case for Defoe is the weaker. The first public notice of the book, in 1786, classified it under the heading
Novels and Romances; this designation applied back to the 1743
edition. Dr. Johnson, in his conversation about the book in
1784, did not know it as a book of English history. Lists among
the supporters of Defoe's authorship: Walter Wilson (1830), John
Gibson Lockhart (1837), William Hazlitt (1840), Thomas Tegg
(1840), William Lowndes (1843), Henry Bohn (1854), George Craik
(1883). Up to 1888, all Queen Anne historians followed Capt.
George Carleton in accounts of the War of the Succession in Spain
as if it were eye-witness history; all collected editions of
Defoe's works included it as if it were fiction. Although the
case for Defoe's authorship does not necessarily require either a
real or a fictitious Carleton, the case for Swift's authorship
does allow an important role for the real-life Carleton. Develops the argument fully for Swift's authorship.

13   PLOMER, HENRY R. "Literature of the Plague." Library 3:209-
     28.
         Surveys plague literature from the Black Death of the
fourteenth century to the present, and makes an effort at class-
ifications. Judges that the largest class consists of medical
works; the next largest, the theological class. Places the Journal of the Plague Year in the fourth class, "general literature,"
the most important of the fictional works: "its author must have
been well acquainted with the literature of the plague."

14   REPPLIER, AGNES. "A Plea for Humor." In Points of View.
     Boston and New York: Houghton, Mifflin & Co., p. 4.
         Objects strenuously to the extended meanings given to Robin-
son Crusoe as "a picture of civilization," by Frederic Harrison,
1888.7, such being destructive to a young boy's reading plea-
sures. Reprinted: 1892, 1893, 1894, 1895, 1896, 1899, 1919.

15   ROE, J[OHN] E[LISHA]. The Mortal Moon; or Bacon and His
     Masks. The Defoe Period Unmasked. New York: Burr Printing
     House, 605 pp. passim.
         Argues the preposterous idea that Francis Bacon wrote all
of the works generally assigned to Defoe, in particular Robinson
Crusoe. Noting the recurring "language characteristics" and
"distinctive Baconian expressions and sentence formation," develops the "theory" that certain Shakespeare plays (The Tempest),
Bunyan's Pilgrim's Progress, some of Addison, all of the "Defoe
literature" (including Lee's "newly discovered writings"), and
Swift's major works were the product of one mind, Lord Bacon's;
and all led to his New Atlantis [1627] as the "capstone." Applies this pseudo-scholarship erratically in three extensive
chapters: "Baconian Framework in Crusoe," "Harley and Defoe,"
and "The Thread of the Labyrinth."

16   SABIN, JOSEPH. <u>A Dictionary of Books Relating to America,</u>
     <u>from Its Discovery to the Present Time</u>. New York: J. Sabin &
     Sons, 19:247.
        Under the entry "Selkirk (A.)," lists <u>Providence Display'd</u>
(1712) by Selkirk himself, and a different book with similar
title (1800) by Isaac James. See also 1873.6; 1888.19.

1892

1   B., J.H. "Defoe (Daniel), b.1661, d.1731." In <u>The New Cal-</u>
     <u>endar of Great Men</u>. Edited by Frederic Harrison. London and
     New York: Macmillan & Co., pp. 323-24.
        Includes Defoe among "the 558 worthies of all ages and
nations in the positivist calendar of Auguste Comte." In this
brief biography, with Minto the only reference cited, comments on
the "strict adherence to reality" in <u>Robinson Crusoe</u>: "The shipwrecked sailor, to all seeming 'out of Humanity's reach,' yet
owes everything to Humanity. . . ."

2   CLERK, SIR JOHN. <u>Memoirs of the Life of Sir John Clerk of Pen-</u>
     <u>icuik</u>. Edited by John M. Gray. Edinburgh: Scottish History
     Society, pp. 63-66, 244-45.
        Defoe's secret activities, in 1706-1707, are clearly known
to one of the Queen's Commissioners for the Treaty of Union: "He
was therefor a Spy amongst us, but not known to be such, other-
ways the Mob of Edin. had pulled him to pieces." On the accuracy
of the <u>History of the Union</u>: "There is not one single fact in it
that I can challenge." Reprinted: London: Nichols & Sons,
1895.

3   CREIGHTON, C. "London after the Great fire." <u>Blackwood's</u>
     <u>Edinburgh Magazine</u> 152, no. 925 (November):739-40, 742-43.
        Uses the <u>Journal of the Plague Year</u> to observe how the new
City arose out of the ashes of the old, except for certain courts
and alleys in parishes like St. Stephen, Coleman Street. In this
parish the dead carts could not come near the houses to fetch bod-
ies. The narrator also dismisses the notion held by "some of our
quaking philosophers" that the seeds of the plague were destroyed
by the great fire of 1666.

4   DNARGEL. "<u>Robinson Crusoe</u>." <u>Notes and Queries</u>, 8th ser. 1,
     no. 5 (30 January):93.
        Replies to 1891.1, with information on Joachim Heinrich
Campe. States that his <u>Robinson der Jungere</u> was translated into
English, 1855; and [incorrectly] that "it is merely <u>Robinson</u>
<u>Crusoe</u> put into dialogues."

*5   GIBB, DOUGLAS. "Notice biographique et litteraire." <u>Daniel</u>
     <u>De Foe. Vie et aventures de Robinson Crusoe</u>. Édition clas-
     sique. Paris: Belin Frères.
        Information from <u>Bibliotheque nationale</u>. See also Mann,
  p. 116.

6 GRIFFINHOOFE, H.G. "New Life of Daniel Defoe." Notes and Queries, 8th ser. 2, no. 47 (19 November):417. Replies to 1892.20. Asks from what painting Freeman made the engraving in Robinson's History of Stoke Newington (1831), and calls attention to the Rev. W. Palin's Stifford and Its Neighborhood [1871] for information on the Foes and the tile factory in Chadwell, St. Mary.

*7 KAMENSKII, A. Daniel' Defo, ego zhizn' i deiatel'nost' [Daniel Defoe, his life and works]. Pavlenkov series. St. Petersburg. In Russian. Reference from Literaturnaia entsiklopediia (Moscow: Publishing Company of the Communist Academy, 1930), 3:231. No copy has been located. (A.L.S.R.)

8 KIPPENBERG, AUGUST. "Robinson in Deutschland bis zur Insel Felsenburg (1731-43). Ein Beitrag zur Litteraturgeschichte des 18. Jahrhunderts." Ph.D. dissertation, Hannover: Norddeutsche Verlagsanstalt O. Goedel, 141 pp. Has chapters on "Robinson" in Germany before Defoe: the English "Robinson" and reasons for its success in Germany; the first translations, with judgment of the work and commendations by individuals; the Robinsonades up to Insel Felsenburg (1731); and Insel Felsenburg. The appendices "Bibliographie" document the findings, with the third, listing Schnabel's work. See also the reviews by J. Bolte, in Archiv für das Studium des neueren Sprachen und Literatur 90, no. 47 (1893):414-16; and Ullrich, 1893.16.

9 MINET, WILLIAM. Some Account of the Huguenot Family of Minet from Their Coming out of France at the Revocation of the Edict of Nantes MDCLXXXVI. London: For the Author, pp. 67, 74, 98, 99, 100, 101, 207. Makes no mention at all of Defoe, but gives evidence of the existence of William Veal, comptroller of the Customs in Kent, and his marriage in 1724 to the widow of Captain William Young who commanded the ship Degrave up to his death in 1701, in Madras, and before it was wrecked on the shores of Madagascar. Quotes the undated manuscript notes of Hughes Minet, great-grandson of Captain Young, in two different copies of Madagascar, which corroborate "the truth of Drury's narrative."

10 MOUNSEY, R.K. "Robinson Crusoe." In A Long Time Ago. Favourite Stories Retold by Mrs. Oscar Wilde & Others. London: Ernest Nister; New York: E.P. Dutton & Co., 3 pp. Follows the well-established tradition of comic verses, this time to Crusoe's discovering the human footprint.

11 NORGATE, FR. "Robinson Crusoe." Notes and Queries, 8th ser. 1, no. 5 (30 January):93. Replies to 1891.1 with more information on Johann Heinrich Campe and his Robinson der Jungere.

12   P., W.G.F. "Robinson Crusoe." Notes and Queries, 8th ser. 1,
      no. 5 (30 January):93.
         Asks for help in dating a copy of Robinson Crusoe in which
both the publishers and illustrators were J. & J. Cunder, London.

13   "Prologue: L'Oeuvre et son auteur." In Aventures de Robinson
      Crusoé. Traduit de l'Anglais de Daniel De Foë. New ed.
      Paris: Bernardin-Béchet & Fils, pp. v-x.
         Stands out from the ordinary run of prefatory obligation in
that while giving the biographical facts, at times erroneously,
(e.g., the birth-year, 1663), it distorts through oversimplifi-
cation. States, for instance, the money gained from the success
of "Le véritable Anglais" was used to pay off creditors; in his
Essay upon Projects Defoe was "one of the creators of political
economy"; with George I's ascending the throne, Defoe was totally
neglected, and so abandoned political life and gave himself
entirely to literary composition. Offers English pronuncia-
tions: Fô, "whih" [Whig], "Robinnsonn Crousô." Concludes that
Robinson was "not just a young shipwrecked Englishman, he is the
humanity, intelligence, will in the struggle with nature or blind
force . . .; the humanity leading to piety, and knowing how to
find God through nature, its splendours, its clouds, and its
tempests."

14   SAINTSBURY, GEORGE, ed. Introductions in Selections from
      Defoe's Minor Novels. Pocket Library of English Literature.
      New York: Macmillan & Co., pp. vii-xvii, 1-2, 135-36, 202,
      203, 243, 320-21, 332.
         Presents the "satellites" of Robinson Crusoe which show
Defoe's "unrivalled talents for description and narrative."
Describes the unique situation in which Defoe, having none of the
usual literary qualities of mind, produces writing which has
everywhere the same "peculiar literary quality." Introduces the
concept of "'disrealizing,'" for which Defoe has been taken to be
"a mere Realist." Assesses that a great part of his popularity
arises from his "sublimated commonplace," in which "what pleases"
stands "just above the mind and taste of the reader." On Captain
Singleton: stresses that Defoe got close to the truth about the
geography of Africa through the use of accounts or maps of some
Portuguese traveller. Praises Moll Flanders as "the most remarkable example of pure realism in literature," and compares Zola
and Defoe as "the difference between talent misled by theory and
genius conducted by art." As inventions, Memoirs of a Cavalier
ranks with Moll Flanders, next to Robinson Crusoe. Roxana, the
"least good" and "one of the most puzzling" of the minor novels,
compares unfavorably with Manon Lescaut and Moll Flanders.

15   _____. Introductions to The Shortest Way with the Dissenters.
      Political Pamphlets. New York: Macmillan & Co., pp. vii-xix,
      23-24.
         Places the Shortest-Way with the Dissenters among the first
pamphlets "of great literary merit," right after Halifax's A Let-

ter to a Dissenter; regards Defoe as among "the Seven Masters of
English political writing." For a part of his life, he was almost exclusively a pamphleteer, his other famous pamphlets being
the Legion Letter and Reasons Against War with France. Discounts
any irony in the Shortest-Way with the Dissenters.

16   SPIELMANN, M.H. "The New Robinson Crusoe." Magazine of Art
     15:47-51.
        Takes the occasion of the publishing a new edition of
     Robinson Crusoe (Cassell's) to examine the illustrated editions
     published to-date. Starts with the Clark and Pine frontispiece
     of the first edition, a "poor production"; and continues with the
     folding map of the second volume, the plates as first used in the
     sixth edition (1722), and the numerous other illustrated editions
     of the eighteenth and nineteenth centuries, ending with the edi-
     tion of perhaps the most successful illustrator, J.D. Watson, and
     the Cassell's edition under review, with Mr. Wal Paget, "easily
     at the head of all Crusoe illustrators."

17   STEPHEN, LESLIE. "De Foe's Novels." In Hours in a Library.
     New ed., enlarged. 3 vols. London: Smith, Elder, & Co.,
     1:1-46.
        Revises 1874.8. Omits a few topical references: the pref-
     erence of Thackeray's Barry Lyndon [1844] to Defoe's writings;
     Capt. George Carleton as no longer acceptable in the canon.
     Relocates a long section and some scattered comments into a new
     conclusion on Defoe's journalism as a part of his novels, on his
     morality, and on Robinson Crusoe as being both Defoe and "the
     typical Englishman of his time." Reprinted: 1892; 1894; 1899;
     1904; 1907; 1909; 1917; in part, Critical Heritage.

18   TOMLINSON, C. "Robinson Crusoe." Notes and Queries, 8th ser.
     1, no. 5 (30 January):93.
        Replies to 1891.1, identifying Campe as author of the in-
     dependent work, Robinson der Jungere, which Tomlinson translated
     and offered to the publisher, J.W. Parker.

19   [WALKLEY, A.B.] "Unabashed Defoe." Daily Chronicle, 17 Feb-
     ruary, p. 3.
        Reviewing Saintsbury (1892.14), deals mainly with Moll
     Flanders as the best of Defoe's novels, "a finer novel than
     'Crusoe,' we think, because a more subtle, more complex." Sin-
     gles out the most striking literary quality of the novels: a
     lack of "construction" or an "amorphousness," found especially in
     the conclusions of Robinson Crusoe, Moll Flanders, and Roxana.
     Assigns external reasons in Defoe's "writing for the market."
     Assigns also internal reasons in the artist's desire to imitate
     life through the "artessness" of his narratives. Strongly
     defends these "qualities, their discontinuity, their décousus,
     their alternate slackening and hurrying of pace, their digres-
     sions, their garrulity, their level tracts of commonplace, in
     following what Mr. Henry James calls 'the strange, irregular

rhythm of life,' [as giving] them the very air of truth." Reprinted, in part: Wright (1894; 1931).

20   WRIGHT, THOMAS. "New Life of Daniel Defoe." Notes and Que-
    ries, 8th ser. 2, no. 43 (22 October):326.
        Announces preparations for his new Life of Defoe which he
intends to make more about the private life than the political.
See replies, 1892.6; 1893.7, 15.

21   ZALSHUPIN, A. "Angliiskii publitsist XVII Veka: Po povodu
    novago izdaniia 'Essays on Projects' Danielia Defoe" [An En-
    glish publicist of the XVIIth century: Concerning a new edi-
    tion of Essays upon Projects by Daniel Defoe]. Nabliudatel'
    [The Observer], no. 6:277-85.
        In Russian. Reacts with special resonance to an Essay upon
Projects, one of six major works included in Morley's Earlier
Life (1889). Admires Defoe throughout his career as a publicist.
Expresses surprise that the author who captivated us in our childhood with Robinson Crusoe was also "an outstanding economist of
his time" in an Essay upon Projects, and dwelt upon social problems we are only now attempting to resolve. Ranks Defoe among
the representatives of "state socialism," and demonstrates how,
in one project after another, he daringly invested the state with
power; how he used financial ideas relating to credit, banks, and
insurance to respond to social questions. Takes a similar approach in resolving the problems of the insane or women's education. Praises the originality and humane far-sightedness of
Defoe's projects.   (A.L.S.R.)

1893

1   AITKEN, GEORGE A. "Defoe and Mist's Weekly Journal." Athe-
    naeum, no. 3435 (26 August):287-88.
        Supplements 1864.7 with additional information from the
Public Record Office on Defoe's "secret management" of Mist's
Weekly Journal, from August, 1717, to the end of 1724. Identi-
fies specific articles by Defoe, and quotes from documents by
Mist and Thomas Warner, and from Defoe's letter to Charles De la
Faye, dated 7 June 1720. See the entry on "Nathaniel Mist" by
Aitken, DNB, 1894.3.

2   BILTZ, KARL. "Magister Ludwig Friedrich Vischer, der erste
    deutsche Robinson-Übersetzer." Archiv für das Studium der
    neueren Sprachen und Literaturen 90:13-26.
        Discovers independently of Kippenberg, whose study had just
appeared (1892.8), that Vischer's Hamburg edition of Robinson Crusoe was the first German translation, not the Frankfurt/Leipzig
edition, as had been presumed by earlier scholars. Supports this
with convincing evidence based on close textual comparison. Provides a brief biographical sketch of the obscure Vischer.
                                         (P.E.C.)

3   CLARKE, F.R. [F.R.C.S.]. Glimpses of Ancient Hackney and
     Stoke Newington. Being a Reprint of a Series of Articles
     Appearing in the "Hackney Mercury," from April 23rd, 1892,
     to November 25th, 1893. London: A.T. Roberts, Son & Co.,
     pp. 270-71.
          Mentions the Assembly Room which now occupies part of the
     site of the garden and house on Defoe Road "where eccentric, but
     talented Daniel Defoe for some years resided." Contains a brief
     biographical sketch of Defoe, but mistakenly refers to the "large
     boys' school . . . kept by one Mr. Marton [Morton] on Stoke
     Newington green," and refers to "part of the old garden wall of
     Defoe's premises" as still standing on Oldfield Road.

4   DICKENS, CHARLES. Letter to Douglas Jerrold, in The Letters
     of Charles Dickens. Edited by His Sister-in-Law and His
     Eldest Daughter. Reprint. The Letters of Charles Dickens.
     Edited by Walter Dexter. Bloomsbury: Nonesuch Press, 1938.
     1:639.
          16 November 1844: expresses irritation to Jerrold with the
     "parrots" who declaim against the railroad "building across the
     water at Venice": "Before God, I could almost turn bloody-mind-
     ed, and shoot the parrots of our island with as little compunc-
     tion as Robinson Crusoe shot the parrots in his."

5   DOBLE, C.E. "The Memoirs of Captain Carleton; Swift or De-
     foe?" Academy 43, no. 1096 (6 May):393-95; no. 1098 (20 May):
     438-39; no. 1099 (27 May):461-62; no. 1100 (3 June):482-83.
          Extends the controversy over Capt. George Carleton one step
     farther by asking who was the author--Swift or Defoe?--of this
     admittedly fabricated work. Agrees with Parnell (1891.12) that
     this important source of information on the War of Succession in
     Spain is not the work of Carleton and therefore historically un-
     reliable; disagrees with him as to the author, finding the case
     for Defoe stronger than for Swift. Presents the argument in four
     divisions: (I) External evidence that Swift could not possibly
     have written Capt. George Carleton, e.g., the given composition
     and publication dates, serious problems with the Dedication as
     the work of Swift; internal evidence, in the use of Latin, Span-
     ish, and French references and allusions. (II) Vocabulary and
     general style, favorite authors cited, repeated "facts and
     ideas," and pungent anecdotes--all more demonstrably "parallel"
     to Defoe's other works than to Swift's. (III) Additional inter-
     nal evidence suggestive of Defoe's authorship in the treatment
     given to Providence, General (later Lord) Stanhope, the memory of
     King William. (IV) Similarities of details in repeated anec-
     dotes, for example, the one about the underground river Guadiana
     and its bridge which, we are told, had a special interest for
     Defoe, appearing in Capt. George Carleton and the Review. Con-
     cludes that Captain Carleton was "simply a cloak for Defoe" and
     that it was certainly Defoe who "worked up Carleton's anecdotes
     and reminiscences into literary shape."

6   GEISSLER, PAUL. "Is Robinson Crusoe an Allegory?" In
    Programm der städtischen Realschule mit Progymnasium. Pirna:
    [n.p.], pp. 1-26.
        Anticipates his inaugural dissertation on the same subject,
    presented in German at Leipzig University (1896.3), and article
    in Anglia (1897). Taking a refreshingly new direction, focuses
    on critical theory by tracing the meanings, in their varied
    contexts, of such terms as invention, parable, emblem, fable,
    allusion, and especially allegory; and by emphasizing Serious
    Reflections . . . of Robinson Crusoe as had never been done
    before. Chronicles the attitudes of critics and scholars who
    pointedly accept Robinson Crusoe as an allegory (Kingsley, Lee),
    and those who certainly do not (Minto, Saintsbury). Starts out
    with the assumption that as a result of the political double life
    led by Defoe (as revealed by the 1864 discovery of letters), he
    was driven to "the fatal turning point of his life . . . a true
    tragedy." Goes boldly farther to suggest that because of the
    "grief in his soul," he took to writing pseudonymously or anon-
    ymously, and groped his way to a theoretical understanding of
    "allegory" far ahead of his time and (under the pressures of con-
    temporary critics like Gildon) to a changing interpretation of
    his own Robinson Crusoe as allegory. Argues that the allegory
    represents the life of a man, but of Defoe himself, not Selkirk
    (as Chalmers, Wilson, and others thought). On his own now, iden-
    tifies three different stages in the meanings assigned to "alle-
    gory" as gradually understood by Defoe: from the story as a
    "just history of fact," to the story as "mere invention," and
    finally to the story which, "though allegorical, is also histor-
    ical." Cautions that in this final meaning we do not put "a
    modern construction upon an argument which cannot bear it"--that
    is, in short, Defoe is not advancing such an aesthetic as "art
    exists for its own sake."

7   HARRISON, D. "New Life of Daniel Defoe." Notes and Queries,
    8th ser. 3, no. 55 (14 January):37.
        Replies to 1892.20; quotes the inscription on the memorial
    obelisk erected in 1870 over Defoe's grave in Bunhill Fields
    cemetery.

8   "The Last of the Defoes." Sketch, 27 September:437.
        On James William Defoe, the great-great-grandson of Defoe,
    descendant through the son Daniel--now a pauper of the Chelmsford
    Union.

9   LATIMER, JOHN. The Annals of Bristol in the Eighteenth Cen-
    tury. [Frome and London]: Printed for the Author, pp. 75-77.
        Tells the story of the "speculative Bristolians" and the
    financing of the privateers Duke and Duchess, but rejects "the
    local tradition" that Defoe obtained Selkirk's papers and produc-
    ed Robinson Crusoe as "an idle fiction."

10 LESEVITCH, V. "Daniel' Defo' kak chelovek, pisatel' i
    obshchestvennyi deiatel': Opyt kharakteristiki" [Daniel Defoe
    as a man, writer and public figure]. Russkoe bogatstvo
    [Russian riches], no. 5: 19-51; no. 7:28-54; no. 8:18-39.
      In Russian. Sums up the current [solid] state of knowl-
    edge, in Russia, about Defoe as a man, writer, and public figure.
    Defines two conflicting "opinions," the first based on a pre-
    Minto position of his having complete moral integrity--"a fighter
    for political and religious tolerance"--and the second, recogniz-
    ing the emergence of "dark spots" in his personality, as early as
    the "plagiarisms" of an Essay upon Projects, and an outright com-
    mitment to duplicity, in George I's time, which "current English
    criticism" has mercilessly unmasked. Uses [Sir Francis] Galton's
    theory of heredity to interpret Defoe's complex personality as
    one constantly turning to action whenever deliberate choices
    present themselves. Demonstrates a "sharp demarcation" between
    the "first bright period" under William III, which produced the
    greatest political pamphlets, and the later sombre one, "which
    presents, in the person of Defoe, another man broken by life."
                                                          (A.L.S.R.)

11 "Notes." Critic, n.s. 20, no. 607 (7 October):233.
      On Defoe's great-great-great-grandson, named after "his
    famous ancestor," once at the Blue Coat School and now "a sailor
    boy on the Atlantic." See also 1896.10.

12 OLIPHANT, M[ARGARET] O[LIPHANT] W[ILSON]. "The Author of Rob-
    inson Crusoe." Century 46, nos. 97-98 (May-October):740-53.
      Locates "the turning point" of Defoe's life in his accep-
    tance of employment with Harley in 1704, and thus interprets the
    well known biographical facts differently. Pursues the view of
    Defoe transformed by Harley into "a dishonest partizan, a paid
    and slippery special pleader and secret agent," into later events
    that include "the most traitorous of employments during the per-
    iod of his supposed retirement" and his ultimate fall like that
    other "father of lies and betrayer of mankind." Judges Defoe the
    writer to be most influential, but the man to be "nothing."
    Expresses a lower esteem for Robinson Crusoe because it lacks
    "dramatic construction" and "any real inspiration of art";
    praises the Journal of the Plague Year as his most distinctive
    achievement--in part, because of a power arising from the com-
    plete absence of any emotion; in part, because of the narrator,
    whom she clearly identifies with Defoe himself. Reprinted, in
    part: 1894.15.

13 PASSY, FRÉDÉRIC. "Robinson et Vendredi ou la naissance du
    capital." Revue économique de Bordeaux (March):1-16.
      In a major address delivered at a conference sponsored by
    the Société industrielle d'Amiens, argues for the condition of
    mutual reenforcement rather than of conflict between labor and
    capital. Taking a cue from the social economist [Claude Fréd-
    éric] Bastiat to define "the birth of capital," makes an extended

use of "the fiction of Robinson and Friday." Creates the para-
digm of Robinson alone, living on the Island of Despair, as representing man having intellectual and moral capital, but without
any material capital; and argues that capital may be described
as the charm of difference separating Robinson and Friday. Expresses one of main points of his polemic: "There's the truth.
There's the finding that we report from our voyage to the Island
of Despair--transformed, thanks to labor and capital, into the
Island of Hope."

*14   SPRATLING, J.R. [Giltspur]. The Story of Church Street, Stoke
      Newington. Stoke Newington: [n.p.], 92 pp.
         Listed in British Museum Catalogue (86:317); no copy has
      been located.

15   T. "New Life of Daniel Defoe." Notes and Queries, 8th ser.
      3, no. 58 (4 February):91.
         Replies to 1892.20. Refers Wright to the Memoirs of Sir
      John Clerk of Penicuik (1892.2) for new information on pamphlets
      attributed to Defoe.

16   ULLRICH, HERMANN. Review of August Kippenberg's Robinson in
      Deutschland bis zur Insel Felsenburg (1731-1743), 1892.
      Zeitschrift für vergleichende Litteraturgeschichte und Renais-
      sance-Litteratur, n.s. 6, no. 2:259-66.
         Shows that Kippenberg made his strongest contribution in
      the chapters on Schnabel's Insel Felsenburg, the early German
      translations of Robinson Crusoe, and the Robinsonades to 1731.
      Points out numerous errors and omissions in the other parts, deal-
      ing with Robinsonades after 1731 and the author J.G. Schnabel.
      Cites locations of many books overlooked by Kippenberg and gives
      readers a preview of his own bibliographical work-in-progress.
                                                              (P.E.C.)

17   WARBURG, KARL. Foreword to Robinson Crusoe af Daniel Defoe
      [Robinson Crusoe of Daniel Defoe]. Trans. Jean Fr. Rossander.
      Göteborg: Torsten Hedlunds Förlag, pp. ix-xvi.
         In Swedish. For this translation in Swedish of Robinson
      Crusoe and the Farther Adventures of Robinson Crusoe (352 pp.),
      Walter Paget did the illustrations. Prints of the foreword were
      generously sent by the Göteburg University Library, but not in
      time to be translated and annotated.

                                1894

1   [AITKEN, GEORGE A.] "De Foe and Malthus." Social Economist
      (Gunton's Magazine) 7 (October):203-10.
         Contrasts at the outset the implications of Malthus's Essay
      on the Principle of Population (1798) and Defoe's Robinson Cru-
      soe, to conclude that the authors are "the chiefs of two anti-
      nomial clans of ideas." But then probes more deeply to reveal

Malthus's basic premise ("man tends to multiply faster than his means of subsistence") is invalid. To set up the initial contrast, makes severely critical generalizations about Defoe's economic writings and his novels, "all of the blasé social type, with a flavor of Tolstoi, Hugo and Zola."

2 AITKEN, GEORGE A. "Defoe in Trouble: 1703." Athenaeum 104, no. 3504 (22 December):862.
    Follows up on the publication of invaluable letters in Wright (1894) with the text of Defoe's moving letter to Lord Nottingham dated 9 January 1703 in which he pleads to be pardoned for his offence in writing the Shortest-Way with the Dissenters. Observes that the letter is dated just one day before the proclamation describing Defoe's features and offering a reward, which appeared in the London Gazette, 11 January 1703. Reprinted: Healey.

3 _____. "Nathaniel Mist." In The Dictionary of National Biography. Edited by Sir Leslie Stephen and Sir Sidney Lee. Reprint. London: Oxford University Press, 1963-1965, 13:500-4.
    Presents new information already reported, so far as it relates to Defoe, 1893.1.

4 BÜLBRING, KARL D. "An Autograph MS. of Defoe's in the British Museum." Academy 46, no. 1171 (13 October):280-81.
    Argues correctly for the separation of the autograph manuscript (British Museum, Add. MS., 32,555) into two distinct works by Defoe: "The Compleat English Gentleman" and "Of Royall Educacion" (see 1890.6 and 1895.16). Previous biographers, Walter Wilson and William Lee, had mistakenly described the contents of "The Compleat English Gentleman" as if they included "Of Royall Educacion." In his editions Bülbring used the textual arrangements he had argued for here.

5 _____. "Concerning Defoe's Character." Academy 46, no. 1180 (15 December):513-14.
    Offers fresh evidence of "deliberate falsehood" on Defoe's part in claiming to have written "Of Royall Educacion" many years earlier and designed the publication for Queen Anne's time. Confirms Minto's view of him as "perhaps the greatest liar that ever lived." See also 1894.4.

6 CRAIK, HENRY, ed. Introduction to English Prose Selections with Critical Introductions by Various Writers and General Introductions to Each Period. New York: Macmillan & Co., 3:1-6.
    Traces the developments in English prose style during the seventeenth century, and identifies the characteristic traits of the "new generation" of stylists. Places Defoe with Bunyan and Swift as writers of "outstanding genius, who defy classification," neither following a "hereditary line" nor transmitting a stylistic individuality, but profoundly affecting our prose style. Reprinted: 1920.

7   DALTON, CHARLES. "Captain Carleton's Memoirs." Academy 46,
    no. 1162 (11 August):104.
        Without entering into the question of authorship for Capt.
    George Carleton, announces the "discovery" from three commissions
    at the War Office that the full name was George Villiers Carle-
    ton, and that the information thus made available agrees substan-
    tially with the memoirs. Corrects Parnell, 1891.12.

8   DENNIS, JOHN. The Age of Pope (1700-1744). Handbooks of
    English Literature. London: George Bell & Sons. Reprint.
    1906, pp. 180-91.
        Observes that only a few readers know the entire range of
    Defoe's labors "as a politician, social reformer, projector,
    pamphleteer, and novelist." Underscores the change of attitude
    toward Defoe since the discovery in 1864 of the six letters by
    Defoe in the State Paper Office and William Lee's researches in
    1869 revealed "the baseness of his conduct." Holds the view that
    if Defoe asserts something to be true in his writing, he is not
    to be trusted. Sees "knavery to some extent in his method of
    workmanship as a man of letters," in the Mrs. Veal story, or an
    "art of mystification." On the novels, judges Robinson Crusoe as
    a "thoroughly healthy book," and Captain Singleton, Moll Fland-
    ers, Colonel Jack, and Roxana presumably as less healthy, incul-
    cating morality by carrying readers "into the worst dens of
    vices"; of these, Roxana, "the most powerful." Ranks the History
    of the Plague in London next to Robinson Crusoe in literary
    merit. In the general assessment of the novelist, links Defoe
    with "a method dear in our day to some of the least worthy of
    French novelists, who while aiming to copy Nature debase her."

9   HALES, JOHN W. "Defoe." In English Prose Selections with
    Critical Introductions by Various Writers and General Intro-
    ductions to Each Period. Edited by Henry Craik. New York:
    Macmillan & Co., 3:355-59.
        Introduces selections "An Academy for Women" from An Essay
    upon Projects, "Selfish Preachers of Toleration" from the Short-
    est-Way with the Dissenters, and from Robinson Crusoe. In the
    short biographical summary, describes Defoe's career beginning
    with his joining Harley in 1704 as "obscure, and his conduct, to
    say the least, highly dubious, and after the accession of George
    I, worse than dubious." Stresses the fluency with which he pro-
    duced mainly ephemeral pamphlets, never with a self-conscious
    style, and novels unsurpassed in "the art of literary deception"
    or "'lying like truth.'" Reprinted: 1920.

10 HIPPE, MAX. "Eine vor-Defoe'sche Englische Robinsonade."
    Englische Studien 19, no. 1:66-104.
        Examines the widely influential Isle of Pines (1668) and
    its author Henry Nevil [i.e., Neville], its affinities with
    Defoe's masterpiece and other Robinsonades, and its many transla-
    tions into several European languages.   (P.E.C.)

11 KLEEMAN, SELMAR. "Zur Geschichte der Robinsonaden." <u>Euphor-
    ion: Zeitschrift für Literaturgeschichte</u> 1:603-4.
        Offers miscellaneous notes on Robinsonades as minor correc-
    tions or amplifications of Kippenberg, 1892.8, in part already
    given by Ullrich, 1893.16.   (P.E.C.)

12 LANGE, PAUL. Review of P. Geissler's <u>Is Robinson Crusoe an
    Allegory?</u> 1893. <u>Anglia. Beiblatt</u> 4, no. 11 (March):329-30.
        Finds the book to be a good study of <u>Robinson Crusoe</u>, gen-
    erally, as an allegory of Defoe's life, but also of mankind's
    cultural progress--an idea traceable to Rousseau.   (P.E.C.)

13 LEWIS, EDWIN HERBERT. <u>The History of the English Paragraph</u>.
    Chicago: University of Chicago Press, 177 pp.
        Originally a Ph.D. dissertation at the University of
    Chicago, gives statistical counts for 200 paragraphs each in <u>An
    Essay upon Projects</u> and <u>Robinson Crusoe</u> for the categories:
    "average words per sentence," "average words per paragraph, av-
    erage sentences per paragraph," and "per cent of single-sentence
    paragraphs." Selects authors that are predominantly English.
    From these data, deduces that Defoe wrote the fewest number of
    sentences per paragraph; in <u>Robinson Crusoe</u> he has the highest
    average of words in a sentence. In all respects Defoe may be
    said to be the worst paragrapher since he makes little or no
    distinction between the sentence and the paragraph.

14 [LYALL, ALFRED C.] Review of Dunlop's <u>History of Fiction</u>, <u>The
    Works of Daniel Defoe</u>, <u>Capt. George Carleton</u>, and other works.
    <u>Quarterly Review</u> 178, no. 355 (January):31-51 passim.
        Reviewer identified in <u>Wellesley Index</u>. Attempts to follow
    the line connecting "the domain of Fable with the domain of His-
    tory." Defoe's romances are counterfeit histories, deliberate
    deceptions; include the <u>Journal of the Plague Year</u>, <u>Memoirs of a
    Cavalier</u>, and <u>Capt. George Carleton</u>.

15 OLIPHANT, M[ARGARET] O[LIPHANT] W[ILSON]. "The Author of <u>Rob-
    inson Crusoe</u>." In <u>Historical Characters of the Reign of Queen
    Anne</u>. New York: Century Co., pp. 129-66.
        Reprinted from 1893.12. Expands here and there with addi-
    tions appropriate to the book format: for instance, comparisons
    with other "historical characters" such as Swift; quotations
    from Defoe's writings; a richer narrative account. Altogether,
    strengthens the sense of major change in Defoe's life due to
    Harley's unfavorable influence.

16 RALEIGH, WALTER. <u>The English Novel</u>. New York: Charles Scrib-
    ner's Sons, 298 pp. passim.
        Places Defoe among writers of fiction from Nash to Paltock.
    Devotes part of chapter 5 "The Beginnings of the Modern Novel" to
    Defoe's inaugurating the new fiction: "the art of grave imper-
    turbable lying, in which art the best instructor is the truth."
    Questioning the presence of irony in the <u>Shortest-Way with the</u>

Dissenters, finds there the same "strength" as in Mrs. Veal and
the future novels. Observes that the "limitations" of Robinson
Crusoe are the means for Defoe to display "his particular talent"
and thus produce "a masterpiece" (Part One) that "marks a new
era in the writing of prose fiction." Nevertheless, in chap. 6,
makes it clear that Defoe's method of narration, while it gave
the reader "common life," fell short of "the freedom and imagination of a great artist" like Fielding. Reprinted: (with minor
revisions) 1895; 1922.

17 ROBERTSON, J. LOGIE. "Daniel Defoe (1661-1731)." In A His-
    tory of English Literature. Edinburgh and London: William
    Blackwood & Sons, pp. 213-15.
        In a literary history intended for secondary schools, under
    the heading "Novelists and Narrative Writers," confirms many of
    the biographical and critical commonplaces for "the father of the
    English novel."

18 ROWLAND, P[ERCY] F[RITZ]. A Comparison, Criticism and Esti-
    mate of the English Novelists from 1700 to 1850. The Chan-
    cellor's Essay. Oxford: B.H. Blackwell; London: Simpkin,
    Marshall, Hamilton, Kent & Co., 28 pp. passim.
        Persistently allows presumed lapses in Defoe's personal
    life to influence critical judgments. Turns to "the first
    English novelist . . . the inimitable and unamiable author of
    Robinson Crusoe." Alleges that there were "repeated failures"
    everywhere: "his whole life-history is one of moral deteriora-
    tion." Claims that Defoe served both political parties in the
    Review; labels Mrs. Veal "a shameless puff . . . to facilitate
    the sale of Drelincourt on Death." On the novels Colonel Jack,
    Moll Flanders, Captain Singleton, and others: recognizes that
    "Defoe was possessed of a thorough sympathy with low life"; in
    Moll Flanders, he dealt with "the sore of society in very much
    the spirit of M. Zola and his followers." Judges the other
    heroes and heroines to be as unattractive as Moll Flanders.
    Marks out an important distinction between Defoe and later novel-
    ists: whereas they wrote fiction, he always pretended to write
    fact. Uses the standard of Minto (1879): "he has been called
    the greatest master of the art of circumstantial lying that ever
    lived." In the rest of the study, introduces comparisons with
    Defoe as he discusses Fielding's Jonathan Wild, Smollett's Count
    Fathom, Edward Bulwer, Charlotte Brontë.

19 SCHWOB, MARCEL, trans. "Daniel Defoe et Moll Flanders."
    Revue hebdomadaire 27 (August):69-76.
        Introduces his serialization in French of Moll Flanders for
    the August, September, and October issues, each of which contain-
    ed four installments. Focuses on Defoe's source for Moll Flan-
    ders: the famous Mary Frith or Moll Cutpurse, who appeared as a
    character in earlier plays. Claims that Defoe's realistic novel
    most closely resembles Goncourts' Germinie lacerteux (1865). See
    the Journal of the Goncourts (1896.4), in the entry for 18 Febru-

ary 1894, where Schwob, a man steeped in "universal knowledge,"
is described reading his translation of this novel "completely
unknown, of the author of Robinson Crusoe." In the anonymous
"Notice" of Schwob's reprinted translation (vol. 5, Oeuvres complètes, Paris: Typographie François Bernouard, 1928, pp. 397-
98), the translation is erroneously identified as being Moll
Flanders, in the entry for 4 March 1894, whereas the Goncourts'
Journal clearly refers to Colonel Jack (9:198-99). Reprinted:
1895.34.

20   SIMONDS, WILLIAM EDWARD. An Introduction to the Study of
      English Fiction. Boston: D.C. Heath & Co., pp. 30, 39-43,
      44, 45, 62.
          Favors Defoe over Richardson as the "first English novel-
ist." Includes biographical facts which are no longer tenable,
for instance that Defoe wrote "a little paper" [Review] out of
his prison cell. Praises him as a writer who had a "knowledge of
men" which surpassed even Shakespeare's, and judges the stories
of Mrs. Veal and the erupting volcano to be "clever inventions,"
just short of lying, but leading to Robinson Crusoe and Journal
of the Plague Year. Quotes Minto admiringly as expressing
Defoe's "dulness of truth." Identifies realism as his special
contribution, and differentiates it from sensationalism.

21   [SYLE, L. DU PONT.] Introduction to History of the Plague in
      London. Eclectic English Classics. New York, Cincinnati,
      Chicago: American Book Co., pp. 7-16.
          Shows the deeply ingrained biases against Defoe both as a
person and a writer, which had set in during the latter part of
the nineteenth century. Identifies among nature's gifts to Defoe
"a special aptitude for chicanery and intrigue." When, in 1710,
the Review supported the Tories, the change is called "his turn-
coating"; after 1714, his conduct is described as "a double part"
of spy for eight years. Severely criticizes him as a writer:
inept in his style, not quite so correct as Dryden, Congreve, or
Swift; "deadly dull" in two thirds of Moll Flanders, Roxana, and
Captain Singleton. Only Robinson Crusoe and a History of the
Plague in London have any readers outside the eighteenth century.
Traces the origin of Robinson Crusoe to the journalistic skills
he had acquired in writing the lives of Jack Sheppard and Avery.
Stresses the appearance of authenticity in the History of the
Plague in London.

22   THOMSON, JOHN A., and CAMPION, ROBERT. The New and Original
      Gorgeous Christmas Pantomime, entitled Robinson Crusoe, His
      Man Friday, and the Cannibal King of the Cokernut Islands.
      Hastings Pier Pavilion, 28 pp.
          "Gorgeous Scenic Tableau, the Levee of Nations . . . Patri-
otic Song Heroes of England." At one point, Robinson says:

          In me behold young Crusoe! As you know
          Immortalised by good old Dan Defoe.

23   TOWNLEY, CHARLES [Geoffrey Thorn]. Rollicking Robinson Cru-
      soe; or, Harlequin Good Man Friday, Who Kept the House Tidy,
      and Pretty Polly of Wapping Old Stairs. [London: Grand
      Theatre], 72 pp.
          Differs from Townley's other pantomimes, 1886.18 and
      1900.13.

24   WRIGHT, THOMAS. The Life of Daniel Defoe. London, Paris &
      Melbourne: Cassell & Co., 453 pp.
          While this full-length biography offers considerable new
      information, it also strains credibility by pushing certain re-
      strictive theories. Holds the view, for instance, that not only
      is Robinson Crusoe an allegory of Defoe's life, the "correspon-
      dence" or parallel between the two extends to the most minute
      details for main events dated 27 years apart in Crusoe's and
      Defoe's lives. Incredulous as Wright's "silence" theory may
      seem (Defoe's vow of silence for 28 years), he has still another
      theory--to explain the mass of publications which appear to be by
      Defoe at a given time. He posits the existence of a collabora-
      tor, a double, a man Friday, who can think and write like his
      master. Such may be the case with the Secret History of the
      White Staff (1714) or Mesnager. Wright relies heavily upon the
      scholarship of Lee and the criticism of William Minto and George
      Saintsbury. His method is to provide a running commentary on
      Defoe's writings, using Lee's list of 254, and to intersperse
      biographical information--part 1 "Pamphleteer and Poet" (229 pp.)
      and part 2 "Novelist and Historian" (165 pp.). Adds only one
      item to the canon, Due Preparations, which Lee had accidentally
      omitted; and gives the biography an important emphasis through
      the twenty-four Defoe letters still surviving, in some instances
      reprinted from Notes and Queries. Not only does Wright use them
      to structure his biography, he prints eight for the first time
      (six of them concerned with the "dowry squabble" of Henry Baker).
      Near the end of the biography, he turns to the manuscript volume
      (seen by no other biographer) in which Henry Baker describes his
      courtship of Defoe's youngest daughter Sophia and which gives
      intimate glimpses of Defoe himself, facing problems still myster-
      ious even to this day. In part 2, he offers some presumed new
      attitudes toward the fiction. On Robinson Crusoe: insists on
      the basis of "new evidence" that a meeting actually took place,
      late in 1711 or early 1712, between Defoe and Selkirk in Bristol,
      at the home of Mrs. Damaris Daniel, the corner house of St. James
      Square--at which time Defoe received all Selkirk's papers "as a
      matter of business." On "the Great Criminal Series" (Moll Flan-
      ders, Colonel Jack, Roxana): Wright does not believe that he
      should, like Aitken before him, explain Defoe's motives in writ-
      ing criminal stories. The novelist's wide-ranging curiosity
      about matters human ought to be reason enough. Above all, Wright
      maintains, Defoe cannot be charged with any coarseness in the
      secondary novels. Although he borrows heavily to comment critic-
      ally on the other novels, he has a special view of Moll Flanders,
      believing that "almost all its features are taken from real

life." From A.B. Walkley (1892.19) he borrows the concept of
"amorphousness," which sets up a conflict between the demands of
art and those of the market, and the argument that "the Great
Criminal Series" need not be defended or justified for the "moral
lessons" which the novels convey: "we enjoy them for their splendid literary quality." See also Wright's revised Bi-Centenary
Edition (London: C.J. Farncombe & Sons, 1931), 427 pp.

1895

1   AITKEN, GEORGE A. "Defoe in Trouble: More State Papers."
    <u>Athenaeum</u>, no. 3507 (12 January):50.
         Discovers among the State Papers Domestic Lord Chief Jus-
    tice Parker's letter of 15 April 1713 to a Secretary of State,
    and quotes liberally from it, to the effect that Defoe should be
    brought to trial for publishing three libelous pamphlets favoring
    the Pretender. Makes a special point of regarding the mixture of
    "banter" and the serious as dangerous. Notes that the letter
    reveals further that Defoe had chambers in the Temple, and that
    both his sons assisted him in his work. Explains that the "Par-
    don to Daniel De Foe of London, Gent." was given by the Earl of
    Oxford on 11 December. From still another State Papers Domestic
    document (28 August 1714), sums up the Attorney-General's case
    against Hurt, Baker, and Defoe for a libel in the <u>Flying Post</u>.

2   _____. "Defoe's <u>Apparition of Mrs. Veal</u>." <u>Nineteenth Century</u>
    37, no. 215 (January):95-100.
         Irrefutably makes the case that <u>Mrs. Veal</u>, long thought to
    be "an early example of Defoe's power of making fiction to appear
    to be fact," can only be (as he said) "'a <u>true</u> relation' of
    'matter of fact.'" Amasses solid evidence to demonstrate the
    real existence of Mrs. Bargrave, Mrs. Veal and her brother, Cap-
    tain Watson, old Mr. Breton; includes a translation of the Latin
    manuscript testimonial (1714) in which Mrs. Bargrave asserts that
    most matters in the narrative were true as stated. But Aitken
    presses to a much more significant conclusion in strong opposi-
    tion to Minto's "scepticism," which extends to Defoe's life and
    character as well as to his novels: "we should be at least as
    likely to arrive at the truth by believing what Defoe says, in
    the absence of proof of the contrary." Reprinted: (with
    changes) 1895.8; 1902.

3   _____. "Defoe's Library." <u>Athenaeum</u>, no. 3527 (1 June):
    706-7.
         Announces the discovery in the British Museum of the fifty-
    three page <u>Catalogue</u> in which the bookseller Olive Payne listed
    for sale, on 15 November 1731, the books in the libraries of
    Defoe and Phillips Farewell. Culls out arbitrarily the items
    which had belonged to Farewell, and presents the rest according
    to size (folios, quartos, octavos) and the special classification
    "Scarce Tracts" (including numerous "Civil War pamphlets"), and

"Libri Omissi" (again, according to format size). Assigns the
theological and classical works, books on canon law, medals, and
coins to Farewell; itemizes and occasionally annotates books on
voyages, travel, history, memoirs, biography, the supernatural,
America, and the rest, which Aitken is fairly certain belonged to
Defoe. For the complete sales catalogue in usable form, with
introduction (35 pp.), full identifications of items, and indexes, see The Libraries of Daniel Defoe and Phillips Farewell:
Olive Payne's Sales Catalogue (1731), ed. Helmut Heidenreich
(Berlin, 1970). See also 1731.7; 1895.39.

4 _____. "Defoe's Silence." Speaker 11 (4 May):490.
       Rejects "the silence theory" proposed by Wright (1894), but
seems to accept the remarkable coincidence of events in Robinson
Crusoe and Defoe's life. Accepts also the modification suggested
by Quiller-Couch, 1895.29, in which Crusoe's shipwreck, now dated
1658, would represent the Monmouth rising. Points out the serious difficulties in describing the twenty-eight odd years 1685-
1714, as secret political work.

5 _____, ed. Introduction and Postscript to The Fortunes and
       Misfortunes of the Famous Moll Flanders. In Romances and
       Narratives, 7:vii-xviii.
       Encounters only obstacles in trying to trace the identity
of Moll Flanders, but does not entirely give up the hope that
success may one day come. Recites "the bold facts" of Moll's
story; links the success of Marcel Schwob's translation during
the past season in Paris with Zola's popularity, but argues that
the realistic details here belong to the eighteenth century
rather than the seventeenth. Praises the novel for "the excellent view it gives us of the manners of the middle classes under
Queen Anne." In the postscript, makes an adjustment in the
matching of incident and date in Robinson Crusoe with a significant event in Defoe's life twenty-eight years later, in accordance with Wright's interpretation of the allegory, as refined by
Arthur Quiller-Couch. Notes that difficulties persist with
Wright's theory. Reprinted: 1902.

6 _____, ed. Introduction to A Journal of the Plague Year. In
       Romances and Narratives, 9:vii-xiii.
       While written in response to public concern over the plague
at Marseilles in 1720-1721, the Journal of the Plague Year suc-
ceeds in being the best source of "popular knowledge" about the
plague. Sums up the information on the narrator, H.F., as Henry
Foe, Defoe's real-life uncle, who in his "journal" has Defoe's
stylistic mannerisms. Considers also as the basis of the narrative Defoe's use of his own recollections and overheard talk
about the plague, and of books (such as Dr. Hodges's) which were
in his library. Observes that Defoe created an imaginary authority on the plague since no person named Dr. Heath can be traced.
Linking the theme with that of Robinson Crusoe, urges that the
novelist now concerns himself with "dire calamity" falling upon a

great city, and not an individual. Concludes that, in general, the impression of the plague here is an accurate one, when compared with other contemporary accounts, five of which appear in the Appendix (extracts from Dr. Hodges's <u>Loimologia</u>, Vincent's <u>God's Terrible Voice in the City</u>, Boghurst's <u>Loimographia</u>, Pepys's and Evelyn's diaries). Reprinted: 1902; 1908.

7   _____, ed. Introduction to <u>A New Voyage Round the World</u>. In <u>Romances and Narratives</u>, 14:vii-x.
     Demonstrates that the <u>New Voyage Round the World</u> (1725) was published at the end of an eight-month interval after <u>Roxana</u>, which included such long works as the <u>Great Law of Subordination Considered</u> and the first part of the <u>Tour</u>. Describes the <u>New Voyage</u> as a book of adventures, but as lacking the unity and "personal interest" of <u>Robinson Crusoe</u> or <u>Captain Singleton</u>. Finds that the <u>New Voyage</u> focuses on the easterly direction taken round the Cape of Good Hope, the lands discovered in the South Sea, and (in the second part) the journey across the Andes. Lists the voyagers whose accounts may have given Defoe the factual bases of his narrative. Reprinted: 1902.

8   _____, ed. Introduction to <u>Due Preparations for the Plague as well for Soul as Body</u> [and other works]. In <u>Romances and Narratives</u>, 15:ix-xxiv.
     Points out that while the first considerably altered printing of <u>Due Preparations for the Plague</u> was by the Reverend John Scott, 1832.3, the first recognition of Defoe's authorship came from Crossley, 1838.2; the work was now being included in a collected edition for the first time. For the second piece, <u>The Dumb Philosopher</u>, believes that Dickory Cronke, the central character, was a real person, but has not found any confirming evidence. To introduce <u>Mrs. Veal</u>, repeats substantially the significant discoveries announced in <u>Nineteenth Century</u>, 1895.2. Concludes with a brief comment on Defoe's delight in the "make-believe," which produced the article, "The Destruction of the Isle of St. Vincent," in <u>Mist's Journal</u> (1718). Reprinted: 1902.

9   _____, ed. Introduction to <u>Memoirs of a Cavalier</u>. In <u>Romances and Narratives</u>, 5:vii-xx.
     On the perennial questions--Who was the Cavalier? Was there a manuscript?--offers little new information, except (first) to devastate on chronological grounds any remaining hope of identifying the Cavalier with Andrew Newport (as stated in "The Publisher of the Second Edition to the Reader" [1740-50?], reprinted here); and (second) to identify the printed sources for both the Thirty Years War and the Civil War portions of the <u>Memoirs of a Cavalier</u>, making the existence of a manuscript unnecessary, but at the same time still leaving the question open. For their bearing on the question of authorship, notes the contradiction between a manuscript discovered in 1651 and concluding in the Restoration, the numerous "anachronisms," the discrepancies

in Civil War history discerned by C.H. Firth, the stylistic
mannerisms of Defoe, the parallels with other works. Comments
on Defoe's method in this re-creation of historical events.
Reprinted: 1902; Everyman's Library, 1908.

10   _____, ed. Introduction to The Fortunate Mistress or a His-
        tory of the Life of the Lady Roxana. In Romances and Narra-
        tives, 12:vii–xii.
            In reviewing the story of Roxana, stresses the abruptness
        of Defoe's conclusion to the novel; surveys the continuations by
        later writers, but allots an inordinate amount of space to dis-
        cussing the continuation in the 1745 edition: it was "very dif-
        ferent" from the rest and "not without merit"; it became the
        basis for Godwin's Faulkener (1807) and drew strong praise from
        Lamb. Contrasting Roxana and Moll Flanders, finds a much greater
        degree of sympathy in the latter. Has special praise for the art
        in Defoe's characterization of Amy, but has to be apologetic for
        the book's "coarseness." In vol. 13, reprints the "Continuation
        (From the 1745 Edition)." Reprinted: 1902.

11   _____, ed. Introduction to The History and Remarkable Life of
        the Truly Honourable Colonel Jack. In Romances and Narra-
        tives, 10:vii–xiii.
            While giving mainly summary of the plot, does direct atten-
        tion away from the pathetic early account of the young Jack to,
        for example, the enlightened treatment of slaves on the Virginia
        plantation. Endeavors to see Colonel Jack as something more than
        "the male counterpart of Moll Flanders." In describing the boy
        Jack as always inquisitive, argues that Defoe is autobiographi-
        cal; we have here "Defoe's own account of how the Memoirs of a
        Cavalier came to be written." Reprinted: 1902.

12   _____, ed. Introduction to The History of the Life and Adven-
        tures of Mr. Duncan Campbell. In Romances and Narratives,
        4:ix–xviii.
            Analyzes the complex relationships of Defoe's Duncan Camp-
        bell (1720) which in some copies of the second edition, published
        August 1720, included Mr. Campbell's Pacquet; Eliza Haywood's A
        Spy upon the Conjuror (1724) and her supplement The Dumb Projec-
        tor (1725); Defoe's The Friendly Daemon (1726); and the Secret
        Memoirs of the late Mr. Duncan Campbell (1732). Summarizes the
        biographical information about Campbell and his broad reputation
        as a public figure known for his "second-sightedness." In addi-
        tion, discusses Defoe's very strong interest, elsewhere, in the
        supernatural, apparitions, and the devil. Reprints Duncan Camp-
        bell, "Remarkable Passage of an Apparition" (1720), and "The
        Friendly Daemon." Admits that Defoe was not the author of the
        "Remarkable Passage of an Apparition," but simply retold vividly
        "a popular legend." For the rejection of all these titles from
        the Defoe canon, see Rodney M. Baine, Daniel Defoe and the Super-
        natural (Athens: University of Georgia Press, 1968).

13   _____, ed. Introduction to <u>The King of Pirates: The Famous</u>
<u>Enterprises of Captain Avery</u> [and other works]. In <u>Romances</u>
<u>and Narratives</u>, 16:ix-xix.
      Places the seven short narratives of pirates and robbers,
reprinted here (six for the first time), in relation to the longer "masterpieces": <u>The King of Pirates</u> (1719); <u>A Narrative of</u>
<u>the Proceedings in France</u> (1724); two accounts of the notorious
Jack Sheppard (1724) and one account each of Jonathan Wild (1725)
and Captain John Gow (1725); and <u>A Brief Historical Account of</u>
<u>the Lives of the Six Notorious Street Robbers</u> (1726). For De-
foe's possible authorship of these pieces, relies on such tests
as his "favorite phrases" and parallels to works accepted as his,
and on his connections with Applebee. Reprinted: 1902.

14   _____, ed. Introduction to <u>The Life, Adventures and Piracies</u>
<u>of the Famous Captain Singleton</u>. In <u>Romances and Narratives</u>,
6:vii- xviii.
      Ranks <u>Captain Singleton</u> below <u>Robinson Crusoe</u> and <u>Journal</u>
<u>of the Plague Year</u> as being somewhat deficient in "unity of pur-
pose," "high tone," and interest in the main character. Accepting Minto's research (1878.5), finds Singleton's trek across the
"dark continent" to be a striking anticipation of discoveries
made by Stanley and others in Central Africa; holds that Defoe's
conception of African geography went beyond that of seventeenth-
century map-makers and such books as De Flacourt's on Madagascar
(1661), Ogilby's on Africa (1670), or Dapper's. Selects for
extended comment the second most important matter in the book,
the characterization of the serio-comic Quaker, William Walters.
Reprinted: 1902; 1904.

15   _____, ed. Preface, General Introduction, and Introduction to
<u>The Life and Strange Surprizing Adventures of Robinson Crusoe</u>.
In <u>Romances and Narratives by Daniel Defoe</u>. 16 vols. London:
J.M. Dent & Co., 1:ix-xi, xiii-xlvii, xlix-lxv.
      States in the preface the principles which guided the solu-
tions of problems relating to classification, authorship, and
text while preparing the first collected edition of the "narratives, real and fictitious." In the "General Introduction," summarizes the important biographical information available to date,
bringing together close analyses of Defoe's writings, Aitken's
own discoveries in the Public Record Office and elsewhere, and
the findings of previous biographers, including the Defoe correspondence and related memoranda published in the Historical Manuscripts Commission Reports; and sympathetically evaluates the
novels (15 pp.). Most important, brings a fresh positive perspective to Defoe's life and writings, alternative to the negative
one that prevailed earlier in the century. Forcefully states the
view [in sharp disagreement with Minto], that "we are most likely
to understand [Defoe] rightly if we believe his statements about
himself to be true, in the absence of evidence to the contrary."
On the novels: stresses the similarity of Defoe's and Crusoe's
isolation, the absence of any real predecessors in the novel,

Defoe's style and method, the possibility that stories which he
asserted to be true may have "at least a foundation of truth,"
and the choice of low characters. Selects as the best known
works Robinson Crusoe, Journal of the Plague Year, Memoirs of a
Cavalier, each with its own "problem of life which it is the business of the novelist to solve." Specifically, on Robinson Crusoe: summarizes the publication of the three parts; the sources,
especially the Alexander Selkirk story (the accounts by Captain
Woodes Rogers, 2d ed., 1718, and Richard Steele, 1713, reprinted
in the appendix to vol. 3). Rejects any suggestion of possible
misappropriation by Defoe of Selkirk's materials and, in particular, the notion of a meeting between the two men in Bristol, as
speculated by Wright (1894). Argues vigorously against Wright's
reading of the incidents in Robinson Crusoe as representing alle-
gorically specific events in Defoe's life; in particular, against
Wright's reading of the entire castaway experience as representing a twenty-eight year long silence imposed by Defoe on his wife
and children. Judging from Crusoe's character and the limits
placed upon the author by the island itself, urges as the theme,
that the reader is constantly aware of "the calamity of being
left alone on a desert island." Reprinted: 1902.

16   BÜLBRING, KARL D., ed. Of Royall Educacion: A Fragmentary
      Treatise by Daniel Defoe. Edited for the First Time, with
      Introduction, Notes, and Index. London: David Nutt, [vii]-
      xix; 72 pp.
            Publishes for the first time an autograph manuscript in
      Defoe's hand (British Museum, Add. MS., 32,555, fols. 67-100)
      entitled "Of Royall Educacion," which is clearly separate from
      the larger work, "The Compleat English Gentleman" (see 1890.6).
      For details on the manuscript and for Bülbring's argument on the
      separation of the two works, see 1894.4. Offers as background
      that Defoe began a treatise, which was mainly historical, on the
      importance and necessity of good education "in the children of
      princes and noblemen, as also of persons of rank, either for
      quality or employment," and proceeded to give historical examples
      from Henry VII "down to the present time." He never got beyond
      Edward VI, and seems to have abandoned the project out of a fear
      that the book "threatened a pointed satyr at his [own] times."
      He pretends that the sheets for "Of Royall Educacion" were writ-
      ten many years earlier, "design'd to be publish'd during the life
      of Her Late Majestie Queen Ann and before Her Majestie's acces-
      sion to the crown, viz., while the Duke of Gloucester was alive
      and for whom the whole scheme was intended." Regards Defoe's
      "misrepresentation" here as "a deliberate falsehood," close to
      Minto's view of him as "perhaps the greatest liar that ever
      lived." More than likely, Defoe began the treatise "some time
      before the year 1728." Out of fear that his writing would be
      suspected of having a political motive, he adopted a new design,
      "the general neglect of the education of the English gentry."
      See the review by Ullrich, 1895.38.

17   CARPENTER, GEORGE RICE, ed. Preface and Introduction to
      Daniel Defoe's Journal of the Plague Year. New York and Lon-
      don: Longmans Green, Green, & Co. Reprint. [Williamstown,
      Mass.]: Corner House Publishers, 1978, pp. v, vii-xix.
          In a textbook, for which the first edition was not avail-
      able, introduces chapter divisions and offers annotations of
      "words, phrases, or allusions as might puzzle a young reader."
      Proceeds from a summary of Defoe's life, in which his isolation
      and estrangement are stressed, to a survey of his works (254
      separate publications) and an examination of the Journal of the
      Plague Year. Explains why Defoe's narrator should appeal to
      Americans, and why the Journal itself should continue to hold
      interest as "one of the most vivid pictures imaginable of the
      varied scenes and experiences of a great national calamity."
      Praises Defoe's style, but also admits its "verbosity" and even
      "slovenliness." Reprinted, with additions: 1896.1.

18   CLEAVER, R.S. "Sir Walter Scott and Mrs. Veal's Ghost."
      Nineteenth Century 37, no. 216 (February):271-73.
          Disagrees with an unnamed contributor (1895.2), that Bal-
      lantyne, and not Walter Scott, was author of the biographical
      notice of Defoe. Quotes Scott's letter of 8 February 1828 to
      Miss Wagner, the aunt of Mrs. Felicia Hemans, in which he dis-
      plays a curious lack of interest in the supernatural. Quotes a
      second letter, for 3 March, in which he requests to know if the
      verses on Friendship were published by the same publisher as for
      Drelincourt on death.

19   DE MORGAN, SOPHIA ELIZABETH. Threescore Years and Ten: Remi-
      niscences of the Late Sophia Elizabeth De Morgan. Edited by
      Mary A. De Morgan. London: Richard Bentley & Son, pp. vii,
      43, 85-86, 97, 108.
          Salvages some rare glimpses of the Defoe house and grounds
      in Stoke Newington, to which Sophia Elizabeth Frend (later Mrs.
      Augustus De Morgan) would come in 1819, at the age of eleven, and
      spend most of her girlhood. Reminisces many years later about
      "the ancient house where Daniel Defoe had lived, and sometime, I
      believe, hid himself from political pursuers . . ."; about the
      "clean, white wainscoted rooms . . . and its large beautiful
      garden full of trees such as we seldom see near London."

20   FITZMAURICE-KELLY, JAMES. "The Picaresque Novel." New Review
      13, no. 74 (July):59-74.
          Traces the picaresque genre mainly as a Spanish develop-
      ment, but includes Moll Flanders (introduced the picara into
      English literature) and Colonel Jack.

21   FULDA, LUDWIG. Robinsons Eiland. Komödie in vier Aufzügen.
      Berlin. Reprint. 2d ed. Stuttgart: I.G. Cotta'schen Buch-
      handlung, 1896, 188 pp.
          Information on the first edition (Berlin, 1895) from
      Ullrich's Robinson und Robinsonaden. Presents upper crust types

from a sunken luxury liner tossed ashore on a desolate Pacific
island and compelled to learn values other than wealth and title.
(P.E.C.)

22   HURLBUT, BYRON SATTERLEE, ed. Defoe's History of the Great
     Plague in London: A Journal of the Plague Year. Boston and
     London: Ginn & Co., 384 pp.
         Text is based on the 1839 edition, reprinted from 1835.4.
     In notes (86 pp.), uses extracts from contemporary publications
     to show "to what extent Defoe was indebted for his material to
     the work of others." Contains all the footnotes, with a few
     omissions, of Brayley's edition. Introduction (18 pp.), says
     Hurlbut, adds nothing new--all derived from Wilson, Lee, Minto,
     Saintsbury, and Wright. Lists books of reference (2 pp.). See
     the objections to this textbook for Defoe's style and content, in
     the Critic, n.s. 25, no. 738 (11 April 1896):258; no. 745 (30 May
     1896):389.

23   "Introductory Sketch." In The Life and Adventures of Robinson
     Crusoe. The Riverside Literature Series. Boston and New
     York: Houghton Mifflin & Co., pp. v-xix.
         Follows upon Aitken's Romances and Narratives from which
     the author takes, and comments upon, biographical information.
     Regards the writing of Robinson Crusoe as the "occasion" to which
     a politically active, but quite lonely, man arrives; and Sel-
     kirk's adventure as comparable to "the rude stories" from which
     Shakespeare composed his plays. Directs scepticism to Wright's
     theory of the chronology, and accepts Defoe's own explanation of
     the allegory in the preface to the Farther Adventures of Robinson
     Crusoe as "a work of pure imagination."

24   L., R.A. "A Chat with Mark Twain." New Zealand Mail, 12 De-
     cember, pp. 51-52.
         Under a column headed "The Interviewer," records Mark
     Twain's answers to R.A.L.'s questions. Recalls that, in 1870,
     "several clever fellows" in New Zealand insisted that Innocents
     Abroad was "vamped out of books of travel and encyclopaedias."
     In response, Twain seemed to emerge from a dream: "You see
     there's a Freemasonry about dealing with things you see yourself
     which can't be counterfeited. There is an ease and certainty of
     touch in describing what you see which you can't get artificial-
     ly." R.A.L. then suggests: "Defoe is the only man in the whole
     range of literature who is credited with the feat which you very
     properly declare impossible." Twain, "laying off his theory with
     unswerving precision," chooses the example of Journal of the
     Plague Year, and argues how well Defoe must have known London,
     "as well as you know this city of Wellington, every spot and cor-
     ner of it." He had no "local colour to supply"; he got all the
     details of the plague at first hand, "from people who had seen."
     To write a book of travel in that way, "you would have to know
     every city in the world as well as Defoe knew his London." Twain
     continues: "Only in that way, could you get the firmness of

touch, the Freemasonry I have spoken of, the thing which depends on your personal observation."

25   M'MURRY, F.M. "The Educational Value of Robinson Crusoe." Public-School Journal (Bloomington, Ill.), January, pp. 252-54.

Explains the pedagogy of a Robinson Crusoe school text which, under the influence of the German Herbartians, is to be used in the second or third school year. Expands upon the merits of the adaptation as "an agent in character development."

26   MANN, MAX FRIEDRICH. Review of Marcel Schwob, trans. Moll Flanders, [1895]. Anglia. Beiblatt 5, no. 11/12 (March/April):330.

Agrees that the realism of Moll Flanders is so "modern" that the novel can safely take its place next to Guy de Maupassant and Prévost. Calls attention to Mary Frith, Moll Cutpurse, as a source.

27   PETER, OTHO B. "The Trebursye Ghost." Launceston Weekly News--Cornwall and Devon Times, 19 October.

Explains in a cover letter that he presents here his own transcription of a manuscript made by James Wakeham, dated 5 February 1730, which in turn was a copy by William Ruddle, the son of John Ruddle, author of "A Remarkable Passage of an Apparition, 1665." Makes no mention of Defoe.

28   Q[UILLER]-C[OUCH], A[RTHUR] T[HOMAS]. "Dorothy Dingley." Speaker 12 (12 October):394-95.

Reviews the claims of Defoe and Rev. John Ruddle to the authorship of the "Remarkable Passage of an Apparition." Finds that Robbins (1895.32) makes "a strong case" that Defoe never wrote the story, but took it "ready-made." Offers, also, the hypothesis that Ruddle's son William made the few corrections in Defoe's manuscript of the narrative (which was, in turn, based on the father's notes). Thus salvages for Defoe one of the best ghost-stories, written in his distinctive style. See also 1895.33.

29   ____. "A Literary Causerie. Defoe's Silence"--I and II. Speaker 11 (13 and 20 April): 411-12, 438-39.

Summarizes "the silence theory" advanced by Wright (1894), which takes the generally accepted view of Robinson Crusoe as a parable or allegory of Defoe's life and narrowly interprets Crusoe's experience as representing twenty-eight years of silence imposed by Defoe upon his wife and children. While still accepting the concept of "coincident events" and even the twenty-seven year separation between them, argues that Crusoe's shipwreck in 1658 most likely represents Jeffreys's sentencing in September 1685 of those who, like Defoe, took part in the Monmouth rising, although the event is not comparable to Crusoe's shipwreck. Reprinted: 1896.12.

30   Review of Aitken's <u>Romances and Narratives</u>, 1895. <u>Athenaeum</u>,
     no. 3518 (30 March):408.
         Praises George A. Aitken's editing of the first three
     volumes and the availability of up-to-date information in the
     "General Introduction," and predicts this will be the standard
     edition of the novels. Expresses strong agreement with Aitken's
     rejection of [Thomas] Wright's theory that Defoe's and Crusoe's
     lives correspond to one another; will wait to read his arguments
     in favor of Defoe's authorship of <u>Memoirs of a Cavalier</u>.

31   Review of Aitken's <u>Romances and Narratives</u>, 1895. <u>Critic</u>,
     n.s. 23, no. 689 (4 May):324-25.
         Disagrees with Aitken's efforts to rehabilitate Defoe's
     character in the "General Introduction." Reaffirms that "Defoe
     always loved a likely lie better than he did truth" and that he
     seems to have been "a clever and none too scrupulous man, living
     in a rough and stupid time, who sometimes profited and sometimes
     suffered by its stupidity." Argues that Aitken falls into "a
     common error" of regarding Defoe's realism as deliberately due to
     "his inartistic habits of composition."

32   ROBBINS, ALFRED F. "Defoe's 'Remarkable Passage of an Appar-
     ition.'" <u>Notes and Queries</u>, 8th ser. 8, no. 195 (21 Septem-
     ber):221-23; and no. 201 (2 November):149-50.
         Argues more emphatically than Aitken's <u>Romances and Narra-
     tives</u>, vol. 4, for the authorship of "A Remarkable Passage of an
     Apparition, 1665," by the Reverend John Ruddle of Launceston
     rather than by Defoe. Among the new information about the Rever-
     end Ruddle: finds evidence of literary capability. Summarizes
     as irrefutable testimonials of Ruddle's authorship the recent pub-
     lication in the <u>Launceston Weekly News</u> of a certified manuscript
     copy of the ghost story as told by the Reverend Ruddle.

33   _____. "Dorothy Dingley and Daniel Defoe." <u>Speaker</u> 12
     (19 October):418-19.
         Responds to 1895.28. Substantiates further the background
     of real events and people in the Rev. John Ruddle's "Remarkable
     Passage of an Apparition." Cites, in particular, evidence of
     Ruddle's writing skill in an account-book written by Ruddle him-
     self. Concludes that the ghost-story was Ruddle's work, and not
     Defoe's.

34   SCHWOB, MARCEL, trans. Preface to <u>Moll Flanders</u>. <u>Traduit de
     l'Anglais de Daniel De Foe</u>. Paris: Paul Ollendorff, pp. i-
     xiii.
         Reprint of 1894.19, with a few minor changes and the addi-
     tion of a penultimate paragraph on Borrow's <u>Lavengro</u> (1851). See
     also the review, 1895.26. Reprinted: in vol. 5, <u>Les Oeuvres com-
     plètes de Marcel Schwob</u> (Paris: Bernouard, [1928]), pp. vii-xv.

35   _____. "R. L. S." <u>New Review</u> 12 (January-June):153-60
     passim.

Argues, in French, that the secret of Stevenson's power has been transmitted from Defoe through Poe. Illustrates the point with "the minute narrative" of <u>Mrs. Veal</u>, Poe's "scrupulous account" in "[The Facts in] the Case of M. Valdemar" (1845), and Stevenson's [The Strange Case of] Dr. Jekyll and Mr. Hyde (1886). Judges the terror to be extreme in the <u>Journal of the Plague Year</u> when the sadler comes upon the leather purse abandoned in the posthouse yard. Selects as the two most terrifying incidents in literature: Robinson's discovery of the single human footprint and Dr. Jekyll's awakening to the realization that his own hand has become the hairy hand of Mr. Hyde.

36   SMITH, JOSIAH RENICK. "New Presentments of Defoe." <u>Dial</u> 19, no. 217 (1 July):14-16.
     Reviews Wright's <u>Life of Daniel De Foe</u> (1894), Aitken's <u>Romances and Narratives</u> (1895), and [G.R. Carpenter's] edition of the <u>History of the Plague in London</u> (Eclectic English Classics, 1895). Expresses most serious reservations about Wright's efforts to penetrate the mystery with which Defoe surrounded his private life, about his idea of a close parallelism between Crusoe and Defoe, and about his view of Defoe as "the man of God." Judges Aitken's "General Introduction" to be "the most satisfactory short memoir . . . that we have seen," but [Carpenter's] introductory sketch in the <u>History of the Plague in London</u> so unfavorable to Defoe as to give "an incorrect idea of his rank in literature."

37   TEXTE, JOSEPH. <u>Jean-Jacques Rousseau et les origines du cosmopolitisme littéraire</u>. Paris: Libraire Hachette, pp. 148-53. Translated by J.W. Matthews. London: Duckworth & Co.; New York: Macmillan Co., 1899, pp. 18, 33, 62, 68, 111, 115, 124-28.
     Traces the influence in eighteenth-century France of <u>Robinson Crusoe</u>, not through the original but through the inaccurate translation into French (1720-1721) by Thémiseul de Saint-Hyacinthe and Justus Van Effen--"undoubtedly," the translation read by Rousseau and praised in his <u>Émile</u> (1762). In chap. 2, discusses Rousseau's "first studies in English," including Locke and Addison; and later Pope, Milton, Richardson's novels, and <u>Robinson Crusoe</u>. Claims that certain critical ideas discussed by Thémiseul de Saint-Hyacinthe and Justus Van Effen in their prefaces assume a larger significance, given the fame Rousseau would bring to <u>Robinson Crusoe</u>; for instance, their recognition in the preface to vol. 2 of the art of creating an illusion of reality. Observes that the readers of the French translation, however, were more under "the spell of marvellous adventure" than of verisimilitude. Makes the point that Defoe the author, as distinct from his book, was completely unknown. In the translation of <u>Robinson Crusoe</u> published at Frankfurt in 1769, the authorship was even assigned to the "celebrated" Richard Steele. Argues that with this background, Rousseau's high praise of <u>Robinson Crusoe</u> takes on an unusual importance: "It was his testimony to

its qualities that gave Daniel Defoe's work a place in the philosophical heritage of humanity."

38 ULLRICH, HERMANN. Review of K.D. Bülbring's edition, Of Roy-
    all Educacion. A Fragmentary Treatise by Daniel Defoe, 1895.
    Literaturblatt für germanische und romanische Philologie 14,
    no. 12 (December):400-1.
        Praises perspicacity of Bülbring in bringing this manu-
    script to light, just as he had the Compleat English Gentleman in
    1890. Expresses hope that Bülbring will turn his "German thor-
    oughness and critical acumen" to the production of a biography of
    Defoe, a fascinating man of "mixed character," so exemplary of
    his era.   (P.E.C.)

39 VOGUE, EUGENE [MARIE] MELCHIOR DE. "Le Livre Anglais: Robin-
    son Crusoé." Revue des deux mondes 131 (1 October):668-81.
        Claims that Robinson Crusoe (in Petrus Borel's translation)
    serves as "a good treatise of historical psychology" about the
    English people, and explores this concept in a full-blown inter-
    pretation of Robinson as "a mythic man." As in Chasles (1833.2),
    stresses resemblances between Robinson Crusoe and Don Quijote.
    Notes the origins in Selkirk of Robinson as "the national and
    historic type par excellence." Traces in Robinson the character-
    istics of mythic man: "the incoercible one escaped from the
    Scandinavian fjords, the lover of the sea . . . who thrusts his
    tiny boat into the ocean . . . the Englishman who is the north-
    man, who remains the wandering Jew of the great waters." Des-
    cribes Robinson Crusoe as "a work of edification, a chapter added
    to the Bible, a second book of Job, purged of the doubts and mur-
    murs which disfigure the first." Uses Chasles's story (1833.2)
    of the Ohio colonist who drew courage from the "divine volume" of
    Robinson Crusoe. But while Robinson has "the ferment of Prome-
    theus," he more nearly represents the average Englishman because
    he submits to reality; he lacks "an excess of sensibility" and
    shows even "something dry and cold in his most tragic despairs";
    he has also the "distinctive national trait" of seeking an emphat-
    ically "comfortable" religion. Carries the mythic interpretation
    even to the point of recognizing that Robinson is aware of "a
    superiority of race." Calls attention to the "symbolic tableau"
    of the prostrate Friday with Robinson's foot planted on his head,
    and gives instances of Robinson as the prototype of the ruthless
    conqueror and empire-builder. Concludes more favorably by reas-
    serting that "there is much to admire, much to learn, in this
    magnificent example of humanity." Reprinted: Histoire et poésie
    (Paris: Armand Colin & Co., 1898), pp. 193-224.

40 WARD, C.A. Defoe's Library." Athenaeum, no. 3529 (15 June):
    773.
        Observes in 1895.3, that some of the books apparently owned
    by Defoe just before his death were published between 1725 and
    1729, and had fine bindings or were otherwise expensive. Assum-
    ing that such books were Defoe's, and not Farewell's, this cir-

cumstance argues against Defoe's having been in "abject poverty"
near the end of his life.

1896

1   CARPENTER, GEORGE RICE, ed. Daniel Defoe's Journal of the
    Plague Year. Longmans' English Classics. 2d ed. New York,
    London, Bombay: Longmans, Green, and Co., pp. v–xxv, 254–72.
       Reprint of 1895.17. Adds in the appendix the paragraphs
    omitted from Carpenter's earlier edition and from editions later
    than Defoe's first edition. The omissions were concerned with
    "religious opinion or feeling and . . . civic administration."

2   DAY, GEORGE. "Daniel Defoe, The Tile-Maker of Tilbury,
    Essex." Essex Review 5:46–59.
       Surveys Defoe's career focusing upon connections with Essex
    county: his pantile business in Tilbury; considerable interest
    in Essex and towns such as Colchester, reflected in the Tour,
    Moll Flanders, and the attributed work The Coffee House Preachers
    (1706); and his use of the verses on the Vicar of Baddow in the
    Political History of the Devil (1726).

3   GEISSLER, PAUL. "Defoes Theorie über Robinson Crusoe. Ein
    Beitrag zur Geschichte der Theorie des Romans." Inaugural
    dissertation, Leipzig University; Halle: Erhardt Karras,
    33 pp. Reprint. Anglia, N.S., 7 (1897):1–33.
       Presented first in English, 1893.6, under considerable
    difficulties due to the lack of a complete satisfactory text of
    Serious Reflections . . . of Robinson Crusoe. In place of the
    hodge-podge of texts, now has the elegant edition of Aitken's
    Romances and Narratives. In addition, must integrate his own
    interpretation of Robinson Crusoe as allegory with Wright (1894).
    Defines Defoe's theory of the novel extracted from the prefaces
    to Part Two of Robinson Crusoe and Serious Reflections by explain-
    ing the meanings of parable, emblem, fable, allusion, allegory,
    truth, and relating them to one another. Rejects Hettner's view
    of Robinson Crusoe as an allegory of man's life (1854.4), and
    finds that aspects of Defoe's own "inner and outer" experiences
    were instead incorporated into a statement, not of concealed auto-
    biography, as Henry Kingsley (1868.16) or Minto (1879.5) would
    have it, but of objective "poetic truth." More systematically
    organizes the material into chapters, and more thoroughly docu-
    ments ideas in the notes.   (P.E.C.)

4   GONCOURT, EDMOND and JULES DE. Journal des Goncourt--Memoires
    de la vie littéraire. 9 vols. Paris: G. Charpentier & Co.,
    1887–1896, 9:196, 198–99.
       In the entry for 18 February 1894, mentions Marcel Schwob
    as he read from his translation of an unidentified novel by Defoe
    [most likely, Moll Flanders] which Edmond de Goncourt refers to
    as being "completely unknown" and as having some resemblance to

Germinie Lacerteux (1865). In the entry for 4 March 1894, Schwob
is described at a dinner with Alphonse Daudet, this time translat-
ing from Colonel Jack--a work written "with all the rigorous documentation and minute detail of a realistic novel of our time."
See also Marcel Schwob, trans., Moll Flanders de Daniel de Foe,
in Les Oeuvres Complète (Paris: Typographie François Bernouard,
1928), 5:vii-xv, 397-98. Reprinted: see National Union Catalog.

5   HOLMES, MRS. BASIL. The London Burial Grounds: Notes on
     Their History from the Earliest Times to the Present Day. New
     York: Macmillan & Co., pp. 121-30, 133-35.
         Takes information on the plague of 1665-1666 from the Jour-
     nal of the Plague Year as if it were a historical document: for
     instance, the locations of plague-pits, burial grounds, and pest-
     houses. Describes also the grave of Defoe in Bunhill Fields,
     City Road.

6   JOHNSON, CHARLES FREDERICK. "Daniel Defoe (1660?-1731)." In
     Library of the World's Best Literature Ancient and Modern.
     Edited by Charles Dudley Warner. Special Edition. New York:
     International Society, 11:4479-84.
         Introduces the selections from Defoe's works by setting up
     three classes: political writings, including "his wretched at-
     tempts at political satire," and journalism; fiction; and "miscel-
     laneous work," including biographies, Journal of the Plague Year,
     Storm, and Mrs. Veal. On Defoe as a journalist, finds that he
     has "a touch of genius"; in his Robinson Crusoe, "the elements of
     universal humanity." But calls his Colonel Jack, Captain Single-
     ton, Moll Flanders, and Roxana "repulsive." Severely criticizes
     the "other novels" as "inartistic"; and Moll Flanders and Roxana,
     while not "harmful or corrupting," as vulgar: "Passion is reduc-
     ed to mere animalism, and is depicted with the brutal directness
     of Hogarth." Accepts Defoe as "the first great realist" only in
     a limited sense. Reprinted: R.S. Peale & J.A. Hill, 1897, 8:
     4479-84.

7   LAYARD, GEORGE SOMES. "Robinson Crusoe and Its Illustrators."
     Bibliographica 2:181-203.
         Surveys the illustrators of Robinson Crusoe, starting with
     the unknown designer of the frontispiece to the first edition and
     concluding with J.B. Yeats of the Dent edition (1895). In a
     rapid overview, touches upon "the artist's habit" seen in both
     the frontispiece and the map of Serious Reflections, of represent-
     ing events simultaneously which occurred over a long period of
     time. Places emphasis on such illustrators as B. Picart (first
     French edition); the engravers Clark and Pine (first English
     edition); the illustrator of two editions (1781, 1790), Thomas
     Stothard; the exceptional designer of the three-volume set (1787)
     in Voyages imaginaires, Clement Pierre Marillier; and the illus-
     trator of two editions (1820, 1831), George Cruikshank. Comments
     briefly on illustrations in a number of other Robinson Crusoe
     editions.

8   LESEVITCH, V. "Po povodu Moll Flenders Danielia Defo" [Con-
     cerning Moll Flanders by Daniel Defoe]. Rosskoe bogatstvo
     [Russian riches], no. 1, pt. 2 (January):1-16.
         In Russian. Introduces the translation by P. Konschalov-
     skii of The Joys and Sorrows of the Famous Moll Flanders, pub-
     lished in installments in Russkoe bogatstvo, no. 1, pt. 1:174-216
     [chaps. 1-6]; no. 2, pt. 1:138-78 [chaps. 7-11]; no. 3, pt. 1:
     143-95 [chaps. 12-17]; no. 4, pt. 1:84-141 [chaps. 17-25]. De-
     fends the reprinting of an old book, Moll Flanders, as part of a
     still lively genre, the picaresque, which continues to produce
     creative variations even in the contemporary novel. Defines the
     picaresque as "the autobiography of a fictitious person which, by
     its condition, belonged to the dregs of society"; and traces its
     descent from Spanish and French, and a few English writers (Head,
     Nashe). Enlarges the definition to allow Defoe to add to Moll
     Flanders from his own Newgate experiences, reading of judiciary
     chronicles, and interviews of criminals--producing results that
     are "quite original." Places Moll Flanders in a "joint role"
     with Colonel Jack and Roxana, and argues that in each of the
     novels Defoe is mainly concerned to establish the authenticity of
     his main character: in Moll Flanders and Colonel Jack, through
     sources of the real in Spanish picaresque novels; in Roxana,
     through the Memoirs of Count Grammont (1715). Emphasizes that
     the picaresque genre constantly undergoes change, as is evident
     in Roxana. Reprinted: 1903.   (A.L.S.R.)

9   LOBBAN, J[OHN] H[AY], ed. Introduction and "Daniel Defoe
     (1661-1731)." In English Essays. The Warwick Library. Lon-
     don: Blackie & Son, pp. ix-lxi passim, 11-20.
         As part of a series, in which each volume is concerned with
     "the development in English literature of some special literary
     form," appraises the essay and reprints selections from Francis
     Bacon to Charles Lamb. Claims, first, that Defoe made a major
     contribution to the essay as a form through the Scandal Club of
     his Review, and that there are interconnections between this work
     and the novels Roxana and Richardson's Pamela; and second, that
     he kept the essay form alive in the interval between the Specta-
     tor and the Rambler through his contribution to Mist's and Apple-
     bee's journals. Reprints and annotates "The Instability of Human
     Glory" from Applebee's Original Weekly Journal, 21 July 1722
     [Lee's Defoe, 3:27-30], and "Descriptions of a Quack Doctor" from
     Mist's Weekly Journal, 5 December 1719 [Lee's Defoe, 2:173- 77].
     See also 1900.12. Reprinted: 1902; Essay Index Reprint Series
     (New York: Books for Libraries Press, 1972).

10   "Notes." Critic, n.s. 26, no. 755 (8 August):97.
         Provides a brief "genealogical table," male descendants of
     Defoe to the recently dead Daniel, in San Francisco. See also
     1893.11.

11   PANCOAST, HENRY S[PACKMAN]. "Daniel Defoe.--1661-1731." In
     An Introduction to English Literature. Reprint. New York:
     Henry Holt & Co., 1899, pp. 215-25.

Holds a consistent view of Defoe as a man, journalist, and
novelist. Characterizes him as a person almost entirely "free
from studious seclusion which is sometimes the badge of the
author's profession." Explains the True-Born Englishman and
the Shortest-Way with the Dissenters as the writings of a "born
fighter" actively engaged in the rough controversy of his day;
and Robinson Crusoe and the other novels as "a natural, although
surprising, outcome of his long career as journalist and pamphleteer." Claims that Defoe as "a man of a new type," having that
journalistic "modernness," was "quite unconsciously feeling his
way toward the novel." Accepts the view that Defoe "interviewed"
Selkirk at Bristol, that he has "the most amazing talent on record for telling lies" (Stephen), that he excelled in depicting
"the outward facts" but was singularly deficient with "the inner
facts and unseen experiences of the spirit, the subtler, or
higher emotions." Closes with especially high praise for the
author's identification with the narrator, Crusoe as "the typical
Englishman" (Daudet), but also the saddler narrator of the Journal of the Plague Year as the Dissenter and tradesman, Defoe.
Reprinted, with major revisions: 1907.13.

12   QUILLER-COUCH, A[RTHUR] T[HOMAS]. "Robinson Crusoe." In his
      Adventures in Criticism. London: Cassell & Co., pp. 77-92.
           Reprint of 1895.29. Includes also Aitken's acceptance of
      this view, 1895.4, 15.

13   RÖTTEKEN, HUBERT. "Weltflucht und Idylle in Deutschland von
      1720 bis zur Insel Felsenburg: Ein Beitrag zur Geschichte des
      deutschen Gefühlslebens. I. Die Robinsonaden." Zeitschrift
      für vergleichende Literaturgeschichte, N.S. 9:1-32.
           Takes issue with Kippenberg (1892.8) and Adolf Stern ["Der
      Dichter der Insel Felsenburg," 1880], who had imputed the motive
      of an escape from the world into an idyllic setting to the
      "emotionally engaged" authors of German Robinsonades 1719-1731.
      Finds this to be true only of Schnabel's Insel Felsenburg (1731),
      whereas the earlier Defoe-imitations evidenced more interest in
      the religious, moralistic, and adventure-novel aspects of the
      work.   (P.E.C.)

14   STEPHENS, KATE, ed. Preface to The Life and Adventures of
      Robinson Crusoe. New York, Cincinnati, Chicago: American
      Book Co., pp. 5-6.
           Prefers to identify Crusoe's island with Tobago, and men-
      tions a legend of a "solitary Frenchman" who lived there alone
      for twenty-one years. Claims that in writing about Crusoe,
      "Defoe wrote of himself. . . ."

15   STORM, JOHAN. "Literatur des achtzehnten Jahrhunderts." In
      Englische Philologie. Anleitung wissenschaftlichen Studium
      der englischen Sprache. 2d ed. Leipzig: O.R. Reisland,
      pp. 920-22.

Includes Defoe among the sources examined in this study of changes in the English language since Shakespeare. See also 1910.12.   (P.E.C.)

16   TRAILL, H[ENRY] D[UFF], ed. Social England. 6 vols. New York: G.P. Putnam's Sons; London: Cassell & Co., 4:557, 577, 593-94, 598; 5:85-88, 126.
       Introduces Defoe as participating directly in social reform through criticism of the Societies for the Reformation of Manners in his Poor Man's Plea (1698) and Reformation of Manners (1702); and later, in the Age of Walpole, as contributing to social history with Robinson Crusoe and the other novels. Refers specifically to Moll Flanders as "'the greatest example of pure realism in literature'" and Roxana as "the last, and, taking it altogether the worst of his novels." Comments also upon Defoe's Essay upon Loans (1710) and its role in Harley's formation of the South Sea Company.

1897

1   FÉRET, CHA[RLE]S JA[ME]S. "Flip Can." Notes and Queries, 8th ser. 12, no. 303 (16 October):308-9.
       Wants to locate Selkirk's flip can and verify the inscription.

2   HALE, EDWARD E[VERETT]. "Robinson Crusoe and Defoe." Outlook 55, no. 16 (17 April):1031-35.
       Accounts for the enormous popularity of Defoe's Robinson Crusoe and his own preference of the original on the grounds that the hero does not succeed in everything he wants to do. Prefers this Crusoe to the versions of Campe, Wyss, and other imitators. Disagrees sharply with D'Israeli [1817.4 on the resemblances between Selkirk and Crusoe, and defends Defoe's originality. While rejecting Wright's "theory of silence" [1894.24], does accept a rough parallelism between Crusoe's chronology and actual Stuart history.

3   HAZLITT, WILLIAM CAREW. The Confessions of a Collector. London: Ward & Downey, p. 9.
       Relates an anecdote about how his father, William Hazlitt the younger, while editing the Works (1840), acquired a copy of Mrs. Veal. The father did not believe in acquiring first editions: "the best standard text was his line."

4   HEADLAM, CECIL. Selections from the British Satirists. With an Introductory Essay. London: F.E. Robinson, pp. 62, 268-71.
       Mistitles the Shortest-Way with the Dissenters, "an amazingly clever burlesque"; includes brief selections from the True-Born Englishman and Hymn to the Pillory.

5   LANDOR, WALTER SAVAGE. <u>Letters and Other Unpublished Writ-</u>
     <u>ings</u>. Edited by Stephen Wheeler. London: Richard Bentley &
     Son, pp. 56, 117, 201-2.
         In "Defence of Dr. Parr" (<u>Imaginary Conversations</u>). remarks
     "what small hearts and twisted heads have some otherwise great
     men. Swift was the reviler of Defoe." Writes in a letter to
     Arthur de N. Walker (3 March [1856]) of a successful appeal to
     the public for funds to benefit a Defoe descendant. In two sep-
     arate verse tributes published for the first time, praises Defoe
     and Crusoe. Reprinted, in part: <u>The Poetical Works of Walter</u>
     <u>Savage Landor</u>, ed. Stephen Wheeler (3 vols. Oxford: Clarendon
     Press, 1937), 2:454; <u>Critical Heritage</u>.

6   <u>The Manuscripts of His Grace the Duke of Portland, Preserved</u>
     <u>at Welbeck Abbey</u>. Edited by J.J. Cartright. Historical
     Manuscripts Commission, Fifteenth Report, Appendix, Part 4.
     London: HMSO, vol. 4, 723 pp. passim.
         Publishes for the first time the largest number of manu-
     script letters and memoranda written by or relating to Defoe, in
     their entire texts, ranging in time from April 1703 to March
     1711. Although the introduction (5 pp.) surveys the Defoe
     letters, an index was not available until vol. 6 of the <u>Portland</u>
     was published in 1901. The introduction notes that the signifi-
     cance of the Defoe-related papers lies in "recording the very
     intimate relations for public purposes, which existed for many
     years between Harley and De Foe," and that the secret of Defoe's
     advisory role was kept for so long is a marvel. All together in
     this one volume there are 112 letters by Defoe, written mainly to
     his benefactor, Robert Harley, Speaker of the House of Commons
     and later Secretary of State; one letter from Harley to Defoe;
     and a number of enclosures which reveal the nature of Defoe's
     work as government agent: "An Abstract of my Journey with casual
     Observations on Public Affairs," "Defoe's Proposals for Scot-
     land," and his "Queries for Management" in Scotland. Quite a few
     of the letters are signed by the alias Alexander Goldsmith or
     Claude Guilot. Not only do the letters illuminate the writer,
     especially during his mission to Scotland in behalf of the Union,
     the numerous letters by other writers provide the larger contexts
     in reconstructing biographical events. Such are the observations
     about Defoe in the letters by Godolphin; John Bell, the post-
     master of Newcastle; Robert Davis, the brother-in-law. See also
     1899.7; 1907.17; <u>Report on the Manuscripts of His Grace the Duke</u>
     <u>of Portland, K.G.. Preserved at Welbeck Abbey</u>, ed. R.F. Isaacson
     (Historical Manuscripts Commission; London: HMSO, 1931), 10:239,
     288-89. Reprinted: Healey.

7   OMOND, [GEORGE W. THOMSON]. "Defoe the Rebel." <u>Athenaeum</u>,
     no. 3632 (5 June):745.
         Rejects suggestion that Defoe may have been with Argyll's
     expedition in the summer of 1685 rather than with Monmouth.

8　"The Speech of Mr. John Checkley upon His Trial." In <u>John
　　Checkley; or the Evolution of Religious Tolerance in Massa-
　　chusetts Bay</u>. Publications of the Prince Society. 2 vols.
　　Boston: Prince Society, 2:19-20.
　　　　Reprinting of 1738.1. The editor annotates in <u>Vox Populi,
　　Vox Dei</u> [which he assigns to Defoe] the idea that the powers of
　　kings derives from the people; claims that such an idea aroused
　　Checkley's disapproval; also corrects Checkley's quotation of
　　three lines as being Defoe's, which are actually from Dryden's
　　<u>Conquest of Granada</u>.

9　STOCKTON, FRANK R. "My Favorite Novelist and His Best Book."
　　<u>Munsey's Magazine</u> 18:351-56.
　　　　Selects two favorites who "calmly" hold their places in
　　front, Defoe and Dickens: the first for his excellent story,
　　and the second for characters superior to his story. Tells an
　　anecdote of the old sea captain who, in hating the fool Robinson
　　Crusoe, gave no thought of the author. Describes Defoe's "prom-
　　inence" as "his ability to transmute a fictional narrative into a
　　record of facts."

10　TAPPERT, WILHELM. Review of Karl Foth's school edition of
　　<u>Robinson Crusoe</u>. Vol. 75, Französische and Englische Schul-
　　bibliothek. Leipzig: Renger, 1893. <u>Anglia. Beiblatt</u> 8,
　　nos. 5-6 (September-October):175-78.
　　　　Praises the school edition mildly; makes numerous correc-
　　tions.　　　　　　　　　　　　　　　　　　　　　　　　　　　(P.E.C.)

11　WRIGHT, THOMAS. <u>The Acid Sisters and Other Poems</u>. Olney:
　　Thomas Wright, pp. 10-11, 14-15, 69-70.
　　　　From his strong interest in Defoe biography (1894.24), pre-
　　sents occasional verses that continued the assessment: "When Jo-
　　seph Reigned at 'Buttons,'" "The Two Defoes," and "Saint Defoe."

1898

1　CLARK, J. SCOTT. "Defoe, 1661(?)-1731." In <u>A Study of En-
　　glish Prose Writers: A Laboratory Method</u>. New York: Charles
　　Scribner's Sons, 1909, pp. 143-67.
　　　　Bases the biographies of the earlier authors on Leslie
　　Stephen's entries in the <u>DNB</u>, and adds a bibliography on Defoe's
　　style (2 pp.).

2　ELLINGER, J. Review of Woldemar Rost's <u>The Heroes of English
　　Literature</u>, 1898. <u>Anglia. Beiblatt</u> 9, no. 4 (September):153-
　　54.
　　　　Provides from well-known compendia brief sketches in En-
　　glish of the life and works of Defoe and forty-one other English
　　and American authors, intended for upper-level school pupils.
　　　　　　　　　　　　　　　　　　　　　　　　　　　　　　　(P.E.C.)

3 FELKIN, HENRY M., and FELKIN, EMMIE. An Introduction to Herbart's Science and Practice of Education. Boston: D.C. Heath & Co., pp. 126-27.

Discusses briefly the attempt to put into practice certain ideas on elementary education held by Johann Friedrich Herbart and, after his death in 1841, continued by Tuiskon Ziller (d.1882). In November 1893, according to D.P. Leinster-Mackay, The Educational World of Daniel Defoe, ELS Monograph Series, no. 23 (University of Victoria, 1981), pp. 9, 84, the School Board of Würzburg came close to adopting a Rousseauistic concept for elementary school students which, by making Robinson Crusoe central to their curriculum during the second year of the program, introduced new material of "a moral-religious character." Reprinted: 1901.

4 "Foë (Daniel De)." In Nouveau Larousse Illustré Dictionnaire universel encyclopédique. Edited by Claude Augé. Paris: Librairie Larousse, 4:576.

Brief, inaccurate in places (e.g., imprisonment in Newgate for two years).

5 HAWTHORNE, JULIAN, ed. "Daniel Defoe." In The Literature of All Nations and All Ages, History, Character and Incident. 10 vols. Philadelphia: W. Finley & Co., 7:301-11.

Appraises Robinson Crusoe as "the accepted self-revelation of the sturdy Anglo-Saxon, destined to subdue wild nature and wilder savages." Accepts the "merited oblivion" of Colonel Jack, Moll Flanders, and Roxana. At the same time, recognizes that with the current interest in realism, Defoe's genius should be more appreciated. Quotes at length from Robinson Crusoe: "The Footprint in the Sand" and "Crusoe and Friday." Reprinted: 1899; 1900; 1901; 1902; The Masterpieces and the History of Literature (New York and Chicago: E.R. DuMont, 1902), 7:301-11; 1903; 1904; 1906; 1910.

6 HEWSON, J. JAMES. Grand Christmas Pantomime Robinson Crusoe, 38 pp.

Performed at the Pavilion Theatre, Mile End, [London], 26 December.

7 LANDMANN, H. "Robinson Crusoe." In Encyklopädisches Handbuch der Pädagogik. Edited by W[ilheim] Rein. Langensalza: Hermann Beyer & Sons, 5:916-22.

Anticipates more detailed analysis by J. Meyer (1919.7) on the usefulness of Robinson Crusoe as a school text, particularly in the Herbart-Ziller schools (in Saxony in the final third of the nineteenth century), where it was the focal point of second-grade instruction. The character of Robinson Crusoe was seen to help younger children navigate between the worlds of fantasy and reality, prepare for the study of history, and develop ethical-religious values. The book can also be recalled to good purpose in higher grades (religion, geography, science). The perfect

school text, properly abridged and annotated, has yet to be produced. Reprinted: 1908.   (P.E.C.)

8   LE BRETON, ANDRÉ. Le Roman au dix-huitième siècle. Nouvelle
     Bibliothèque Littéraire. Paris: Societé Française d'Impri-
     merie et de Librairie, pp. 358-67.
        Brings an openly nationalistic bias to a discussion of Rob-
inson Crusoe and certain earlier French works, Marivaux's Effets
supprenantes de la sympathie (1713) and Voyages et avantures de
Jacques Massé (1710). Analyzes Jacques Massé at length, pointing
out some of the "numerous and striking analogues" to Robinson
Crusoe. Complains that Defoe has become "popular in France from
one day to the next, and has been regarded as an initiator while
Jacques Massé's book disappeared to the depths of our libraries,
under a thick bed of dust." Urges that Robinson Crusoe should be
read by children at the ages of twelve or fourteen, but also reread "at a more advanced age": its first merit being "an air of
authenticity" as the author merges himself into a Scotsman; and
its second merit, the high-minded morality worthy of "a second
Odyssey."

9   MARSHALL, ED. "Robinson Crusoe." Notes and Queries, 9th ser.
     2, no. 39 (24 September):248.
        Inquires about the edition of Robinson Crusoe published in
Paris, 1783, but not the French translation; has only praise for
the concept of the translation into Latin by F.J. Goffaux as
revised in London, 1823.

10   OBER, FREDERICK A. Crusoe's Island: A Bird-Hunter's Story.
     Appleton's Home Reading Series. New York: D. Appleton & Co.,
     279 pp. passim.
        States in the preface (3 pp.) that in 1878 the American
ornithologist Ober concluded a Smithsonian-sponsored investigation of the Lesser-Antilles, and then fulfilled a dream of his
youth by searching out the truth, in the island of Tobago, dif-
ferentiating his fictional hero Robinson Crusoe from the real
Alexander Selkirk. Now presents conclusive evidence that Tobago,
not Juan Fernandez, was "the veritable island" and that Friday
was a Carib stolen from the island of Trinidad. Contends that
while Defoe, in the main, described the natives accurately, he
fell into one of his many anachronisms when he claims they heard
firearms for the first time (1719). In the appendix, has a section, "Evidence in Support of Tobago as the True Crusoe's Island"
(10 pp.). In another section, "In Defense of Selkirk. Perhaps
Apocryphal," quotes an anonymous passage about Daniel Foe, "who
was now a penny-a-liner for small newspapers," as having broke
his "compact" with Selkirk and as having written Robinson Crusoe
alone; he dishonestly used Selkirk's adventures, and thus made
the errors of inconsistency and contradiction noted in the narrative.

11   P., C.M. "Defoe." Notes and Queries, 9th ser. 1, no. 7
     (12 February):133.
          Replies to 1898.18. The earliest external evidence con-
     firming that Defoe wrote the Journal of the Plague Year in 1722:
     Chalmers's Life of Daniel De Foe.

12   POWELL, F. YORK. "Daniel Defoe." Quarto, 4th ser., pp. 23-
     37.
          Finds Defoe most energetic in "the whole field of the Vita
     Activa," deficient in "the Vita Contemplativa." Among the
     "scattered scraps of testimony" which admirers have assembled
     "into something like a complete biography," accepts the legend
     of Selkirk's having sold his "papers" to Defoe in Bristol, in
     1711, and of Defoe's composing Robinson Crusoe from these papers;
     the idea of a writing "colleague" kept "in constant employment";
     and the political motivation for Defoe's isolation at the end
     of his life. On the charm of his "homespun style," on the blem-
     ishes of his style, on his art, on his resemblances to Balzac
     ("circumstantial detail") or Diderot ("an indefatigable encyclo-
     paedist")--offers insights which conclude with the view of Defoe
     as a "contradiction in terms, a bourgeois genius . . . one of the
     noblest Philistines that ever lived." Reprinted: Frederick York
     Powell: A Life and a Selection from His Letters and Occasional
     Writings, ed. Oliver Elton, 2 vols. (Oxford: Clarendon Press,
     1906), 2:281-97.

13   ROBBINS, ALFRED F. "A Cornish Ghost Story." Cornish Magazine
     1 (July-December):283-97.
          Starts with brief summary by the editor, Arthur T. Quiller-
     Couch, and reprints "A Remarkable Passage of an Apparition, Re-
     lated by the Rev. Dr. Ruddle, of Launceston, in Cornwall, in the
     Year 1665." States the case for the Rev. John Ruddle as the
     author and Defoe as the editor and publisher of the narrative,
     which first appeared in Mr. Campbell's Pacquet, in the second
     edition of the History of the Life and Adventures of Mr. Duncan
     Campbell (August, 1720).

*14 ROST, WOLDEMAR. "Daniel Defoe." In The Heroes of English
     Literature. Aus englischen Originalen ausgewählt und für den
     Schulgebrauch erklärt. Berlin: R. Gaertners, [pp. unknown].
          Chap. 11, on Defoe, is drawn, in English, from well known
     older and newer compendia. See the review by Ellinger, 1898.2.
                                                            (P.E.C.)

15   SAINTSBURY, GEORGE. A Short History of English Literature.
     New York: Macmillan Co. Reprint. 1900, pp. 546-48.
          After a biographical summary, comments on Defoe's achieve-
     ments in verisimilitude. Only the last step remained: "the
     final projection of character."

16   ULLRICH, HERMANN. <u>Robinson und Robinsonaden. Bibliographie,</u>
     <u>Geschichte, Kritik. Ein Beitrag zur vergleichenden Litteratur-</u>
     <u>geschichte, im Besonderen zur Geschichte des Romans und zur</u>
     <u>Geschichte der Jugendlitteratur. Teil 1. Bibliographie.</u>
     Litterarhistorische Forschungen, 7. Weimar: Emil Felber,
     263 pp.
          Presents only the first part of a long-planned larger work
     investigating "the history of the world-book <u>Robinson Crusoe</u>."
     In this most compendious bibliography of 718 items, covering
     "originals" and translations in some twenty-three languages,
     lists and briefly annotates (section 1) the editions of originals
     (196); (section 2) translations (110); (section 3) adaptations
     (115); (section 4) imitations (233 "actual" Robinsonades, 44
     pseudo-Robinsonades); (appendix) apocryphal Robinsonades (10)
     and "Robinsonstuff" on the stage (9); and (supplement) imitation
     (1). In the preface (11 pp.), stresses that the motivation behind
     the work was a lifelong admiration of <u>Robinson Crusoe</u>, and out-
     lines his ambitious plan for examining this world-book and the
     continuity of the "Robinson-motif." Innovates by substituting
     his own definition of the true Robinsonade, abandoning the old
     criterion of "Robinson" in the title of a work, and identifying
     the island experience of Part One as "the controlling factor."
     Discusses a dozen sources or so, at times severely, as with
     Hettner (worthless, "since he had probably never actually seen
     the works about which he wrote"). Lists the important libraries
     and collections used. As the bibliography represents many years
     of work, it was already partially eclipsed by one of these
     sources, Kippenberg (1892.8). For additions and corrections to
     the bibliography, see Ullrich, 1907-1908.1; and for the dis-
     agreement with Staverman, see his <u>Robinson Crusoe in Nederland</u>,
     1907.20. See reviews, 1898.17; 1899.5; 1901.13. Reprinted:
     Kraus Reprints (Nendeln, Liechtenstein: Kraus-Thomson Organ-
     ization, 1977).

17   VON ZOBELTITZ, FEDOR. "Eine Bibliographie der Robinsonaden"
     <u>Zeitschrift für Bücherfreunde</u> 2, pt. 2, nos. 8/9 (November-
     December):386-88.
          Heaps praise on Ullrich's <u>Robinson und Robinsonaden</u>. Sug-
     gests some slightly different bibliographical data on the basis
     of his own modest collection of Robinsonades. Differs with both
     Ullrich and Kippenberg (1892.8) on specifics in the confusing
     question of German translations of <u>Robinson Crusoe</u> and who was
     copying whom.   (P.E.C.)

18   Y., X. "Defoe." <u>Notes and Queries</u>, 9th ser. 1, no. 3
     (15 January):47.
          Asks for early external evidence that Defoe wrote the
     <u>Journal of the Plague Year</u>. See 1898.11.

1899

1   CHANDLER, FRANK WADLEIGH. Romances of Roguery: An Episode
     in the History of the Novel. Part I, The Picaresque Novel in
     Spain. New York and London: Macmillan Co., pp. 63, 239, 367.
         Mentions briefly Moll Flanders and Colonel Jack in the
     development of the picaresque novel.

2   CROSS, WILBUR L. "Daniel Defoe." The Development of the En-
     glish Novel. New York: Macmillan Co.; London: Macmillan &
     Co., pp. 27-32.
         Places Defoe in a chapter "From Arthurian Romance to Rich-
     ardson," and not in the next chapter, "The Eighteenth-Century
     Realists." Finds the main distinction between the older picar-
     esque story and Robinson Crusoe to be "a sense of reality," with
     which Defoe invested his narrative, and "humanized [his] adven-
     ture." Praises his secondary novels as reaching a standard of
     realism or naturalism (Moll Flanders), but makes no mention of
     Colonel Jack or Roxana. Reprinted: 1902; in part, Daniel Defoe:
     Moll Flanders, ed. J. Paul Hunter, Crowell Critical Library (New
     York: Thomas Y. Crowell Co., 1970), p. 276.

3   ELTON, OLIVER. "The English Augustan Writers." In The Augus-
     tan Age. Edinburgh and London: William Blackwood & Sons,
     pp. 291-94.
         In a chapter, which by design excludes the novel, takes the
     view of Defoe as playing with "unequalled relish the part of the
     picaresque hero as man of letters." Follows and extends Minto's
     Defoe (1879), maintaining that falsehood is to Defoe "'no casual
     mistress, but a wife' whose value he respects profoundly" and
     that "the seam between his facts and fancies" cannot easily be
     detected. Under this rubric, subsumes also his politics--the
     secret and later underhanded dealings, which Lee has only partly
     unravelled. On the Review, describes the effects of an "English
     bourgeois" writer on a class he understood well, as compared with
     Swift impersonating the Draper.

4   HADDEN, J. CUTHBERT. "The Making of Robinson Crusoe." Cen-
     tury Magazine, n.s. 36, no. 48:387-95.
         Reviews the facts and myths about Selkirk, centering upon
     his solitary experience on Juan Fernandez and comparing him with
     Robinson Crusoe. Assesses and rejects the charges against Defoe
     for plagiarism and misappropriation of money from Selkirk.

5   HIPPE, M. Review of Ullrich's Robinson und Robinsonaden.
     Englische Studien 26, no. 3:405-11.
         Reviews the newly published, long awaited "model" bibli-
     ography, first installment of Ullrich's Robinson und Robinson-
     aden, the promised three-part study of the famous novel and its
     sources, editions, translations, adaptations, and imitations.
     Adds thirty-five works to the Bibliography, mostly in Slavic

languages, which Ullrich seems to have largely passed over.
Praises the work highly, especially for performing the thankless
task of trying to include pertinent juvenile literature, but
wishes Ullrich had cited locations of rare editions and provided
an alphabetical index.   (P.E.C.)

6   "A Masterly Lie." Academy 57 (9 September):256-57.
     Analyzes the narrative skill with which Defoe imposed his
"masterly lie" about the blowing up of the island of St. Vincent,
for some three weeks, upon readers of Mist's Journal, 5 July
1718.

7   Report on the Manuscripts of His Grace the Duke of Portland,
     Preserved at Welbeck Abbey. Edited by J.J. Cartright. Histor-
     ical Manuscripts Commission. London: HMSO, vol. 5, 692 pp.
     passim.
     Continues the publication of letters and memoranda, 1711 to
1724, selected from the Robert Harley papers; includes 65 letters
by Defoe to Harley and one letter to Defoe from T.P. (1711). Of
special interest are the enclosures: advice on the position of a
third secretary for public affairs in Scotland (1711); two statements (1711) giving respectively, his "thoughts" on the South
Seas trade and "a proposal for a settlement upon the coast of
America"; an account of a huge assembly of Cameronians gathered
for fasting (1712); and Defoe's indictment of Richard Steele's
writings for sedition in a statement, "Collection of Scandal"
(1714). See also 1897.6. Reprinted: Healey.

8   SANDERS, HERBERT M. "Literature in Captivity." Temple Bar
     118 (September):30-32.
     Discusses the conditions under which "prison-born litera-
ture" was produced. For Defoe, starts with the Shortest-Way with
the Dissenters, which got him into prison through its irony; continues with Hymn to the Pillory, Challenge of Peace (1703), Storm
(1704), Review [six months in Newgate, common mistake on the
release date]; briefly mentions the use of his prison experience
later in the novels.

9   STEVENSON, ROBERT LOUIS. Letter to Sidney Colvin, July 1884.
     In The Letters of Robert Louis Stevenson. Edited by Sidney
     Colvin. New York: Charles Scribner's Sons, pp. 377-78.
     Colvin had reported to Stevenson a remark by Edward
Burne-Jones on an "analogy" between a passage of Defoe and one
in Treasure Island. Stevenson guesses the Defoe book was Cap-
tain Singleton, which he had never read; he admits that Treasure
Island came partly from "the great Captain Johnson's History of
Notorious Pirates." [He was not aware that "Captain Johnson"
was a pseudonym for Defoe.] See also Stevenson's letter to W.E.
Henley, 1923.20.

1900

1   BATESON, THOMAS. "The Relations of Defoe and Harley."
     English Historical Review 15, no. 58 (April):238-50.
        Makes use for the first time of the largest number of let-
    ters and memoranda written by or relating to Defoe, available
    now in print (1897.6), toward an interpretation of the complex
    relations between Robert Harley and Defoe from 1703 to 1711.
    While correcting Lee who "rather suspected than understood"
    these relations, moves in the opposite direction by suggesting
    that Defoe's motivation was as much personal as it was political,
    and by describing the relationship as a "degradation of charac-
    ter" for Defoe. Clarifies the two "intelligence" missions in
    1704 and 1705, the services through the Review, and the secret
    work in Edinburgh for the union. Removes the confusion about
    the date of Defoe's release from Newgate (May, not August, 1704),
    and graphically documents his difficulties in obtaining funds
    and instructions from Harley, and his frequent disappointments
    in gaining an official position or some reward for his hard
    work.

2   BESANT, WALTER. Introduction to A Journal of the Plague Year
     by Daniel Defoe. Century Classics. New York: Century Co.,
     pp. v-xx.
        Admittedly having no interest in party warfare, rushes over
    the early career of Defoe, to focus on the five novels, all works
    of the imagination, which he rates as equal in merit. Praises
    the Journal of the Plague Year for its grasp of the whole situ-
    ation, simple style relying heavily upon repetition, and choice
    of "a strong subject." Contrasts Pepys with Defoe to convey the
    sense in the latter of the plague as horror. In this respect,
    the Journal of the Plague Year is also "a true history."

3   COCKBURN, JAMES D. "Daniel Defoe in Scotland." Scottish
     Review 36 (October):250-69.
        Uses the considerable new information made available in
    the Historical Manuscripts Commission publication of the Port-
    land Papers, including many of Defoe's letters (1897.6; 1899.7),
    to confirm and extend Minto's charges that Defoe was essentially
    a liar. Argues that as in the 1864 discovery of the letters
    revealing his role "in gagging a Tory Press," the new materials
    show him engaged in similar duplicity leading to a "final degrad-
    ation" some time after the death of Queen Anne; they may even
    necessitate the rewriting of his biography. Narrates from these
    letters accounts of Defoe's work as "government spy," especially
    during the first of four visits to Scotland, and quotes exten-
    sively the letters concerned with the Union. Notes certain dif-
    ferences between the letters and such published accounts as in
    his History of the Union. Reaches strong conclusions about
    Defoe's "moral myopia" and total alienation from family and
    society.

4 G., E.L. "Daniel Defoe." Notes and Queries, 9th ser. 6,
   no. 139 (25 August):156.
      On the picture of Defoe in the pillory at Temple Bar, at
   the recent Guildhall Exhibition. See also 1900.5-6.

5 GNOMON [pseud.]. "Daniel Defoe." Notes and Queries, 9th ser.
   6, no. 145 (6 October):270-72.
      Takes issue with 1900.4 on his insistence that the picture
   by Eyre Crowe of Defoe in the pillory at Temple Bar should have
   shown the heads of traitors on three iron spikes.

6 HOPE, HENRY GERALD. "Daniel Defoe." Notes and Queries,
   9th ser. 5, no. 129 (16 June):483-84; 9th ser. 6, no. 139
   (25 August:156; 9th ser. 6, no. 142 (15 September):219.
      Draws information about Defoe's bankruptcy in 1692 and re-
   covery, from Forster's biography (1843, 1860). See also 1900.9.
   In the second note, collects the praises of Robinson Crusoe; in
   the third, responds to 1900.4, referring to Eyre Crowe's painting
   of Defoe in the pillory at Temple Bar, first exhibited in 1862.

7 MASTERMAN, J. HOWARD B. Introduction to Robinson Crusoe.
   Pitt Press Series. Cambridge: University Press, pp. v-x.
      Links the popularity of Robinson Crusoe to the spirit of
   adventure prevailing then, and the story itself to Selkirk's
   experiences. Finds the "charm" of the book to consist in the
   qualities of the hero that made Great Britain "the greatest colon-
   izing power in the world." As for the other works, most are now
   forgotten.

8 RHEAD, LOUIS. "Introduction to the Present Edition." In The
   Life and Strange Surprising Adventures of Robinson Crusoe.
   New York and London: Harper & Brothers, pp. v-vi.
      Numerous decorations of the flora, fauna, and scenes des-
   cribed throughout the book have been made especially in the West
   Indies. Maintains that Crusoe's island is now known as Tobago,
   and provides a map of its location.

9 ROBBINS, ALFRED F. "Daniel Defoe." Notes and Queries, 9th
   ser. 5, no. 120 (14 April):285.
      As an illustration of Defoe's difficulties in recovering
   from his bankruptcy of 1692, summarizes the "Merchant Insurers
   (War with France) Bill," which the Commons had passed early in
   1694, but which failed to emerge from committee. As one of nineteen persons specifically named as having met with "many losses
   from the present war with France," who would be assisted in satis-
   fying their creditors, Defoe stood to gain greatly by the passage
   of the Bill. See also 1900.6.

10 ROWE, ARTHUR F. "Daniel Defoe." Notes and Queries, 9th ser.
   6, no. 148 (27 October):337.
      On further evidence, in 1766, of two heads of traitors
   stuck on spikes at Temple Bar. See also 1900.4-5.

11   SHARP, R. FARQUHARSON. "Defoe." In <u>Architects of English Lit-</u>
<u>erature: Biographical Sketches of Great Writers from Shake-</u>
<u>speare to Tennyson.</u> London: Swan Sonnenschein & Co., pp. 43–
53.
      Offers standard biographical fare with a few unusual em-
phases. Reproduces in facsimile the conclusion of Defoe's letter
to Lord Halifax in autograph manuscript; notes a "strain of very
sound patriotism" running through most of the nonfictional writing; accepts Saintsbury's view that Defoe was "strictly honest,"
but had "a rather blunt moral perception"; stresses that <u>Robinson</u>
<u>Crusoe</u> and "the less famous novels" were distinguished from other
fictions by Defoe's inventive powers. Suspects that in the later
novels "the central idea was suggested by some incident that had
arrested public attention."

12   STARKWEATHER, CHAUNCEY C., ed. "Daniel Defoe (1661–1731)."
In <u>Essays of British Essayists, Including Biographical and Cri-</u>
<u>tical Sketches.</u> Rev. ed. 2 vols. New York: Colonial Press,
1:138–47.
      Borrows heavily in the brief introduction from 1896.9; re-
prints and annotates Defoe's two essays from this source.

13   TOWNLEY, CHARLES [Geoffrey Thorn]. <u>Grand Christmas Pantomime</u>
<u>Robinson Crusoe: or Harlequin Man Friday, Gal Topsy, and Pret-</u>
<u>ty Polly Perkins.</u> [London]: Grand Theatre Islington, 33 pp.
      Differs from Townley's other pantomimes, 1886.18 and
1894.23.

14   ULLRICH, HERMANN. "Unbekannte Übersetzungen von Schriften Daniel Defoés." <u>Zeitschrift für Bücherfreunde</u> 4, no. 1 (April):
32–35.
      Identifies as Defoe's works a dozen or so anonymous German
translations, some as well known as <u>Moll Flanders</u>, <u>Political His-</u>
<u>tory of the Devil</u>, <u>Treatise Concerning the Use and Abuse of the</u>
<u>Marriage Bed</u> (1727), <u>Memoirs of a Cavalier</u>, and <u>Roxana</u>. (P.E.C.)

15   V., Q. "Daniel Defoe." <u>Notes and Queries</u>, 9th ser. 6,
no. 148 (27 October):337.
      Calls attention to Defoe's letters published in the two
most recent volumes of the Historical Manuscripts Commission,
Duke of Portland's papers (1897, 1899). See also 1900.6.

*16   VERNE, JULES. "Seconde Patrie." <u>Magasin d'éducation et de</u>
<u>récréation</u>, 2d ser. 11 (1 January)–12 (15 December). Reprint.
<u>Seconde Patrie</u> (2 parts). Paris: J. Hetzel, 1900.
      Information on publications from Edward J. Gallagher, <u>Jules</u>
<u>Verne: A Primary and Secondary Bibliography</u> (Boston, Mass.:
G.K. Hall & Co., 1980), p. 29. For Verne's debt to Defoe and
J.R. Wyss, see his foreword to the original French work (1900)
and I.O. Evans, <u>Jules Verne and His Work</u> (London: Arco Publications, 1965), p. 114. Reprinted: 1923; 1924.

17   WELSH, CHARLES. "The Children's Books That Have Lived."
      Library, 2d ser. 1:314-23.
         Takes view that children adapt themselves to the classics.
      Selects four books written before the end of the eighteenth
      century, among them Robinson Crusoe, which while never intended
      for children have been appropriated by them. Quotes Lady [Eliza-
      beth] Eastlake, writing "over sixty years since," that "the best
      juvenile writing will not fail to delight those who are no longer
      children," including Robinson Crusoe.

18   WHITE, DOUGLAS. "Robinson Crusoe's Island." Overland Monthly
      36, no. 212 (August):161-69.
         Recalls the history of Juan Fernandez, in particular its
      association with Alexander Selkirk, on the occasion of a visit
      there by the U.S.S. Hartford, two years after an earthquake.
      Revives [the completely apocryphal] story of Selkirk's leaving
      the island with "an extensive notebook" about his experiences,
      which he gave to Defoe, to become the basis of Robinson Crusoe.

19   WHITTEN, WILFRED. Daniel Defoe. The Westminster Biographies.
      Boston: Small, Maynard & Co., 129 pp.
         Provides a compact end-of-the-century summation of biog-
      raphy and criticism, with a portrait, chronology, and brief
      secondary bibliography. Fulfills the aim of the Westminster
      Biographies series, to give accounts of Englishmen "whose
      personalities have impressed themselves most deeply on the
      character and history of their country" and to use "the best
      contemporary point of view." While absorbing the views of
      Chalmers, Wilson, Chadwick, Minto, and Aitken, and correcting
      Lee and Wright, still makes strong independent judgments. About
      Defoe as a person: draws conclusions cautiously, from his re-
      semblance to Robinson Crusoe and Colonel Jack. From the large
      number of "details of place" in the novels and works like the
      Tour: concludes that he was a "born topographer." Takes a
      commonsensical and balanced view of Defoe's secret work for the
      government, 1715-1726; comments briefly on selected major non-
      fictional works, such as the Complete English Tradesman or the
      Family Instructor (1715). Observes that the secret for his
      phenomenal output was that "he wasted no emotion in his work,"
      and refused to make "fastidious distinctions" between journal-
      istic and creative writing. On Moll Flanders, Roxana, Colonel
      Jack, Captain Singleton: reveals no apparent bias, while prais-
      ing his talent for making "fiction look like sworn evidence" and
      "the photographic vividness of all the episodes, and the pathos
      of a few." In Robinson Crusoe, finds "little real imagination,
      little realism," but a triumph won by simply satisfying "the
      craving to be done with psychology and the overlays of a refined
      civilisation, and picture the natural man who builds, bakes,
      contrives, loves, and prays." Reprinted: London: Kegan Paul,
      Trench, Trubner & Co., [1900].

<u>1901</u>

1   BRETHERTON, RALPH HAROLD. "<u>The Apparition of Mrs. Veal</u>." <u>Gentleman's Magazine</u>, n.s. 67 (December):531-43.
      Without any apparent awareness of Aitken's discovery (1895.2), persists in arguing that in <u>Mrs. Veal</u> Defoe gave an account of an apparition, which he pretended to be true, but which was "really a complete fiction." Stresses that <u>Mrs. Veal</u> was written as an introduction to a religious work, Drelincourt on death. Analyzes Defoe's habit of deliberately departing from ordinary storytelling in order to strengthen the piece as fiction.

2   BRINK, JAN TEN. "Daniel Defoe en zijn gewolg." In <u>Romans in Prosa</u>, part 7. Leiden: E.J. Brill, pp. 413-48.
      In Dutch. Listed in Gove, p. 405, and cited elsewhere. The copy in the Hubbard Imaginary Voyage Collection (Department of Rare Books and Special Collections, University of Michigan Library) does not have a title page for part 7 and therefore no date.

3   CLARK, THOMAS ARKLE, ed. <u>Daniel Defoe</u>. Biographies of Great English Authors. Taylorville, Ill.: C.M. Parker, 32 pp.
      Publishes a school text for "pupils of intermediate and grammar grades," intended as the best and cheapest supplementary reading. Contains an elementary biography (16 pp.) and selections "London in the Plague," with brief introduction and questions (6 pp.), and "The Raft" from <u>Robinson Crusoe</u> (11 pp.). Observes in the biography that of his more than 250 works, only the <u>History of the Great Plague</u> and <u>Robinson Crusoe</u> are worth knowing.

4   CLAYTON, HERBERT B. "The Last Male Descendant of Daniel Defoe." <u>Notes and Queries</u>, 9th ser. 7, no. 177 (18 May):395.
      See 1901.8.

5   DAVIDSON, FRANK S. <u>Robinson Crusoe Dramatized by Frank S. Davidson</u>. [n.p.], 54 pp.
      The first two acts of this dramatization bring Crusoe together with assorted characters who have no counterparts whatsoever in the original story. The father of Annie Blythe, "the pet of the port," tries to coax her into marrying the wealthy shipbuilder, Felix Blackthorn, instead of Robinson Crusoe. Xury does make an appearance in act 2 on board Crusoe's ship. In the third and final act, Crusoe has been living on the island for twenty-eight years, but he now has Annie on his mind. In one scene Friday enters the cave and narrates how "Massa" rescued him. The play concludes with the happy reunion of Robin and Annie.

6   H., A. "The Last Male Descendant of Daniel Defoe." <u>Notes and Queries</u>, 9th ser. 7, no. 166 (2 March):177 and no. 177 (18 May):395.

Continues the information of Defoe descendants; some taken from Lee's Defoe (1869) prove incorrect. See 1901.8.

7   HALE, EDWARD EVERETT. "From Edward Everett Hale." Outlook 69, no. 14 (7 December):876-78.
Lists the qualities he expects in books for children, including both Robinson Crusoe and The Swiss Family Robinson, personally preferring the former, but recognizing the latter as "the most popular book with children."

8   HIBGAME, FREDERICK T. "The Last Male Descendant of Daniel Defoe." Notes and Queries, 9th ser. 7, no. 162 (2 February):86.
Identifies James William Defoe. See also 1901.4, 6, 10-11, 14.

9   HOWELLS, W.D. "Some Nineteenth-Century Heroines in the Eighteenth Century." In Heroines of Fiction. New York and London: Harper & Brothers, pp. 2-5.
Derives nineteenth-century fiction from Defoe "in some things that are best in it, especially in that voluntary naturalness and instructed simplicity which are the chiefest marks of modernity." Places him with Zola; ranks him higher and more modern as an artist than Fielding or Richardson. Yet he cannot be used to begin the study of nineteenth-century heroines "because of his matter, and not because of his manner or motive."
Reprinted: 1903.

10   KING, CHARLES. "The Last Male Descendant of Daniel Defoe." Notes and Queries, 9th ser. 7, no. 172 (13 April):297; and no. 177 (18 May):395.
Makes corrections to 1901.6, 8. Quotes the article "The Last of the Defoes" in the Sketch of 27 September 1893 about the Daniel Defoe who attended Christ's Church Blue Coat School and became a sailor; he died at the age of twenty-two, in 1896, in San Francisco.

11   M.A. OXON. "The Last Male Descendant of Daniel Defoe." Notes and Queries, 9th ser. 7, no. 172 (13 April):297-98.
See 1901.8.

12   SCHNEIDER, ARNO. "Die Entwickelung des Seeromans in England im 17. und 18. Jahrhundert." Inaugural-dissertation, Leipzig University; Leipzig: Druck von August Pries, pp. 12-26.
In this slim study of the "novel of the sea," Defoe merits a chapter, the conclusion of which is to place him on the boundary between this "genre" and that of the "adventure novel."
(P.E.C.)

13   STRAUCH, PHILIPP. Review of Ullrich's Robinson und Robinsonaden. Anzeiger fuer deutsches Altertum und deutsche Literatur 27:245-48.

Laudatory, though critical of high-priced format and dearth of information on locations of hard-to-find items.   (P.E.C.)

14   SWEETING, W.D. "The Last Male Descendant of Daniel Defoe." Notes and Queries, 9th ser. 7, no. 172 (13 April):298.
Corrects the name of the village where the Foes lived: Etton, in the county of Northamptonshire. See 1901.8.

1902

1   BARNARD, GEORGE W.G. "Pedigree of the Family of Cruso." Genealogist, n.s. 18:246-52.
Makes no mention of Defoe's famous character; in each listing the name is spelled without a final "e." A considerable number of persons named "Cruso" lived in the Norwich area.

2   "Chronicle and Comment." Bookman 16 (October):107-9.
Brings together critical comment on Robinson Crusoe from a recent issue of the Academy (1902.18): the true mystery of the book as being its "unique affinity" between Defoe's mind, the chance subject of the castaway, and its readers being adults whose interests are defined by the beliefs and traits of Crusoe himself. Uses an unidentified source in the Biographie universelle (1854.9) to repeat "a delightful story" of Madame de Talleyrand's mistaking her dinner guest, the famous Egyptologist Denon, for Robinson Crusoe. Versions of this anecdote appear also in 1816.7; 1853.15; 1870.24.

3   CLARKE, WM. A. "Robinson Crusoe." Notes and Queries, 9th ser. 9, no. 212 (18 January):48.
Continues noting textual discrepancies in early editions of Robinson Crusoe, as in his 1889.6. Now calls attention to "dispatched" in the first edition, "disputed" in later editions; changes in the frontispiece of the fifth edition, 1720. Seeks communication.

4   DIXON, RONALD. "Defoe at Tooting." Notes and Queries, 9th ser. 9, no. 225 (19 April):318; and "Defoe." Notes and Queries, 9th ser. 10, no. 237 (12 July):32.
Confirms 1902.12 that Defoe did not live at Tooting-Graveney in 1688 or at any other time in his career. In the second note, quotes a notice of the death of Miss Mary Ann Defoe of Croydon, the last lineal descendant of Defoe. See also 1902.9.

5   HENDERSON, JOHN. Pantomime Robinson Crusoe and His Adventures. London: Roberts & Newton, 23 pp.
Presents familiar characters, such as Crusoe and Atkins, on the island of Juan Fernandez, following an exotic story line.

6   MÉLIÈS, GEORGES. Director of film (French). Robinson Crusoe. See Filmographic Dictionary of World Literature.

7   MILLAR, J[OHN] H[EPBURN]. <u>The Mid-Eighteenth Century</u>. Peri-
     ods of European Literature, 9. New York: Charles Scribner's
     Sons, pp. 127-28, 143-47, 157, 313, 317.
          Dismisses quickly the life and career of "this arrant dou-
     ble dealer." States that Defoe "stands outside the main line of
     development followed by the English novel." In <u>Robinson Crusoe</u>,
     emphasizes the plainness of narrative and use of details to cre-
     ate "an illusion of absolute veracity"; still accepts the work as
     an allegory of the author's self. In the other novels, singles
     out "crime or vice, or both" as the strikingly different subject-
     matter. While he notes similarities to Bunyan, particularly his
     <u>Mr. Badman</u>, nevertheless regards Defoe mainly as a journalist,
     even a "gutter journalist," who wrote only for the market, and
     his "view of life" <u>bourgeois</u> and "his moral code . . . of no very
     lofty order."

8   MOULTON, CHARLES WELLS, ed. "Daniel Defoe / 1661?-1731."
     In <u>The Library of Literary Criticism of English and American</u>
     <u>Authors</u>. Buffalo, N.Y.: Moulton, 3:22-51.
          Includes fairly long extracts from numerous older works
     difficult to locate as well as briefer "personal" items which are
     mainly biographical.

9   PAGE, JOHN T. "Defoe." <u>Notes and Queries</u>, 9th ser. 10,
     no. 242 (16 August):137-38.
          In reply to 1902.4, cites a newspaper notice concerning
     Defoe's descendants through his daughter Sophia and Henry Baker.

10   PERRY, BLISS. <u>A Study of Prose Fiction</u>. Boston and New York:
     Houghton, Mifflin & Co., pp. 161-62, 184, 189, 212, 232.
          Offers critical observations on the rare use of "natural
     scenery" (before Rousseau) in a Stevenson-like passage of <u>Captain</u>
     <u>Singleton</u>; an imagination focussed upon "things as they are"; a
     special public shared with Stockton; and <u>Roxana</u>, "an absolutely
     realistic exposition of the sober, terribly earnest, Protestant
     theme that the wages of sin is death." Reprinted: 1920.

11   POE, EDGAR ALLAN. <u>The Complete Works of Edgar Allan Poe</u>.
     Edited by James A. Harrison. Croxley Edition. New York:
     Society of French & English Literature, 1:383-92; 3:259-72;
     8:234-35; 10:119-21, 123, 218; 11:7, 205; 16:183; 17:341-42.
          For Poe's critical comments on Defoe, see 1836.9-10;
     1841.10-11; 1843.5; 1844.4; 1848.1. For his letter to Evert A.
     Duyckinck, dated 8 March 1849, see <u>The Letters of Edgar Allan</u>
     <u>Poe</u>, ed. John Ward Ostrom (Cambridge, Mass.: Harvard University
     Press, 1948), 2:433-34: on his "Von Kempelen and His Discovery"
     as written "in the plausible or verisimilar style" for the delib-
     erate purpose of deceiving readers, as compared with <u>Mrs. Veal</u>
     and <u>Robinson Crusoe</u>, written in the same style, but for different
     purposes. See especially Burton R. Pollin, "Poe and Daniel De-
     foe: A Significant Relationship," <u>Topic: 30</u> 16 (1976):3-22, for
     an examination of Poe's developing concept of "verisimilitude."

12   R., S.K. "Defoe at Tooting." Notes and Queries, 9th ser. 9,
      no. 220 (15 March):207.
         On the tradition that Defoe lived at Tooting-Graveney
      around 1688 and formed the first Nonconformist congregation
      there: no supporting evidence can be found, including Morden's
      History of Tooting-Graveney (1897). See also 1902.4.

13   ROBBINS, ALFRED F. "Defoe and the St. Vincent Eruption of
      1718." Notes and Queries, 9th ser. 9, no. 233 (14 June):461-
      62.
         Provides ample evidence that Defoe's account of the volcan-
      ic eruptions and complete disappearance of the island of St. Vin-
      cent, given in Mist's Journal for 5 July 1718, was not invented,
      but factual.

14   ROSCOE, E[DWARD] S[TANLEY]. Robert Harley, Earl of Oxford,
      Prime Minister 1710-1714: A Study of Politics and Letters in
      the Age of Anne. London: Methuen & Co., pp. 40, 49-74, 78-
      79, 99, 101, 129-32, 149-51, 160-61, 186-87.
         For the first time, makes use of the Harley Papers (now
      published as part of the Portland Papers by the Historical Manu-
      scripts Commission) to describe the relationship between Defoe
      and Robert Harley from 1703 to 1714. Adds considerable new
      information: corrected date for Defoe's release from Newgate
      (November, 1703, rather than August, 1704); his participation in
      parliamentary battles against the bill to prevent occasional con-
      formity or against the Schism Bill; his actions in major events
      such as those leading to the union with Scotland. Acknowledges
      principal creative roles for Defoe in designing Harley's "intel-
      ligence" system, and in starting the South Sea Scheme. Assesses
      the collaboration of the two men as being "business-like" and
      especially beneficial to Harley.

15   SCHOTT, EMIL. "Der erste deutsche Uebersetzer des Robinson--
      ein Kind des württembergischen Schwarzwaldes." Aus dem
      Schwarzwald 9:176-78, 194-96.
         Continues the interest in Ludwig Friedrich Vischer, the
      first German translator of Robinson Crusoe, begun by Kippenberg
      (1892.8) and Biltz (1893.2). Presents here the little that could
      be learned about his fellow native Swabian, in an address to the
      Antiquarian Society of Cannstatt.   (P.E.C.)

16   [TRENT, WILLIAM PETERFIELD.] "Defoe, Daniel (c.1661-1731)."
      In The New International Encyclopaedia. Edited by Daniel Coit
      Gilman, Harry Thurston Peck and Frank Moore Colby. New York:
      Dodd, Mead & Co., 5:750.
         At still an early stage of his researches into the biogra-
      phy and canon, presents here a conventional summary, without the
      force of his later theory (namely, that Defoe steadily deterio-
      rated in character because of his experience in the pillory) and
      without the breadth he would later achieve. See also 1914.13.
      Reprinted: 1904, 1905, 1906, 1907, 1909, 1911.

17 ULLRICH, HERMANN, ed. Introduction to <u>Die Insel Felsenburg</u>
    <u>von Johann Gottfried Schnabel</u>. <u>Erster Theil (1731)</u>. Deutsche
    Litteraturdenkmale des 18. und 19. Jahrhunderts, nos. 108-20,
    n.s. nos. 58-70. Berlin: B. Behr, pp. iii-liv.
         Explains what is characteristic, what is unique about
    <u>Robinson Crusoe</u>, hitting upon many aspects that were later to
    be examined in depth by other scholars (economic, religious,
    social, political). Explores the external and internal sources
    of the Robinson material; sees in the novel several telling
    parallels to Defoe's autobiography, which he feels are more
    important than the external influences for that aura of verisi-
    militude the work exhibits. Traces five probable literary in-
    fluences on Schnabel's <u>Insel Felsenburg</u> (excluding Defoe's work),
    all of which this novel surpasses in most respects. Compares
    the religious element in Defoe's and Schnabel's famous novels,
    and its relationship to sensual elements. Provides additional
    information concerning <u>Insel Felsenburg</u> and its author Schnabel.
                                                       (P.E.C.)

18 W., W. "Robinson Crusoe." <u>Academy and Literature</u> 63,
    no. 1579 (9 August):159-60.
         Takes the occasion of reviewing the World's Classics edi-
    tion of <u>Robinson Crusoe</u> to reassess its current status as a liter-
    ary work. Considers the authorship of the book and its place of
    writing as no longer mysteries. Regards the work and its success
    as still mysterious--as continuing to defy any relationship to
    "some sort of literary process." Admits to being baffled by "the
    unique autocracy of the book" and by its solitary genius. Views
    <u>Robinson Crusoe</u>, compared with the other novels, as inferior "in
    mere range over human feeling"; agrees with William Minto and
    Leslie Stephen as to Defoe's limited artistic intention and
    achievement in Part One of <u>Robinson Crusoe</u>. Extends the mystery
    of <u>Robinson Crusoe</u> through considering its broad appeal, as Gil-
    don predicted, to "poor, world-wrecked people." Quoted heavily
    in 1902.2.

19 WHEATLEY, HENRY B. "Coleridge's Marginalia in a Copy of <u>Robin-</u>
    <u>son Crusoe</u>." <u>Hampstead Annual</u>, pp. 98-107.
         Lamb's comment does apply here: Coleridge returns bor-
    rowed books "with usury; enriched with annotations tripling their
    value." In Henry Gilman's copy of <u>Robinson Crusoe</u>, 1812.5, are
    the marginalia which were first reproduced in 1836.4, according
    to Raysor, "with the usual garblings." Mistakenly believes
    that the marginalia had not previously been published. Praises
    highly the "real addition to our knowledge of Coleridge's
    opinions," and asserts a preference of Defoe over Swift. Re-
    printed: <u>Coleridge's Miscellaneous Criticism</u>, ed. Thomas Middle-
    ton Raysor (Cambridge, Mass.: Harvard University Press, 1936),
    pp. 292-300.

1902-1904

1   HAZLITT, WILLIAM. The Collected Works of William Hazlitt.
     Edited by A.R. Waller and Arnold Glover. 12 vols. London:
     J.M. Dent & Co.; New York: McClure, Phillips & Co., 4:277,
     334; 5:13-15; 6:50, 413; 10:355-85, 431-33; 12:142, 400, 403.
     Reprints of 1818.2; 1821.2; 1825.1; 1827.1; 1830.2-3.

1903

1   AITKEN, GEORGE A. Introduction to Later Stuart Tracts. In
     An English Garner. Edited by Edward Arber. 12 vols. West-
     minster: Archibald Constable & Co., 8:vii-xxix.
         Makes selections, from the works of Sir William Petty, John
     Arbuthnot, and Defoe. For Defoe, reprints items in An English
     Garner, vol. 2 (1879.1) and vol. 7 (1883.3), and places emphasis
     upon the Review as "the forerunner of all political reviews of
     to-day"; the Essay upon Projects as showing the influence of
     Petty's Political Arithmetic (1690); and the "masterly" Appeal to
     Honour and Justice as shedding light upon some of the pamphlets
     being reprinted. Includes also such rare items as The History of
     the Kentish Petition (1701). Adds the preface to vol. 8 of the
     Review, reprinted for the first time.

2   GOSSE, EDMUND, and GARNETT, RICHARD. English Literature: An
     Illustrated Record. 4 vols. New York: Grosset & Dunlop,
     3:252-58.
         Treats Defoe and Mandeville as writers who were "kept out-
     side the sacred ring of the Anne wits." Manages to convey a
     remarkable bias against Defoe for his "vulgarization of English"
     in the earlier non-fictional writings. Recognizes the freshness
     of Robinson Crusoe on its first appearances and its greater influ-
     ence upon French than English writers, compared with the almost
     furtive status in England of Defoe's "bourgeois romances." Con-
     tains a number of biographical misconceptions.

3   JESSUP, ALEXANDER, and CANBY, HENRY SEIDEL, eds. "The Appari-
     tion of Mrs. Veal." In The Book of the Short Story. New York
     and London: D. Appleton & Co., pp. 191, 195-96.
         Classifies the Mrs. Veal [mistakenly] as one of "the gen-
     eral realistic type" of short stories written in the eighteenth
     century "which attempt to make fiction appear to be fact." In an
     earlier listing of "representative tales and short stories," in-
     cludes "The Destruction of the Isle of St. Vincent" (1718), the
     stories in A System of Magic (1726), and the "ghost stories" in
     An Essay on the History and Reality of Apparitions (1727).

4   LAMB, CHARLES. The Works of Charles and Mary Lamb. Edited by
     E.V. Lucas. 7 vols. New York: G.P. Putnam's Sons; London:
     Methuen & Co., 1:127-32, 280-83, 325-27, 523-24; 5:67-70, 123.
     Reprinting of 1807.2; 1811.2; 1825.2-3; 1830.4-6.

5   LUBIN, STEGMUND. Robinson Crusoe (film).
       Listed in Howard Lamarr Walls, Motion Pictures 1894-1912
   (Washington, D.C.: Library of Congress, 1953), p. 52.

6   MAYNADIER, G.H., ed. Introduction to Captain Singleton. In
   The Works of Daniel Defoe. 16 vols. New York: Thomas Y.
   Crowell, 6:vii-xiv.
       Notes the resemblances between Defoe's works, The King of
   Pirates: Being an Account of the Famous Enterprises of Captain
   Avery and Robinson Crusoe, on the one hand, and Captain Single-
   ton, on the other. Finds little variety in Singleton's piracies.
   Praises Defoe's advanced knowledge of Africa's geography, and his
   skill in character-drawing with Quaker William, but the other
   characters generally remain "wooden." Reprinted: Freebooters
   and Buccaneers: Novels of Adventure and Piracy (New York: Dial
   Press, 1935), pp. vii-xiv.

7   _____, ed. Introduction to Memoirs of a Cavalier. In Works
   of Daniel Defoe, 5:ix-xxiii.
       Concentrates the discussion on the question of authorship
   which arose in the preface to the first edition with the "editor's" claim of a manuscript base for the Memoirs, and continued
   in the undated second edition of Leeds with the publisher's
   identification of the author with Andrew Newport, Esq., second
   son to Richard Newport, of High Ercall. In the 1792 edition, the
   name "Newport" became a part of the title. Concludes that the
   social class represented in the Memoirs, although a higher one
   than that of any other novel, nevertheless remains within Defoe's
   range. Rejects the possibility of a manuscript base, certainly
   not for the second part dealing with the Cavalier's own country;
   and finds that all questions can be answered by assuming that
   Defoe wrote the Memoirs.

8   _____, ed. Introduction to Moll Flanders and Appeal to Honour
   and Justice. In Works of Daniel Defoe, 7:vii-xv.
       Conveys a high critical regard for Moll Flanders as the
   Defoe character who, with the possible exception of Roxana, comes
   closest to having "the life and individuality of the people created by our great novelists." Finds in her characterization "more
   psychological interest and more imagination" than is usually the
   case with Defoe's fictions. While she takes on serious vices,
   she never steps outside the range of "our sympathy." Claims that
   Defoe falls short of Fielding in producing "the English novel of
   real life"; in Moll Flanders he shows qualities "unfortunately
   rare" in his fiction. On the Appeal to Honour and Justice
   (1715): explains Defoe's political stance, and incidentally
   criticizes Defoe severely, not for his support of ministerial
   policy, but for "his underhand method." Calls attention to the
   style here in describing the relationship to Harley.

9   _____, ed. Introduction to Mr. Duncan Campbell. In Works of
   Daniel Defoe, 4:xi-xxi.

Assigns to Defoe the History of the Life and Adventures of Mr. Duncan Campbell (1720), but rejects A Spy upon the Conjuror (1724), The Dumb Projector (1725), the second part of The Friend-ly Demon (1726), and Secret Memoirs of the Late Mr. Duncan Camp-bell (1732). Although reprinted here, A Remarkable Passage of an Apparition was probably supplied by Defoe, but written by the Reverend John Ruddle, first published in 1720. Until recently, it was attributed to Defoe.

10   ____, ed. Introduction to Robinson Crusoe (three parts). In Works of Daniel Defoe, 1:ix-xxviii.
As the general introduction to the works, summarizes cur-rent biographical information and assesses the narratives, in particular Robinson Crusoe. Takes a strong negative attitude on Defoe's alleged vulgarity. On the novels: places Robinson Crusoe among the picaresque novels, and praises it for its ex-pressions of weariness with civilization and (in Part One) "the intense reality of its scenes." Finds that the characters lack individuality mainly because they lack emotions, and that there-fore critics do not always regard his fictions as novels. Al-though Defoe's stories have a compelling interest for their "humble realism," we turn to Fielding for the novel as "a lit-erary form unsurpassed for picturing actual life."

11   MONTAGUE, F.C. "War of the Succession in Spain, January, 1833: Note on the Essay." In Thomas Babington Macaulay, Critical and Historical Essays Contributed to the Edinburgh Review. 3 vols. New York: G.P. Putnam's Sons; London: Methuen & Co., 1:483-84.
In his review of Lord Mahon's History of the War of the Succession in Spain (1832), Macaulay does not mention Defoe. Macaulay's account of the war was "incorrect in outline as well as in detail," and his hero "little better than an impostor." He drew information about the war from a work he regarded as authentic, Capt. George Carleton, first published under the title Memoirs of an English Officer (1728) and republished as recently as 1809 in Sir Walter Scott's edition. At no time was Defoe as-sociated with Capt. George Carleton as the author until Wilson's Memoirs of Defoe (1830). In 1888 and again in 1891, Colonel Arthur Parnell argued the case for Swift as the author. For a summary of the authorship controversy, see Secord, 1924.20.

12   PURVES, W. LAIDLAW. "The Authorship of Robinson Crusoe," 1 and 2. Athenaeum, no. 3940 (2 May):563-64; no. 3941 (9 May): 595-96.
Pursues the argument in favor of Lord Oxford's authorship of Robinson Crusoe (vol. 1) beyond the manuscript anecdote of Thomas Warton (1788.3; 1843.2). Argues that Lord Oxford could have amused himself in writing a work like Robinson Crusoe; he could have avoided his own name and used a pseudonym; he could have used someone like Defoe to deliver the manuscript to the publisher. Cites evidence in the "0" edition of Robeson Cruso which appears to corroborate Defoe's role of editor. In section

2, moves the argument farther by demonstrating that <u>Memoirs of a</u>
<u>Cavalier</u> was published within thirteen months of <u>Robinson Crusoe</u>.
The improbability of Defoe's having written an incredibly large
number of pages becomes reduced if we accept his own statements
that in these two works, <u>Robinson Crusoe</u> and <u>Memoirs of a Cava-</u>
<u>lier</u>, he was only the editor, and not the author.

13   _____. "The 'O' Edition of <u>Robeson Cruso</u>," 1 and 2. <u>Athen-</u>
   <u>aeum</u>, no. 3937 (11 April):465-66; no. 3938 (18 April):498.
      Identifies as a unique edition of <u>Robeson Cruso</u> the one
having a title page with the name spelled as here; lists and
analyzes a selection of textual changes from the first fourteen
pages of Taylor's first edition; argues that the changes made
from the "O" edition were not made by a pirate, but by an author
or editor, and that the unique copy of the "O" edition was therefore run on the press of one of Defoe's journals before or after
its acceptance for publication by William Taylor. See also
1903.12, 14; 1913.17-20; Hutchins's, <u>"Robinson Crusoe" and Its</u>
<u>Printing</u> (1925), pp. 167-82.

14   Review of Purves's "The 'O' Edition of <u>Robeson Cruso</u>," 1903.
   <u>Bibliographer</u> 2, no. 5 (May):351-52.
      Summarizes Purves's evidence (1903.13) that the <u>Robeson</u>
<u>Cruso</u> or "O" edition was the first.

15   [STEPHEN, LESLIE.] "Defoe, Daniel (1661?-1731)." In <u>The Dic-</u>
   <u>tionary of National Biography. The Concise Dictionary, Part</u>
   <u>I</u>. Reprint. London: Oxford University Press, 1961, p. 330.
      Epitomizes 1888.20. Corrections were made in the 1953
impression. See also the three revisions in <u>Corrections and Addi-</u>
<u>tions to the Dictionary of National Biography</u> (Boston: G.K. Hall
& Co., 1966), p. 57. Reprinted: 1906; 1920; 1924; 1925; 1930;
1938; 1942; 1948; 1953.

16   ULLRICH, HERMANN. "Zur Textgeschichte von Defoes <u>Robinson</u>
   <u>Crusoe</u>." <u>Archiv für das Studium der neueren Sprachen und</u>
   <u>Litteraturen</u> 111, nos. 1/2:93-105.
      Corrects J. Storm's faulty scholarship on Defoe's use of
language (in <u>Englische Philologie</u>, 2d ed., 1892 and 1896), since
it was based on insufficient bibliographical information. Disputes notion that Defoe had to search long and hard for a publisher of <u>Robinson Crusoe</u>, and that the publisher William Taylor
dealt with material of inferior quality. Makes a close comparison of three passages from the first four Taylor editions, along
with seven newer ones and a facsimile, to ascertain which (if
any) should be exclusively consulted in investigating Defoe's use
of language. Posits the existence of more than one version of
the first edition. Decides that no single edition should be used
in researching the language; rather, an ecclectic approach, along
with comparisons to Defoe's other writings, will give a better
picture. None of the newer editions was found to follow such a
method, and hence none deserved to be called philologically
definitive.   (P.E.C.)

17 WAGNER, H[ERMANN] F. Robinson und die Robinsonaden in unserer Jugendliteratur. Literaturgeschichtliche Studie. Vienna: [Author], 20 pp.

A true juvenile literature exists only since the time of the Enlightenment. It is a useful cultural yardstick, but was ignored by scholarship in Germany until the 1880's. Comments on the reception of Robinson Crusoe in Germany from the time of Bodmer and Breitinger (1720's) to more recent times. The book was read by youthful contemporaries of Goethe even before the efforts of Rousseau and Campe. In Adelung's Leipziger Wochenblatt für Kinder (1773-1775), Defoe was reported to have betrayed Selkirk's trust, which alleged misdeed served as ample grounds for the pedagogues to cleanse and reorient Defoe's text to their good purposes. Offers a glimpse into the Wezel-Campe rivalry in their competing adaptations of Defoe's work. Compares their motivations and methods. Explores the continuation of Wezel's and (more commonly) Campe's work by others. Retraces the pedagogical discussion as to the role and value of Robinson Crusoe as children's literature and in the schools. Traces juvenile literature of more or less Robinsonian character through James Fennimore Cooper up to Karl May, with special attention to what was appearing in Austria.   (P.E.C.)

18 WEBSTER, DANIEL. "The Dignity and Importance of History, February 23, 1852." In The Writings and Speeches of Daniel Webster. Vol. 13, Addresses on Various Occasions Hitherto Uncollected, vol. 1. Boston: Little, Brown & Co., p.480.

In an address before the New York Historical Society: gives the example of Defoe among English prose writers who have "the same skill" to write powerfully as poets like Thomas Gray. "No boy doubts that everything told of Robinson Crusoe is exactly true, because all is so circumstantially told." Recalls his own "distress and perspiration" when, at the age of about ten, he read of Crusoe's plight in trying to manoeuvre the boat within the currents. On the Journal of the Plague Year: "No man doubts, until he is informed of the contrary, that the historian of the plague of London actually saw all that he described, although De Foe was not born until a subsequent year." Generalizes that both true and fictitious history should make "skillful use of circumstance."

1903-1906

1 ARBER, EDWARD, ed. The Term Catalogues, 1668-1709. 3 vols. London: Privately printed, 3:742 pp.

Records rare bibliographical information on authors, titles, and publishers, as well as year and month of publication, from the contemporary serials Mercurius Librarius and Catalogues of Books, for the years 1668-1682 in vol. 1, 1683-1696 in vol. 2, and 1697-1709 in vol. 3. Indexes the term catalogues--"quarterly Advertising Sheet[s] of New Books and

Reprints"--for varied works related to English literature. From
this vast storehouse of new information, draws conclusions in
the preface, on contemporaries such as Charles Leslie, or on
the books that were popular (voyages and travels). In vol. 3,
assigns to Defoe twenty-six individual works generally acknowledged to be his, and three works no longer acknowledged as his
(e.g., History of Addresses); identifies also six works that are
"answers" to Defoe or attacks on him.

1903–1908

1   RUSKIN, JOHN. The Works of John Ruskin. Edited by E.T. Cook
     and Alexander Wedderburn. Library Edition. 39 vols.
     London: George Allen; New York: Longmans, Green, & Co.,
     1904, 12:536; 1905, 19:138-40; 1907, 27:167, 28:170, 199,
     673-74, 29:590; 1908, 35:13.
         See entries 1851.18; 1866.10; 1871.13; 1874.6; 1876.10;
     1885.10; 1907.18.

1904

1   COLLINS, FRANCIS ARNOLD. "Robinson Crusoe's Island (Two Hun-
     dred Years Later)." St. Nicholas 31, no. 6 (April):499-505.
         Compares places such as "the cave" and "the lookout" on
     Juan Fernandez as they are described on Crusoe's island; finds
     impressive similarities. Summarizes Selkirk's story as told by
     Dampier and Rogers, and quotes liberally from Robinson Crusoe.

2   CONWAY, MONCURE D. "My Hawthorne Experience." Critic 45,
     no. 1 (July):21-25. Reprint. Hawthorne Among His Contempo-
     raries. Edited by Kenneth Walter Cameron. Hartford, Conn.:
     Transcendental Books, 1966, p. 482.
         Retells in more expanded form the anecdote first told in
     1869.2. Specifies now that the time was "not long after the
     dread outbreak of war," and that Hawthorne talked "rather volubly
     of Defoe and belief in ghosts" and asked about "the negro ghost-
     lore in Virginia."

*2-b COOPER, NASARVANJI MANECJI. See p. 399.

3   COWPER, WILLIAM. "Robinson on His Island." In Robinson Cru-
     soe for Boys and Girls. Adapted by Lida B. McMurray and Mary
     Hall Husted. Rev. ed.; Bloomington, Ill.: Public School
     Publishing Co., 1923, pp. 120-21.
         The title of Cowper's poem has been unwarrantably changed
     from "Verses Supposed to Be Written by Alexander Selkirk during
     His Solitary Abode in the Island of Juan Fernandez," showing the
     identification of Selkirk with Robinson Crusoe. Cowper's fourth
     stanza on "Religion" has also been omitted.

4   DALTON, CHARLES, ed. English Army Lists and Commission
    Registers, 1661-1714. 6 vols. London: Eyre & Spottis-
    woode. Reprint. London: Francis Edwards, 1960, 6:vii-viii,
    268.
        Calls attention to the name Daniel Defoe listed as "Capt.-
    Lieut." in Colonel John Desbordes's Regiment of Dragoons, accord-
    ing to a "List of Half-Pay Officers," 1714, found at the War
    Office. Claims (for the first time) that this person was the
    famous author, and that he may never have joined the regiment in
    Portugal. Records that Defoe's name appears on a similar list
    for 1722. See also 1905.5.

5   _____, ed. Introduction to A Journal of the Plague Year. In
    Works of Daniel Defoe, 9:ix-xii.
        Taking advantage of the earlier date assigned to Defoe's
    birth, argues that in 1665 he was old enough to experience and
    remember the deep sense of gloom which filled the city. Re-
    gards the Journal as "a remarkable fabric of fact and fiction,"
    based on Defoe's own recollections of the experience itself
    and the stories he heard as he grew up. Stresses that the
    Journal was the most "artistic" of all Defoe's narratives be-
    cause it had the "easy" unity which subject matter provides,
    as in Robinson Crusoe. In the appendix, quotes extracts from
    contemporary writers on the plague (Hodges, Vincent, Boghurst,
    Allin, Pepys, Evelyn) to show that Defoe did not exaggerate the
    gloom.

6   _____, ed. Introduction to A New Voyage Round the World.
    In Works of Daniel Defoe, 14:vii-ix.
        As the last of the "largely imaginative" stories Defoe
    would write, the New Voyage Round the World (1724) shows almost
    no interest in character, but relies on incidents related in
    Defoe's manner. He made use of old material "in substantially
    the same old way." Reprinted: Freebooters and Buccaneers:
    Novels of Adventure and Piracy (New York: Dial Press, 1935),
    pp. vii-ix.

7   MAYNADIER, G.H., ed. Introduction to Colonel Jack, the True-
    born Englishman, and the Shortest-Way with the Dissenters. In
    Works of Daniel Defoe, 10:vii-xviii.
        Asks why Colonel Jack continued to be popular as late as
    1748 (Smollett's Roderick Random, chap. 62) or even today. The
    story seems no more than an "inorganic tale of the simplest
    kind"; the main character, quite unattractive. Launches into the
    severe criticism of Colonel Jack as being like thousands of to-
    day's "clever, prosy, cold-blooded business-men," and of Defoe as
    "the Yankee trader of the Queen Anne writers." The popularity
    may be owing to the Colonel's "successful trading" or to the
    "circumstantial vividness" of the narrative. Unsurpassed in the
    eyes of everyone is the sympathetic first part dealing with the
    neglected young thief.

8   _____, ed. Introduction to Due Preparations for the Plague,
     and other writings. In Works of Daniel Defoe, 15:ix-xvi.
          Although Due Preparations for the Plague was not listed by
     Lee as being by Defoe, he was definitely the author, but it is
     not known whether it was published before or after the Journal
     of the Plague Year. Clearly it reads like a continuation of the
     Journal, and has the same "public-spirited motives," but one
     should not discount "the shrewd commercial sense "of publishing
     two works on a current issue like the plague. The other writings
     introduced here are The Dumb Philosopher (1719), about a totally
     unknown person named Dickory Cronke; Mrs. Veal, where Aitken's
     discoveries (1895.2) concerning the diminished use of "inventive
     powers" are assessed; and "The Destruction of the Isle of St. Vin-
     cent" (1718), which may be all Defoe's invention.

9   _____, ed. Introduction to seven accounts of notorious con-
     temporary criminals. In Works of Daniel Defoe, 16:ix-xiii.
          Introduces graphically written accounts which are reprinted
     in this volume: The King of Pirates (1719), An Account of the
     Cartoucheans in France (1724), The History of the Remarkable Life
     of John Sheppard (1724), A Narrative of All the Robberies, Es-
     capes, &c. of John Sheppard (1724), The Life and Actions of the
     Late Jonathan Wild (1725), Adventures of Captain John Gow (1725),
     Lives of Six Notorious Street-Robbers (1726). Disagrees with
     Lee; believes the purpose of the pamphlets was "to catch pennies"
     rather than "to save souls." The Lives of the Six Notorious Rob-
     bers was not assigned to Defoe by Lee; it has all the "internal
     evidence" of being "almost certainly Defoe's." Reprinted: Free-
     booters and Buccaneers: Novels of Adventure and Piracy (New
     York: Dial Press, 1935), pp. ix-xiii.

10   _____, ed. Introduction to The Fortunate Mistress (Roxana).
     In Works of Daniel Defoe, 12:vii-xiii.
          Judges Roxana to be closer to a novel than Moll Flanders be-
     cause more of its characters are "real": the Prince, Quakeress,
     Dutch Merchant, "unfortunate daughter," and especially Amy and
     Roxana. Calls attention to the only continuation (in the 1745
     edition) which has been attributed to Defoe, but demonstrates
     that although it has merit (and is reprinted here), it cannot be
     his on the evidence of stylistic differences. Expresses surprise
     that Defoe, "the vulgarest of all our great men of letters in the
     early eighteenth century," understood "a woman's heart better
     than a man's." Roxana also, on occasion, seems to be a character
     out of "a 'problem' play or novel of our day."

11   NORTHROP, W.B. "The Author of Robinson Crusoe." St. Nicholas
     31, no. 6 (April):495-99.
          A brief popularized account of Defoe's life contains some
     egregious errors, such as Defoe's being in prison when the Review
     was published simultaneously in Edinburgh and London, his theft
     of "many letters belonging to Selkirk," his travels all over
     Europe as government agent. The couplet and signature reproduced
     at the end of the article are not Defoe's "autograph."

12   ULLRICH, HERMANN. "Der Robinson-Mythus." <u>Zeitschrift für</u>
      <u>Bücherfreunde</u> 8, no. 1 (April):1-10.
            Seeks to dispell frequently cited untruths as to the author-
      ship, originality, circumstances of publication, narrative "over-
      sights," allegorical interpretation, and place of authorship of
      <u>Robinson Crusoe</u>.
                                                                    (P.E.C.)

                                    <u>1905</u>

1   BALDWIN, JAMES. "To Daniel Defoe, Esq." In <u>Robinson Crusoe</u>
      <u>Written Anew for Children</u>. New York, Cincinnati, Chicago:
      American Book Co., pp. 187-91.
            Extends the highest praise for "the harmless entertainment
      of mankind." Although "faulty" in the externals, <u>Robinson Crusoe</u>
      had "the internal quality to become a favorite of the common
      people. In writing the abridgement, the "translator" has pre-
      served the simplicity of the style.

2   BERGMEIER, F. "Ein Beitrag zur Quellenuntersuchung von Daniel
      Defoes <u>Journal of the Plague Year</u>." <u>Archiv für das Studium</u>
      <u>der neueren Sprachen und Litteraturen</u> 59, no. 114:87-91.
            Is the <u>Journal of the Plague Year</u> at all based on written
      sources? This question has never been satisfactorily answered.
      Refutes Bullen and Jusserand in their surmise that Dekker's <u>Won-</u>
      <u>derful Year</u> was a source, and suggests instead stronger resem-
      blances to <u>The Meeting of Gallants at an Ordinaire: or the</u>
      <u>Walkes in Powles</u> (1604).
                                                                    (P.E.C.)

3   DAWSON, W[ILLIAM] J[AMES]. "The Father of English Fiction."
      In <u>The Makers of English Fiction</u>. London: Hodder & Stough-
      ton, pp. 1-11.
            Explains that designating Defoe "the father of English fic-
      tion" may be uniquely appropriate because his novels first met a
      demand, as did Shakespeare's drama, for the presentation of "a
      transcript of life." In the <u>Shortest-Way with the Dissenters</u> he
      "stumbled upon the truth rather than discovered it." Following
      upon Minto, states as "the primary principle of fiction, that
      fiction is a kind of lie, and that it is useless to lie unless
      you can lie so like the truth that you are believed." Regards
      this inauspicious moment as the beginning of "modern fiction,"
      and sees its further development in the art of creating "an air
      of credibility" in <u>Mrs. Veal</u>. In <u>Robinson Crusoe</u>, the main
      appeal is "by mere truthfulness of detail in common things."
      Disputes the typical judgment which places <u>Robinson Crusoe</u> above
      the secondary novels; argues that <u>Moll Flanders</u> and <u>Roxana</u> are
      greater works, having "a unique value as human documents and
      records of contemporary life," and defends even their unsavoury
      details. Hesitates to say how far Defoe wrote these novels with
      a moral purpose; makes an important distinction: "The question
      of coarseness must not be confounded with the question of immo-
      rality." Finds Defoe's chief fault to be his "lack of discrim-

ination in incident," his habit of writing "in the spirit of a
police-court journalist." Assesses the "wonderful" later fictions with genuine enthusiasm for their scenery and analyses of
women characters. Compares Defoe with writers like Kipling whose
"power of vision" surpass "their power of artistic combination."

4   DAY, THOMAS. The History of Little Jack. In Old-Fashioned
    Tales. Edited by E.V. Lucas. London: Wells, Gardner, Dar-
    ton, pp. 1-40.
        In his "Introduction" (pp. vi-vii) Lucas discusses the ex-
    tent to which the authors of the nineteen stories collected here,
    including Thomas Day's The History of Little Jack, show "single-
    mindedness (single-mindedness in the wish to give the nursery a
    good time)." Robinson Crusoe seems to be an exception, "which
    certainly (one may urge) was not written to give the nursery a
    good time. And yet Robinson supports it too; for never was a
    book more single-mindedly conceived and written." The case for
    Robinson Crusoe is made on the grounds that Defoe aimed the story
    at the reader "with a love of adventure and circumstantial minute
    description"--a love that begins in, and never leaves, the nur-
    sery. See also 1788.2.

5   "Defoe as a Soldier." Academy 69, no. 1745 (14 October):1077.
        Traces the "internal evidence" of Defoe's knowledge of "the
    art of war" and military tactics, especially in Memoirs of a Cava-
    lier, and hails with delight the recent announcement by Charles
    Dalton [1904.4] that the Daniel Defoe listed as "captain-lieuten-
    ant" in Colonel Desborde's dragoons was indeed the famous author.

6   HILL, WILLIAM N. "Defoe: Political Economist." Tom Watson's
    Magazine (New York) 3, no. 2 (December):187-92.
        Looks upon Robinson Crusoe as "a work of profound philo-
    sophy written by one of the greatest political thinkers of the
    English-speaking race"; seeks to understand it by exploring De-
    foe's personality and career. Urges the view that Defoe, in his
    Robinson Crusoe and political essays, did pioneer work in "politi-
    cal economy." Suggests that he had an interest in "the welfare
    of the masses" and "republican proclivities." Compares Defoe as
    a prolific writer with Balzac and Dumas. Commends Colonel Jack
    for its Maryland setting and description of "the business and
    social customs of the colonial period," and hints at a connection
    between the English and American revolutions through Defoe's
    influence upon Benjamin Franklin.

7   MATHIESON, WILLIAM LAW. Scotland and Union: A History of
    Scotland from 1695 to 1747. Glasgow: James Maclehose & Sons,
    pp. 55, 135, 136-37, 158-59, 184-85, 280, 376.
        Makes use of Defoe's letters published with the Duke of
    Portland manuscripts (1897, 1899), as well as his History of the
    Union (1709), to narrate the events leading to the legislative
    Union. Quotes or refers to Defoe as an authority on support for
    the colony of Darien in 1699, the general and specific strategies

for passing articles, the behavior of "great men" posting to London just before the Union.

8   RANGER [pseud.]. "Daniel Defoe." Bookman 29, no. 170 (November):67-68, 70.
       Approaches Defoe from William Minto's perspective (1879), finding "mystification" everywhere, the novels as "by the greatest liar that ever lived," autobiographical statements always requiring verification. Has respect for Defoe's fighting spirit. Admires his achievements in journalism, essay, and novel. Concludes with an attempt to define Defoe's uniqueness as a novelist in his realism and "complete illusion"; praises the general application and "national characteristics" of Robinson Crusoe.

9   TRENT, W[ILLIAM] P. "A New Edition of Defoe." Forum 36 (April):625-34.
       In a review of G.H. Maynadier's edition (1903-1904), regrets the lack of any fairly complete reprinting of Defoe's works; surveys the editions to date and their shortcomings, and notes that the Aitken edition (1895) and the Maynadier (1902-1904) reprint the same novels and differ only slightly in the choices of other works. Favors the publication of "a cheap edition of all the products of his marvellous pen that the public can be induced to buy," but clearly perceives that for the American public the emphasis will fall upon Robinson Crusoe (Part I), Journal of the Plague Year, Moll Flanders, and Roxana. Describes the second great lack in Defoe scholarship as a satisfactory biography: one which explores fully the biographical view (which Trent will develop later) of Defoe as a person forced by hard circumstances to change morally, to grow gradually into "a consummate casuist," whose actions are at times veiled in mystery, a complex personality--definitely not the "unmitigated liar" whom Minto and others invented. See also 1913.23.

10   ULLRICH, HERMANN. Introduction to Leben und Abenteuer des Robinson Crusoe von Daniel Defoe. Neu aus dem Englischen übersetzt und mit literarhistorischer Einleitung verschen von Dr. Hermann Ullrich. Halle: Otto Hendel, pp. v-xvi.
       In [J.H. Schutt's] "Hermann Ullrich: A Bibliography" (English Studies 13 [1931]:88), this item is dated 1906. Provides a literary-critical introduction to his translation, which he claims surpasses the previous best German version by Altmüller (1869) in several respects. Includes also a summary of the work and a brief analysis of its pedagogical and religious motivations and certain symbolic features, followed by a biographical sketch. Points out common shortcomings of would-be imitators and inept interpreters of the novel. Reprinted: Bibliothek der Gesamtliteratur, nos. 1912-1915, Neuer verbesserter Abdruck (Berlin: Hillger, 1923).   (P.E.C.)

11   WATSON, THOMAS E. "Robinson Crusoe and My Insurance Policy."
      Tom Watson's Magazine (New York) 3, no. 2 (December):139-42.
            In an enigmatic editorial Watson directs heavy humor
      against Tom Ryan's Equitable insurance society. Introduces a
      certain Robinson D. Crusoe, secretary of the Southern Guarantee
      Loan Company, who writes a letter to Watson in which he asks hard
      questions about the terms of an insurance policy and the huge sur-
      plus created. In a cartoon by Gordon Nye, Crusoe is shown in his
      goatskins, on Equitable Island, watching a dirigible depart which
      has the label $80,000,000 Surplus." For Watson's bid for the
      U.S. presidency in 1904, see the Dictionary of American Biography
      (1936).

12   WELLS, CHARLES. "Defoe and Selkirk at Bristol." Academy 69,
      no. 1756 (30 December):1357-58.
            More information on the legend of a meeting by Defoe and
      Selkirk in the home of Mrs. Caysgarne, later Mrs. Daniells, St.
      James Square, Bristol. A variation of the legend, which appears
      in Seyer's Memoirs of Bristol (1823) taken from the Gentleman's
      Magazine (1787.7), has the lady giving assurances from William
      Dampier that Defoe received the Selkirk papers, and from them
      wrote Robinson Crusoe.

13   WHERRY, ALBINIA. Daniel Defoe. Bell's Miniature Series of
      Great Writers. London: George Bell & Sons, 128 pp. Reprint.
      Folcroft Library Editions, 1973.
            Four biographical chapters cover Defoe's life sketchily,
      with little or no new information and a few old errors and myths;
      tend to simplify the issues or controversies in political tracts
      selected from an "Abbreviated List" (62 items) of his works.
      More important are the five remaining chapters. In "Writings
      Economical, Social, and Didactic," makes fresh observations: for
      instance, Defoe's high regard for women in the Essay upon Pro-
      jects, "considering the character of the heroines in his novels,"
      or the individualized comments on certain places of the Tour,
      "probably no true pilgrimage, but a kind of potpouri" from many
      sources. The chapter "Various Fictitious Writings" expresses a
      strong bias against the "secondary novels," a change of taste
      since the days of Charles Lamb. Asserts that Defoe can no longer
      be accepted as "the father of the English novel" since it is not
      even certain he wrote novels. Notes "a family likeness" in
      Singleton, Roxana, Moll, and Jack: "the outcasts from a society
      system of whose sins and follies they are at once the cause and
      the result." In the chapter on "Robinson Crusoe," lavishes
      praise on the "English classic" for "the appeal it makes to the
      most deeply-rooted sentiments of the national character" and for
      its hero, "the 'True born Englishman,' no cross bred mongrel, but
      a man in whom are united the qualities of many races, Briton,
      Saxon, Norseman, and Dane." An entire chapter, next, considers
      Serious Reflections as "a philosophic treatise" which holds the
      key to the allegory of Robinson Crusoe and gives insight into the
      personality of Defoe through Crusoe's story. A final chapter

assesses "His Style," and states the current critical judgment
which views Defoe primarily as "past master" in telling lies.
Reprinted: 1910.

1906

1   BAKER, E[RNEST] A. Introduction to The Fortunes and Misfor-
    tunes of the Famous Moll Flanders: Also The Fortunate Mis-
    tress or the Lady Roxana. London: George Routledge & Sons;
    New York: E.P. Dutton & Co., pp. vii-xxiii.
       Treats more expansively, with some repetition, the same
    Zolaesque naturalism discussed in 1906.2. Claims that Moll
    Flanders and Roxana reveal "the trains of causes and effects by
    which character is moulded and transformed," operating within a
    physical universe. They prove actual social conditions. Defoe,
    like a sociologist, has Mauppassant's aim of mirroring life. The
    resemblance to the romances of roguery is only superficial, not
    genealogical. Judges Octave Mirbeau's Journal d'une femme de
    chambre to be like Moll Flanders and especially Roxana. Argues
    that Defoe had no "special intuition" into women characters. For
    Roxana, includes the sequel "by some inferior hand," found in the
    1745 edition.

2   _____. "A Literary Causerie: Defoe as Sociological Novel-
    ist." Academy 70 (26 May):502-3.
       Gives a fairly extended Zolaesque reading to Captain Single-
    ton, Moll Flanders, Roxana, and Colonel Jack. Interprets Defoe
    as "the first naturalist in modern literature," the novels as
    essentially "chapters in the natural history of the race," the
    subject of each novel "a victim of social injustice." Under
    severe scrutiny: marriage irregularities before the Hardwick Act
    (1753) in Moll Flanders; women in subjection in Roxana.

3   CHAPLIN, HOLROYD. "Defoe on the Vicar of Baddow." Notes and
    Queries, 10th ser. 5, no. 127 (2 June):428.
       Asks about the story of the vicar of Baddow, mentioned in
    Defoe's Political History of the Devil (pt. 2, chap. 4). See
    1882.9.

4   ELTON, OLIVER, ed. Frederick York Powell: A Life and a
    Selection from His Letters and Occasional Writings. 2 vols.
    Oxford: Clarendon Press, 1:261, 271-72; 2:281-97.
       Assesses Powell's essay on "Daniel Defoe," first printed
    in 1898.12. Notes how much he admired Defoe, "a bourgeois genius
    . . . the noblest Philistine that ever lived," since in general
    he detested the bourgeois and the Philistine. In a letter to
    Elton, 10 October 1899, Powell again treats an imperfect Defoe
    generously: "His novels are excellent, and exceedingly modern
    in part." He prefers him to Thackeray because he had character.

5 GARNETT, EDWARD. Preface to <u>Captain Singleton</u>. Everyman's
   Library. London: J.M. Dent & Sons, pp. vii-xiv.
      Observes that changes in taste have made <u>Captain Single-</u>
   <u>ton</u>--as well as <u>Memoirs of a Cavalier</u>, <u>Colonel Jack</u>, and <u>Moll</u>
   <u>Flanders</u>--into a little-read classic. Explains that "Defoe's
   plain and homely realism" has been judged "vulgar"; and the
   works of Defoe and Hogarth, "the two most English of Englishmen,"
   not acceptable to polite society. While critics continue to
   confuse "an artist's subject with his treatment of it," they now
   do so less confidently. Holds the view that in <u>Captain Single-</u>
   <u>ton</u> Defoe's "descriptions of 'low life' are artistically as
   perfect as any descriptions of 'higher life' in the works of
   the English novelists." Praises among other things the sense
   of "actuality" as comparable to Robert Drury's in <u>Madagascar</u>,
   the "dryly satiric" touches, Quaker William as "a masterpiece
   of shrewd humour," the second lieutenant as "worthy of Tolstoy,"
   the style as perfect as that in <u>Robinson Crusoe</u>. Reprinted:
   1922; 1951.

6 GRANDIDIER, ALFRED, and GRANDIDIER, GUILLAUME, eds. <u>Collec-</u>
   <u>tion des ouvrages anciens concernant Madagascar</u>. Vol. 4, <u>Les</u>
   <u>Aventures de Robert Drury pendant ses quinze années de capti-</u>
   <u>vité à Madagascar et son second voyage dans cette ile (1701-</u>
   <u>1717 et 1719-1720)</u>. Paris: Comité de Madagascar, 436 pp.
   passim.
      Translates into French <u>Madagascar</u> (411 pp.) from the text
   of S. Pasfield Oliver with occasional references to his notes
   (1890.15), and includes a "Malagasy vocabulary" (17 pp.) of words
   in Drury's spelling, the correct spelling, and their French translations. In the preface, while the Grandidiers show a full knowledge of <u>Madagascar</u>, its publishing history, and all the testimon-
   ials relating to the work, they also have personal information of
   the geographical area. They emphatically reject Defoe as either
   the author or editor, taking positions quite different from Lee,
   Blanchard, and Oliver; and assert an "absolute trust" in <u>Madagas-</u>
   <u>car</u> and complete acceptance of the narrator's veracity and the
   authenticity of his actions. They admit that there were "inventions" (e.g., p. 371n) added by an editor or "transcriber," but
   never refer to him as Defoe. On the Grandidiers's edition, see
   also Gove, pp. 274-75, and Arthur W. Secord, <u>Robert Drury's Jour-</u>
   <u>nal and Other Studies</u> (Urbana: University of Illinois Press,
   1961), pp. 62-71.

7 LIVINGSTONE, LUTHER S. "The Bibliophile." <u>Evening Post</u> (New
   York), 10 February.
      Responds to Purves's claim (1903.12-13) that his recently
   purchased copy of the "O" edition, entitled <u>Robeson Cruso</u>, was
   printed before the William Taylor first edition. Demonstrates
   point by point, by comparison of texts, that this "botch" of a
   printing job must have been printed from Taylor's second or later
   edition.

8   LYNN, W.T. "Robinson Crusoe's Island." Notes and Queries,
     10th ser. 6, no. 143 (22 September):225.
          Calls attention to problems in identifying Crusoe's island
     with either Juan Fernandez or Tobago.

9   "Robinson Crusoe's Island." Bookman (New York) 24 (October):
     92.
          Briefly notes the disappearance of Juan Fernandez in an
     earthquake--the scene of "probably the most dramatic single
     incident in all fiction--the finding by Crusoe of the footprint
     in the sand."

10   SECCOMBE, THOMAS. Introduction to George Borrow's L'Avengro--
     The Scholar--The Gypsy--The Priest. Everyman's Library. Lon-
     don and Toronto: J.M. Dent & Sons; New York: E.P. Dutton &
     Co., pp. xxiv-xxvi.
          Places Defoe among the "unfashionable authors" with whom
     Borrow was intimately acquainted, and describes Borrow's singular
     achievement as a modification of "old novela picaresca as modi-
     fied by Defoe." Reprinted: [frequently to] 1925.

11   SECCOMBE, THOMAS, and NICOLL, W. ROBERTSON. "Defoe." In The
     Bookman Illustrated History of English Literature. 2 vols.
     London: Hodder & Stoughton, 2:241-45, 274.
          With political concerns waning in 1719, Defoe turned the
     "power" which he had started to develop in The Storm (1704), Mrs.
     Veal (1705), and "a queer imaginary history of an earthquake in
     St. Vincent" to Robinson Crusoe. Comments: on Moll Flanders and
     Colonel Jack as "the most distinctly picaresque" and Robinson Cru-
     soe as "a national novel." Observes that "Defoe's style is a per-
     fect mirror of the most positive-minded of our writers." Later,
     argues that Robinson Crusoe, in turning the novel to "ordinary hu-
     man concern and everyday experience," reverted to the picaresque.

12   TRENT, W[ILLIAM] P. "Defoe's Tracts." Notes and Queries,
     10th ser. 6, no. 134 (21 July):47.
          In England, requests help in locating copies of seven
     tracts listed by William Lee.

13   ULLRICH, HERMANN. "Die Berechtigung einer neuen Robinson-
     übersetzung." Englische Studien 36:394-403.
          Justifies further his translation of Robinson Crusoe than
     was possible in the introduction (1905.10), taking issue with
     Karl Altmüller's edition (1869) for numerous inaccuracies and
     with A. Tuhten (1886) for her uncritical dependence on Altmüller,
     these being the only two other translations still generally avail-
     able in German. For listings of the two editions, see Ullrich's
     Robinson und Robinsonaden (p. 53).   (P.E.C.)

14   WATTS-DUNTON, THEODORE. Introduction to Captain Singleton.
     World's Classics, 82. London and New York: H. Frowde. Re-
     print. London et al.: Oxford University Press, 1924, pp. v-
     xviii.

Although ostensibly an introduction to <u>Captain Singleton</u>, ranges widely to assess the qualitative differences (and some similarities) between Defoe and Balzac (5 pp.), Godwin, Austen, Scott, Dickens, Zola; and to provide insights into Defoe's method and style, "illusion," influence, adventures which are true as contrasted with those which are fictitious, Balzac's "relative" vision compared with Shakespeare's and Defoe's "Absolute Vision," the lapses in the requirements of the "autobiographic form" as in <u>Captain Singleton</u>.

1907

1   BARNETT, P.A., ed. "Epistle Dedicatory and Explanatory." In
    G.F. Goffeaux, <u>The Story of Robinson Crusoe in Latin</u>. London:
    Longmans, Green & Co., pp. i-xii.
        Explains the practice of the Frenchman, G.F. Goffeaux, who
    discovered sixty or seventy years ago that the Latin language bet-
    ter engaged the interests of boys when used to tell the history
    of Robinson Crusoe than of Caesar, Cicero, or Virgil. Goffeaux,
    however, takes his adaptation from J.H. Campe's <u>Robinson der
    Jungere</u> rather than <u>Robinson Crusoe</u>.

2   CHANDLER, FRANK WADLEIGH. <u>The Literature of Roguery</u>. 2 vols.
    Boston and New York: Houghton, Mifflin & Co., 584 pp. passim.
        Comments significantly on Defoe's application of the "obser-
    vational method to native materials," on the increased importance
    of characterization relative to his picaresque predecessors, and
    on his advance toward the modern novel. In the eighteenth-cen-
    tury English revival of the picaresque, ranks Defoe important for
    his "naturalism and character drawing." Specifically, in the
    chapter on Defoe (16 pp.), judges that Robinson Crusoe lacks any
    definite character, spiritual conflicts, or ethical development.
    Slightly in <u>Robinson Crusoe</u>, emphatically in <u>Captain Singleton</u>,
    Defoe was drawn to "the romantic side of roguery." Focuses upon
    Defoe's three major picaresque novels: deals with <u>Roxana</u>, in
    which the characters are found to be psychologically deficient,
    the incidents dominant; with <u>Colonel Jack</u>, in which interest in
    character begins to emerge; and finally with the picaresque
    triumph, <u>Moll Flanders</u>, in which he significantly sets himself
    apart from his picaresque forebearers: ". . . Defoe at a blow
    changed a comic and satirical fiction to one, in some sense, of
    character."

3   CHRISTY, MILLER. "Brick-Making and Tile-Making," in chapter
    on "Industries." In <u>Essex</u>. Victoria Histories of the Coun-
    ties of England. Edited by William Page. [London]: Archi-
    bald Constable. Reprint. University of London, Institute of
    Historical Research. William Dawson & Sons, 1977, 2:456.
        Summarizes information on Defoe's association with a com-
    pany, first as secretary and then as proprietor, formed to manu-
    facture bricks and pantiles at Tilbury. Wrongly gives the date
    1701 for the start of the company, instead of 1696.

4   DAVIS, ANDREW MCFARLAND. "A Search for the Beginnings of
      Stock Speculation." In Transactions 1904-1906. Publications
      of the Colonial Society of Massachusetts. Boston: Published
      by the Society, 10:278-310.
           Traces the term "stock-jobbing" and the early use of the
      practice through the Anatomy of Exchange Alley (1719), [which is
      here not recognized to be Defoe's], and through the Essay upon
      Projects, Essay upon Loans (1710), and Consolidator. The hostil-
      ity toward stock-jobbing led to a bill which was passed by the
      Commons and became law in April 1697.

5   DUFF, E. GORDON. "Defoe's Novels Issued in Parts." Notes and
      Queries, 10th ser. 7, no. 107 (18 May):389.
           Raises questions about method of publication of a later edi-
      tion of Defoe's New Voyage Round the World (Chester: W. Cooke),
      folio, issued in forty-four parts.

6   DUTT, WILLIAM A. Some Literary Associations of East Anglia.
      New York: McClure, Phillips & Co.; London: Methuen & Co.,
      pp. 197-98, 237, 258-60.
           Mainly Defoe's comments on places in East Anglia, in the
      Tour: Yarmouth, Scole, and Bury St. Edmunds.

7   LANG, ANDREW. A History of Scotland from the Roman Occupa-
      tion. 4 vols. New York: Dodd, Mead, & Co.; Edinburgh and
      London: William Blackwood & Sons, 4:109-50 passim.
           In chap. 5 on "The Union" and chap. 6 on "Jacobite Move-
      ments," respectfully makes full use of Defoe's History of the
      Union as perhaps the most important authority on the negotiations
      from February, 1706, through 1711, giving details, names, policy
      summaries. Provides an account, also, of Defoe as a participant
      in the negotiations, "Harley's spy," engaging directly in the
      dangerous proceedings, reporting his experiences in letters to
      Harley, and giving influential opinions.

8   MATTHEWS, ALBERT. "Defoe and Woodward." Nation 85, no. 2198
      (15 August):140.
           Questions the assumption by Trent (1907.22) that Defoe did
      not write the Account of the Societies for the Reformation of
      Manners (1699). Since it can be shown that the author was not
      Josiah Woodward, why may it not have been Defoe?

9   MILDEBRATH, BERTHOLD. "Die deutschen 'Avanturiers' des
      achtzehnten Jahrhunderts." Inaugural dissertation, Würzburg
      University; Gräfenhainichen: C. Schulze & Co., 137 pp.
           Carefully sorts out the commonly confused labels "Robin-
      sonade" and "Avanturier." The latter are shown to be the last
      carry-overs from the seventeenth-century "rogue novels," some-
      times containing Robinsonesque elements, but not dominated by
      them. Of the works analyzed, eleven "Avanturiers" fall into this
      category, five others do in fact qualify as Robinsonades, and
      four (despite their titles) satisfy the criteria for neither

group. Of interest is a frequency list of the motifs found in
the "Avanturier" novels.   (P.E.C.)

10   MILLE, PIERRE. "En Passant: Court Conversation entre Gulli-
     ver et Robinson Crusoé." Temps, no. 16,742 (25 April).
        Creates an imaginary situation and dialogue in which Crusoe
and Gulliver comment generally upon their respective authors and
particularly about the Lilliputians. When Crusoe protests that
"an air of irony, I would say almost of wickedness," seems to be
at odds with his friend's gentleness, Gulliver offers fresh new
memories of how incoherent and feeble were the minds of the poor
Lilliputians. Continues the political allegory of the war between Lilliput and Blefuscu into a current controversy, the main
outlines of which now seem to be lost.

11   OPPENHEIM, M. "Maritime History." In Essex. Victoria His-
     tories of the Counties of England. Edited by William Page.
     [London]: Archibald Constable. Reprint. University of Lon-
     don, Institute of Historical Research. William Dawson & Sons,
     1977, 2:291 and note.
        After 1694, repairs and improvements were needed at Tilbury
Fort, with the intention of making it "the central artillery
arsenal." Quotes Defoe's Tour on Tilbury's armaments as being
"upwards of 100 guns." Notes that "many of Defoe's statements
will not bear examination, and this particular one is not in
accordance with such official documents as are known to the
writer.

12   PAIN, BARRY ERIC ODELL. Robinson Crusoe's Return. London:
     Hodder & Stoughton. Reprint. Supernatural and Occult Fic-
     tion. New York: Arno Press, 1976, 168 pp.
        Parodying the style and method of Robinson Crusoe, comments
severely on the theme of civilization. As a Robinsonade in
reverse, takes Crusoe back to England in his raft, and shows him
making bitter discoveries about human nature in the modern civilized world. Crusoe is first deceived by a character named
George Rats, and goes through a series of adventures in which he
encounters one "insanity" after another. Tricked by George Rats
a second time, Crusoe reflects that "a prolonged residence on a
desert island had made me too ready to think well of men, the
common cannibal being higher on the moral scale than those whom I
had now encountered in a state of civilization." Unable any
longer to cope with life in England, he embarks in his raft for
new shores.

13   PANCOAST, HENRY S[PACKMAN]. "Daniel Defoe (1659?-1731)."
     In An Introduction to English Literature. Reprint. 3d ed.,
     enlarged. New York: Henry Holt & Co., [n.d.], pp. 363-71.
        Revises 1896.11. Incorporates some of the new scholar-
ship in the extensive additions, for instance, on Defoe's secret
work for the government in and after 1704: while he was "a master of the art of deception, and his character seems to have been

a singular mixture of courage and duplicity," he nevertheless
maintained "a basis of conscience and stubborn integrity." On
Robinson Crusoe: changes the "interview" of Selkirk to a possible visit in Bristol. Now sees the book, in Pope's "artificial
time," as emerging "suddenly the story of a far-away world: the
story of a man in an almost primitive relation to nature. . . ."
Continues to regard the Journal of the Plague Year as unique and
"perhaps never surpassed"; now it is not a work of art, but
nature, "our daily commonplace life in its hours of tragic crisis, in those unexpected dramatic situations which seem beyond
the fancies of the romancer."

14 PRIDEAUX, W.F. "Defoe's Colonel Jacque." Notes and Queries,
    10th ser. 8, no. 188 (3 August):87.
        Query: Information on the first edition of Colonel Jack
    with the date 1722 on the title page. See 1907.15.

15 _____. "Defoe's Colonel Jacque." Notes and Queries, 10th
    ser. 8, no. 204 (23 November):411-12.
        Replies to his own query, 1907.14, giving his reasons for
    believing that the title page of the first edition of Colonel
    Jack was postdated 1723. In over thirty years of collecting, has
    never met with a copy having 1722 on the title page.

16 PROTHERO, ROWLAND E. "The Growth of the Historical Novel."
    Quarterly Review 206, no. 410 (January):25, 44-45.
        In a review of Jonathan Nield's A Guide to the Best His-
    torical Novels and Tales (3d ed., 1904) explains that of English
    literature before 1748 only Pilgrim's Progress and Robinson
    Crusoe are still read, and that "the first historical novel" was
    published in 1814. Richard Head's The English Rogue (1665) forms
    the only English link to Defoe's Captain Singleton, Colonel Jack,
    and Moll Flanders. Defoe's novels are a class apart: "They are
    intended to deceive, to pass as real histories."

17 Report on the Manuscripts of His Grace the Duke of Portland,
    K.G., Preserved at Welbeck Abbey. Edited by A. Maxwell-Lyte
    and S.C. Lomar. Historical Manuscripts Commission. London:
    HMSO, 8:135-39, 141, 240-41, 297-98, 310, 354.
        Publishes for the first time the manuscript enclosure, "Of
    the Fleet and Sir George Rook" (July? 1704), containing Defoe's
    bold attack on the Admiral for the cowardly conduct of the navy.
    Calendars, but does not reprint, "the case of the paying the
    Equivalent in Exchequer bills" (20 February 1708). Both items
    are printed in Healey. Important comment about Defoe may be
    found in letters to Harley from James Stancliffe (23 August 1704)
    and William Carstares (18 November 1707). Two additional items
    are calendared, but not reprinted: a long anti-Union pamphlet in
    manuscript, sent from Edinburgh, which is addressed to the
    Dissenters in England and which Harley endorsed to Goldsmith
    [Defoe], 29 August 1706; and a petition and address (1707) from
    Scottish merchants trading with England who are now addressing

a grievance to the Queen with Defoe's help. Healey does not
print either document. Reprinted, in part: Healey.

18   RUSKIN, JOHN. Letter of August 1877 to Mr. T.C. Horsfall, in
      Appendix to Fors Clavigera. In The Works of John Ruskin.
      Edited by E.T. Cook and Alexander Wedderburn. London: George
      Allen; New York: Longmans, Green, & Co., 29:590.
          Claims that usury is "a sin of the same unnatural class
      as Cannibalism"--a remark which leads to further comment on how
      wrong Robinson Crusoe's Friday must be.

19   SAINTSBURY, GEORGE. "A Pioneer of Realism." Bookman 82,
      no. 192 (September):202.
          Reviews E.A. Baker's introduction to Moll Flanders and
      Roxana, 1906.1, and takes issue with the comparison of Defoe's
      "Realism" or "Naturalism" with Mirbeau's and Maupassant's.
      Compares Moll Flanders and Roxana as women copied from real
      life, and thus serving the purpose of Realism or Naturalism.

20   STAVERMAN, W.H. Robinson Crusoe in Nederland. Een bijdrage
      tot de geschiedenis van den roman in de XVIIIe eeuw [Robinson
      Crusoe in the Netherlands: A contribution to the history of
      the novel in the XVIII century]. Groningen: Academisch Proef-
      schrift, 191 pp.
          In Dutch. Presented originally as a dissertation at
      Groningen University, offers introduction (5 pp.); chapters on
      Robinson Crusoe (38 pp.); Robinsonades before Robinson Crusoe,
      including Hai Ebn Yokdan, Krinke Kesmes, Historie der Sevarambes,
      and others (17 pp.); Robinsonades translated into Dutch (29 pp.)
      original Dutch Robinsonades (33 pp.); summary (2 pp.); and bibli-
      ography (53 pp.).   (P.T.)

21   TRENT, W[ILLIAM] P. "Bibliographical Notes on Defoe--I."
      Nation 84, no. 2188 (6 June):515-18.
          While preparing his own bibliography, makes here the first
      of two analyses of the standard "Chronological Catalogue" in
      Lee's Defoe (1869)--the first concentrating on the errors of
      commission; the second, on the errors of omission. Among sources
      of new information, finds James Crossley's notes, lent by Aitken,
      so helpful as alone to be responsible for "fully half of the addi-
      tions I shall propose." Next, states his method which includes
      special tests for Defoe's authorship and general reliance upon in-
      ternal evidence resulting from Trent's complete disillusion with
      Defoe's integrity in any comments on his own authorship. Reduces
      Lee's total of 254 items to 230; eliminates seven more items as
      erroneously assigned. Scrutinizes the remaining "suspicious
      items," one by one, and assigns reasons for accepting, rejecting,
      or still questioning them. See also 1907.22-23.

22   _____. "Bibliographical Notes on Defoe--II." Nation 85,
      no. 2193 (11 July):29-32.
          Takes up Lee's omissions of Defoe's works from his "Chrono-
      logical Catalogue" in two groups. First, the writings listed in

earlier bibliographies (e.g., Wilson, Hazlitt, Bohn's additions
to Lowndes's Bibliographer's Manual [1858]) which Lee rejected,
and should now be included in the canon on the basis of Trent's
tests; and second, additions drawn from the British Museum Catalogue and especially the sixty-one tracts, added by James Crossley whom Trent regards as "the greatest of all authorities on
what is perhaps the most tangled subject in English bibliography." Meticulously analyzes seriatim the remaining fifty-two
Crossley items, each annotation containing an important judgment
relating to authorship. See also 1907.21, 23.

23   _____. "Bibliographical Notes on Defoe--III." Nation 85,
       no. 2200 (29 August):180-83.
       Places thirty-six new items as "more or less positive"
additions to Lee's list of writings by Defoe, and eighteen new
items in the category of those which he is "on the verge of
attributing to our voluminous author." Lee's revised list now
stands at 220, to which Trent has made additions and subtrac-
tions, bringing the total to 289. The final bibliography should
list no less than 350 works by Defoe. See also 1907.21-22.

24   _____. "To the Editor of the Nation." Nation 85, no. 2198
       (15 August):140.
       Replies to 1907.8, sustaining the judgment that he can find
no reason for assigning the Account of the Societies for the
Reformation of Manners (1699) to Defoe.

25   WARNER, G.F. "An Unpublished Political Paper by Daniel
       De Foe." English Historical Review 32, no. 85 (January):
       130-43.
       Announces the discovery of an important autograph manu-
script (British Museum, Lansdowne MS. 98, fols. 223-46) addressed to Robert Harley shortly after he became secretary of state
on 18 May 1704. The autograph is without a title or any indica-
tion of authorship or date. An endorsement in a later hand reads
"Maxims and Instructions for Ministers of State, seemingly written about the end of the reign of Q. Anne for the use of some
great man." The date is given much earlier, by Warner, as May or
June, 1704; and by Healey as "July-August 1704?" So far as is
known, the autograph manuscript has not been published before
1907. The manuscript is organized around four main heads: (1)
"a step to confirm your friends in the belief of what they hope
for from you . . .," (2) "Of popularity," (3) "Of making the
Secretarys of State an inner cabinett to the Queen," and (4)
"Some consideracions with relation to the affaires of Hungaria
and Poland." Here Defoe shows himself, writing pithily at times,
in a statesmanlike role, confidentially and forthrightly advising
Harley how as secretary of state he can make himself prime minister, and even suggesting for Defoe himself, at times brazenly,
the role of a privy councillor to help Harley accomplish this
end. He displays a breadth of reading, for example, in the life
of Richelieu, and an awareness of statesmen in the past whom he

admires, both French and English. He has a mastery of contemporary information about continental politics, as in the section
"the affaires of Hungaria and Poland." Defoe appears to be offering himself for some new role, of which he only vaguely hints.
He writes about the necessity for the secretary of state's office
to be "an abridgement of all Europe" and to have detailed "intelligence" about every facet of life in the towns and counties of
England, and about Scotland. With brutal honesty, he informs
Harley how he is perceived by his friends. Without any apparent
sense of infidelity for himself, he advises him how he can garner
credit to himself, from the Dissenters, by deceiving them: "they
are to be pleas'd with words." Altogether, the autograph manuscript reveals, perhaps better than any published work, the sup-
pleness of Defoe's mind and his capacity to understand the mind
of his patron.

26 WELFORD, RICHARD. "Joseph Saywell, 1710." In "Early New-
castle Typography, 1639-1800." Archaeologia Aeliana: or
Miscellaneous Tracts Relating to Antiquity, 3d ser. 3:16-18.
   All the information we have about the relationship between
Defoe and Joseph Button, bookseller on Tyne Bridge, appears in
Button's letter which survives with No. 65 of The Newcastle
Gazette, or the Northern Courant (23-25 December 1710) in the
Advocates' Library in Edinburgh. Mentions the tradition of
Defoe's having lived in Gateshead and written one of his books
there. The letter also refers to the printer, Joseph Saywell.
See 1837.7; Healey.

1907-1908

1 ULLRICH, HERMANN. "Zur Bibliographie der Robinsonaden.
Nachträge und Ergänzungen zu meiner Robinson-Bibliographie."
Zeitschrift für Bücherfreunde 11:444-56, 489-98.
   Using the same classification system of his bibliography
(1898.16), makes many unnumbered additions and corrections.
                                                    (P.E.C.)

1908

1 A., N.M.&. "Defoe: The Devil's Chapel." Notes and Queries,
10th ser. 9, no. 219 (7 March):187.
   Gives earlier versions by other writers of the first two
lines of the True-Born Englishman, as do also 1908.2, 5, 12, 14,
18.

2 APPERSON, G.L. "Defoe: The Devil's Chapel." Notes and Queries, 10th ser. 9, no. 222 (28 March):255.
   See 1908.1.

3   BARING-GOULD, S[ABINE]. "The Botathen Ghost." In <u>Cornish</u>
      <u>Characters and Strange Events</u>. First Series. London: John
      Lane, The Bodley Head. Reprint. 1925, pp. 72-82.
         Sums up the problem of authorship for "The Remarkable Pas-
     sage of an Apparition." Rejects the ghost story as an "invention
     of Defoe," and reaffirms it as "a genuine narrative" by John
     Ruddle, as Alfred Robbins demonstrated (1898.13). Quotes exten-
     sively from the narrative; makes the curious mistake of saying
     that Defoe changed Dorothy Dingley into Mrs. Veale [sic]; and
     surmises that Defoe obtained the manuscript when he was in Laun-
     ceston "acting as a spy" for Harley in August, 1705.

4   _____. "Captain John Avery." In <u>Devonshire Characters and</u>
      <u>Strange Events</u>. First Series. London: John Lane, The Bodley
      Head. Reprint. 1926, pp. 375-89.
         Of the four biographical accounts of Captain Avery cited,
     judges the most reliable to be "The Life of Captain Avery" in
     Captain Charles Johnson's <u>General History of the Robberies and</u>
     <u>Murders of [the Most] Notorious Pyrates</u> (1724), and bases the
     narrative given here on this account. Specifically rejects <u>The</u>
     <u>King of Pirates</u> (1720) "supposed to be by Daniel Defoe" as having
     no authority, and is not aware that Captain Johnson is a pseudo-
     nym for Defoe, as John Robert Moore would demonstrate in <u>Defoe in</u>
     <u>the Pillory</u> (1939), pp. 126-88. Near the close of the account,
     notes certain difficulties in accepting "Johnson's" narrative,
     especially when it disagrees with Adrian von Broeck's (1709).

5   BAYNE, THOMAS. "Defoe: The Devil's Chapel." <u>Notes and Que-</u>
      <u>ries</u>, 10th ser. 9, no. 222 (28 March):255.
         See 1908.1.

6   BULLEN, FRANK T. "Robinson Crusoe." <u>Bibliophile</u> 1:243-48.
         A seaman, writer, and editor of sea-stories for a magazine,
     attests to his belief in the reality of Crusoe's "doings," both
     when he read the story at the age of six and recently at the age
     of fifty. Especially in the re-reading, finds impressive Defoe's
     ability to make "the creatures of his fancy live." Believes
     Tobago to be Crusoe's island, and so feels compelled to look for
     Crusoe "marks of identification," when he visited the harbour of
     Scarborough. Does not identify with the author Defoe, only with
     his hero Robinson Crusoe. Remembers reading the "Great Storm of
     1704" and feeling uneasy about its passing as historical fact.

7   COUPER, W[ILLIAM] J[AMES]. <u>The Edinburgh Periodical Press</u>
      <u>Being a Bibliographical Account of the Newspapers, Journals,</u>
      <u>and Magazines Issued in Edinburgh from the Earliest Times to</u>
      <u>1800</u>. 2 vols. Sterling: Eneas Mackay, 1:22, 39, 91, 97,
      234-38, 244-46, 247-48.
         Pauses briefly, in this still authoritative introduction
     (141 pp.), to identify the press in the College at the Kirk o'
     Field, Edinburgh, from which Mrs. Anderson may have reprinted
     Defoe's <u>Review</u> during 1709-1710. Stresses the importance of the

Englishman's contribution to the periodical press, his support
for the removal of a Privy Council in Scotland after the Union,
his direct participation in the publication of the second Edinburgh Courant (1710). In the bibliography proper: gives entries
for newspapers which Defoe published in Edinburgh. For the Review, with parallel issues beginning Edinburgh, 25 March 1709,
and London, 5 April 1709, a question exists as to "whether it
was not the London edition that was really the reprint, and not
the Edinburgh." During that year [1709-1710?], Defoe lived in
Edinburgh, and "corrected every paper himself." For the Edinburgh Courant, Defoe had the authorization to publish from the
Edinburgh Town Council dated 1 February 1710, but produced only
a few numbers, and had to return to London at the end of March.

8   FILON, AUGUSTIN. "Daniel Defoe, precurseur du naturalisme."
     Journal des débats: politiques et litteraires, 22 July:1-2.
          Elaborating on E.A. Baker (1906.1), reenforces the view of
     Moll Flanders as a naturalistic novel, but more in the tradition
     of the masters--Flaubert, Zola, Goncourt--than of Maupassant
     and Octave Mirbeau. Argues that in writing a picaresque novel,
     Defoe intended to produce "a novel of observation." Analyzes
     the patterns of love and marriage, and of thefts, in terms of
     the novel as a social document.

9   GOODRICK, A.T.S. "Robinson Crusoe, Impostor." Blackwood's
     Magazine 183, no. 1111 (May):672-85.
          Focuses upon desert island narratives (real or fictional)
     which preceded Robinson Crusoe, and makes these the basis of the
     plagiarism charge: Ibn Tophail, Peter Serrano's story, Island
     of Pines, Simplicissimus, Leguat's narrative, Jacques Sadeur's
     adventures. Concludes that even if Defoe were a plagiary,--for
     its "matchless charm," humanity, and "brilliant presentation
     of common happenings"--Robinson Crusoe would be "the greatest
     romance the world has ever seen."

10   JACKSON, HOLBROOK. "Daniel Defoe." In Great English Novel-
     ists. London: Grant Richards, pp. 17-38. Reprint. Phila-
     delphia: George W. Jacobs & Co., [1908].
          Sums up Defoe's life to show that he emerged after the Pur-
     itan revolution "to take full advantage of the new view of life"
     that was being created. Places emphasis upon him as a publicist
     and journalist, arguing even that "the original matter eventually
     worked up into narrative fiction is to be found in the various
     journals he either owned or edited." Prefers to describe Defoe
     as "the creator of the imaginative biography or history." Even
     this designation does not do justice to his great gift of plausi-
     bility, best seen in Robinson Crusoe.

11   LECKIE, JOHN D. "A Spanish Robinson Crusoe." Chambers's Jour-
     nal, 6th ser. 11, no. 554 (11 July):510-12.
          Summarizes a source for Robinson Crusoe--the account of
     Peter Serrano, stranded for seven years on "a mere sandbank" of

an island in the Caribbean Sea, as told in the words of the Spanish historian, Garcilasso de la Vega, in his Commentarios reales,
translated into English, 1688.

12   MCKERROW, R.B. "Defoe: The Devil's Chapel." Notes and Que-
      ries, 10th ser. 9, no. 222 (28 March):255.
          See 1908.1.

13   MURET, MAURICE. "Pedro Serrano le vrai Robinson Crusoé."
      Journal des débats 15, no. 2:595-96
          Pedro Serrano, and not Alexander Selkirk, was "the true
      prototype of Robinson Crusoe," according to a recent discovery in
      an English translation (1688) of the Commentarios reales by Garci-
      lasso de la Vega.

14   PICKFORD, JOHN. "Defoe: The Devil's Chapel." Notes and Que-
      ries, 10th ser. 9, no. 226 (25 April):331.
          See 1908.1.

15   QUILLER-COUCH, A[RTHUR] T[HOMAS], ed. Introduction to Daniel
      Defoe: Selections. Oxford: Clarendon Press, pp. 2-4.
          Summarizes Defoe's life up to the age of sixty when he be-
      gan writing the novels: he was "an honest man; but at the best
      he ate a great deal of dirt in the course of his irrepressible
      career." With Robinson Crusoe, his genius broke out of the
      "squalor." Among Englishmen he remains unique for "his marvel-
      lous gift of visualizing." Selections are from Robinson Crusoe,
      Memoirs of a Cavalier, Captain Singleton, New Voyage Round the
      World, Colonel Jack, and Journal of the Plague Year.

16   "Robinson Crusoe for Grown-Ups." Nation 87, no. 2270 (31
      December):647-48.
          Reviews the just-issued Houghton Mifflin edition, and de-
      fends Robinson Crusoe as a powerful tale of adventure for adult
      readers. Modifies Frederic Harrison's praise of the book (1888)
      as "a work on social philosophy to the mature . . . a picture of
      civilization." Argues that Defoe aimed "to tell a good story,"
      and did it so well "we can discern in it all sorts of profundi-
      ties which we dignify by such terms as historical evolution."
      Admires especially the characterization ("the fine stoicism with
      which he inflexibly faces the world as it is") and the absorbing
      incidents.

17   SAMPSON, GEORGE. "Daniel Defoe." Bookman 34, no. 201 (June):
      93-99.
          Of the 250 works in William Lee's "heroic bibliography"
      all that remains is Robinson Crusoe "cherished as a treasure,
      and a few others, cherished for Robinson's sake, or for histori-
      cal rather than literary value." In his novels, as with his
      journalism, Defoe succeeded "because he had instinctively gauged
      the capacity of the man in the street." His method is that of
      journalism--"realising and intensifying the probable with circum-

stantial and corroborative detail." Although limited in what he could do with characters, he nevertheless had "the gift of incident" and "the gift of honest prose." Two illustrations show the Old Manor House near Tooting Junction "where Defoe wrote Robinson Crusoe."

18   SOUTHAM, HERBERT. "Defoe: The Devil's Chapel." Notes and Queries, 10th ser. 10, no. 242 (15 August):134.
      See 1908.1.

19   TRENT, W[ILLIAM] P. "New Light on Defoe's Life." Nation 87, no. 2255 (17 September):259-61.
      Summarizes new findings on Defoe's life from the examination of the sixty-six volumes in the Nichols Collection of Newspapers at the Bodleian Library: (1) more exact information on his arrest, 20 May 1703, and on the length of his confinement in Newgate; (2) evidence that as early as 1705 Defoe was possibly writing for two papers at the same time as he would do in the years 1717-1724; (3) the "scandal" about the duel between Samuel Tuffley and a certain Captain John Silk on 10 September 1711, yielding an early clue to the identity of Defoe's wife, Mary Tuffley; (4) more accurate circumstances of his prosecution and imprisonment in 1713 for writing the supposedly Jacobite tracts.

20   ULLRICH, HERMANN. "Robinson und Robinsonaden in der Jugendliteratur." In Encyklopädisches Handbuch der Pädagogik. Edited by W. Rein. Reprint. 2d ed. Langensalza: H. Beyer, 7:567-76.
      Describes factors in the character Robinson Crusoe with which most younger readers readily identified. Notes that pronouncements on usefulness of the novel to young readers can be traced back to J. Vernet of Geneva, prior to Rouseau (quoted in Haken's Bibliothek der Robinsone, 1805-1808). Discusses early adaptations that lean toward Rousseau's view: Feutry (1766), Savin (1768), Wezel (1778-1779), Campe (1779-1780) which in turn had 120 editions and twenty-five translations, Geiger (1794), Gräbner (1864) who was "completely ignorant of the original text," and Zimmerman (1904) "very acceptable." Discusses Robinsonade-adaptations for youth, including various Insel Felsenburg versions between 1788 and 1876. Finally, lists several Robinsonades written expressly for young people, almost without commentary.   (P.E.C.)

21   _____. "Zu den Quellen des Robinson." Das literarische Echo 11, no. 1 (1 October):153.
      In a brief note, protests the newly announced discovery in a Frankfurt newspaper (referring to Chambers's Journal) of a Robinson Crusoe source (Serrano) to be neither a new finding nor a true source.   (P.E.C.)

22   WALLING, R.A.J. George Borrow: The Man and His Work.
     London: Cassell & Co. Reprint. Folcroft Library Editions,
     1977, pp. 13-15, 26, 134, 297, 303, 343.
          Assesses the influence of Defoe--along with the Bible and
     Shakespeare, one of the "classics"--on Borrow.

23   WILLIAMS, RALPH OLMSTED. "Robinson Crusoe's Island." Modern
     Language Notes 23, no. 23 (March):85-87.
          Notes the persistent identification in reference works of
     Crusoe's island with Juan Fernandez and the discrepancy with the
     geographical location as given in authoritative texts and the
     map of the fourth edition. Explains the mistake as resulting
     from the association of Crusoe with Selkirk who was abandoned on
     Juan Fernandez. See also the correction to this note--American
     Review of Reviews 37, no. 6 (June, 1908):739--which rightly
     states that "Crusoe's island itself existed only in Defoe's
     imagination."

                                  1909

1   ABRAHAMS, ALECK. "Robinson Crusoe's Literary Descendants."
     Notes and Queries, 10th ser. 12, no. 288 (3 July):7.
          Adds to 1909.3: The Adventures of Philip Quarll, the
     English Hermit, with folding hand-coloured frontispiece dated
     1823.

2   AITKEN, G.A. "Daniel Defoe's Wife." Notes and Queries, 10th
     ser. 11, no. 287 (26 June):516.
          Corrects 1909.9: information concerning Defoe's wife
     already given in 1890.1-2.

3   AXON, WILLIAM E.A. "Crusoe Richard Davis." Notes and Que-
     ries, 10th ser. 11, no. 283 (29 May):425.
          Describes the "lesser known" literary descendant of Robin-
     son Crusoe, probably published in 1801, without an author given:
     The Voyages and Discoveries of Crusoe Richard Davis. The influ-
     ence comes more immediately from Robert Paltock's Peter Wilkins
     (1750). See also 1909.1, 4, 16.

4   B., W.C. "Robinson Crusoe's Literary Descendants." Notes and
     Queries, 10th ser. 12, no. 291 (24 July):79.
          Adds to 1909.1 on Philip Quarll, 1727 or "perhaps a year or
     two before."

5   BROWN, P. HUME. History of Scotland. Vol. 3, From the Revo-
     lution of 1689 to the Disruption, 1843. Cambridge Historical
     Series. Cambridge: University Press, p. 113.
          Describing the different alignments with regard to the
     treaty of Union, places "the indefatigable Daniel Defoe" first
     among the champions outside Parliament. Reprinted: 1911; 1912;
     1929.

6   BURTON, RICHARD. Masters of the English Novel: A Study of
     Principles and Personalities. New York: Henry Holt & Co.,
     pp. 46-47, 119, 225, 309.
          Uses Defoe's novels as example or contrast: for instance,
     to show the distance which separates Robinson Crusoe and Gulli-
     ver's Travels from Richardson's Pamela in characterization. Moll
     Flanders, although picaresque, still has greater "psychological
     value" than Robinson Crusoe. On Jane Austen: Defoe demonstrated
     that you can have "a powerful story" without any love interest.
     On Stevenson's grasp of the vernacular: "it reminds of Defoe or
     Swift, at their best."

7   CANBY, HENRY SEIDEL. "Daniel Defoe." In The Short Story in
     English. New York: Henry Holt & Co., pp. 184-88.
          Describes Defoe's contribution to realism as the "correct-
     ing the manners of the time," and illustrates his style of plain
     narrative and verisimilitude from "a library of short stories" in
     [An Essay on the] History and Reality of Apparitions (1727), Jour-
     nal of the Plague Year, and Mist's and Applebee's Journals (1716-
     1722). Explicates Mrs. Veal strictly as fiction. Reprinted:
     [1926].

8   CHARLTON, J.E. "De Foe--The Journalist." Methodist Review 91
     (March):219-30.
          Stresses throughout two qualities possessed by Defoe which
     were especially "beneficial to a newspaper man": courage and
     "facility of resource." Illustrates them, in writing about
     "things which occurred in his absence," such as the Journal of
     the Plague Year, or things which occurred while he was in prison,
     among "the low and deficient," as in Roxana, Moll Flanders, and
     Colonel Jack. Also, illustrates the second quality [erroneously]
     in The Storm (1704) where he wrote about things he could not have
     observed and in the Review which, [we are told incorrectly], was
     started and written for "nearly two years" in Newgate. Analyzes
     the aim of the Review in handling the affairs of France and
     Europe; and in the introduction of amusements in the section
     "Mercure Scandale or Advice from the Scandal Club," Defoe's use
     of "yellow journalism," his ethics as a newspaperman generally,
     his inclusion of Scotland in the Review, his themes in general.

9   DIEGO [pseud.]. "Daniel Defoe's Wife." Notes and Queries,
     10th ser. 11, no. 285 (12 June):466.
          Repeats the information already given by Aitken (1890.1-2)
     about the allegations for marriage licenses issued on 28 December
     1683 to Daniel Foe and Mary Tuffley; and about Defoe's year of
     birth, 1659.

10   GÜNTHER, MAX "Entstehungsgeschichte von Defoe's Robinson
     Crusoe." Inaugural dissertation, Königlichen University;
     Greifswald: Julius Abel, 79 pp.
          Offers a largely uninspired compiling of information from
     a handful of studies, dealing with sources, publishing history,

reception, and several motifs shared with certain works of travel
literature. Ullrich finds this work a meagre beginning toward a
true scholarly examination of the making of Robinson Crusoe ("Zur
Robinson-Literatur," Literaturblatt für germanische und romanische Philologie 33, nos. 3–4 (March–April, 1912):109–10.
                                                        (P.E.C.)

11   HARFORD, ALICE. Annals of the Harford Family. London: West-
      minster Press, p. 34.
            Explains that Joseph Harford obtained the information about
      Selkirk's placing "his papers in the hands of Defoe" from Mrs.
      Damaris Daniel, daughter of Major [Nathaniel] Wade who had been
      wounded at Sedgemoor. Repeats the words of the Gentleman's Maga-
      zine editor (1787.7): "Mr. Harford has thus proved what was
      always believed to be the case, namely, that Daniel Defoe wrote
      Robinson Crusoe from Selkirk's papers."

12   HOOGEWERFF, G.J. "Een Nederlandsche bron van den Robinson
      Crusoe" [A Dutch source of Robinson Crusoe]. Onze Eeuw 9,
      no. 3 (September):360–412.
            In Dutch. Describes Hendrik Smeeks's Beschrijvinge van het
      Koningrijk Krinke Kesmes (Amsterdam, 1708) in detail, and argues
      strongly that the similarities between this work and Robinson
      Crusoe cannot be ascribed to chance. Since there are no known
      translations into English of Krinke Kesmes, Defoe must have been
      able to read the Dutch language. Indications that he knew Dutch
      are that he uses the phrase "Den wild zee"; he probably traveled
      to the Netherlands; he describes Rotterdam; and he had Dutch con-
      tacts in the court of William III, who was himself Dutch. Dis-
      cusses possible sources of Krinke Kesmes: the apparently true
      story by Schouten about a shipwreck; the History of the Sevar-
      ambes (1677–1679) by Sieur Denis Vairasne d'Allais, a book appar-
      ently known to Smeeks, about the shipwreck of a vessel bound for
      Batavia. Reprints the fragment of an episode from Krinke Kesmes
      (14 pp.). See also 1921.10.   (P.T.)

13   HORTEN, FRANZ. "Studien über die Sprache Defoe's. I. Ortho-
      graphie." Inaugural dissertation, Rheinischen Friedrich
      Wilhelms University; Bonn: Peter Hanstein, 105 pp.
            Examines Defoe's orthography in the first printing of his
      Robinson Crusoe, with sections on "Vocalismus," "Consantismus,"
      "Zeichensetzung," and "Gross- und Kleindruck." See also the con-
      siderably expanded version, 1914.5.

14   K., L.L. "Robert Drury, Mariner." Notes and Queries, 10th
      ser. 11, no. 270 (27 February):162–63.
            Questions the DNB's acceptance of Robert Drury's "life" as
      given in his Madagascar. Captain S. Pasfield Oliver (1890.15)
      concluded that Drury was a real person, but his later history was
      questionable. Earlier William Lee, although allowing some role
      for Defoe as a possible editor, had rejected Madagascar from the
      canon. Alfred and Guillaume Grandidier, in their annotated

French translations of works about Madagascar (1906.6), found
evidence to corroborate certain incidents of Madagascar. Produces evidence here, from Albert Pitot's T'Eylandt Mauritius
(Port Louis, 1905), that corroborates an incident relating to
the pirate John Bowen, and identifies his ship. The Grandidiers
had blamed the "unknown editor" for any blunders and inaccuracies
in the narrative. Now L.L.K. specifically refers to "Defoe or
one of his imitators" as responsible for the expansion and editing of the narrative.

*15   KINNOSUKE, NATSUME [Natsume Sōseki]. Bungaku Hyoron [Eigh-
      teenth-century English literature]. Tokyo: Shunyodo.
         In Japanese. A translation in English of Sōseki's lec-
      ture (1907) on five neo-classical writers (Addison and Steele,
      Swift, Pope, and Defoe) has not been located. A discussion
      does appear in Beongcheon Yu, Natsume Soseki (TWAS. New York:
      Twayne Publishers, 1969), pp. 35-38; and more fully, with gener-
      ous quotations, in Matsui Sakuko, "A Criticism of Literature:
      'Daniel Defoe and the Structure of the Novel,'" in Natsume Sōseki
      As a Critic of English Literature (East Asian Cultural Studies
      Series, no. 16. Tokyo: Centre for East Asian Cultural Studies,
      1975), pp. 254- 78, 340-45. Using Sōseki's own words, Sakuko
      describes his attitude as generally unfavorable to Defoe, but
      one in line with critics of the day (Masson, Stephen, Minto,
      E.M. Forster) and his own "non-naturalist" view of the novel.
      Sōseki severely criticizes the novels generally, and Robinson
      Crusoe and Moll Flanders particularly, as deficient in structure,
      coherence, "unity for development," and plot. To Sōseki, the
      novels are only biographies or "life histories"; the pace of
      Robinson Crusoe, "like a rickshaw man with a heavy load"; the
      writing "detailed, exhaustive and detective-like but very vul-
      gar." Defoe is not "an expert in realism," as Sōseki understands
      the term.

16   MCMAHON, MORGAN. "Robinson Crusoe's Literary Descendants."
     Notes and Queries, 10th ser. 12, no. 308 (20 November):417.
        Adds to 1909.1, 4: The Adventures of Capt. Robert Boyle
     "suggested in the eighteenth century by Defoe's masterpiece,"
     named by Charles Lamb as one of his "classics," read in Ireland
     when the author was a boy.

17   MASEFIELD, JOHN. "Daniel Defoe." Fortnightly Review, n.s. 85
     (January):65-73.
        Brings together a composite of interpretations: the "una-
     bashed" quality in Defoe's features as reflected in his portrait,
     his "personal peculiarities," his admiration for the industry of
     man (thus his limited sensitivity to natural beauty), attitude
     toward the sea, care about clothes, fondness for wine, love of
     horses and horse-racing, his two marriages [incorrect]. On Defoe
     the novelist: finds him seriously flawed and lacking as a pro-
     fessional artist, quickly bored with his characters who "never
     develop . . . never become more engaging, more interesting, more

human"; fond of creating "external situations" and artificially
keeping them alive. Identifies his noblest emotion as "honest
indignation," which turns into "ironical humour" in the Review;
and his strongest emotion as the fear of death, which appears
"meaningly" in most novels. Singles out as the one feature which
differentiates Defoe from all other writers: his "gift of invent-
ing realities." Compared with his tracts, the novels show only
one side of him, "a lively but stunted part of him." Reprinted:
"Appreciation," in the introduction to 1909.18.

18   _____, ed. Defoe. Masters of Literature. London: George
        Bell & Sons, 415 pp.
        The introduction consists of both a biographical section
(13 pp.) and an "appreciation" (12 pp.), the latter having·been
first published as 1909.17. The biographical account dutifully
traces the high points of Defoe's life, ending with a critique of
the novels which ranks Colonel Jack as "the best work of fiction
ever done by him." In part 1, the "romances" are introduced by
short critical assessments of a page or less, with strong sociological overtones. The excerpts are of varied lengths from eight
novels, including Duncan Campbell. Part 2 consists of the "Lesser Works, Pamphlets, and Occasional Papers."

19   PRICA, ZORA. "Daniel Defoe's Robinson Crusoe und Robert Pal-
        tock's Peter Wilkins." Inaugural dissertation, University of
        Zurich; Budapest: Serbische Buchdruckerei, 58 pp.
        Discusses briefly Robinson Crusoe, fourteen Robinsonades
before Peter Wilkins, that Robinsonade, and fourteen imitations.
See the review by Hermann Ullrich, "Zur Robinson-Literatur,"
Literaturblatt für germanische und romanische Philologie 33, nos.
3-4 (March-April, 1912):112-13.   (P.E.C.)

20   RANSOME, ARTHUR. A History of Story-Telling: Studies in the
        Development of Narrative. London: T.C. & E.C. Jack, pp. 114,
        132-35, 140, 155.
        Sketches the transition from Elizabethan fiction to Defoe,
using mainly Charles Lamb's comments, and referring only to
Robinson Crusoe and Journal of the Plague Year. Notes especially
the differences in narrative manner during the transition.

21   Review of John Masefield's edition of Defoe, 1909. TLS,
        no. 409 (11 November):417-18.
        Elaborates upon (and challenges) some of Masefield's cri-
tical comments expressed in his introduction: Defoe's abject
closeness to "the normal intelligence and experience of mankind";
his apparent lack of self-awareness "as the insensitive superfi-
ciality of his men and women would seem to imply"; the absence in
the novels of "the psychological aura, the halftones, the subcon-
scious syllabling of the 'naturalist,'" the solitudes and the
silences of Robinson Crusoe, Captain Singleton, and Journal of
the Plague Year.

22   ROBINSON, CHARLES NAPIER. <u>The British Tar in Fact and Fic-</u>
     <u>tion: The Poetry, Pathos, and Humour of the Sailor's Life</u>.
     London and New York: Harper & Brothers. Reprint. Detroit:
     Singing Tree Press, 1968, pp. 71, 112, 250, 259-64, 270, 284,
     301, 303..
         Ultimately, expresses disappointment in Defoe's novels
     since the author finds there very little pathos, humour, and
     sense of patriotic duty. Notes Defoe's opposition to impressment
     in the <u>Essay upon Projects</u> and <u>Review</u> (1705); the possibility he
     used talk taken directly from seafaring people; treatment of
     naval affairs in the <u>Review</u>; preoccupation with, and "unimagin-
     ative" depicting of, mariners and pirates. Deals not only with
     <u>Robinson Crusoe</u>, but also with <u>The King of Pirates</u> (1719) and
     <u>Captain Singleton</u>; later with Jane Porter's <u>Sir Edward Seaward's</u>
     <u>Narrative of His Shipwreck</u> (1831), found to be very much like
     <u>Robinson Crusoe</u>.

23   SMITH, ARTHUR LIONEL. "English Political Philosophy in the
     Seventeenth and Eighteenth Centuries." <u>The Cambridge Modern</u>
     <u>History</u>. Edited by A.W. Ward, G.W. Prothero, Stanley Leathes.
     New York: Macmillan Co., 6:815-17.
         Names Defoe as "the most thorough-going exponent" of Whig
     principles in the reigns of William III and Queen Anne, and his
     Lockean tract <u>The Original Power of the Collective Body of the</u>
     <u>People of England</u> (1701) as his chief contribution to political
     theory. Among other contributions, "permanent in their histori-
     cal importance": <u>True-Born Englishman</u> and <u>Shortest-Way with the</u>
     <u>Dissenters</u>; "work of the first value": the <u>Review</u>.

24   ULLRICH, HERMANN. "Nachwort des Herausgebers." In <u>Das Leben</u>
     <u>und die gantz ungemeine begebenheiten des weltberühmten Engel-</u>
     <u>länders, Robinson Crusoe</u>. Translated by Ludwig Friedrich
     Vischer. 2 vols. Leipzig: Insel Verlag, 2:409-43.
         As an afterword to Vischer's influential translation of the
     two parts of <u>Robinson Crusoe</u> into German (1731), surveys the en-
     tire field of the "Robinsonades" by applying the term loosely and
     indiscriminately, for instance, to "our national epic 'Gudrun,'"
     the twelfth-century narrative of Hai Ebn Yoktan, the fifteenth-
     century collection <u>Thousand and One Nights</u> including the adven-
     tures of the seafarer Sinbad, Queen Margaret of Navarre's <u>The</u>
     <u>Heptameron</u>, Grimmelshaussen's <u>Simplicissimus</u>, Garcillasso de la
     Vega's <u>Peter Serrano</u>, and so on—even to the inclusion of the
     Selkirk story as a Robinsonade, though it is a true one. Con-
     tains important information about the "Third Hamburg Edition"
     (reprinted here), the translator Ludwig Friedrich Vischer, the
     translations of <u>Robinson Crusoe</u> into many other languages during
     the eighteenth century, the adaptations for young readers, pub-
     lications relating to <u>Robinson Crusoe</u> by the original Hamburg
     publisher Thomas Wiering, significant imitations such as the
     German <u>Insel Felsenburg</u> (1731-1743) by Johann Gottfried Schnabel
     and the English <u>Life and Adventures of Peter Wilkins</u> (1750) by
     Robert Paltock.

25   WACKWITZ, FRIEDRICH. "Entstehungsgeschichte von D. Defoes
      Robinson Crusoe." Inaugural dissertation, Friedrich Wilhelms
      University; Berlin: Mayer & Müller, 77 pp.
         Attempts to enumerate all the possible sources for Robinson
      Crusoe (English tales of men stranded on islands, the tradition
      of seafarers' reports, Selkirk's experiences, adventure novels,
      Pietist I-form journals, socio-political novels, autobiogra-
      phies), but not in-depth enough to make a convincing argument
      that these are true sources. See also the review by Hermann
      Ullrich, "Zur Robinson-Literatur," Literaturblatt für germanische
      und romanische Philologie 33, nos. 3/4 (March-April, 1912):105-
      13.   (P.E.C.)

                                 1910

1   BLOM, AUGUST. Director of film (Danish). Robinson Crusoe.
      See Filmographic Dictionary of World Literature.

2   CLAPP, JOHN M. "An Eighteenth-Century Attempt at a Critical
      View of the Novel: The Bibliothèque Universelle Des Romans."
      PMLA, n.s. 18, no. 1:60-96.
         Analyzes an important source of information on the broad
      range of pre-Revolutionary French interest in serious fiction,
      Bibliothèque universelles des romans, published from July, 1775,
      to June, 1789. Comments specifically, with no mention of Defoe
      as author, on the lengthy review (143 pp.) given to the French
      translation (1768) of Robinson Crusoe, as compared with reviews
      of other eighteenth-century novelists. Includes in the appendex
      a listing of "Eighteenth-Century Collections of Prose Fiction."
      See also 1787.11.

3   DAVIS, ANDREW MCFARLAND. A Bibliographical Puzzle. Cam-
      bridge, Mass.: J. Wilson & son. Reprint. Publications of
      the Colonial Society of Massachusetts: Transactions 13
      (1912):2-15.
         In Massachusetts, during the years 1720-1721, certain
      publications imprinted from "Cruso's Island" were alleged to be
      libellous for reflecting severely on members of the House of Rep-
      resentatives. Only remotely connected with these pamphlets, if
      at all, is the eight-page News from the Moon. A Review of the
      State of the British Nation, which we now know was published in
      1721 for the Boston bookseller, Benjamin Gray. For advertising
      this pamphlet while he was under indictment, Gray was unsuccess-
      fully prosecuted. Some evidence exists that J. Franklin was the
      printer. The pamphlet reprints, with minor changes, Defoe's
      Review, no. 14, dated 2 May 1710, in the Edinburgh edition--a
      witty satire of the tailor in the lunar regions who was dragged
      to court for making "a Character-Coat" which everyone thought
      fitted him. Just how or why this particular Review should have
      any bearing on Massachusetts "polemics" of 1721 remains still a
      puzzle. See also 1911.3.

4   DAWSON, WILLIAM J., and DAWSON, CONINGSBY W. <u>The Great</u>
     <u>English Short-Story Writers</u>. 2 vols. New York and London:
     Harper & Brothers, 1:24-25; 2:4.
         In the evolution of the short story (chap. 1), places <u>Mrs.</u>
     <u>Veal</u> first, and reprints it (chap. 2), claiming the narrative to
     be "an almost perfect example of the most modern method of han-
     dling a ghost-tale." Praises the story for its "<u>verisimilitude</u>"
     and the references to Drelincourt's <u>Book on Death</u> as "a master-
     stroke of genius."

5   DIBELIUS, WILHELM. <u>Englische Romankunst</u>. <u>Die Technik des</u>
     <u>englischen Romans im achtzehnten und zu Anfang des neunzehnten</u>
     <u>Jahrhunderts</u>. Reprint. Palaestra 92 and 98. 2d ed. 2 vols.
     Berlin and Leipzig: Mayer & Müller, 1922, 1:406 pp.; 2:471
     pp. passim.
         Devotes a full chapter to Defoe (1:31-53), and in the other
     chapters links him to Fielding, Godwin, Scott, and Marryat. Sum-
     marily treats Defoe's novels as largely picaresque narrations
     whose characterization (earliest beginnings of individual psycho-
     logical portrayal), plot (loosely structured, but with incipient
     concentration of material), and narrative techniques (tradition-
     al, with subjective and objective elements) combine in a highly
     didactic manner. See also Paula van Beeck for an elaboration on
     the psychology didaxis dualism--"Der psychologische Gehalt in der
     Romanen Defoes" (Inaugural dissertation, Westfälischen Wilhelms
     University; Quackenbrück: Robert Kleinert, 1931, 68 pp.). Re-
     viewed severely, in English, by A.J. Tieje, <u>Journal of English</u>
     <u>and Germanic Philology</u> 11 (1912):626-35.   (P.E.C.)

6   HAMEL, FRANK. "English Books in the Indexes 'Librorum
     Prohibitorum et Expurgandorum.'" <u>Library</u>, 3d ser. 1, no. 4
     (October):374.
         In a section discussing the eighteenth-century novelists,
     lists <u>Robinson Crusoe</u> as being in the Spanish Index, although it
     was not prohibited at Rome. The <u>Political History of the Devil</u>
     appears in the Catalogue [Expurgandorum] under a decree of 1743.

7   HIBGAME, FREDERICK T. "Defoe Methodist Chapel, Tooting."
     <u>Notes and Queries</u>, 11th ser. 2, no. 52 (24 December):505.
         Quotes the announcement of the sale of the Defoe Primitive
     Methodist Chapel, Tooting, in the 9 December issue of the <u>Daily</u>
     <u>Chronicle</u>. States that the chapel was founded by the author of
     <u>Robinson Crusoe</u>; incorrectly asserts that Defoe is buried in a
     small burying-ground at the rear of the chapel. See also 1911.9,
     12, 16.

8   HOVELAQUE, ÉMILE. "L'Enseignement des langues vivantes dans
     de deuxième cycle." <u>Revue universitaire</u> 19, pt. 2, no. 7:
     101-6.
         On the teaching of Puritanism, the Inspector General of
     Public Instruction turns from <u>Paradise Lost</u> with the observation:
     "you will meet Satan again in this excellent Robinson Crusoe, not

because of their specific sins, but because they are both children of the same race." Explains next that although Robinson
Crusoe seems to be "a simple narrative for children," it also
suggests "the most profound thoughts" to the philosopher or
sociologist because nowhere else has a clearer light been cast
on "the psychology of a race" or a better explanation given of
"material destinies." Shows in some detail how Robinson Crusoe
fits into this theory of race, apparently derived from Taine and
linked here with Kipling's "White Man's Burden" and Ruskin's
aesthetics. See also 1915.1.

9   "Introductory Note." In The Shortest-Way with the Dissenters
     and "The Education of Women." In English Essays from Sir Phil-
     ip Sidney to Macaulay. Edited by Charles W. Eliot. Harvard
     Classics. New York: P.F. Collier & Son, 27:131-51.
         Reprints the entire Shortest-Way with the Dissenters and
     the section on women from the Essay upon Projects. In the brief
     note (1 p.), describes the Essay upon Projects as "remarkable for
     the number of schemes suggested in it which have since been
     carried into practice." Otherwise, generally repeats prevailing
     [mis]conceptions, such as Defoe's having been "thoroughly dis-
     credited as a politician" and regarded "a mere hireling journal-
     ist" for the latter part of his career.

10   JERROLD, WALTER, ed. "Robinson Crusoe: The Story of This
     Book." In Robinson Crusoe. London: Ernest Nister; New York:
     E.P. Dutton & Co., pp. 6-8.
         Publication date is not given on the title page; may be
     1911, according to the National Union Catalog. Summarizes quick-
     ly the broad interest in Robinson Crusoe as a children's classic
     and pantomime. Rejects entirely the view that Robinson Crusoe is
     an allegory of the author's life; regards it as just "a delight-
     ful story."

11   LANNERT, GUSTAF L:SON. A Few Remarks Concerning a "Rejected"
     Doctor's Treatise. Uppsala: Almqvist & Wiksells Boktryck-
     eri-A.-B., 9 pp.
         Summarizes the reasons why the dissertation (1910.12) was
     rejected at the University of Uppsala while approved at the
     University of Lund. One of the examiners raised questions about
     the adequacy of studying "the flexional part" of Robinson Crusoe
     for a doctor's treatise and about the use of investigating the
     differences between all the editions.

12   _____. An Investigation into the Language of "Robinson Cru-
     soe" as Compared with That of Other 18th Century Works. Ph.D.
     dissertation, University of Lund (rejected); Uppsala: Alm-
     qvist & Wiksells, 162 pp.
         Using a method of statistical counts and representative
     samplings, examines the language of Robinson Crusoe closely, and
     makes elaborate comparisons of linguistic phenomena here and in
     other works by Defoe, his contemporaries, and Fanny Burney

(Evelina, 1778). Determines that for his purpose, only the first
two editions of Robinson Crusoe are relevant, and rules out all
the other early editions, piracies, and modern reprints--especial-
ly, the venerable ones (e.g., Lee's, 1869) claiming to derive
their texts exactly from the original edition. Compares usage in
Robinson Crusoe with that of the Compleat English Gentleman (manuscript, proofsheet), Of Royall Education (1895), Robinson Crusoe
(Part 2), Moll Flanders, Captain Singleton, and Journal of the
Plague Year; and with that of Swift's Tale of a Tub (1704), letters, and Polite Conversation (1883 ed.); the Tatler; Spectator;
and Burney's Evelina. In addition relates the practice by Defoe
and his contemporaries with the theory as reflected in the early
grammars, such as J. Wallis's Grammatica Linguae Anglicanae
(1674). Organizes the presentation around an introduction which
includes an important section "General Remarks on the Language of
RC" (16 pp.); and chapters on "Orthography" (2 pp.), "Some Phono-
logical Notes" (4 pp.), "Accidence" (91 pp.; on indefinite article, substantives, adjectives, numerals, pronouns, verbs, the
adjectival adverb), and an index of key words (6 pp.). Throws
new light on Defoe's habits of composition and all aspects of
language in Robinson Crusoe, but expecially on the currency of
his usage vis-à-vis archaic language and colloquial or vulgar
speech, on Defoe's style as it relates to his language, on the
use of foreign words in Robinson Crusoe and Journal of the Plague
Year, on characteristic or favorite phrases. See also 1910.11.
Reprinted: Folcroft Press, 1969; Norwood Editions, 1976; in part
Robinson Crusoe, ed. Michael Shinagel, Norton Critical ed. (New
York: W.W. Norton & Co., 1975), pp. 303-6.

13   LIDDELL, A.C., ed. "Editor's Introduction" and "Notes." In
     The Life and Adventures of Robinson Crusoe. Oxford: Claren-
     don Press, pp. iii-xvi, 287-332.
        Presents a factually accurate biographical summary, but
reveals also a definite bias, taking cues from Leslie Stephen
("'we cannot deny that Defoe descended into very dirty practices
in his old age'") and William Minto. In this perspective,
Memoirs of a Cavalier and Journal of the Plague Year are "excellent examples of Defoe's power 'to lie like truth.'" Reserves
special praise for Robinson Crusoe: for its "wonderful air of
reality" arising from Defoe's capacity of "lying like truth,"
for the situation that strongly appeals to the imagination, for
the attractiveness of Crusoe as a hero. Observes also that most
of Defoe's remaining 250 works are already forgotten.

14   NABER, S.P. L'HONORÉ. "Nog eens de Nederlandsche Bron van den
     Robinson Crusoe." Onze Eeuw 10:427-48.
        In Dutch. While it has not been possible to obtain a trans-
lation of this article, its general purport seems to be that it
accepts Krinke Kesmes as a source of Robinson Crusoe. See also
Gove, pp. 213-16.

15   O'DONOGHUE, FREEMAN. "Defoe, Daniel; political writer and
     novelist; 1661?-1731." In Catalogue of Engraved British
     Portraits Preserved in the Department of Prints and Drawings
     in the British Museum. London: British Museum, 2:27.
         Lists seven engraved portraits: one by painter J. Richard-
son and engraver J. Hopwood for the plate to Cooke's Classics
(1797); five identified by engravers M. Van der Gucht, H. Barnett, H. Rothwell, R. Graves, T. Medland; and one, anonymous.
"None of the engravings of Defoe have any claim to authenticity."

16   PANCOAST, HENRY S., and SHELLY, PERCY VAN DYKE. A First Book
     in English Literature. New York: Henry Holt & Co., pp. 263-
     65.
         Links the "sketches of individual characters, and of social
manners in London: by Addison and Steele with the development of
the "modern" novel. On Robinson Crusoe, makes the point that in
the "artificial time" of Pope and the rest, "there comes suddenly
the story of a far-away world; the story of a man in an almost
primitive relation to nature." Quotes Lamb's judgment on the
"secondary novels" which make Defoe's later years "the most brilliant literary period of his life."

17   PLUMMER, ALFRED. The Church of England in the Eighteenth
     Century. London: Methuen & Co., pp. 8-11, 33, 42-44, 58-59.
         Places Defoe's prosecution for libel in his Shortest-Way
with the Dissenters within the history of the Church of England.
The titles of his numerous tracts suggest that he and Harley
stood for moderation in religion. Quotes Defoe's amusing account
[source not given] of the enthusiasm of women in 1710 for the
priest, Henry Sacheverell.

18   SAINTSBURY, GEORGE. "Defoe, Daniel (c1659-1731)." In The
     Encyclopaedia Britannica. 11th ed. Cambridge: University
     Press, 7:927-31.
         Revises 1878.9 to bring the biography up-to-date, and re-
tells more fully the controversies involving Defoe by introducing
information from new items of the canon. Assesses the novels
other than Robinson Crusoe as strongly as in 1878, but waxes less
enthusiastic for Moll Flanders, and harsher for Roxana.

19   WALKER, EMERY. "Portraits Wanted." Notes and Queries, 11th
     ser. 2, no. 42 (15 October):307-8.
         Requests information on the present owner of the portrait
of Defoe by Kneller said to have been acquired by J.C. Laud
(1882.4).

1911

1   CHENEY, DAVID MACGREGOR. A Collection of "Robinson Crusoes"
    Wherein Are Set Forth Sundry Diverting Adventures in the
    Library of George A. Hough of New Bedford, with the Great

Adventurer, Himself, As a Guide. New Bedford, Mass.: [n.p.],
10 pp.
    Reprinted from the New Bedford Sunday Standard, 17 December
1911. Presents the colorful characters in the engravings and
illustrations of Robinson Crusoe editions in Hough's invaluable
collection as people whom Cheney meets in a dream.

2   CROSS, WILBUR L., ed. Introduction to Defoe's Robinson Cru-
     soe. English Readings for Schools. New York: Henry Holt &
     Co., pp. vii-xxx.
    Presents a full account of Defoe's life and writings as
well as some strongly held new convictions. Describes, in part
1, the main transition of his career as a turning to "real and
imaginary biography, in which truth and fiction are sometimes so
cleverly blended that a reader may be in doubt which is the
author's main purpose." Argues for the view [no longer tenable]
that Defoe displays his "peculiar gift of mystification" in The
Storm (1704), written while he was in Newgate, and in Mrs. Veal.
For Memoirs of a Cavalier and Captain Singleton, extends "a
secondary immortality," but acknowledges Moll Flanders to be "a
disagreeable but powerful novel." In part 2, specifically on
Robinson Crusoe (11 pp.), notes that certain key differences
between Selkirk and Crusoe (e.g., the introduction of the shipwreck) chiefly determine the course taken by Robinson Crusoe; and
so argues that self-preservation as an instinct serves as the
theme of the novel and the symbol of Defoe's life.

3   DAVIS, ANDREW MCFARLAND. Reprints and notes in Colonial Cur-
     rency Reprints 1682-1751. Boston: Prince Society, 2:109-37,
     257-77.
    Comments upon satirical pamphlets that made use of "Cruso's
Island" as a disguise for the place of publication during the
controversy over the election of speaker to the house of representatives in the spring of 1720. Reprints Reflections upon
Reflections: or, More News from Robinson Cruso's Island (1720),
attributed to Elisha Cooke, as a response to News from Robinson
Cruso's Island (1720), possibly written by Increase or Cotton
Mather. Probably unconnected with this controversy is News from
the Moon (1720), itself a reprint of Defoe's Review (2 May 1710).
What the connection might be between this piece and Boston polem-
ics of the day, no one seems to know. See also Davis, "Currency
and Banking in the Province of the Massachusetts-Bay," Publications of the American Economic Association, 3d ser. 1, no. 4
(December, 1900):68n; 1910.3.

4   ERNST, OTTO. "An den Leser!" Daniel Defoes Robinson Crusoe.
     Stuttgart, Berlin, Leipzig: Union Deutsche Verlagsgesell-
     schaft, pp. v-vi.
    Recalls what it was like to read the old "Robinson" forty
years ago and to share fully his feelings. Intends to give German youth, not a textbook in this edition, but "an experience."
"What one experiences in his innermost soul, there one learns
entirely from himself."

5   ESCOTT, T.H.S. Masters of English Journalism--A Study of Per-
    sonal Forces. London: T. Fisher Unwin. Reprint. Westport,
    Conn.: Greenwood Press, 1970, pp. 48-83, 86-87, 284-85.
       Claims Defoe as "the real creator of the English newspaper"
    with whom the English newspaper first became "in reality as well
    as in name, a Fourth Estate." Utilizes biographical details to
    show that the young journalist had received an appropriately
    "modern" education at Morton's academy; boldly speculates that
    Defoe had fled to Lisbon after the Monmouth "adventure," spent
    his time making "the grand tour" from Madrid to Moscow, and re-
    turned "a seasoned man of the world with a knowledge of foreign
    politics picked up on the spot, and with his natal patronymic im-
    proved into Defoe." Argues that in the Essay upon Projects Defoe
    set out on a "newspaper programme" which placed the different
    "causes" in a chronological sequence for "social progress"; and
    that later he would have an equally strong political influence
    through the Legion Memorial and the True-Born Englishman. To
    King William, Defoe was "the English Teniers of the pen." He was
    the first journalist to give the newspaper a national role, a cer-
    tain respectability, and an influence comparable to parliament's.

6   HALSEY, ROSALIE V. Forgotten Books of the American Nursery:
    A History of the Development of the American Story-Book.
    Boston: Charles E. Goodspeed & Co. Reprint. Detroit: Sing-
    ing Tree Press, 1969, pp. 79, 90, 118, 129, 130, 159.
       Offers sketchy evidence for the availability of Robinson
    Crusoe and Moll Flanders among imported books advertised in Bos-
    ton, around 1781, as well as for the prominence among domestic
    publications for children of Robinson Crusoe, especially the
    edition (1794) of Isaiah Thomas.

7   HASTINGS, WILLIAM T. "Misprints in Defoe." Nation 92,
    no. 2394 (18 May):501.
       Corrects three misprints in texts of Robinson Crusoe which
    should be corrected for the sense, although the incorrect read-
    ings appear in the older editions. Finds also that the text of
    the Aitken edition (as well as Maynadier's, which is "apparently
    a direct reprint") is unreliable both for Robinson Crusoe and
    Duncan Campbell.

8   JACKS, L[AWRENCE] P[EARSALL]. "The Castaway." In Among the
    Idolmakers. London: Williams & Norgate, pp. 1-23 passim.
       Allows the narrator to characterize himself in "this auto-
    biographical piece" as one having "an unconventional, nay, a
    capricious, standard of truth," which comes close to outright
    lying. Describes the narrator's lifelong obsession with the
    castaway experience on a Desolate Island as starting in March
    1868 with his father's purchase for him of Robinson Crusoe.

9   K., L.L. "Defoe Methodist Chapel, Tooting." Notes and Que-
    ries, 11th ser. 3, no. 56 (21 January):54.
       See 1910.7.

10   A MEMBER FOR HULL [pseud.].   "Dickens and Defoe, or the
     Dickens Fellowship in Hull."   Dickensian 7, no. 4 (April):
     96-98.
          Tries to establish relationships between Dickens and Defoe,
     with little success, except for the character Joe Toddyhigh in
     Master Humphrey's Clock, "once a poor boy who had gone to sea
     from Hull," as had Robinson Crusoe.   Little Nell and Barnaby
     Rudge have other sailings from Hull.

11   MORGAN, CHARLOTTE E.   The Rise of the Novel of Manners: A
     Study of English Prose Fiction between 1600 to 1740.   Columbia
     University Studies in English.   New York: Columbia University
     Press, 271 pp. passim.
          States in the preface that this study, originally a disser-
     tation directed by William P. Trent, only clears the ground "in a
     field where little has been done and much remains to be accom-
     plished."   Differentiates in the introduction between literary
     and popular fiction; describes the merging of readers into one
     general public by the end of the seventeenth century.   Mentions
     Defoe throughout the book, and frequently cites him as author or
     possible author in the appendix, "Chronological List of the Prose
     Fiction Printed in England Between 1600 and 1740."   Devotes a
     separate section (9 pp.) of chap. 4, "The Popular Fiction," to
     his contributions.

12   PAGE, JOHN T.   "Defoe Methodist Chapel, Tooting."   Notes and
     Queries, 11th ser. 3, no. 56 (21 January):54.
          See 1910.7.

13   PICKETT, LA SALLE CORBELL.   Literary Hearthstones of Dixie.
     Philadelphia and London: J.B. Lippincott Co., pp. 15-18.
          During the young Poe's stay in Stoke-Newington, in 1824,
     imagines him finding inspiration by gazing at the "massive walls"
     of Defoe's house, "within which the immortal Robinson Crusoe
     sprang into being and found that island of enchantment."

14   RYAN, JAMES, ed.   Preface to Robert Knox, An Historical Rela-
     tion of Ceylon.   Glasgow: MacLehose & Sons, p. xxii.
          Reprints Knox's An Historical Relation of Ceylon (1681)
     from the manuscript found last year in the Bodleian Library,
     along with his autobiography.   Claims briefly that Defoe knew
     Knox, quoted the Historical Relation extensively in Captain
     Singleton, and may have modeled Quaker William after him.

15   SALLEY, ALEXANDER S., JR., ed.   Introduction to "Party-Tyran-
     ny, By Daniel Defoe, 1705."   In Narratives of Early Carolina
     1650-1708.   Original Narratives of Early American History.
     New York: Charles Scribner's Sons, pp. 221-23.
          Provides background for Defoe's stating the case, to the
     English parliament in 1705, on behalf of Dissenters of South Caro-
     lina and against the provincial government seeking to deprive the
     Dissenters of the right to sit in the Commons House.   Reprints

with notes the entire pamphlet, <u>Party-Tyranny: or, An Occasional</u>
<u>Bill in Miniature; As now Practised in Carolina</u> (41 pp.).

16   TAYLOR, HENRY. "Defoe Methodist Chapel, Tooting." <u>Notes and</u>
      <u>Queries</u>, 11th ser. 3, no. 56 (21 January):54.
           See 1910.7.

17   WILLIAMS, HAROLD. "Daniel Defoe (1661?-1731)." In <u>Two Cen-</u>
      <u>turies of the English Novel</u>. London: Smith, Elder & Co.,
      pp. 12-32.
           Devotes an entire chapter to Defoe as an index of his im-
      portance. In addition to the expected biographical and critical
      commentary, introduces startlingly fresh observations, as for
      instance, on Defoe's art (or lack of it) and on the qualities of
      the novels. Denies that in <u>Robinson Crusoe</u> or any other novel
      there was any "artistic craftsmanship," "dramatic sense," psycho-
      logical effects, or even lifelike conversation. Defoe is totally
      deficient in the modern interests of psychology and local colour.
      What the novelist had, as Carlyle noted, was "clearness of sight"
      upon the world as "a stage for action" and "a fine sense of pro-
      portion" which made him attentive to the minute details requisite
      for verisimilitude. Sums up Defoe's art by referring to its
      effects: "his novels pulse with restless energy and life."

1912

1   ARKLE, A.H. "Statue of the Piper in the Plague of London."
      <u>Notes and Queries</u>, 11th ser. 5, no. 109 (27 January):67.
           Reprints the anecdote of the drunken bagpiper which is,
      as the editor explains, "a variant or an expansion of the story
      related by Defoe" in the <u>Journal of the Plague Year</u>. See also
      1912.4.

2   BASTIDE, CH[ASLES]. "Le traducteur de <u>Robinson Crusoé</u>:
      Thémiseul de Saint-Hyacinthe. "In <u>Anglais et Français du</u>
      <u>XVIIe siècle</u>. Paris: Félix Alcan, pp. 321-53.
           Narrates the lively events in the life of the young cavalry
      officer, Chevalier de Thémiseul, who in 1715 achieved some ac-
      claim with the publication of his <u>Chef-d'oeuvre d'un inconnu</u>
      under the pseudonym Doctor Matanasius, and whose scandalous life
      thereafter seems to have gotten progressively worse. While life
      was at its "blackest," he began translating <u>Robinson Crusoe</u>
      (1720), but wearied of the task and left it to Justus van Effen
      to complete. See the translation into English, 1914.1.

3   BELL, WALTER GEORGE. <u>Fleet Street in Seven Centuries</u>.
      London: Sir Isaac Pitman & Sons, pp. 390-92.
           Tells briefly of Defoe's association with Temple Bar at
      the far end of Fleet Street, his "unabashed" appearance on the
      pillory, his triumph on 31 July 1703.

4   BRASSINGTON, W.S. "Statue of the Piper in the Plague of Lon-
     don." Notes and Queries, 11th ser. 5, no. 113 (24 February):
     153.
          Replies to 1912.1. Locates the famous statue of "the piper
     and his dog," by Caius Gabriel Cibber, at Welcombe, Stratford-
     upon-Avon, the home of Sir George and Lady Trevelyan.

5   E. "Defoe: 'Royal Gin.'" Notes and Queries, 11th ser. 5,
     no. 117 (23 March):228.
          Queries where Defoe eulogized "Royal Gin." Repeats a con-
     versation, recorded in an essay by Paul Léautaud, in which Marcel
     Schwob reads: "Royal Gin, surprising of color and 'humour,' of
     the quintessence of Baudelaire."

6   ESDAILE, ARUNDELL. A List of English Tales and Prose Romances
     Printed before 1740. London: Bibliographical Society,
     pp. 201-10.
          In part 2 (1643-1739), lists alphabetically under Defoe the
     titles of twenty-seven fictional works available at the British
     Museum with their pressmarks, or by the number in William Lee's
     catalogue, giving publisher's name, and identifying the edition.
     See review by Prothero, 1924.14.

7   FEA, ALLAN. The Real Captain Cleveland. London: Martin
     Secker, 256 pp. passim.
          Relates the story of John Gow, the real Captain Cleveland
     of Scott's The Pirate (1821), as given in Defoe's Account of
     the Conduct and Proceedings of the late John Gow alias Smith
     (1725). Argues, in turn, that Captain Singleton seems to have
     been "Gow's prototype"; and continues using the Account and
     other sources to characterize the real John Gow and describe
     his adventures.

8   GUIMARAENS, A.J.C. "Daniel Defoe and the Family of Foe."
     Notes and Queries, 11th ser. 5, no. 118 (30 March):241-43.
          Summarizes newly discovered legal documents: (1) Henry
     Foe's will corroborating details concerning the narrator H.F.
     in the Journal of the Plague Year; (2) the legal dispute in
     1724 between Defoe the plaintiff and John Ward over the lat-
     ter's tenancy of a farm near Colchester, the property of Hannah
     Defoe; (3) Defoe's bill in Chancery, 1728 and 1730, against
     Mary Brooke, creditrix, in countersuit to her charges in the
     King's Bench or Exchequer for recovery of debts owed many years
     earlier by Defoe to James and Samuel Stancliffe. See also
     James R. Sutherland, "A Note on the Last Years of Defoe,"
     Modern Language Review 29 no. 2 (April, 1934):137-41; "Down
     Chancery Lane," Evidence in Literary Scholarship: Essays in
     Memory of James Marshall Osborn, ed. René Wellek and Alvaro
     Ribeiro (Oxford: Clarendon Press, 1979), pp. 170-74.

9   HACKWOOD, FREDERICK WILLIAM. <u>William Hone: His Life and</u>
<u>Times</u>. London: T. Fisher Unwin; Leipzig: Inselstrasse,
pp. 210, 276, 292-93, 320, 364.
    For Hone, in a letter dated 3 February 1819 to the "radi-
cal" printer John Childs: "Old De Foe is a man after my own
heart, respecting whom and his works I know more, perhaps, than
any other living admirer of him--his 'Jure Divino' is indeed
a famous old book, and yet I fear would not (I wish it would)
bear re-printing"; refers also to William Hazlitt [senior] as
"a De Foeite." In the "Bibliography," Hone's <u>The Right Divine</u>
<u>of Kings to Govern Wrong</u> (1821) is described as "a Rifacimento
of one of De Foe's works, with a Preface by Hone." Reprinted:
New York: Burt Franklin, [n.d.]

10   HASTINGS, WILLIAM T. "Errors and Inconsistencies in Defoe's
<u>Robinson Crusoe</u>." <u>Modern Language Notes</u> 27, no. 6 (June):161-
66.
    Examines here minutely the errors and inconsistencies in
the chronology of <u>Robinson Crusoe</u> as important toward countering
any possible allegory of Defoe's life in Crusoe's story. Analyzes the textual problems arising from contradictory statements on
the time for the disappearance of the wreck, the month and the
year for Crusoe's first sight of the cannibals, the length of Friday's stay with Crusoe before others join them, the overall time-
span for the "captivity" (27 or 28 years). Itemizes the discrepancies in Crusoe's experiences as revealed by Charles Gildon in
1719. Reaches conservative conclusions with regard to the text,
recognizing the inconsistencies, but leaving the text unchanged.

11   HOLLIDAY, CARL. <u>English Fiction from the Fifth to the Twen-</u>
<u>tieth Century</u>. New York: Century Co., 445 pp. passim.
    Provides "a study of the story-telling <u>instinct</u> among the
English people." Unlike Swift or Addison, Defoe described "men
as they are." Particularly with Robinson Crusoe, he gave people
what they wanted, "one of their own at the common daily tasks of
life." Under the influence of Minto, sets out three stages of
Defoe's development: "real persons in real scenes"; "fictitious persons in real scenes"; "fictitious persons in fictitious
scenes." Finds "a certain cold-bloodedness" in Defoe's manner;
vivid portrayal of character, but no development. Casts doubt on
any moral purpose in <u>Moll Flanders</u>, <u>Colonel Jack</u>, <u>Captain Single-</u>
<u>ton</u>. Views Moll's manner as showing "some lack of conscience in
himself"; <u>Roxana</u> as "in part downright corrupt; and his "masterpiece," <u>Robinson Crusoe</u>, as falling short of "the complete nature
of a novel."

12   JEFFERSON, MARK. "Winds in <u>Robinson Crusoe</u>." <u>Journal of</u>
<u>Geography</u> 11, no. 1 (September):23-25.
    Follows up on 1912.13, displaying evidence from <u>Robinson</u>
<u>Crusoe</u> that Defoe knew about wind changes around Sallee for one
part of the story, and in the area just north of the equator for
another part.

13   MARTZOEFF, C.L. "Robinson Crusoe—A Study in the New Geog-
      raphy." Journal of Geography 10, no. 9 (May):295-97.
         In showing that Robinson Crusoe is consonant with "more mod-
      ern conceptions of geography and its teaching," traces main out-
      lines of the story as epitomizing "the experiences of the race."

14   PILON, EDMOND. "Daniel De Foë." Nouvelle Revue Française
      7:141-217.
         Takes the form of a fictionalized biography, a moving
      tribute addressed to Defoe as a monologue. Creates imaginary epi-
      sodes, even characters, out of a few facts or myths and legends
      which are unsubstantiated. Although on occasion the interpreta-
      tion may be provocative or a critical insight, the overall effect
      is impressionistic. Fictionalized events include the incident of
      the Kentish petition; the trial and punishment on the pillory,
      with comment on the crucifixion overtones; the despair and ill-
      ness recorded in the Appeal to Honour and Justice (1715); the
      subsequent departure from London, apoplexy, sale of the Robinson
      Crusoe manuscript to William Taylor; the meeting in Bristol with
      Selkirk; the death in a public house in Islington. Not infre-
      quently, commits outright errors. Benefits from the positive
      influences of Philarète Chasles and Marcel Schwob; warmly appre-
      ciates the social differences between Swift and Pope, on the one
      hand, and Defoe, on the other; has a keen awareness of Defoe's
      other novels by reminding us intermittently that jostling Defoe
      on London streets or in Newgate are people who would become poor
      Jacques, Bob Singleton, Moll Flanders, Lady Roxana. Reprinted:
      Portraits de Sentiment, 2d ed. (Paris: Mercure de France, 1913),
      pp. 9-92.

15   POLLARD, ALFRED W. Fine Books. Connoisseur's Library. New
      York: G.P. Putnam's Sons; London: Methuen, p. 294.
         Identifies the engravers "Clark and Pine" for the plates of
      the first edition of Robinson Crusoe as John Clark (1688-1736)
      and John Pine (1690-1756).

16   PURVES, W. LAIDLAW. "The Literary Output of Daniel Defoe."
      Library, 3d ser. 3, no. 11 (July):333-35.
         Gives the statistics in numbers of pages to document De-
      foe's "marvellous and almost incredible fertility": from 1719 to
      1728, a total of 11,453 octavo pages. Asks if Defoe might not
      have had "one or more imitators," or if he might not have been at
      times the editor and not the author.

17   TIEJE, ARTHUR J. "The Expressed Aim of the Long Prose Fiction
      from 1579 to 1740." Journal of English and Germanic Philology
      11:402-32.
         For the five expressed aims of pre-Richardsonian fiction,
      selects Defoe to introduce "social purpose" ("the humanitarianism
      of Dickens" anticipated by Colonel Jack); religious purpose (The˙
      Storm, 1704; Robinson Crusoe); and moral purpose, including
      "purity of phrase" (Roxana, Moll Flanders).

18   TRENT, W[ILLIAM] P. "Defoe--The Newspaper and the Novel." In
     Cambridge History of English Literature. Edited by A.W. Ward
     and A.R. Waller. 14 vols. New York: G.P. Putnam's Sons; Cam-
     bridge: University Press, 9:1-28, 463-82.
         Deals briefly with Defoe's predecessors in journalism
     (e.g., Roger L'Estrange, Henry Care, John Dunton); concentrates
     upon biography and a reappraisal of the writings, to uphold the
     thesis that the novelist evolved out of the journalist and mis-
     cellaneous writer. Builds a fresh perspective of Defoe out of a
     revised listing of works in the canon (365 items plus 19 news-
     papers), the first thoroughgoing revision since Lee's Defoe
     (1869). Stands out from earlier biographers in forthrightly
     arguing that it is impossible now to view the man as favorably
     as he was regarded in the nineteenth century. As a consequence
     of his persecution for the Shortest-Way with the Dissenters, he
     underwent changes in personality and character which allowed him
     even to betray Harley, as in the publication of Atalantis Major
     (1711). Determines the turning point of Defoe's life and career
     to be in the pillorying. Views him as a writer, not as "a shame-
     less and wholesale liar," but as "a consummate casuist who was
     often his own chief dupe." In the role of journalist, he was "a
     treacherous mercenary"; but in any other role, he was "a pious,
     philanthropical, fairly accurate and trustworthy man and citi-
     zen." On the novels (10 pp.), praises Robinson Crusoe as "the
     most indisputable English classic of modern times" because it has
     "the power to make alive"; Captain Singleton, Moll Flanders, and
     Roxana as displaying "a power of characterization"; Roxana as
     showing the "greatest advance, not a very great one after all,
     toward the construction of a well-ordered plot." Credits Defoe
     with the role of "the shaper" in both the Capt. George Carleton
     and Madagascar. Regards Defoe the writer as "second only to
     Swift, if even to him" and as "the greatest of plebeian genius-
     es." See also 1912.19. Reprinted: 1932.

19   ____. "A Talk About Defoe." In Papers of the Hobby Club
     of New York City, 1911-1912. Cambridge, Mass.: Riverside
     Press, pp. 28-50.
         Describes his work on "the man who has literally haunted
     me, whom I can truly characterize as the most interesting and
     perplexing, though far from the most inspiring, personality I
     have ever studied." Started eight years ago investigating the
     canon of Defoe, and expanded Lee's 250 items to double that
     number through five collecting visits to England and the devel-
     opment of "tests of style" for Defoe as reenforcements of the
     evidence from contemporaries. During the second visit to En-
     gland, abandoned every "confidence in Defoe's probity," and came
     to believe that the pillorying of 1703 was the main turning-
     point in Defoe's career, converting him to a "mercenary trickster
     and scribbler," one given to dissimulation and deception. As
     a man, Defoe remained "a most interesting and likable person";
     as a novelist, "the greatest of plebeian geniuses." See also
     1912.18.

20   WHITTEN, WILFRED. A Londoner's London. Toronto: Bell &
     Cockburn, pp. 95, 100-1.
         Briefly associates Defoe ("son of the Fore Street butcher")
     with London places such as Tokenhouse Yard and Freeman's Court.

                              1913

1   BARRIE, J[AMES] M[ATTHEW]. Preface to R.M. Ballantyne's The
     Coral Island. London: James Nisbet & Co., pp. v-viii.
         On the subject of being a castaway: Robinson Crusoe and
     Wyss's Swiss Family Robinson.

2   BLACK, WILLIAM GEORGE. "Glasgow Cross and Defoe's Tour."
     Notes and Queries, 11th ser. 8, no. 201 (1 November):349.
         Query: In the description of the marketplace in Glasgow,
     do the words appear in the first edition of the Tour: "In the
     centre stands the cross"? In which edition were they first omit-
     ted? Who, if not Defoe, was the author of the Scottish portion
     of the Tour? See replies, 1913.9, 12; 1914.11.

3   BRANDL, LEOPOLD. "Vordefoesche Robinsonaden in der Weltliter-
     atur." Germanisch-Romanische Monatsschrift 5:233-61.
         Draws upon Ullrich (1909.24) in presenting characteristic
     variants of the "Robinsonades" before Defoe. Observes that the
     treatment of the motif was less fabulous in the writings of sea-
     faring peoples (Dutch, French, English) than among the Germans.
     Consists largely of plot-summaries of works from Sophocles to
     Leguat.   (P.E.C.)

*4   CHESTERTON, G.K. Defoe [Selections].
         Listed in CBEL and New CBEL (1971), but not in Payne's
     "Annotated Bibliography" (1975). No copy has been located.

5   CHINARD, GILBERT. L'Amérique et le rêve exotique dans la
     littérature française au XVIIe et au XVIIIe siècle. Paris:
     Hachette, pp. 248-52, 347, 393.
         So widely read was Robinson Crusoe among us in the eigh-
     teenth century that "we almost have the right to consider it a
     French work." Although the source generally cited for the Sel-
     kirk narrative is given here as Woodes Rogers, Chinard insists
     that Esquemeling had told the story earlier in an edition of
     Buccaneers of America (1704). From this source Defoe had taken
     "the primitive idea" of Robinson Crusoe; from the Adventures of
     Ravenau de Lussan (published in the 1689 edition of Buccaneers
     of America) he had clearly taken inspiration for Part One of
     Robinson Crusoe. Comments on the reception given Robinson Crusoe
     in France at the time of Rousseau: readers had not recognized
     "in the Puritan style of Defoe and under Robinson's goatskin cap,
     the revolutionary accent of our Utopian novelists and the pictur-
     esque features of buccaneers and adventure-hunters." Reprinted:
     Paris: E. Droz, 1934.

6   COUPER, W.J., ed. Appendix: "Memorial for Mr. Watson, Print-
    er, 1713." In Watson's Preface to the "History of Printing,"
    1713. Edinburgh: Darien Press, p. 76.
        Describes the efforts made in Edinburgh as early as March
    1711--on the part of the printer James Watson, the bookseller
    Robert Freebairn, and the printer John Baskett--to wrest the
    printing monopoly in Scotland away from Mrs. Anderson and her
    family, and have it assigned to the appellant, Freebairn. Into
    the long-protracted, at times embittered controversy, Defoe was
    drawn, as here, when Mrs. Anderson was attacked as "a woman who
    printed the seditious reviews of Defoe (in the very time she was
    soliciting for the renewing of her gift of Sovereign's Printer)
    containing unparalleled reproaches against the Queen and her
    present ministers, and who lately printed the seditious 'Season-
    able Warning.'"

7   CURRY, FRANK. "De Foe and Napoleon Bonapart." Notes and
    Queries, 11th ser. 7 (24 May):405-6.
        Receives "sudden shock" at discovering the substitution
    in the text of Defoe's [Political] History of the Devil (London:
    Joseph Smith, 1837) the name of Napoleon Bonaparte. The succes-
    sion described here is from Nimrod the first through a number
    of ambitious princes. Instead of the expected George I appears
    Napoleon Bonaparte. See reply, 1913.16.

8   _____. "Defoe's Weekly Review." Notes and Queries, 11th ser.
    8, no. 206 (6 December):448-49.
        Identifies the James Crossley copy of the Review as the
    only "perfect" one now in existence, and strongly urges that
    "this valuable commentary on affairs between 1704 and 1713" be
    reprinted, and distributed among important British libraries.
    See reply, 1914.7.

9   _____. "Glasgow Cross and Defoe's Tour." Notes and Queries,
    11th ser. 8, no. 208 (20 December):492-93.
        Replies to 1913.2. Summarizes the changes in the text of
    the Tour after the first edition; cites the evidence from Defoe's
    preface and Wright (1894) on his responsibility for the Scottish
    portion of the Tour. Accepts the statements in Defoe's Great Law
    of Subordination (1724) that he visited Scotland during his
    travels, 1684-1688.

10 _____. "Two Anonymous Works: Eighteenth Century." Notes and
    Queries, 11th ser. 8, no. 187 (26 July):69.
        Asks for help in identifying the authorship of Secret His-
    tory of Arlus and Odolphus (1710) and Way to Bring the World to
    Rights (1711), both assigned to Defoe in a current bookseller's
    catalogue.

11 "Daniel Defoe and a Forth Naval Base." Times (London), 10
    January, p. 11.

Notes that in the Dunfermline Journal Defoe's views are
quoted in his "Proposals for Scotland" to Harley on 5 September
1710, in which he favors a naval base in the Firth of Forth as
opposed to one at Leith.

12   G. "Glasgow Cross and Defoe's Tour." Notes and Queries, 11th
      ser. 8, no. 204 (22 November):417.
          Replies to 1913.2 that it is difficult to decide on Defoe's
      responsibility for the Scottish portion of the Tour.

13   GREENOUGH, CHESTER N. "John Dunton's Letters from New En-
      gland." In Publications of the Colonial Society of Massachu-
      setts. Vol. 14, Transactions 1911-1913. Boston: Published
      by the Society, pp. 212-57 passim.
          Demonstrates that Dunton's "Letters from New England,"
      published first in his Life and Errors (1705), must have been
      written much later than 1686, and is more fiction than history.
      Draws evidence from Dunton's quoting of, and alluding to, Defoe's
      More Reformation (1703).

14   GUTHKELCH, A.C. "Defoe's True-Born Englishman." In Essays
      and Studies by Members of the English Association, vol. 4.
      Collected by C.H. Herford. Oxford: Clarendon Press,
      pp. 101-50.
          Introduces (4 pp.), reprints (1st ed., 1700, 42 pp.), and
      annotates (4 pp.) the True-Born Englishman. For the first time,
      prints the text with the original heading for Sir Charles Dun-
      comb's "Fine Speech" and with the attack on John Tutchin. The
      verses are separately paged and the lines numbered.

15   HASTINGS, WILLIAM T., ed. Introduction to The Life and
      Strange Surprising Adventures of Robinson Crusoe. Lake En-
      glish Classics. Chicago and New York: Scott, Foresman & Co.,
      pp. 7-38.
          Although described on the title page as "edited for school
      use," this critical edition of Part One shows a high level of
      quality, incorporating the author's earlier research on the
      errors and inconsistencies in Robinson Crusoe and providing a
      useful textual apparatus. In "The Life of Defoe" (11 pp.), gives
      more attention to his political career than to his personal life;
      scrutinizes carefully every bit of biographical information.
      Finds in "Defoe As Journalist and Pamphleteer" (4 pp.), that the
      tracts and verses are less important than the Review. In "Defoe
      As a Writer of Prose Fiction" (15 pp.), discusses his predeces-
      sors and his own narrative experiments, and turns to Robinson
      Crusoe with fresh insights on the reasons for its success: for
      instance, the comments on Crusoe as "in part an unconsciously
      drawn portrait of Defoe's inner man, only less competent and more
      stupid"; on the lack of any clash between character and action;
      on the autobiographical form as allowing "certain apparent errors
      in literary craftsmanship" which increase the plausibility of
      the narrative. As to "Defoe's Later Narratives," rates the four

autobiographies of "presumably fictitious criminals" as among Defoe's best achievements; singles out <u>Roxana</u> as representing a definite advance in structure, plot, and character-development.

16   JONAS, ALFRED CHAS. "De Foe and Napoleon Bonaparte." <u>Notes and Queries</u>, 11th ser. 7 (28 June):514.
      Replies to 1913.7, with the information that the 1793 edition of the <u>Political History of the Devil</u> has Louis XIV in place of the original George I.

17   POLLARD, ALFRED W. "Notes. . . ." <u>Library</u>, 3d ser. 4, no. 15 (July):351-52.
      Gives four brief notes in reply to Purves, 1913.20, which repeat earlier arguments (1913.18) concerning the "O" edition. Now three copies of the <u>Robeson Cruso</u> have been discovered. Calls for a reprinting of at least part of the O edition with a collation of the first four Taylor editions. See Hutchins's <u>"Robinson Crusoe" and Its Printing</u> (1925), pp. 167-82.

18   <u>   </u>. "Robeson Cruso." <u>Library</u>, 3d ser. 4, no. 14 (April): 204-20.
      Revives the discussion of the "O" edition, <u>Robeson Cruso</u>, which Purves began in 1903.13. General agreement exists that the O edition represents a state of the text which is earlier than the Taylor first edition (T^1), and therefore has readings in common with this text, but it also shares readings with the Taylor third edition (T^3). Offers the plausible theory, which answers to the data of textual comparisons, that the O edition was printed, "in whole or in part, from the uncorrected first proofs of T^1, and that T^3 was printed, in whole or in part, from the corrected proofs or revises." Some of the variant readings, discussed here, between O, T^1 and T^3 were most likely the work of Defoe himself. Argues finally that the O edition was a piracy from "a stolen set of first proofs" and that T^3 was printed from "a nearly correct set of second proofs or revises of the Taylor First Edition." See also 1913.17, 19-20; Hutchins's <u>"Robinson Crusoe" and Its Printing</u> (1925), pp. 167-82.

19   PURVES, W. LAIDLAW. <u>The Bibliographical Puzzle of "Robeson Cruso."</u> London: Alexander Moring, 19 pp.
      Follows up on the revived interest in the "O" edition, <u>Robeson Cruso</u>, when a second copy was purchased by the British Museum and discussed by Pollard, 1913.18, expressing both agreement and disagreement with Purves, 1903.13. Claims to be reprinted from the <u>Library</u>, July, 1913, but the original article has not been found there. Reproduces facsimiles of title pages of the O edition and the Taylor first edition; the Map of the World from the Fourth edition, and the <u>Farther Adventures</u>; and the title page of <u>Serious Reflections</u>--all to illustrate the continuing spelling of "Cruso" in 1719 texts. Shows that the advertisements in early newspapers reflect the change from "Cruso" to "Crusoe" on 12 May 1719. Includes tables showing "variations" beteen the O edition

and the Taylor first edition (8 pp.), and presents evidence that
the O edition and the four Taylor editions were set up separately, and that the O edition was printed from its own manuscript,
and was not a piracy.

20 _____. "Robeson Cruso. A Rejoinder." Library, 3d ser. 4,
no. 15 (July):338-51.
   Reasserts his general agreement with Pollard, 1913.18, that
the text of the "O" edition, Robeson Cruso, preceded the four
editions published by William Taylor in 1719. Develops his disagreement, point by point, particularly with the view that the
O edition was a piracy of the Taylor first edition, by offering
"feasible explanations" for Pollard's overly elaborate ones.
Repeats his main point that many questions arising from the O edition copy as "a disgraceful specimen of printing" are answered if
one assumes that the ingenious Defoe had Robeson Cruso printed on
one of his journal presses--Mist's Journal or Whitehall Evening
Post--as "typed proof" which he might then show to several publishers. See also 1903.12, 14; 1913.17-19; Hutchins's "Robinson
Crusoe" and Its Printing (1925).

21 SAINTSBURY, GEORGE. "From Lyly to Swift." In The English
Novel. London: J.M. Dent & Sons. Reprint. London: J.M.
Dent & Sons; New York: E.P. Dutton & Co., 1931, pp. 64-72.
   Decries the little criticism written about Defoe's novels
and the tendency of "occasional eccentrics" to belittle him as a
novelist. Moves rapidly to consider the "picaresque romances"--
Captain Singleton, Moll Flanders, Colonel Jack, and Roxana.
Assesses the quality of Defoe's contribution to the novel, the
"Story-Interest," as being especially high. Then examines "the
Four Elements of the novel" (Plot, Character, Description, and
Dialogue) and the suitability of style to method. Concludes that
Defoe was "the first of the magicians--not the greatest by any
means, but great and almost alone in the peculiar talent of
making uninteresting things interesting . . . by serving them
'simple of themselves' as though they actually existed."

22 TIEJE, ARTHUR JERROLD. "A Peculiar Phase of the Theory of
Realism in Pre-Richardsonian Fiction." PMLA 28, no. 2:213-52
passim.
   Places Defoe's theoretical statements in the prefaces of
his fictional narratives, which relate to the expressed aim of
achieving realism or forcing belief upon the reader, in the
larger context of French and English fiction before Richardson.
Specifically relies upon the Storm (1704) for Defoe's insistence
on "sufficient authority" to vouch for a story; upon Avery,
Moll Flanders, and Roxana, for the device of the elaborate
preface; upon Mrs. Veal and Robinson Crusoe, for assertions of
the author's attempts to gain the truth; upon Memoirs of a Cavalier, for the ploy of the discovered manuscript; upon Part Two
of Robinson Crusoe, for providing "geographical definiteness."
Makes the case that the theoretical statements are part of an

important movement which had structural and stylistic effects
upon narrative.

23   TURNER, OTIS. Director of film (American). Robinson Crusoe.
        Cast includes Robert Z. Leonard as Robinson. See Filmo-
graphic Dictionary of World Literature.

24   WYATT, EDITH. "The Author of Robinson Crusoe." North Ameri-
        can Review 198, no. 692 (July):87-92.
        Recapitulates the biography of Defoe from secondary sources
and "personal references" in his works; includes a few misstate-
ments. Discusses the major novels (5 pp.) where for eleven years
he "exercised in fresh fields his ruling passion for original designs." Offers fresh observations on the novels. For instance:
in Journal of the Plague Year and Memoirs of a Cavalier, Defoe
shows his genius for "writing like Legion." Moll Flanders, Colonel Jack, and Roxana are like the novels of Zola, "indecent but
moral." You turn away from Defoe's novels as you would "from
mountain forests in the morning light--refreshed with new wonder
and courage."

                              1913-1914

1   "Defoe, Daniel." The Everyman Encyclopaedia. Edited by An-
        drew Boyle. London: J.M. Dent & Sons; New York: E.P. Dutton
        & Co., 5:18-19.
        Concludes the biographical summary with the comment that
"perhaps his fecundity, his vivid imagination, his almost unpar-
alleled versatility as a man of letters and his impressive style
have been somewhat obscured by the unheroic, unromantic character
of his moral standard and beliefs, as also by his offensive,
though by no means unique, political inconsistencies."

                                1914

1   BASTIDE, CHARLES. "The Strange Adventures of the Translator
        of Robinson Crusoe, the Chevalier de Thémiseul." In The
        Anglo-French Entente in the Seventeenth Century. London:
        John Lane; New York: John Lane Co.; Toronto: Bell & Cock-
        burn. Reprint. New York: Burt Franklin, 1971, pp.207-27.
        Translation of 1912.2.

2   BAYLEY, A.R. "A Note on Sheridan." Notes and Queries, 11th
        ser. 10 (25 July):61-63.
        Includes a letter dated 7 November 1825 from William Linley
to Thomas Moore, who was one of R.B. Sheridan's early biographers, in which the Robinson Crusoe pantomime (1781.4) is assigned to Mrs. Sheridan as the author. See also 1781.1.

3   BERNBAUM, ERNEST. The Mary Carleton Narratives 1663-1673:
     A Missing Chapter in the History of the English Novel. Cam-
     bridge, Mass.: Harvard University Press; London: Oxford
     University Press, 106 pp. passim.
         Examines closely the relationship of the English novel and
     criminal biographies. Makes the case that the closest approach
     to Defoe, "the father of the English novel," is to be found in
     Francis Kirkman's The Counterfeit Lady Unveiled (1673)--one of
     some twenty narratives dealing with Mary Carleton, published
     between 1663 and 1732. Demonstrates that all the novelistic
     techniques, especially the blending of fact and fiction, were
     already present in the popular criminal biographies. In chap. 6,
     "The Historical Significance of The Counterfeit Lady Unveiled,"
     attempts to demolish "three cardinal doctrines about the origin
     of the modern novel." For the second of these doctrines, argues
     that Defoe's realistic fiction was not so much an "imitation of
     records" as it was of "records that falsely pretended to be truth-
     ful"; further, that Defoe was "thoroughly schooled in unscrupu-
     lous mendacity." In these "methods of fabrication," Defoe was
     not so much the inventor as the consummate "master of the art."
     See the review "A Famous Adventuress," TLS, no. 956 (13 May
     1920):292; and The Counterfeit Lady Unveiled and Other Criminal
     Fiction of Seventeenth-Century England, ed. Spiro Peterson (New
     York: Doubleday & Co., 1961), pp. 3-8.

4   BRÜGGEMANN, FRITZ. Utopie und Robinsonade. Untersuchungen zu
     Schnabels "Insel Felsenburg" (1731-1743). Forschungen zur
     neueren Literaturgeschichte, 46. Weimar: Alexander Duncker
     Verlag, 208 pp.
         Substantiating earlier suggestions of a utopian flavor in
     this work, claims Insel Felsenburg to be the only fully developed
     utopian Robinsonade. Analyzes Insel Felsenburg in detail along
     with Robinson Crusoe; discusses briefly Insel Felsenburg motifs
     found in other Robinsonades before 1731 and in earlier utopian
     works since Thomas More. Reprinted: Hildesheim: Gerstenberg
     Verlag, 1978.   (P.E.C.)

5   HORTEN, FRANZ. Studien über die Sprache Defoe's. Nebst einem
     Anhang. Bonn: Peter Hanstein, 253 pp.
         Expands the dissertation (1909.13) by adding an eight-page
     forward and an entirely new second part ("Words") and a new third
     part ("Syntax"). Attempts to compare Defoe's grammar, syntax,
     and orthography with modern practice. Notes the changes in mean-
     ings of words, and gives a brief account of the differences be-
     tween manuscript and print versions of the Compleat English Gen-
     tleman (1890), Of Royall Education (1895), and Robinson Crusoe.
     See the review by Hermann Ullrich in Zeitschrift für franzosichen
     und englischen Unterricht 16 (1917):230-32.

6   HOWARD, CLIFFORD. "Crusoe's Real Island." Bookman 39, no. 5
     (July):505-11.

Makes the case for Tobago, and not Juan Fernandez, as Crusoe's island. Cites title page of Robinson Crusoe and the places
in the narrative which seem to confirm the geographical location.
Argues that Selkirk was not the original of Crusoe, but Defoe was
himself; bases this view on [Wright's] theory of the story as an
allegory of Defoe's twenty-eight years of silence.

7   MATTHEWS, ALBERT. "Defoe's Weekly Review." Notes and Que-
    ries, 11th ser. 9, no. 214 (31 January):95-96.
        Replies to 1913.8. Notes that Trent had made the sugges-
tion for reprinting the Review in 1913.23; advises future editor
of such a reprint to study carefully the Edinburgh connections
of the Review in vols. 6 and 7 available in the United States.

8   PARKER, IRENE. Dissenting Academies in England: Their Rise
    and Progress and Their Place among the Educational Systems of
    the Country. Cambridge University Press, pp. 56, 58-63, 126.
        Describes the high educational quality of the Dissenting
Academies, such as Newington Green Academy, which Defoe attended,
under the tutor Charles Morton. In their curriculum and standards, the academies rivalled the universities which were closed
to Dissenters; in their willingness to introduce new subject-mat-
ter and teaching techniques (for both innovations Defoe praised
Morton), they surpassed the universities. Defoe gives considerable information about his school and tutor in one of the
Reviews. Along with praise, he mentions one shortcoming: "a
want of conversation." Even a hostile critic of the Dissenting
Academies, Samuel Wesley, has only admiration for the discipline
there for students "to avoid the debaucheries of the universities." The influence of a Dissenting education was great--on
Defoe, on English thought ("a modified Puritanism"), on English
education.

9   POLAK, LÉON. "A Source of Defoe's Robinson Crusoe." Notes
    and Queries, 11th ser. 9, no. 234 (20 June):486.
        Calls attention of English scholars to his article,
1914.10, on the Dutch source, Krinke Kesmes (Amsterdam, 1708).

10   . "Vordefoesche Robinsonaden in den Niederlanden."
    Germanisch-Romanische Monatsschrift 6:304-7.
        Calls attention to the omission by Brandl (1913.3) of Hen-
drik Smeeks's Dutch Robinsonade, Beschrijvinge van het Magtig
Koningrijk Krinke Kesmes (1708), and of the presence there of an
episode which shows "the Robinson motif in its purest form" and
is next to Selkirk's adventures the most significant source of
Robinson Crusoe. Cites errors (such as the date, 1721) in Hettner's literary history [1865] and Harnack's revision to explain
the neglect in Germany of "the Dutch Robinson"; notes the late
recognitions by Hoogewerff (1909) and Naber (1910). Presents a
comparison to show Smeeks's episode as a source.

11   R., J.F. "Glasgow Cross and Defoe's <u>Tour</u>." <u>Notes and Que-</u>
      <u>ries</u>, 11th ser. 9, no. 211 (10 January):32.
           Replies to 1913.2. The words "in the centre stands the
      cross" do not appear in the description of the Glasgow market-
      place in the <u>Tour</u> (first ed.).

12   RICHARDSON, R.R. "Daniel Defoe: A Great Journalist." <u>Papers</u>
      <u>of the Manchester Literary Club</u> 40:452-60.
           Observes that Defoe has "considerable claim" to the titles
      of "the father of English journalism" and "the greatest of all
      journalists," but does not focus on specific works in any detail,
      to demonstrate his point that literature and journalism are not
      necessarily "antagonistic in spirit." Accepts the view that the
      "duplicity" which he practiced in his government role as a
      journalist [after 1715], his "cynical delight in imposing upon
      people," the enjoyment he received from writing with irony and
      verisimilitude--"this method of work" served him well when he
      began writing novels. Characterizes the novels harshly as, for
      instance, lacking in "the spiritual and the romantic," entirely
      concerned with "worldly and material things," filled with "low
      utilitarian" moralizings. As a person, Defoe himself is neither
      admirable nor lovable.

13   TRENT, WILLIAM PETERFIELD. "Defoe, Daniel (c.1660-1731)." In
      <u>The New International Encyclopaedia</u>. 2d ed. New York: Dodd,
      Mead & Co., 6:605-7.
           Compared with Trent's entry in the earlier <u>Encyclopaedia</u>
      (1902.16), reflects a dramatic increase in more accurate bio-
      graphical content, knowledge of the canon expanded mainly by his
      own researches (375 titles and other "plausible attributions"
      swelling the total to 500), and the rich variety of publications.
      Sums up by saying that Defoe's achievements lie in creating
      "lifelikeness" through the use of minute details and in mastery
      of the "homely vernacular."

14   _____. "William Pittis: The Difficulties of a Pamphleteer
      and Biographer," I and II. <u>Nation</u> 98, no. 2554 (11 June):692-
      94; no. 2555 (18 June):722-24.
           Brings together for the first time biographical and histori-
      cal information on the minor Jacobite pamphleteer, William Pittis
      (1674-1724). Lists as by Pittis the <u>History of the Mitre and</u>
      <u>Purse</u> (1714), which replies to Defoe's defence of his patron Lord
      Oxford in the <u>Secret History of the White Staff</u>; and the <u>History</u>
      <u>of the Mitre and Purse Continued--Part II</u>. In Pittis's <u>Queen</u>
      <u>Anne Vindicated</u> (1715), the <u>Secret History of the Secret History</u>
      <u>of the White Staff, Purse and Mitre</u> (1715) and the <u>Memoirs of the</u>
      <u>Conduct of Her Late Majesty</u> (1715) are added to Defoe's writings.
      The account given by Defoe in his <u>Secret History</u>, about scrib-
      blers like Pittis, is said to be outstanding.

1915

1   HOVELAQUE, ÉMILE. "Les Sentements allemands pour l'Angle-
     terre." Revue de Paris 22, no. 2 (1 April):524-58.
        In a long exposé of the German penchant for "systems,"
     turns in section 5 (pp. 555-56) to Robinson Crusoe as one of
     the most important expressions of Puritanism and the psychology
     of the English race, which Hovelaque had already formulated
     (1910.8); and adapts his "theory of race" now to an eloquent
     statement of the democratic ideal as embodied in the concept of
     the British empire, which, as a living force, will always prevail
     over German "mechanism." Reprinted: Bulletin de la société
     autour du monde, no. 2 (July, 1915):36-69.

2   LLOYD, WILLIAM S. Catalogue of Various Editions of "Robinson
     Crusoe" and Other Books by and Referring to Daniel Defoe.
     Library of William S. Lloyd, Germantown, Philadelphia. Phil-
     adelphia, Penn.: Shaw Printing Co., 43 pp.
        Lists by year, from 1719 to 1913, some 277 editions of
     Robinson Crusoe, not all of which are separates, including two
     issues of the first edition, copies of all four editions pub-
     lished by August 1719, altogether representative copies of some
     seventy-eight editions between 1719 and 1819. Lays the "ground-
     work" for the preparation of a bibliography. In a facsimile
     letter which serves as an introduction (4 pp.), W.P. Trent
     praises the collection as "your superb assembly of Crusoes," but
     does find a few gaps.

3   MINET, WILLIAM. "Daniel Defoe and Kent: A Chapter in Capel-
     le-Ferne History." Archaeologia Cantiana 31:61-75.
        Characterizes Mrs. Veal as a "pure romance" built on the
     foundation of "real people," identified here through external
     evidence as William Veal (Controller of the Customs at Dover)
     and his wife Elizabeth. Verifies the existence of the ship
     Degrave which figures prominently in Madagascar. Demonstrates
     the connection between Captains William Young, father and son,
     and Mrs. Elizabeth Veal, formerly the widow Mrs. Hughes and
     daughter of Captain Young, and thus between Madagascar and Mrs.
     Veal. The evidence confirms Defoe's role as "transcriber" and
     thus author of Madagascar. Quotes manuscript notes by Hughes
     Minet, written in 1811, attesting to "the truth of Drury's narra-
     tive" on the basis of conversations he remembers having with his
     mother, Alice Minet.

4   PHELPS, WILLIAM LYON. "The Advance of the English Novel"
     (part 2). Bookman 42, no. 3 (November):281-88 passim.
        Emphasizes the novel in the rehabilitation of Augustan
     literature over the past fifteen years. No prose fiction, ex-
     cept for Mallory's Morte Darthur, seems worth reading before
     Defoe. Among the realists, he had "a telescopic imagination,
     and a microscopic eye." His subject-matter in Robinson Crusoe
     was "wildly romantic"; his method and style were "studiously
     realistic." Without any reservation about their morality,

praises Moll Flanders and Roxana--"slum stories"--as "shining
examples of absolute realism": even if he had never written
Robinson Crusoe, they would have made Defoe the first English
novelist. Captain Singleton most resembles Stevenson's Master
of Ballantrae. The Journal of the Plague Year, according to
findings that Watson Nicholson would announce later (1919.9), is
not a work of the imgination, but "history narrated by a great
artist." Compares Defoe with Bunyan and Swift (early prose
fiction), Gissing (realism), Flaubert and Guy de Mauppasant
(objectivity). Reprinted: The Advance of the English Novel (New
York: Dodd, Mead, & Co., 1922), pp. 35-47; 1927.

5   WALKER, HUGH.   The English Essay and Essayists.   London and
    Toronto: J.M. Dent & Sons; New York: E.P. Dutton, pp. 99-
    105, 168, 185.
       Makes the point that just as Defoe gave hints to Richard
Steele and Joseph Addison in the Mercure Scandale of his Review
and in his separate Little Review, which are important in the development of the essay, he also received hints from the Spectator
and Tatler for the 350 or so essays and letters "disinterred from
forgotten journals" (1716-1729) and published in Lee's Defoe
(1869). Comments also on the suitability of Defoe's temperament
to be an essayist, on the subjects that are "pure Defoe," on the
comparable productivity of later essayists such as Leigh Hunt.

6   WHICHER, GEORGE FRISBIE.   The Life and Romances of Mrs. Eliza
    Haywood.   New York: Columbia University Press, pp. 12, 13,
    76, 77-91, 119, 126, 201-4.
       Contrasts the methods of narration, styles, and subject-
matter of Defoe, representing "the triumphant culmination of the
picaresque," and Mrs. Eliza Haywood, producing "mere vague in-
choations of a form as yet to be produced." Primarily, on the
basis of internal evidence, resolves complex problems of authorship in chap. 3 "The Duncan Campbell Pamphlets" (15 pp.). Concludes that Duncan Campbell was "written largely by Defoe," with
the uncharacteristic touches supplied by William Bond whose name
appeared on the title page of the reprint, The Supernatural Philosophy (1728). Assigns A Spy upon the Conjuror (1724) and The
Dumb Projector (1725) to Mrs. Haywood; The Friendly Daemon (1726)
to Defoe; and the Secret Memoirs of the Late Mr. Duncan Campbell
(1732) to both writers--a version left unfinished by Defoe in
1731, and revised and supplemented by Mrs. Haywood.

1916

1   Calendar of State Papers, Domestic Series, of the Reign of
    Anne. Preserved in the Public Record Office.   Volume 1 (1702-
    1703). Edited by Robert Pentland Mahaffy. London: HMSO,
    pp. 532-33, 726.
       Summarizes Defoe's letter to Daniel Finch, second Earl of
Nottingham, dated 9 January 1703, published by Aitken, 1894.2;

reprinted: Healey. Prints Nottingham's letter (25 May 1703) to the Lord Treasurer, Godolphin, requesting payment of the £50 reward to anyone giving information leading to the arrest of Defoe.

2   CURRY, GUNNER F. "First Illustrated English Novel." <u>Notes and Queries</u>, 12th ser. 2, no. 34 (19 August):153.
        Replies to 1916.4 by correcting the reference to <u>Robinson Crusoe</u> from the second volume to the first volume, published 25 April 1719. Describes the frontispiece as by Clark and Pine. See also 1916.8.

3   "De Foe, Dan." In <u>Deutsches Bücherverzeichnis: Eine Zussamenstellung der im deutschen Buchhandel erschienenen Bücher, Zeitschriften und Landkarten</u>. Leipzig: Börsenverein der deutschen Buchhändler, 1:537.
        Covers listings of Defoe's novels in German, 1911-1914: <u>Captain Singleton</u>, <u>Moll Flanders</u>, <u>Robinson Crusoe</u>.

4   GRIME, R. "First Illustrated English Novel." <u>Notes and Queries</u>, 12th ser. 2, no. 31 (29 July):90.
        Asks if the second volume of <u>Robinson Crusoe</u>, published 20 August 1719, was the first novel published with an illustration, in this instance, a map. See replies, 1916.2, 8.

5   MCKEE, JOHN. <u>Robinson Crusoe</u> (film). Henry W. Savage, Inc.
        Listed in <u>Motion Pictures 1912-1939</u> (Washington, D.C.: Library of Congress, 1951), p. 720.

6   MANN, WILLIAM EDWARD. <u>Robinson Crusoé en France: Étude sur l'influence de cette oeuvre dans la littérature française</u>. Ph.D. dissertation, University of Paris. Paris: Typographie A. Davis, 290 pp.
        Despite its age, this study has not been supplanted, remains invaluable for its store of information from books and periodicals unavailable in the United States. Covers the vast, complex influence of <u>Robinson Crusoe</u> through the translations, imitations, adaptations, criticisms, and theatrical productions from 1720 to 1908, including the parallel or related developments in England and Germany (e.g., Robinsonades). Focuses upon the influences radiating also from such exceedingly popular adaptations as the <u>Swiss Robinson</u>. Amidst many complex details, holds the "universal significance" of <u>Robinson Crusoe</u> as a constant. Starts with an analysis of the work, its origins, its publication in France (32 pp.); and continues with the translations (35 pp.), adaptations (38 pp.), "<u>Robinson Crusoe</u> and the Novel of the Eighteenth Century" (52 pp.), <u>Swiss Robinson</u> (20 pp.), nineteenth-century imitations (26 pp.), and "<u>Robinson Crusoe</u> in the Theatre" (56 pp.). Offers finally two appendices dealing with "Religious Scruples of Crusoe: How the Translators Interpret Them" (2 pp.) and "Notes on the Literary Quarrel between Madame Tastu and Pétrus Borel" (2 pp.); and a comprehensive bibliography (6 pp.). Provides European perspectives on <u>Robinson Crusoe</u> and

the changing tastes which vary significantly from their English
counterparts. Opens up an entire galaxy of new continental per-
sonages: translators (Thémiseul de Saint-Hyacinthe, Mme. Tastu,
Pétrus Borel, Mme. Panckoucke), critics (Philarète Chasles,
Borel, La Harpe, Feutry, Freron, Hillebrand), adaptors (Johann
Heinrich Campe, Johann Rudolf Wyss), and dramatists (d'Arnould,
Pixérecourt, Brazier, Girard, Sardou). Parallels almost every
Robinson Crusoe interest or fashion in England with counterparts
in France, earlier or later: for instance, the Selkirk contro-
versy, the value of Part Two of Robinson Crusoe, the issues of
Rousseauistic natural education and the mechanical arts, the
question of whether Robinson Crusoe can stand alone in the
theatre as "monodrama" (pantomime).

7   SCHREIBER, MARIANNE. "Daniel Defoe, sein Leben und seine
    Werke." Part I. In 12. Jahresbericht des 6-klassigen
    Mädchen-Lyzeums . . . in Salzburg über das Schuljahr 1915/16.
    Salzburg, pp. 5-25.
        A pleasingly written "term paper," without any sources
cited.   (P.E.C.)

8   SPARKE, ARCHIBALD. "First Illustrated English Novel." Notes
    and Queries, 12th ser. 2, no. 34 (19 August):153.
        Replies to 1916.4. Identifies the engravers of the plates
for the first edition of Robinson Crusoe, Part I, as John Clark
(1688-1736) and John Pine (1690-1756).

9   STEVENS, DAVID HARRISON. Party Politics and English Journal-
    ism 1702-1742. Menasha, Wis.: Collegiate Press, pp. 23-24,
    47-60, 71, 104-17.
        In chap. 4, "Defoe and the Earl of Oxford," analyzes
Defoe's roles, in his changes of party, as pamphleteer, author
and editor of the Review, and government agent during two periods
of service for Robert Harley and one period for Godolphin. The
intricate relationships between Harley and Defoe included the
publication of the Review as a party organ from 1704 to 1713;
Defoe's work in an advisory capacity (e.g., his written proposals for the establishment of a secret service in England and the
continent; his secret agent activities in Scotland during the
Union negotiations); and Defoe's successful efforts at disqual-
ifying Steele from parliamentary service. In the discussion of
the amounts and frequency of payments received, makes the judgment that Harley and Godolphin gave fair treatment. In chap. 7,
"Defoe and Walpole in the Service of George I," places Defoe's
efforts at weakening Tory journals in the general context of
Robert Walpole's concerted designs for controlling the Oppositon
writers and press.

10 TIEJE, ARTHUR JERROLD. The Theory of Characterization in
    Prose Fiction Prior to 1740. University of Minnesota Studies
    in Language and Literature, 5. Minneapolis: University of
    Minnesota, pp. 78-79, 123, 125, 127.

Comments only on the brief theory of reform in the preface
to Moll Flanders. In the bibliography, places most of Defoe's
fictional works under "The Picaresque Tale"; Memoirs of a Cavalier under "The Historical-Psychological Novel"; Robinson Crusoe,
Voyages of Richard Falconer, Captain Singleton, and New Voyage
Round the World under "The Voyage Imaginaire."

11   TRENT, WILLIAM P[ETERFIELD]. Daniel Defoe: How to Know Him.
     Indianapolis: Bobbs Merrill Co., 329 pp.
     Not since the "General Introduction" to Aitken's Romances
and Narratives (1895) has there been so comprehensive a biographical, bibliographical, and critical assessment. After ten years
of research into the life and writings of this "Proteus both in
literature and affairs," and this "titanic genius," presents in
eleven chapters one of the most wide-ranging selections from the
works, to date, and a running commentary that introduced considerable new information. For instance: confirms the year of birth
as either 1659 or 1660; suggests a residence in Spain before marriage, and travel to Italy, Bavaria, France; corrects the long-
standing error of the first imprisonment as lasting five or six
months (not eighteen), and thus eliminates the legend that the
Review had been started in Newgate, and the misjudgment that the
Storm was necessarily imaginary; clarifies the times when Defoe
was present in Scotland during the years 1706-1712; demolishes
the view that Defoe retired from politics in 1715; elaborates on
new biographical evidence from legal documents, such as pertain
to William Hurt, printer of the Flying Post, and John Ward, mer-
cer of Coleshill in Warickshire; and describes credibly Defoe's
relationship with Nathaniel Mist and John Applebee, and his
mysterious last two years. Collects a vast amount of new information, but also organizes it into a pattern which he had first
outlined in 1912.18 and 1912.19, namely, the view that because he
underwent the traumatic experience of the pillory, and financial
ruin, he lost every semblance of "intellectual honesty," accepted
any disguise or duplicity, became a "social outcast" and "human
chameleon." Unlike Minto (1879.5), however, Trent avoids a
necessary linkage of mendacity in personal life with "lying" in
the fictional writings. In chap. 10 (38 pp.), partly on Robinson
Crusoe, analyzes the personality of the "aging man of genius,"
publications such as A Continuation of Letters Written by a Turkish Spy at Paris (1718) and their revelations about the author of
Robinson Crusoe, and the reasons for the book's popularity. Rejects emphatically the myths of Defoe's misappropriation of the
Selkirk manuscript, Robert Harley as author of Part One, and the
narrative as "an allegory of its author's life." In chap. 11 (46
pp.), on the "Other Works of Fiction," reiterates and amplifies
critical positions stated earlier for the ten other novels, with
most attention being paid to the Journal of the Plague Year ("an
English classic") and Memoirs of a Cavalier ("a rather low form
of art"). While continuing the bias toward Moll Flanders and Roxana, Trent judges that Defoe reached the height of his "powers of
characterization" and "realistic presentation" in the former, and

produced his most "complicated plot" in the latter. Among the
miscellaneous writings discussed in chap. 12, claims for Defoe
three narratives in which he had a hand as author or editor: The
Four Years Voyages of Capt. George Roberts (1726), Capt. George
Carleton, and Madagascar. See also the review, 1918.2. Reprinted: New York: Phaeton Press, 1971.

12 _____, ed. The Life and Strange Surprising Adventures of
     Robinson Crusoe. Boston, Mass.: Ginn & Co., 392 pp.
          Includes a "Prefatory Note" (1 p.) which describes the text
     as "somewhat modernized," an important introduction which divides
     into a section on "The Writer" (18 pp.) and another on "The Book"
     (9 pp.), the text of Part One (334 pp.), and invaluable "Notes"
     (24 pp.) which are both textual and commentary. The introduc-
     tion, conservative and commonsensical, serves as a summing-up of
     previous research into Defoe's life, the canon which now stands
     at "over four hundred well authenticated titles," and a critical
     assessment of the novels. Identifies an apparently new theme in
     the biographical portion, namely, that as a result of his punish-
     ment for the Shortest-Way with the Dissenters and subsequent
     financial ruin, Defoe became "a consummate casuist, whose state-
     ments must be closely scrutinized, and a political and journal-
     istic intriguer, whose conduct often seems indefensible." Again
     later, from 1708 to 1710, as "a pilloried social outcast," he
     could not serve openly in public office, but was well qualified
     to be a government spy: "throughout this period his moral nature
     was deteriorating and his health was suffering." While Trent
     repeatedly removes long-standing biographical puzzles, solves a
     problem, or affixes accurate dates to events, he also continues
     this theme of Defoe as a consummate casuist into his assessment
     of the novels and even into the Notes. On the novels other than
     Robinson Crusoe, only two are designated "masterpieces of their
     kind"--Moll Flanders and Journal of the Plague Year. All are
     surpassed by "the best works of later novelists"; all have merits
     which "regretfully" are "more than counterbalanced for many read-
     ers by a coarseness inseparable from the realistic fiction of a
     coarse age." In the section on "The Book," Trent "settles" for
     Robinson Crusoe the problems of authorship, place of composition,
     immediate sources, reprintings, Crusoe's island, and critical
     interpretation.

1917

1   COUPER, W.J. "Mrs. Anderson and the Royal Prerogative in
     Printing." Proceedings of the Royal Philosophical Society
     at Glasgow 48:79-102.
          Deals briefly (pp. 98-99) with the first printing of De-
     foe's Review in Edinburgh by Mrs. Anderson and the subsequent
     reprinting in London, issues from 25 March 1709 to 23 March 1710.
     Traces the history of Mrs. Anderson's monopoly of printing,
     obtained by Charles II's appointment of her husband, Andrew

Anderson, as King's Printer for Scotland. On his death in 1676, she took over the royal patent; in her hands it became oppressive, "a dead stroke" to printing, as her archrival, the printer James Watson, declared. In 1713 Watson denounced Mrs. Anderson, "a woman who printed the seditious Reviews of Defoe"; and Mrs. Anderson responded with a defense which hints at Defoe's whereabouts and his methods in distributing the Review. See also 1908.7; 1913.6.

2   Robinson Crusoe (film). Universal Film Manufacturing Co.
     Listed in Motion Pictures 1912-1939 (Washington, D.C.:
Library of Congress, 1951), p. 720.

3   SAINTSBURY, GEORGE. A History of the French Novel (to the
     Close of the 19th Century). 2 vols. London: Macmillan,
     1:292, 329, 358, 456; 2:287-88, 362.
     Touches upon resemblances between Defoe and Furetière,
Lesage, Prévost, and Restif. Places Defoe with Fielding, Richardson, Lesage and others in using a "mimesis" which imitated or copied an actual, recognizable personality, as compared with Laclos and Dumas fils who "proceeded by synthesis."

4   WILLIAMS, ANEURIN. "Cassell's Illustrated Robinson Crusoe."
     Notes and Queries, 12th ser. 3, no. 59 (10 February):110.
     Asks who were the illustrators and engravers of the Robinson Crusoe edition published by Cassell & Co. "some decades back." Separate replies are given by J. Makham, R.J. Parker, J. Foster Palmer, and John B. Wainewright in Notes and Queries, 12th ser. 3, no. 63 (10 March):194-95; and by Cassell & Co., in Notes and Queries, 12th ser. 3, no. 68 (May):308.

                              1918

1   BASTIDE, CHARLES, ed. Daniel Defoe: Oeuvres choisies. Tra-
     duction nouvelle avec une introduction et des notes. Les Cent
     Chefs-d'Oeuvres étrangers. Paris: La Renaissance du Livre,
     197 pp.
     Presents in the introduction (27 pp.) a view of Defoe the man as we see him "in the light of the most recent discoveries," playing a most ambiguous role, at times even carrying out inappropriate business, analogous to "that of nocturnal scavengers." Locates the turning point of his life in two well-documented "capitulations." The first: his "corruption" by Harley in 1704, leading ultimately to the complete "deformation of his professional conscience" during the Mesnager affair. The second: his work for the Whig government after 1715 in which he "blunted" Tory journals, such as Mist's and at least five others. In the light of these new findings, interprets Defoe as a narrative writer. Argues that he rarely invents and so cannot be judged a liar. Describes his imagination as one "proper to positive men" and his "air of realism" as arising from a reality in Defoe's

experience. Sees the method essentially the same in <u>Mrs. Veal</u>,
<u>Robinson Crusoe</u>, <u>Moll Flanders</u>, <u>Roxana</u>, and <u>Journal of the Plague
Year</u>. Interprets <u>Robinson Crusoe</u> as an "allegory" in which Robinson and Defoe are identified as one. Claims also that Crusoe is
"the symbol of navigators and English colonists who, by their
perseverance, tenacity, and calm courage, have given to the
mother country so beautiful a crown of territories beyond seas,"
and that his narrative assumes "the proportion of an epic poem."
Ultimately, forgives Defoe his "moral shortcomings" revealed by
recent discoveries on account of our love for Crusoe during childhood. Reprints for the first time in France extracts from the
<u>Journal of the Plague Year</u> (34 pp.) and <u>Mrs. Veal</u> (13 pp.), in
addition to extracts from <u>Robinson Crusoe</u> (87 pp.), <u>[Political]
History of the Devil</u> (14 pp.), and Marcel Schwob's translation
(1895) of <u>Moll Flanders</u> (19 pp.).

2   C[HEW], S[AMUEL] C. Review of William P. Trent's <u>Defoe: How
to Know Him</u>, 1916. <u>Modern Language Notes</u> 33, no. 2 (February):127.
    Judges that aside from the <u>Journal of the Plague Year</u> and a
few other pieces, Defoe's works are "dead, utterly dead," and
that the present volume will do nothing for the general reader.

3   NEWTON, A. EDWARD. <u>The Amenities of Book-Collecting and Kin-
dred Affection</u>. Reprint. 4th ed. Boston: Atlantic Monthly
Press, 1922, pp. 43, 44, 99-101, 102, 122, 226.
    Preserves invaluable comments on rare books in his personal
library, such as the three-volume edition of <u>Robinson Crusoe</u>, two
volumes of which were "once the property of 'Mr. William Congreve.'" Describes also the extremely rare edition published in
the <u>Original London Post</u>, and includes also W.P. Trent's analysis
of the bibliographical "points" of a "first issue" of <u>Robinson
Crusoe</u>. For many of his purchases, takes the book-collector's
pride in quoting prices paid.

4   WHITEFORD, ROBERT NAYLOR. <u>Motives in English Fiction</u>. New
York and London: G.P. Putnam's Sons, pp. 60-75, 278-80.
    Investigates patterns of motives which provide strong moral
linkages between Bunyan's <u>Pilgrim's Progress</u> (1678) and the <u>Life
and Death of Mr. Badman</u> (1680) with Defoe's novels and Thackeray's <u>Vanity Fair</u>. The Newgate scenes of <u>Moll Flanders</u> look back
to <u>Mr. Badman</u>, and forward to Fielding, Smollett, Goldsmith,
Henry Brooke, Dickens (<u>Pickwick</u>), and Thackeray (<u>Barry Lyndon</u>).
Friday's ethics resemble those of Aphra Behn's Oroonoko; his questions about God and the Devil have links with <u>Pilgrim's Progress</u>
and Nashe's <u>The Unfortunate Traveller</u> (1594). Moll's fear of
child-labor and Colonel Jack's pathetic childhood were doubtless
motivated by Defoe's use of fiction "to favor reforms in the social system." More independent in his motives, Defoe introduces
spontaneous humor in the characterization of Quaker William, "a
delightful figure of fun in hypocrisy"; pathetic humor in Colonel
Jack's placing his money in a hollow tree; and satirical pathos
as when he shows tears in the eyes of Moll and Roxana.

1918-1919

1   DIBELIUS, WILHELM. "Zum Jubiläum des Robinson Crusoe."
    <u>Velhagen & Klasings Monatshefte</u> 33, no. 2:209-13.
       After a biographical sketch of Defoe, enumerates reasons
for the popularity of <u>Robinson Crusoe</u> from its first appearance:
clever promotion; appropriateness to the taste of the times;
psychological realism; interesting, clear style for bourgeois
readers.   (P.E.C.)

1919

1   ARDAGH, J. "Defoe and Alexander Selkirk." <u>Notes and Queries</u>,
    12th ser. 5, no. 94 (July):177.
       Corrects the <u>DNB</u> article on Selkirk by reproducing notes by
E.A. after a conversation with W.P. Lunell (May, 1834) on Defoe's
meeting Selkirk in the home of Mrs. Daniells in James's Square,
Bristol.

2   BELL, WALTER GEORGE. "Letters from London during the Great
    Plague." In <u>Unknown London</u>. London and New York: John Lane,
    pp. 213-30.
       Reproduces letters on the plague written by John Allin,
Anglican minister ejected in 1662 from his living in Rye, and
residing in London. Of his 190 letters over a ten-year period,
those graphically describing the plague are written to friends
back in Rye, Philip Fryth, a solicitor, and Samuel Jeake, historian of the Cinque Ports; and are dated irregularly from 26 May to
26 December 1665. Allin deserves attention "as fact," in contrast to Defoe's <u>Journal of the Plague Year</u> "given to the world
as fiction." Reprinted: 1920; also ed. E.R. Withersett (London:
Spring Books, 1966).

3   DEKOBRA, MAURICE, trans. "Daniel De Foë." In <u>L'Étonnante</u>
    <u>Vie du Colonel Jack</u>. Paris: L'Édition Française Illustrée,
    pp. vii-xii.
       Tells an anecdote of meeting, in 1908, a young woman of the
streets (named Winnie) who read <u>Roxana</u> and discoursed upon Defoe's ability to depict manners. Finds himself now haunted by
this memory as he writes the "astonishing life" of Defoe, to
introduce his translation of <u>Colonel Jack</u>. Senses the same combination of the visionary and the real in Defoe's life and writ-
ings--the novels, in particular. Compares and contrasts <u>Moll</u>
<u>Flanders</u> and <u>Roxana</u>. Generalizes that all the novels have "the
charm of an unlimited imagination and the attraction of a style
whose originality makes everything a pleasure."

4   "In Praise of <u>Robinson Crusoe</u>." <u>Athenaeum</u>, no. 4643 (25
    April):229-30.
       Expresses the view that "luckily for England, <u>Robinson Cru-</u>
<u>soe</u> is a classic of the nursery." Although not itself art, the

book is "the product of an attitude upon which great art depends, and sound living also." Emphasizes and demonstrates briefly that like Crusoe, one should be "a romantic in action," but practical in thought.

5   KIRKLAND, WINIFRED. "Robinson Crusoe Reread." Outlook 123,
     no. 5 (1 October):202-3.
        Contrasts Crusoe with the shipwrecked heroes of today, the original island with current islands, the old struggle (with surroundings) with the new one ("of soul with soul-stuff"). Prefers the old pattern.

6   LATHROP, HENRY BURROWES. The Art of the Novelist. New York:
     Dodd, Mead & Co. Reprint. London: George G. Harrap & Co.,
     1921, pp. 17, 39-40, 52-54, 69, 110, 201-2, 255-56.
        Scattered comments on Defoe's novels: "A mere piece of fictitious history" would not be a novel, such as "the Adventures of a Cavalier" [Memoirs of a Cavalier]. As the novel "approaches the actual," it becomes "merely fictitious biography," such as Defoe's. Even his criminals and pirates do not have any "imaginative life" from the start. On Robinson Crusoe and Journal of the Plague Year: the observations are more positive; notes in both instances the distinctions of "strangeness" from the commonplace or ordinary.

7   MEYER, JOHANNES. Robinson Crusoe. Seine Geschichte, Eigenart
     und pädagogische Bewertung zum 200. Jahrestage seines Erscheinens. Friedrich Mann's Pädagogisches Magazin, no. 724. Langensalza: Hermann Beyer & Son, 53 pp.
        A highly idiosyncratic jumble of information in a shallow introduction to Defoe's work is followed by a discussion of older and newer children's editions of Robinson Crusoe for school and nursery, and their pedagogical usefulness. Includes an in-depth examination of the use to which the novel was put in the Herbart-Ziller schools since the 1860's: second-graders derived moral-religious instruction from an animated presentation of the didacticized Robinson material three hours weekly, but it also strengthened their concentration, their will, and their industriousness. The centerpiece of Ziller's pedagogical plan was the "Kulturstufentheorie," believed since Rousseau to inform the novel, to which second graders, it was held, were unusually receptive. See also 1898.7.   (P.E.C.)

8   MOFFAT, JAMES. "The Religion of Robinson Crusoe." Contemporary Review 115 (June):664-99.
        Upon rereading Robinson Crusoe, discovers that the large amount of moralizing is both "vital" and "organic," as revealed in Crusoe's religion (which is essentially Defoe's). Analyzes Crusoe's Protestantism, the role of the devil, the working of a general Providence (no word occurs more often in Robinson Crusoe), and special Providence.

9   NICHOLSON, WATSON. The Historical Sources of Defoe's
     "Journal of the Plague Year". Boston, Mass.: Stratford Co.,
     190 pp.
         Claims to establish, finally, that in its design and execu-
     tion the Journal of the Plague Year is history, and not fiction.
     Makes the case emphatically in three long chapters, a "Summary,"
     twelve appendices, and a bibliography. In chap. 1 "Origins and
     Parallels of the Stories in Defoe's Journal" (47 pp.), demon-
     strates that "there is not a single essential statement . . . not
     based on historic facts"; differentiates the method and style of
     Due Preparations as being closer than the Journal to fiction
     ("admonitory"); and argues that the Journal of the Plague Year
     cannot match such sources as Thomas Vincent's God's Terrible
     Voice in the City (1667) in "tragic pathos and graphic portray-
     al." In chap. 2 "The Historical Sources of the Journal" (34
     pp.), analyzes Defoe's use of the Bills of Mortality, Orders of
     the Mayor, Royal Proclamations, newspapers, and Nathaniel Hod-
     ges's Loimologia (1672; trans., 1720) to create the "framework"
     for his entire narrative; and his manner of introducing "illustra-
     tive stories" (e.g., Solomon Eagle) to produce the overwhelming
     effect of calamity and desolation. Having established as Defoe's
     purpose to write a saleable book, describes in chap. 3 "Errors in
     the Journal" (15 pp.), his desperate efforts to pad the manu-
     script by ineptly using first-person narrative "to cover up the
     most egregious faults known to literature,--digressions, incoher-
     encies, involved and cumbrous expressions, tiresome repetitions.
     . . ." Condemns the Journal, in its style and art, as the work
     "execrable"; even the famous story of the sailor, soldier, and
     joiner as narrated in a "methodless fashion." In the concluding
     "Summary" (4 pp.), makes the important distinction between two
     kinds of sources: printed and manuscript; and Defoe's own
     memories of the Plague as well as those of survivors. Reproduces
     parts of the twelve sources in the appendices (77 pp.) on which
     he built the case for the Journal of the Plague Year as "authen-
     tic history." See the reviews, 1920.3; and W.V. Maanen, in En-
     glish Studies 3 (1921):19-20. Reprinted: Kennikat Press, 1966.

10   ULLRICH, HERMANN. "Der zweihundertste Geburtstag von Defoes
     Robinson (25 April 1919)." Zeitschrift für Bücherfreunde,
     n.s. 11, no. 1:35-41.
         Assesses uniqueness of Robinson Crusoe. The early imita-
     tors ignored the "panorama of cultural development" incorporated
     in the original. Recounts sources, publication circumstances of
     the novel. Discusses briefly the editions, translations, adapta-
     tions, and influences. Concurs with Brüggemann (1914.4) on the
     importance of Insel Felsenburg among the Robinsonades. (P.E.C.)

11   [WOOLF, VIRGINIA.] "The Novels of Defoe." TLS, no. 901
     (24 April):217-18.
         Celebrates the bi-centenary of Robinson Crusoe, but sur-
     prisingly devotes most of the article to a sympathetic reading of
     Moll Flanders and Roxana: "among the few English novels which
     we can call indisputably great." After some refreshing insights

into Moll Flanders, observes that Defoe was not, "as he has been
accused of being, a mere journalist and literal recorder of facts
with no conception of the nature of psychology." Extends the
sympathy to admiration of Moll Flanders and Roxana as the "patron
saints" of women's rights advocates in "problem novels" of their
day; recognizes that this element is subordinate to the appeal
of their "natural veracity." See also B.J. Kirkpatrick, A Bibliography of Virginia Woolf (London: Rupert Hart-Davis, 1957),
pp. 18-21, 101. Reprinted: 1919.12; "Defoe," in The Common
Reader [First Series] (London: Hogarth Press, 1925), pp. 125-35;
New York: Harcourt, Brace & Co., 1948; other impressions in
1927, 1930, 1933, 1942, 1944, 1948, and 1954. The essay is generally reprinted from The Common Reader, as in collections of
critical essays edited by Louis Kronenberger, Novelists on Novelists (New York: Doubleday & Co., 1962); Robert C. Elliott,
Twentieth Century Interpretations of Moll Flanders (Englewood
Cliffs, N.J.: Prentice-Hall, 1970); J. Paul Hunter, Daniel
Defoe: Moll Flanders (New York: Thomas Y. Crowell Co., 1970);
Moll Flanders, ed. Edward Kelly (New York: W. W. Norton & Co.,
1973); Max Byrd, Daniel Defoe: A Collection of Critical Essays
(Englewood Cliffs, N.J.: Prentice-Hall, 1976).

12   _____. "Two Hundred Years of Defoe." Living Age 301, no.
       3909 (7 June):619-24.
       Reprint of 1919.11.

1919-1920

1   PRICE, LAWRENCE MARSDEN. English-German Literary Influences:
    Bibliography and Survey. University of California Publica-
    tions in Modern Philology. Berkeley: University of Califor-
    nia Press, 1 (Bibliography):21, 30-31; 2 (Survey):174-77, 283.
       In a study of the broad "relations" of English to German
    literature, and not German to English, lists in part 1 (Bibliog-
    raphy), the section "Defoe in Germany," the work of Hettner, Kip-
    penberg, Biltz, Kleemann, Rötteken, Ullrich, Mildebrath, Schott;
    in the section "Defoe and Schnabel": Rötteken, Halm, Brüggeman;
    and in the section "Defoe in Austria": Wagner. Examines in part
    2 (Survey) the relations of Defoe (exclusively his Robinson
    Crusoe) to the first translator Vischer and imitators Schnabel,
    Campe, and others. Denies that the many imitations necessarily
    mean "literary influence" or that Defoe made any contribution to
    the Bildungsroman in Germany.

1920

1   ATKINSON, GEOFFROY. The Extraordinary Voyage in French Lit-
    erature before 1700. New York: Columbia University Press,
    pp. xiii, 94, 96, 105, 142, 164-65.
       Defines the novel of the "Extraordinary Voyage," and ex-
    plains its emergence as part of the rationalistic spirit in

French literature of the seventeenth and eighteenth centuries.
Of the three Extraordinary Voyages examined here, L'Histoire des
Sévarambes (1677-1679) by Denis Vairasse bears some resemblance
to Robinson Crusoe. Influences on Defoe may also be found in Ibn
Thofaïl's Hayy ben Yaqdhan, Baltasar Gracián's L'Homme détrompé,
ou le Criticon (first part, 1696), and Les Voyages et aventures
de François Leguat et ses compagnons (1708). The kinship of
Robinson Crusoe to the Extraordinary Voyages seems recognized in
the Nouvelles littéraires of Amsterdam (December, 1719), in the
comment that Robinson Crusoe was "in the taste of L'Histoire des
Sévarambes and Jacques Sadeur." Reprinted: New York: AMS
Press, 1966.

2   BELLESORT, ANDRÉ. "Les Romans Picaresques de Daniel De Foé."
     Revue politique et littéraire: Revue bleue 58, no. 14 (17
     July):442-45.
        Rejoices over the current availability, in faithful French
     translations, of Moll Flanders (Marcel Schwob), Roxana (George
     Garnier), Colonel Jack (Maurice Dekobra), and the forthcoming
     translations of the Journal of the Plague Year and Captain Sin-
     gleton. Places the first three in "the picaresque genre of
     England"; analyzes them according to a broad definition of the
     "picaresque." Allows in the definition for Defoe's use of his
     personal experience (Newgate) or for the "bases" in facts, pre-
     tended or real, of the narratives. Argues that the three novels
     abound in "improbabilities, psychological and moral," which make
     them most unlike "art," and bring Defoe close to Balzac. Points
     to moving scenes, but also to "defects," in the three novels.

*2-b BLONDOT, J. See p. 399.

3   "Defoe As Historian." TLS, no. 963 (1 July):418.
        Reviews 1919.9. Observes that Nicholson's study of the
     Journal of the Plague Year moves in the same direction as Bern-
     baum (1914.3) and Aitken [1895.2] in that it reduces Defoe's
     reputation for "inventiveness." But the Journal becomes even
     more "the classic work on the Great Plague" with its art based on
     truth rather than on fiction.

4   FERNSEMER, O.F.W. "Daniel Defoe and the Palatine Emigration
     of 1709." Journal of English and Germanic Philology 19:94-
     124.
        Finds "the Selkirk theory" unsatisfactory in explaining the
     origins of Robinson Crusoe; prefers to identify as the source
     "the Robinson-idea" among the colonization schemes, to which De-
     foe contributed in the issues of the Review for July and August,
     1709. Interprets this idea to mean relocation to a place where
     "the poor and heavy laden of all Europe" might find, with dig-
     nity, "liberty and freedom of conscience" and a livelihood. In
     this instance, some 13,000 to 14,000 Palatine emigrants were
     seeking asylum in England or the colonies of New York and North
     Carolina. Although Defoe's scheme for "home colonization" was

not followed, and the relocations abroad turned out to be traps
for the colonists, the journalist Defoe was nevertheless deeply
engrossed in this controversy. Similarities between the shipwrecked mariner and the Palatine exiles seeking their "islands"
of refuge suggest what may be the true origin of Robinson Crusoe.

5   "A Forgotten Satire of Defoe." TLS, no. 944 (19 February):
    128.
        Reports on a manuscript letter in a lot sold by the Ander-
son Galleries in New York on 9 February. Dated in May, 1709, the
four-page letter by G. Haviland transcribes Defoe's "lost" satire
"Parson Plaxton of Barwick in ye Country of York turn'd inside
out" and George Plaxton's "Retort." For additional comment on
Plaxton, see TLS, no. 946 (4 March 1920): 159. For the full text
of the letter (written actually by George Staniland) and satire,
as well as an analysis, see Spiro Peterson, "Defoe's Yorkshire
Quarrel," Huntington Library Quarterly 19, no. 1 (November,
1955):57-79.

6   FREEMAN, LEWIS R. "Where Is Robinson Crusoe's Island?"
    Travel 34, no. 4 (February):27-30, 53.
        Describes in considerable detail the two islands which are
generally regarded as the prime candidates for being Crusoe's island, each with its own model for Robinson Crusoe: Tobago (Pedro
Serrano) and Mas-a-Tierra, one of two islands known as Juan Fernandez (Alexander Selkirk). Landmarks on each island are named
after Robinson Crusoe. Of special interest: the panque plant,
apparently indigenous in Juan Fernandez, has such large leaves
that for protection from rain, the inhabitants do not need to
carry umbrellas.

7   FURNISS, EDGAR S. The Position of the Laborer in a System
    of Nationalism: A Study in the Labor Theories of the Later
    English Mercantilists. Boston and New York: Houghton Mifflin
    Co. Reprint. Economic Classics. New York: Augustus M.
    Kelley, 1965, pp. 16, 35, 53, 86, 99-100, 103, 129, 141, 223,
    241.
        Uses Defoe's social writings (particularly, Giving Alms No
Charity, 1704) to sum up early eighteenth-century theory regarding the laborer and the poor.

8   GARDNER, GILSON. A New Robinson Crusoe: A New Version of His
    Life and Adventures with an Explanatory Note. New York: Har-
    court, Brace & Howe, 109 pp.
        In the "Explanatory Note" (6 pp.), reports the discovery of
a manuscript purportedly written by Daniel Defoe and Alexander
Selkirk, and alleged to be the original version of Robinson Crusoe. In place of "the religious homiletics," which we now read,
one finds "the economic problem of an individual in Selkirk's
situation." Here we have "his island world . . . an economic
microcosm wherein he found, reduced to simplest terms, all the
elements of the problems which make up the economics of the most

elaborate civilization." All of this, if the reader has not already caught on, is of course a preposterous hoax, but the analysis of the economics seems to be seriously intended.

9   HÜBENER, GUSTAV. "Der Kaufmann Robinson Crusoe." Englische
    Studien 54, no. 3:367-98.
        Explores differences between the cultural philosophical
    view of Defoe as an idealized heroic figure, prevalent in Germany
    (e.g., Hettner, 1854.4), and the realistic, even unflattering
    view represented in Anglo-American scholarship (e.g., Gosse,
    1889.9). Traces back to Rousseau's influence the "erroneous"
    Kulturstufentheorie, or the view of mankind's cultural develop-
    ment, which Ullrich (1919.10) and others claim to see exemplified
    in Robinson Crusoe. Also finds shortcomings among the Anglo-
    American realists who see Robinson Crusoe simply within the
    context of the European adventure novel. Posits a third, zeit-
    geist-oriented interpretation of Robinson (and Defoe) as models
    of the early middle class: a capitalist (calculating, mercan-
    tile, cautiously entrepreneurial) spirit combined with an
    artisan's contented self-sufficiency. Further, the religious
    component of the novel underscores this: God directs Robinson
    toward the path of reason, moderation, and solid bourgeois
    industry, and away from wild speculation. See the response by
    Ullrich, 1921.18.   (P.E.C.)

10 LÜTHI, ALBERT. "Daniel Defoe und seine Forsetzungen zu Robin-
    son Crusoe. The Farther Adventures und Serious Reflections."
    Inaugural dissertation, Zurich University; Stuttgart: Druck
    der Aktien Gesellschaft Deutsches Volksblatt, 76 pp.
        Follows Minto's call (1879.5) for further study of the
    continuations, Farther Adventures of Robinson Crusoe and Serious
    Reflections . . . of Robinson Crusoe, in the light of Defoe's
    biography and with special focus on his religious beliefs (chap.
    3) and morality (chap. 4). Brings together Robinson Crusoe and
    Serious Reflections, and the life and works (chap. 5); examines
    "the question of allegory in Robinson Crusoe" in a separate sec-
    tion of this chapter. All together, the findings do not reflect
    well on his character.   (P.E.C.)

11 REYNOLDS, GEORGE F., and GREEVER, GARLAND. "Daniel Defoe
    (c1659-1731)." In The Facts and Backgrounds of Literature:
    English and American. New York: Century Co.. 1922, pp. 104-
    5, 110-11.
        Entirely in outline form, continues some of the most tena-
    cious misconceptions of Defoe as, for example, "the Yankee trader
    of the Queen Anne writers," "member of the lower classes."

12 ULLRICH, HERMANN. "Einfuhrung in das Studium Daniel Defoes."
    Zeitschrift für Französischen und Englischen Unterricht
    19:6-28.
        Annotates a bibliography of the editions of Defoe's col-
    lected works, followed by the biographies with their strengths

and weaknesses, and a particularly lengthy, critical review of
the newly published essay by Trent (1913.23). Describes projects
Ullrich wishes to see undertaken by German scholars of Defoe, including a detailed account of the origins and history of <u>Robinson
Crusoe</u> (and its great influence on German literature), a study
that he had once contemplated doing himself. He calls also for
several detailed studies of Defoe's other novels, offering useful
insights which future scholars might pursue, and urges various
studies devoted to Defoe's other writings.   (P.E.C.)

13   WISE, THOMAS J., ed. <u>A Catalogue of the Library of the Late
     John Henry Wrenn</u>. Compiled by Harold B. Wrenn. 5 vols.
     Austin: University of Texas, 1;ix-xii, 2:14-45.
         In the preface, describes his collaboration with John H.
Wrenn in collecting books by selected authors including Defoe.
Lists chronologically 119 books and pamphlets dated from 1680 to
1730 as "by and attributed" to Defoe, giving for each the title
and facts of publication, information on the edition, collation,
and alternative authorship (if any). For at least two items,
mentions documents attached in which William Lee certifies Defoe's authorship. Certain items are clearly not by Defoe. See
also the review by Draper, 1922.5.

14   WYETH, N.C. "Illustrator's Preface." In <u>Robinson Crusoe by
     Daniel Defoe</u>. New York: Cosmopolitan Book Corp., pp. i-ii.
         Describes the special appeal of <u>Robinson Crusoe</u> to himself
personally as "the remarkably sustained sensation one enjoys of
Crusoe's contact with the elements." Reproduces the paintings in
the thirteen illustrations given here.

                              1921

1   ARMSTRONG, T. PERCY. "Robinson Crusoe's Island." <u>Notes and
     Queries</u>, 12th ser. 8, no. 162 (21 May):415.
         Replies to 1921.5, by citing evidence favoring Tobago as
Crusoe's island. Concludes that the island must have been an
imagined one.

2   ATKINSON, GEOFFROY. "A French Desert Island Novel of 1708."
     <u>PMLA</u> 36, no. 4 (December):509-28.
         Establishes that the <u>Voyage et avantures de François
Leguat</u>, published with a London imprint in 1708 and translated
into English in the same year, was thought to be "a true story"
for over 200 years, one very much like <u>Robinson Crusoe</u> in certain
of its themes. The 1792 Leignitz edition even bears the title
<u>Der Französischer Robinson</u>. Now the <u>Voyage</u> can be shown to be "a
desert island novel" made up, not of firsthand travels and observations by Lequat, but "a mosaic of the observations of many
travelers in both Africa and America." The author of its preface
and the general editor: Maximilien Misson.

3   BENSLY, EDWARD. "Daniel Defoe in the Pillory." <u>Notes and Que-</u>
<u>ries</u>, 12th ser. 8, no. 147 (5 February):118.
       Replies to the query, 1921.14, and the reply, 1921.7.
States that in spite of Pope's line in the <u>Dunciad</u> (2:147), Defoe
never suffered mutilation (i.e., loss of his ears), according to
W.J. Courthope, <u>Pope's Works</u>.

4   BULLOCH, J.M. "Defoe's Relations." <u>Notes and Queries</u>, 12th
ser. 8, no. 163 (28 May):432.
       Query as to Defoe's remote connection with the family of
William Gordon, M.D., Kingston-upon-Hull, 1801-1849.

5   CONSTANT READER [pseud.]. "Robinson Crusoe's Island." <u>Notes</u>
<u>and Queries</u>, 12th ser. 8, no. 159 (30 April):415.
       Raises question of Crusoe's island: Juan Fernandez or an
island "in the estuary of the Orinoco"? See replies, 1921.1, 19.

6   DE RICCI, SEYMOUR. <u>The Book Collector's Guide: A Practical</u>
<u>Handbook of British and American Bibliography</u>. Philadelphia
and New York: Rosenbach Co., pp. 159-61.
       Lists prices for first and other editions of <u>Robinson Cru-</u>
<u>soe</u> (including the "O" edition), <u>Moll Flanders</u>, <u>Journal of the</u>
<u>Plague Year</u>, <u>Roxana</u>, and <u>Conjugal Lewdness</u> (1727).

7   DRUETT, W.W. "Daniel Defoe in the Pillory." <u>Notes and Que-</u>
<u>ries</u>, 12th ser. 8, no. 145 (22 January):78.
       Replies to 1921.14 by quoting an item in the <u>London Ga-</u>
<u>zette</u>, no. 3936 (2 August 1703), giving the dates and locations
for Defoe's standing in the pillory, and other details about his
punishment.

8   ESDAILE, ARUNDELL. "Author and Publisher in 1727: <u>The En-</u>
<u>glish Hermit</u>." <u>Library</u>, 4th ser. 2, no. 3 (December):185-92.
       Describes an issue II of <u>The English Hermit</u> (1727) which
has different preliminaries from issue I. Both issues have prefaces which refer to Defoe's novels (<u>Robinson Crusoe</u>, <u>Moll Flan-</u>
<u>ders</u>, <u>Colonel Jack</u>) in strikingly different ways. The preface of
I, probably the work of a hack, contrasts Defoe's readers ("lower
Rank") with those of Swift's <u>Gulliver's Travels</u> ("the superior
Class of Mankind"), while the preface of II was probably written
later by the author, Peter Longueville, and badly garbles the
reference to Defoe's three novels. Reconstructs the transaction
which led to the differences between I and II.

9   GIRADOUX, JEAN. <u>Suzanne et le Pacifique</u>. Translated by Ben
Ray Redman. New York & London: G.P. Putnam's Sons, 1923,
286 pp. passim.
       Not only does Suzanne the narrator experience a Robinson-
ade in many respects deliberately different from Crusoe's, she
also uses the narrative to comment directly upon the original.
Late in the story, she finds the pages of books owned by the
Frenchman, her predecessor in the second of the three islands.

The last of the masterpieces thus preserved--after <u>Don Quixote</u>, <u>Montaigne</u>, <u>Jacques le Fataliste</u>, <u>Gil Blas</u>, and so on--is "one whose title was such that I remained motionless for a moment as above a mirror: Robinson Crusoe!" She then gives an extended comment (7 pp.) on Crusoe, "a whiner and incoherent." Inter-mingled with Suzanne's adventures on three islands, which are patterned upon a rising evolutionary scale, is the constant awareness of a comparison and contrast between herself and "classic shipwrecked adventurers" including Robinson Crusoe.

10   HUBBARD, LUCIUS L. <u>A Dutch Source for "Robinson Crusoe."</u>
     <u>The Narrative of the El-Ho "Sjouke Gabbes" (Also Known As</u>
     <u>Henrich Texel). An Episode from the Description of the</u>
     <u>Mighty Kingdom of Krinke Kesmes, Et cetera by Hendrik</u>
     <u>Smeeks 1708. Translated from the Dutch and Compared with</u>
     <u>the Story of Robinson Crusoe</u>. Ann Arbor: George Wahr,
     212 pp.
          Surveys in the introduction (34 pp.) the scholarship
     leading to Hubbard's conviction that <u>Robinson Crusoe</u>--"in its
     setting, in many of the incidents which it chronicles, and in
     the traits and activities of its hero"--strongly resembles the
     story of the Dutch boy, Sjouke Gabbes, as it appears in Hendrik
     Smeeks's <u>Description of the Mighty Kingdom of Krinke Kesmes</u>
     (1708). Minimizes the contributions to the <u>Robinson Crusoe</u> story
     of Woodes Rogers and Alexander Selkirk, and claims to identify in
     the Dutch source "the earlier conception of the so-called Robin-
     son motif" as well as to clear up certain inconsistencies and
     contradictions in Defoe's text by recourse to Smeeks's narrative.
     Claims the turning point in the scholarship of <u>Krinke Kesmes</u>
     came with the announcement by W.H. Staverman (1907.20) that the
     episode in Smeeks's book was a pre-Robinsonade, not an imitation
     of <u>Robinson Crusoe</u>, and with the elaborations by G.J. Hoogewerff
     (1909.12), S.P. L'Honoré Naber (1910.14), and Leon Polak
     (1914.9). In addition, Hubbard provides a comparison (108 pp.)
     through parallel passages of the episode from <u>Krinke Kesmes</u> and
     <u>Robinson Crusoe</u>, and the Dutch text (64 pp.) of "De Historie van
     den El-Ho (Sjouke Gabbes)." For a review article which extends
     Hubbard's argument in favor of the Dutch source, see 1923.13;
     for the case against the Dutch source, see Krutch, 1922.10; and
     Arthur H. Nethercott, in <u>Modern Language Notes</u> 39, no. 4 (April,
     1924):235-41.

*11 JACOB, ERNST GERHARD. <u>Defoe's Projekts, Ein Beitrag zur</u>
     <u>Characteristik Defoe's und seiner Zeit</u>. Leipzig.
          Although listed in Dottin's <u>Daniel De Foe et ses romans</u>,
     p. 866 (under "G.E. Jacob) and Stoler, p. 327, I have not been
     able to locate a copy.

12   LEPRIEUR, GASTON. Director of film (French). <u>Les Aventures</u>
     <u>de Robinson Crusoé</u>.
          Cast includes Mario Dani as Robinson, Claude Mérelle,
     Armand Numès. See <u>Filmographic Dictionary of World Litera-</u>
     <u>ture</u>.

13   "L'Ile de Robinson Crusoë." <u>Mercure de France</u> 150 (15 August):280-81.

       Reasserts the claim of Juan Fernandez to be "the true island of the hero of Daniel Defoe." The island of Tobago seems, at this time, to be gaining ground in claiming the honor. See also 1922.2, 11.

14   M., G.B. "Daniel Defoe in the Pillory." <u>Notes and Queries</u>, 12th ser. 8, no. 142 (1 January):12.

       Asks for information on Defoe's "mutilation" (e.g., Pope's charge that his ears were cut off) and offence when he was put in the pillory on 29, 30 and 31 July 1703. See replies, 1921.3, 7.

15   MAANEN, W. VAN. "Defoe and Swift." <u>English Studies</u> 3 (June): 65-69.

       Traces the parallel early developments in the careers of Swift and Defoe in order to describe the "first crossing" of their lives. Argues that Defoe, recovering from the effects of the pillory upon his finances, intended to write a saleable book, and chose Swift's <u>Tale of a Tub</u> (1704) as a model. Comments on three passages in the <u>Consolidator</u> (1705): the first showing Defoe's "grudge" against the <u>Tale of a Tub</u>, the second hinting that he knew the identity of the author, and the third explaining the engine called in the lunar language "concionazimiz"--with a play on the word "vessel" clearly connected to a passage in the <u>Tale of a Tub</u>, which Defoe (rightly or wrongly) took to be a jibe at his being pilloried.

16   NAISH, CHARLES E. "Defoe and Africa." <u>Notes and Queries</u>, 12th ser. 8, no. 154 (26 March):251.

       Refers to the atlas published by Abraham Ortelius in Antwerp (1574) as showing the tributaries of the Nile, Niger, and Congo and of the great lakes. Asks if such a map might be Defoe's source for <u>Captain Singleton</u>.

17   <u>Robinson Crusoe Hours (A Post Nature Picture)</u>. Post Pictures Corp.

       Listed in <u>Motion Pictures 1912-1939</u> (Washington, D.C.: Library of Congress, 1951), p. 720.

18   ULLRICH, HERMANN. "Zum Robinson-Problem." <u>Englische Studien</u> 55:231-36.

       Responds to Hübener's article (1920.9), refuting his economic interpretation of <u>Robinson Crusoe</u> almost entirely. Hübener counters this response in 1923.14. Both are highly polemic.

                                              (P.E.C.)

19   WAINEWRIGHT, JOHN B. "Robinson Crusoe's Island." <u>Notes and Queries</u>, 12th ser. 8, no. 162 (21 May):415-16.

       Replies to 1921.5. Explains why Mas-a-Tierra (Juan Fernandez), as the island on which Selkirk was left and rescued, became known as Crusoe's island.

1922

1 ATKINSON, GEOFFROY. The Extraordinary Voyage in French Literature from 1700 to 1720. Paris: Champion, pp. 6, 26, 35, 37,
   48-49, 67, 71.
        Sporadically refers to Robinson Crusoe as a type of fiction-
   al writing which was, upon first publication, quickly categorized
   as being "in the style of the Histoire des Sévarambes and of
   Jacques Sadeur" (Nouvelles littéraires, Amsterdam, December,
   1719). Like Robinson Crusoe were also such predecessors as Misson's Voyage et avantures de François Leguat (1708), now shown to
   be "a fictional desert island novel," and Tyssot de Patot's Voyages et avantures de Jacques Massé (1710), discussed at an early
   date by André LeBreton (1898).

2 B., Dr. E. "L'Ile de Robinson Crusoe." Mercure de France 156
   (1 June):568.
        Notes that M.A. Hyatt Verril, Clifford Howard, and Elisée
   Reclus had already pressed the claim of Tobago to be Crusoe's
   island.

3 CODMAN, JOHN S. "Robinson Crusoe Up-To-Date." Freeman 5,
   no. 126 (9 August):514-16.
        Imagines Robinson Crusoe rewritten "in the light of
   present-day industrial conditions," and the changes necessary to
   give modern versions of Crusoe the landowner, tenant and employ-
   er, and employee or wage-earner. The "object" for retelling the
   story: to argue for private ownership of land and its natural
   resources, but also for the requirement of appropriate payment by
   the owners as assurance that the use of the land will not be
   denied to industry.

4 DOTTIN PAUL. "L'Ile de Robinson." Mercure de France 160
   (15 November):112-19. Translated by Paul Dottin, in Living
   Age 315, no. 4094 (23 December):776-80.
        Summarizes and assesses the comparative claims of Tobago
   and Juan Fernandez to be identified with Crusoe's island, and
   rejects both locations. Offers an explanation for placing the
   island in the mouth of the Orinoco River, in terms of the novel's
   origin. Argues that Defoe deliberately gave vague descriptions
   of the location since it was basically an island of the imagination.

5 DRAPER, JOHN W. Review of A Catalogue of the Library of the
   Late John Henry Wrenn, 1920. Modern Language Notes 37, no. 4
   (April):237-43.
        Among the "multiplicity of errors" found in the Catalogue,
   includes listings for the "Defoe collection . . . the special
   boast of the editor," Thomas J. Wise. Particularly criticizes
   the new attributions to Defoe, and places the blame, not on Wise,
   but on unscrupulous booksellers. Claims that for scholarly
   purposes, the five elegant volumes of the Catalogue are not
   reliable.

6   ELLIOTT, L[ILLIAN] E[LWYN]. "Crusoe's Island. The Pacific
     Group of Juan Fernandez: The Journalist and the Marooned
     Man." Pan-American Magazine 34 (May):29–38.
          Derives the Robinson Crusoe story mainly from Alexander
     Selkirk's adventure of having been marooned on Juan Fernandez.
     Recapitulates the geographical description of the Juan Fernandez
     group of islands, the Selkirk story, and Defoe's career as a
     writer.

7   HAWKINS, H.K., ed. Introduction to Selections from Daniel
     Defoe. Methuen's English Classics. London: Methuen & Co.,
     pp. 1–21.
          Although the book aims "to encourage students to break new
     ground," the Introduction barely mentions Moll Flanders and Rox-
     ana. Chooses as "selections" portions of Colonel Jack, Memoirs
     of a Cavalier, Captain Singleton, Journal of the Plague Year, and
     An Essay upon Projects ("An Academy for Women"); and the complete
     Mrs. Veal and Shortest-Way with the Dissenters. All the selec-
     tions are intended to show the author "a brilliant journalist."
     In section 1 "Defoe's Literary Works" (10 pp.), provides a criti-
     cal overview of the "selected" works. Defines Defoe's achieve-
     ment as "the air of sober truth" he gave to all his fiction,
     noting (for instance) the frequent acceptance of the Memoirs of
     a Cavalier and the Journal of the Plague Year as authentic docu-
     ments. Endeavors to relate Defoe's preparation for the role of
     novelist to the training he received from his pamphleteering and
     journalism. On characterization, makes the observation that De-
     foe relied upon "a sound general knowledge of human nature based
     on years of observation and experiment," but he had little "curi-
     osity" about individuals or their psychology: "The mind which he
     had studied with deepest interest was the collective mind of the
     British public." Summarizes in section 2 "the life and times of
     Daniel Defoe" (11 pp.).

8   HILL, ROBERT F. Director of film (American). Robinson
     Crusoe.
          Cast includes Harry C. Myers as Robinson, Noble Johnson as
     Vendredi, Gertrude Olmsted. See Filmographic Dictionary of World
     Literature.

9   JACKSON, HENRY E. Robinson Crusoe Social Engineer: How the
     Discovery of Robinson Crusoe Solves the Labor Problem and
     Opens the Path to Industrial Peace. New York: E.P. Dutton
     & Co., 301 pp.
          Quests after the secret of Robinson Crusoe's popularity for
     over 200 years. Discovers that the usual elements of romance are
     missing; instead it romanticizes the commonplace by introducing
     "the charm of uncertainty." Above all, Crusoe has "a true per-
     spective on the relative value of things," as evident in his
     soliloquy on money or in his observations on things taken from
     the wreck. In his control over the emotions, acceptance of
     circumstances, indomitable courage, he shows a unique "mental

attitude." At the high point of part 1, "The Secret of Robinson
Crusoe's Popularity," makes the tenuous connection that Crusoe
"represents the type of man produced in England previous to the
English Industrial Revolution," and reenforces the view later by
adding that he was "in first hand contact with realities and real
processes." In part 2, "Robinson Crusoe's Challenge to Modern
Industry," describes the conditions up to World War I that have
turned workmen into machines. In part 3, "How Robinson Crusoe
Solves the Labor Problem," builds up to "the audacious proposi-
tion" by noting a significance in Crusoe's keeping a journal: he
not only makes things (ink, pottery, boats), he also balances
good and evil, and so is "a time-binder." Although mainly concerned with a highly idiosyncratic scheme for industrial peace,
identifies Robinson Crusoe as the seminal work. Tells an anecdote of a manufacturer who as president and part-owner of "a
typical American factory" was experiencing problems of workers'
unrest after World War I, and adopted "a revolutionizing idea"
from a rereading of Robinson Crusoe; gave his workmen "moral
equality," and thus transformed them into well-satisfied Crusoes.

10   KRUTCH, JOSEPH WOOD. "Source of Crusoe?" New York Evening
        Post Literary Review, 9 September:12.
           Reviews The Narrative of El-Ho (1921.10); maintains that
Hubbard overstated the case for Defoe's imitating the Dutch
source in his Robinson Crusoe; and that American scholarship (as
in Trent, 1916.12) was well aware of both the Dutch book and
Defoe's alleged debt.

11   "L'Ile de Robinson Crusoe." Mercure de France 155 (1 May):
        860-61.
           Refers to the communication on Crusoe's island, 1921.13,
and cites the view of M.A. Hyatt Verrill in favor of Tobago's
claim.

12   LILJEGREN, S.B. "Defoes Robinson." Englische Studien 56,
        no. 2:281-86.
           Strong defense of Hübener (1920.9) against Ullrich
(1921.18). Stresses capitalistic features of Robinson Crusoe as
stemming from the zeitgeist, not from Defoe's aesthetic intention. Makes observations on Defoe's ironic treatment of religion, his utilitarian (not abstract) mode of thought, and the
"experimental ethics" of Robinson (judging goodness by measure of
success) as an early stage of utilitarian ethics.   (P.E.C.)

13   NIEHAUS, AGNES. "Defoes Einfluss auf Swifts 'Gulliver.'" In
        Jahrbuch der philosophischen und naturwissenschaftlichen Facul-
        tat Munster i. W. fur 1920. Pederborn: Ferdinand Schoningh,
        pp. 71-75.
           A student essay enumerating the many situational, composi-
tional, and stylistic similarities that lead to the conclusion:
Swift was looking over Defoe's shoulder.   (P.E.C.)

14   SCHÖFFLER, HERBERT. <u>Protestantismus und Literatur: Neue
     Wege zur englischen Literatur des achtzehnten Jahrhunderts</u>.
     Leipzig: B. Tauchnitz. Reprint. Gottingen: Vandenhoeck &
     Ruprecht, 1958, 242 pp.
          Offers insights into the interrelationship between the
     weakening of the protestant (including dissenter) hold on its
     member population, the rise of the Enlightenment, and the grad-
     ual shift from homiletic to belletristic production by key
     adherents of protestantism (among them clergy, their offspring,
     and candidates for the clergy)--true both of England and Germany.
     Places particular emphasis on Bunyan, Defoe, and Richardson.
     Argues that more attention needs to be paid to <u>Serious Reflec-
     tions</u> since it shows clearly, in retrospect, Defoe's indebtedness
     to the great stream of edifying literature of the seventeenth
     century. Sees in the "Puritan ethic" the link between his and
     Hübener's accurate but too exclusively economic observations
     (1920.9), representing the other side of this sociologically
     oriented view of literary developments. Blames narrowly liter-
     ature-historical approaches (of Ullrich and others) for their
     misinterpreting the sudden popularity of Defoe's and Richardson's
     novels.   (P.E.C.)

                              1923

1   ALBERT, EDWARD. <u>A History of English Literature</u>. New York:
     Thomas Y. Crowell Co. Reprint. 1925, pp. 249-51, 268, 272-
     73, 339-40, 557.
          Using a textbook and literary history format, sums up the
     life (Defoe, poor and disreputable) and the prose (divided into
     political writings and fiction). Finds the plan of each novel to
     be "slatternly and unequal" and the style "unpolished to the
     verge of rudeness," but the overall effect in realism "rarely
     approached by the most ardent of modern realists." Reprinted:
     1955; 1971.

2   BENNETT, HANNAFORD. "Biographical Introduction." In <u>A Jour-
     nal of the Plague Year</u>. Carlton Classics. London: John
     Long, pp. 5-15.
          Except for the next to the last paragraph listing the
     novels, shows Defoe engaged in political activities for which he
     was reviled.

3   BIRRELL, AUGUSTINE. "<u>Moll Flanders</u>." <u>Nation & the Athenaeum</u>
     33 (16 June):363-64.
          Reviews the Constable reprint (1923) of <u>Moll Flanders</u>.
     Comments randomly upon the popularity and literary reputation of
     <u>Moll Flanders</u>, from the admiration of George Borrow in <u>Lavengro</u>
     (1851) to the neglect of "critical pundits" or the quick dismis-
     sals of William Hazlitt (the elder), Charles Lamb, and Walter
     Scott.

                              384

4   DAVIES, W.H. Review of <u>Moll Flanders</u>, published by Constable, 1923. <u>New Statesman</u> 21 (23 June):330.
     Describes Defoe's almost exclusive concern with human characters. As for style: he has "scracely a purple passage in all his works"; relies on monosyllables to create an effect of intense feeling. Illustrates the style by offering a poem as Defoe would have written it for Moll Flanders.

5   DEFOE, DANIEL. <u>The Fortunes and Misfortunes of the Famous Moll Flanders</u>. London: Constable & Co., 423 pp.
     See the reviews of this reprint (1st ed.), 1923.3-4, 6, 12.

6   "Defoe and Moll Flanders." <u>TLS</u>, no. 1118 (21 June):418.
     Reviews the Constable reprint (1923) of <u>Moll Flanders</u>. Finds "the genius of reality" to be the distinguishing quality of this novel and <u>Robinson Crusoe</u>. To achieve it, Defoe used a method "poles apart" from Zola's or the French naturalists. He wrote from "hints," creating Robinson Crusoe from Alexander Selkirk and Moll Flanders from Moll Cutpurse in Middleton's play. In addition, because Defoe recognized the "hard necessity" of life, his Robinson Crusoe and Moll Flanders have in common the constant need to wrestle an existence from harsh surroundings.

7   DOTTIN, PAUL. "Daniel De Foe et les sciences occultes." <u>Revue anglo-américaine</u> 1, no. 2 (December):102-19.
     Comprehensively surveys Defoe's attitudes toward the supernatural, the occult sciences, and the devil. Covers first the works in which his primary aim was to make money such as the pamphlets in which the second-sighted highlander sets forth political predictions for each year ahead (1711-1715), or the Duncan Campbell publications; second, the series of important works in which his attitude toward the supernatural and the occult sciences clearly changed: "the old Puritan ideas which he had inherited from his ancestors seized possession of his soul." His changed attitude toward spirits, oracles, dreams was first evident in <u>Serious Reflections . . . of Robinson Crusoe</u>, and more systematically expanded in the <u>Political History of the Devil</u> (1726), <u>System of Magic</u> (1726), <u>An Essay on the History and Reality of Apparitions</u> (1727). The titles are misleading; the works are, actually, "weighty volumes . . . a violent press-campaign against the general taste for occultism." Of special interest with respect to the novels is Defoe's attack, in the <u>Political History of the Devil</u>, on the usual locations assigned to Hell and on the usual depictions of the devil. In <u>A System of Magic</u> he best ridiculed the occult sciences. Altogether he has a strange mélange of beliefs which are at times apparently contradictory: mysticism, "practical mentality," ridicule of popular conceptions, open acceptance of superstitions (e.g., "secret hints," dreams).

8   _____. "Daniel De Foe mystificateur ou les faux mémoires de
Mesnager." Revue germanique 14 (July):269–82.
       With Queen Anne's death in August 1714, the collapse of the
ministry, and the imprisonment of Robert Harley for high treason,
Defoe began a series of "mystifications" designed to rescue his
former patron. So effective was the strategy of the anonymous
Mesnager that Harley's trial ended in his triumphant acquittal.
Demonstrates conclusively that the Mesnager was not authentic
memoirs; cites the evidence from Abel Boyer's Political State of
Great-Britain (30 June 1717) that the "forger" was "the hack"
whom he clearly identifies as Defoe, as well as by specific references to his Newington home and his recent publications. Explains Defoe's denials of authorship of the Mesnager in the July
1717 number of Mercurius Politicus and the Saint James Post, but
his use of the Mesnager as an authority for his Memoirs . . . of
his Grace the D. of Shrewsbury (1718). Concludes harshly by
admitting "the duplicity of this hired libellist," but suggests
that the novels are like the Mesnager, "in the vein of mystification."

9   _____. Robinson Crusoe Examin'd and Criticis'd or A New Edition of Charles Gildon's Famous Pamphlet Now Published with an
Introduction and Explanatory Notes Together with an Essay on
Gildon's Life. London and Paris: J.M. Dent & Sons, 189 pp.
       In "The Life of Charles Gildon" (42 pp.), provides for the
first time essential information about the first extensive commen-
tator on Defoe's Robinson Crusoe, in The Life and Strange Surprizing Adventures of Mr. D..... De F..., of London, Hosier (1719).
Makes available also an exact reprint of Gildon's rare pamphlet
(66 pp.). In addition, glosses, at times extensively, obscure
passages and allusions to Defoe's novel (52 pp.). Offers also
"A Chronological List of Gildon's Works" (7 pp.), indexes to both
Gildon's life and the pamphlet, and an introduction to Gildon's
pamphlet (8 pp.) which discusses his motivation in writing the
pamphlet. With clearly a pejorative intent, Gildon endeavors to
connect "the chief events of Crusoe's life with De Foe's past" in
order to show the author more ridiculous than his hero. Sees
Robinson Crusoe as an allegory of Defoe's life, a view along with
Gildon's use of the word "parable" that would have repercussions
in later criticism of Defoe's novel. Among the biographical details preserved by Gildon, includes the assertion that Robinson
Crusoe was written at Stoke Newington, and not at four other cit-
ies laying claim to being the place where the novel was written.
Reprinted: Folcroft Library Editions, 1974.

10   EDDY, WILLIAM A. Gulliver's Travels: A Critical Study.
Princeton, N.J.: Princeton University Press, pp. 8, 23–24,
33–35.
       Originally, a Ph.D. dissertation, Princeton University.
Examines the little known Consolidator, "a Fantastic Voyage" that
anticipated Swift's Gulliver's Travels in using the made-up language of the Lunarians; it has never before been mentioned as a

source. Describes <u>Captain Singleton</u>, also, as having the same
realistic method as <u>Gulliver's Travels</u>.

11   EVANS, S[YLVIA] HOPE. <u>The Book of Nailsea Court</u>. Bristol:
     St. Stephen's Press, pp. 67, 90.
        In a history of this ancient west country manor house
     located in Somerset ten miles east of Bristol, deals incidental-
     ly, for the first time in print, with the connection between
     Defoe's participation in the Duke of Monmouth rebellion shortly
     after 11 June 1685 where he met and perhaps served with one of
     the leaders, Major Nathaniel Wade, and the meeting of Selkirk and
     Defoe at Nailsea Court. Indicates that the two men got together
     probably at some time before 1717, the year in which Wade died,
     according to the frequent recollection of Mrs. Damaris Daniel,
     Wade's daughter, about the meeting; and "from that had arisen the
     writing of <u>Robinson Crusoe</u>."

12   FREEMAN, JOHN. "The Autobiography of Mrs. Flanders." <u>Specta-</u>
     <u>tor</u> 131, no. 4963 (11 August):192-93.
        Reviews the Constable reprint (1923) of <u>Moll Flanders</u>.
     Analyzes the differences in style between the preface and the
     "autobiography" itself, and concludes the preface to be the more
     sophisticated, even showing "a concern for aesthetics." Suggests
     that Defoe edited out some of the wicked language for a reason
     never mentioned in the preface—out of admiration for the woman
     named Moll. Notes, on the one hand, the strengthening of "auto-
     biography" through incidents such as the stealing of the horse,
     which reads like "plain fact"; and, on the other, the non-autobio-
     graphical practice of almost completely omitting all names.

13   GOEBEL, JULIUS. "The Dutch Source of <u>Robinson Crusoe</u>."
     <u>Journal of English and Germanic Philology</u> 22, no. 2:302-13.
        Review of Hubbard, 1921.10. Adds strong additional support
     to the view that Defoe was far more indebted to the episode in
     Hendrik Smeeks's <u>Krinke Kesmes</u>, the Dutch Utopia published at Am-
     sterdam in 1708, than to the Selkirk sources. Extends Hubbard's
     comparison of Smeeks and Defoe to include Selkirk; demonstrates
     how Defoe gathered some of the psychological perceptions for Rob-
     inson Crusoe from the Dutch cabin boy of Smeeks's narrative. Ar-
     gues also that certain Utopian elements in the Dutch source have
     left traces in <u>Robinson Crusoe</u>, as for example, Crusoe's allowing
     religious tolerance in his small colony.

14   HÜBENER, GUSTAV. "Zu Ullrich's Aufsatz 'Zum Robinson-prob-
     lem.'" <u>Englische Studien</u> 57, no. 2:316-18.
        Responds to several of Ullrich's criticisms of Hübener
     (1921.18) who had presented an economic interpretation of <u>Robin-</u>
     <u>son Crusoe</u> (1920.9). Suggests willful misinterpretation, out-
     dated methodology, selective amnesia and breakdown in logic.
     Offers no new insights.   (P.E.C.)

15   "The Lesser Defoe." TLS, no. 1127 (23 August):534.
     Reviews the Constable reprint (1923) of Roxana. In his mas-
terpiece Robinson Crusoe, Defoe balanced "the genius, the journalist, and the moralist." In Roxana he has only the journalist and
the moralist, and neglects the artist. Among the reasons cited
for the novel's failure: Lady Roxana lacks any "development" in
her history; she does not establish causal connections between
her actions and her moral comments, and thus becomes "no more
than a puppet." Now and then, introduces favorable judgments as,
for example, on Defoe's style or language, but on the whole—
severe.

16   LILJEGREN, S.B. "Bemerkung zu Ullrichs Ausführungen." En-
     glische Studien 57, no. 2:315-16.
     A Further swordstroke in the duel between the new sociolo-
gists of literature and Ullrich, the enfeebled master of the old
school.   (P.E.C.)

17   MARR, GEORGE S. The Periodical Essayists of the Eighteenth
     Century. London: James Clarke & Co., pp. 11, 15-19, 22, 33,
     46, 65-66, 79. Reprint. Folcroft, Pa.: Folcroft Library
     Editions, 1974.
     In the first exclusive study of the periodical essay since
Nathan Drake (1805), discusses the Review—its Scandal Club,
style, and techniques such as the question-and-answer, mock
trial, and "vision"—as precursor of the Tatler and Spectator.
In 1720 and later Defoe contributed "letters introductory" to
Appleby's moderately Tory Original Weekly Journal and Mist's
Jacobite Weekly Journal. Reprinted: D. Appleton & Co., 1924.

18   MULDER, ARNOLD. "Was Robinson Crusoe Written by a Hollander?"
     Outlook 135 (17 October):277-78, 280.
     Cautiously accepts the theory advanced by Hubbard in A
Dutch Source of Robinson Crusoe (1921.10) that Hendrik Smeeks's
Description of the Mighty Kingdom of Krinke Kesmes (1708) directly inspired Robinson Crusoe, or it stimulated Defoe to make use
of the Selkirk story. Equally probable, although not as likely,
is the alternative that the two authors worked with the Selkirk
material independently of one another. Much more harm fell upon
Robinson Crusoe from the incessant abridgements and adaptions.

19   SARGENT, GEORGE H. "Rescuing Robinson Crusoe." Antiques 3,
     no. 1 (January):35-37.
     On book-collecting, rare Robinson Crusoe editions as in the
collections of William S. Lloyd and William P. Trent, the bibliographical "points" of the first edition, and early American
editions.

20   STEVENSON, ROBERT LOUIS. Letter to W.E. Henley, July 1884.
     In The Letters of Robert Louis Stevenson. Edited by Sidney
     Colvin. New ed. 4 vols. New York: Charles Scribner's Sons,
     2:223-26.

Adds to 1899.9. After his letter to Colvin, Stevenson
writes to Henley also in July, 1884, and expresses enthusiasm
upon reading Captain Singleton for the first time and upon rereading Colonel Jack (superior to Robinson Crusoe).

21   ULLRICH, HERMANN. "Zum Defoe-Problem." Englische Studien 57,
      no. 2:309-15.
           Responds to Hübener (1920.9) and Liljegren (1922.12), cri-
      ticizing above all their faulty knowledge of Defoe and his works,
      and their haste in (mis)applying general observations from the
      history of ideas.   (P.E.C.)

22   UTTER, ROBERT PALFREY. "On the Alleged Tediousness of Defoe
      and Richardson." University of California Chronicle 25, no. 1
      (January):175-93.
           Staunchly defends the quantity of details on grounds that
      the reader shares the "hoarding instinct" of Crusoe, and the
      repetitions on grounds that they add heroic stature or "the color
      of a myth." Similarly, defends the repetitions of Captain
      Singleton, but cannot make the case for Moll Flanders or Roxana.
      Instead, "the piling up of details" in these two books makes
      possible one of their finest qualities, the effect of watching
      "motion pictures of Defoe's England flashing and changing before
      your eyes." Of the three qualities essential to the artist,
      Defoe has been charged with having dominant "the sense of fact"
      or realism, but with totally lacking "the sense of form." Re-
      printed: Pearls & Pepper (New Haven: Yale University Press,
      1924), pp. 200-27.

23   VAN DOREN, CARL, ed. Introduction to The Fortunes and Misfor-
      tunes of the Famous Moll Flanders. Borzoi Classics. New
      York: A.A. Knopf, pp. xi-xv.
           Sympathetically interprets Moll Flanders, a realistic novel
      whose author was deeply "sincere" and whose chief character, a
      prostitute and theif, was deemed worth writing about. Describes
      Defoe's moral system "as absolute as it was simple" and Moll's
      conflict, between "virtue and instinct," as powerfully dramatic.
      Asserts that the only conflict possible for Moll must be at the
      economic level, never the speculative one. Compliments, finally,
      Marcel Schwob's translation, appearing at the high point of
      French naturalism: it justified "a method and an attitude which
      are possibly bourgeois but which are singularly immortal." See
      also the review by Littell, 1924.13.

                                1924

1   ATKINSON, GEOFFROY. Les Relations de voyages du XVIIe siècle
      et l'évolution des idées. Paris: Librairie Ancienne Édouard
      Champion, pp. 59, 63, 182-83.
           Mentions briefly Henri du Quesne and his Recueil de quelque
      mémoires servans d'instruction pour l'établissement de l'isle

d'Éden (1689), the aim of practicing Plato's political virtues on a Crusoe-like desert island and thus creating an Utopian state. Makes a passing reference to Defoe's contribution to a leading idea of the French Revolution, "the good savage." In the "Conclusion," recognizes a gap between the ideas of Defoe, Rousseau, and Voltaire, which the public readily accepted, and those of Pascal and Bossuet.

2   BELL, WALTER GEORGE. The Great Plague in London in 1665. London: John Lane; New York: Dodd, Mead & Co., 387 pp. passim.
        Although Bell takes on the entire subject of the Plague of 1665 in general, he must constantly deal with only one antagonist, "my great predecessor," whose Journal of the Plague Year he can only regard as "an historical novel," not as the "authentic history" of Watson Nicholson. The Plague graphically depicted here [Bell's book] cannot be Defoe's: "this picture . . . of a city in its agony is more terrible than all that Defoe imagined." The two books [Bell's and Defoe's], "in method as in purpose," differ greatly from one another. Points out the places in which Defoe shows "all too frequent inaccuracy," as in the number of pest-houses; or in which his picture is "delusive," as in the general non-compliance of the public with the Mayor's Orders; or in which he commits outright errors, as in claiming there was actually a parish officer with the title of "Examiner" whose specific function was "to search for Plague in the dwellings." He found Defoe to be "entirely careless" with history. The Journal of the Plague Year was "a fictional work"; and although its author used history, he was "not an historical writer." See also the revised edition (London: John Lane, 1951) which adds some new material.

3   Calendar of State Papers, Domestic Series, of the Reign of Anne. Preserved at the Public Record Office. Volume II (1703-1704). Edited by Robert Pentland Mahaffy. London: HMSO, pp. 53, 54, 60, 66, 473, 476.
        Publishes or summarizes manuscript documents relating to the pursuit, arrest, and punishment of Defoe for "high crimes and misdemeanors" in publishing the Shortest-Way with the Dissenters. The extracts from State Papers Domestic, Entry Book 350, 352, 104 are dated from 3 January to 27 July 1703; and include letters from the Earl of Nottingham.

4   CAREY, ANDREW. Review of Moll Flanders editions published by Grant Richards and Guy Chapman. Spectator, no. 5035 (27 December):1027-29.
        Assesses Defoe as neither a great writer nor a great man, and makes observations on "the peculiar turn to his spirit" which he identifies as "an openness and honesty of intelligence" in novels such as Moll Flanders.

5   CATHER, WILLA. Introduction to <u>The Fortunate Mistress</u>.
     Borzoi Classics. New York: Alfred A. Knopf, pp. vii-xiii.
          States the view that Defoe, the "practical journalist,"
     looked upon the writing of narratives as a trade much like being
     a hosier. The peculiar circumstances of <u>Robinson Crusoe</u>, such as
     the author's "literal method" or Crusoe's having the entire scene
     to himself, worked in its favor. But in <u>The Fortunate Mistress</u>
     the effects are different. Given all its "inflammatory materi-
     al," the novel "remains so dull." Defoe has ready invention, but
     lacks imagination. He cannot command "scene" as well as Bunyan,
     or provide "atmosphere." He does not adequately differentiate
     cities, countries, "physical surroundings," and so forth. The
     novel amasses "the evidence of a curious insensibility in Roxanna
     [misspelled throughout] and her author." The two care only about
     her clothes. Roxana does have "enough sense of character for her
     purpose," particularly with regard to her servant Amy. So strong
     is her verisimilitude that one "never doubts that this is a
     woman's actual story, told by a woman." Neither Roxana nor her
     author make any pretensions to feelings; the book has "mental
     integrity": it is "as safe as serilized gauze." Reprinted: "De-
     foe's <u>The Fortunate Mistress</u>" in <u>On Writing: Critical Studies on
     Writing as an Art</u> (New York: Alfred A. Knopf, 1949), pp. 75-88;
     1953.

6   DAVIES, W.H. Introduction to <u>Moll Flanders</u>. Abbey Classics,
     21. London: Simpkin, Marshall, Hamilton, Kent & Co.,
     pp. ix-xiii.
          Tells why, as a writer, he turned to reading one of the
     Masters, starting with his <u>Moll Flanders</u> and continuing with <u>Rob-
     inson Crusoe</u> and <u>Journal of the Plague Year</u>. Finds the language
     "so simple and direct," the style "bare and quiet" conveying
     intense feeling, the action rich and central, the concentration
     upon "human character" almost exclusive of everything else. See
     the brief but severe criticism by Paul Dottin, in <u>Revue anglo-
     américaine</u> 2, no. 5 (1925):445. Reprinted: The Bibliophilist
     Society, 1931.

7   DOTTIN, PAUL. <u>Daniel De Foe et ses romans</u>. 3 vols. Paris:
     Presses Universitaires de France; London: Oxford University
     Press, 1:3-289; 2:293-546; 3:549-891.
          A monumental work in its breadth and influence, stands out
     as perhaps the most important piece of French scholarship and
     criticism. Divides the subject into, first, a biography which
     freshly interprets all the information available; second, a his-
     torical and critical study of <u>Robinson Crusoe</u>; and third, a cri-
     tique of "the secondary novels." Bases analyses and conclusions
     on a new investigation of the canon, the first since Trent's
     (1912.18), and raises the total to 359 writings confirmed by
     external evidence and fifty-eight, confirmed by internal evidence
     (51 pp.). In vol. 1, <u>The Life and Strange and Surprising Adven-
     tures of Daniel Defoe</u> (289 pp.), reacts to previous biographers
     by taking his subject as he was, without making him a national

hero or deifying him. Deduces shrewdly certain dates, hitherto
not known, such as the year of Defoe's birth or the years when he
could most logically have traveled in England or abroad. Reconstructs the early years by personally visiting places, especially
in London, associated with Defoe; and by borrowing "evidence"
from the novels [on a few occasions, the reconstruction has ludi-
crous results]. Presents a less known personal side of Defoe, in
conflict with his Puritanism: the pleasure-loving gallant who
mimicked the ways of noblemen like Lord Rochester, attended horse-
races, and kept a mistress. Places emphasis on Defoe's role of
confidant and spy to William III. Correlates biographical and
fictional events, with helpful cross-references in the footnotes.
In vol. 2, Robinson Crusoe: Historical and Critical Study (254
pp.), continues the reconstruction "to show the genesis of the
work in the mind of Defoe." As a historian, examines Robinson
Crusoe as the carrying out of a dream that began with plans he
submitted to William III for ·the conquest of Spain in America,
and revived in 1711. Locates the genesis of Robinson Crusoe,
not with Alexander Selkirk or Juan Fernandez, but with the region
near the mouth of the Orinoco River. As a literary critic,
applies a concept from Maupassant concerning the "pure psychology" of the modern novel, and sees the novels as places where
Defoe puts on different "masks" of himself: preacher, non-con-
formist, tradesman, politician, and journalist. Reconstructs
Defoe's method as one in which he brought the broad outlines or
plan of a novel to the bookseller(s), gained approval, and then
wrote--hastily, without correcting or rewriting. For Robinson
Crusoe, makes the case that here he has the four essential conditions of the modern novel: credibility, presence ("interior
vision given with the precision of photography"), an important
subject ("verities," such as the White Man's burden and other
symbolic meanings), and finally the recreation of life. Makes
the point repeatedly and especially in the conclusion (4 pp.)
that "Defoean characters" are essentially reincarnations of himself, the novels are autobiographical fictions, and the ideas
spring from his own innermost being. Most daringly challenges
the critical "tradition" in vol. 3, The Secondary Novels of
Daniel De Foe (250 pp.), where Dottin presents the most lengthy
and most minute examination to-date of the secondary novels, as
Lamb uses the term. Confronts and overturns sacrosanct notions.
Argues that all Defoe's novels are underrated: Memoirs of a Cavalier and Journal of the Plague Year start the new genre of the
historical novel; Captain Singleton undeniably bears "the imprint
of authenticity"; Colonel Jack and the other social novels never
have a chance against "Victorian prudery"; and Roxana, venturing
into an entirely new genre ("the roman galant"), pushes the novel
beyond known limits. Affirms boldly that artistically Moll Flanders surpasses Robinson Crusoe, which belongs in the domain of
children's literature; and takes certain subjects "out of the
closet," such as the incest and pornography in Moll Flanders, and
the feminism in Roxana. Claims that already the evolution in
literary taste has taken place. Working with a new conception of

the man and novelist, introduces stylistic analyses which recognize the centrality of Defoe's sense of mystery in the novels; a
prevailing mode of autobiography which now and then is violated;
repetitions, contradictions, anachronisms, errors; digressions
and "parentheses"; and a rhetoric that takes each novel as
"speaking" rather than written art. Vol. 1 was translated by
Louise Ragan as The Life and Strange and Surprising Adventures of
Daniel De Foe (New York: Macaulay, 1929; reprinted, 1971), which
includes chap. 11 "Defoe's Novels," but omits Dottin's documentation for vol. 1 and drastically reduces the contents of vols. 2
and 3. See also the reviews by Oliver Elton, French Quarterly 7
(1925):89-92; Hermann Ullrich, Englische Studien 6 (1925-1926):
364-70; W.H. Staverman, English Studies 8 (1926):189-93.

8   DOTTIN, PAUL. "Le Robinson Suisse." Mercure de France 169
     (1 January):114-26.
        Describes the low fortunes of Robinson Crusoe in France for
the period just before Émile (1762) and its revival as the book
of education for young people. Campe, in 1779, carried out the
task of reducing Robinson to "the state of nature" and of recast-
ing the narrative to remove all the benefits to Crusoe of civilization. His Nouveau Robinson was translated into twenty-seven
languages, and only now has fallen into general neglect, except
in Germany. In 1812, the Robinson suisse of Johann David Wyss
took the Robinsonade in the direction of the family, away from
the solitary hero; the capable translator of this volume into
French, Madame de Montolieu, published the Continuation du Robinson Suisse (1824) before Wyss brought out his own continuation
(1827). In 1855, a popular romancer named Paul Adrien tried to
replace Wyss with a book now entirely forgot, Pilote Willis.

9   _____. "Salomon Eagle, le quaker nu de la peste de Londres."
     Revue Anglo-Américaine 1, no. 6 (August):532-34.
        Corrects critics who overemphasize the role of imagination
in Defoe's novels. Demonstrates, for instance, that behind the
"enthusiast" Salomon Eagle, who runs naked through the streets of
London in the Journal of the Plague Year, is the real-life person
Salomon Eccles--a musician who turned Quaker and engaged in an-
tics not very different from those described by Defoe.

10   FISCHER, WALTHER. "Defoe und Milton." Englische Studien
     58:213-17.
        In his Political History of the Devil, Defoe accuses Milton
of revealing heterodoxy (Arianism) and faulty logic in Paradise
Lost, but most of the criticism was of the carping, polemical
kind. Moreover, a carelessness on Defoe's part is sometimes difficult to distinguish from tongue-in-cheek comment.   (P.E.C.)

11   JAMES, MONTAGUE R. Introduction to Ghosts and Marvels:
     A Selection of Uncanny Tales from Daniel Defoe to Algernon
     Blackwood. Edited by V.H. Collins. World's Classics, 284.
     London: Oxford University Press, pp. v-xiii.

Refers to Scott's explanation for the publication of the
fictitious <u>Mrs. Veal</u> as a means of stimulating the sales of
<u>Drelincourt on Death</u>; also remembers Andrew Lang's belief that
the narrative was "an attempt to record an occurrence believed
to be real."

12   LEGOUIS, É[MILE], and CAZAMIAN, L[OUIS]. "De Foe." In
     <u>Histoire de la littérature anglaise</u>. Paris: Hachette,
     pp. 749-54.
     Summarize compactly the factual information known about
Defoe and the broad continental attitudes towards his works.
Group the diverse writings around "certain themes and tendencies," and move toward generalizations. Tend to see Defoe as
giving voice for the first time to "the average bourgeoisie."
The generalizations extend from the personal (e.g., "psychological disorder" accompanies "this type of bourgeois search
for balance") to the literary/critical (e.g., <u>Robinson Crusoe</u>
as "the symbolic drama of the rude and patient effort through
which civilization is born"). Reprinted: 1925; 1929; 1939;
1946; 1949; 1951; translated into English: 1926-1927 and others
to 1948.

13   LITTELL, ROBERT. Review of <u>Moll Flanders</u>, with Introduction
     by Carl Van Doren, 1923. <u>New Republic</u> 37, no. 474 (2 Janu-
     ary):152.
     Compares Defoe with the French naturalists; finds an
essential difference in that he is not cerebrally preoccupied
with method, having "as little mind as the lens of a camera."

14   PROTHERO, ROWLAND EDMUND, FIRST BARON ERNLE. "A Book-Box of
     Novels (1688-1727)." <u>Edinburgh Review</u> 240, no. 490 (October):
     309-29.
     With Arundell Esdaile's <u>List of English Tales and Prose
     Romances</u> (1912) as a base, comments upon the new direction given
to the novel by Defoe's realism, verisimilitude, and "natural
genius for journalism." Still intensely active and not retired,
he turned to novel-writing seeking in the reading public that
was forming "a market for a new kind of prose fiction." Most of
his novels are "<u>pièces de circonstance</u>," based on actual happen-
ings; <u>Moll Flanders</u> and <u>Roxana</u> are independent of circumstances;
four are "in the picaresque style"; two simulate history. Spec-
ulates, finally, on why <u>Robinson Crusoe</u> was a success: ". . .
Defoe has realised a type of the men who, among solitudes, hard-
ships, and dangers, have been pioneers and builders of the
British Empire."

15   "Robinsonaden." In <u>Deutsches Bücherverzeichnis: Eine Zus-
     sammenstellung der im deutschen Buchhandel erschienenen Bücher,
     Zeitschriften und Landkarten</u>. Leipzig: Börsenverein der
     deutschen buchhändler, 6, pt. 2:1279-80.
     Covers listing of Robinsonades in German, 1915-1920.

16   Robinson Crusoe. Hysterical History Comedies (film). Univer-
      sal Pictures Corp.
         Listed in Motion Pictures 1912-1939 (Washington, D.C.:
      Library of Congress, 1951), p. 720.

17   ROSS, ERNEST C. The Development of the English Sea Novel from
      Defoe to Conrad. Ph.D. dissertation, University of Virginia;
      Ann Arbor, Mich.: Edwards Brothers, 1926, 112 pp. passim.
         Begins and ends with the statement that the recognition of
      the novel as a literary form and the introduction of "the seaman
      in the salty sense of the term" happened simultaneously, and not
      coincidentally. In a special section (5 pp.), discusses Robinson
      Crusoe, King of the Pirates (1719), Captain Singleton, New Voyage
      Round the World, and An Account of . . . the late John Gow
      (1725); reaches the conclusion that while Defoe sent "the tale of
      adventure seaward, or to an island," it was Smollett who sent a
      seaman with it. Comments briefly on the mention of Robinson
      Crusoe in Cooper's The Crater (1848), Dana's Two Years Before the
      Mast (1840), Melville's Typee (1846), Russell's Frozen Pirate
      (1880), and London's Sea-Wolf (1904). Reprinted: Folcroft
      Press, 1969.

18   SCHMIDT, RICHARD. Der Volkswille als realer Faktor des Verfas-
      sungslebens und Daniel Defoe. Berichte über die Verhandlungen
      der Sächsischen Akademie der Wissenschaften zu Leipzig. Leip-
      zig: S. Hirzel, 36 pp.
         Deals with Defoe's agitations for constitutional reform and
      his work on behalf of the government to limit the power of parlia-
      ment and more fairly reflect the will of the people.   (P.E.C.)

19   SCHÜCKING, LEVIN L. "Die Grundlagen des Richardson'schen
      Romans. I." Germanisch-romanische Monatsschrift 12:21-42
      passim.
         Views Defoe as a precursor of Richardson in intimately de-
      tailed spiritual portraits of the family, particularly the female
      characters. Cites works, Family Instructor (1718) and Religious
      Courtship.   (P.E.C.)

20   SECORD, ARTHUR WELLESLEY. Studies in the Narrative Method of
      Defoe. University of Illinois Studies in Language and Litera-
      ture, 9. Urbana, Ill.: University of Illinois Press, 248 pp.
         Describes Defoe's art and method of composition generally,
      in long fictitious narratives, and does not merely hunt for
      sources; and specifically, in Robinson Crusoe, Captain Singleton,
      and Capt. George Carleton. In chap. 1, "The Defoe Problem," ex-
      amines four explanations of the origins (picaresque, journalism,
      criminal biography, moral treatises), and finds them all defi-
      cient. Analyzes the three long narratives, each in a chapter,
      with a thoroughness and attention to details never before seen
      in Defoe scholarship. In "The Composition of Robinson Crusoe,"
      changes the direction of critical study away from sources which
      are exclusively about man alone on a small island to sources

which narrate "every sort of experience under primitive conditions." Out of extensive research, beyond Hakluyt and Purchas,
offers a table summary (p. 107) which shows at a glance, for each
"portion" of Part One, sources which are "certain," "probable,"
or "possible." Selkirk continues to be the person who suggested
to Defoe the idea of the desert island story, but now among the
"certain" sources are the equally important Robert Knox, who provided "a concrete embodiment of that idea" in his Historical Relation of Ceylon (1681) and manuscript "Autobiography," and William
Dampier, who supplied "a large storehouse of details of life
under unusual circumstances" in his Voyages (1697, 1699, 1703,
1709). Unravels the complex indebtedness of the Farther Adventures of Robinson Crusoe to Louis Le Comte's Memoirs and Observations Made in a late Journey through the Empire of China (1697)
and E. Ysbrant Ides's Three Years Travels from Moscow overland to
China (1706). On the art and method of composition in Captain
Singleton, Secord opposes a number of set positions. Argues that
the problem of sources, as related to method, becomes complex
because given the two narratives (the African journey and the
piracy adventures), each has its own distinct set of sources.
For the "earlier adventures," Defoe used the Voyages and Travels
of J. Albert de Mandelslo in Adam Olearius's Voyages and Travels
of the Ambassadors (1682) and Maximilien Misson's New Voyage of
François Leguat (1707). Although not able to locate any specific
source for "the most striking feature of the story, namely, the
journey across Africa," Secord severely castigates William Minto
for his geographical "blunders" (1878.5) which have seriously
misled scholars, and concludes that Defoe's knowledge of Africa's
geography was not "uncanny" or drawn "from unpublished Portuguese
sources," but obtained readily from books in English. For the
pirate adventures which were Defoe's original and primary interest in Captain Singleton, he elaborated upon his own King of the
Pirates (1719), published six months earlier. A rough sketch for
Quaker William in Captain Singleton and his prececessor in King
of the Pirates Defoe had found in the Quaker Highwayman, Jacob
Halsey, in Captain Alexander Smith's Highwaymen (1714). From
Exquemelin's Bucaniers of America (1684, 1685) he borrowed the
incident of the ship drifting at sea without mast and without
crew, and from Dampier's Voyages he had gotten the information to
send Singleton through the Bass Strait, in the belief that Tasman-
ia was an island. He had not located any source for Singleton's
"hollow-tree encounter" with the natives, but had "suggestions"
to offer from Dampier's descriptions of natives in New Guinea and
parallel accounts of powder explosions in other writings by
Defoe. Elucidates the closely related problems of authorship and
composition in Capt. George Carleton. Argues, without reservation, that "Defoe fabricated the whole story from the slightest
suggestions of Carleton's activity"; and so ranges himself with
Wilson, Lockhart, Lowndes, Craik, Doble, and Trent, who viewed Defoe as the author—as against Carleton himself or Jonathan Swift.
Makes a strong case that Capt. George Carleton is "a history of
the times," and not "a book of reminiscences"; it is written from

the larger perspective of a general or a historian, and not of an individual campaigner. More precisely, the Capt. George Carleton draws upon Abel Boyer's History of William III (1702-1703) and Life of Her Late Majesty Queen Anne (1721), the London Gazette and other periodicals. For the latter half of the book, the author borrows heavily from Countess d'Aulnoy's Ingenious and Diverting Letters of the Lady's--Travels into Spain (1708). All the discoverable sources of Capt. George Carleton were already in print by 1728; there was no need to hypothesize the role of an author named Carleton who had to rely on his memory or a diary for the composition of Capt. George Carleton. In the final chapter, "Defoe's Method of Composition," Secord summarizes, cautiously and painstakingly, the advances which his research has made toward an understanding of Defoe's workmanship. See also reviews by Hermann Ullrich, in Englische Studien 59, no. 3 (1925):457-67; Howard Buck, in Modern Language Notes 42, no. 2 (February, 1927): 121- 24; Henry Clinton Hutchins, in Journal of English and Germanic Philology 28, no. 3 (July, 1929):443-52.

21   SWINNERTON, FRANK. "A Note on the English Novel." Bookman (New York) 60, no. 4 (December):398-403.
      Begins the novel "genuinely," with Defoe's "plain narrative" and Richardson's "psychological novel": the former having "at least his faithfulness" in common with Arnold Bennett, the latter "his interminable examinations of the heart" in common with Henry James. While Defoe was neglected for one hundred and fifty years, Richardson started "a new movement in literature." Together they are responsible for the two traits which comprise "all that is best in the English novel": an "honest faithfulness" which they shared, and the "serious sentiment" or sensibility which Richardson contributed.

22   ULLRICH, HERMANN. Defoes "Robinson Crusoe": Die Geschichte eines Weltbuches für den weiteren Leserkreis. Leipzig: O.R. Reisland, 116 pp.
      This long-awaited study was actually completed in 1919, but the publication delayed. Presents a brief overview as in part a commentary on the subject-matter covered in the general headings of his Bibliography (Robinson und Robinsonaden Bibliographie, 1898) and Supplement/Bibliographie (1907-1908), and some of the more interesting works listed there, as well as an introduction to certain of the most important concerns of Defoe scholars over the years. While not the second volume (after the Bibliography) of the major Defoe work he had once envisioned, the study is aimed rather at an educated general reading public, and presents sketches of Defoe, Robinson Crusoe (its genesis, precursors, style and content, motifs, influence, etc.), and various adaptations (Robinsonades and pseudo-Robinsonades) throughout the world. The fairly detailed synopsis of the contents allows for ready consultation. As reviewers noted, Ullrich continues to hold the view that Robinson Crusoe is largely a product of Defoe's literary imagination colored strongly by his autobio

graphical circumstances, thus playing down theories of direct
influence from other sources. Defines the work as a "character
novel," depicting above all the moral and spiritual development
of the castaway hero. Critics were generally favorable, except
with regard to Ullrich's unfailing loyalty to Defoe's "spotless
character" and his tendency to overlook or discount later scholarship in certain cultural/historical (e.g., religious and economic) aspects of the subject. See also the review, in English, by
Erwin G. Gudde, Journal of English and Germanic Philology 25
(1926):132-34.   (P.E.C.)

[192-]

1   FR, V. "Defo (Defoe), Daniel." Entsiklopedicheskii slovar'
    [Encyclopedia]. Moscow: Granat, 18:284-86.
        In Russian. Makes the claim that Defoe lived in poverty
    until the profits came in from Robinson Crusoe; and that he was a
    "brilliant economist" in an Essay upon Projects. On the novels:
    Defoe wrote one adventure type "in the spirit of Spanish novella
    picaresca"; another type, in the direction of the later English
    novel of manners. Claims that Robinson Crusoe preached "humane-
    ness, religious tolerance, and civil liberty"; and had enormous
    pedagogical value. Defoe was not so much concerned with artistic
    goals as with moral goals: "a brilliant representative of the
    liberal English bourgeoisie of the eighteenth century."
                                                        (A.L.S.R.)

[19--]

1   "Biographical Notice of the Author of Robinson Crusoe." In
    Life and Adventures of Robinson Crusoe by Daniel De Foe. In-
    cluding A Memoir of the Author and an Essay on His Writings.
    New York: Fifth Avenue Publishing Co., pp. vii-viii.
        Omits a separate "Essay on His Writings." Combines a bio-
    graphical summary containing errors (e.g., Defoe's death in 1781)
    and the assertions of his "poverty and neglect" and his advocacy
    of principles, with an emphasis on two works of fiction that have
    "a value and a significance quite irrespective of time and
    place"--History of the Plague of 1665 and Adventures of Robinson
    Crusoe.

[n.d.]

1   BUNTING, J.F. Robinson Crusoe, a Grand Spectacular, Comical,
    Nonsensical, Aesthetical Burlesque. Tottenham: Herald
    Office, 15 pp.

Writings Omitted in the Regular Order

1904

*2-b   COOPER, NASARVANJI MANECJI, ed. <u>John Bull's Failings.</u>
     <u>Being Selections from Daniel Defoe's "The True-born English-</u>
     <u>man.</u>" London: Simpkin, Marshall & Co.; Bombay: K. & J.
     Cooper, 20 pp.
          Listed in the British Library <u>General Catalogue</u>, but not
     examined. According to Dottin's <u>Daniel De Foe et ses romans</u>
     (p. 90), this item was a Hindu propaganda against British
     oppressors.

1920

*2-b   BLONDOT, J. <u>En Lisant Robinson</u>. Paris: Coquemard.
          Surveying the "great ideas" in <u>Robinson Crusoe</u>, Dottin's
     <u>Daniel De Foe et ses romans</u> (p. 480) cites this excellent hand-
     book on the practice of the primary schools.

Author and Title Index

A., G., 1886.1
A., M., 1859.1
A., N.M. &, 1908.1
About Old Story-Tellers, 1878.6
Abrahams, Aleck, 1909.1
Abrégé chronologique ou histoire
    des découvértes faites par les
    Européens, 1756.1; 1765.2;
    1767.2
The Acid Sisters and Other Poems,
    1897.11
An Account of the Conduct and
    Proceedings of the Pirate Gow,
    1890.22
Adams, Henry Cadwallader, 1877.1
Adams, William Henry Davenport,
    1871.1; 1886.2
Adventures in Criticism, 1896.12
The Adventures of a French
    Serjeant, 1826.3
The Adventures of Roderick Random,
    1748.3
The Age of Pope (1700-1744),
    1894.8
Aikin, Lucy, 1868.1
Aimé-Martin, Louis, 1818.1
Ainsworth, William Harrison,
    1841.1, 11
Aitken, George A., 1889.1-2;
    1890.1-2; 1893.1; 1894.1-3;
    1895.1-15, 30-31; 1903.1;
    1909.2
Albert, Edward, 1923.1
Album Verses, 1830.5
Allibone, S. Austin, 1858.1
Alonzo, 1889.3
Alpha, 1850.3; 1889.4; 1890.3-4
The American Cyclopaedia, 1874.2
Among the Idolmakers, 1911.8

Analecta Scotica, 1837.7
Anatol, 1851.1
Anderson, James, 1787.1
Anderson, Mrs., 1917.1
Anderson, Wm., 1883.1
Anecdotes, Observations, and
    Characters of Books and Men,
    1820.6
Anecdotes of British Topography,
    1768.2
Angell, James Burrill, 1857.1
"Angliiskii publitsist XVII Veka,"
    1892.21
The Anglo-French Entente in the
    Seventeenth Century, 1914.1
Annales maritimes et coloniales,
    1819.2
Annales typographiques, 1762.1
The Annals of Bristol in the
    Eighteenth Century, 1893.9
The Annual Register, 1771.1
"Anticipations of Modern Ideas by
    Defoe," 1851.7, 16, 20
Apperson, G.L., 1908.2
Apperson, George L., 1883.2;
    1884.1
Arber, Edward, 1879.1; 1883.3;
    1903.1; 1903-1906.1
Architects of English Literature,
    1900.11
Ardagh, J., 1919.1
Arkle, A.H., 1912.1
Armstrong, T. Percy, 1921.1
Arnould, Jean François Mussot,
    1787.2
The Art of the Novelist, 1919.6
Artois, Francois Victor Armand D',
    1817.1
Atkinson, Geoffroy, 1920.1;
    1921.2; 1922.1; 1924.1
Aufrere, Anthony, 1817.6
Augé, Claude, 1898.4
The Augustan Age, 1899.3
Austen, Jane, 1821.4; 1861.9
An Author to Be Lett, 1732.3
Axon, William E.A., 1868.2;
    1871.2; 1909.3
Ayscough, S., 1787.10
'Aλιεύς, 1854.1

The English Essay and Essayists,
1915.5
English Essays, 1896.9
An English Garner, 1879.1; 1883.3;
1903.1
English-German Literary Influ-
ences, 1919-1920.1
The English Hermit, 1921.8
English Lands, Letters, and Kings,
1890.13
English Literature: An Illus-
trated Record, 1903.2
English Literature in the
Eighteenth Century, 1883.13
English Merchants, 1866.1
English Newspapers, 1887.1
The English Novel, 1894.16;
1913.21
The English Novelists, 1874.3
English Plays of the Nineteenth
Century, 1860.1
English Political Philosophy,
1909.23
"Engraved Portrait," 1851.15
En Lisant Robinson, 1920.2-b
Entick, John, 1757.1
Entsiklopedicheskii slovar',
192-.1
Epictetus, 1869.9
Erler, Gotthard, 1879.3
Ermel, Alexander, 1889.8
Ernst, Otto, 1911.4
Escott, T.H.S., 1911.5
Esdaile, Arundell, 1912.6; 1921.8
Espinasse, Francis, 1860.3
Essays, Biographical, Critical,
and Historical, 1805.3
Essays, Moral and Political,
1832.4
Essays Biographical and Critical,
1857.10
Essays of British Essayists,
1900.12
Essex, 1896.2; 1907.3, 11
Ethica, 1860.10
Études religieuses, 1862.9
Evans, I.O., 1888.24
Evans, Mary Ann, 1860.4
Evans, Sylvia Hope, 1923.11
The Everyman Encyclopaedia,
1913-1914.1

The Exploits of Robinson Crusoe,
179-.1
The Extraordinary Voyage in French
Literature, 1920.1; 1922.1

F., T., 1885.5
The Facts and Backgrounds of
Literature, 1920.11
Fama, 1880.5
The Family Robinson Crusoe, 1812-
1813.1
Farnie, Henry Brougham, 1886.9
Farrar, Eliza Ware Rotch, 1830.1
"The Fate of the Mouse," 1748.2
A Father's Instructions, 1793.2
Faulkener: A Tragedy, 1807.1, 3
Fea, Allan, 1912.7
Felkin, Emmie, 1898.3
Felkin, Henry M., 1898.3
Feller, François Xavier de, 1848.3
The Female American, 1767.1
Female Robinson Crusoe, 1837.3
Fèret, Charles James, 1897.1
Fernsemer, O.F.W., 1920.4
Feutry, Aimé Ambroise Joseph,
1766.3-4; 1769.4; 1775.2-3
Field, E.M., 1891.7
Fielding, Henry, 1749.1
Filon, Augustin, 1908.8
A First Book in English Liter-
ature, 1910.16
Fischer, Hugo, 1890.10, 25
Fischer, Walther, 1924.10
Fitzhopkins, 1868.9
Fitzmaurice-Kelly, James, 1895.20
Fleet Street in Seven Centuries,
1912.3
"Flip Can," 1897.1
Foa, Eugénie Rodrigues-Gradis,
1858.5
Foe, E., 1800.1
Foote, Samuel, 1764.2; 1820.7
Ford, J. Herbert, 1887.4
Forgotten Books of the American
Nursery, 1911.6
"Forgotten Periodical Publica-
tions," 1866.4
"A Forgotten Satire of Defoe,"
1920.5
Forman, H. Buxton, 1876.5
Fors Clavigera, 1871.13; 1874.6;
1876.10; 1907.18

Trent, William Peterfield,
1902.16; 1905.9; 1906.12;
1907.21-24; 1908.19; 1912.18-
19; 1914.13-14; 1916.11-12;
1918.2
Trevelyan, George Otto, 1875.7
Trimmer, Mrs. Sarah, 1804.2-3
Trollope, T.A., 1888.23
"The True History of Robinson
Crusoe," 1778.1
Trusov, Yakov, 1762-1764.1
Ts, 1851.24
Tuckerman, Bayard, 1882.11
Tuckerman, Henry Theodore,
1854.12; 1857.10
Turner, Otis, 1913.23
Two Centuries of the English
Novel, 1911.17
"Two Hundred Years of Defoe,"
1919.12
Two Years' Holiday, 1888.24
Typee, 1846.5

Ullrich, Hermann, 1885.13;
1890.25-26; 1893.16; 1895.38;
1898.16; 1899.5; 1900.14;
1901.13; 1902.17; 1903.16;
1904.12; 1905.10; 1906.13;
1907-1908.1; 1908.20-21;
1909.24; 1919.10; 1920.12;
1921.18; 1923.21; 1924.22
"Unabashed Defoe," 1892.19
"The Uncommercial Traveller,"
1860.2
Uneda, 1872.3; 1881.6
The Universal Songster, 1797.1
Unknown London, 1919.2
"An Unpublished Political Paper by
Daniel De Foe," 1907.25
Utopie und Robinsonade, 1914.4
Utter, Robert Palfrey, 1923.22

V., Q., 1900.15
V., V.H.I.L.I.C.I., 1875.8
Valbert, G. See Cherbuliez,
Victor
Van Doren, Carl, 1923.3; 1924.13
Van Laun, Henri, 1863.5
Venable, William H., 1885.14
Verne, Jules, 1874.9; 1882.12;
1888.24; 1900.16

"Verses, Supposed to be written by
Alexander Selkirk," 1782.2
Viator, 1864.20
The Vicar of Wakefield, 1766.5
Vinet, Alexandre, 1844.5
Vischer, Ludwig Friedrich, 1893.2;
1909.24
Vitruvius, 1820.8
Vogüe, Eugène Marie Melchior de,
1895.39
Voiart, Élise, 1841.8
Von Zobeltitz, Fedor, 1898.17
Voyages imaginaires, songes,
visions, et romans cabalis-
tiques, 1787.5; 1787-1789.1
Les Vrais Robinson, 1863.2

W., 1790.7
W., A.E., 1869.27
W., E., 1868.25
W., J.W., 1869.28
W., W., 1788.3; 1902.18
Wackwitz, Friedrich, 1909.25
Wagner, Hermann F., 1886.19;
1903.17
Wainewright, John B., 1921.18
Walford, E., 1881.7; 1888.25
Walker, Emery, 1910.19
Walker, Hugh, 1915.5
Walker, Peter, 1850.11
Walkley, A.B., 1892.19
Waller, A.R., 1818.2; 1821.2;
1825.1; 1902-1904.1; 1912.18
Walling, R.A.J., 1908.22
Wallis, Alfred, 1888.26
Walter, John, 1790.8
Warburg, Karl, 1893.17
Ward, A.W., 1909.23; 1912.18
Ward, C.A., 1875.9; 1876.11;
1886.20; 1895.40
Warner, Charles Dudley, 1896.6
Warner, G.F., 1907.25
The War of the Succession in
Spain, 1888.16
Warren, C.F.S., 1884.12
Warter, John Wood, 1850.9; 1851.21
Watson, J., 1868.26
Watson, James, 1913.6
Watson, John, 1775.6
Watson, Thomas E., 1905.11
Watt, Robert, 1824.3

Subject Index

Bunyan, John, 1791.2; 1813.1;
  1833.5; 1858.14; 1860.7;
  1871.3; 1887.10; 1894.6;
  1902.7; 1918.4; 1922.14
Burnet, Gilbert, 1869.21
Burney, Fanny, 1910.12
Burns, Robert, 1828.1
Burton, James F., 1864.13; 1878.5
Butler, Benjamin Franklin, 1891.8
Button, Joseph, 1837.7; 1866.8;
  1907.26
Byrd, Max, 1919.11

Cadell, T., 1820.4
Caleb Williams, 1815.3
Caledonia, 1780.1; 1861.1
Campe, Friedrich, 1862.14
Campe, Joachim Heinrich,
  1779-1780.1; 1853.11; 1862.14;
  1864.14; 1879.3; 1892.4, 11,
  18; 1897.2; 1903.17; 1907.1;
  1908.20; 1916.6; 1919-1920.1;
  1924.8

Capt. George Carleton, 1785.5;
  1791.1; 1808.3; 1830.9;
  1833.1; 1837.6; 1840-1841.1;
  1840-1843.1; 1844-1845.1;
  1848.4; 1854-1865.1; 1857.5;
  1858.4; 1859.2-3, 9-10, 12,
  16, 18; 1864.10, 17; 1868.20;
  1869.16; 1870.8; 1873.1;
  1876.13; 1880.1; 1888.16;
  1889.13-14; 1890.23, 27;
  1891.12; 1892.17; 1893.5;
  1894.7, 14; 1903.11; 1912.18;
  1924.20
-attitudes of renowned persons,
  1791.1; 1840-1841.1; 1868.20
-authorship, 1869.16; 1888.16;
  1890.3; 1893.5
-character George Carleton,
  1858.4; 1859.9-10; 1864.10;
  1893.5; 1894.7

Captain Singleton
-Africa, 1864.13, 20; 1865.1;
  1878.5; 1887.10; 1895.14;
  1921.16; 1924.7, 20
-attitudes of renowned persons,
  1813.1; 1830.4; 1864.13;

  1868.16, 20; 1878.9; 1899.9;
  1923.20
-authorship, 1787.12; 1790.4
-character Captain Singleton,
  1825.2
-characterization, 1912.18
-comparisons with other books,
  1830.9; 1833.1; 1864.5, 18;
  1869.16; 1871.4; 1880.1;
  1882.11; 1887.3; 1888.15;
  1890.17; 1895.7; 1900.19;
  1907.2, 16; 1912.11; 1915.4;
  1923.10, 22; 1924.17
-editions, 1776.1; 1790.4; 1840.3;
  1840-1843.1; 1887.9; 1895.14;
  1903.6; 1906.5, 14
-French criticism, 1870.1; 1877.2;
  1920.2; 1924.7
-geography, 1840.3; 1851.1, 20;
  1864.13, 20; 1865.1; 1878.5,
  9; 1892.14; 1903.6; 1924.20
-imaginary voyage, 1916.11
-language, 1910.12
-low life, 1830.3; 1884.1; 1894.8,
  18; 1906.5
-method, 1924.20
-neglected, 1882.7
-other references, 1858.14;
  1859.4; 1909.22; 1911.2
-picaresque, 1877.2; 1913.21
-pirates, 1924.20
-Quaker character, 1895.14;
  1911.14
-selections, 1908.15
-sources, 1864.20; 1865.1; 1878.5;
  1911.14; 1912.7; 1921.16;
  1924.20
-style, 1887.10; 1894.21; 1902.11;
  1906.5; 1909.21; 1922.7
-translations, 1916.3
-Zolaesque reading, 1906.2

Care, Henry, 1912.18
The Careless Husband, 1764.1;
  1782.1; 1812.2
Carleton, George Villiers, 1894.7
Carlyle, Thomas, 1887.3; 1889.17
Carpenter, G.R., 1895.36
Casanova de Seingalt, Giovanni
  Jacopo, 1889.17

-portraits, 1793.1; 1806.2;
  1836.3; 1840-1843.1; 1851.6,
  15; 1858.7; 1868.19; 1876.5-6,
  11; 1882.4; 1910.15, 19
-religion, 1883.1
-residences, 1775.6; 1850.9;
  1851.17, 22; 1865.11; 1871.11;

  1889.16; 1893.3; 1895.19;
  1911.13
-silence, 1894.24; 1895.4, 29;
  1897.2
-spy, 1892.2
-verses on Defoe, 1741.2; 1748.2;
  1820.2; 1851.6, 15; 1885.14;
  1886.6; 1897.5, 11
-wife, 1845.4; 1890.1-2; 1908.19;
  1909.2
-Writings
--amorphousness, 1892.19; 1894.24
--characterization, 1856.9; 1887.7
--compared with other writers,
  1818.4; 1821.4; 1826.5;
  1836.7, 9-10; 1837.4; 1841.1,
  7; 1843.1, 6; 1844.4; 1853.10;
  1855.8; 1856.3, 9; 1860.2, 4,
  7; 1863.5; 1866.10; 1868.7,
  16; 1875-1876.1; 1876.9-10;
  1877.3; 1883.3
--father of the English novel,
  1853.13; 1854.12; 1857.10;
  1877.3; 1894.17-18, 20;
  1905.3, 13; 1914.3
--fictions, deceptions, lies,
  1821.4; 1830.8; 1833.4;
  1841.3, 6; 1844.2; 1849.5;
  1856.9; 1860.7; 1862.20;
  1868.20; 1875-1876.1; 1879.5;
  1881.2; 1889.5, 9, 17;
  1893.10, 12; 1894.5, 8-9, 14,
  16, 18, 20; 1895.13, 16;
  1896.11; 1899.3, 6; 1900.3;
  1905.3; 1905.8-9, 13; 1907.16;
  1910.13; 1911.8; 1912.18;
  1914.3; 1916.11; 1918.1
--general criticism of Defoe as
  novelist,1743.2; 1783.1-2;
  1785.2; 1791.2; 1814.2-4;
  1815.3; 1816.4; 1817.2;
  1820.4; 1821.1, 4; 1822.2;
  1823.4; 1825.2-3; 1827.2;

  1828.1; 1830.3-6; 1831.4;
  1833.1-2; 1834.2; 1844.2;
  1844-1845.1; 1845.4; 1853.13;
  1854.12; 1855.1-2, 8; 1856.3,
  9, 11; 1857.5, 7, 10; 1859.11;
  185-.1; 1860.9; 1862.5;
  1863.5; 1864.2, 18; 1868.16;
  1868.20-22; 1870.18; 1871.1,
  4; 1872.2; 1874.1-3, 8; 1875-
  1876.1; 1877.2-3; 1878.9;
  1879.5; 1882.6, 11, 18;
  1883.12-13; 1886.2, 14;
  1887.3, 7-8, 10; 1889.5, 9;
  1891.8; 1892.19; 1894.8-9,
  16-18, 20-21, 24; 1895.15;
  1896.3, 11; 1900.11; 1901.1,
  9, 12; 1902.7, 10, 18; 1903.6-
  8, 10; 1904.6, 10; 1905.3, 8,
  13; 1906.1-2, 4; 1907.2, 16;
  1908.17; 1909.17, 21-22;
  1910.5; 1911.17; 1912.18-19;
  1913.15, 21-22, 24; 1914.3,
  12; 1915.4; 1916.12-13;
  1917.2; 1918.1, 4; 1919.6;
  1922.7; 1923.1; 1924.7, 13-14,
  21-22; 192-.1
--"genius for 'lying like truth,'"
  1879.5
--imagination, 1856.9; 1860.9;
  1862.5; 1871.1
--morality or immorality of the
  novels, 1808.1; 1813.1;
  1814.2; 1830.3, 9; 1845.4;
  1853.3; 1854.12; 1855.1;
  1856.3, 9; 1857.5; 1860.9;
  1864.18; 1869.11; 1870.18;
  1871.4, 8; 1875.7; 1884.1;
  1894.8; 1902.7; 1912.11, 17;
  1913.24; 1913-1914.1; 1915.4;
  1916.12; 1924.7; 192-.1
--novels parallel to life, 1879.5
--pattern in the novels, 1882.11
--style, 1872.2; 1881.1; 1882.11;
  1887.7; 1924.7

Defoe, Daniel (descendant),
  1893.11; 1901.10
Defoe, Hannah, 1912.8
De Foe, James, 1859.6, 17
Defoe, James William, 1893.8;
  1901.8

Godwin, William, 1807.1-2; 1848.4; 1886.12; 1895.10; 1906.14; 1910.5

Goffaux, J.F., 1881.6-7; 1898.9

Goffeaux, G.F., 1907.1

Goldsmith, Oliver, 1855.3; 1891.10; 1918.4

Goncourt, Edmond and Jules, 1908.8

Good Advice to the Ladies, 1878.6

Goodale, Hannah, 1866.7

Gordon, John, 1882.9

Gordon, William, 1921.4

Gosse, Edmund, 1920.9

Gow, John, 1895.13

Gracián, Baltasar, 1920.1

Grandidier, Alfred, 1909.14

Grandidier, Guillaume, 1909.14

Grant, James, 1872.3

Graves, R., 1910.15

Gravesend, 1850.3, 7

Gray, Benjamin, 1910.3

"the greatest of plebeian geniuses," 1912.18-19

The Great Law of Subordination Consider'd, 1850.3, 5; 1851.8; 1895.7; 1913.9

"the great Middle-class English Character," 1845.4

"Great Storm of 1704," 1908.6

Grimmelshausen, Hans Jakob, 1888.15

Groans of Europe, 1859.4

Gulliver, 1907.10

Gulliver's Travels, 1750.1; 1814.4; 1844-1845.1; 1856.3; 1865.12; 1921.8; 1922.13

Hackney, 1893.3

Haggard, Sir Henry Rider, 1887.3

Halifax, 1868.26

Halifax, Charles Wood, 1892.15

Hallier, Emil, 1862.14

Halm, 1919-1920.1

Hannibal at the Gates, 1868.26

Hardy, Thomas, 1875-1876.1

Harford, Joseph, 1909.11

Harley, Robert, 1732.2; 1735.2; 1851.9; 1854.10; 1855.3; 1859.4; 1863.4; 1869.16; 1870.24; 1876.13; 1879.5; 1883.12; 1893.12; 1894.9, 15;

1896.16; 1897.6; 1899.7; 1900.1; 1902.14; 1903.8, 12; 1907.7, 17, 25; 1908.3; 1910.17; 1912.18; 1913.11; 1916.10, 12; 1923.8

Harnack, Otto, 1914.10

Harris, William, 1847.3

Harrison, Frederic, 1891.14; 1908.16

Harte, Walter, 1873.4

Haviland, G., 1920.5

Hawthorne, Nathaniel, 1869.2; 1904.2

Hayward, John, 1820.8

Haywood, Eliza, 1895.12; 1915.6

Hazlitt, William, 1807.1; 1833.1; 1840-1843.1; 1841.4; 1855.2; 1869.16; 1891.12; 1897.3; 1912.9; 1923.3

Hazlitt, William (the younger), 1845.3-5; 1907.22

Head, Richard, 1907.16

Hearne, Samuel, 1882-1883.2

Hearne, Thomas, 1885.9

Herbart, Johann Friedrich, 1898.3

Herbert, George, 1864.6

The Hermit, 1873.2

Hettner, Hermann, 1877.3; 1886.19; 1890.10; 1914.10; 1919-1920.1; 1920.9

High Church, 1854.5

The Highland Rogue, 1869.16; 1870.3, 8, 13-14

Hillebrand, Karl, 1916.6

Hirst, William, 1772.1; 1853.3; 1885.8

historian's view, 1890.21

historical novel, 1883.12; 1916.10

History of Addresses, 1836.2; 1883.10

History of . . . John Sheppard, 1904.9

History of Mademoiselle de Beleau. See Roxana

History of Notorious Pirates, 1899.9

History of the Civil Wars, 1857.6

History of the Devil, 1860.4; 1869.14, 28; 1872-1874.1; 1881.5. See also The Political History of the Devil

Pepys, Samuel, 1900.2; 1904.5
Pepys's Diary, 1858.7
Perto, Silva, 1864.20
Peter Wilkins, 1823.3; 1909.3, 19
Petzholdt, Herren Julius, 1862.14
photographer's art and novels,
    1868.20; 1871.4; 1886.2;
    1900.19; 1924.7, 13
picaresque, 1827.2; 1877.2;
    1879.3; 1883.13; 1887.7;
    1895.20; 1896.8; 1899.1, 3;
    1906.10-11; 1907.2; 1908.8;
    1909.6; 1910.5; 1913.21;
    1915.6; 1916.10; 1920.2;
    1924.7, 14, 20; 192-.1. See
    also individual novels
Picart, Bernard, 1896.7
The Pilgrim's Progress, 1791.2
Pine, John, 1892.16; 1896.7;
    1912.15; 1916.2, 8
Pirate Gow, 1890.22; 1895.13;
    1912.7
Pitot, Albert, 1909.14
Pitt, William, 1st Earl of
    Chatham, 1830.9; 1868.16
Pittis, William, 1914.14
Pixerécourt, René Charles Guilbert
    de, 1916.6
plagiarisms, 1864.6, 15, 19;
    1868.9, 12, 17; 1908.9
"Plague in London with suitable
    Thoughts," 1864.8
"Plague in Newcastle, 1710:
    Daniel De Foe," 1866.8
A Plan of the English Commerce,
    1859.8; 1866.1
Plaxton, George, 1920.5
The Pleasant and Surprizing Adven-
    tures of Robert Drury, 1826.2;
    1872.1
Poe, Edgar Allan, 1831.2; 1835.2;
    1848.1; 1849.1-2; 1863.5;
    1887.3; 1895.35; 1911.13
poems, verse satires. See verses
Polak, Leon, 1921.10
political and social tracts,
    1746.1; 1753.1; 1769.1, 4-5,
    7; 1785.1; 1787.6, 9; 1813-
    1814.1; 1829.2; 1838.7; 1840-
    1843.1; 1844.6; 1854.12;
    1868.20; 1883.3; 1891.9;

    1892.15; 1906.12; 1909.23;
    1910.9; 1911.15; 1920.7
political economy, 1891.12
The Political History of the
    Devil, 1860.4; 1869.14, 28;
    1872-1874.1; 1881.5; 1882.2,
    9; 1896.2; 1900.14; 1906.3;
    1910.6; 1913.7, 16; 1923.7;
    1924.10
The Political State of Great
    Britain, 1869.3
Pollard, Alfred, 1913.20
The Poor Man and the Lady,
    1875-1876.1
The Poor Man's Plea, 1833.2;
    1889.12; 1896.16
"Poor Old Robinson Crusoe,"
    1850.10
"Poor Robinson Crusoe," 1864.3;
    1884.8
Pope, Alexander, 1753.1; 1770.1;
    1820.6; 1831.3; 1845.4;
    1851.11; 1855.3; 1869.14;
    1871.13; 1895.37; 1910.16;
    1912.14; 1921.3, 14
Porter, Jane, 1909.22
Portland Manuscripts, 1897.6;
    1899.7; 1902.14; 1907.17
Post Boy, 1865.8
The Postman, 1866.7
The Present State of Jacobitism
    Considered, 1746.1
Pretender, 1735.2
Prévost d'Exiles, Antoine
    François, 1917.3
Prévost, Marcel, 1895.26
Priestly, Nathaniel, 1775.6
Prior, Matthew, 1870.18
prison experience, 1871.3; 1899.8
Proteus, 1746.1; 1916.11
Providence Displayed, 1880.7
Purves, W. Laidlaw, 1903.14;
    1906.7; 1913.17
Puttick and Simpson, 1849.7

Quaker William, 1911.14
Quarll, Philip, 1873.2; 1909.1, 4
Queen Anne, 1859.4; 1890.13;
    1909.23; 1923.8
Quiller-Couch, Arthur Thomas,
    1895.4; 1898.13

Ragan, Louise, 1924.7
Ralph, James, 1813-1814.1
Rats, George, 1907.12
realism, theory of, 1913.22
Reasons Against War with France, 1892.15
Reclus, Elisée, 1922.2
Reed, Charles, 1870.5, 17
Reed, Isaac, 1782.1
Reeve, Clara, 1823.4
"Reflections in the Pillory," 1864.2
Reflections upon Reflections, 1911.3
Reformation of Manners, 1753.1; 1808.1; 1896.16
Reichard, Heinrich A.O., 1811.1
Religious Courtship, 1789.1; 1817.5; 1820.5; 1823.2; 1836.2; 1855.3, 6; 1865.6; 1924.19
"Remarkable Passage of an Apparition," 1850.12; 1884.9; 1895.27-28, 32-33; 1898.13
Restif, Nicolas Edme, 1870.18; 1917.3
Review, 1796.2; 1805.3; 1808.1-2; 1830.9; 1833.6; 1834.1; 1836.2; 1840.2; 1845.4; 1855.3; 1856.3; 1857.8; 185-.1; 1866.4, 8; 1871.9; 1874.1; 1876.4; 1878.6; 1880.1, 3, 5-6; 1881.1; 1884.10; 1887.1, 10; 1890.9, 11, 14; 1891.9; 1893.5; 1894.18, 20-21; 1896.9; 1899.3, 8; 1900.1; 1903.1; 1904.11; 1908.7; 1909.8, 17, 22-23; 1910.3; 1911.3; 1913.8, 15; 1914.7-8; 1915.5; 1916.10, 12; 1917.1; 1920.4; 1923.17
Reynald, Hermile, 1878.2
Richardson, J., 1910.15
Richardson, Samuel, 1769.6; 1813.1; 1828.1; 1834.2; 1853.10; 1855.1; 1856.9; 1868.17, 23; 1874.8; 1877.3; 1883.13; 1884.1; 1887.3, 7, 10; 1889.5; 1895.37; 1896.9; 1901.9; 1909.6; 1912.17; 1913.22; 1917.2; 1922.14; 1923.22; 1924.19, 21

"The Right divine of Kings to govern wrong," 1851.11
Rippon, John, 1885.11
River Don, 1879.2
Robbins, Alfred, 1908.3
Robert Drury's Journal. See Madagascar
"Robeson Cruso," 1913.17-20
Robinnsonn Crousô, 1892.13
"Robinson" (meaning), 1883.2, 4, 17
Robinson (name), 1888.21-22, 25
Robinson, Sir Thomas, 1870.24
Robinson, William, 1892.6
Robinsonades before Defoe, 1913.3; 1922.1. See also Robinson Crusoe/-Robinsonades, immitations, adaptations
Le Robinson Chrétien, 1852.5
"Robinson Cruso," 1886.1, 3-4, 6, 10-11, 17, 20; 1888.1, 3, 17, 21-22, 25

Robinson Crusoe
-adventures, 1748.3; 1883.8
-allegorical interpretations, symbolism, parable, 1762.1; 1868.16; 1876.12; 1878.8; 1893.6; 1894.12, 24; 1895.4-5, 15, 23, 29; 1896.3; 1902.7; 1905.13; 1910.10; 1912.10; 1914.6; 1916.11; 1918.1; 1921.10; 1923.9; 1924.7
-amorphousness, 1892.19
-Anglo-Saxon race personified, 1863.5; 1866.3; 1877.2; 1883.8; 1910.8; 1915.1
-Arabic translation, 1883.11
-attitudes of renowned persons, 1737.1; 1749.1; 1762.2; 1764.2; 1766.4; 1783.1-2; 1785.1; 1791.1-2; 1810.1, 4; 1813.1; 1816.8; 1818.2, 4; 1819.4; 1820.6; 1825.1; 1828.4; 1829.2; 1830.2, 6; 1831.3; 1836.10; 1841.10-11; 1843.1, 5; 1847.1; 1848.1, 4; 1849.5; 1849-1850.1; 1851.3, 14, 19; 1853.7-8; 1859.11; 1860.2; 1862.13; 1866.10; 1867.6; 1868.16, 20; 1869.10;

1921.10; 1922.6, 10; 1923.6,
11, 13, 18; 1924.7, 20
-style, 1783.1; 1784.2; 1814.2, 4;
1827.2; 1830.3; 1838.5;
1853.10; 1855.8; 1856.3;
1869.16, 20; 1878.6; 1882.7;
1893.12; 1900.19; 1902.2, 11;
1903.10; 1905.8, 13; 1908.10;
1909.21; 1912.11; 1913.15;
1915.4; 1923.6
-Swedish criticism, 1893.17
-teaching text, 1868.1; 1862.10;
1881.6-7; 1882.5; 1884.7;
1887.4; 1895.25; 1898.2-3, 7;
1901.3; 1919.7
-textual studies. See Defoe,
Daniel/-Bibliography
-themes, 1793.1; 1844.6; 1849-
1850.1; 1884.4; 1895.6, 15;
1898.5; 1910.16; 1911.2;
1919.4-5
-translations, 1762.1; 1762-
1764.1; 1766.3; 1769.4;
1775.2; 1787.11; 1787-1789.1;
1800.3-4; 1835.7-8; 1836.3, 5,
7; 1842.1; 1843.3; 1862.10,
13; 1862-1865.1; 1874.1, 7;
1875.1; 1877.2; 1878.2, 8;
1881.6-7; 1882.5, 8; 1883.6,
11; 1884.7; 1888.13, 19;
1892.5; 1893.17; 1898.16;
1906.13; 1907.2; 1909.24;
1910.2; 1912.2; 1916.3;
1919.10
-universality, 1738.2; 1836.4;
1840.4; 1844.5; 1887.10;
1896.6; 1912.13; 1916.6
-veraciousness, 1737.1; 1753.1;
1770.1; 1833.3; 1835.5;
1845.4; 1849.4; 1852.6;
1855.2; 1856.9; 1862.1;
1870.24; 1886.5; 1892.1;
1899.2; 1902.7; 1905.3
-verisimilitude, 1827.2; 1854.12;
1857.10
-Verne, Jules. See separate entry
-verse, 1787.3; 1793.2; 1816.2;
1820?.1; 1821.5; 1826.4;
1831.1; 1844.1; 1845.1;
1850.10; 1853.11-12; 1862.8;
1870.2; 1880.11; 1882.1;

1884.8; 1892.10; 1897.5;
1904.3
-verse in, 1871.7
-voyages imaginaires romanesques,
1787-1789.1
-Welsh translation, 1882.8
-world-book, 1888.27; 1898.16;
1924.22

Robinson dans son isle, 1879.8
Robinson der Jüngere, 1892.4, 11,
18
"Robinson on His Island," 1782.2
Robinson the Younger, 1779-1780.1
Rob Roy, 1870.3, 8, 13-14
Rochester, Lord. See Wilmot,
John, 2d Earl of Rochester
Roe, William, 1868.12
Rogers, Captain Woodes, 1744.1;
1745.1; 1756.2; 1757.1;
1765.1; 1766.2; 1767.2;
1779.1; 1781.2; 1796.1;
1805.2, 4; 1810.5; 1812.6;
1824.2; 1826.4; 185-.1;
1871.12; 1873.2; 1877.1;
1881.3; 1883.12; 1888.9;
1895.15; 1913.5; 1921.10
Rothwell, H., 1910.15
Rötteken, Hubert, 1919-1920.1
Rousseau, Jean-Jacques, 1766.3;
1768.1; 1769.4; 1779-1780.1;
1784.6; 1804.1-2; 1812.5;
1812-1813.1; 1816.8; 1835.7;
1865.4; 1871.1; 1874.1;
1879.3; 1891.11; 1894.12;
1895.37; 1898.3; 1908.20;
1916.6; 1919.7; 1920.9; 1924.1
"the Rousseau of the gutter,"
1870.18

Roxana
-amorphousness or lack of
construction, 1892.19
-Amy, 1924.5
-attitudes of renowned persons,
1775.1; 1807.1, 3; 1830.4, 6;
1845.4; 1848.4; 1868.20;
1875.7; 1878.9; 1906.1;
1910.18; 1919.11; 1924.5
-authenticity, 1896.8
-authorship, 1787.12

Sherwin, William, 1851.15
Shiells, William, 1787.4
Shiels, Robert, 1766.6; 1775.2;
    1787.12
Short and Easy Method with the
    Deists, 1738.1
Short Discourse Concerning Pesti-
    lential Contagion, 1744.2

Shortest-Way with the Dissenters,
    1735.2; 1753.1; 1785.1;
    179-.1; 1808.1; 1818.3;
    1830.8; 1838.5; 1851.12;
    1853.13; 1856.3; 1857.7;
    1859.4; 1868.16; 1869.11, 13;
    1871.15-16; 1874.1; 1875-
    1876.1; 1876.13; 1878.6;
    1880.1; 1885.13; 1886.13;
    1887.12; 1889.4, 7, 12, 14;
    1890.4; 1891.9; 1892.15;
    1894.2, 9, 16; 1896.11;
    1897.4; 1899.8; 1905.3;
    1909.23; 1910.9, 17; 1912.18;
    1916.13; 1922.7; 1924.3
-editions, 1885.13; 1892.15;
    1904.7; 1910.9

A Short History of English Litera-
    ture, 1898.15
A Short Narrative . . . of John
    Rhinholdt Count Patkul,
    1869.16
Shrewsbury, 1825.5
"A Shropshire Inscription," 1864.4
Simplicissimus, 1888.15; 1908.9;
    1909.24
Sir Edward Seaward's Narrative of
    His Shipwreck, 1909.22
Six Distinguishing Characters of a
    Parliament Man, 1769.5, 7
Skelton, William, 1876.11
Smeeks, Hendrik, 1914.10; 1921.10;
    1923.13, 18
Smith, Alexander, 1924.20
Smollett, Tobias, 1789.1; 1821.1;
    1834.2; 1855.8; 1877.3;
    1886.8; 1889.5; 1890.12;
    1894.18; 1918.4; 1924.17
social reformer, 1862.5; 1883.13
Some Considerations on a Law for
    Triennial Parliaments, 1852.2

Somerville, Thomas, 1830.9
South Carolina, 1911.15
Southern, Henry, 1769.2
Southerne, Thomas, 1775.1
South Sea Scheme, 1902.14
Spanish picaresque, 1883.13
Speculum Crape-Gownorum, 1845.4;
    1850.11; 185-.1; 1864.18;
    1868.16
Speke, John Henning, 1864.13;
    1865.1; 1878.5
spiritual knocking, 1853.12, 18;
    1854.1, 6; 1855.3
The Spy upon the Conjuror, 1915.6
Stancliffe, James, 1912.8
Stancliffe, Samuel, 1912.8
Standerwick, Sophia, 1784.5;
    1785.2
Stanhope, James, 1870.21
Stanhope, Philip Henry, 1890.27
Staniland, George, 1920.5
Stanley, Henry Morton, 1878.5
statue of the piper, 1912.1, 4
Staverman, W.H., 1921.10; 1924.7
Stebbing, H., 1862.8
Stebbing, William, 1890.3
Steele, Richard, 1766.3-4; 1769.4;
    1775.2-3; 1787-1789.1; 1800.4;
    1805.2; 1817.4; 1834.2;
    1835.7; 1848.3-4; 1870.18;
    1877.1; 1883.3, 12; 1886.13;
    1887.1; 1889.2; 1895.15, 37;
    1899.7; 1910.12, 16; 1915.5;
    1916.10
Stephen, Fitzjames, 1883.9
Stephen, Leslie, 1871.1; 1875.1;
    1883.12; 1886.2; 1896.11;
    1898.1; 1902.18; 1909.15;
    1910.13
Stephens, William, 1885.9
Stern, Adolf, 1896.13
Sterne, Laurence, 1887.7; 1889.5
Stevenson, Robert Louis, 1887.3;
    1895.35; 1909.6; 1915.4
Stifford, 1871.11
stock-jobbing, 1907.4
Stoke Newington, 1820.5; 1851.17,
    22; 1865.11; 1866.6; 1868.25;
    1869.19; 1870.24; 1886.10;
    1889.16; 1893.3, 14; 1895.19;
    1911.13; 1923.9